Fodor's First Edition

Brazil

The complete guide, thoroughly up-to-date

Packed with details that will make your trip

The must-see sights, off and on the beaten path

What to see, what to skip

Mix-and-match vacation itineraries

City strolls, countryside adventures

Smart lodging and dining options

Essential local do's and taboos

Transportation tips, distances and directions

Key contacts, savvy travel tips

When to go, what to pack

Clear, accurate, easy-to-use maps

lon, Sydney, Auckland

Fodor's Brazil

EDITOR: Laura M. Kidder

Editorial Contributors: Karen Bressler, Karla Brunet, Deb Carroll, Shane Christensen, Joyce Dalton, Mary Dempsey, Marilene Felinto B. de Lima, Wilma Felinto B. de Lima, José Fonseca, Althea Gamble, Melisse Gelula, Amy Karafin, Christina Knight, Chelsea Mauldin, Charles Runnette, Carlos Henrique Severo, Carlos Tornquist, Brad Weiss

Editorial Production: Melissa Klurman, Rebecca Zeiler

Maps: David Lindroth, Inc., Mapping Specialists Ltd., *cartographers;* Rebecca Baer and Bob Blake, *map editors*

Design: Fabrizio La Rocca, *creative director;* Guido Caroti, *art director;* Jolie Novak, *photo editor*

Cover Design: Pentagram

Production/Manufacturing: Bob Shields

Cover Photograph *(zoo in Manaus, the Amazon)*: Andrea Pistolesi/The Image Bank

Copyright

First Edition

ISBN 0–679–00459–9

ISSN 0163–0628

Special Sales

Fodor's Travel Publications are available at special discounts for bulk purchases for sales promotions or premiums. Special editions, including personalized covers, excerpts of existing guides, and corporate imprints, can be created in large quantities for special needs. For more information, contact your local bookseller or write to Special Markets, Fodor's Travel Publications, 201 East 50th Street, New York, NY 10022. Inquiries from Canada should be directed to your local Canadian bookseller or sent to Random House of Canada, Ltd., Marketing Department, 2775 Matheson Boulevard East, Mississauga, Ontario L4W 4P7. Inquiries from the United Kingdom should be sent to Fodor's Travel Publications, 20 Vauxhall Bridge Road, London SW1V 2SA, England.

PRINTED IN THE UNITED STATES OF AMERICA

10 9 8 7 6 5 4 3 2 1

Important Tip

Although all prices, opening times, and other details in this book are based on information supplied to us at press time, changes occur all the time in the travel world, and Fodor's cannot accept responsibility for facts that become outdated or for inadvertent errors or omissions. So **always confirm information when it matters,** especially if you're making a detour to visit a specific place.

CONTENTS

Maps

ON THE ROAD WITH FODOR'S

THE TRIPS YOU TAKE THIS YEAR and next are going to be significant trips, if only because they'll be your first in the new millennium. So, we've pulled out all stops in preparing *Fodor's Brazil*. To guide you in putting together your Brazilian experience, we've created multiday itineraries and neighborhood walks. And to direct you to the places that are truly worth your time and money in these important years, we've rallied the team of endearingly picky know-it-alls we're pleased to call our writers. If you knew them, you'd poll them for tips yourself.

Karen Bressler rolled up her veteran travel writer's sleeves and helped to fine-tune the Salvador, Recife, and Fortaleza chapter. Karen has written for *Condé Nast Traveler, Honeymoon,* and *Elegant Bride* and is a correspondent for Condé Nast's online travel publication.

Mary Dempsey, a former UPI reporter/editor, was bitten by the travel bug 15 years ago while working at a newspaper in Venezuela. Time spent writing from Peru and Puerto Rico solidified her wanderlust. Mary, who worked on the Rio chapter, has written about South America and the Caribbean for the *Los Angeles Times, Condé Nast Traveler,* and *Travel & Leisure.*

Shane Christensen, who updated the Minas Gerais chapter, has written about Argentina, Ecuador, and Paraguay for *Fodor's South America.* Shane is based in Washington, D.C., where he's the bureau chief for On the Road, Inc.

Marilene Felinto B. de Lima—a São Paulo–based freelancer who contributes to the city's large daily newspaper, *Folha*—helped to expand the Salvador, Recife, and Fortaleza chapter. Her sister, Wilma, assisted her in covering this vast region.

Charles Runnette has been a writer/editor for *New York Magazine,* Microsoft's Sidewalk, and the *New York Times* Electronic Media. He also worked for StarMedia.com and covered Chile in *Fodor's South Amer-*

ica. For this guide, Charles updated his shots and went off to western Brazil and the Pantanal.

São Paulo chapter writer **Carlos Henrique Severo** is a journalist who has put his talents to work on the Internet since 1995. He was assisted by **Karla Brunet,** a photographer who studied art in San Francisco, CA. Both live in São Paulo.

Carlos Tornquist, who covered the south, is a soil scientist who is highly qualified to write about his native turf. When he's not teaching in the agronomy department of a university in southern Brazil, he's traveling. Carlos has also seen much of the New World—from the U.S.–Canada border to the tip of Patagonia.

Fluent in both Portuguese and Spanish, English-teacher, translator, and intrepid traveler **Brad Weiss** put his language skills to work on the Amazon chapter of this guide and the Litoral chapter of *Fodor's Argentina.*

We'd also like to thank Continental Airline, particularly Thomas Anderson; Stela Maris Dallari of the Brazilian Consulate in New York; Mary Lamberti of Pro-Brazil, Inc.; Natalia Zapatero and Mario Brito of RioTur; Maria Taraboulous, Kreps & Adams, and the Inter-Continental hotels; and Tom Dovidas at Varig Airlines.

Don't Forget to Write

Keeping a travel guide fresh and up-to-date is a big job. So we love your feedback—positive and negative—and follow up on all suggestions. Contact the Brazil editor at editors@fodors.com or c/o Fodor's, 201 East 50th Street, New York, New York 10022. And have a wonderful trip!

Karen Cure

Karen Cure
Editorial Director

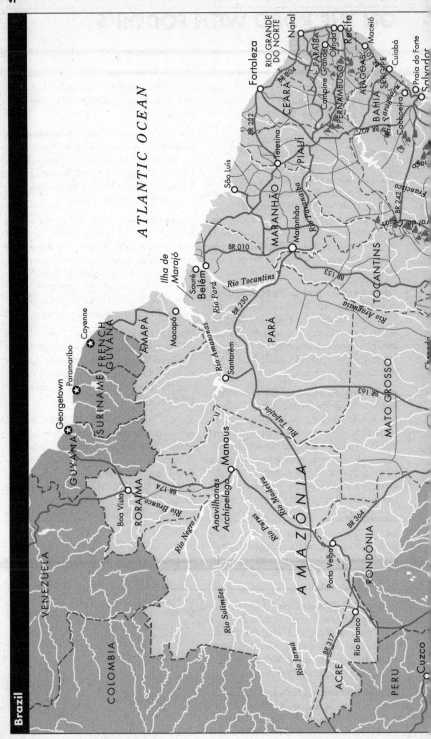

ATLANTIC OCEAN

Fortaleza

RIO GRANDE
DO NORTE
Natal

Recife
PARAÍBA
Olinda
Maceió

CEARÁ
Campine Grande
PERNAMBUCO
ALAGOAS
SERGIPE
Cuiabá
Praia do Forte
Salvador

BR 222
Teresina
PIAUÍ
BAHIA
Cachoeira

São Luís
MARANHÃO
BR 242

BR 010
Maranhão
TOCANTINS
Francisco

Ilha de
Marajó
Souré
Belém
Rio Pará
Rio Tocantins

BR 230
PARÁ
Rio Araguaia

Cayenne
AMAPÁ
Macapá
Rio Amazonas

Paramaribo
Santarém

Georgetown
SURINAME
FRENCH
GUYANA

GUYANA
Rio Tapajós
MATO GROSSO
BR 163

VENEZUELA
Manaus
Anavilhanas
Archipelago

Boa Vista
RORAIMA
BR 174
Rio Branco
Rio Madeira
Rio Purus

Rio Negro
AMAZÔNIA
BR 364
RONDÔNIA

COLOMBIA
Rio Solimões
Porto Velho

Rio Juruá
BR 317
Rio Branco
ACRE

PERU
Cuzco

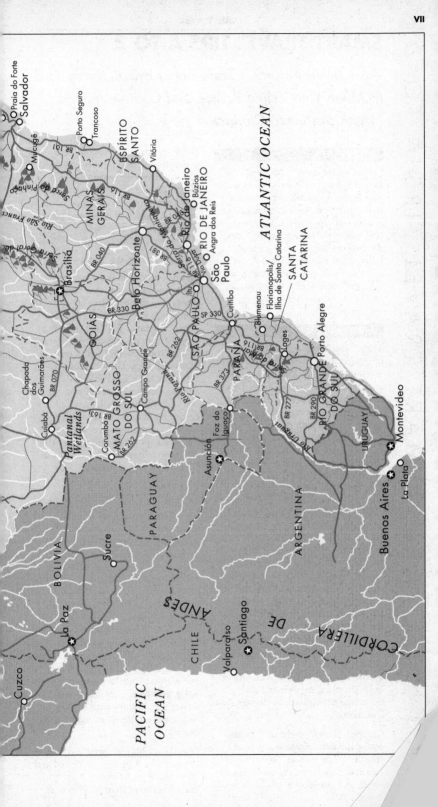

SMART TRAVEL TIPS A TO Z

Basic Information on Traveling in Brazil, Savvy Tips to Make Your Trip a Breeze, and Companies and Organizations to Contact

ADDRESSES

In Portuguese *avenida* (avenue) and *travessa* (lane) are abbreviated (as *Av.* and *Trv.* or *Tr.*) while other common terms such as *estrada* (highway) and *rua* (street) often aren't. Street numbers follow the names; postal codes are widely used. In some parts of Brazil street numbering still doesn't enjoy the wide popularity that it has achieved elsewhere, hence, you may find the notation "s/n," meaning "no street number."

AIR TRAVEL

There's regular jet service between all of the country's major cities and most medium-size cities. Remote areas are also quite accessible—as long as you don't mind small planes. Flights can be long, lasting several hours on trips to the Amazon with stops en route. The most widely used service is the Ponte Aérea (Air Bridge), the Rio–São Paulo shuttle, which departs every half-hour from 6 AM to 10:30 PM (service switches to every 15 minutes during morning and evening rush hours). It costs $90–$140 each way; reservations aren't necessary.

AIRPORTS & TRANSFERS

Chicago, Houston, Los Angeles, Miami, and New York are the major gateways for flights to Brazil from the United States and Canada. Several airlines fly directly from London, but there's no direct service from Sydney, Australia or Auckland, New Zealand. The two biggest Brazilian gateways are Rio de Janeiro and São Paulo. For details on airports in these and other Brazilian cities, *see* Arriving and Departing By Airplane *in* chapter A to Z sections.

Getting to and from the airport may not be the most pleasant aspect of your Brazilian journey. Subway transit to the airports is nearly nonexistent, and bus service, while often cheap, can require a serious time commitment. Taxi fares to city centers vary from the reasonable to a steep $20–$35. To ensure that your city destination is understood, write it down on a piece of paper and present it to bus or taxi drivers, most of whom don't speak English.

BOOKING YOUR FLIGHT

When you book **look for nonstop flights** and **remember that "direct" flights stop at least once.** Try to avoid connecting flights, which require a change of plane. Within a country as big as Brazil, it's especially important to plan your itinerary with care. Try to arrange trips with one stopover—for example, in São Paulo or Brasília—instead of seven stops in cities between, say, Salvador and Belém. Book as far in advance as possible, particularly for weekend travel. Planes tend to fill up on Friday, especially to or from Brasília or Manaus.

CARRIERS

Major U.S. carriers serving Brazil include American Airlines (which flies nonstop from New York and Miami to Rio and São Paulo), Continental Airlines (which flies from Houston and Newark to Rio and São Paulo), and United Airlines (with flights from Chicago, New York, and Miami to São Paulo, and from Miami to Rio). Delta serves Rio and São Paulo directly from Atlanta. Canadian Airlines flies direct from Toronto to São Paulo. It also offers connecting flights with American and United Airlines and with the Brazilian carriers TAM, Varig, and Vasp. Air Canada has service partnerships with Brazil's largest carrier, Varig, as well as with United.

From London's Heathrow Airport you can take American or United and fly to Brazil via Miami or New York. Varig has flights from Heathrow to both Rio and São Paulo. British Airways has nonstop service from London's Gatwick Airport to Rio and São Paulo. Continental flies from Gatwick to Newark and on to both Rio and São Paulo.

From Sydney, Australia, you can take Qantas to Los Angeles, pick up an American Airlines flight to Miami, and then complete your trip to Rio on Varig. Other options include Sydney to Buenos Aires to Rio, or a trip to Rio that's routed through Papeete and Santiago, Chile, which should only be considered if you want to spend a couple days on a plane. Air New Zealand offers flights to major Brazilian cities through their partnership with Varig. Direct flights to Los Angeles—where you transfer to Varig—depart from Auckland once or twice a day.

TAM, Transbrasil, Varig, and VASP are the Brazil-based carriers. TAM, which has an agreement with American Airlines that allows passengers to accumulate AA miles and awards, flies nonstop from Miami to São Paulo, with connections to 22 other cities. (TAM is small and expensive but has garnered praise from flyers for good service and food, among other things; however, there have also been reports that the airline is poorly organized.) Transbrasil's nonstops run from Miami and Orlando to São Paulo; the carrier also flies from Chicago; Los Angeles; New York; and Washington, D.C. São Paulo is Transbrasil's hub, and from there you can catch flights to Belo Horizonte, Brasília, Rio, Salvador and 17 other cities, either on Transbrasil or on its partner carrier, Intrabrasil.

Varig, Brazil's largest international carrier and traditionally the best one with which to travel, has service to Rio and São Paulo from Chicago, Los Angeles, Miami, and New York. Some of these flights may be on United, Varig's U.S. partner carrier. Varig also serves Manaus, Recife, Fortaleza, and Belém from Miami. VASP flies from Miami, New York, and Los Angeles to São Paulo and Rio; and from Miami to Recife and Brasília.

➤ BRAZILIAN CARRIERS: **TAM** (☎ 888/235–9826 in the U.S.), **Transbrasil** (☎ 800/872–3153 in the U.S.), **Varig** (☎ 800/468–2744 in the U.S.), **VASP** (☎ 800/732–8277 in the U.S.).

➤ NORTH AMERICAN CARRIERS: **Air Canada** (☎ 800/776–3000 or 800/361–8620 in Canada), **American Airlines** (☎ 800/433–7300 in North America), **Canadian Airlines** (☎ 800/665–1177 in Canada or 800/426–7000 in the U.S.), **Continental Airlines** (☎ 800/231–0856 in North America), **Delta Airlines** (☎ 800/241–4141 in the U.S.), **United Airlines** (☎ 800/241–6522 in North America).

➤ FROM AUSTRALIA AND NEW ZEALAND: **Air New Zealand** (☎ 0396/703–700 in Australia; 0800/737–000 or 09/357–8900 in New Zealand), **Qantas** (☎ 13–13–13 in Australia or 0800/808–767 in New Zealand).

➤ FROM THE U.K.: **American Airlines** (☎ 0345/789–789), **British Airways** (☎ 0345/222–111), **Continental Airlines** (☎ 0800/776464), **United Airlines** (☎ 0845/844–4777), **Varig** (☎ 020/7287–3131).

CHECK-IN & BOARDING

Assuming that not everyone with a ticket will show up, airlines routinely overbook planes. When that happens, airlines ask for volunteers to give up their seats. In return these volunteers usually get a certificate for a free flight and are rebooked on the next flight out. If there aren't enough volunteers, the airline must choose who will be denied boarding. The first to get bumped are passengers who checked in late and those flying on discounted tickets, so **get to the gate and check in as early as possible,** especially during peak periods.

Always **bring a government-issued photo ID to the airport.** You may be asked to show it before you're allowed to check in. **Be prepared to show your passport when leaving Brazil and to pay hefty airport taxes.** Fees on international flights can run as high as $40; even domestic flights incur $10 in additional charges. You should **plan to pay taxes with local currency.**

CUTTING COSTS

The least expensive airfares to Brazil must usually be purchased in advance and are nonrefundable. It's smart to **call a number of airlines, and when you are quoted a good price, book it on the spot**—the same fare may not be available the next day. Always **check different routings** and look into using different airports. International flights are also sensitive to season: try to **fly in the off season** for the cheapest fares. Travel agents, especially low-fare specialists (☞ Discounts & Deals, *below*), are helpful.

Consolidators are another good source. They buy tickets for scheduled international flights at reduced rates from the airlines, then sell them at prices that beat the best fare available directly from the airlines, usually without restrictions. Sometimes you can even get your money back if you need to return the ticket. Carefully read the fine print detailing penalties for changes and cancellations, and **confirm your consolidator reservation with the airline.**

Look into discount passes. If you plan to travel a lot within Brazil, buy an airpass from Transbrasil or Varig before you leave home (these can only be purchased externally). Varig, which has the better service and flies to more cities, offers three versions: for $490, you get 5 flights within the country over a period of 21 days; for $350, you can travel between 4 destinations in the south, southeast, and central west; $290 buys you 4 flights within the northeast, and you can begin or end your trip in Rio or São Paulo. In high season (Dec.–Feb. and July), prices are higher.

If your itinerary includes destinations in Argentina, Chile, Paraguay, and/or Uruguay as well as Brazil, the MER-COSUR (Southern Common Market) pass may work for you. It can save you money, but it has very tricky requirements. It's also very difficult to get reliable information about this pass from the participating airlines, which include the flag carriers of each of the nations involved. A better bet is to contact a travel agent who specializes in open-jaw or round-the-world tickets, and even then, be patient.

➤ CONSOLIDATORS: **Cheap Tickets** (☎ 800/377–1000), **Discount Airline Ticket Service** (☎ 800/576–1600), **Unitravel** (☎ 800/325–2222), **Up & Away Travel** (☎ 212/889–2345), **World Travel Network** (☎ 800/409–6753).

ENJOYING THE FLIGHT

For more legroom **request an emergency-aisle seat.** Don't sit in the row in front of the emergency aisle or in front of a bulkhead, where seats may not recline. If you have dietary concerns, **ask for special meals when booking.** These can be vegetarian, low-cholesterol, or kosher, for example. On long flights try to maintain a normal routine to help fight jet lag. At night **get some sleep.** By day **eat light meals, drink water** (not alcohol), and **move around the cabin** to stretch your legs.

Travel between the Americas is a bit less wearing than to Europe or Asia because there's far less jet lag. (Rio is 3 hours behind Greenwich Mean Time: if it's 5 PM in London, it's noon in New York, and it's 2 PM in Rio; Manaus is an hour behind Rio.) Flights to Rio de Janeiro generally depart after dark; you're in luck if you sleep well while flying. Southbound, the best views are usually out windows on the left side of the plane.

FLYING TIMES

The flying time from New York is 8½ hours to Rio, 9½ hours to São Paulo. From Miami, it's 7 hours to Rio, 8 hours to São Paulo. Most flights from Los Angeles go through Miami, so add 5 hours to the Miami times given; direct flights to São Paulo from Los Angeles take about 11 hours. From London, it's 7 hours to São Paulo.

Within Brazil, it's 1 hour from Rio to São Paulo or Belo Horizonte, 1½ hours from Rio to Brasília, 2 hours from Rio to Salvador, and 2½ hours from Rio to Belém or Curitiba. From São Paulo it's 4 hours to Manaus and 1½ hours to Iguaçu Falls.

HOW TO COMPLAIN

If your baggage goes astray or your flight goes awry, complain right away. Most carriers require that you **file a claim immediately.**

➤ AIRLINE COMPLAINTS: U.S. Department of Transportation **Aviation Consumer Protection Division** (✉ C-75, Room 4107, Washington, DC 20590, ☎ 202/366–2220), **Federal Aviation Administration (FAA) Consumer Hotline** (☎ 800/322–7873).

RECONFIRMING

Always **reconfirm your flights,** even if you have a ticket and a reservation. This is particularly true for travel within Brazil and throughout South America, where flights tend to operate at full capacity—usually with passengers who have a great deal of baggage to process before departure.

BIKE TRAVEL

Riding a bike will put you face to face with the people and landscapes of Brazil. However, the oft-rugged terrain and varying road conditions pose considerable challenges. **Consider a mountain bike,** since basic touring bikes are too fragile for off-road treks. Many tour operators within South America offer bike trips—sometimes including equipment rental—that range in length from a half-day to several days. Always remember to **lock your bike when you make stops.** Although some cities, such as Rio, have places that are perfect for a bike ride, for the most part you should **avoid riding in congested urban areas,** where it's difficult (and dangerous) enough getting around by car let alone by bike.

BIKES IN FLIGHT

Most airlines accommodate bikes as luggage, provided they're dismantled and boxed. For bike boxes, often free at bike shops, you'll pay about $5 (it's at least $100 for bike bags). International travelers can sometimes substitute a bike for a piece of checked luggage at no charge; otherwise, the cost is about $100. Domestic airlines charge $25–$50.

BUS TRAVEL

The nation's *ônibus* (bus) network is affordable, comprehensive, and efficient—compensating for the lack of trains and the high cost of air travel. Every major city can be reached by bus as can most of the small- to medium-size communities.

On well-traveled routes, service is especially frequent and inexpensive.

Lengthy bus trips anywhere will involve travel over some bad highways, an unfortunate fact of life in Brazil today. Trips to northern, northeastern, and central Brazil tend to be especially trying; the best paved highways are in the south and southeast, so trips to and within this region may go more smoothly. When traveling by bus, **bring water, toilet paper, and an additional top layer of clothing** (the latter will come in handy if it gets cold, or it can serve as a pillow). Travel light, dress comfortably, and **keep a close watch on your belongings**—especially in bus stations.

CLASSES

Various classes of service are offered, with each increase in price buying plusher seats and more leg room. (If you're over 5′10″ buy the most expensive ticket available and try for front-row seats; otherwise, be prepared for knee pain.)

Buses used for long trips are modern and comfortable (bathrooms and air-conditioning are common amenities), and they stop regularly at reasonably clean roadside cafés. Sleeper buses have fewer seats, permitting the seats to recline more and allowing more space for each passenger to stretch out. Note that regular buses used for shorter hauls may be labeled AR CONDICIONADO (AIR-CONDITIONED) but often are not.

CUTTING COSTS

Bus fares are substantially cheaper than in North America or Europe. Between Rio and São Paulo (6½–7 hours), for example, a bus departs every ½ hour and costs about $15 (a night sleeper, about $28). Sometimes, competing companies serve the same routes, so it can pay to shop around.

PAYING AND RESERVATIONS

Tickets are sold at bus-company offices and at city bus terminals. Note that in larger cities there may be different terminals for buses to different destinations, and some small towns may not have a terminal at all (you're picked up and dropped off at the bus line's office, invariably in a central location). **Expect to pay with** cash as credit cards aren't accepted everywhere. Note that reservations or advance-ticket purchases generally aren't necessary except for trips to resort areas during high season—particularly on weekends—or during major holidays (Christmas, Carnival, etc.) and school-break periods. In general, **arrive at bus stations early, particularly for travel during peak seasons.**

BUSINESS HOURS

BANKS & OFFICES

Banks are, with exceptions every now and again, open weekdays 10–4. Office hours are generally 9–5.

GAS STATIONS

Within cities and along major highways, many gas stations are open 24 hours a day, 7 days a week. In smaller towns, they may only be open during daylight hours Monday–Saturday.

MUSEUMS

Many museums are open from 10 or 11 to 5 or 6 (they may stay open later one night a week). Some museums, however, are only open in the afternoon, and many are closed on Monday. Always check ahead.

SHOPS

Generally, small shops are open weekdays from 9 to 6 and on Saturday from 9 to 1 or 2. Centers and malls are often open from 10 to 10. Some centers, malls, and pharmacies are open on Sunday.

CAMERAS & PHOTOGRAPHY

Brazil, with its majestic landscapes and varied cityscapes, is a photographer's dream. Brazilians seem amenable to having picture-taking tourists in their midst, but you should always **ask permission before taking pictures in churches or of individuals.** If you're bashful about approaching strangers, **photograph people with whom you interact:** your waiter, your desk clerk, the vendor selling you crafts. Even better, have a traveling companion or a passerby photograph you *with* them.

To avoid the blurriness caused by hand shake, **buy a mini tripod**—they're available in sizes as small as 6 inches. **Get a small beanbag to support your camera on uneven surfaces.** If you plan to take photos on some of the country's many beaches **bring a skylight (81B or 81C) or polarizing filter** to minimize haze and light problems. If you're visiting the Amazon or Pantanal, **bring high-speed film** to compensate for low light under the tree canopy and **invest in a telephoto lens** to photograph wildlife; standard zoom lenses of the 35–88 range won't capture enough detail.

Casual photographers should **consider using inexpensive disposable cameras** to reduce the risks inherent in traveling with sophisticated equipment. One-use cameras with panoramic or underwater functions are also nice supplements to a standard camera and its gear.

➤ PHOTO HELP: **Kodak Information Center** (☎ 800/242–2424), *Kodak Guide to Shooting Great Travel Pictures,* available in bookstores or from Fodor's Travel Publications (☎ 800/533–6478; $16.50 plus $4 shipping).

EQUIPMENT PRECAUTIONS

Always **keep your film and tape out of the sun** and on jungle trips **keep your equipment in resealable plastic bags** to protect it from dampness. As petty crime is a problem throughout Brazil, particularly in the cities, **keep a close eye on your gear. Carry an extra supply of batteries,** and **be prepared to turn on your camera or camcorder** to prove to security personnel that the device is real. Always **ask for hand inspection of film,** which becomes clouded after successive exposures to airport X-ray machines, and **keep videotapes away from metal detectors.**

FILM

Bring your own film. It's expensive in Brazil and is frequently stored in hot conditions. Plan on shooting a minimum of one 36-exposure roll per week of travel. If you don't want the hassle of keeping a shot log, **make a quick note whenever you start a new roll**—it will make identifying your photos much easier when you get home.

CAR RENTAL

In cities, driving is chaotic at best, mortally dangerous at worst; in the countryside, the usually rough roads, lack of clearly marked signs, and language difference are discouraging (☞ Car Travel, *below*). Further, the cost of renting can be steep. All that said, certain areas are most enjoyable when explored on your own in a car: the beach areas of Búzios and the Costa Verde (near Rio) and the nearby Belo Horizonte region; the North Shore beaches outside São Paulo; and many of the inland and coastal towns of the south, a region with many good roads.

Always **give the rental car a once-over** to make sure that the headlights, jack, and tires (including the spare) are in working condition.

➤ MAJOR AGENCIES: **Alamo** (☎ 800/ 522–9696; 020/8759–6200 in the U.K.), **Avis** (☎ 800/331–1084; 800/ 879–2847 in Canada; 02/9353–9000 in Australia; 09/525–1982 in New Zealand), **Budget** (☎ 800/527–0700; 0144/227–6266 in the U.K.), **Dollar** (☎ 800/800–6000; 020/8897–0811 in the U.K., where it's known as Eurodollar; 02/9223–1444 in Australia), **Hertz** (☎ 800/654–3001; 800/ 263–0600 in Canada; 0990/90–60– 90 in the U.K.; 02/9669–2444 in Australia; 03/358–6777 in New Zealand), **National InterRent** (☎ 800/227–3876; 0345/222525 in the U.K., where it's known as Europcar InterRent).

CUTTING COSTS

Fly/drive packages are rare in Brazil. To make arrangements before you leave home, **book through a travel agent who will shop around.** Although international car-rental agencies have better service and maintenance track records than local firms (they also provide better breakdown assistance), your best bet at getting a good rate is to **rent on arrival, particularly from smaller, local companies.** Only reserve ahead (and check that a confirmed reservation guarantees you a car) if you plan to rent during a holiday period.

Consider hiring a car and driver through your hotel concierge, or

make a deal with a taxi driver for some extended sightseeing at a longer-term rate. Often, drivers charge a set hourly rate, regardless of the distance traveled. You'll have to pay cash, but you'll often spend less than you would for a rental car.

Look into wholesalers, companies that don't own fleets but rent in bulk from those that do and often offer better rates than traditional car-rental operations. Payment must be made before you leave home.

➤ LOCAL AGENCIES: For details on local agencies, *see* Getting Around By Car *in* chapter A to Z sections.

➤ WHOLESALER: **Auto Europe** (☎ 207/842–2000 or 800/223–5555, FAX 800–235–6321).

INSURANCE

When driving a rented car you're generally responsible for any damage to or loss of the vehicle and for any property damage or personal injury that you may cause. Before you rent see what coverage your personal auto-insurance policy and credit cards already provide.

REQUIREMENTS & RESTRICTIONS

In Brazil, the minimum driving age is 18. Your own driver's license is acceptable—sort of (☞ Car Travel, *below*). An International Driver's Permit, available from automobile associations, is a *really* good idea. If you do plan to drive in Brazil, confirm in advance with a car rental agency the proof of insurance you may need to carry.

SURCHARGES

Before you pick up a car in one city and leave it in another **ask about drop-off charges or one-way service fees,** which can be substantial. Note, too, that some rental agencies charge extra if you return the car before the time specified in your contract. To avoid a hefty refueling fee **fill the tank just before you turn in the car,** but be aware that gas stations near the rental outlet may overcharge.

CAR TRAVEL

Brazil has more than 1.65 million km of highway, about 1/10 of it paved.

Recent developments and construction are improving the situation, but independent land travel in Brazil definitely has its liabilities (one expat referred to it as "downright hazardous"). In addition, Brazilian drivers are, to say the least, daredevils. For these reasons, you may find it easier to rely on taxis and buses for short distances and on planes for longer journeys.

Some common-sense rules of the road: before you set out **establish an itinerary** and **ask about gas stations.** Be sure to **plan your daily driving distance conservatively** and **don't drive after dark.** Always **obey speed limits and traffic regulations.**

AUTO CLUBS

➤ IN AUSTRALIA: **Australian Automobile Association** (☎ 02/6247–7311).

➤ IN CANADA: **Canadian Automobile Association** (CAA, ☎ 613/247–0117).

➤ IN NEW ZEALAND: **New Zealand Automobile Association** (☎ 09/377–4660).

➤ IN THE U.K.: **Automobile Association** (AA, ☎ 0990/500–600). **Royal Automobile Club** (RAC, ☎ 0990/722–722 for membership; 0345/121–345 for insurance).

➤ IN THE U.S.: **American Automobile Association** (☎ 800/564–6222).

EMERGENCY SERVICES

The Clube Automótivel do Brasil (Automobile Club of Brazil) provides emergency assistance to foreign motorists in cities and on highways, but only if they're members of an automobile club in their own nation.

➤ CONTACTS: **Clube Automótivel do Brasil** (⊠ Rua do Passeio 90, Rio de Janeiro ☎ 021/297–4455).

GASOLINE

Gasoline in Brazil costs around $1.30 a liter ($5 a gallon). Unleaded gas is called *especial* and carries the same price. Brazil also has an extensive fleet of ethanol-powered cars. Ethanol fuel is sold at all gas stations, and costs a little less than gasoline. However, such cars get lower mileage, so

they offer little advantage over gas-powered cars. Stations are plentiful both within cities and on major highways, and many are open 24 hours a day. In smaller towns, few stations take credit cards, and their hours may be more limited.

PARKING

Finding a parking space in most cities—particularly Rio, São Paulo, Belo Horizonte, and Salvador—is a major task. It's best to **head for a garage or a lot** and leave your car with the attendant. Should you find a space on the street, you'll probably have to pay a fee. There are no meters; instead, there's a system involving coupons that allow you to park for a certain time period (usually two hours) and that you post in your car's window. You can buy them from uniformed street-parking attendants or at newsstands.

No-parking zones are marked by a capital letter "E" (which means *estacionamento,* the Portuguese word for "parking") that is crossed out. These zones are, more often than not, filled with cars, which are rarely bothered by the police.

ROAD CONDITIONS

Although Brazil's federal highways were, for the most part, built fairly recently (between 1964 and 1976), maintenance on them was nearly nonexistent in the 1980s. The country's highway department estimates that 40% of the federal highways (including those with either the designation "BR" or a state abbreviation such as "RJ" or "SP"), which constitute 70% of Brazil's total road system, are in a dangerous state of disrepair. Evidence of this is everywhere: potholes, lack of signage, inadequate shoulders, etc. Landslides and flooding after heavy rains are frequent and at times shut down entire stretches of key highways. Increasing traffic adds to the system's woes, as does the fact that neither speed limits nor the most basic rules of safety seem to figure in the national psyche. The worst offenders are bus and truck drivers. For these reasons, if you drive, do so with the utmost caution.

ROAD MAPS

Quatro Rodas offers atlases, books, and maps of different sizes for states, regions, and cities. They are *the* name for maps of Brazil. If you're a beach aficionado, look for this company's beautiful, four-color book of topographical maps of all the nation's beaches.

RULES OF THE ROAD

Brazilians drive on the right, and in general, traffic laws are the same as those in the United States. The use of seat belts is mandatory. The national speed limit is 80 kph (48 mph), but is seldom observed. In theory, foreign drivers licenses are acceptable. In practice, however, police (particularly highway police) have been known to claim that driving with a foreign license is a violation in order to shake down drivers for bribes. It's best to **get an international driver's license,** which is seldom challenged. If you do get a ticket for some sort of violation—real or imagined—don't argue. And plan to spend longer than you want settling it.

CHILDREN IN BRAZIL

Children are welcomed in hotels and in restaurants, especially on weekends, when local families often go out for lunch. Having yours along may prove to be your special ticket to meeting the locals.

Let older children join in on planning as you outline your trip. **Scout your library for picture books, story books, and maps about places you'll be going.** Try to **explain the concept of foreign language**; some kids, who may have just learned to talk, are thrown when they can't understand strangers and strangers can't understand them. On sightseeing days try to **schedule activities of special interest to your children.** If you're renting a car don't forget to **arrange for a car seat** when you reserve.

FLYING

If your children are two or older **ask about children's airfares.** As a rule, infants under two not occupying a seat fly at greatly reduced fares or even for free. When booking **confirm carry-on allowances** if you're traveling with infants. In general, for babies charged 10% of the adult fare, you're allowed one carry-on bag and a collapsible stroller; if the flight is full the stroller may have to be checked or you may be limited to less.

Experts agree that it's a good idea to use safety seats aloft for children weighing less than 40 pounds. Airlines set their own policies: U.S. carriers usually require that the child be ticketed, even if he or she is young enough to ride free, since the safety seats must be strapped into regular seats. Do **check your airline's policy about using safety seats during take-off and landing.** And since safety seats aren't allowed just everywhere in the plane, get your seat assignments early.

When reserving, **request children's meals or a freestanding bassinet** if you need them. But note that bulkhead seats, where you must sit to use the bassinet, may lack an overhead bin or storage space on the floor.

LODGING

Many hotels in Brazil allow children under a certain age to stay in their parents' room at no extra charge. Others charge for them as extra adults; be sure to **find out the cutoff age for children's discounts.**

PRECAUTIONS

Any person under the age of 18 who isn't traveling with both parents or legal guardian(s) must provide a notarized letter of consent signed by the non-accompanying parent or guardian. The notarized letter must be authenticated by the Brazilian embassy or consulate and translated into Portuguese.

Children must have all their inoculations up to date (those between the ages of 3 months and 6 years must have an international polio vaccination certificate) before leaving home. Make sure that health precautions, such as what to drink and eat, are applied to the whole family. Not cramming too much into each day will keep the whole family healthier while on the road.

SIGHTS & ATTRACTIONS

Places that are especially good for children are indicated by a rubber duckie icon in the margin.

SUPPLIES & EQUIPMENT

Pack things to keep your children busy while traveling. For children of reading age, **bring books from home**; locally, literature for kids in English is hard to find.

COMPUTERS ON THE ROAD

If you're traveling with a laptop, carry a spare battery, a universal adapter plug, and a converter if your computer isn't dual voltage. **Ask about electrical surges** before plugging in your computer. **Keep your disks out of the sun** and **avoid excessive heat for both your computer and disks.** In Brazil, carrying a laptop computer signals wealth and could make you a target for thieves; **conceal your laptop in a generic bag, and keep it close to you at all times.**

Internet access is surprisingly widespread. In addition to business centers in luxury hotels and full-fledged cybercafés, look for computers set up in telephone offices. Rates range from $1 to $10 an hour. Dial-up speeds are variable, though they tend toward the sluggish—don't expect to find a T1.

CONCIERGES

Concierges, found in many urban hotels, can help you with theater tickets and dinner reservations. A good one with connections—which are always key in Brazil—may be able to get you seats for a hot show or a table at the restaurant of the moment. You can also turn to your concierge for help with travel arrangements, sightseeing plans, services ranging from aromatherapy to zipper repair, and emergencies. **Always tip** a concierge who has been of assistance.

CONSUMER PROTECTION

Whenever shopping or buying travel services in Brazil, **pay with a major credit card** so you can cancel payment or get reimbursed if there's a problem. If you're doing business with a particular company for the first time, **contact your local Better Business Bureau and the attorney general's offices** in your state and the company's home state, as well. Have any complaints been filed? Finally, if you're buying a package or tour, always **consider travel insurance** that includes default coverage (☞ Insurance, *below*).

➤ LOCAL BBBs: **Council of Better Business Bureaus** (✉ 4200 Wilson Blvd., Suite 800, Arlington, VA 22203, ☎ 703/276–0100, FAX 703/525–8277).

CRUISE TRAVEL

Cruise itineraries to Brazil change from ship to ship, from line to line (or tour operator to tour operator), and from year to year, so contact a travel agent or the cruise company to get the most recent information. In the past, the tour operator Abercrombie & Kent has offered a 3,200-km (2,000-mi) Amazon River tour. Crystal Cruises has had 14- and 16-day trips from Barbados to Buenos Aires and from Buenos Aires to Puerto Rico that may include Fortaleza, Rio de Janeiro, and Florianópolis. On its cruise from Buenos Aires to Miami, Cunard often makes stops in Florianópolis, Rio, Salvador, Belém, Barbados, Puerto Rico, and St. Thomas. Holland America has offered a whopping 33-day South American itinerary that departs from Ft. Lauderdale, travels through the Panama Canal, rounds Cape Horn, and culminates in Rio. One of Princess Cruise's 12-day tours departs from Manaus and calls at Boca de Valeria and Santarém before continuing to Trinidad, Caracas, and Curaçao and ending in Puerto Rico. Royal Olympic has offered a similar 13-day cruise that begins in Manaus and proceeds to Boca da Valeria, Santarém, Trinidad, St. Vincent, Antigua, St. Thomas, and Ft. Lauderdale. Silversea has had cruises that round Cape Horn, stop in the Falkland Islands, proceed up the coast of Argentina, and end in Brazil. Other operators who have offered Brazilian cruises in the past include Amazon Tours and Cruises, Radisson Seven Seas Cruises, and Seabourne Cruise Lines.

➤ CRUISE LINES: **Abercrombie & Kent** (☎ 800/323–7308), **Amazon Tours and Cruises** (☎ 800/423–2791), **Crystal Cruises** (☎ 800/446–6620), **Cunard** (☎ 800/5–CUNARD), **Holland America Line** (☎ 800/426–0327), **Princess Cruises and Tours** (☎

800/421–0522), **Radisson Seven Seas Cruises** (☎ 800/285–1835), **Royal Olympic Cruises** (☎ 800/872–6400), **Seabourne Cruise Lines** (☎ 800/929–9595), **Silversea Cruises**, (☎ 800/277–6655).

CUSTOMS & DUTIES

When shopping, **keep receipts** for all purchases. Upon reentering the country, **be ready to show customs officials what you've bought.** If you feel a duty is incorrect or object to the way your clearance was handled, note the inspector's badge number and ask to see a supervisor. If the problem isn't resolved, write to the appropriate authorities, beginning with the port director at your point of entry.

IN BRAZIL

Formerly strict import controls have been substantially liberalized as part of the Brazilian government's efforts to open up the nation's economy to competition. In addition to personal items, you're now permitted to bring in, duty-free, up to $500 worth of gifts purchased abroad, including up to 2 liters of liquor. If you plan to bring in plants, you may do so only with documentation authenticated by the consular service.

IN AUSTRALIA

Australia residents who are 18 or older may bring home $A400 worth of souvenirs and gifts (including jewelry), 250 cigarettes or 250 grams of tobacco, and 1,125 ml of alcohol (including wine, beer, and spirits). Residents under 18 may bring back $A200 worth of goods. Prohibited items include meat products. Seeds, plants, and fruits need to be declared upon arrival.

➤ INFORMATION: **Australian Customs Service** (Regional Director, ✉ Box 8, Sydney, NSW 2001, ☎ 02/9213–2000, FAX 02/9213–4000).

IN CANADA

Canadian residents who have been out of Canada for at least 7 days may bring home C$500 worth of goods duty-free. If you've been away less than 7 days but more than 48 hours, the duty-free allowance drops to C$200; if your trip lasts 24–48 hours, the allowance is C$50. You may not pool allowances with family members. Goods claimed under the C$500 exemption may follow you by mail; those claimed under the lesser exemptions must accompany you. Alcohol and tobacco products may be included in the 7-day and 48-hour exemptions but not in the 24-hour exemption. If you meet the age requirements of the province or territory through which you reenter Canada, you may bring in, duty-free, 1.14 liters (40 imperial ounces) of wine or liquor or 24 12-ounce cans or bottles of beer or ale. If you are 16 or older you may bring in, duty-free, 200 cigarettes and 50 cigars. Check ahead of time with Revenue Canada or the Department of Agriculture for policies regarding meat products, seeds, plants, and fruits.

You may send an unlimited number of gifts worth up to C$60 each duty-free to Canada. Label the package UNSOLICITED GIFT—VALUE UNDER $60. Alcohol and tobacco are excluded.

➤ INFORMATION: **Revenue Canada** (✉ 2265 St. Laurent Blvd. S, Ottawa, Ontario K1G 4K3, ☎ 613/993–0534; 800/461–9999 in Canada).

IN NEW ZEALAND

Homeward-bound residents 17 or older may bring back $700 worth of souvenirs and gifts. Your duty-free allowance also includes 4.5 liters of wine or beer; one 1,125-ml bottle of spirits; and either 200 cigarettes, 250 grams of tobacco, 50 cigars, or a combination of the three up to 250 grams. Prohibited items include meat products, seeds, plants, and fruits.

➤ INFORMATION: **New Zealand Customs** (Custom House, ✉ 50 Anzac Ave., Box 29, Auckland, New Zealand, ☎ 09/359–6655, FAX 09/359–6732).

IN THE U.K.

From countries outside the EU, including Brazil, you may bring home, duty-free, 200 cigarettes or 50 cigars; 1 liter of spirits or 2 liters of fortified or sparkling wine or liqueurs; 2 liters of still table wine; 60 ml of perfume; 250 ml of toilet water; plus £136 worth of other goods, including gifts and souvenirs. If returning from outside the EU, prohibited items

SMART TRAVEL TIPS A TO Z

include meat products, seeds, plants, and fruits.

➤ INFORMATION: **HM Customs and Excise** (⊠ Dorset House, Stamford St., Bromley Kent BR1 1XX, ☎ 020/7202–4227).

IN THE U.S.

U.S. residents who have been out of the country for at least 48 hours (and who have not used the $400 allowance or any part of it in the past 30 days) may bring home $400 worth of foreign goods duty-free.

U.S. residents 21 and older may bring back 1 liter of alcohol duty-free. In addition, regardless of your age, you are allowed 200 cigarettes and 100 non-Cuban cigars. Antiques, which the U.S. Customs Service defines as objects more than 100 years old, enter duty-free, as do original works of art done entirely by hand, including paintings, drawings, and sculptures.

You may also send packages home duty-free: up to $200 worth of goods for personal use, with a limit of one parcel per addressee per day (and no alcohol or tobacco products or perfume worth more than $5); label the package PERSONAL USE and attach a list of its contents and their retail value. Do not label the package UNSOLICITED GIFT or your duty-free exemption will drop to $100. Mailed items do not affect your duty-free allowance on your return.

➤ INFORMATION: **U.S. Customs Service** (inquiries, ⊠ 1300 Pennsylvania Ave. NW, Washington, DC 20229, ☎ 202/927–6724; complaints, ⊠ Office of Regulations and Rulings, 1300 Pennsylvania Ave. NW, Washington, DC 20229; registration of equipment, ⊠ Registration Information, 1300 Pennsylvania Ave. NW, Washington, DC 20229, ☎ 202/927–0540).

DINING

The restaurants (all of which are indicated by an ✕) that we list are the cream of the crop in each price category. Properties indicated by an ✕⊡ are lodging establishments whose restaurant warrants a special trip. Price categories are as follows:

CATEGORY	COST*
$$$$	over $35
$$$	$25–$35
$$	$15–$25
$	under $15

per person for an appetizer, entrée, and dessert, excluding tax, tip, and beverages

MEALS & MEALTIMES

Mealtimes vary according to locale. In Rio and São Paulo, lunch and dinner are served later than in the United States. In restaurants, lunch usually starts around 1 and can last until 3. Dinner is always eaten after 8, and in many cases, not until 10. In Minas Gerais, the northeast, and smaller towns in general, dinner and lunch are taken at roughly the same time as in the States.

Note that you'll be hard-pressed to find breakfast outside a hotel restaurant; it's just not a Brazilian thing. At lunch and dinner, portions are large. Often a single dish will easily feed two people; no one will be the least surprised if you order one entrée and two plates. In addition, some restaurants automatically bring a *couberto* (an appetizer course of such items as bread, cheese or pâté, olives, quail eggs, and the like). You'll be charged extra for this, and you're perfectly within your rights to send it back if you don't want it. (For details on the country's many food and drink specialties, *see* Dining *in* Pleasures and Pastimes *in* Chapter 1 and at the start of each chapter.)

RESERVATIONS & DRESS

Reservations are always a good idea: we mention them only when they're essential or aren't accepted. Book as far ahead as you can, and reconfirm as soon as you arrive. We mention dress only when men are required to wear a jacket or a jacket and tie.

DISABILITIES & ACCESSIBILITY

Although international chain hotels in large cities have some suitable rooms and it's easy to hire private cars and drivers for excursions, Brazil isn't very well equipped to handle travelers with disabilities. There are few ramps and curb cuts, and it takes effort and planning to negotiate cobbled city streets, get around museums and other buildings, and explore the countryside. City centers such as Rio de Janeiro are the most comfortable to visit.

LODGING

When discussing accessibility with an operator or reservations agent **ask hard questions.** Are there any stairs, inside *or* out? Are there grab bars next to the toilet *and* in the shower/tub? How wide is the doorway to the room? To the bathroom? For the most extensive facilities meeting the latest legal specifications **opt for newer accommodations.**

TRANSPORTATION

➤ COMPLAINTS: **Disability Rights Section** (✉ U.S. Department of Justice, Civil Rights Division, Box 66738, Washington, DC 20035-6738, ☎ 202/514–0301; 800/514–0301; 202/514–0301 TTY; 800/514–0301 TTY; FAX 202/307–1198) for general complaints, **Aviation Consumer Protection Division** (☞ Air Travel, *above*) for airline-related problems, **Civil Rights Office** (✉ U.S. Department of Transportation, Departmental Office of Civil Rights, S-30, 400 7th St. SW, Room 10215, Washington, DC 20590, ☎ 202/366–4648, FAX 202/366–9371) for problems with surface transportation.

TRAVEL AGENCIES

Although the Americans with Disabilities Act requires that U.S. travel firms serve the needs of all travelers, some agencies specialize in working with people with disabilities.

➤ TRAVELERS WITH MOBILITY PROBLEMS: **Access Adventures** (✉ 206 Chestnut Ridge Rd., Rochester, NY 14624, ☎ 716/889–9096), run by a former physical-rehabilitation counselor; **CareVacations** (✉ 5-5110 50th Ave., Leduc, Alberta T9E 6V4, ☎ 780/986–6404 or 877/478–7827, FAX 780/986–8332), which has group tours and is especially helpful with cruise vacations; **Flying Wheels Travel** (✉ 143 W. Bridge St., Box 382, Owatonna, MN 55060, ☎ 507/451–5005 or 800/535–6790, FAX 507/451–1685); **Hinsdale Travel Service** (✉ 201 E. Ogden Ave., Suite 100, Hinsdale, IL 60521, ☎ 630/325–1335, FAX 630/325–1342).

DISCOUNTS & DEALS

Be a smart shopper and **compare all your options** before making decisions. A plane ticket bought with a promotional coupon from travel clubs, coupon books, and direct-mail offers may not be cheaper than the least expensive fare from a discount ticket agency. And always keep in mind that what you get is just as important as what you save.

DISCOUNT RESERVATIONS

To save money **look into discount-reservations services** with toll-free numbers, which use their buying power to get a better price on hotels, airline tickets, even car rentals. When booking a room, always **call the hotel's local toll-free number** (if one is available) rather than the central reservations number—you'll often get a better price. Always ask about special packages or corporate rates.

When shopping for the best deal on hotels and car rentals **look for guaranteed exchange rates,** which protect you against a falling dollar. With your rate locked in, you won't pay more, even if the price goes up in the local currency.

➤ AIRLINE TICKETS: ☎ 800/FLY-4–LESS. ➤ HOTEL ROOMS: **Steigenberger Reservation Service** (☎ 800/223–5652).

PACKAGE DEALS

Don't confuse packages and guided tours. When you buy a package, you travel on your own, just as though you had planned the trip yourself.

ECOTOURISM

Ecotourism is a fast-growing and ever more popular form of tourism. However, as with any industry, some operators are more trustworthy than others. In addition to those named throughout this guide, the Brazilian Institute of Ecotourism (IEB) is greatly respected and is a fine resource for special-interest tours.

➤ INFORMATION: **Brazilian Institute of Ecotourism** (✉ Rua Wandderlei 750, São Paulo, ☎ FAX 011/262–2069).

ELECTRICITY

The current in Brazil isn't regulated: In São Paulo and Rio, it's 110 or 120 volts, 60 cycles alternating current (the same as in the United States and Canada); in Recife and Brasília it's 220 volts (the same as in Europe); and in Manaus and Salvador, it's 127 volts. **Bring a converter.** Wall outlets take Continental-type plugs, with two round prongs. **Consider buying a universal adapter;** the Swiss-Army-knife of adapters, a universal has several types of plugs in one handy unit. If your appliances are dual-voltage (as many laptops are), you'll need only an adapter. Don't use 110-volt outlets, marked FOR SHAVERS ONLY, for high-wattage appliances such as blow-dryers.

EMBASSIES & CONSULATES

➤ IN AUSTRALIA: **Brazilian Embassy** (✉ Box 1540, Canberra, ACT 2601, ☎ 616/273–2372).

➤ IN BRAZIL: **American Embassy** (✉ Lote 3, Unit 3500, Av. das Nações, 70403-900, Brasília, DF, ☎ 061/321-7272), **Australian Embassy** (✉ SES, Quadra 09 Conjunto 16, Casa 01, 70469-900, Brasília, DF, ☎ 061/248–5569), **British Embassy** (✉ SES, Quadra 801, Loto 8, Conjunto K, 70408-900, Brasília, DF, ☎ 061/225–2710), **Canadian Embassy** (✉ SES, Av. das Nações, Lote 16, 70410-900, Brasília, DF, ☎ 061/321–2171), **New Zealand Consulate-General** (✉ Rua Hungria 888-6, 01455, São Paulo, SP, ☎ 011/212–2288).

➤ IN CANADA: **Brazilian Embassy** (✉ 450 Wilbrod St., Ottawa, Ontario, K1P 6M8, ☎ 613/237–1090).

➤ IN THE U.K.: **Brazilian Embassy** (✉ 32 Green St., London, W1Y 4AT, ☎ 020/7499–0877).

➤ IN THE U.S: **Brazilian Embassy** (✉ 3006 Massachusetts Ave. NW, Washington, DC 20008, ☎ 202/745–2700).

FURTHER READING

On the nonfiction front, Joseph A. Page provides a fascinating, highly readable overview of Brazilian history and culture in his book *The Brazilians.* Along the same lines is Marshall C. Eakin's *Brazil: The Once and Future Country.* Social anthropologist Claude Lévi-Strauss discusses his research of Amazonian peoples in *Tristes Tropiques,* a book that's part travelogue, part scientific notebook—with many interesting observations and anecdotes. Chris McGowan's *The Brazilian Sound: Samba, Bossa Nova, and the Popular Music of Brazil* provides an overview of the country's 20th-century music. Christoper Idone's *Brazil: A Cook's Tour* has more than 100 color photos and 100 recipes.

Fiction lovers should try John Grisham's captivating *The Testament,* in which a lawyer voyages to the Pantanal Wetlands to search for a missionary who has inherited a fortune. In *Brazil,* John Updike puts a Rio twist on the classic tale of Tristan and Isolde. Several Jorge Amado titles, which are usually set in his native Bahia, are available in English, including *Dona Flor and Her Two Husbands; Gabriela, Clove and Cinnamon;* and *The War of the Saints.*

GAY & LESBIAN TRAVEL

Brazil is South America's most popular destination for gay and lesbian travelers, and major cities such as Rio de Janeiro, São Paulo, and Salvador have numerous gay bars, organizations, and publications. Outside these destinations, however, gay and lesbian travel can be difficult due to conservative religious and cultural norms. Use discretion and common sense about public displays of affection.

➤ GAY- AND LESBIAN-FRIENDLY TRAVEL AGENCIES: **Different Roads Travel** (✉ 8383 Wilshire Blvd., Suite 902, Beverly Hills, CA 90211, ☎ 323/651–5557 or 800/429–8747, FAX 323/651–3678); **Kennedy Travel** (✉ 314 Jericho Turnpike, Floral Park, NY 11001, ☎ 516/352–4888 or 800/237–7433, FAX 516/354–8849); **Now Voyager** (✉ 4406 18th St., San Francisco, CA 94114, ☎ 415/626–1169 or 800/255–6951, FAX 415/626–8626); **Skylink Travel and Tour** (✉ 1006 Mendocino Ave., Santa Rosa, CA 95401, ☎ 707/546–9888 or 800/225–5759, FAX 707/546–9891), serving lesbian travelers.

HEALTH

DIVERS' ALERT

Don't fly within 24 hours of scuba diving. Neophyte divers should have a complete physical exam before undertaking a dive. If you have travel insurance that covers evacuations, **make sure your policy applies to scuba-related injuries,** as not all companies provide this coverage.

FOOD & DRINK

If you've got just two weeks, you don't want to waste a minute stuck in your hotel room battling Montezuma's Revenge, so **watch what you eat and drink**—on and off the beaten path. **Drink only bottled water** or water that has been boiled for at least 20 minutes. Stay away from ice, uncooked food, and unpasteurized milk and milk products. Peel or thoroughly wash fresh fruits and vegetables.

MEDICAL PLANS

No one plans to get sick while traveling, but it happens, so **consider signing up with a medical-assistance company.** Members get doctor referrals, emergency evacuation or repatriation, hot lines for medical consultation, cash for emergencies, and other assistance.

➤ MEDICAL-ASSISTANCE COMPANIES: **AEA International SOS** (✉ 8 Neshaminy Interplex, Suite 207, Trevose, PA 19053, ☎ 215/245–4707 or 800/523–6586, FAX 215/244–9617; ✉ 12 Chemin Riantbosson, 1217 Meyrin 1, Geneva, Switzerland, ☎ 4122/785–6464, FAX 4122/785–6424; ✉ 331 N. Bridge Rd., 17-00, Odeon Towers, Singapore 188720, ☎ 65/338–7800, FAX 65/338–7611).

OVER-THE-COUNTER REMEDIES

Mild cases of diarrhea may respond to Imodium (known generically as loperamide) or Pepto-Bismol (not as strong), both of which can be purchased over the counter; paregoric, another antidiarrheal agent, doesn't require a doctor's prescription in South America. Drink plenty of purified water or *chá* (tea)— *camomila* (chamomile) is a good folk remedy. In severe cases, rehydrate yourself with a salt–sugar solution: ½ teaspoon *sal* (salt), and 4 tablespoons *açúcar* (sugar) per quart of *agua* (water). The word for aspirin is *aspirinha*; Tylenol is pronounced *tee-luh-nawl.*

PESTS & OTHER HAZARDS

Bichos de pé, parasites found in areas where pigs, chickens, and dogs run free, embed themselves in humans' feet. To avoid these parasites, never walk barefoot in areas where animals are loose.

Sunshine, limes, and skin don't mix well. The oil in lime skin juice, if left on human skin and exposed to the sun, will burn and scar. If you're using lime and will be exposed to a lot of sun, be sure to wash well with soap and water. Should spots appear on skin areas that have been exposed, pharmacies will know which creams work best to heal the burns. (Note that affected areas shouldn't be exposed to the sun for three months following the burn.)

A 1998 publication issued by Brazil's Ministry of Health estimated that there were as many as 500,000 cases of AIDS and HIV in the country. Aside from the obvious safe-sex precautions, keep in mind that Brazil's blood supply isn't, overall, subject to the same intense screening as it is in North America, western Europe, Australia, or New Zealand. If you need a transfusion and circumstances permit it, ask that the blood be screened. Insulin-dependent diabetics or those who require injections should take the appropriate supplies with them—syringes, needles, disinfectants—enough to last the trip. In addition, you might want to resist the temptation to get a new tattoo or body piercing while you're in Brazil.

Women traveling for an extended time in Brazil may find that their menstrual cycles are thrown off schedule. This is due to crossing the equator and shouldn't be cause for undue alarm. Home pregnancy tests are available in pharmacies but are more expensive and less reliable than blood tests by laboratories that are easily located in big cities.

SMART TRAVEL TIPS A TO Z

SHOTS & MEDICATIONS

All travelers should have up-to-date tetanus boosters, and a hepatitis A inoculation can prevent one of the most common intestinal infections. If you're heading to tropical regions, you should get yellow fever shots, particularly if you're traveling overland from a yellow-fever country (Peru, Bolivia, etc.). Children must have current inoculations against measles, mumps, rubella, and polio.

According to the Centers for Disease Control (CDC) there's a limited risk of cholera, typhoid, malaria, hepatitis B, dengue, and chagas. While a few of these can be contracted in any area, most cases occur in jungle areas. If you plan to visit remote regions or stay for more than six weeks, **check with the CDC's International Travelers' Hot Line.** In areas with malaria and dengue, which are both carried by mosquitoes, take mosquito nets, wear clothing that covers the body, apply repellent containing DEET, and use a spray against flying insects in living and sleeping areas. The hot line recommends chloroquine (analen) as an antimalarial agent. (Note that in parts of northern Brazil, a particularly aggressive strain of malaria has become resistant to chloroquine and may be treated with mefloquine, an expensive alternative that can also have some rather unpleasant side effects—from headaches, nausea, and dizziness to psychosis, convulsions, and hallucinations.) No vaccine exists against dengue.

➤ HEALTH WARNINGS: **National Centers for Disease Control** (National Center for Infectious Diseases, Division of Quarantine, Traveler's Health Section, ✉ 1600 Clifton Rd. NE, M/S E-03, Atlanta, GA 30333, ☎ 888/232–3228, FAX 888/232–3299).

HOLIDAYS

Major national holidays include: New Year's Day (Jan. 1); Epiphany (Jan. 6); Carnaval, the week preceding Ash Wednesday (which falls on March 8 in 2000 and Feb. 28 in 2001), Good Friday (Apr. 21, 2000; Apr. 13, 2001); Easter (Apr. 23, 2000; Apr. 15, 2001), Tiradentes Day (Apr. 21), Labor Day (May 1), Corpus Christi (June 22, 2000; June 14, 2001);

Independence Day (Sept. 7); Our Lady of Aparecida Day (Oct. 12); All Souls' Day (Nov. 1); Declaration of the Republic Day (Nov. 15); Christmas (Dec. 25).

INSURANCE

The most useful travel insurance plan is a comprehensive policy that includes coverage for trip cancellation and interruption, default, trip delay, and medical expenses (with a waiver for preexisting conditions). Without insurance you'll lose all or most of your money if you cancel your trip, regardless of the reason. Default insurance covers you if your tour operator, airline, or cruise line goes out of business. Trip-delay covers expenses that arise because of bad weather or mechanical delays. Study the fine print when comparing policies.

If you're traveling internationally, a key component of travel insurance is coverage for medical bills incurred if you get sick on the road. Such expenses are not generally covered by Medicare or private policies. U.K. residents can buy a travel insurance policy valid for most vacations taken during the year in which it's purchased (but check pre-existing-condition coverage). British and Australian citizens need extra medical coverage when traveling overseas.

Always **buy travel policies directly from the insurance company**; if you buy it from a cruise line, airline, or tour operator that goes out of business you probably won't be covered for the agency or operator's default, a major risk. Before you make any purchase **review your existing health and home-owner's policies** to find what they cover away from home.

➤ TRAVEL INSURERS: In the United States **Access America** (✉ 6600 W. Broad St., Richmond, VA 23230, ☎ 804/285–3300 or 800/284–8300), **Travel Guard International** (✉ 1145 Clark St., Stevens Point, WI 54481, ☎ 715/345–0505 or 800/826–1300). In Canada **Voyager Insurance** (✉ 44 Peel Center Dr., Brampton, Ontario L6T 4M8, ☎ 905/791–8700; 800/668–4342 in Canada).

➤ INSURANCE INFORMATION: In the United Kingdom the **Association of British Insurers** (⊠ 51–55 Gresham St., London EC2V 7HQ, ☎ 020/7600–3333, ℻ 0171/696–8999). In Australia the **Insurance Council of Australia** (☎ 03/9614–1077, ℻ 03/9614–7924).

LANGUAGE, CULTURE, AND ETIQUETTE

The language in Brazil is Portuguese, not Spanish, and Brazilians will appreciate it if you know the difference. The two languages are distinct, but common origins mean that many words are similar, and fluent speakers of Spanish will be able to make themselves understood. English is spoken among educated Brazilians and, in general, by at least some of the staff at hotels, tour operators, and travel agencies. Store clerks and waiters may have a smattering of English; taxi and bus drivers won't. As in many places throughout the world, you're more likely to find English-speaking locals in major cities than in small towns or the countryside.

Although Brazil is a predominately Catholic country, in many places there's an anything-goes outlook. As a rule, coastal areas (particularly Rio and parts of the northeast) are considerably less conservative than inland areas and those throughout the south. People dress nicely to enter churches, and hats are frowned upon during mass.

Whether they tend toward the conservative or the risque, Brazilians are a very friendly lot. Don't be afraid to smile in the streets, ask for directions, or strike up a conversation with a local (be aware, however, that a Brazilian may give you false directions before admitting that he or she doesn't know where to point you). The slower pace of life in much of the country reflects an unwavering appreciation of family and friendship (as well as a respect for the heat); knowing this will help you understand why things may take a little longer to get done.

Throughout the country, use the "thumbs up" gesture to indicate that something is OK. The gesture created by making a circle with your thumb and index finger and holding your other fingers up in the air has a very rude meaning.

LODGING

When you consider your lodgings in Brazil, add these three terms to your vocabulary: *pousada* (inn), *fazenda* (farm), and "flat" or "block" hotel (apartment-hotel). Flat hotels are popular with Brazilians, particularly with families and groups and particularly in cities. Some have amenities such as pools, but for most folks, their biggest draw is affordability: with kitchen facilities and room for a group, flat hotels offer more for the money.

In the hinterlands, it's good to **look at any room before accepting it;** expense is no guarantee of charm or cleanliness, and accommodations can vary dramatically within one hotel. Also, **be sure to check the shower:** some hotels have electric-powered shower heads, rather than central hot-water heaters. In theory, you can adjust both the water's heat and its pressure. In practice, if you want hot water, you have to turn the water pressure down; if you want pressure, expect a brisk rinse. Careful! Don't adjust the power when you're under the water—you can get a little shock.

If you ask for a double room, you'll get a room for two people, but you're not guaranteed a double mattress. If you'd like to avoid twin beds, **ask for a cama de casal** ("couple's bed"; no wedding ring seems to be required).

The lodgings (all indicated with 🏨) that we list are the cream of the crop in each price category. We always list the facilities that are available—but we don't specify whether they cost extra: When pricing accommodations, always ask what's included. All hotels listed have private bath unless otherwise noted. Properties indicated by ✕🏨 are lodging establishments whose restaurant warrants a special trip.

Assume that hotels operate on the European Plan (**EP,** with no meals) unless we specify that they're all-inclusive (including all meals and most activities) or use the Breakfast Plan (**BP,** with a full breakfast daily),

SMART TRAVEL TIPS A TO Z

Continental Plan (**CP,** with a Continental breakfast daily), or Modified American Plan (**MAP,** with breakfast and dinner daily). For destination-specific information, *see* Lodging *in* Pleasures and Pastimes at the start of each chapter. Price categories are as follows:

CATEGORY	COST*
$$$$	over $150
$$$	$100–$150
$$	$50–$100
$	under $50

for a double room in high season, excluding taxes

APARTMENT & VILLA RENTALS

If you want a home base that's roomy enough for a family and comes with cooking facilities **consider a furnished rental.** These can save you money, especially if you're traveling with a group. Home-exchange directories sometimes list rentals as well as exchanges.

➤ INTERNATIONAL AGENTS: **Hideaways International** (✉ 767 Islington St., Portsmouth, NH 03801, ☎ 603/430–4433 or 800/843–4433, FAX 603/430–4444; membership $99).

HOSTELS

No matter what your age you can **save on lodging costs by staying at hostels.** There are about 100 hostels scattered across Brazil, all of them affiliated with Hostelling International (HI). Many Brazilian hostels' names are preceded by the letters "AJ" (Albergues de Juventude). The Federação Brasileira dos Albergues de Juventude (FBJA; Brazilian Federation of Youth Hostels) is based in Rio.

Membership in any HI national hostel association, open to travelers of all ages, allows you to stay in HI-affiliated hostels at member rates (one-year membership is about $25 for adults; hostels run about $10–$25 per night). Members also have priority if the hostel is full; they're eligible for discounts around the world, even on rail and bus travel in some countries.

➤ ORGANIZATIONS: **Australian Youth Hostel Association** (✉ 10 Mallett St., Camperdown, NSW 2050, ☎ 02/9565–1699, FAX 02/9565–1325),

Federação Brasileira dos Albergues de Juventude (✉ Rua da Assembleia 10, Sala 1211, Centro, Rio De Janeiro, 20011 RJ, ☎ 021/531–2234 or 021/531–1302), **Hostelling International—American Youth Hostels** (✉ 733 15th St. NW, Suite 840, Washington, DC 20005, ☎ 202/783–6161, FAX 202/783–6171), **Hostelling International—Canada** (✉ 400–205 Catherine St., Ottawa, Ontario K2P 1C3, ☎ 613/237–7884, FAX 613/237–7868), **Youth Hostel Association of England and Wales** (✉ Trevelyan House, 8 St. Stephen's Hill, St. Albans, Hertfordshire AL1 2DY, ☎ 01727/855215 or 01727/845047, FAX 01727/844126), **Youth Hostels Association of New Zealand** (✉ Box 436, Christchurch, New Zealand, ☎ 03/379–9970, FAX 03/365–4476).

Membership in the U.S. $25, in Canada C$26.75, in the U.K. £9.30, in Australia $44, in New Zealand $24.

HOTELS

Hotels listed with EMBRATUR, Brazil's national tourist board, are rated using stars. Note, however, that the number of stars awarded appears to be based strictly on the number of amenities, without taking into account intangibles such as service and atmosphere.

Carnaval (Carnival), the year's principal festival, occurs during the four days preceding Ash Wednesday. For top hotels in Rio, Salvador, and Recife—the three leading Carnaval cities—you must make reservations a year in advance. Hotel rates rise 20% on average for Carnaval. Not as well known outside Brazil but equally impressive is Rio's New Year's Eve celebration. More than a million people gather along Copacabana Beach for a massive fireworks display and to honor the sea goddess Iemanjá. To ensure a room, book at least six months in advance.

Hotels accept credit cards for payment, but first ask if there's a discount for cash. Try to bargain hard for a cash-on-the-barrel discount, then pay in local currency.

➤ TOLL-FREE NUMBERS: **Best Western** (☎ 800/528–1234), **Hilton** (☎ 800/

445–8667), **Holiday Inn** (☎ 800/ 465–4329), **Inter-Continental** (☎ 800/327–0200), **Le Meridien** (☎ 800/ 543–4300), **Renaissance Hotels & Resorts** (☎ 800/468–3571), **Sheraton** (☎ 800/325–3535).

MAIL & SHIPPING

Post offices are called *correios,* and branches are marked by the name and a logo that looks something like two interlocked fingers; most are open weekdays 8–5 and Saturday until noon. Mailboxes are small yellow boxes marked CORREIOS that sit atop metal pedestals on street corners. Airmail from Brazil takes at least 10 or more days to reach the United States, possibly longer to Canada and the United Kingdom, definitely longer to Australia and New Zealand.

OVERNIGHT SERVICES

Brazil has both national and international express mail service, the price of which varies according to the weight of the package and the destination. International express mail companies operating out of Brazil include Federal Express and DHL.

POSTAL RATES

An airmail letter from Brazil to the United States and most parts of Europe, including the United Kingdom, costs about $1. Aerograms and postcards cost the same.

RECEIVING MAIL

Mail can be addressed to "poste restante" and sent to any major post office. The address must include the code for that particular branch. American Express will hold mail for its cardholders.

MONEY MATTERS

The mid-1994 anti-inflation program that accompanied the currency change resulted in a strong real (R$; plural: *reais,* though it's sometimes seen as *reals*) against the dollar, and in general terms, the country became more expensive. Recent economic developments, however, have seen the dollar and the pound strengthen significantly against the real. Still the winds of change blow fast in this part of the world—and they might take the good exchange rates with them; check before you travel.

Top hotels in Rio and São Paulo go for more than $200 a night, and meals can—but do not have to—cost as much. Outside Brazil's two largest cities and Brasília, prices for food and lodging tend to drop considerably. Self-service salad bars where you pay per weight (per kilo) are inexpensive alternatives in all cities and towns, though be sure to choose carefully among them. Taxis can be pricey. City buses, subways, and long-distance buses are all inexpensive; plane fares definitely aren't.

Due to the relative instability of the real, we don't list specific admission prices. The word "admission" appears where an entry fee is charged, and the word "free" where one is not. Occasionally, we cite sample prices for cab fares and sports-equipment rental; these are in U.S. dollars based on exchange rates at press time.

ATMS

Nearly all the nation's major banks have automated teller machines. MasterCard and Cirrus are rarely accepted (some airport Banco Itau ATMs are linked to Cirrus); Visa and Plus cards are. American Express card holders can make withdrawals at most Bradesco ATMs marked 24 HORAS. To be on the safe side, carry a variety of cards. Note also that if your PIN is more than four digits long and/or uses letters instead of numbers, it might not work; talk to your bank. Finally, for your card to function on some ATMs, you may need to hit a screen command that roughly translates to "foreign client."

ATM Locations: **MASTERCARD CIRRUS** (☎ 800/424–7787). **VISA PLUS** (☎ 800/843–7587).

CREDIT CARDS

In Brazil's largest cities and leading tourist centers, restaurants, hotels, and shops accept major international credit cards. Off the beaten track, you may have more difficulty using them. Many gas stations in rural Brazil don't take credit cards.

For costly items use your credit card whenever possible—you'll come out ahead, whether the exchange rate at which your purchase is calculated is the one in effect the day the vendor's bank abroad processes the charge or the one prevailing on the day the charge company's service center processes it at home.

Throughout this guide, the following abbreviations are used: **AE**, American Express; **DC**, Diner's Club; **MC**, Master Card; and **V**, Visa.

CURRENCY

One real has 100 centavos (cents). There are notes worth 1, 5, 10, 50, and 100 reais, together with coins worth 1, 5, 10, 25, and 50 centavos, and 1 real, all of which feel and look similar.

CURRENCY EXCHANGE

For the most favorable rates, **change money through banks.** Although ATM transaction fees may be higher abroad than at home, ATM rates are excellent because they're based on wholesale rates offered only by major banks. You won't do as well at exchange booths in airports or rail and bus stations, in hotels, in restaurants, or in stores.

At press time, the real was at 2.89 to the pound sterling, 1.82 to the U.S. dollar, 1.20 to the Canadian dollar, 1.17 to the Australia dollar, and 0.95 to the New Zealand dollar. For an average week in a Brazilian city, a good strategy is to convert $500 into reais. This provides sufficient cash for most expenses, such as taxis and small purchases and snacks. To avoid lines at airport exchange booths **get local currency before you leave home.** (Don't wait until the last minute to do this as many banks—even the international ones—don't have reais on hand and must order it for you. This can take a couple days.) Outside of larger cities, changing money in Brazil becomes more of a challenge. It's best when leaving a large city for a smaller town to travel with enough cash.

➤ EXCHANGE SERVICES: **International Currency Express** (☎ 888/842–0880 on East Coast; 888/278–6628 on West Coast). **Thomas Cook Currency Services** (☎ 800/287–7362 for phone orders and retail locations).

TRAVELER'S CHECKS

Do you need traveler's checks? If you're going to rural areas and small towns, go with cash; traveler's checks are best used in cities. Lost or stolen checks can usually be replaced within 24 hours. To ensure a speedy refund, buy your own checks—don't let someone else pay for them: irregularities like this can cause delays. The person who bought the checks should make the call to request a refund.

Traveler's checks can be exchanged at hotels, banks, *casas de câmbio* (exchange houses), travel agencies, and shops in malls or stores that cater to tourists. Many small tradesmen are at a total loss when faced with traveler's checks. Note, however, that the rate for traveler's checks is lower than that for cash, and hotels often change them at a rate that's lower than that available at banks or casas de câmbio.

PACKING

If you're doing business in Brazil, you'll need the same attire you would wear in U.S. and European cities: for men, suits and ties; for women, suits for day wear and cocktail dresses or the like for an evening out. For sightseeing, casual clothing and good walking shoes are appropriate; most restaurants don't require very formal attire. For beach vacations, you'll need lightweight sportswear, a bathing suit, a sun hat, and really good sunscreen.

Travel in rain forest areas will require long-sleeve shirts, long pants, socks, sneakers, a hat, a light waterproof jacket, a bathing suit, and plenty of insect repellent. Other useful items include a screw-top water container that you can fill with bottled water, a money pouch, a travel flashlight and extra batteries, a Swiss Army knife with a bottle opener, a medical kit, binoculars, a pocket calculator, and lots of extra film. A sarong or a light cotton blanket makes a handy beach towel, picnic blanket, and cushion for hard seats, among other things.

In your carry-on luggage **bring an extra pair of eyeglasses or contact lenses** and **enough of any medication you take** to last the entire trip. You may also want your doctor to write a spare prescription using the drug's generic name, since brand names may vary from country to country. In luggage to be checked, **never pack** prescription drugs or valuables. To avoid customs delays, carry medications in their original packaging. And don't forget to copy down and carry addresses of offices that handle refunds of lost traveler's checks.

CHECKING LUGGAGE

How many carry-on bags you can bring with you is up to the airline. Most allow two, but not always, so make sure that everything you carry aboard will fit under your seat, and get to the gate early. Note that if you have a seat at the back of the plane, you'll probably board first, while the overhead bins are still empty.

If you're flying internationally, note that baggage allowances may be determined not by piece but by weight—generally 88 pounds (40 kilograms) in first class, 66 pounds (30 kilograms) in business class, and 44 pounds (20 kilograms) in economy.

Airline liability for baggage is limited to $1,250 per person on flights within the United States. On international flights it amounts to $9.07 per pound or $20 per kilogram for checked baggage (roughly $640 per 70-pound bag) and $400 per passenger for unchecked baggage. You can buy additional coverage at check-in for about $10 per $1,000 of coverage, but it excludes a rather extensive list of items, shown on your airline ticket.

Before departure itemize your bags' contents and their worth, and label the bags with your name, address, and phone number. (If you use your home address, cover it so that potential thieves can't see it readily.) Inside each bag pack a copy of your itinerary. At check-in make sure that each bag is correctly tagged with the destination airport's three-letter code. If your bags arrive damaged or fail to arrive at all, file a written report with the airline before leaving the airport.

PASSPORTS & VISAS

When traveling internationally carry a passport even if you don't need one (it's always the best form of ID), and make two photocopies of the data page (one for someone at home and another for you, carried separately from your passport). If you lose your passport promptly call the nearest

embassy or consulate and the local police.

ENTERING BRAZIL

To enter Brazil, all U.S. citizens, even infants, must have both a passport and a tourist visa (valid for five years). To obtain one, you must submit the following to the Brazilian Embassy or to the nearest consulate: a passport that will be valid for six months past the date of first entry to Brazil; a passport-type photo; a photocopy of your round-trip ticket or a signed letter from a travel agency with confirmed round-trip bookings or proof of your ability to pay for your stay in Brazil; and cash, a money order, or a certified check for $45 (there's also a $10 handling fee if anyone other than the applicant submits the visa).

If you're a business traveler, you may need a business visa (valide for 90 days). It has all the same requirements as a tourist visa, but you'll also need a letter on company letterhead—addressed to the embassy or consulate and signed by an authorized representative (other than you)—stating the nature of your business in Brazil, itinerary, business contacts, dates of arrival and departure, and that the company assumes all financial and moral responsibility while you're in Brazil. The fee is $105 (plus the $10 fee if someone other than you submits the visa). In addition to the forms of payment detailed above, a company check is also acceptable.

Canadian nationals, Australians, and New Zealanders also need visas to enter the country. For Canadians, the fee is US$40; for New Zealanders, US$20; and for Australians, there's no charge. Citizens of the United Kingdom don't need a visa.

In the United States, there are consulates in Atlanta, Boston, Chicago, Houston, Los Angeles, Miami, New York, San Francisco, and San Juan. To get the location of the Brazilian consulate to which you must apply, contact the Brazilian Embassy (☞ Embassies, *above*). Note that some consulates don't allow you to apply for a visa by mail. If you don't live near a city with a consulate, consider hiring a concierge-type service to do

SMART TRAVEL TIPS A TO Z

your legwork. Many cities have these companies, which not only help with the paperwork for such things as visas and passports, but also send someone to wait in line for you.

PASSPORT OFFICES

The best time to apply for a passport or to renew is during the fall and winter. Before any trip, check your passport's expiration date, and, if necessary, renew it as soon as possible.

➤ AUSTRALIAN CITIZENS: **Australian Passport Office** (☎ 131–232).

➤ CANADIAN CITIZENS: **Passport Office** (☎ 819/994–3500 or 800/ 567–6868).

➤ NEW ZEALAND CITIZENS: **New Zealand Passport Office** (☎ 04/494– 0700 for information on how to apply; 04/474–8000 or 0800/225– 050 in New Zealand for information on applications already submitted).

➤ U.K. CITIZENS: **London Passport Office** (☎ 0990/210–410) for fees and documentation requirements and to request an emergency passport.

➤ U.S. CITIZENS: **National Passport Information Center** (☎ 900/225– 5674; calls are 35¢ per minute for automated service, $1.05 per minute for operator service).

REST ROOMS

The word for "bathroom" is *banheiro,* though the term *sanitários* (toilets) is also used. *Homens* means "men" and *mulheres* means "women." Around major tourist attractions and along the main beaches in big cities, you'll find public rest rooms. In other areas you may have to rely on the kindness of local restaurant- and shop-owners. If a smile and polite request (*"Por favor, posso usar o banheiro?"*) don't work, become a customer—the purchase of a drink or a knickknack might just buy you a trip to the loo. Rest areas with relatively clean, well-equipped bathrooms are plentiful along major highways. Still, carry a pocket-size package of tissues in case there's no toilet paper. Bathroom attendants will *truly* appreciate a tip of a few spare centavos.

SAFETY

By day, the countryside is quite safe. Although there has been a real effort to crack down on tourist-related crime, particularly in Rio, petty street thievery is still prevalent in urban areas, especially in places around tourist hotels, restaurants, and discos. **Avoid flashing money around.** To safeguard your funds, **lock traveler's checks and cash in a hotel safe,** except for what you need to carry each day. Money (and important documents) that you do carry are best tucked into a money belt or carried in the inside pockets of your clothing. Wear the simplest of timepieces and **do not wear any jewelry you aren't willing to lose**—stories of travelers having chains and even earrings yanked off them aren't uncommon. **Keep cameras in a secure camera bag,** preferably one with a chain or wire embedded in the strap. Always **remain alert for pickpockets,** particularly in market areas, and **follow local advice about where it's safe to walk.**

Note that Brazilian law requires everyone to carry official identification with them at all times. You should always have a copy (leave the original in the hotel safe) of your passport's data page and the visa stamp.

LOCAL SCAMS

Most tourist-related crimes occur in busy public areas: beaches, sidewalks or plazas, bus stations (and on buses, too). In these settings, pickpockets, usually young children, work in groups. One or more will try to distract you while another grabs a wallet, bag, or camera. **Be wary of children who suddenly thrust themselves in front of you** to ask for money or who offer to shine your shoes. Another member of the gang may strike from behind, grab whatever valuable is available, and disappear in the crowd. It's best not to protest if you're mugged. Those on the take are sometimes armed or will tell you that their backup is, and although they're often quite young, they can be dangerous.

WOMEN IN BRAZIL

Although women are gradually assuming a more important role in the nation's job force, machismo is still a strong part of Brazilian culture. Nonetheless, women should have no fear of traveling unaccompanied.

SENIOR-CITIZEN TRAVEL

There's no reason that active, well-traveled senior citizens shouldn't visit Brazil, whether on an independent (but prebooked) vacation, an escorted tour, or an adventure vacation. Before you leave home, however, determine what medical services your health insurance will cover outside the United States; note that Medicare doesn't provide for payment of hospital and medical services outside the United States. If you need additional travel insurance, buy it (☞ Insurance, *above*).

The country is full of good hotels and competent ground operators who will meet your flights and organize your sightseeing. To qualify for age-related discounts **mention your senior-citizen status up front** when booking hotel reservations (not when checking out) and before you're seated in restaurants (not when paying the bill). When renting a car **ask about promotional car-rental discounts**, which can be cheaper than senior-citizen rates.

➤ EDUCATIONAL PROGRAMS: **Elderhostel** (⌧ 75 Federal St., 3rd fl., Boston, MA 02110, ☎ 877/426–8056, FAX 877/426–2166).

SHOPPING

Centers and malls—many based on the American model—abound, though well-to-do Brazilians prefer the personal attention they get in smaller shops. Price and quality vary dramatically; as a rule, you get what you pay for, though shops that cater to tourists invariably charge more. Prices in department stores are fixed, but in smaller shops and boutiques there might be some room for discussion, and some stores give discounts for cash. At outdoor fairs and markets, bargaining is a way of life. If you wish to haggle, the Portuguese phrase for "that's too expensive" is *"está muito caro."*

SIGHTSEEING GUIDES

If you're in Olinda and want to be shown around, the guides with official ID badges in the Praça do Carmo may be the way to go. Under any other circumstances, though, **don't hire sightseeing guides who approach you on the street.** Hire one through the museum or sight you're visiting (once you get inside), a tour operator, the tourist board, your hotel, or a reputable travel agency—and no one else.

STUDENTS IN BRAZIL

Although airfares to and within Brazil are high, you can take buses to most destinations for mere dollars, and you can usually find safe, comfortable (if sparse) accommodations for a fraction of what it might cost back home (☞ Hostels, *above*). Most Brazilian cities also have vibrant student populations.

➤ STUDENT IDs & SERVICES: **Council on International Educational Exchange** (CIEE, ⌧ 205 E. 42nd St., 14th floor, New York, NY 10017, ☎ 212/822–2600 or 888/268–6245, FAX 212/822–2699) for mail orders only, in the U.S. **Travel Cuts** (⌧ 187 College St., Toronto, Ontario M5T 1P7, ☎ 416/979–2406 or 800/667–2887) in Canada.

TAXES

Hotel taxes at press time were roughly 8%; meal taxes, 15.25%; car rental taxes, 12.5%. Taxes on international flights from Brazil aren't always included in your ticket and can run as high as $40; domestic flights may incur $10 in additional charges. Although U.S. dollars are accepted in some airports, be prepared to **pay departure taxes in reais.**

TELEPHONES

Telephone numbers in Brazil don't always have the same number of digits. Public phones are everywhere and are called *orelhões* (big ears) because of their shape. To use them, buy a phone card, *cartão de telefone,* at a *posto telefônico* (phone office), newsstand, or post office. Cards come with a varying number of units (each unit is usually worth a couple of minutes), which will determine the price.

Buy a couple of cards if you don't think you'll have the chance again soon.

Even with a phone card, you may not be able to make long-distance calls from some pay phones—and the logic behind which ones will and which ones won't allow such calls varies from region to region, making it as baffling as it is Brazilian. First, do as the locals do: shrug your shoulders and smile. Second, do as the locals say: ask the staff at your hotel for insight.

Commercial establishments don't usually have public phones, although a bar or restaurant may allow you to use its private phone for a local call if you're a customer. Phone offices are found at airports, many bus stations, and in downtown neighborhoods of large cities.

COUNTRY & AREA CODES

To call Brazil from overseas, dial the country code, 55, and then the area code, omitting the first 0. The area code for Rio is 021, for São Paulo, 011. Other area codes for all parts of the country are listed in the front of the phone directory and in chapter A to Z sections throughout this guide.

DIRECTORY & OPERATOR INFORMATION

For local directory assistance, dial 102. For directory assistance in another Brazilian city, dial the area code of that city plus 121.

LONG-DISTANCE CALLS

Long-distance calls within and international calls to and from Brazil are extremely expensive. Hotels also add a surcharge, increasing this cost. For operator-assisted international calls, dial 000111. For international information, dial 000333.

With the privatization of the Brazilian telecommunications network, everyone now has a choice of long-distance companies. Hence, to make direct-dial, long-distance calls you must find out which companies serve the area you're calling from and then get their access codes—the staff at your hotel can help. (Note, however, that some hotels have already made the choice for you, so you may not need an access code when calling from the hotel itself.) For international calls

dial 00 + the long-distance company's access code + the country code + the area code and number. For long-distance calls within Brazil dial 0 + the access code + the area code and number. AT&T, MCI, and Sprint operators are also accessible from Brazil.

LONG-DISTANCE SERVICES

Before you go, **find out the local access codes** for your destinations. AT&T, MCI, and Sprint access codes make calling long distance relatively convenient, but you may find the local access number blocked in many hotel rooms. First ask the hotel operator to connect you. If the hotel operator balks ask for an international operator, or dial the international operator yourself. One way to improve your odds of getting connected to your long-distance carrier is to travel with more than one company's calling card (a hotel may block Sprint, for example, but not MCI). If all else fails call from a pay phone—if you can find one that allows international calls, that is.

➤ ACCESS CODES: **AT&T USADirect** (☎ 800/874–4000), **MCI Call USA** (☎ 800/444–4444), **Sprint Express** (☎ 800/793–1153).

TIME

Although Brazil technically covers several time zones, most Brazilian cities are three hours behind GMT (Greenwich Mean Time), which means that if it's 5 PM in London, it's noon in New York, and it's 2 PM in Rio. Manaus is an hour behind Rio.

TIPPING

At restaurants that add a 10% service charge onto the check, it's customary to give the waiter an additional 5% tip. If there's no service charge, leave 15%. In deluxe hotels, tip porters 50¢ per bag, chambermaids 50¢ per day, $1 for room and valet service. Tips for doormen and concierges vary, depending on the services provided. A good tip would be $10 or higher, average $5. For moderate and inexpensive hotels, tips tend to be minimal (salaries are so low that virtually anything is well received). If a taxi driver helps you with your luggage, a per-bag charge of about 35¢ is levied in addition to the fare. In general, tip taxi drivers 10% of the fare.

At the barber shop or beauty salon, a 10%–20% tip is expected. If a service station attendant does anything beyond filling up the gas tank, leave him a small tip of a nickel or dime. Tipping in bars and cafés follows the rules of restaurants, although at outdoor bars Brazilians rarely leave a tip if they had only a soft drink or a beer. In general, tip washroom attendants and shoe-shine boys about one-third what you would tip at home. At airports and at train and bus stations, tip the last porter who puts your bags into the cab (50¢ a bag at airports, 25¢ a bag at bus and train stations). In large cities you will often be accosted on the street by children looking for handouts; 25¢ is an average "tip."

TOURS & PACKAGES

On a prepackaged tour or independent vacation everything is prearranged so you'll spend less time planning—and often get it all at a good price.

BOOKING WITH AN AGENT

Travel agents are excellent resources. But it's good to collect brochures from several agencies because some agents' suggestions may be influenced by relationships with tour and package firms that reward them for volume sales. If you have a special interest **find an agent with expertise in that area**; the American Society of Travel Agents, or ASTA (☞ Travel Agencies, *below*), has a database of specialists worldwide.

Make sure your agent knows the accommodations and other services of the place they're recommending. Ask about the hotel's location, room size, beds, and whether it has a pool, room service, or programs for children, if you care about these. Has your agent been there in person or sent others whom you can contact? Do some homework on your own, too: Local tourism boards can provide information about lesser-known and small-niche operators, some of which may sell only direct.

BUYER BEWARE

Each year consumers are stranded or lose their money when tour opera-tors—even large ones with excellent reputations—go out of business. So **check out the operator.** Ask several travel agents about its reputation, and try to **book with a company that has a consumer-protection program.** (Look for information in the company's brochure.) In the United States, members of the National Tour Association and United States Tour Operators Association are required to set aside funds to cover your payments and travel arrangements in case the company defaults. It's also good to choose a company that participates in ASTA's Tour Operator Program (TOP); ASTA will act as mediator in any disputes between you and your tour operator.

Remember that the more your package or tour includes the better you can predict the ultimate cost of your vacation. Make sure you know exactly what's covered, and **beware of hidden costs.** Are taxes, tips, and transfers included? Entertainment and excursions? These can add up.

Tour-Operator Recommendations: ASTA (☞ Travel Agencies, *below*), National Tour Association (NTA, ✉ 546 E. Main St., Lexington, KY 40508, ☎ 606/226–4444 or 800/ 682–8886), United States Tour Operators Association (USTOA, ✉ 342 Madison Ave., Suite 1522, New York, NY 10173, ☎ 212/599–6599 or 800/468–7862, FAX 212/599– 6744).

THEME TRIPS

Among companies that sell theme-trip tours to Brazil, the following are well known, have a proven reputation, and offer plenty of options.

➤ Amazon River Trips: **Abercrombie & Kent** (✉ 1520 Kensington Rd., Suite 212, Oak Brook, IL 60523, 630/954–2944 or 800/323–7308, www.abercrombiekent.com), **Brazil Nuts** (✉ 1854 Trade Center Way, Suite 101B, Naples, FL 34109, ☎ 941/593–0266 or 800/553–9959, www.brazilnuts.com), **Clipper Cruise Line** (✉ 7711 Bonhomme Ave, St. Louis, MO, 63105, ☎ 314/727–2929 or 800/325–0010, www.clipper-cruise.com), **Explorers Travel Group** (✉ 1 Main St., Suite 304, Eatontown, NJ 07724, ☎ 732/542–9006 or 800/

631–5650, explorers@monmouth. com), **Journeys International** (✉ 107 April Dr., Suite 3, Ann Arbor, MI 48103, ☎ 313/665–4407 or 800/ 255–8735, www.journeys-intl.com), **Marine Expeditions** (✉ 30 Hazelton Ave., Toronto, Ontario, M5R 2E2 Canada, ☎ 416/964–9069 or 800/ 263–9147, www.marineex.com), **Nature Expeditions International** (✉ 6400 E. El Dorado Center, Suite 210, Tucson, AZ 85715, ☎ 520/721–6712 or 800/869–0639, www.naturexp. com), **Tara Tours** (✉ 6595 N.W. 36th St., Suite 306, Miami Springs, FL 33166, ☎ 305/871–1246 or 800/ 327–0080, www.taratours.com), and **Travcoa** (✉ 2350 S.E. Bristol St., Newport Beach, CA 92660, ☎ 949/ 476–2800 or 800/992–2003, 800/992– 2004 in California, www.travcoa.com).

➤ BIRD-WATCHING: **Field Guides, Inc.** (✉ Box 160723, Austin, TX 78716, ☎ 512/327–4953 or 800/728–4953, www.fieldguides.com), **Focus Tours** (✉ 403 Moya Rd., Santa Fe, NM 87505, ☎ 505/466–4688, www.fo-custours.com), **Swallows and Amazons** (✉ Box 771, Eastham, MA 02642, ☎ 508/255–1886, www.over-lookinn.com/swallows.html), **Victor Emanuel Nature Tours** (✉ Box 33008, Austin, TX 78764, ☎ 512/ 328–5221 or 800/328–8368, www.ventbird.com).

➤ CANOEING: **Swallows and Amazons** (☞ Bird-Watching, *above*).

➤ CRUISING: For cruise ships that sail to South America, including the Amazon, *see* Cruising, *above*.

➤ CULTURE: **Amizade, Ltd.** (✉ 7612 N. Rogers Ave., Chicago, IL 60626, ☎ 773/973–3719, www.amizade.org) and **Swallows and Amazon** (☞ Bird-Watching, *above*).

➤ FISHING: **Fishing International** (✉ Box 2132, Santa Rosa, CA 95405, ☎ 707/542–4242 or 800/950–4242, www.fishinginternational.com), **Frontiers** (✉ Box 959, 305 Logan Rd., Wexford, PA 15090, ☎ 724/ 935–1577 or 800/245–1950, www.frontierstrvl.com), **Quest Global Angling Adventures** (✉ 3595 Canton Hwy., Suite C11, Marietta, GA 30066, ☎ 770/971–8586 or 888/ 891–3474, www.fishquest.com), and **Rod and Reel Adventures** (✉ 566

Thomson La., Copperopolis, CA 95228, ☎ 209/785–0444 or 800/ 356–6982, www.rodandreeladv.com.

➤ PHOTOGRAPHY: **Close-Up Expeditions** (✉ 858 56th St., Oakland, CA 94608, ☎ 510/654–1548 or 800/ 457–9553, qcuephotog@aol.com), **Joseph Van Os Photo Safaris** (✉ Box 655, Vashon Island, WA 98070, ☎ 206/463–5383, FAX 206/463–5484, www.photosafaris.com).

➤ TREKKING: **Amazon Tours and Cruises** (✉ 8700 W. Flagler St., Suite 190, Miami, FL 33174, ☎ 305/227– 2266 or 800/423–2791, amazon-cruz@aol.com), **Brazil Nuts** (☞ Amazon Cruises *above*), **Explorers Travel Group** (✉ 1 Main St., Suite 304, Eatontown, NJ 07724, ☎ 732/ 542–9006 or 800/631–5650, explorers@monmouth.com), **Naturequest** (✉ 30872 S. Coast Hwy., Suite 185, Laguna Beach, CA 92561, ☎ 949/ 499–9561 or 800/369–3033, www.naturequesttours.com), **Safaricentre** (✉ 3201 N. Sepulveda Blvd., Manhattan Beach, CA 90266, ☎ 310/546–4411 or 800/223–6046, www.safaricentre.com), **Southwind Adventures** (✉ Box 621057, Littleton, CO 80162, ☎ 303/972–0701 or 800/377–9463, www.southwindadventures.com), and **Swallows and Amazons** (☞ Bird-Watching, *above*).

TRAIN TRAVEL

Brazil has an outdated and insufficient rail network, the smallest of any of the world's large nations. Although there are commuter rails to destinations around major cities, don't plan on taking passenger trains between major cities. There's one exception: the ride from Curitiba to Paranaguá—in the southern state of Paraná—offers spectacular vistas of ravines, mountains, and waterfalls from bridges and viaducts (☞ Arriving and Departing by Train *under* The South A to Z *in* Chapter 4).

TRAVEL AGENCIES

A good travel agent puts your needs first. Look for an agency that has been in business at least five years, emphasizes customer service, and has someone on staff who specializes in your destination. In addition **make sure the agency belongs to a profes-**

sional trade organization. ASTA, with 27,000 agents in some 170 countries, is the largest and most influential in the field. Operating under the motto "Integrity in Travel," it maintains and enforces a strict code of ethics and will step in to help mediate any agent-client disputes if necessary. ASTA also maintains a Web site that includes a directory of agents. Note that if a travel agency is also acting as your tour operator, *see* Buyer Beware *in* Tours & Packages, *above*.

➤ LOCAL AGENT REFERRALS: American Society of Travel Agents (ASTA, ☎ 800/965–2782 24-hr hot line, FAX 703/684–8319, www.astanet.com), Association of British Travel Agents (✉ 68–271 Newman St., London W1P 4AH, ☎ 020/7637–2444, FAX 020/7637–0713), Association of Canadian Travel Agents (✉ 1729 Bank St., Suite 201, Ottawa, Ontario K1V 7Z5, ☎ 613/521–0474, FAX 613/521–0805), Australian Federation of Travel Agents (✉ Level 3, 309 Pitt St., Sydney 2000, ☎ 02/9264–3299, FAX 02/9264–1085), Travel Agents' Association of New Zealand (✉ Box 1888, Wellington 10033, ☎ 04/499–0104, FAX 04/499–0786).

VISITOR INFORMATION

EMBRATUR, Brazil's national tourism organization, doesn't have offices overseas, though its Web site is helpful. For information in your home country, your best bet is to contact the Brazilian Embassy or the closest consulate—some of which have Web sites and staff dedicated to promoting tourism. RioTur, the city of Rio's tourist board, has offices in New York and Los Angeles. An organization called Pro-Brazil, Inc., which has an office in New York, represents the Brazilian states of Bahia, Rio, and São Paulo.

Cities and towns throughout Brazil have local tourist boards, and some state capitals also have state tourism offices. (For local tourist board information, *see* the A to Z sections in each chapter.)

➤ BRAZILIAN TOURIST INFORMATION: Pro-Brazil, Inc. (✉ 554 5th Ave., 4th floor, New York, NY 10036, ☎ 212/997–4070), RioTur (✉ 3601 Aviation Blvd., suite 2100, Manhattan Beach, CA 90266, ☎ 310/643–2638; ✉ 201 E. 12th St., Suite 509, New York, NY 10003, ☎ 212/375–0801).

U.S. Government Advisories: U.S. Department of State (✉ Overseas Citizens Services Office, Room 4811 N.S., 2201 C St. NW, Washington, DC 20520; ☎ 202/647–5225 for interactive hot line; 301/946–4400 for computer bulletin board; FAX 202/647–3000 for interactive hot line); enclose a self-addressed, stamped, business-size envelope.

WEB SITES

Do check out the World Wide Web when you're planning. You'll find everything from up-to-date weather forecasts to virtual tours of famous cities. Fodor's Web site www.fodors.com, is a great place to start your on-line travels.

Be prepared to really surf. For good information, you may have to search by region, state, or city—and hope that at least one of them has a comprehensive official site of its own. Don't rule out foreign-language sites; some have links to sites that present information in more than one language, including English. On Portuguese-language sites, watch for the name of the region, state, or city in which you have an interest. The search terms for "look," "find" and "get" are *olhar/achar, buscar,* and *pegar*; "next" and "last" (as in "next/last 10") are *próximo* and *último/anterior*. Keep an eye out for such words as: *turismo* (tourism), *turístico* (tourist-related), *hoteis* (hotels), *restaurantes* (restaurants), *governo* (government), *estado* (state), and *cidade* (city).

The following sites should get you started: www.embratur.gov.br (the official Brazilian tourist board site, with information in English), www.varig.com (Varig Airline's site, with English information), www.consuladobrasilny.org (the official consular Web site in New York, with details about other consulates and the embassy as well as travel information and links to many other sites).

WHEN TO GO

CLIMATE

Seasons below the Equator are the reverse of the north—summer in Brazil runs from December to March and winter from June to September. The rainy season in Brazil occurs during the summer months, but this is rarely a nuisance. Showers can be torrential but usually last no more than an hour or two, after which the sun reappears. The areas of the country with pronounced rainy seasons are the Amazon and the Pantanal. In these regions, the rainy season runs roughly November to May and is marked by heavy downpours that usually occur twice a day.

Prices in beach resorts invariably are higher during the high season (Brazilian summer). If you're looking for a bargain, stick to the off-season (May–June and August–October; July is school-break month). In Rio and at beach resorts along the coast, especially in the northeast, these months offer the added attraction of relief from the often oppressive summer heat, although in Rio the temperature can drop to uncomfortable levels for swimming in June through August.

Rio de Janeiro is on the Tropic of Capricorn, and its climate is just that—tropical. Summers are hot and humid, with temperatures rising as high as 105°F (40°C), although the average ranges between 84°F and 95°F (29°C–35°C). In winter, temperatures stay in the 70s (20s C), occasionally dipping into the high 60s (15°C–20°C). The same pattern holds true for all of the Brazilian coastline north of Rio, although in general temperatures are slightly higher year-round in Salvador and the coastal cities of the northeast. In the Amazon region where the equator crosses the country, temperatures in the high 80s to 90s (30s C) are common throughout the year. In the south, São Paulo, and parts of Minas Gerais, winter temperatures can fall to the low 40s (5°C–8°C). In the southern states of Santa Catarina and Rio Grande do Sul, snowfalls occur in winter, although they're seldom more than dustings.

➤ FORECASTS: **Weather Channel Connection** (☎ 900/932–8437), 95¢ per minute from a Touch-Tone phone.

The following are the average daily maximum and minimum temperatures for Rio de Janeiro.

Jan.	84F	29C	**May**	77F	25C	**Sept.**	75F	24C
	69	21		66	19		66	19
Feb.	85F	29C	**June**	76F	24C	**Oct.**	77F	25C
	73	23		64	18		63	17
Mar.	83F	28C	**July**	75F	24C	**Nov.**	79F	26C
	72	22		64	18		68	20
Apr.	80F	27C	**Aug.**	76F	24C	**Dec.**	82F	28C
	69	21		64	18		71	22

The following are the average daily maximum and minimum temperatures for Salvador.

Jan.	87F	31C	**May**	80F	27C	**Sept.**	78F	26C
	76	24		70	21		69	21
Feb.	88F	31C	**June**	80F	27C	**Oct.**	80F	27C
	76	24		67	19		69	21
Mar.	87F	31C	**July**	78F	26C	**Nov.**	83F	28C
	77	25		66	19		72	22
Apr.	84F	29C	**Aug.**	80F	27C	**Dec.**	86F	30C
	73	23		67	19		77	25

1 DESTINATION: BRAZIL

A LAND OF CONTRAST AND DIVERSITY

THE MATCH AGAINST FRANCE to decide the 1998 World Cup was about to start when the news hit that *futebol* (soccer) superstar Ronaldo had had an epileptic seizure and wouldn't play. Brazilians reacted as though an earthquake had hit. During the crisis, Brazilian sports commissioners rushed to the locker room in the packed Parisian stadium and came out seconds later with new plans. Ronaldo played, but Brazil lost, and the country's dream of winning the World Cup for the fifth time went down the drain. A national catastrophe, the incident monopolized public and private attention in Brazil for several months, eliciting media analyses and solemn discussions on radio programs and TV talk shows.

In Brazil, sports heroes are like royalty. They rivet the country's attention, forming an emotional chain across this spread-out land, linking its 160 million people. Even the lesser princes, such as Gustavo "Guga" Kuerten—the first Brazilian to rank among the world's top 10 tennis players—are met by cheering crowds throughout the country. In 1994, when race car driver Airton Senna died in a crash, the president declared three days of official mourning. The funeral in São Paulo was attended by a record 1 million people, and the whole country seemed to fall into a deep depression.

Brazilians rarely unite in so passionate a manner behind weightier issues, but when they do, the effects are awesome. No one who was in the country in 1984 can forget the months of nationwide marches that nudged the military regime toward holding democratic elections for a president after 20 years of dictatorship. Little more than a decade later, the movement to impeach the corrupt president, Fernando Collor de Mello, brought out similar crowds—not only politically organized groups but also citizens going about their everyday affairs. Housewives donned black as a sign of protest when they did their weekly shopping, and students made up their faces using Indian war paint when they attended classes. Involving very little direct confrontation—and even less violence—these events seemed more like Carnaval (Carnival) than political revolution. But this is a style that makes sense in Brazil.

In this gigantic territory, larger than the continental United States and 250 times the size of Holland, contrasts are overwhelming. Brazil is a fabulously rich land, but it's full of inequalities. You're as apt to see five-star hotels and resorts as you are shanty towns. Shopping malls, McDonald's restaurants, and international banks stand side-by-side with street vendors peddling homemade foods and herbal medicines. Brazil's GNP is nearly US\$470 billion (more than half that of Latin America as a whole), yet it also has a relatively high infant mortality rate (10% of the nation's babies don't reach the age of one) and one of the world's worst distributions of wealth. The nation has more than 100 million acres of arable land; unequaled reserves of iron, bauxite, manganese, and other minerals; and mammoth hydroelectric power plants. Yet reckless mining and agricultural procedures—particularly in the Amazon—have poisoned rivers, created deserts, and dislodged entire Indian tribes. Further, the racial democracy for which Brazil is often praised is more evident in the bustling downtown markets than in the plush salons of suburban socialites.

It has been said that in this radiant land live a sad people, and certainly the feeling of *saudade* (nostalgia) is latent in much Brazilian poetry and music. Yet this plaintive tone vanishes as soon as the Carnaval season begins. In the heat of the South American summer (February or March based on the Easter calendar) the country explodes in gaiety. From such cities as Rio de Janeiro, Salvador, and Recife—where hundreds of thousands dance in street parades—to the small towns of Pará or Goiás, Brazil comes alive. Carnaval season involves not only the days right before Lent (Friday through Ash Wednesday), but also months of rehearsal beforehand. And the sparks of passion flow over into other events throughout the year: religious festivals, ball games, weekend dances.

If you examine Brazil's demographics, you'll find other stark contrasts. You can drive through vast regions in the central *cerrados* (savannas), the southern pampas, or the northeastern *sertão* (arid interior) without seeing a soul, and then, paradoxically, spend hours stuck in traffic in a major city. The bloated urban areas harbor nearly 75% of the population. They're like cauldrons containing a stew of many races that's seasoned by regional customs and accents. Although Brazil is considered a Latin country—and the Portuguese language does, indeed, help to unify it—any type of person can fit the Brazilian "mold." The country's racial composition reflects the historical contact between native Indian peoples; Portuguese colonizers; African slaves; and immigrants from Germany, Italy, Japan, and even the United States.

In terms of diversity, religion runs a close second to ethnicity. Although the almanac will tell you that Brazil is 70% Catholic, the people's tastes are much more eclectic. Some estimates put the number of spiritualists—followers of the 19th-century Belgian medium, Alan Kardec—at 40 million. Candomblé, Macumba, Umbanda, and other cults inspired by African religions and deities abound. And, recently, Pentecostal sects have opened one church after another, performing exorcisms and miraculous cures in front of packed auditoriums. Most of these churches and cults welcome visitors of any creed or culture. Brazilians, it seems, are anything but sectarian.

Brazil is truly a land of contrasts, and any visit here is likely to be a sensuous adventure. A variety of cultures, beliefs, and topographies make this warm nation a showcase of diversity. An array of nature's bounty—from passion fruit and papaya to giant river fish and coastal crabs—has inspired chefs from all over the world to come and try their hands in Brazilian restaurants (adding lightness and zest to the country's already exquisite cuisine). Spas—with bubbling mineral water and soothing hot springs—all over the land offer the best that both nature and technology can offer. Whether you travel to the Amazon rain forest, the mountain towns of Minas Gerais, the urban jungle of São Paulo, or the immense central plateau surrounding Brasília, you'll plunge into an exotic mix of colors, rhythms, and pastimes.

Historical Notes

Colonial Days

Brazil was officially "discovered" in 1500, when a fleet commanded by Portuguese diplomat Pedro Álvares Cabral, on its way to India, landed in Porto Seguro, between Salvador and Rio de Janeiro. (There is, however, strong evidence that other Portuguese adventurers preceded him. Duarte Pacheco Pereira, in his book *De Situ Orbis,* tells of being in Brazil in 1498, sent by King Manuel of Portugal.)

Brazil's first colonizers were met by Tupinamba Indians, one group in the vast array of the continent's native population. Lisbon's early goals were simple: monopolize the lucrative trade of *pau-brasil,* the red wood (valued for making dye) that gave the colony its name, and establish permanent settlements. There's evidence that the Indians and Portuguese initially worked together to harvest trees. Later, the need to head farther inland to find forested areas made the pau-brasil trade less desirable. The interest in establishing plantations on cleared lands increased and so did the need for laborers. The Portuguese tried to enslave Indians, but, unaccustomed to toiling long hours in fields and overcome by European diseases, many natives either fled far inland or died. (When Cabral arrived, the indigenous population was believed to have been more than 3 million; today the number is scarcely more than 200,000.) The Portuguese then turned to the African slave trade for their workforce.

Although most settlers preferred the coastal areas (a preference that continues to this day), a few ventured into the hinterlands. Among them were Jesuit missionaries, determined men who marched inland in search of Indian souls to "save," and the infamous *bandeirantes* (flag bearers), tough men who marched inland in search of Indians to enslave. (Later they hunted escaped Indian and African slaves.)

For two centuries after Cabral's discovery, the Portuguese had to periodically deal with foreign powers with designs on Brazil's resources. Although Portugal and

Spain had the 1494 Treaty of Tordesillas—which set boundaries for each country in their newly discovered lands—the guidelines were vague, causing the occasional territory dispute. Further, England, France, and Holland didn't fully recognize the treaty, which was made by Papal decree, and were aggressively seeking new lands in pirate-ridden seas. Such competition made the Lusitanian foothold in the New World tenuous at times.

The new territory faced internal as well as external challenges. Initially, the Portuguese Crown couldn't establish a strong central government in the subcontinent. For much of the colonial period, it relied on "captains," low ranking nobles and merchants who were granted authority over captaincies, slices of land often as big as their motherland. By 1549 it was evident that most of the captaincies were failing. Portugal's monarch dispatched a governor-general (who arrived with soldiers, priests, and craftspeople) to oversee them and to establish a capital (today's Salvador) in the central captaincy of Bahia.

At the end of the 17th century, the news that fabulous veins of emeralds, diamonds, and gold had been found in Minas Gerais exploded in Lisbon. The region began to export 30,000 pounds of gold a year to Portugal. Bandeirantes and other fortune hunters rushed in from all over, and boat loads of carpenters, stonemasons, sculptors, and painters came from Europe to build cities in the Brazilian wilderness.

In 1763, the capital was moved to Rio de Janeiro for a variety of political and administrative reasons. The country had successfully staved off invasions by other European nations and it had roughly taken its current shape. It added cotton and tobacco to sugar, gold, and diamonds on its list of exports. As the interior opened so did the opportunities for cattle ranching. Still, Portugal's policies tended toward stripping Brazil of its resources rather than developing a truly local economy. The arrival of the royal family, who were chased out of Portugal by Napoléon's armies in 1808, initiated major changes.

The Empire and the Republic

As soon as Dom João VI and his entourage arrived in Rio, he began transforming the city and its environs. Building projects were set in motion, universities as well as a bank and a mint were founded, and investments were made in the arts. The ports were opened to trade with other nations, especially England, and morale improved throughout the territory. With the fall of Napoléon, Dom João VI returned to Portugal, leaving his young son, Pedro I, behind to govern. But Pedro had ideas of his own: he proclaimed Brazil's independence on September 7, 1822, and established the Brazilian empire. Nine years later, following a period of internal unrest and costly foreign wars, the emperor stepped aside in favor of his five-year-old son, Pedro II. A series of regents ruled until 1840, when the second Pedro was 14 and Parliament decreed him "of age."

Pedro II's daughter, Princess Isabel, officially ended slavery in 1888. Soon after, disgruntled landowners united with the military to finish with monarchy altogether, forcing the royal family back to Portugal and founding Brazil's first republican government on November 15, 1889. A long series of easily forgettable presidents, backed by strong coffee and rubber economies, brought about some industrial and urban development during what's known as the Old Republic. In 1930, after his running mate was assassinated, presidential candidate Getúlio Vargas seized power via a military coup rather than elections. In 1945 his dictatorship ended in another coup. He returned to the political scene with a populist platform and was elected president in 1951. However, halfway through his term, he was linked to the attempted assassination of a political rival; with the military calling for his resignation, he shot himself.

The next elected president, Juscelino Kubitschek, a visionary from Minas Gerais, decided to replace the capital of Rio de Janeiro with a grand, new, modern one (symbolic of grand, new, modern ideas) that would be built in the middle of nowhere. True to the motto of his national development plan, "Fifty years in five," he opened the economy to foreign capital and offered credit to the business community. When Brasília was inaugurated in 1960, there wasn't a penny left in the coffers, but key sectors of the economy (such as the auto industry) were functioning at full steam. Still, turbulent times were ahead. Kubitschek's successor Jânio Quadros, an eccentric, spirited carouser who had risen from high school teaching to politics, resigned after seven months in office. Vice-president João "Jango" Goulart, a Vargas man with leftist leanings, took office only to be overthrown by the military on March 31, 1964, after frustrated attempts to impose socialist reforms. Exiled in Uruguay, he died 13 years later.

Military Rule and Beyond

Humberto Castello Branco was the first of five generals (he was followed by Artur Costa e Silva, Emílio Médici, Ernesto Geisel, and João Figueiredo) to lead Brazil in 20 years of military rule that still haunt the nation. Surrounded by tanks and technocrats, the military brought about the "economic miracle" of the 1970s. However, it did not last. Their pharaonic projects—from hydroelectric and nuclear power plants to the conquest of the Amazon—never completely succeeded, and inflation soared. Power was to go peacefully back to civil hands in 1985.

All hopes were on the shoulders of Tancredo Neves, a 75-year-old democrat chosen to be president by an electoral college. But, just before his investiture, Neves; he died of a general infection days later. An astounded nation followed the drama on TV. Vice-president José Sarney, a former ally of the military regime, took office. By the end of his five-year term, inflation was completely out of hand. Sarney did, however, oversee the writing of a new constitution, promulgated in 1988, and Brazil's first free presidential elections in 30 years.

Fernando Collor de Mello, a debonair 40-year-old from the state of Alagoas, took office in March 1990. Dubbed "the maharajah hunter" (an allusion to his promises to rid the government of idle, highly paid civil servants), Mello immediately set about trying to control inflation (his first step was to block all savings accounts in Brazil). His extravagant economic plans only became clear two years later with the discovery of widespread corruption involving his friend and campaign manager Paulo César "P. C." Farias. After an impeachment process, Collor was ousted in December 1992, and Brazil's leadership fell to Vice-President Itamar Franco. With his "Plano Real" Franco brought inflation under control.

In 1994, Franco was replaced by Fernando Henrique Cardoso, the former Secretary of the Treasury. Following the dictates of the International Monetary Fund, Cardoso brought about relative economic stability, but at the price of recession, cuts in health and educational programs, and a soaring national debt. His policy of selling state-owned industries—from banks to mines to phone companies—was riddled with irregular practices.

In October 1998, taking advantage of a constitutional amendment that he personally engineered allowing for reelection, Cardoso won a second term, running against Workers Party candidate Luis Inácio "Lula" da Silva. He based his campaign on propaganda that promised a return to economic growth and an end to unemployment. Cardoso managed to avoid draconian economic measures and a 35% currency devaluation until the day after the election. Then, new taxes and budget cuts were announced, recession settled in, and unemployment soared. In 1999, Cardoso's popularity was at a record low, causing nationwide calls for his resignation. But Brazilians show amazing resilience even under political and economic stress. Recovery may be slow and difficult, but it's almost impossible to lose faith in such a rich land. And in the midst of all the uncertainty, most Brazilians are sure about one thing: winning soccer's 2002 soccer World Cup will be a cinch.

–by José Fonseca

Born and raised in Minas Gerais, José Fonseca left Brazil at the start of the military dictatorship, earned a masters in journalism from the University of Kansas, and then spent over 10 years in Europe and West Africa before returning to Brazil. Working as a freelance environmental journalist and translator, he now lives in Porto Alegre with his anthropologist wife, children, and cats and dogs.

WHAT'S WHERE

Rio de Janeiro dangles from the south-central edge of the state by the same name. The city cascades down and between dramatic hump-topped mountains and out to beaches that ribbon the metropolitan area. Rio de Janeiro State bulges from Brazil's southeast coast, just at the point where the country starts to narrow. Although Rio is best known for its coastline and sandy stretches, inland you'll find several historical towns in refreshingly cool (relatively speaking) and lush mountainous settings.

Just south of Rio de Janeiro State is the coastal state of **São Paulo.** Its huge, eponymous capital is on a plateau just 72 km (46 mi) from the coast. The large port of Santos, several beautiful beaches, and some ecological preserve areas—including some patches of the Mata Atlântica (Atlantic Forest)—run along its shores. Like the state of Rio, São Paulo's inland includes mountainous regions bedecked with charming historical and resort towns.

The **South**'s three states—Paraná, just below São Paulo, followed by Santa Catarina and Rio Grande do Sul—run along the coast as well as stretching inland to the border of Uruguay, Argentina, and Paraguay. Together they fill up the narrowest section of Brazil's mass, covering 570,000 square km—an area about the size of France. Curitiba, the capital of Paraná, is on a plateau 80 km (50 mi) from the sea. Santa Catarina's capital of Florianópolis literally straddles the Atlantic—its coastal mainland portion is connected by bridge to its offshore island portion. Rio Grande do Sul's capital, Porto Alegre, is halfway between São Paulo and Buenos Aires (about a 1½-hr flight to either destination). Inland you'll find both mountainous regions and flat grasslands famous for their *gaúchos* (South American cowboys). Far to the west are the mighty Foz de Iguaçu (Iguaçu Falls).

To the northwest of the Rio de Janeiro and São Paulo states is the large (roughly the size of Spain), inland state of **Minas Gerais**, which is known for its amazing mineral wealth. It has several historical cities (known as the Gold Towns), the most famous of which is Ouro Prêto, as well as several mineral spa towns. The Gold Towns are a short drive from one another southeast of the capital, Belo Horizonte, and in the Serra do Espinhaço.

Brasília, the nation's capital, lies in the geographical center of the country in a vast, flat region dominated by the *cerrado*, the Brazilian savanna. The cerrado extends **west** through the sparsely populated "frontier" states of Goiás, Tocantins, Mato Grosso, and Mato Grosso do Sul. The massive, untamable Pantanal—one of the world's largest swamps—is the dominant feature of the far west both in terms of geography and tourist appeal.

In the northeast, the nation's most curvaceous bit of coast is adorned with three urban jewels: **Salvador,** capital of Bahia State at the south of the region; **Recife,** capital of Pernambuco State slightly to the north; and **Fortaleza,** capital of Ceará State and just below the Amazon region. These cities are at once lively with the ambience of contemporary Brazilian beach culture, austere with the history of colonial struggles, and exotic with a mix of African and European traditions. Between them they have hundreds of miles of beaches lapped by warm waters and caressed by cooling breezes.

The **Amazon** coincides with the region generally referred to as the north. Although the area is laced with more than 1,000 jungle-lined rivers, the main communities are, for the most part, along the gargantuan Amazon River itself. The city of Manaus has a longitudinal location that's almost exactly in the center of the continent. Santarém sits just under 800 km (500 mi) downriver, nearly halfway between Manaus and the Atlantic. Before reaching the ocean, the river splits. Its northeastern branch leads to Macapá; its eastern branch, to Belém. The two are separated by nearly 300 km (200 mi) and Ilha do Marajó, the world's largest river island.

NEW AND NOTEWORTHY

Throughout Brazil, city, state, and federal governments have been working hard to better serve visitors by pumping out new, improved brochures and maps. And just in time, too, as the real has weakened, resulting in a favorable rate of exchange for North American and European travelers. In mid-1999, the U.S. dollar was worth 1.82 reais, though analysts predicted that the currency would stabilize at 1.60 reais to the dollar.

Crime in **Rio de Janeiro** is on the decline thanks to a greater police presence (including police kiosks along the city's beaches). A new bike path along the beaches and into Centro is nearly finished, two *metrô* (subway) lines have been expanded, and a new traffic code—the first revision in the laws since 1966—aims to bring more calm to the oft-chaotic roadways.

São Paulo's metrô subway system is being expanded. The green line, which runs under Avenida Paulista, has two new stations on its west side, Sumaré and Vila Madalena; the blue line has three new stations—Jardim São Paulo, Parada Inglesa, and Tucuruvi—to the north; more work is being done to the lines along the Marginal Pinheiros; and several new stations now connect the neighborhoods of Pinheiros and Santo Amaro. At the same time, in attempts to cut down on traffic jams and reduce pollution, new city and state traffic laws have been enacted.

Cities in the **South** have been blessed with several new attractions. Curitiba's Estação Plaza Show entertainment complex has opened in a renovated rail terminal. Here you'll find live-music performances, a cineplex, dozens of bars and restaurants, indoor amusement parks, shops, and a train museum. Two museums have recently been added to Porto Alegre's list of attractions: The Museu de Arte do Rio Grande do Sul (Art Museum of Rio Grande do Sul) reopened in late 1998 after several years of renovation and the Memorial do Rio Grande do Sul—which depicts the state's history—opened in early 1999. After extensive improvements, the Parque Nacional dos Aparados da Serra—a nature reserve that contains several canyons—has been reopened.

In **Brasília,** the Federal District government has initiated a lakefront development project—the Projeto Orla—that will include landscaping improvements and new hotels, marinas, bike lanes, trails, and other facilities. The kiosks north of Palácio do Planalto are already open, and, at press time, two world-class hotels were about to open.

In the **Amazon,** the state of Pará and its capital of Belém have made tourism a high priority. Projects under way include building restoration, new museums, a new airport, a dock for tourist excursions, and an enormous glass visitors complex. On the transportation front, a paved road now connects Manaus with Venezuela, and two new high-speed boats now have routes between Manaus and Santarém and Macapá and Belém.

PLEASURES AND PASTIMES

Architecture

Although Brazilian architecture has seen many periods, in this land of contrasts it comes as no surprise that the field is dominated by two wildly different styles—baroque and modernist. In the 17th century, to ensure their control of the mining industry when gold was discovered in Minas Gerais, the Portuguese exiled the traditional religious orders, which led to the formation of lay or "third" orders. Attempts by these lay brothers to build churches on European models resulted in improvisations (they had little experience with or guidance on such matters) and, hence, a uniquely Brazilian style of baroque. Many churches from this period have simple exteriors that belie interiors whose gold-leaf-encrusted carvings are so intricate they seem like filigree. As the gold supply diminished, facades became more elaborate—with more sophisticated lines, elegant curves, and large round towers—and their interiors less so as murals were used more than carvings and gold leaf. Today you can see several outstanding examples of baroque architecture in Ouro Prêto (where there are 13 such churches, including the exceptional Igreja São Francisco de Assis) and the other Gold Towns of Minas.

At the other end of the spectrum is modernism. In the middle of the 20th century, Brazilian leaders longed for ways to express a "nation of the future" outlook. They found it in the works of such architects as Lúcio Costa and Oscar Niemeyer (as well as in those of landscape designer Roberto Burle Marx). Their linear buildings epitomize functionality and simplicity (of design) and economy (of building materials); they also embody the vastness of Brazil. Many are set upon huge concrete *pilotis* (pillars), leaving large open areas beneath them. Enormous glass facades and reflecting pools (some are really more the size of small lakes) often add to the sense of space; organic-looking sculptures—either as plump and curvaceous as a cluster of coconuts or as willowy and elongated as palm fronds—add touches of softness. Although the thoroughly planned capital, Brasília, is a mecca for modernist fans, you can see examples of this style in Rio de Janeiro (Catedral de São Sebastião, Monumento aos Pracinhas, Museu de Arte Moderna), in São Paulo (Edifício Copan, Museu de Arte de São Paulo, Memorial da América Latina), and elsewhere.

Beaches

Brazil's Atlantic coast runs more than 7,300 km (4,600 mi), edging the country with sandy, palm-lined shores as well as some dramatic, rugged stretches. Many northeastern *praias* (beaches) offer sweeping, isolated expanses of gloriously high dunes; warm, aquamarine waters; and constant breezes. Of course Rio's famous beaches seem to embody the Brazilians themselves: vibrant, social, joyful, and beautiful. São Paulo's cleanest and best sands are along the North Shore, where mountains and bits of Atlantic forest hug small, sandy coves. In the south, some glorious sands and slightly cooler climes can be found in Paraná State as well as on Ilha de Santa Catarina; still farther south the Mata Atlântica gives way to cliffs that run into the sea. Not all the best beaches are on the ocean. The banks of the Amazon and its tributaries also have splendid sandy stretches.

Carnaval

Carnaval (Carnival) is the biggest party of the year. In some areas, events begin right after Reveillon (New Year's) and continue beyond the four main days of celebration (just before the start of Lent) with smaller feasts and festivities. At Carnaval's peak, businesses close throughout the country as Brazilians don costumes—from the elaborate to the barely there—and take to the streets singing and dancing. These four explosive days of color see formal parades as well as spontaneous street parties fueled by flatbed trucks that carry bands from neighborhood to neighborhood.

In Rio de Janeiro

The *cariocas* (citizens of Rio) unleash a passion that sweeps across the city in over-the-top parades, pulsating street parties, and galas—all with the frenetic samba beat sizzling in the background. The highlight is the judging of the city's *escolas de samba* (samba schools or clubs) in two nights of glittering parades. These com-petitions draw some of Rio's best percussionists, dozens of lavish floats, and thousands of marchers, including statesmen, beauty queens, veteran samba musicians, soccer personalities, and would-be celebrities (even a few seconds of TV exposure marching with a samba school is enough to launch a modeling or acting career). They all weave through the aptly named Sambodromo from sunset to dawn. The floats have themes that run the gamut from political to playful; in past years they've included dark commentaries on the country's poor and silly tributes to plastic surgery.

In Salvador

Bahia's distinctive *axé* music has gained popularity around the country, and Salvador now competes with Rio's more traditional celebrations. Here, Carnaval means street dancing—night after night—to the music of the *trios elétricos* (bands on special sound trucks). It means watching parades of groups such as the Filhos de Gandhi (Sons of Gandhi), a Carnaval association founded by striking stevedores in 1949 and whose members dress in white tunics and turbans—the relics of Africa's Muslim conversions. And it means ridding yourself of your inhibitions and moving freely to ancient, mesmerizing rhythms produced by such famous percussion groups as Ilê Aiyê and Casa do Olodum.

In Recife and Olinda

In Recife, people attend *bailes* (dances) and *bloco* (percussion group) practice sessions for two months prior to the main festivities. Here the beat of choice is *frevo* (a fast-paced, frenetic music that normally accompanies a lively dance performed with umbrellas). Galo da Madrugada, the largest of Recife's estimated 500 blocos, officially opens Carnaval and has been known to draw 20,000 costumed revelers. Throughout the festivities the blocos are joined by escolas de samba, escolas de frevo, the *caboclinhos* (who dress in traditional Indian garb and bright feathers), and the *maracatus* (African processions accompanied by percussionists), among others. In Olinda, Carnaval lasts a full 11 days. Highlights include the opening events—led by a bloco of more than 400 "virgins" (men in drag)—and a parade of huge dolls (likenesses of famous northeasterners) made of Styrofoam, fabric, and papier-mâché.

Dining

Eating is a national passion, and the portions are huge. In many restaurants, plates are prepared for two people; when you order, ask if one plate will suffice. In major cities, the variety of eateries is staggering: Restaurants of all sizes and categories, snack bars, and fast-food outlets line downtown streets and fight for space in shopping malls. In São Paulo, for example, Italian eateries—whose risottos rival those of Bologna—sit beside Pan-Asian restaurants, which, like the chicest spots in North America and Europe, serve everything from Thai satay to sushi to Vietnamese summer rolls. In addition, there's excellent Portuguese, Chinese, Japanese, Arab, Hungarian, and Spanish cuisine. Outside the cities you'll find primarily typical, low-cost Brazilian meals that consist simply of *feijão preto* (black beans) and *arroz* (rice) served with beef, chicken, or fish. Manioc, a root vegetable that's used in a variety of ways, and beef are adored everywhere. Note that Brazilians eat few vegetables, and these often must be ordered separately.

Specialties

Between the extremes of sophistication and austere simplicity, each region has its own cuisine. You'll find exotic fish dishes in the Amazon, African spiced dishes in Bahia, and well-seasoned bean mashes in the mining country of Minas Gerais.

Many Brazilian dishes are adaptations of Portuguese specialties. Fish stews called *caldeiradas* and beef stews called *cozidos* (a wide variety of vegetables boiled with different cuts of beef and pork) are popular, as is *bacalhau*, salt cod cooked in sauce or grilled. *Salgados* (literally "salteds") are appetizers or snacks served in sit-down restaurants as well as stand-up *lanchonetes* (luncheonettes). Dried salted meats form the basis of many dishes from the interior and northeast of Brazil, and pork is used heavily in dishes from Minas Gerais. The national dish of Brazil is *feijoada* (a stew of black beans, sausage, pork, and beef), which is often served with arroz, shredded kale, orange slices, and manioc flour or meal—called *farofa* if it's coarsely ground, *farinha* if finely ground—that has been fried with onions, oil, and egg.

One of the most avid national passions is the *churrascarria*, where meats are roasted on spits over an open fire, usually *rodízio*-style. Rodízio means "going around," and waiters circulate nonstop carrying skewers laden with charbroiled hunks of beef, pork, and chicken, which are sliced onto your plate with ritualistic ardor. For a set price you get all the meat and side dishes you can eat.

The mainstay of *comida mineira* (the cuisine of Minas) is *tutu*, a tasty mash of black beans, bacon, and manioc meal served with meat dishes. Another bracing favorite is *feijão tropeiro,* a combination of brown beans, bacon, and manioc meal. Among meat dishes, pork is the most common, in particular the famed *lingüiça* (Minas pork sausage) and *lombo* (pork tenderloin). The most typical chicken dish is *frango ao molho pardo,* broiled chicken served in a sauce made with its own blood. The region's very mild white cheese is known throughout Brazil simply as *queijo do Minas* (cheese from Minas).

Seafood is the thing in Bahia, in great variety and quantity, prepared either Bahian style or using more traditional Continental recipes. A happy mix of African and local ingredients has come down the centuries from the hands and hearts of slave women, and then maids, working in Bahian kitchens.

The basic raw materials are coconut milk, lemon, coriander, tomato, *dendê* (palm oil), onions, dried shrimp, salt, and hot chili peppers. The ubiquitous *moqueca,* which has all these ingredients plus the seafood catch of the day, is cooked quickly in a clay pot over a high flame. Other main dishes include *vatapá,* a fish purée made of bread, ginger, peanuts, cashews, and olive oil; *caruru,* okra mashed with ginger, dried shrimp, and palm oil; *ximxim de galinha,* chicken with peanuts and coconut; and *efo,* a bitter chicorylike vegetable cooked with dried shrimp. Most restaurants serve hot pepper sauce on the side, as well as farofa or farinha, which do a delicious job of soaking up sauces. (Note that palm oil is high in cholesterol and hard to digest; you can order these dishes without it. And most Bahian restaurants are happy to prepare simpler fish or shrimp dishes even if they're not on the menu.)

Brazilian *doces* (desserts), particularly those of Bahia, are very sweet, and many are descendants of the egg-based custards and puddings of Portugal and France.

Cocada is shredded coconut caked with sugar; *quindim* is a small tart made from egg yolks and coconut; *doce de banana* (or any other fruit) is banana cooked in sugar; ambrosia is a lumpy milk and sugar pudding.

Coffee is served black and strong with sugar in demitasse cups and is called *cafezinho*. (Note that requests for *descafeinado* [decaf] will be met with a firm shake of the head "no," a blank stare, or outright amusement—it's just not a Brazilian thing.) Coffee is taken with milk—called *café com leite*—only at breakfast. Bottled mineral water is sold in two forms: with and without bubbles (*com gas* and *sem gas*, respectively).

The national drink is the *caipirinha*, made of crushed lime, sugar, and *pinga* or *cachaça* (sugarcane liquor). When whipped with crushed ice, fruit juices, and condensed milk, the pinga/cachaça becomes a *batida*. A *caipivodka*, or *caipiroska*, is the same cocktail with vodka instead of cachaça. Some bars make both drinks using fruit other than lime, like kiwi and *maracujá* (passion fruit). Brazil's best bottled beer is Cerpa, sold at most restaurants. In general, though, Brazilians prefer tap beer, called *chopp*, which is sold by all bars and some restaurants. Be sure to try the carbonated soft drink *guaraná*, made using the Amazonian fruit of the same name.

Futebol

South Americans in general are passionate about *futebol* (soccer), but Brazilians are virtually hysterical about it. Here, it's the stuff of myth and legend, with top players treated in a manner befitting minor deities. The world's most famous player, Pele, is Brazilian, and though he retired more than 20 years ago, he's still revered as a national hero. *O jogo bonito* (the beautiful game) is considered an art form. The best players are considered to possess the quality known as *jinga*, which translates roughly as a feline, almost swaggering grace. However, the professional game, although avidly followed throughout the country, suffers from chronic lack of funding; many of the country's best players leave to display their superlative skills abroad. Nevertheless, the national team is a repeat World Cup title holder, and you can catch some outstanding games in larger cities such as Rio and São Paulo. If you do attend a match, expect to see Brazilian fans at their passionate best and, alas, sometimes worst.

Lodging

Variety is the catchword in Brazil, where you can stay in world-class urban high-rises, "flat" (apartment) hotels, quaint *pousadas* (inns), rustic *fazendas* (farms or ranches), or jungle lodges. Just remember, however, that top prices aren't always indicators of deluxe accommodations. Embratur, the national tourism agency, has a rating system that often seems to merely take into consideration the amenities offered by a hotel without evaluating such vital intangibles as the quality of service and the upkeep.

Make reservations for stays in high-end establishments well in advance, particularly if you're planning a trip during peak season or special events. (Unless you're part of a tour, reservations in the best hotels must be made at least a year ahead for stays during Carnaval.) If possible, before you take a room in an inexpensive or moderate establishment, ask to see it. If you want a quieter room, a better view, or a *cama de casal* (a "couple's," or double, bed) instead of two singles, be sure to ask. Note that "motels" in Brazil are usually rented out for the hour, afternoon, or overnight. A pousada is always more advisable.

Music

Even a short list of Brazilian musical styles—which are as often linked to rhythms and dances as they are to tunes and lyrics—rolls off the tongue like an ancient chant: *axé, bossa nova, forró, frevo, lundu, maxixe, samba, tropicalismo*. Many of these are themselves divided into subcategories, with varying types of lyrics, singing styles, arrangements, and instrumentation. Some also fall into the supercategory of *música popular brasileira* (MPB; Brazilian popular music). Most fill the ear with a seamless and enchanting blend of European, African, and regional Brazilian sound.

The music for which Brazil is most famous, samba, has its roots in lundu (a Bantu rhythm that's reminiscent of a fandango yet is characterized by a free-form, hip-swiveling style of dance) and maxixe (a mixture of polka as well as Portuguese and African rhythms). The more mournful samba (from the Bantu word *semba,* meaning "gyrating movement") originated in Rio de Janeiro in the early 20th century but wasn't refined until the 1940s, when Rio's Carnaval competitions began. Contributions by performers in Bahia led to further transformations. Today its many forms include the pure samba *de morro* (literally "of the hill," figuratively "of the poor neighborhood"), which is performed using only percussion instruments, and the samba *cançao* (the more familiar "samba song").

From the samba came two more MPB genres: The bossa nova (a slang term that's akin to "new way" or, even, "new wave") and tropicalismo. Bossa nova—a blend of mellow samba, cool American jazz, and French impressionism—began in the late 1950s in Rio's chic Zona Sul neighborhoods of Copacabana, Ipanema, and Leblon. Its innovators included the classically trained composer, Tom Jobim; the poet and diplomat, Vinícius de Morais; and the northeastern guitarist, João Gilberto, and his wife and singer, Astrud Gilberto. The politically turbulent '60s and '70s saw the development of tropicalismo. Such northeastern musicians and intellectuals as Caetano Veloso, Chico Buarque, and Giberto Gil combined contemporary instruments (including the electric guitar and keyboard) and avant-garde experimentation with samba and other traditional rhythms. Often the tunes were upbeat even though the lyrics were highly critical of social injustice and political tyranny. The tropicalismo movement, though popular with the people, was frowned upon by the military regime. Some of its performers were arrested; others, including Veloso and Buarque, had to live abroad for several years.

In addition to being linked with tropicalismo, Brazil's northeast is known for several other musical styles. Many of these have gained popularity throughout the country. Among them are forró (which uses the accordion to its best—and most rhythmic—advantage), axé (a Bahian blend of samba and reggae), and frevo (a fast-paced dance music most associated with Recife's Carnaval).

FODOR'S CHOICE

Beaches

★ **Barra do Sahy, São Paulo.** Families in search of relief from the big city favor this beach on a North Shore bay.

★ **Barra da Tijuca, Rio de Janeiro.** The citizens of Rio adore this urban stretch of sand for its clean, refreshing waters; its cool breezes; and its many nearby amenities.

★ **Boa Viagem, Recife.** The aquamarine waters along this urban stretch form tidal pools near the *arrecifes* (reefs) that give the city its name. You'll also find cool breezes and plenty of Brazilian beach atmosphere.

★ **Búzios, Rio de Janeiro.** Just two hours from the city, this resort community and its string of gorgeous sands attract the chic and savvy from around the world.

★ **Canoa Quebrada, near Fortaleza.** Dunes, red cliffs, and palm groves are among this northeastern stretch's many charms.

★ **Ilha do Mel (South).** You must hike to the unspoiled beaches of this island, where cars aren't allowed and the number of visitors is limited each day.

★ **Ilha de Santa Catarina (South).** Any of the 42 beaches on this, the "Magic Island," will charm you immediately.

★ **Prainha and Grumari, Rio de Janeiro.** These two tiny crescents, just beyond Barra da Tijuca Beach, are so isolated that it's hard to believe they're part of the city.

★ **Stella Maris, Salvador.** *The* Salvador beach attracts both sun worshipers and surfers to its sands and shores; the famous food kiosks here also entice.

Comforts

★ **Bonaparte Hotel Residence, Brasília.** Stylish decor, spacious guest rooms, and outstanding business services are among the draws here. *$$$$*

★ **Caiman Ecological Refuge, Pantanal (West).** The deluxe ranch that pioneered the concept of sustainable land use and ecological awareness in the Pantanal remains one of the region's top lodges. *$$$$*

⭐ **Copacabana Palace, Rio de Janeiro.** Old World elegance and charm join contemporary amenities and excellent service at this grande dame. The guest list reads like a Who's Who of the last seven decades—Marlene Dietrich, Fred Astaire, Ginger Rogers, and Princess Di all stayed here. $$$$

⭐ **Costão do Santinho Resort, Florianópolis (South).** This comfortable, sophisticated resort enjoys a privileged location on a lovely beach as well as a solid roster of amenities. $$$$

⭐ **Fazenda Carmo Camará, Ilha do Marajó (Amazon).** A stay on this vast Amazonian buffalo farm makes for a memorable experience. You'll undoubtedly ride, drive, paddle, and swim by and amid the abundant wildlife. $$$$

⭐ **Gran Meliá São Paulo.** Location—near the business center and the exit to the beach—is a big draw here. There are also lots of creature comforts and amenities—including some of the high-tech variety. $$$$

⭐ **Hotel das Cataratas, Foz de Iguaçu (South).** The location itself—within the national park facing the falls—would put the Cataratas on any best-of list. Just the same, the ambience is unique, and the service is excellent. $$$$

⭐ **Lago Salvador, near Manaus (Amazon).** One of the famed jungle lodges near Manaus offers a sense of seclusion and unity with the forest as well as simple comforts. $$$$

⭐ **Naoum Plaza Hotel, Brasília.** Diplomats, politicians, and royalty have opted to stay at the Naoum for its sophistication, luxury, and service. $$$$

⭐ **Ouro Minas Palace Hotel, Belo Horizonte (Minas Gerais).** Outside the city center, this fine hotel offers elegant surroundings, excellent service, and many amenities. $$$$

⭐ **Solar Nossa Senhora do Rosário, Ouro Prêto (Minas Gerais).** One of the state's top hotels is housed in a beautiful baroque building and counts elegant guest rooms, impeccable service, and an outstanding French restaurant in its list of offerings. $$$$

⭐ **Solar da Ponte, Tiradentes (Minas Gerais).** This charming colonial inn has quiet, comfortable rooms, an immaculate English garden, and such enjoyments as afternoon tea. $$$$

⭐ **Academia de Tênis Resort, Brasília.** What started as a tennis club has grown into a full-fledged lakefront resort, with guest chalets and plenty of opportunities for swimming (in one of eight pools) or a tennis match (on one of 25 courts). $$$

⭐ **Caesar Towers, Porto Alegre (South).** Porto Alegre's finest hotel is in a pleasant, quiet neighborhood with views of the Rio Guaíba. $$$

⭐ **Maison Joly, São Paulo.** This Ilhabela establishment offers sophisticated service and amenities, which include a heliport and an outstanding restaurant. $$$

⭐ **Pousada dos Pireneus, Pirenópolis (West).** Well-heeled families from Brasília leave the starkness of their planned concrete-and-asphalt city for this beautifully landscaped resort on the outskirts of a colonial city. $$$

⭐ **Pousada do Principe, Rio de Janeiro.** As its name implies, this is the inn of a prince—literally. The great-grandson of Dom Pedro II runs this charming hotel in the enchanting colonial coastal town of Parati. $$

⭐ **Manacá, Belém (Amazon).** Confusion sets in when you see how little this attractive, comfortable, well-situated hotel actually costs. $

Flavors

⭐ **Le Coq d'Or, Ouro Prêto (Minas Gerais).** Here the executive chef (who trained at the prestigious Cordon Bleu in Paris) brings French inspiration to Brazilian cuisine. $$$$

⭐ **Troisgros, Rio de Janeiro.** A delicate use of Brazilian ingredients, and chefs whose creativity knows no end, result in dishes that are out of this world. $$$$

⭐ **Antigamente Lago Sul.** A lakefront setting and delicious Brazilian fare make a meal here memorable. $$$

⭐ **Boulevard, Curitiba (South).** In this top French restaurant, you might actually forget that you're in Brazil rather than France. $$$

⭐ **Caso do Ouvidor, Ouro Prêto (Minas Gerais).** The city's most popular restaurant serves the best in typical mineira food. $$$

★ **Chalezinho, Belo Horizonte (Minas Gerais).** This romantic, chalet-style restaurant in the hills above the city attracts couples in search of magical fondues and light evening music. $$$

★ **La Chaumiere, Brasília.** This has been the capital's finest French restaurant for years on end. $$$

★ **Famiglia Mancini, São Paulo.** The atmosphere here is jovial, the decor unique, and the Italian food delicious. $$$

★ **Il Gattopardo Ristorante, Porto Alegre (South).** The city's beautiful people regularly choose this restaurant for its fine Italian cuisine and its sophisticated ambience. $$$

★ **Marina Ponta da Areia Restaurant, Ilha da Santa Catarina (South).** Locals are fond of this seafood spot (the shrimp dishes are a particular treat) with its superb location overlooking the Lagoa da Conceição. $$$

★ **Porcão, Rio de Janeiro.** This restaurant embodies the boisterous churrascaria experience: harried waiters zip among tables, slicing sizzling chunks of tender grilled beef, pork, and chicken onto the plates of hungry diners. $$$

★ **Quatro Sete Meia, Rio de Janeiro.** The seafood treats from the top-class kitchen of this restaurant, which is in a fishing village just outside the city, are served indoors or outside in a garden that offers a stunning coastal panorama. $$$

★ **La Via Vechia, Brasília.** Here you can join politicians and other notables for an eclectic, though truly elegant, feast. $$$

★ **Lá em Casa, Belém (Amazon).** The outstanding interpretations of indigenous Amazon dishes have given this restaurant an international renown. $$

★ **Canto da Paixada (Manaus).** This restaurant's popularity stems from its masterful preparation of river fish, the staple of the Amazon. $$

★ **Galpão, São Paulo.** Don't come expecting a traditional pizzeria. The decor here is modern, reflecting the good taste of the architect-owner, and the delicious pies tend toward the nouveau. $$

★ **Minha Deusa, Ilha do Marajó (Ama-**zon). In a remote part of a tiny city on a remote island, this restaurant serves buffalo meat that's out of this world. $

Monumental Structures

★ **Basílica de Nazaré, Belém (Amazon).** Built entirely of marble, this spectacular church can hold its own next to any of the Old World's finest. It's no wonder, as most of the materials—except for the abundant gold—used to build it came from Europe.

★ **Catedral Metropolitana Nossa Senhora Aparecida, Brasília.** Oscar Niemeyer's audacious masterpiece honors Brazil's patron saint with a structure resembling a crown of thorns.

★ **Corcovado and Christo Redentor, Rio de Janeiro.** The statue of Christ the Redeemer—bathed in sunlight by day and in spotlight by night—gazes out benevolently from Corcovado Mountain, creating the city's most recognizable landmark.

★ **Edifício Itália, São Paulo.** The top of this building offers an incredible 360-degree view, making it one of the few places where you can get a sense of how big this city really is.

★ **Hidrelétrica de Itaipú (South).** The world's largest dam—truly a civil-engineering masterpiece—tames the mighty Rio Paraná.

★ **Igreja Bom Jesus do Matosinho, Congonhas do Campo (Minas Gerais).** It's not the church, but rather the twelve Old Testament prophets— carved from soapstone by the legendary Aleijadinho—standing before it that are among Brazil's most cherished artworks.

★ **Igreja de São Francisco, Salvador.** The ornate carvings and gold leaf of this church's interior will leave you breathless, particularly if you have a chance to see it all in natural light.

★ **Igreja São Francisco de Assis, Ouro Prêto (Minas Gerais).** This brilliant, baroque church with lavishly carved altars and soapstone sculptures is considered Aleijadinho's masterpiece.

★ **Memorial JK, Brasília.** Immerse yourself in the pyramid that contains displays on the city's history and is the final resting place of Juscelino Kubitschek, the man who made it all happen.

☆ **Palácio Catete, Rio de Janeiro.** The building's magnificent details (look at the ceilings) are almost as incredible as its history: the presidential residence until Brasília became the capital, it was, among other things, the place where Brazil signed a declaration of war against Germany in World War II and the spot where President Getúlio Vargas committed suicide in 1954.

☆ **Palácio do Itamaraty, Brasília.** This modernist structure houses Brazil's foreign ministry, an impressive collection of art, and an interior tropical garden designed by Roberto Burle Marx, who also created its memorable exterior waterscape.

☆ **Teatro Amazonas, Manaus (Amazon).** No other structure better represents the opulence and splendor of the Amazon's rubber boom.

Museums

☆ **Centro de Preservação da Arte, Cultura, e Ciências Indigena, near Santarém (Amazon).** The brilliantly assembled collection here does, indeed, help to preserve the art, culture, and science of indigenous peoples from throughout Latin America.

☆ **Museu de Arte Naïf do Brasil, Rio de Janeiro.** The canvases that grace the walls here bring to art what Brazilians bring to life: verve, color, and joy.

☆ **Museu de Arte de São Paulo.** MASP is the pride of São Paulo, and its image is linked to the city in the same way that the Eiffel Tower is linked to Paris.

☆ **Museu Chácara do Céu, Rio de Janeiro.** Situated atop a hill in an enchanting, breezy neighborhood, this museum's location is almost as appealing as its collection of modern art.

☆ **Museu Emílio Goeldi, Belém (Amazon).** In this small chunk of rain forest you'll find some of the Amazon's most interesting flora and fauna as well as an excellent museum with Indian artifacts.

☆ **Museu da Inconfidência, Ouro Prêto (Minas Gerais).** This museum commemorates Brazil's first attempt at independence, which was led by the courageous but ultimately unsuccessful Tiradentes.

☆ **Museu da Mineralogia e das Pedras, Ouro Prêto (Minas Gerais).** The large collections here illustrate Minas's gold and the wealth and variety of its gems.

☆ **Museu Republicano, São Paulo.** To learn how Brazil's Republican movement began, you should visit this museum in the town of Itu. Its many 19th-century documents and furnishings tell the tale.

Parks and Preserves

☆ **Pantanal Wetlands (West).** About the same size as the United Kingdom, this vast flood plain of the Rio Paraguay and its tributaries is considered the best place to see wildlife outside of sub-Saharan Africa. The savannas, forests, and swamps that make up the Pantanal are home to more than 600 species of birds as well as giant anteaters, anacondas, jaguars, otters, monkeys, and other creatures.

☆ **Parque da Pedreira, Curitiba (South).** Here, impressive landscaping and unique structures have given an abandoned quarry new life.

☆ **Parque Nacional do Iguaçu (South).** This naturalist's paradise has one of the world's most fantastic waterfalls and so much more.

☆ **Parque Nacional dos Aparados da Serra (South).** The awe-inspiring Paraná pine–fringed canyons here are often hidden by fog, evoking an other-worldly atmosphere.

☆ **Sítio Roberto Burle Marx.** Nestled on the outskirts of Rio de Janeiro's urban sprawl and just inland amid mangrove swamps and tropical jungle, this museum pays tribute to Brazil's finest landscape designer.

FESTIVALS AND SEASONAL EVENTS

Note that country-wide events and celebrations related to Brazil's biggest festival, Carnaval, start in January and peak in the days preceding Lent, sometime in February or March. Holy Week, in March or April, is marked by many events throughout the country, including Passion plays. Remember: the country's seasons are the reverse of those in the Northern Hemisphere.

WINTER

➤ MAY: Many communities throughout Brazil celebrate the **Festa do Divino Espírito Santo,** with food donations for the poor, processionals, and folkloric festivals. The central-west town of Pirenópolis observes the holiday with the *cavalhadas,* equestrian events that reenact battles between Christians and Moors.

➤ JUNE: The **Festas Juninas** is a cycle of celebrations throughout the month honoring various saints. The festivals are particularly noteworthy in Rio de Janeiro State and in several interior regions of the northeast. In São Paulo, the annual **Carlton Dance Festival** starts in June and continues through July. During Brasília's **Festa dos Estados,** held the last weekend of June, each of the nation's 26 states gets a chance to showcase its culture and traditions. Outside of Salvador, the

town of Cachoeira celebrates the **Feast of St. John** (June 23–24), which commemorates the harvest season. There are many special music and dance activities, and the children dress up in traditional garb. The **Paratins Folk Festival** (June 28–30) takes place 400 km (250 mi) downriver from Manaus and is the Amazon's largest folkloric festival. The chief event is the *boi bumba* dancing competition between two groups—the Garantidos (who wear red) and the Caprichosos (who wear blue)—that have slightly different styles. Among the more than 40,000 spectators, all wearing the color of their favorite group, there's a mania not unlike that of a soccer match.

➤ JULY: The **Festival de Inverno,** in Campos do Jordão, São Paulo, is one of Brazil's most important classical musical events. Young musicians can learn from more experienced ones, and everyone can watch performances at the Auditório Cláudio Santoro. On Ilhabela, July sees the **Semana da Vela,** which brings sailors from throughout Brazil to the island for competitions. During Ouro Prêto's week-long **winter festival** in mid-July the town is overtaken by musical and theatrical performances. In the west the **Chapada dos Guimarães Festival de Inverno** takes place the last week of July. Young hippies flock here for the variety of bands that perform and because this town—as the uncontested geodesic center of South

America—has some really good vibes. During Fortaleza's **Regata de Jangadas,** held in late July, you can watch fishermen race their *jangada* boats between Praia do Meireles and Praia Mucuripe. **Fortal,** Fortaleza's lively out-of-season Carnaval, is held the last week of the month.

➤ AUG.: São Paulo's Museu da Imagem e do Som sponsors the **International Short Film Festival** in August. The month also sees São Paulo's annual, three-day **Free Jazz Festival.** During Ilhabela's **Festival do Camarão,** restaurants get together to organize cooking contests and offer lectures. Salvador's **Festin Bahia** is a three-day international music festival held every August or September featuring foreign and local performers; past participants have included Maxi Priest, Youssou N'Dour, China Head, Carlinhos Brown, Pepeu Gomes, and Olodum. Many of the events are free. In Cachoeira, west of Salvador, the Irmandade da Boa Morte (Sisterhood of the Good Death; once a slave women's secret society) holds a **half-Candomblé, half-Catholic festival** August 14–16 honoring the spirits of the dead. In Fortaleza each August 15 the **Iemanjá Festival,** honors the water goddess on Praia do Futuro. In addition, August 22–29 sees Fortaleza's **Semana do Folclore,** the city's folklore week.

SPRING

➤ SEPT.: Ouro Prêto's giant, week-long **Julibeu do Senhor Ben Jesus do Matosinhos** religious festival is held in mid-September. One of Belém's two out-of-season Carnavals, **Paráfolia,** takes place at the end of September. The most interesting and eagerly awaited week on Ilha do Marajó (Amazon) comes in September when Soure hosts the annual **ExpoBúfalo.** The finest water buffalos in Brazil are brought here to compete in such categories as the prettiest and the best milk producer. The week-long **Cairé Festival,** held in Alter do Chão (Amazon) the second week of September, features folkloric music and dance presentations.

➤ OCT.: Not only is October 12 the official day (celebrated all over the country and particularly in Aparecida in São Paulo State) of Brazil's patron saint **Nossa Senhora da Aparecida,** but it's also **Children's Day.** São Paulo's international film festival, **Mostra Internacional de Cinema,** is held in October. The world-renowned biennial art exhibition (South America's largest), the **São Paulo Biennial,** is held from mid-October to mid-December in each even-numbered year in Ibirapuera Park. Porto Alegre's month-long **Feira do Livro** (Book Fair) is the largest and most famous event of its kind in Brazil. Blumenau's **Oktoberfest** lasts three weeks and emulates the original in Munich. The citizens of Recife repeat Carnaval in the weekend-long **Recifolia** festival; dates vary each year. On the second Sunday in October, thousands of worshipers flock to Belém for the **Círio de Nazaré** processional honoring the city's patron saint. There's also a procession on the river involving hundreds of boats bedecked in flowers.

➤ NOV.: In November Ouro Prêto's **Aleijadinho Week** honors the great 18th-century sculptor, whose work adorns many of the city's churches. The second of Belém's out-of-season Carnavals, **Carnabelém,** takes place in mid-November.

SUMMER

➤ JAN.: On **Ano Novo** (New Year's Eve) followers of Macumba (a spiritualist cult) honor Iemanjá, goddess of the sea, with fireworks, songs, rituals, and offerings along Rio's beaches, particularly Copacabana. Salvador's four-day **Festival of the Good Lord Jesus of the Seafarers** starts on the first Sunday of the month. It features samba and capoeira performances, feasts of Bahian food, and a processional—with hundreds of small vessels—along the coast to Boa Viagem Beach.

➤ FEB.: In Salvador the **Festival of Iemanjá** is held on the second Sunday of February. Devotees of the Afro-Brazilian Candomblé cult begin singing the sea goddess's praises at the crack of dawn along the beaches.

AUTUMN

➤ MARCH: The **Formula I Grand Prix** is held during March in São Paulo. In Salvador March sees **PanPerc,** a percussion festival in which such music notables as Gilberto Gil and Caetano Veloso perform alongside percussion groups. In Macapá (Amazon) the most important local holiday is the **Festa de São José,** a week-long celebration honoring the city's patron saint. The festivities, which consist mostly of traditional music and dance presentations, end on March 19.

➤ APRIL: The 21st is **Tiradentes Day,** a national holiday honoring the father of Brazil's 18th-century independence movement, the Inconfidência. On this date Joaquim José da Silva Xavier, known as Tiradentes ("tooth-puller") because he was a dentist, was executed for treason by the Portuguese crown in Ouro Prêto. The city celebrates over a four-day period (April 18–21) with many ceremonies.

2 RIO DE JANEIRO

The spectacular beauty of Rio is compelling. This glamorous metropolis is kissed by the sun, scalloped by gorgeous wide beaches, and dotted with dramatic mountains. Yet its history marked it not as a playground but as an important port—for the shipment of gold, gemstones, and coffee—and as a seat of colonial power.

Updated and
expanded by
Mary A.
Dempsey

RIO WAS NAMED—OR MISNAMED—BY the crew of a Portuguese ship that arrived in what is now the city on January 1, 1502. (Portuguese navigator Gonçalo Coelho as well as Amerigo Vespucci and Gaspar de Lemos—all members of the expedition—are alternatively credited with discovering the city.) Thinking they had found the mouth of a river, instead of the bay that became known as the Baía de Guanabara (Guanabara Bay), they dubbed the spot Rio de Janeiro (January River). Sixty-five years later, on the feast of St. Sebastian, the city was founded with the official name of São Sebastião do Rio de Janeiro.

In 1736, Brazil's colonial capital was moved to Rio from Salvador and, in 1889 when the country became independent, Rio was declared the capital of the Republic of Brazil. It held this title until 1960 when the federal government was moved to Brasília.

Today, this pulsating city is synonymous with the girl from Ipanema, the dramatic Pão d'Açucar (Sugarloaf) Mountain, and the wild and outrageous Carnaval (Carnival) celebrations. But Rio is also a city of stunning architecture, good museums, and marvelous food; it's a teeming metropolis where the very rich and the very poor live in uneasy proximity and where enthusiasm is boundless—and contagious.

As you leave the airport and head to your hotel, you'll be tossed onto a massive, chaotic, not-so-scenic urban roadway. But, by the time you reach breezy, sunny Avenida Atlântica—flanked on one side by white beach and azure sea, and on the other by the pleasure-palace hotels that testify to the city's eternal lure—your heart will leap with expectation. Now you're truly in Rio, where the 10 million wicked angels and shimmering devils known as *cariocas* dwell.

The term "carioca" comes from the country's early history, when it meant "white man's house" and was used to describe a Portuguese trading station. Today the word defines more than birthplace, race, or residence: It represents an ethos of pride, a sensuality, and a passion for life. Much of the carioca verve comes from the sheer physical splendor of a city blessed with seemingly endless beaches and sculpted promontories.

Prepare to have your senses engaged and your inhibitions untied. You'll be seduced by a host of images: the joyous bustle of vendors at Sunday's Feira Hippie (Hippie Fair); the tipsy babble at sidewalk cafés as patrons sip their last glass of icy beer under the stars; the blanket of lights beneath Pão d'Açucar; the bikers, joggers, strollers, and power walkers who parade along the beach each morning. Borrow the carioca spirit for your stay; you may find yourself reluctant to give it back.

Pleasures and Pastimes

Beaches

Rio's beaches define its culture: vibrant, joyful, beautiful. From infants to women in barely-there string bikinis—known as *tangas*—and thong-wearing men to senior citizens, the beach culture seduces all. The strands of tawny sand are exercise centers, gathering places, lovers' lanes—in effect, the city's pulse points. And every beach has its own flavor: from grande dame Copacabana with its volleyball nets and outdoor cafés to the seductive Ipanema; from São Conrado with its hang gliders to the hip, expansive Barra da Tijuca. And a day at the beach doesn't necessarily mean just a day of swimming. Although cariocas wander into the water to surf or cool off, most spend their time crammed on the sand, sunning and socializing. (Note: beach vendors aren't supposed to charge more than R$5.50 for a beer or other alcoholic beverage, R$4.50 for a coconut water, or R$3 for a mineral water.)

Carnaval

Of the great carnivals of the world—Venice in Europe, Trinidad and Tobago in the Caribbean, and Mardi Gras in New Orleans—the most amazing may be Brazil's. And while Carnaval celebrations unfold all over this South American country, there's none more glittery, glitzy, or downright decadent than Rio's. During the four official days of the celebration, which ends the day before Lent begins, *escolas de samba* (samba schools, which are actually neighborhood groups, not schools at all) compete in opulent parades, and costumed revelers writhe at street parties and gala balls to the seductive samba beat. "Costume" is a relative term: some are wildly elaborate; others are barely there. The joyous free-for-all infects even the most staid.

Dining

With more than 900 restaurants, Rio's dining choices are broad, from savory Middle Eastern to exceptional Italian and French. There are casual walk-up kiosks where sandwiches and fresh juices are the mainstays, and there are elegant eateries with posh decor, award-winning kitchens, and first-class service. Be sure to sample some local fare such as that found at the *churrascarias* (steak houses specializing in grilled meats). *Feijoada* (a hearty black bean and pork meat stew) is the national dish. Wash it down with a *chopp* (the local draft beer; pronounced *shop*, as in "born to") or a *caipirinha* (made with crushed lime, crushed ice, and a potent sugarcane liquor called *cachaça*). For price categories, *see* Dining *in* Smart Travel Tips A to Z.

Lodging

From luxury high-rise hotels gazing out over the beaches and ocean, to small inland inns, to aparthotels (apartments with hotel service that are popular with business travelers), you'll find a range of lodging options here. You may also find prices high, but that surprise will be softened by the top-rate service that's synonymous with carioca hospitality. Many hotels have computers and business services, and some include generous breakfast buffets in their rates; the concierges are more than willing to help you nab samba show tickets, tables at the best eateries, or a reliable, English-speaking tour guide. If you plan to spend time at the beach, your best bet is a hotel along Copacabana, Ipanema, or Barra da Tijuca. (Copacabana has the advantage of being on the *metrô,* or subway, line.) For price categories, *see* Lodging *in* Smart Travel Tips A to Z.

Side Trips

As tantalizing as Rio is, you'll have a far richer taste of Brazil—of its imperial past and its jet-setting present—if you wander outside town. A scenic road leads to Petrópolis and the opulent imperial palace that was the summer home of Brazil's emperor. Swiss-settled Novo Friburgo peeks from a lush valley speckled with waterfalls. Sailboat-jammed Cabo Frio is a popular coastal resort, and although Brigitte Bardot in a bikini may have put Búzios on the map, it is really its 23 beaches, temperate weather, and sophisticated ambience that have kept it there. Southwest of Rio, on Brazil's Costa Verde (Green Coast), Angra dos Reis is the jumping off point for 365 islands that pepper a picturesque bay. One of the loveliest, Ilha Grande, is lapped by emerald waters and retains an unspoiled flavor despite its popularity. The most amazing gem, however, is the coastal town of Parati and its 18th-century architecture; the lovely cays sprinkled along its bay have attracted the likes of British rocker Mick Jagger and Brazilian actress Sonia Braga.

EXPLORING RIO DE JANEIRO

Cariocas divide their city into three sections: Zona Norte (North Zone), Zona Sul (South Zone), and the "downtown" area that separates them, called Centro. Except for some museums, churches, and historical sights, most of the tourism activity is in the beach- and hotel-laden Zona Sul. To sense the carioca spirit, spend a day on Copacabana and walk from the Avenida Atlântica to Ipanema. The western extension of Ipanema, Leblon, is an affluent, intimate community flush with good, small restaurants and bars (sadly, the water is polluted). The more distant southern beaches, beginning with São Conrado and extending past Barra da Tijuca to Grumari, become richer in natural beauty and increasingly isolated.

Although Rio's settlement dates back nearly 500 years, it's in every respect a modern city. Most of the historic structures have fallen victim to the wrecking ball, though a few churches and villas are still tucked in and around Centro. As these colonial vestiges are far flung, consider seeing them on an organized walking or bus tour. However, you can use the metrô (and comfortable walking shoes) to explore on your own. The bus is another option; just be sure to know where you're going and memorize some key phrases in Portuguese as bus drivers don't speak English. Police have put a dent in the crime, but as in any large city, be discreet and aware.

Great Itineraries

IF YOU HAVE 3 DAYS

If you only have three days, you must visit Rio's two most famous peaks: try Pão d'Açucar your first morning and Corcovado—and the nearby Museu de Arte Naif do Brasil—that afternoon. In between, swing by the little Museu Carmen Miranda to see the Brazilian bombshell's costumes, jewelry, and wild headdresses. In the evening, join the fun at a samba show. Set your second day aside for exploring historic Rio—perhaps having lunch in Centro at the opulent Café do Teatro—and for shopping. By your third day, the sun and sand will be irresistible. Explore Copacabana and Ipanema, or settle in under a beach umbrella on breezy Barra da Tijuca. In the evening, try the national dish at Ipanema's Casa da Feijoada.

IF YOU HAVE 5 DAYS

On your first day, explore Centro, take the cable car to Pão d'Açucar, and head to a samba show at Plataforma. The next day, jump on the cogwheel train to Corcovado and set aside time for the captivating Museu de Arte Naif do Brasil near its base before indulging in a Brazilian barbecue at Mariu's or Porcão. Bike or walk off that lunch at Lagoa Rodrigo de Freitas, then slide into a shopping center. On your third day, stroll from Copacabana to Ipanema, stopping en route to order a tropical pizza at Bar Garota de Ipanema, or grab an icy drink on Barra da Tijuca. Take an organized *favela* (shantytown) tour in the afternoon and, in the evening, dine on feijoada or churrasco. On the fourth day, head for Petrópolis to see the Imperial Palace, or make the 40-minute drive to Sítio Roberto Burle Marx to see the country house and gardens of Brazil's most famous landscaper. Have your concierge check the evening schedule at the Banco do Brasil Cultural Center. On your last day, take the Santa Teresa trolley to the charming neighborhood with the Museu Chácara do Céu before you hop the metrô to the opulent Palácio Catete. Wind up the day at the kitschy Museu Carmen Miranda.

Begin in the Flamengo and Botafogo neighborhoods and Pão d'Açucar; work in visits to the Museu Carmen Miranda and the Museu de Arte Moderna. On the second day, wander through Centro and head for the Palácio Catete. Then take the trolley to Santa Teresa and the Museu Chácara do Céu. On the third day, beach-hop by bus early in the day and then do some shopping. On your fourth day, slide out of town to Petrópolis or down the coast to Angra dos Reis or Parati for a day or two. When you return to Rio, visit Corcovado and the nearby Museu de Arte Naïf do Brasil; spend the afternoon roaming through the Jardim Botânico or biking around Lagoa Rodrigo de Freitas. Your final days could include an escape to Prainha and Grumari beaches and the Sítio Roberto Burle Marx or a favela tour. In the evenings, catch a samba revue or bossa nova or jazz show or head out dancing. If you're in the city on Sunday, wander through Ipanema's Feira Hippie.

When to Tour

Carnaval is the best time to soak in the city's energy. Arrive a few days before the celebrations begin (or stay a few days after they end) to enjoy the museums and other sights that close for the four days of revelry. Be sure to book your hotel and flight at least one year in advance. To tour the city at a quieter time with gentler temperatures (it usually stays in the 90s during Carnaval) and lower prices, the off season runs from May to October (Brazil's winter).

Centro and Environs

What locals generally refer to as Centro is a sprawling collection of several districts that contain the city's oldest neighborhoods, churches, and most enchanting cafés. Rio's beaches, broad boulevards, and modern architecture may be impressive, but its colonial structures and old narrow streets and alleyways in leafy inland neighborhoods are no less so.

Numbers in the text correspond to numbers in the margin and on the Rio Centro and Environs map.

A Good Tour (or Two)

Start at the **Mosteiro de São Bento** ① for your first taste of Brazilian baroque architecture. From here, move south into the heart of Centro. At the beginning of Avenida Presidente Vargas you'll find the solid **Igreja de Nossa Senhora da Candelária** ②. From this church there are several options: Soccer fans can take a cab or the metrô to **Maracanã** soccer stadium, where the *jogo bonito* (beautiful game) is played; those who prefer a more bucolic setting can head (by cab or metrô) to **Quinta da Boa Vista;** and history buffs can walk south along Avenida 1 de Março, crossing it and heading west to a network of narrow lanes and alleys highlighted by the **Beco do Comércio** ③, a pedestrian street. After wandering this area, return to Avenida 1 de Março and walk southeast to the Praça 15 de Novembro, a square that's dominated by the **Paço Imperial** ④. A few blocks away is the large **Museu Histórico Nacional** ⑤.

From the Museu Histórico Nacional, follow Rua Santa Luzia southeast to Avenida Rio Branco, Centro's main thoroughfare. North one block is the Victorian **Biblioteca Nacional** ⑥, and one block up from it is the French neoclassical **Museu Nacional de Belas Artes** ⑦. In the middle of the next block up, and across Rio Branco, you'll find the **Teatro Municipal** ⑧ and its elegant café. Continue north on Rio Branco and turn left on Avenida Almirante Barroso. A short walk northwest brings you to the Largo da Carioca, a large square near the Carioca metrô stop. Atop a low hill overlooking it are the **Igreja de São Francisco da Penitência** ⑨ and the **Convento do Santo Antônio** ⑩. The architecturally striking (or absurd, depending on your viewpoint) **Catedral de São Sebastião do Rio de Janeiro** ⑪ is just south of here (off Avenida República do Chile), as is the station where you can take a *bonde* (trolley) over the **Aqueduto da Carioca** ⑫ and along charming Rua Joaquim Murtinho into Santa Teresa. This eccentric neighborhood is famed for its cobblestone streets and its popular **Museu Chácara do Céu** ⑬, whose works are displayed in a magnificent former home with beautiful city views.

TIMING AND PRECAUTIONS
Although you can follow this tour in a day if you set out early, you might want to break it up into two days or be selective about which museums you fully explore. You can also mix some of the southernmost sights in with those (the Aterro do Flamengo, Museu de Arte Moderna, or Monumento aos Pracinhas) in the Flamengo, Botafogo, and Pão d'Açucar tour (☞ *below*). However you organize your day, you'll need plenty of energy to get everything in. Leave your camera at your hotel if you're planning to use public transportation. Wear no jewelry, and keep your cash in a money belt or safe pocket.

Sights to See

⑫ **Aqueduto da Carioca.** The imposing Carioca Aqueduct, with its 42 massive stone arches, was built between 1744 and 1750 to carry water from the Rio Carioca in the hillside neighborhood of Santa Teresa to Centro. In 1896 the city transportation company converted the then-abandoned aqueduct to a viaduct, laying trolley tracks along it. Since then, Rio's distinctive trolley cars (called "bondes" because they were financed by foreign bonds) have carried people between Santa Teresa and Centro. (Guard your belongings particularly closely when you ride the open-sided bondes; the fare is about 50¢.) *Metrô: Carioca or Cinelândia.*

❸ **Beco do Comércio.** A network of narrow streets and alleys is the setting for this pedestrian thoroughfare. The area is flanked by restored 18th-century homes, now converted to offices. The best known is the Edifício Telles de Menezes. A famous arch, the Arco dos Telles, links this area with Praça 15 de Novembro. ⊠ *Praça 15 de Novembro No. 34, Centro. Metrô: Uruguaiana.*

❻ **Biblioteca Nacional.** Corinthian columns flank the neoclassical National Library (built between 1905 and 1908), the first such establishment in Latin America. Its original archives were brought to Brazil by King João VI in 1808. Today it contains roughly 13 million books, including two 15th-century bibles; New Testaments from the 11th and 12th centuries; first-edition Mozart scores as well as scores by Carlos Gomes (who adapted the José de Alencar novel about Brazil's Indians, *O Guarani,* into an opera of the same name); books that belonged to the Empress Teresa Christina; and many other manuscripts, prints, and drawings. Tours aren't available in English, but the devoted staff of docents will work something out to accommodate English-speaking book lovers. ⊠ *Av. Rio Branco 219,* ☎ *021/262–8255.* ⊡ *Admission.* ☉ *Weekdays 9–8, Sat. 9–3. Tours: Weekdays at 11, 1, 3, and 5. Metrô: Cinelândia.*

⑪ **Catedral de São Sebastião do Rio de Janeiro.** The exterior of this metropolitan cathedral (circa 1960), which looks like a concrete beehive, can be off-putting. (The daring modern design stands in sharp contrast to the baroque style of other churches.) But don't judge until

Rio Centro and Environs

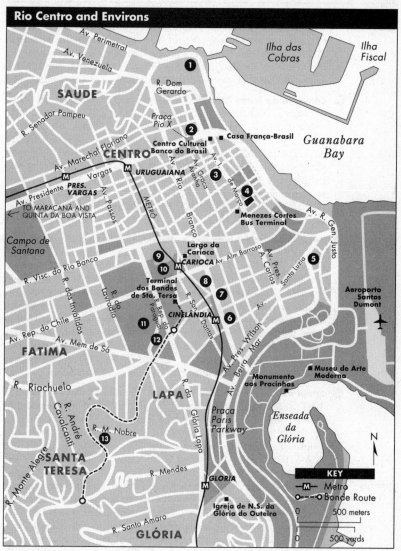

Av. Perimetral

Av. Venezuela

SAUDE

R. Dom Gerardo

R. Senador Pompeu

Praça Pio X

Ilha das Cobras

Ilha Fiscal

❶

❷ Centro Cultural Banco do Brasil

Casa França-Brasil ■

Guanabara Bay

Av. Marechal Floriano

CENTRO

M Vargas

Av. Presidente

PRES. VARGAS

Av. Passos

TO MARACANÃ AND QUINTA DA BOA VISTA

M **URUGUAIANA**

Av. Graça Aranha

Av. Rio Branco

MÉTRÔ

Av. 1 de Março

❸

❹

Menezes Cortes Bus Terminal

Av. R. Gen. Justo

Campo de Santana

R. Visc. do Rio Banco

R. dos Invalidos

Av. Rep. do Chile

R. da Lavadio

Largo da Carioca

CARIOCA

❾

❿

Terminal dos Bondes de Sta. Tersa

❽

Av. Alm Barroso

A. Carlos

Av. Pres. Carlos

Santa Luzia

❺

Aeroporto Santos Dumont

R. Rep. do Paraguai

❼

R. Santa Danias

❻

M **CINELÂNDIA**

Av. Mem de Sá

FATIMA

⓫

⓬

R. Riachuelo

R. André Cavalcanti

LAPA

R. da Glória Lapa

Av. Pres. Wilson

Av. Beira Mar

Monumento aos Pracinhas

Museu de Arte Moderna ■

R. M. Nobre

⓭

Praça Paris Parkway

Enseada da Glória

N

R. Monte Alegre

SANTA TERESA

R. Mendes

M **GLORIA**

KEY

M — Métro

o–●–o Bonde Route

R. Santo Amaro

GLÓRIA

Igreja de N.S. da Glória do Outeiro ■

0   500 meters

0   500 yards

Aqueduto da Carioca, **12**

Beco do Comércio, **3**

Biblioteca Nacional, **6**

Catedral de São Sebastião do Rio de Janeiro, **11**

Convento do Santo Antônio, **10**

Igreja de Nossa Senhora da Candelária, **2**

Igreja de São Francisco da Penitência, **9**

Mosteiro de São Bento, **1**

Museu Chácara do Céu, **13**

Museu Histórico Nacional, **5**

Museu Nacional de Belas Artes, **7**

Paço Imperial, **4**

Teatro Municipal, **8**

you've stepped inside. Outstanding stained-glass windows transform the interior—which is 96 m (315 ft) in diameter and 80 m (263 ft) high—into a warm, yet serious, place of worship that accommodates up to 20,000 people. An 8½-ton granite rock lends considerable weight to the concept of an altar. ⊠ *Av. República do Chile 245,* ☎ *021/240–2869.* ☒ *Free.* ☉ *Daily 7–5:30. Metrô: Carioca or Cinelândia.*

🔟 **Convento do Santo Antônio.** The Convent of St. Anthony was completed in 1780, but some parts date from 1615, making it one of Rio's oldest structures. (At press time, the convent was being thoroughly restored.) Its baroque interior contains priceless colonial art—including wood carvings and wall paintings—and the sacristy is covered with *azulejos* (Portuguese tiles). Note that the church has no bell tower: its bells hang from a double arch on the monastery ceiling. An exterior mausoleum contains the tombs of the offspring of Dom Pedro I and Dom Pedro II. ⊠ *Largo da Carioca 5,* ☎ *021/262–0129.* ☒ *Free.* ☉ *Weekdays 2–5. Metrô: Carioca.*

❷ **Igreja de Nossa Senhora da Candelária.** The classic symmetry of Candelária's white dome and bell towers casts an unexpected air of sanity over the chaos of downtown traffic. The church, which supports 630 tons of stonework on its foundation, was built on the site of a chapel founded in 1610 by Antônio de Palma after he survived a shipwreck; paintings in the present dome tell his tale. Construction on the church in its present state began in 1775, and although it was formally dedicated by the emperor in 1811, work on the dome wasn't completed until 1877. The sculpted bronze doors were exhibited at the 1889 world's fair in Paris. ⊠ *Praça Pio X,* ☎ *021/233–2324.* ☒ *Free.* ☉ *Weekdays 7:30–noon and 1–4:30, weekends 8–1. Metrô: Uruguaiana.*

❾ **Igreja de São Francisco da Penitência.** The church was completed in 1737, nearly four decades after it was started. Today it's famed for its wooden sculptures and its rich gold-leaf interior. The nave contains a painting of St. Francis, the patron of the church—reportedly the first painting in Brazil done in perspective. ⊠ *Largo da Carioca 5,* ☎ *021/262–0197.* ☉ *By appointment. Metrô: Carioca.*

OFF THE
BEATEN PATH

MARACANÃ – From the Igreja de Nossa Senhora da Candelária, you can walk 3½ blocks to the Uruguaiana station and take the metrô to the world's largest soccer stadium. Officially called Estádio Mario Filho after a famous journalist, but best known as Maracanã for the neighborhood in which it's situated (and a nearby river), this 178,000-seat stadium (with standing room for another 42,000) went up in record time to host the 1950 World Cup. Brazil lost its chance at the cup by losing a match 2–1 to Uruguay—a game that's still analyzed a half century later. It was here that soccer star Pelé made his 1,000th goal in 1969. The smaller 17,000-seat arena in the same complex hosts events featuring such notables as Madonna, Paul McCartney, and Pope John Paul II. Stadium tours are offered daily (except on match days). ⊠ *Rua Prof. Eurico Rabelo,* ☎ *021/264–9962 or 021/242–8806 (group tours). Metrô: Maracanã.*

❶ **Mosteiro de São Bento.** Just a glimpse of this church's main altar will fill you with awe. Layer upon layer of curvaceous wood carvings—coated in gold—create a sense of movement. Spiral columns whirl upward to capitals topped by cherubs so chubby and angels so purposeful that they seem almost animated. Although the Benedictines arrived in 1586, they didn't begin work on this church and monastery until 1617. It was completed in 1641, but such artisans as Mestre Valentim (who designed the silver chandeliers) continued to add details almost through to the 19th century. On some Sundays, mass here is accompanied by Gregorian chant. ⊠ *Rua Dom Gerardo 32,* ☎ *021/291–7122.* ⊠ *Free.* ⊙ *Weekdays 8–11 and 2:30–5:30.*

★ **⑬** **Museu Chácara do Céu.** With its cobblestone streets and bohemian atmosphere, Santa Teresa is a delightfully eccentric neighborhood. Gabled Victorian mansions sit beside alpine-style chalets as well as more prosaic dwellings—many hanging at unbelievable angles from the flower-encrusted hills. Set here, too, is the quaintly named Museum of the Small Farm of the Sky whose outstanding collection of mostly modern works were left—along with the hilltop house that contains it—by one of Rio's greatest arts patrons, Raymundo de Castro Maya. Included are originals by such 20th-century masters as Pablo Picasso, Georges Braque, Salvador Dalí, Edgar Degas, Henri Matisse, Amedeo Modigliani, and Claude Monet. The Brazilian holdings include priceless 17th- and 18th-century maps and works by leading modernists. The grounds afford fine views of the aqueduct, Centro, and the bay. ⊠ *Rua Murtinho Nobre 93,* ☎ *021/507–1932.* ⊠ *Free.* ⊙ *Wed.–Mon. noon–5.*

NEED A BREAK?
Santa Teresa's has attracted artists, musicians, and intellectuals to its eclectic slopes. Their hangout is **Bar do Arnaudo** (⊠ Rua Almirante Alexandrino 316-B, ☎ 021/252–7246), which is always full.

---

❺ **Museu Histórico Nacional.** The building that houses the National History Museum dates from 1762, though some sections—such as the battlements—were erected as early as 1603. It seems appropriate that this colonial structure should exhibit relics that document Brazil's history. Among its treasures are rare papers, Latin American coins, carriages, cannons, and religious art. ⊠ *Praça Marechal Ancora,* ☎ *021/550–9266.* ⊠ *Free.* ⊙ *Tues.–Fri. 10–5:30, weekends 2–6. Metrô: Carioca or Cinelândia.*

❼ **Museu Nacional de Belas Artes.** Works by Brazil's leading 19th- and 20th-century artists fill the space at the National Museum of Fine Arts. Although the most notable canvases are those by the country's best-known modernist, Cândido Portinari, be on the lookout for such gems as Leandro Joaquim's heart-warming, 18th-century painting of Rio. (At once primitive and classical, the small oval canvas seems a window on a time when fishermen still cast nets in the waters below the landmark Igreja de Nossa Senhora da Glória do Outeiro.) After wandering the picture galleries, consider touring the extensive collections of folk and African art. ⊠ *Av. Rio Branco 199,* ☎ *021/240–0068.* ⊠ *Free.* ⊙ *Tues.–Fri. 10–6, weekends 2–6. Metrô: Carioca or Cinelândia.*

❹ **Paço Imperial.** This two-story colonial building is notable for its thick stone walls and entrance, and its courtyard paved with huge stone slabs. It was built in 1743, and for the next 60 years it was the headquarters for Brazil's captains (viceroys), appointed by the Portuguese court in Lisbon. When King João VI arrived, he made it his royal palace. After Brazil's declaration of independence, the emperors Pedro I and II called the palace home. When the monarchy was overthrown, the building became Rio's central post office. Restoration work in the 1980s transformed it into a cultural center and concert hall. The third floor has a restaurant and a ground-floor shop sells stationery and CDs. The square, **Praça 15 de Novembro,** on which the palace is set has witnessed some of Brazil's most significant historical moments. Known in colonial days as Largo do Paço, it was here that two emperors were crowned, slavery was abolished, and Emperor Pedro II was deposed. Its modern name refers to the date of the declaration of the Republic of Brazil: November 15, 1889. ⊠ *Praça 15 de Novembro 48, Centro,* ☎ *021/533–4407.* ⊠ *Free.* ⊙ *Tues.–Sun. noon–6:30.*

OFF THE
BEATEN PATH
QUINTA DA BOA VISTA – West of downtown, set amid the entrancing, landscaped grounds of a former royal estate, you'll find pools and marble statues as well as the **Museu Nacional** and the **Jardim Zoológico.** Housed in what was once the imperial palace (circa 1803), the museum has exhibits on Brazil's past and on its flora, fauna, and minerals—including the biggest meteorite (5 tons) found in the Southern Hemisphere. At the zoo, you can see animals from Brazil's wilds in re-creations of their natural habitats. One of the highlights is the Nocturnal House, where you can spot such night creatures as bats and sloths. *Entrance at corner of Av. Paulo e Silva and Av. Bartolomeu de Gusmão,* ☎ *021/ 568–7400 (museum) and 021/569–2024 (zoo).* ⊠ *Admission.* ⊙ *Tues.–Sun. 9–4:30. Metrô: San Cristóvão.*

8 **Teatro Municipal.** Carrara marble, stunning mosaics, glittering chandeliers, bronze and onyx statues, gilded mirrors, German stained-glass windows, brazilwood inlay floors, and murals by Brazilian artists Eliseu Visconti and Rodolfo Amoedo make the Municipal Theater opulent, indeed. Opened in 1909, it's reportedly a scaled-down version of the Paris Opera House. The main entrance and first two galleries are particularly ornate. As you climb to the upper floors, the decor becomes more ascetic—a reflection of a time when different classes entered through different doors and sat in separate sections. The theater seats 2,357—with outstanding sightlines—for its dance performances and classical music concerts. Tours are available by appointment. ⊠ *Praça Floriano 210,* ☎ *021/297–4411. Metrô: Cinelândia or Carioca.*

NEED A
BREAK?
Elegance joins good food in the lower level of the Teatro Municipal at the charming **Café do Teatro** (⊠ Praça Floriano 210, ☎ 021/297–4411). Have a light lunch (weekdays 11–3) or coffee and a pastry (served at lunch and during evening performances) as you drink in the atmosphere. Taking center stage is the Assyrian motif, replete with columns and wall mosaics that look like something out of a Cecil B. De-Mille epic. The bar resembles a sarcophagus, and two sphinxes flank the sunken dining area. Note that this is one of the few cafés where you may be turned away if you're dressed too shabbily.

Flamengo, Botafogo, and Pão d'Açucar

These neighborhoods and their most famous peak—Pão d'Açucar—are like a bridge between the southern beach districts and Centro. Several highways intersect here, making it a hub for drives to Corcovado, Copacabana, Barra, or Centro. The metrô also travels through the area. Although the districts are largely residential, you'll find Rio Sul, one of the city's most popular shopping centers, as well as good museums and fabulous public spaces.

The eponymous beach at Flamengo no longer draws swimmers (its gentle waters look appealing but are polluted; the people you see here are sunning, not swimming). A marina sits on a bay at one end of the beach, which is connected via a busy boulevard to the smaller beach (also polluted) at Botafogo. This neighborhood is home to the city's yacht club, and when Rio was Brazil's capital, it was also the site of the city's glittering embassy row. The embassies were long ago transferred to Brasília, but the mansions that housed them remain. Among Botafogo's more interesting mansion- and tree-lined streets are Mariana, Sorocaba, Matriz, and Visconde de Silva.

Botafogo faces tiny sheltered Urca, which is separated by Pão d'Açucar from a small patch of yellow sand called Vermelha. This beach is, in turn, blocked by the Urubu and Leme mountains from the 1-km (½-mi) Leme Beach at the start of the Zona Sul (☞ *below*).

Numbers in the text correspond to numbers in the margin and on the Rio de Janeiro City map.

A Good Tour

Start at the northern end of the lovely, landscaped **Aterro do Flamengo** and the **Museu de Arte Moderna (MAM)** ⑭. Nearby is the **Monumento aos Pracinhas** ⑮, which honors the dead of World War II. Wander south along the Aterro before hopping a cab and heading inland to the hilltop **Igreja de Nossa Senhora da Glória do Outeiro** ⑯. From the church, walk south along Rua da Glória da Lapa (or get on the metrô at the Glória station and take it one stop to the Catete terminal). At the corner of the Rua da Catete you'll find the **Palácio Catete** ⑰. From here you can either return to the Aterro by cab and walk south to the **Museu Carmen Miranda** ⑱ or you can take the metrô to the Botafogo stop and the nearby **Casa Rui Barbosa** ⑲. Finish the tour by riding the cable car up the **Pão d'Açucar** ⑳ for panoramic views of the bay and the neighborhoods you've just explored.

TIMING AND PRECAUTIONS

This tour takes a full day and involves a lot of walking and time outdoors. You can shorten the itinerary by taking a cab to sights off the Aterro do Flamengo and/or from one end of the Aterro to the other. As always, keep your money and other valuables out of sight while strolling.

Sights to See

Aterro do Flamengo. This waterfront park flanks Baía de Guanabara from the Glória neighborhood to Flamengo. It gets its name from its location atop an *aterro* (landfill), and was designed by landscape architect Roberto Burle Marx. Paths used for jogging, walking, and biking wind through it, and there are also playgrounds and public tennis and basketball courts. On weekends the freeway beside the park is closed to traffic, and the entire area becomes one enormous public space.

⑲ **Casa Rui Barbosa.** Slightly inland from the Aterro is a museum in what was once the house of the 19th-century Brazilian statesmen and scholar, Rui Barbosa (a liberal from Bahia State, Barbosa drafted one of Brazil's early constitutions). The pink mansion dates from 1849 and contains memorabilia of Barbosa's life, including his 1913 car and an extensive library that's often consulted by scholars from around the world. ⊠ *Rua São Clemente 134, Botafogo,* ☎ *021/537–0036.* ◫ *Admission.* ◷ *Tues.–Fri. 9–4, weekends 2–5. Metrô: Botafogo.*

⑯ **Igreja de Nossa Senhora da Glória do Outeiro.** Set atop a hill, the baroque Glória Church is visible from many spots in the city, making it a landmark that's truly cherished by the cariocas. Its location was a strategic point in the city's early days. Estácio da Sá took this hill from the French in the 1560s and then went on to expand the first settlement and found a city for the Portuguese. The church, which wasn't built here until 1739, is notable for its octagonal floor plan, large dome, ornamental stonework, and vivid tilework. ⊠ *Praça Nossa Senhora da Glória 135, Glória,* ☎ *021/557–4600.* ◫ *Free.* ◷ *Tues.–Fri. 9–noon and 1–5, weekends 9–noon. Tours by appointment 1st Sun. of the month. Metrô: Glória.*

⑮ **Monumento aos Pracinhas.** The Monument to the Brazilian Dead of World War II (the nation sided with the Allies during the conflict) is

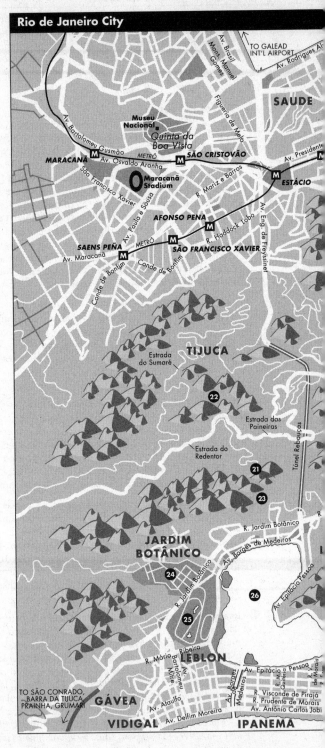

Rio de Janeiro City

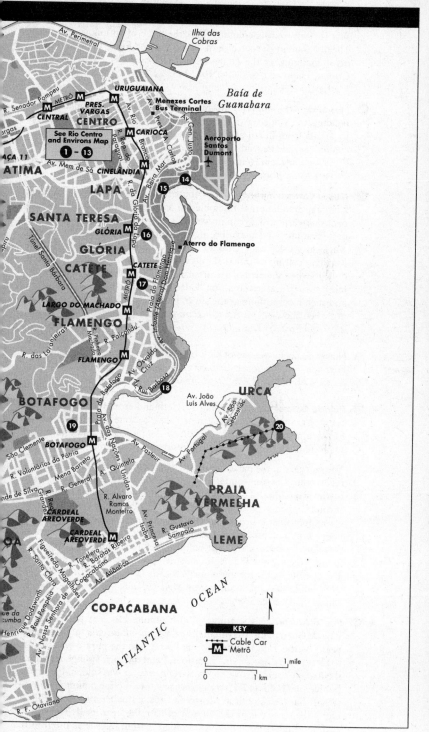

Av. Perimetral

Ilha das Cobras

R. Senador Pompeu

METRÔ

URUGUAIANA

CENTRAL

PRES. VARGAS

Menezes Cortes Bus Terminal

CENTRO

Baía de Guanabara

rgas

See Rio Centro and Environs Map

1 - 13

Av. Mem de Sá

ATIMA

CARIOCA

CINELÂNDIA

Aeroporto Santos Dumont

LAPA

14

15

SANTA TERESA

GLÓRIA

Túnel Santa Bárbara

16

GLÓRIA

CATETE

Aterro do Flamengo

CATETE

17

LARGO DO MACHADO

FLAMENGO

R. das Laranjeiras

R. Paissandu

FLAMENGO

Av. Osvaldo Cruz

18

Av. Rui Barbosa

Av. João Luis Alves

URCA

BOTAFOGO

19

Av. Pasteur

20

BOTAFOGO

São Clemente

A. Quintela

R. Voluntários da Pátria

Nações Unidas

PRAIA VERMELHA

Mena Barreto

R. General

R. Álvaro Ramos Monteiro

CARDEAL AREOVERDE

R. Gustavo Sampaio

LEME

CARDEAL AREOVERDE

R. Tonelero

R. Barata Ribeiro

R. Santa Clara

Av. Atlântica

COPACABANA

ATLANTIC OCEAN

N

KEY

Cable Car

M Metrô

0 ——— 1 mile
0 ——— 1 km

R. F. Otaviano

actually a museum and monument combined. It houses military uniforms, medals, stamps, and documents belonging to soldiers in World War II. Two soaring columns flank the tomb of an unknown soldier. The first Sunday of each month, Brazil's armed forces undertake a colorful changing of the guard here. ⊠ *Parque Brigadeiro Eduardo Gomes, Flamengo,* ☎ *021/240–1283.* 🎟 *Free.* ⊙ *Tues.–Sun. 10–4. Metrô: Cinelândia.*

⑭ Museu de Arte Moderna (MAM). Set in a striking concrete and glass building, the Modern Art Museum has a collection of some 1,700 works by artists from Brazil and elsewhere. It also hosts significant special exhibitions, and its wildly popular cinema shows a broad range of films. ⊠ *Av. Infante Dom Henrique 85, Flamengo,* ☎ *021/210–2188.* 🎟 *Free.* ⊙ *Tues.–Sun. noon–6. Metrô: Cinelândia.*

⑱ Museu Carmen Miranda. This tribute to the Brazilian bombshell is in a circular building that resembles a concrete spaceship (its door even opens upward rather than outward). On display are some of the elaborate costumes and incredibly high platform shoes worn by the actress, who was viewed as a national icon by some and as a traitor to true Brazilian culture by others. Hollywood photos of Miranda, who was only 46 when she died of a heart attack in 1955, show her in her trademark turban and jewelry. You'll also find her records, movie posters, and such memorabilia as the silver, hand-held mirror she was clutching when she died. ⊠ *Av. Rui Barbosa 560, Flamengo,* ☎ *021/551–2597.* 🎟 *Free.* ⊙ *Tues.–Fri. 11–5, weekends 10–4. Metrô: Flamengo.*

NEED A
BREAK?   Flamengo contains some of Rio's better small restaurants. For authentic Brazilian fare, the bohemian community heads to **Lamas** (⊠ Rua Marques de Abrantes 18, ☎ 021/556–0799).

★ ⑰ Palácio Catete. Once the villa of a German baron, the elegant, 19th-century, granite-and-marble Catete Palace became the presidential residence after the 1889 coup overthrew the monarchy and established the Republic of Brazil. Eighteen presidents lived here.

You can gaze at the palace's gleaming parquet floors and intricate bas-relief ceilings as you wander through its **Museu da República** (Museum of the Republic). The permanent—and frank—exhibits include a shroud-draped view of the bedroom where President Getúlio Vargas committed suicide in 1954 after the military threatened to overthrow his government, presidential memorabilia, and furniture and paintings that date from the proclamation of the republic to the end of Brazil's military regime in 1985. A small contemporary art gallery and theater also operate within the museum. ⊠ *Rua do Catete 153, Catete,* ☎ *021/ 225–4302.* 🎟 *Admission; free on Wed.* ⊙ *Tues.–Sun. noon–5, weekends 2–6. Metrô: Catete.*

★ ⑳ Pão d'Açucar. This soaring 1,300-ft granite block at the mouth of Baía de Guanabara was originally called *pau-nh-acugua* (high, pointed peak) by the Tupi Indians. To the Portuguese the phrase was similar to their *pão de açucar,* or "sugarloaf," and the rock's shape reminded them of the conical loaves in which refined sugar was sold. Italian-made bubble cars holding 75 passengers each move up the mountain in two stages. The first stop is at Morro da Urca, a smaller mountain (705 ft high); the second is at the summit of Pão d'Açucar itself. The trip to each level takes three minutes. In high season, long lines often form for the cable-car; the rest of the year, the wait is seldom more than 30 minutes. ⊠ *Between Urca and Praia Vermelha.* 🎟 *Admission.* ⊙ *Daily 8 AM–10 PM.*

Zona Sul

Rio is home to 23 *praias* (beaches), an almost continuous 73-km (45-mi) ribbon of sand. All are public and are served by buses and taxis. At intervals along the beaches at Copacabana and Ipanema are small *postes* with washrooms, showers, and changing rooms that can be used for a small fee. Kiosks manned by police also pepper the avenues running parallel to the beach, and crime has dropped dramatically as a result.

A Good Beach Strategy

Although the circuit starts to the northeast at the beaches of Flamengo, Botafogo, Urca, and Vermelha, the waters off their shores are often polluted. The best sands are farther south. Leme, which is popular with senior citizens, runs into the city's grande dame, **Copacabana.** Its 3-km (2-mi) stretch is lined by a sidewalk whose swirling pattern was designed by Roberto Burle Marx. You'll also find outdoor cafés, high-rise hotels, and juice kiosks. At the end, cut around via small Arpoador—a beach favored by surfers—or Avenida Francisco Otaviano to **Ipanema.** Note that the final leg of this beach, called Leblon, is polluted; swimming here isn't recommended.

Beyond Ipanema and Leblon, mountains again form a natural wall separating you from the next beach, little Vidigal. Still more mountains block it from **São Conrado,** a beach where hang gliders land after leaping from a nearby peak. A highway through a mountain tunnel forms the link between São Conrado and the long, spectacular **Barra da Tijuca.** Its waters are clean and cool, and its far end, known as Recreio dos Bandeirantes, was home to a small fishing village until the late 1960s. Beyond are **Prainha,** whose rough seas make it popular with surfers, and the lovely **Grumari,** whose copper sands are often packed. Just before Prainha, you can take a slight detour to visit the **Museu Casa do Pontal,** Brazil's largest folk-art museum. It's worth continuing down the hill beyond Grumari to the **Sítio Roberto Burle Marx,** for an in-depth look at one of Brazil's greatest artists.

City buses and small green minivans pick you up and drop you off wherever you request along the shore. If you're brave enough to drive, the city has established small, affordable parking lots (look for attendants in green and yellow vests) along waterfront avenues. There are several organized tours that take in the beaches, and agents at Turismo Clássico (☞ Tour Operators and Travel Agents *in* Rio de Janeiro A to Z, *below*) can arrange for drivers and/or guides.

TIMING AND PRECAUTIONS

Although you can tour the shoreline in several hours, consider spending a full day just wandering from Copacabana to Ipanema or sunbathing on Barra da Tijuca. Remember that Rio's beaches aren't just about sunning and swimming, they're also about volleyball games, strolling, biking, and people-watching.

Don't shun the beaches because of reports of crime, but *do* take precautions. Leave jewelry, passports, and large sums of cash at your hotel; avoid wandering alone and at night; and be alert when groups of friendly youths engage you in conversation. (Sometimes they're trying to distract you while one of their cohorts snatches your belongings.) The biggest danger is the sun. From 10 to 3, its rays are merciless making heavy-duty sunscreen, hats, cover-ups, and plenty of liquids essential. (You can also rent a beach umbrella from a vendor or your hotel.) Hawkers stroll the beaches with beverages—take advantage of their services. Lifeguard stations are found once every kilometer.

Sights to See

★ **Barra da Tijuca.** Cariocas consider the beach here to be Rio's best, and the 18-km-long (11-mi-long) sweep of sand and jostling waves certainly is dramatic. Pollution isn't a problem and, in many places, neither are crowds. Barra's water is also cooler and its breezes more refreshing than those at other beaches. However, the waves can be strong in spots, and this attracts surfers, windsurfers, and jet-skiers; swim with caution. The beach is set slightly below a sidewalk, where cafés and restaurants beckon. Condos have also sprung up here, and the city's largest shopping centers and supermarkets have made inland Barra their home.

At the far end of Barra's beachfront avenue, Sernambetiba, is **Recreio dos Bandeirantes,** a 1-km (½-mi) stretch of sand anchored by a huge rock, which creates a small protected cove. Its quiet seclusion makes it popular with families. The calm, pollution-free water, with no waves or currents, is good for bathing, but don't try to swim around the rock—it's bigger than it looks.

Copacabana. Maddening traffic, noise, packed apartment blocks, and a world-famous beach—this is Copacabana, a Manhattan with bikinis. A walk along the neighborhood's classic crescent is a must. Here you'll see the essence of Rio beach culture, a cradle-to-grave lifestyle that begins with toddlers accompanying their parents to the water and ends with graying seniors walking hand in hand along the sidewalk. It's here, too, that athletic men play volleyball using only their feet and heads, not their hands. As evidenced by all the goal nets, soccer is also popular. (Copacabana hosts the world beach soccer championships every January and February.) You can swim here, although pollution levels and a strong undertow can sometimes be discouraging.

At the Pão d'Açucar end is **Leme,** really no more than a natural extension of Copacabana. A rock formation juts into the water here, forming a quiet cove that's less crowded than the rest of the beach. Along a sidewalk, at the side of the mountain overlooking Leme, anglers stand elbow-to-elbow with their lines dangling into the sea.

Copacabana's privileged live on beachfront **Avenida Atlântica,** famed for its wide mosaic sidewalks, hotels, and cafés. On weekends, two of the avenue's lanes are closed to traffic and are taken over by joggers, roller bladers, cyclists, and pedestrians. Two blocks inland from and parallel to the beach is **Avenida Nossa Senhora de Copacabana,** the main commercial street, with shops, restaurants, and sidewalks crowded with the colorful characters that give Copacabana its flavor.

NEED A
BREAK?
Stop in for a drink at one of Avenida Atlântica's few air-conditioned cafés. The windows of **Manoel & Juaquim** (⊠ Av. Atlântica 1936, Copacabana, ☎ 021/236–6768) face the sands so you can settle in with a cold draft beer or a light meal (the garlic potatoes are unbeatable) while watching carioca life unfold. Bring cash; this eatery takes no credit cards.

Ipanema. As you stroll along this beach, you'll catch a cross section of the city's residents, each favoring a particular stretch. There's an area dominated by families; a spot near Copacabana, known as **Arpoador,** that tantalizes surfers; and even a strand favored by the gay community. Ipanema, nearby Leblon (off whose shores the waters are too polluted for swimming), and the blocks surrounding Lagoa Rodrigo de Freitas are part of Rio's money belt. For a close-up look at the posh apartment buildings, stroll down beachfront **Avenida Vieira Souto** and its extension, **Avenida Delfim Moreira,** or drive around the lagoon on **Avenida Epitácio Pessoa.** The tree-lined streets between Ipanema

---

Close-Up

RITES ON THE BEACH

ALTHOUGH RIO'S ANNUAL Carnaval is an amazing spectacle, there is perhaps no stranger sight than that which takes place on the beaches each New Year's Eve. Under the warm, tropical sky and with the backdrop of the modern city, thousands of Macumba (one of Brazil's spiritualistic religions) practitioners honor Iemanjá, the goddess of the sea.

The advent of the new year is a time for renewal and to ask for blessings. The faithful—of all ages, colors, and classes—determined to start the year off right, pour onto the beaches at around 10 PM. Some draw mystic signs in the sand. Others lay out white tablecloths and set up gifts befitting a proud, beautiful goddess: combs, mirrors, lipsticks, hair ribbons, perfumes, wines. Still others bring flowers with notes asking for favors tucked amid the blossoms. Worshipers chant and sing over their offerings and set candles around them.

By 11:30 PM, the beaches are a mass of white-clad believers and flickering candles, and the shore looks as if it has been invaded by millions of fireflies. At midnight, the singing, shrieking, and sobbing is accompanied by fireworks, sirens, and bells. The faithful rush to the water for the moment of truth: If the goddess is satisfied with an offering, it's carried out to sea and the gift giver's wish will come true. If, however, Iemanjá is displeased with an offering, the ocean will throw it back, and the gift giver must try again another year.

Beach and the lagoon are as peaceful as they are attractive. The boutiques along **Rua Garcia D'Avila** make window shopping a sophisticated endeavor. Other chic areas near the beach include **Praça Nossa Senhora da Paz,** which is lined with wonderful restaurants and bars; **Rua Vinícius de Morais;** and **Rua Farme de Amoedo.**

NEED A BREAK?	Have you ever wondered if there really *was* a girl from Ipanema? The song was inspired by schoolgirl Heloisa Pinheiro, who caught the fancy of songwriter Antônio Carlos (a.k.a. Tom) Jobim and his pal lyricist Vinícius de Morais as she walked past the two bohemians sitting in their favorite bar. They then penned one of the century's classics. That was in 1962, and today the bar has been renamed **Bar Garota de Ipanema** (⊠ Rua Vinícius de Morais 49-A, Ipanema, ☎ 021/267–8787).

OFF THE BEATEN PATH	**MUSEU CASA DO PONTAL –** If you're heading toward Prainha or beyond to Grumari, consider taking a detour to Brazil's largest folk-art museum. One room houses a wonderful mechanical sculpture that represents all of the escolas de samba that march in the Carnaval parades. Another mechanical "scene" depicts a circus in action. This private collection is owned by a French expatriate, Jacques Van De Beuque, who has been collecting Brazilian treasures—including religious pieces—since he arrived in the country in 1946. ⊠ *Estrada do Pontal 3295, Grumari,* ☎ *021/490–3278 or 021/539–4914.* ☜ *Admission.* ⊙ *Tues.–Sun. 9–5.*

★ **Prainha and Grumari.** The length of two football fields, Prainha is a vest-pocket beach favored by surfers, who take charge of it on weekends. Set about 35 minutes west of Ipanema on a road that hugs the coast, you need a car to get here. The swimming is good, but watch out for surfboards. About 5 minutes farther down the road is Grumari, a beach that seems an incarnation of paradise. What it lacks in amenities (you'll find only a couple groupings of thatch-roof huts selling drinks and snacks) it makes up for in natural beauty: the glorious red sands of its quiet cove are backed by low, lush hills. On weekdays, especially in the off season, these beaches are almost empty; on weekends, particularly in peak season, the road to and from them is so crowded that it almost becomes a parking lot.

<table>
<tr><td>

NEED A
BREAK?

</td><td>

From Grumari, the road climbs up through dense forest, emerging atop a hill above the vast Guaratiba flatlands. Here you'll find the **Restaurante Pont de Grumari,** an eatery that's famed for grilling fish to perfection. With its shady setting, glorious vistas, and live music performances (samba, bossa nova, jazz) it's the perfect lunch spot (open daily 11:30–7) after a morning on the beach and before an afternoon at the Sítio Roberto Burle Marx or the Museu Casa do Pontal. ⊠ *Estrada do Grumari 710, Grumari,* ☎ *021/410–1434. AE, DC, MC, V.*

</td></tr>
</table>

São Conrado. In Leblon, at the end of Ipanema where the imposing Dois Irmãos Mountain stands, Avenida Niemeyer snakes along rugged cliffs that offer spectacular sea views on the left. The road returns to sea level again in São Conrado, a natural amphitheater surrounded by forested mountains and the ocean. Development of what is now a mostly residential area began in the late '60s with an eye on Rio's high society. A short stretch along its beach includes the condominiums of a former president, the ex-wife of another former president, an ex-governor of Rio de Janeiro State, and a one-time Central Bank president. In the middle of the small valley is the exclusive Gávea Golf and Country Club. The far end of São Conrado is marked by the towering **Pedra da Gávea,** a huge flattop granite block. Next to it is Pedra Bonita, the mountain from which the gliders depart. (Although this beach was the city's most popular a few years ago, contaminated water has discouraged swimmers.)

Ironically, though, the neighborhood is surrounded by shantytowns. Much of the high ground has been taken over by Rio's largest favela, **Rocinha,** where an estimated 200,000 people live. This precarious city within a city seems poised to slide down the hill. It, and others like it, are the result of Rio's chronic housing problem coupled with the refusal by many of the city's poor to live in distant working-class neighborhoods. Though the favelas are dangerous for the uninitiated, they have their own internal order, and their tremendous expansion has even upper-class cariocas referring to them not as slums but as neighborhoods. Notice that the favelas enjoy prime vistas, and most of the structures in them are constructed of brick.

<table>
<tr><td>

OFF THE
BEATEN PATH

</td><td>

SÍTIO ROBERTO BURLE MARX – Beyond Grumari the road winds through mangrove swamps and tropical forest. It's an apt setting for the plantation-turned-museum where Brazil's famous landscape designer, Roberto Burle Marx, is memorialized. Marx, the mind behind Rio's mosaic beachfront walkways and the Aterro do Flamengo, was said to have "painted with plants" and was the first designer to use Brazilian flora in his projects. More than 3,500 species—including some discovered by and named for Marx as well as many on the endangered list—flourish at this 100-acre estate. Here he grouped his plants not only according to their soil and light needs but also according to their shape and texture. Marx also liked to mix modern things with old ones—a recurring

</td></tr>
</table>

theme throughout the property. The results are both whimsical and elegant. In 1985 he bequeathed the farm to the Brazilian government, though he remained here until his death in 1994. His house is now a cultural center full of his belongings, including collections of folk art. The grounds also contain his large, ultramodern studio (he was a painter, too) and a small, restored, colonial chapel dedicated to St. Anthony. *Estrada da Barra de Guaratiba 2019, Guaratiba,* ☎ *021/410–1412 or 021/410–1171.* ✉ *Admission.* ◷ *Daily 9–4. Tours by appointment.*

The Lush Inland

Beyond the sand and sea in the Zona Sul are lush parks and gardens as well as marvelous museums, seductive architecture, and tantalizing restaurants. You can't say you've seen Rio until you've taken in the view from Corcovado and then strolled through its forested areas or beside its inland lagoon—hanging out just like a true carioca.

Numbers in the text correspond to numbers in the margin and on the Rio de Janeiro City map.

A Good Tour

Head first to the imposing **Corcovado** ㉑ and its hallmark Cristo Redentor statue. As you slide up the side of the steep mountain in the train, you'll pass through the lush forested area known as **Floresta da Tijuca** ㉒. (If you want to explore the forest more, you'll need to hire a cab or join a tour that offers both Corcovado and Floresta da Tijuca.) Back down the hill and at the train station again, stroll downhill a short distance to the **Museu de Arte Naif do Brasil** ㉓, which houses a renowned collection of "naive" art from around the world. The same street leads uphill to the delightful colonial square called Largo do Boticário—a good place to rest your feet. From here, grab a taxi and journey west to the inviting **Jardim Botânico** ㉔, across from which is the **Jóque Clube** ㉕. The botanical gardens are walking distance to the **Lagoa Rodrigo de Freitas** ㉖, the giant saltwater lagoon that serves as one of the city's playgrounds—for children and adults alike.

TIMING AND PRECAUTIONS

You can see these sights in a day if you start early. Try to visit Corcovado on a clear day, as clouds often obscure the Christ statue on its summit. You can join an organized tour or hire a cabbie to take you out for the day (public transportation doesn't conveniently reach these sights). The security is good at Corcovado and Floresta da Tijuca, so you can usually carry your camera without worry. At the Jardim Botânico and the Lagoa Rodrigo de Freitas, however, be alert. Throughout this tour, keep valuables in a money belt or somewhere else out of sight.

Sights to See

★ ㉑ **Corcovado.** There's an eternal argument about which view is better, that from Pão d'Açucar or that from here. Corcovado has two advantages: At 2,300 ft it's nearly twice as high as and offers an excellent view of Pão d'Açucar itself. The sheer 1,000-ft granite face of Corcovado (the name means "hunchback" and refers to the mountain's shape) has always been a difficult undertaking for climbers. There are two ways to reach the top: by cogwheel train (originally built in 1885) or by winding road. The train provides delightful views of Ipanema and Leblon (from an absurd angle of ascent) as well as a close look at the thick vegetation and the butterflies and birds it attracts. (You may wonder what those oblong medicine balls hanging from the trees are, the ones that look like spiked watermelons tied to ropes. They're *jaca,* or jack fruit.) Trains leave the **Cosme Velho station** every 20 minutes, daily 8:30–6:30, for the steep, 5-km (3-mi), 20-minute ascent. Late-afternoon trains are the most popular; on weekends be prepared for a long wait. ⊠ *Rua Cosme Velho 513, Cosme Velho,* ☎ *021/558–1329.* ☜ *Admission.*

Whether you arrive by train, tour bus, or car, there's a climb up steep staircases to the summit, where the statue and viewpoints are (there are no elevators or ramps for wheelchairs). You'll pass little cafés and shops selling film and souvenirs along the way. Once at the top, all of Rio stretches out before you.

It wasn't until 1921, the centennial of Brazil's independence from Portugal, that someone had the idea of placing a statue atop Corcovado. A team of French artisans headed by sculptor Paul Landowski was assigned the task of erecting a statue of Christ with his arms apart as if embracing the city. (Nowadays, mischievous cariocas say Christ is getting ready to clap for his favorite escola de samba.) It took 10 years, but on October 12, 1931, the **Cristo Redentor** (Christ the Redeemer) was inaugurated. The sleek, modern, figure rises more than 100 ft atop a 20-ft pedestal and weighs 700 tons. A powerful lighting system transforms it into a dramatic icon in the evenings.

㉒ Floresta da Tijuca. Surrounding Corcovado is the dense, tropical Tijuca Forest. Once part of a Brazilian nobleman's estate, it's studded with exotic trees and thick jungle vines and has a delightful waterfall, the **Cascatinha de Taunay.** About 200 yards beyond the waterfall is the small pink and purple **Capela Mayrink** (Mayrink Chapel), with painted panels by the 20th-century Brazilian artist, Cândido Portinari. From several points along this national park's 96 km (60 mi) of narrow, winding roads the views are breathtaking. Some of the most spectacular are from **Dona Marta,** on the way up Corcovado; the **Emperor's Table,** supposedly the site where Brazil's last emperor, Pedro II, took his court for picnics; and, farther down the road, the **Chinese View,** an area where Portuguese King João VI allegedly located the first Chinese settlers who came to Brazil in the early 19th century to develop tea plantations. A great way to see the forest is by Jeep; you can arrange tours through a number of Rio agencies (☞ Tour Operators and Travel Agents *in* Rio de Janeiro A to Z, *below*). *Entrance at Praça Afonso Viseu 561, Tijuca,* ☎ *021/492–2253.* ☜ *Admission.* ☉ *Daily 7–7.*

㉔ Jardim Botânico. The 340-acre Botanical Garden contains more than 5,000 species of tropical and subtropical plants and trees, including 900 varieties of palms (some more than a century old) and more than 140 species of birds. The cool (its temperature is usually a good 10° lower than on the street), shady garden was created by Portuguese King João VI in 1808, during his exile in Brazil. In 1842 the garden gained its most impressive adornment, the **Avenue of the Royal Palms,** an 800-yard-long double row of 134 soaring royal palms. Elsewhere in the gardens, the **Casa dos Pilões,** an old gunpowder factory, has been restored and displays objects that pertained to both the nobility and to their slaves. Also on the grounds are a library, a small café, and a gift shop that sells souvenirs with ecological themes (the shop is a product of the Earth Summit that was held in Rio in 1992). ⊠ *Rua Jardim Botânico 1008,* ☎ *021/294–6012.* ☜ *Admission.* ☉ *Daily 8–5.*

NEED A BREAK?   Cool off with some homemade ice cream featuring a tropical twist. The flavors at **Mil Frutas Sorvetes** (⊠ Rua J. J. Seabra, Jardim Botânico, ☎ 021/511–2550) are concocted using such local fruits as *acerola* and *jaca.*

㉕ **Jóque Clube.** The Jockey Club's landmark racetrack is hard to miss owing to its opulent Louis XV style. In addition to horse races, the complex is used for shows and receptions. Its El Turf nightclub is popular on weekends. ✉ *Praça Santos Dumont 31, Gávea,* ☎ *021/512–9988.*

㉖ **Lagoa Rodrigo de Freitas.** Under the watchful gaze of the Cristo Redentor, active Rio residents congregate in the park that encircles this saltwater lagoon. The many facilities here include playgrounds, a roller skating rink, and tennis courts; on weekends, you can rent paddleboats. Take advantage of the new food kiosks (each one offers a different type of cuisine—everything from Japanese to Italian to Middle Eastern). There are frequently lakeshore music performances in the evenings. While exploring the area, look for the **Parque da Catacumba,** a pleasant statue-filled park off the western edge of Avenida Epitácio Pessoa, the road around the lagoon.

★ ㉓ **Museu de Arte Naif do Brasil.** More than 8,000 naive works by Brazil's best artists (as well as works by other self-taught painters from around the world) grace the walls of this lovely colonial mansion that was once the studio of painter Eliseu Visconti. The pieces in what is reputedly the world's largest and most complete collection of primitive paintings date from the 15th century through contemporary times. Don't miss the colorful, colossal (7×4-m/23×13-ft) canvas that depicts the city of Rio; it reportedly took five years to complete. This museum sprang from a collection started decades ago by a jewelry designer who later created a foundation to oversee the art. A small gift shop sells postcards, T-shirts, and other items. ✉ *Rua Cosme Velho 561, Tijuca,* ☎ *021/ 205–8612 or 021/205–8547.* 💷 *Admission.* ⊙ *Tues.–Fri. 10–6, weekends noon–6.*

NEED A BREAK?	A few blocks uphill from the Museu de Arte Naif on Rua Cosme Velho is the picturesque, cobblestone **Largo do Boticário** (✉ Rua Cosme Velho 822), a square with seven pastel colonial residences. They were reconstructed on a spot that was once home to a *boticário* (apothecary) to the royal family. Music and other cultural events are often held here.

DINING

Meat lovers will be mesmerized by the succulent offerings in Rio's churrascarias, especially those that serve *rodízio*-style (the meat is brought to your table on skewers continuously—until you can eat no more). Hotel restaurants often offer feijoada on Saturday (sometimes Friday, too). Vegetarians will appreciate the abundance of seafood restaurants and salad bars, where you pay for your greens by the kilo. (Note that it's perfectly safe to eat fresh produce in clean, upscale places; avoid shellfish in all but the best restaurants.)

Cariocas have scaled back on *almoço* (lunch), which used to be a full meal, and have turned more to *lanche,* meaning a sandwich. Dinner is a late affair; if you arrive at 7, you may be the only one in the restaurant. Popular places seat customers until well after midnight on weekends, when the normal closing hour is 2 AM. Cariocas love to linger in bar-choperias that also serve food (☞ Bars, Choperias, and Lounges *in* Nightlife and the Arts, *below*), and such establishments abound. Most of them serve dishes in the $–$$ range, and portions are large enough for two people to share.

Many restaurants offer a special fixed-price menu as well as à la carte fare. Many also include a "cover charge" for the bread and other appetizers placed on the table. As for tipping, check your bill: A 10%

38

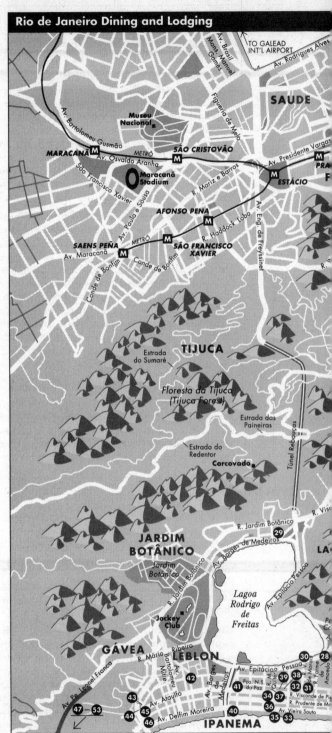

Rio de Janeiro Dining and Lodging

service charge is often added, and it's customary to leave up to an additional 5%. Take note that some restaurants don't accept credit cards, many are closed on Monday, and dress is almost always casual.

Brazilian

$$$ ✗ **Casa da Feijoada.** Brazil's savory national dish is the specialty here,
★ where huge pots of the meat and stew concoction simmer every day. The restaurant does a superb job with desserts as well, whipping up a lovely selection of traditional sweets. Note that this restaurant has joined up with the famous Mangueira Escola de Samba to present weekly feijoada-samba and feijoada-pagode shows at the Centro Cultural de Mangueira (✉ Rua Frederico Silva 85, Centro)). The cost is about $13 per person. Call the restaurant for details. ✉ *Rua Prudente de Morais 10, Ipanema,* ☎ *021/267–4994 or 021/247–2776. AE, DC, MC, V.*

$$$ ✗ **Geraes.** On a cobbled street near Praça 15, this airy restaurant is a
★ cool respite from Centro's hot, busy boulevards. Its cavernous space has a contemporary feel that's offset with such rustic touches as grand archways, tile floors, and white-washed stone walls. *Mineiro* (from Minas Gerais) dishes bubble in large black pots on the buffet table. Waiters dart efficiently between well-spaced tables, taking orders for drinks or items from the à la carte menu. Be sure to try the *feijão tropeiro* (brown beans, bacon, and manioc) with your *lingüiça* (Minas pork sausage). For dessert, have some fruit and the very mild, white *queijo do Minas* (Minas cheese). Although Geraes serves only lunch, you can stop by for drinks and live music 6 PM–midnight Wednesday–Friday. ✉ *Rua do Ouvidor 26-28, Centro,* ☎ *021/242–8610 or 021/224–6480. AE, DC, MC, V. No dinner.*

$$$ ✗ **Mariu's.** This highly regarded churrascaria serves more than a dozen types of sizzling meats. Its popularity sparked the opening of a second restaurant in Leme. Reservations are a good idea. ✉ *Rua Francisco Otaviano 96, Ipanema,* ☎ *021/521–0500. DC, MC, V.* ✉ *Av. Atlântica 290–A, Leme,* ☎ *021/542–2393. DC, MC, V.*

$$$ ✗ **Porcão.** Waiters at these quintessential rodízio-style churrascarias
★ fly up and down between rows of wooden, linen-draped tables wielding giant skewers laden with sizzling barbecued beef, pork, and chicken. All the branches resonate with the good humor that seems to accompany this slightly primitive form of eating. Save room if you can: The papaya creme pudding topped by a bit of cassis shouldn't be missed. ✉ *Rua Barão da Torre 218, Ipanema,* ☎ *021/522–0999. Reservations not accepted. AE, DC, MC, V.* ✉ *Av. Armando Lombardi 591, Barra da Tijuca,* ☎ *021/492–2001. Reservations not accepted. AE, DC, MC, V.*

$$ ✗ **Baby Beef Paes Mendonça.** This traditional churrascaria occupies a top spot among the city's grills. Its huge rooms, seating a total of 600, are packed seven nights a week—an impressive testimony to the quality of the charbroiled meats served here. Portions are equally impressive. ✉ *Av. das Américas 1510, Barra da Tijuca,* ☎ *021/494–2187. AE, DC, MC, V.*

$$ ✗ **Barra Grill.** Informal and popular, this steak house serves some of the best meat in town and is a favorite stop after a long day at the beach. ✉ *Av. Ministro Ivan Lins 314, Barra da Tijuca,* ☎ *021/493–6060. Reservations not accepted. AE, DC, MC, V.*

$ ✗ **Terra Brasilis.** Large windows overlooking a tree-lined street, cool white ceramic tile, and stucco walls painted buttercup yellow and celery green give this "weigh-and-pay" restaurant a cheery atmosphere. You simply help yourself to the Brazilian buffet (including a good selection of salads) and head to a counter where your plate is weighed. It works out to about $8 a kilo, but it's really hard to eat that much

($2.75–$5.50 is average for a main course, $1–$2 for dessert; drinks are extra). And, yes, they do take the plate's weight into account. ⊠ *Rua Humberto de Campos 699, Leblon,* ☏ *021/274–4702. AE, DC, MC, V. No dinner.*

Cafés

$$ ✕ **Café da Praça.** On Ipanema's Praça Nossa Senhora da Paz, this
★ bustling café with high ceilings and large windows is filled with friendly people. The menu includes quiches, pastas, salads, and sandwiches, as well as fish, fowl, and meat dishes. Note that the café is open for breakfast, lunch, tea, and dinner. ⊠ *Rua Maria Quitéria 91, Ipanema,* ☏ *021/247–6984. AE, V. Closed Mon.*

$ ✕ **Colombo.** At the turn of the century, this Belle Epoque structure was
★ Rio's preeminent café, the site of afternoon teas for high-society *senhoras* and a center of political intrigue and gossip. Jacaranda-framed mirrors from Belgium and stained-glass from France add to the artnouveau decor. Portions are generous, but you can also just stop by for a pastry and coffee while you absorb the opulence. ⊠ *Rua Gonçalves Dias 32, Centro,* ☏ *021/232–2300. Reservations not accepted. No credit cards. No dinner. Closed Sun. Metrô: Carioca.*

Eclectic

$$$$ ✕ **Mostarda.** Elegant and understated, this restaurant overlooking the
★ lagoon has great food, indoor and outdoor seating, and a chic club upstairs that opens after midnight. It's best to go with a Brazilian so that he or she can explain the menu's carioca puns to you. (A Ricardo, for example, is a cocktail of champagne and minced fresh fruits, but it's also what husbands say their wives have when the women have taken a lover.) Good salads and interesting entrées are often seasoned with mustard (hence, the restaurant's name), and there's an array of mustards on the table for real fanatics. The wine list includes an ample South American selection. ⊠ *Av. Epitácio Pessoa 980/990, Lagoa,* ☏ *021/ 523–1747 or 021/523–1629. AE, V.*

$$$ ✕ **Alho & Óleo.** On Ipanema's Praça Nossa Senhora da Paz, this restau-
★ rant features an eclectic menu with a hint of Italy. Interesting fowl dishes include partridge with dates and grilled duck with apricots; the arugula salad with eggplant, mushrooms, and sea bass is also recommended. Homemade pasta dishes include a farfalle with seafood and artichokes. ⊠ *Rua Barao da Torre 348, Ipanema,* ☏ *021/523–2703. AE.*

$$$ ✕ **Spices.** A Caribbean flair presides over Spices' creative menu. An extensive array of mixed drinks includes the Nêga Sings the Blues (a variation of the caipirinha made with cachaça, lime, ginger, and honey). The entrées have similarly offbeat names and many of the seafood, fowl, and meat dishes employ fruits and nuts in their preparation. Try the ginger tuna with mango or the grilled beef with gorgonzola and pumpkin purée. Spices has some of the best-looking salads in town as well. ⊠ *Av. Epitácio Pessoa 864, Lagoa,* ☏ *021/259–1041. AE.*

$ ✕ **Garfo Livre.** The by-the-kilo buffets at this eatery two blocks from the beach give economical eating a new twist. As you enter, you're given a card on which the items you select are marked. Grab a plate, help yourself to the buffet—which has many Middle Eastern dishes—get your plate weighed, and then pay on your way out. The salad bar has a large selection that includes beans, hummus, and steamed and raw veggies. Commuters come here on weeknights beginning at 7—trading rush hour for happy hour. ⊠ *Av. Nossa Senhora de Copacabana 1003, Copacabana,* ☏ *021/522–1041. AE, DC, MC, V.*

French

$$$$ ✕ **Monseigneur.** Modern and traditional French cuisine meet here, where the grand decor matches the meals—two striking lighted columns of translucent crystal dominate the center of the restaurant. The disadvantage is that this is a bit off the beaten path, requiring a cab ride to the Inter-Continental Rio hotel (☞ Lodging, *below*). ✉ *Av. Prefeito Mendes de Morais 222, São Conrado,* ☎ *021/322–2200. Reservations essential. AE, DC, MC, V. No lunch.*

$$$$ ✕ **Le Saint Honoré.** Le Saint Honoré offers diners French cuisine and an extraordinary view of Copacabana Beach from atop Le Meridien hotel (☞ Lodging, *below*). Brazilian fruits and herbs are tucked into dishes to produce such gems as *les pièces du boucher marquées sauces gamay et béarnaise,* a fillet with both béarnaise and red-wine sauces. A jacket and tie are advised. ✉ *Av. Atlântica 1020, Copacabana,* ☎ *021/275–9922. Reservations essential. AE, DC, MC, V.*

$$$$ ✕ **Troisgros.** Many consider this Rio's finest restaurant, though Claude
★   Troisgros himself has left and Chef Antônio Costa is now at the helm. The menu is famed for nouvelle cuisine relying entirely on Brazilian ingredients. Every dish—from the crab or lobster flan to the chicken, fish, or duck prepared with exotic herbs and sauces—is pure pleasure, and always exceptionally light. The dessert menu is headed by a to-die-for passion-fruit mousse. ✉ *Rua Custódio Serrão 62, Jardim Botânico,* ☎ *021/537–8582. Reservations essential. AE, DC.*

Italian

$$$$ ✕ **Cipriani.** The Copacabana Palace hotel's (☞ Lodging, *below*) restaurant offers a superb dining experience. Start with a Cipriani—really a Bellini—a drink of champagne with fresh peach juice. The snook carpaccio with apple and fennel is a marvelous appetizer; so is the salad of endive marinated in red wine. The pastas must be imported from heaven, and the meat and fish entrées are, appropriate to their surroundings, fit for kings. None of this, of course, comes cheaply. ✉ *Av. Atlântica 1702, Copacabana,* ☎ *021/545–8747. Reservations essential. AE, DC, MC, V.*

$$$$ ✕ **Margutta.** The pasta, fish, and risottos are all top drawer and al-
★   ways fresh. A good wine list complements the cuisine. ✉ *Av. Henrique Dumont 62, Ipanema,* ☎ *021/259–3887 or 021/259–3718. AE, DC, V. No lunch weekdays.*

$$$ ✕ **Alfredo.** The mainstay here is the pasta, especially the fettuccine Alfredo. Start your meal with a selection from the ample cold buffet of antipasti, which may include traditional pastas served with a variety of sauces. The restaurant is in the Inter-Continental hotel (☞ Lodging, *below*), and has a view of the pool area. ✉ *Av. Prefeito Mendes de Morais 222, São Conrado,* ☎ *021/322–2200. AE, DC, MC, V.*

$ ✕ **La Mole.** This popular chain of Italian restaurants is a good budget bet for lunch or dinner. For the prices, the food is surprisingly good—particularly the lasagna, fettuccine, and gnocchi dishes—and the servings are hearty. ✉ *Rua Dias Ferreira 147, Leblon,* ☎ *021/294–0699. Reservations not accepted. No credit cards.* ✉ *Av. Nossa Senhora de Copacabana 552, Copacabana,* ☎ *021/235–3366. Reservations not accepted. No credit cards.* ✉ *Praia de Botafogo 228, Botafogo,* ☎ *021/ 553–2467. Reservations not accepted. No credit cards. Metrô: Flamengo.* ✉ *Av. Armando Lombardi 175, Barra da Tijuca,* ☎ *021/494–2625. Reservations not accepted. No credit cards.*

Mexican

$$ ✕ **Guapo Loco.** The bustling crowds here feast on tamales, enchiladas, and other Mexican favorites until closing time at 3 AM. Tequila has

garnered quite a following among the young in Rio, and the margaritas here are good. ⊠ *Rua Rainha Guilhermina 48, Leblon,* ☎ *021/ 294–2915. AE, DC, MC, V. No lunch weekdays.*

Portuguese

$$$$ ✕ **Antiquarius.** This much-loved establishment is as famous for its flaw-
★ less—and award-winning—rendering of Portuguese classics as for its high prices. Wander through the antiques shop at the restaurant before settling in at a table. A recommended dish is the *cozido,* a stew with a multitude of ingredients, including bananas. The *cataplana,* a seafood stew with rice, is also marvelous, and the *perna de cordeiro* (leg of lamb) is the most requested dish on the menu. The wine list impresses even Portuguese gourmands. ⊠ *Rua Aristides Epínola 19, Leblon,* ☎ *021/294–1049. Reservations essential. DC.*

Seafood

$$$$ ✕ **Satyricon.** This Italian seafood restaurant, which also has a branch
★ in Búzios, is rumored to have been Madonna's favorite. The *bacalhau* (fish baked in rock salt) is a specialty, and the sushi and sashimi are well loved. It's expensive, but it has some of the best seafood in town. ⊠ *Ruá Barão da Torre 192, Ipanema,* ☎ *021/521–0627. DC, MC, V.*

$$$–$$$$ ✕ **Tiberius.** Although it overlooks the action-packed beachfront of Ipanema, the mood at this Caesar Park hotel (☞ Lodging, *below*) restaurant is one of quiet elegance. For sheer indulgence, order the imperial seafood platter—a meal for two with lobster, shrimp, shellfish, and three types of fish fillets, all grilled and served with herb butter. ⊠ *Av. Antônio Carlos Jobim 460, Ipanema,* ☎ *021/525–2525. AE, DC, MC, V. No lunch.*

$$$ ✕ **Quatro Sete Meia.** Internationally renowned, this restaurant is one
★ hour by car west of Copacabana, at the end of a highway that offers stunning coastal views. Simplicity is the soul of the restaurant—whose name in Portuguese is its street number—and the village in which it's set. There are only 11 tables: 5 indoors and 6 in a garden at water's edge. The menu carries seven delicious options, including *moquecas* (seafood stews), grilled seafood, and curries. ⊠ *Rua Barros de Alarcão 476, Pedra da Guaratiba,* ☎ *021/395–2716. Reservations essential. No credit cards. Closed Mon.–Tues. No dinner Wed.–Thurs.*

$$$ ✕ **Shirley.** Homemade Spanish seafood casseroles and soups are the
★ draw at this traditional Copacabana restaurant tucked onto a shady street. Try the *zarzuela,* a seafood soup, or *cazuela,* a fish fillet with white wine sauce. Don't be turned off by the simple decor (a few paintings hung on wood-paneled walls): The food is terrific. ⊠ *Rua Gustavo Sampaio 610, Leme,* ☎ *021/275–1398. Reservations not accepted. No credit cards.*

Vegetarian

$$ ✕ **Celeiro.** What may be Rio's sole organic restaurant is always full. The buffet offers about 40 salads as well as a broad selection of pastas. ⊠ *Rua Dias Ferreira 199, Leblon,* ☎ *021/274–7843. No dinner.*

LODGING

Most hotels are in Copacabana and Ipanema. Copacabana hotels are close to the action (and the metrô), but the neighborhood is noisier than Ipanema (which is itself noisier than São Conrado and Barra da Tijuca). Note that Rio's "motels" aren't aimed at tourists. They attract couples looking for privacy, and usually rent by the hour.

In the days just prior to and during Carnaval already peak-season rates can double, or even triple. Expect to pay a premium for a room with a view. Many hotels include breakfast in the rate, but the quality varies from a full buffet to a hard roll with butter. Remember that if you're traveling during Carnaval or other peak periods, make reservations as far in advance as possible. Note that air-conditioning is standard in most hotels, as are room safes. Room service is available in all $$$–$$$$ establishments; in $$–$$$$ hotels, you'll find concierges or, at the very least, reception personnel who perform concierge duties.

$$$$ ⊞ **Caesar Park.** This beachfront hotel has established itself as a favorite
★   of business travelers, celebrities, and heads of state, who appreciate its impeccable service. To assist business guests, the hotel provides secretarial services, as well as fax machines and laptops for in-room use. The Caesar Park is home to the elegant Tiberius restaurant (☞ Dining, above), and is also the site of a good Saturday feijoada. ⊠ *Av. Vieira Souto 460, Ipanema 22120,* ☎ *021/525–2525 or 800/223–6800 in the U.S.,* ℻ *021/521–6000. 186 rooms, 32 suites. Restaurant, bar, pool, beauty salon, massage, sauna, exercise room, baby-sitting, laundry service, business services, meeting rooms. AE, DC, MC, V.*

$$$$ ⊞ **Copacabana Palace.** Built in 1923 for the visiting King of Belgium,
★   this was the first luxury hotel in South America. To this day, it retains more soul and elegance than any other Rio hotel. Igor Stravinsky, Marlene Dietrich, Orson Wells, Eva Peron (who reportedly showed up with 100 suitcases in tow), Robert DeNiro, and Princess Di are just a few of the luminaries who have stayed here. It also served as the set for much of the 1933 Fred Astaire and Ginger Rodgers film *Flying Down to Rio.* A recent face-lift restored its facade and left the individually decorated guest rooms with such luxurious touches as inlaid agate and mahogany and computer, fax, and modem facilities. The Copa also has a rooftop tennis court and Rio's largest hotel pool. The Saturday feijoada is a social event bar none except for, perhaps, the gala Carnaval ball held here each year. ⊠ *Av. Atlântica 1702, Copacabana 22021,* ☎ *021/548–7070 or 800/237–1236 in the U.S.,* ℻ *021/235–7330. 122 rooms, 102 suites. 2 restaurants, 2 bars, in-room modem lines, pool, sauna, tennis court, health club, theater, business services, meeting rooms. AE, DC, MC, V. Metrô: Cardeal Arcoverde.*

$$$$ ⊞ **Inter-Continental Rio.** One of the city's only resorts, a member of the respected Inter-Continental chain, is in São Conrado, next to the Gávea Golf and Country Club and on its own slice of beachfront. Attractions include a cocktail lounge, a discotheque, the Monseigneur French restaurant and the Alfredo Italian restaurant (☞ Dining, *above*), business facilities, and golf privileges. Every room has an original tapestry done by a Brazilian artist and a balcony overlooking the ocean. The nearby mall is much less crowded than those with more central locations. ⊠ *Av. Prefeito Mendes de Morais 222, São Conrado 22600,* ☎ *021/322–2200 or 800/327–0200 in the U.S.,* ℻ *021/322–5500. 391 rooms, 20 cabanas, 53 suites. 5 restaurants, 2 bars, piano bar, 3 pools, beauty salon, sauna, golf privileges, 3 tennis courts, health club, shops, dance club, nightclub, business services, convention center, travel services, car rental. AE, DC, MC, V.*

$$$$ ⊞ **Le Meridien.** Of the leading Copacabana hotels, the 37-story French-owned Meridien is the closest to Centro, making it a favorite of business travelers. Rooms are done in pastel tones with dark wood furniture. If you have work to do, the hotel has a complete executive center. Afterward, relax over a meal in Le Saint Honoré restaurant (☞ Dining, *above*) and then head for the jazz bar, which books some of the best

acts in town. ✉ *Av. Atlântica 1020, Copacabana 22012,* ☎ *021/275–9922,* ℻ *021/275–9922. 443 rooms, 53 suites. 3 restaurants, bar, pool, beauty salon, sauna, business services. AE, DC, MC, V.*

$$$$ ⊞ **Rio Atlântica.** Though it's not luxurious, the Atlântica is well appointed and well maintained, offering rooftop sunbathing and swimming, a health club, and a bar with a view of Copacabana Beach. Although breakfast isn't included in the rates, standard rooms are (relatively) reasonably priced, and the service is superb. Business travelers will appreciate the meeting rooms and the secretarial support, which includes such services as simultaneous translation. ✉ *Av. Atlântica 2964, Copacabana 22070,* ☎ *021/548–6332,* ℻ *021/255–6410. 108 rooms, 120 suites. Restaurant, 2 bars, pool, health club, business services, meeting rooms. AE, DC, MC, V.*

$$$$ ⊞ **Rio Othon Palace.** The flagship of the Brazilian Othon chain, this 30-story hotel is a Copacabana landmark. The high point, literally, is the rooftop pool-bar and sundeck, offering a prime view of Copacabana's distinctive black-and-white sidewalk mosaic. The hotel has an Executive Floor, with secretarial support, fax machines, and computer hookups. ✉ *Av. Atlântica 3264, Copacabana 22070,* ☎ *021/522–1522,* ℻ *021/522–1697. 554 rooms, 30 suites. 2 restaurants, 2 bars, pool, sauna, health club, nightclub, business services. AE, DC, MC, V.*

$$$$ ⊞ **Sheraton Rio Hotel & Towers.** Built so that it dominates Vidigal, between Leblon and São Conrado, this is the only hotel in Rio with its own private beach (it's set on a bluff above the water and has a stairway down to the sand). Guest rooms are decorated in pastels, and all have beach views. Four floors in a section called The Towers are reserved for business travelers, who receive separate check-in service and have access to a private lounge, a business center, a buffet breakfast, and around-the-clock butler service. The landscaping out by the pools is fabulous, and though the hotel isn't long on intimacy, the beach views are sublime. Be prepared for numerous taxi rides from this prime, though isolated, location. ✉ *Av. Niemeyer 121, Vidigal 22450,* ☎ *021/274–1122 or 800/325–3589 in the U.S.,* ℻ *021/239–5643. 561 rooms, 22 suites. 4 restaurants, 2 bars, 3 pools, sauna, 3 tennis courts, exercise room, shops, nightclub, business services, meeting rooms, travel services, car rental. AE, DC, MC, V.*

$$$$ ⊞ **Sofitel Rio Palace.** Anchoring one end of Copacabana Beach, this hotel has been given a top-to-bottom face-lift (and new management) and is, once again, one of the best on the strip. The building's H-shape gives all rooms views of the sea, the mountains, or both; all rooms have balconies. One of the pools here gets the morning sun, the other afternoon rays. The rooftop bar areas are always lively. ✉ *Av. Atlântica 4240, Copacabana 22070,* ☎ *021/525–1232 or 800/763–4835 in the U.S.,* ℻ *021/525–1200. 388 rooms, 12 suites. 2 restaurants, 2 bars, tea shop, 2 pools, sauna, health club, shops, nightclub, business services, convention center. AE, DC, MC, V.*

$$$ ⊞ **Everest Rio.** With standard service but one of Rio's finest rooftop views (a postcard shot of Corcovado and the lagoon), this hotel is in the heart of Ipanema's shopping and dining district, a block from the beach. Back rooms offer sea views. ✉ *Rua Prudente de Morais 1117, Ipanema 22420,* ☎ *021/523–2282,* ℻ *021/521–3198. 156 rooms, 11 suites. Restaurant, bar, pool, sauna, business services. AE, DC, MC, V.*

$$$ ⊞ **Excelsior.** This hotel, part of the Windsor chain, may have been built in the 1950s but its look is sleek and contemporary—from the sparkling marble lobby to the guest room closets paneled in gleaming *jacarandá* (Brazilian redwood). Service here is top rate. The expansive breakfast buffet—free for guests—is served in the hotel's window-banked restaurant facing the avenue and beach. (The equally elaborate lunch or dinner buffets cost roughly $10.) The rooftop bar–pool area offers a gentle escape from the hustle and bustle. Ask for a room with a water view. ⊠ *Av. Atlântica 1800, Copacabana 22000,* ☎ *021/257–1950 or 800/44–UTELL in the U.S.,* ☏ *021/257–1850. 230 rooms. Restaurant, 2 bars, pool, health club, meeting rooms. AE, DC, MC, V. Metrô: Cardeal Arcoverde.*

\$\$\$ ⚏ **Guanabara Palace Hotel.** Another member of the Windsor chain, the recently renovated Guanabara is one of the only solid hotel choices right in Centro. Rooms are of a reasonable size and are tastefully done in brown and beige tones. Like its sister hotel, the Excelsior (☞ *above*), the restaurant serves elaborate buffet meals, and breakfast is included in the rate. The contemporary rooftop pool area, with its stunning views of Guanabara Bay, absolutely gleams thanks to its pristine white tiles, white trellises, and white patio furnishings. ⊠ *Av. Presidente Vargas 392, Centro 22071,* ☎ *021/518–0333,* ☏ *021/516–1582. 326 rooms. Restaurant, bar, minibars, room service, pool, sauna, health club, business services, meeting rooms, parking. AE, DC, MC, V. Metrô: Uruguaiana.*

\$\$\$ ⚏ **Leme Othon Palace.** Large rooms and a quiet beachfront location have made this a hotel of choice with repeat visitors. It has a subdued, conservative air. ⊠ *Av. Atlântica 656, Leme 22010,* ☎ *021/275–8080. 168 rooms, 26 suites. Restaurant, bar. AE, DC, MC, V.*

\$\$\$ ⚏ **Miramar Palace.** The beachfront Miramar is a strange mix of old and new. Rooms are among the largest in Rio, and public areas are dominated by classic touches, from the Carrara marble floor of the lobby to the spectacular glass chandeliers that light the two restaurants. The hotel's 16th-floor bar is notable for its unobstructed view of the entire sweep of Copacabana; after 6 live Brazilian music adds a touch of romance. ⊠ *Av. Atlântica 3668, Copacabana 22010,* ☎ *021/521–1122,* ☏ *021/521–3294. 133 rooms, 11 suites. 2 restaurants, 2 bars, coffee shop, tea shop. AE, DC, MC, V.*

\$\$\$ ⚏ **Rio Internacional.** The red frame of this beachfront hotel has become a Copacabana landmark. Swiss-owned and aimed at business travelers, the hotel offers a rarity for Copacabana: All rooms have balconies with sea views. ⊠ *Av. Atlântica 1500, Copacabana 22010,* ☎ *021/543–1555,* ☏ *021/542–5443. 117 rooms, 12 suites. Restaurant, 2 bars, pool, sauna, business services. AE, DC, MC, V.*

\$\$ ⚏ **Atlântico Copacabana.** The large lobby—with its marble walls, red carpeting, black leather furniture, and mirrors—will look modern to some, pretentious to others. Guest rooms are slightly larger than average. The Atlântico is in a residential area four blocks from the beach. ⊠ *Rua Siqueira Campos 90, Copacabana 20000,* ☎ *021/548–0011,* ☏ *021/235–7941. 97 rooms, 18 suites. Restaurant, 3 bars, pool, beauty salon, sauna. AE, DC, MC, V. Metrô: Cardeal Arcoverde.*

\$\$ ⚏ **Copa D'Or.** Rio's largest non-beachfront hotel has an excellent reputation owing to its service and amenities. Businesspeople are well served because of the hotel's location on a thoroughfare to Centro. Sun worshipers will appreciate the free transportation to Copacabana Beach, five blocks away. ⊠ *Rua Figueiredo Magalhães 875, Copacabana 22060,* ☎ *021/235–6610,* ☏ *021/235–6664. 195 rooms, 20 suites. Restaurant, 2 bars, pool, sauna, health club, convention center. AE, DC, MC, V.*

\$\$ ⚏ **Debret.** This former apartment building scores points for keeping its prices moderate despite having a beachfront location. The decor honors Brazil's past: the lobby has baroque statues and prints depicting colonial scenes, and the rooms are furnished in dark, heavy wood. The hotel has a loyal following among diplomats and businesspeople who are more interested in functionality and low prices than elegance. ⊠ *Av. Atlântica 3564, Copacabana 22041,* ☎ *021/522–0132,* ☏ *021/521–0899. 90 rooms, 10 suites. Restaurant, bar. AE, DC, MC, V.*

$$ 🏨 **Glória.** A grande dame of Rio's hotels, this classic was built in 1922 and is full of French antiques. What makes it a draw for business travelers (it's a five-minute cab ride from Centro) may discourage sun worshipers (it's a slightly longer cab ride from the beaches). ⊠ *Rua do Russel 632, Glória 22210,* ☎ *021/205–7272,* FAX *021/555–7282. 596 rooms, 20 suites. 4 restaurants, 3 bars, 2 pools, sauna, exercise room, meeting rooms. AE, DC, MC, V. Metrô: Glória*

$$ 🏨 **Grandville Ouro Verde.** For three decades, folks have favored this hotel for its efficient, personalized service. The tasteful Brazilian colonial decor and dark wood furniture are in step with the emphasis on quality and graciousness. All front rooms face the beach; those in the back on the 6th to 12th floors have a view of Corcovado. ⊠ *Av. Atlântica 1456, Copacabana, 22041,* ☎ *021/543–4123,* FAX *021/542–4597. 61 rooms, 5 suites. Restaurant, bar, library. AE, DC, MC, V.*

$$ 🏨 **Praia Ipanema.** This hotel isn't deluxe, but it has a great location and a view of the sea from all of its rooms. You can take in the dramatic beach view from the pool area on the roof of this 15-story building. You can also catch a breeze from your private balcony (every room has one). ⊠ *Av. Vieira Souto 706, Ipanema, 22420,* ☎ *021/239–9932,* FAX *021/239–6889. 105 rooms. Bar, pool, beach. AE, DC, MC, V.*

$$ 🏨 **Royalty Copacabana.** Among the draws here are the moderate prices and a good location; set three blocks from the beach, it's convenient for beachgoers yet removed enough to satisfy those looking for peace and quiet. The back rooms from the third floor up are the quietest and have mountain views; front rooms face the sea. ⊠ *Rua Tonelero 154, Copacabana, 22030,* ☎ *021/548–5699,* FAX *021/255–1999. 130 rooms, 13 suites. Restaurant, bar, pool, sauna, exercise room. AE, DC, MC, V. Metrô: Cardeal Arcoverde.*

$$ 🏨 **Sol Ipanema.** Another of Rio's crop of tall, slender hotels, this one has a great location, anchoring the eastern end of Ipanema Beach. All rooms have motel-style beige carpets and drapes and light-color furniture; deluxe front rooms have panoramic beach views, while back rooms, which are the same size, have views of the lagoon and Corcovado from the eighth floor up. ⊠ *Av. Vieira Souto 320, Ipanema 22420,* ☎ *021/523–0095,* FAX *021/247–8484. 66 rooms, 12 suites. Restaurant, bar, pool. AE, DC, MC, V.*

$ 🏨 **Arpoador Inn.** This pocket-size hotel occupies the stretch of sand known as Arpoador. Here surfers ride the waves and pedestrians rule the roadway—a traffic-free street allows direct beach access. The hotel is simple but comfortable. At sunset the view from the rocks that mark the end of the beach is considered one of Rio's most beautiful. The spectacle is visible from the hotel's back rooms; avoid the front rooms, which are on the noisy side. ⊠ *Rua Francisco Otaviano 177, Ipanema 22080,* ☎ *021/523–6090,* FAX *021/511–5094. 46 rooms, 2 suites. Restaurant, bar. AE, DC, MC, V.*

$ 🏨 **Ipanema Inn.** This small, no-frills hotel was built for those who want to stay in Ipanema but who have no interest in paying the high prices of a beachfront hotel. Just a half block from the beach, it's convenient not only for sun-worshipers but also for those seeking to explore Ipanema's varied nightlife. ⊠ *Rua Maria Quitéria 27, Ipanema 22410,* ☎ *021/523–6092,* FAX *021/511–5094. 56 rooms. Bar. AE, DC, MC, V.*

$ 🏨 **Toledo.** Although it has few amenities, the Toledo goes the extra mile to make the best of what it does have. The staff is friendly, the service is efficient, and the location—on a quiet back street of Copacabana, a block from the beach—isn't bad either. Back rooms from the 9th to the 14th floors have sea views and sliding floor-to-ceiling windows. ⊠ *Rua Domingos Ferreira 71, Copacabana 22050,* ☎ *021/522–0443,* FAX *021/287–7640. 87 rooms, 8 suites. Bar, coffee shop. DC, MC, V.*

$ ⌖ **Vermont.** This hotel is clean, reliable, and just two blocks from the beach—a good choice for budget travelers. Its only drawback is its location on the main street of Ipanema, which means incessant noise during the day (it tends to quiet down at night after the shops close). ⊠ *Rua Visconde de Pirajá 254, Ipanema, 22410,* ☎ *021/522–0057,* FAX *021/267–7046. 54 rooms. Bar. AE, DC, MC, V.*

NIGHTLIFE AND THE ARTS

Rio's nightlife is as hard to resist as its beaches. Options range from samba shows shamelessly aimed at visitors, to sultry dance halls called *forrós,* a rhythmic music style that originated in Brazil's northeast during World War II. (American GIs stationed at refueling stops opened up their clubs "for all," which, when pronounced with a Brazilian accent, becomes "forró.") You'll find spots that feature the sounds of big band, rock, and everything in between. One of the happiest mediums is *música popular brasileira* (MPB), the generic term for popular Brazilian music, which ranges from pop to jazz. Note that establishments in this carefree city often have carefree hours; call ahead to confirm opening times.

There are also many performing arts options, including opera, theater, music, dance, and film. For current listings, pick up the bilingual *Rio Guia,* published by Riotur, the city's tourist board; *Este Mês no Rio/This Month in Rio* or similar publications are available at most hotels, and your hotel concierge is also a good source of information. The entertainment sections of the Portuguese-language newspapers *Jornal do Brasil* and *O Globo* both publish schedules of events in their Friday editions.

Nightlife

Bars, Choperias, and Lounges

Bars and lounges often ask for a nominal cover in the form of either a drink minimum or a music charge. Plain but pleasant bars called *choperias* attract an unattached crowd. An ice-cold chopp or Brazilian draft beer, is the order of the day—or night.

Bar Bofetada (⊠ Rua Farme de Amoedo 87/87A, Ipanema, ☎ 021/522–9526 or 021/523–3992) has two floors: downstairs the tables flow out onto the street; upstairs large windows open to the sky and afford a good view of the action below. The young, energetic crowd downs chopp and caipirinhas and delicious seafood (the owners are Portuguese) or meat platters large enough to share.
Bar Garota de Ipanema (⊠ Rua Vinícius de Morais 39, Ipanema, ☎ 021/267–5757) is the choperia where regulars Tom Jobim and Vinícius de Morais, authors of *The Girl from Ipanema,* sat and longingly watched the song's heroine head for the beach. (See if you can guess where they usually sat. Hint: it's a table for two near a door.)
Barril 1800 (⊠ Av. Antônio Carlos Jobim 110, Ipanema, ☎ 021/287–0085) is an unpretentious beachfront choperia—an Ipanema landmark usually jammed with people—in which to grab an icy beer or cocktail and a snack before an evening at nearby Jazzmania (☞ *below*).
Cervantes (⊠ Av. Prado Júnior 335, Copacabana, ☎ 021/275–6174) is a great place for sandwiches after a movie. The chopp goes well with the meat and pineapple combo dishes for which Cervantes is famous.
Chico's Bar (⊠ Av. Epitácio Pessoa 1560, Lagoa, ☎ 021/523–3514) is owned by Rio nightspot entrepreneur Chico Recarey. Both the bar and the adjoining restaurant, Castelo da Lagoa, are big with affluent carioca singles and couples.

Hipódromo (⊠ Praça Santos Dumont, Gávea, near the Jóque Clube, ☎ 021/294–0095) has good chopp, honest food, and many young, happy people.

Jazzmania (⊠ Av. Rainha Elizabeth 769, Ipanema, ☎ 021/227–2447) is one of better jazz clubs in town. If you arrive before nightfall, you get a superb view of Ipanema Beach at sunset.

Mistura Fina (⊠ Av. Borges de Medeiros 3207, Lagoa Rodrigo de Freitas, Lagoa, ☎ 021/537–2844) combines fine jazz with excellent food and is open from midnight to 3 AM.

Cabarets and Nightclubs

Variety is the byword of the cabaret scene, which provides visual and sensual stimulation to suit all tastes. Many establishments are walking distance from the Meridien hotel at the end of Copacabana. Although many nightclubs serve food, their main attraction is live music; it's best to eat elsewhere earlier.

Barbarela's (⊠ Av. Princesa Isabel 165, Copacabana) offers the best of the many burlesque, striptease, and sex shows along Avenida Princesa Isabel near the Meridien. It has a reputation for extremely beautiful women.

Canecão (⊠ Av. Venceslau Brás 215, Botafogo, ☎ 021/543–1241) is the city's largest nightclub. It seats up to 5,000 people at the tiny tables in its cavernous space, making it the logical place for some of the biggest names on the international music scene to hold concerts. Reserve a table up front.

Circo Voador (⊠ Aquaduto da Lapa, Lapa, ☎ 021/220–1496) presents top MPB artists in a circus-tent setting, and after the concert you can stay and dance. Seating is limited, so be sure to reserve in advance or you may wind up sitting on the dance floor.

Pão d'Açucar (⊠ Av. Pasteur 520, Praia Vermelha, ☎ 021/541-3737) is definitely a touristy place to see a samba show, but its location—atop Pão d'Açucar—is so appealing, that it doesn't matter. There are two shows a night, 8:30 and 11. When you're finished watching the exuberantly costumed dancers, you can turn your attention to the spectacular view of the sparkling city below.

Plataforma (⊠ Rua Adalberto Ferreira 32, Leblon, ☎ 021/274–4022) holds the most spectacular of Rio's samba shows, with elaborate costumes and a variety of Brazilian musical numbers including samba and rhumba. A two-hour show costs about $38.50, drinks not included. Downstairs is a hangout for many local luminaries and entertainers. Upstairs you can eat at Plataforma's famed barbecue restaurant.

Vinícius (⊠ Rua Vinícius de Morais 39, Ipanema, ☎ 021/287–1497). You may rightly associate sultry bossa nova with Brazil, but it's increasingly hard to find venues that offer it. This club is one. Along with nightly live samba, jazz, popular music, or bossa nova, this club has a good kitchen.

Cybercafé

El Turf Cyber Bar (⊠ Av. Lauro Müller 116, Loja D91, Botafogo, ☎ 021/541–1006) has plenty of terminals, snacks, and a zippy connection—making it the best place to get your E-mail while in Rio. You'll pay about $6 per hour and access is available daily from noon until the last customer leaves. El Turf is in an entertainment complex at the very top of the Rio Sul shopping center (☞ Shopping, *below*).

Dance Clubs

Rio's *danceterias* (discos) offer flashing lights and loud music. At a number of places, including samba clubs, you can dance to live Brazilian music. *Gafieiras* are old-fashioned ballroom dance halls, usually patronized by an equally old-fashioned clientele. Upon entry to some clubs you're given a card to carry with you and each successive drink is marked on it. You pay on departure for what you've consumed.

Asa Branca (⊠ Av. Mem de Sá 17, Lapa, ☎ 021/252–4428) is Chico Recarey's large nightclub, where the decor combines modern, geometric designs with old-fashioned fixtures. Big bands and popular Brazilian musicians keep the crowd moving till dawn.

Biblo's Bar (⊠ Av. Epitácio Pessoa 1484, Lagoa, ☎ 021/521–2645) is *the* place for live music and dancing, particularly if you're single.

El Turf (⊠ Praça Santos Dumont 31, Gávea, ☎ 021/274–1444) is a hot spot with a cool location in the Jóque Clube. Its large space often fills up with the young and the beautiful, and it's open late.

Estudantina (⊠ Praça Tiradentes 79, Centro, ☎ 021/232–1149) was opened as a dance hall in 1932 and has become an eternally popular nightclub. On weekends, it packs in as many as 1,500 people.

Hippopotamus (⊠ Rua Barão da Torre 354, Ipanema, ☎ 021/247–0351) is one of Rio's exclusive (and expensive) discos, requiring membership (available to guests of the better hotels) and a stiff cover to get in. The disco is often closed for private parties, so be sure to call.

Le Maxim's (⊠ 116 Rua Lauro Muller, Botafogo, ☎ 021/541–9342), in the Rio Sul shopping center, has emerged as one of the top nightspots for professional cariocas. The city's movers and shakers are frequently seen hitting the dance floor here; many stay right until closing at 4 AM.

Sôbre as Ondas (⊠ Av. Atlântica 3432, Copacabana, ☎ 021/521–1296) overlooks Copacabana Beach. You can dance to live music, usually MPB or samba, and dine at the Terraço Atlântico restaurant downstairs.

Gay and Lesbian Clubs

Rio is a relatively gay-friendly city; the community even has its own gala during Carnaval. **Style Travel** sometimes has information on local happenings (☞ Gay and Lesbian Information *in* Rio de Janeiro A to Z). **Le Boy** (⊠ Rua Paul Pompeia 94, Copacabana, ☎ 021/521–0367) is a gay disco that draws an upscale crowd. **Barra Gaiviota** (⊠ Rua Rodolfo de Amoedo 343) is reportedly popular with lesbians.

"Baixos Gay," the Botafogo neighborhood around Rua Visconde Silva and Rua Real Grandeza, has the city's highest concentration of lesbian and gay bars and cafés. Try **Queen Victoria** (⊠ Rua Visconde Silva 30, ☎ 021/530–5332), a small pub with a sushi restaurant upstairs. Extremely popular with both women and men, it's often packed on weekends and every night past 11 PM. Across the street from Queen Victoria, **Acesso** is the best women's dance bar around; drink and dance all night for a small cover. **Tamino** (⊠ Rua Arnaldo Quintela 26, ☎ 021/295–1849) is a cozy, romantic bar-restaurant with live acoustic music.

The Arts

Although MPB may have overshadowed música *erudita* (classical music), Rio has a number of orchestras. The Orquestra Sinfônica Brasileira and the Orquestra do Teatro Municipal are the most prominent. Tickets to performing arts events are inexpensive by international standards and may be purchased at the theater or concert hall box offices. Dress is generally smart casual, although the conservative upper crust still likes to dress elegantly for the Teatro Municipal. Just don't wear valuable jewelry or carry lots of cash.

Rio has an avid film-going public and a well regarded film industry. (You may catch a flick here that later hits the international movie circuit.) Films are screened in small *cineclubes,* or state-of-the-art movie theaters (many in shopping malls). Foreign movies are shown in their original language with Portuguese subtitles (only children's films are dubbed). After dark, exercise caution in Cinelândia, where there's a large concentration of theaters.

In addition to its many museums, Rio has several privately funded cultural centers. These host changing, often exceptional art and photography exhibits as well as film series, lectures, and children's programs.

Venues

Centro Cultural Banco do Brasil (✉ Rua 1 de Março 66, Centro, ☎ 021/216–0237 or 021/216–0626). This six-story domed building with marble floors was constructed in 1888 and was once the headquarters of the Bank of Brasil. In the late 1980s it was transformed into a cultural center where art exhibitions and music recitals are held. The state-of-the-art complex features a library, two theaters, four video rooms, an auditorium, and a permanent display of Brazilian currency. Its gift shop is full of stunning coffee-table-type tomes on art and history—some of which are in English. It's open Tuesday–Sunday 10–8.

Fundacão Casa França–Brasil (✉ Rua Visconde de Itaboraí 78, Centro, ☎ 021/253–5366). This center, just steps away from Banco do Brasil Cultural Center, links France and Brazil in a cultural and artistic exchange. The interior of what was once a customs house has been completely restored, leaving an elegant, neoclassical space of gracious columns and arcades. Exhibits have included everything from photography and painting to displays on Carnaval and Brazil's environment. Musical shows (Gilberto Gil was a recent performer), poetry readings, and lectures round out the events. The center's hours are Tuesday–Sunday 10–8.

Metropolitan (✉ Av. Ayrton Senna 3000, Barra da Tijuca, ☎ 021/385–0516 for tickets or 021/285–3773 for schedules). When this posh performance center opened in the Via Parque shopping complex, its premiere was marked with a concert by Diana Ross. Although shows by top-name performers are certainly one of its mainstays, the 4,500-seat venue also hosts theatrical and dance performances.

Sala Cecilia Meireles (✉ Largo da Lapa 47, Centro, ☎ 021/232–4779) is a center for classical music.

Teatro Dulcina (✉ Rua Alcindo Guanabara 17, Centro, ☎ 021/240–4879) is a 600-seat theater that features classical opera and concerts.

Teatro João Caetano (✉ Praça Tiradentes, Centro, ☎ 021/221–0305) offers nightly variety shows—comedy, music, and dance—in a large theater setting.

Teatro Municipal (Praça Floriano, Centro, ☎ 021/297–4411). The city's main performing arts venue hosts dance, opera (an opera company puts on superb productions and often attracts international divas as guest artists), and theater events year-round, although the season officially runs from April to December. The theater's symphony orchestra has a very good reputation and includes many 19th- and 20th-century works in its program. The theater also has its own ballet company and is the site of an international ballet festival during April and May.

Teatro Paço Imperial (✉ Praça 15 de Novembro 48, Centro, ☎ 021/533–4407), like the Teatro Municipal, features a varied schedule of theatrical, musical, and dance performances.

OUTDOOR ACTIVITIES AND SPORTS

Participant Sports

Bicycling and Running

Bikers and runners share the boulevards along the beach and, for cooler and quieter outings, the path around Lagoa Rodrigo de Freitas. On weekends many cariocas also bike or run along the stretch of Floresta da Tijuca road that becomes pedestrian-only. Although hotels can arrange bike rentals, it's just as easy to rent from stands along beach-front avenues or the road ringing the lagoon. Rates are about $7 for two hours. You're usually asked to show identification and give your hotel name and room number, but deposits are seldom required. (Note that helmets aren't usually available, so bring your own.)

Boating and Sailing

Captain's Yacht Charters (⊠ Rua Conde de Lages 44, Glória, ☎ 021/224–0313) charters all types of crewed vessels for any length of time. You can arrange an afternoon of water-skiing with a speedboat or a weekend aboard a yacht.

Golf

Three golf courses are open to non-members (greens fees run as much as $50): the 18-hole **Gávea Golf Club** (⊠ Estrada da Gávea 800, São Conrado, ☎ 021/322–4141); the three-par, six-hole greens at **Golden Green Golf Club** (⊠ Av. Canal de Marapendi 2901, Barra da Tijuca, ☎ 021/433–3950); and the 27-hole **Itanhanga Golf Club** (⊠ Estrada da Barra, Barra da Tijuca, ☎ 021/494–2507).

Hang Gliding

Superfly (⊠ Estrada das Canoas 1476, Casa 2, São Conrado, ☎ 021/332–2286) offers hang-gliding classes and tandem flights with in-structors. To prove that you really made the leap, you can arrange to have your photo taken while airborne. The cost is about $80.

Hiking

Centro Excursionista Brasileiro (⊠ Av. Almirante Barroso 2–8, Centro, ☎ 021/252–9844) provides guides, maps, and gear for hiking expe-ditions throughout the metropolitan area.

Tennis

City tennis courts and clubs that allow visitors to play include **Akxe Club** (⊠ Av. Canal de Marapendi 2900, Barra da Tijuca, ☎ 021/325–3232) and **Rio Sport Center** (⊠ Av. Ayrton Senna 2541, Barra da Ti-juca, ☎ 021/325–6644; ⊠ Rua Visconde de Pirajá 161, Ipanema, ☎ 021/267–4192). Court time runs from $10 to $25 an hour; you can also rent equipment and arrange lessons.

Spectator Sports

Auto Racing

Brazilian race car drivers rank among the world's best and frequently compete in international events. In Rio, you'll get a taste of the speed if you watch the checkered flag drop on competitions in the Formula I Grand Prix circuit named after one of the country's most famous rac-ers, Emerson Fittipaldi. The racetrack is the **Autodromo Internacional Nelson Piquet** (⊠ Av. Embaixador Abelardo Bueno, Jacarepagua, ☎ 021/441–2158).

Futebol

You can watch a match at the **Estádio Maracanã** (⊠ Rua Prof. Eurico Rabelo, Maracanã, ☎ 021/264–9962). The fans are half the specta-cle. During the season the top game is played each Sunday at around 5 PM. The three most popular teams are Flamengo, Fluminense, and Vasco da Gama. Play between any of them is soccer at its finest.

Horse Racing

Races are held year-round in the **Jóque Clube** (⊠ Praça Santos Dumont 31, Gávea, ☎ 021/512–9988) beginning Monday and Thursday at 7 PM and weekends at noon. The big event of the year, the Brazilian Derby, is held the first Sunday of August.

THE BEAUTIFUL GAME

BRAZILIANS ARE MAD ABOUT *futebol* (soccer), and players here are fast and skillful. Some of their ball-handling moves are so graceful and fluid that they seem more akin to ballet—or at least to the samba—than to a sport; others are so acrobatic that they appear to defy the laws of physics; all are beautiful to watch.

The sport is believed to have been introduced here in the late 19th century by employees of British-owned firms. By the early 20th century upper-class Brazilians had formed their own leagues, as had the nation's European immigrants, who were already familiar with the game. As it requires little equipment, it also found a following in Brazil's poor communities. Today you can see young *brasileiros* everywhere practicing—bouncing a ball off a knee or a head and kicking it backward with a bare foot. Any of these boys could be a future futebol hero. Not only has Brazil turned out many international stars—the most famous of them Pelé—but it's consistently included in World Cup competitions and is a repeat title holder.

Soccer-mad fans come to games with musical instruments, flags, banners, streamers, firecrackers, and talcum powder. There's no better spot to witness the spectacle than at the world's largest soccer stadium, Rio's Estádio Maracanã. Here, you and as many as 219,999 other people can make music and make merry. Even if you don't have a great view of the field, you'll certainly be a part of the event.

SHOPPING

From sophisticated jewelry and Euro-style clothes to teeny tangas and funky tie-dyed dresses, the selection in Rio is broad. You can stroll down streets lined with fashionable boutiques, barter with vendors at street fairs, or wander through one of more than two dozen air-conditioned malls. The devaluation of the currency in early 1999 meant bargains were available again, especially in leather (note that larger shoe sizes, once difficult to find in Rio, are now common), suede, and jewelry. Good bets also include cool summer clothing in natural fibers, appropriate for the climate; coffee; samba and bossa nova CDs; and art.

Ipanema is Rio's most fashionable shopping district. Its many exclusive boutiques are in arcades, the majority of which are along Rua Visconde de Pirajá. In Copacabana you'll find souvenir shops, bookstores, and branches of some of Rio's better shops along Avenida Nossa Senhora de Copacabana and the streets just off it. If upscale jewelry catches your fancy, head for Avenida Atlântica.

Brazil is one of the world's largest producers of gold and the largest supplier of colored gemstones, with important deposits of aquamarines, amethysts, diamonds, emeralds, rubellites, topazes, and tourmalines. To get an idea of what's available, figure out what stones interest you, and compare their quality and price at various shops. If you're making a big investment, stick with shops that offer certificates of authenticity and quality. (If you're planning to go to Minas Gerais, save your jewelry shopping for there.)

Centers and Malls

Barra Shopping (⊠ Av. das Américas 4666, Barra da Tijuca, ☎ 021/431–9922) is one of South America's largest complexes. Although it's slightly out of the way, shoppers from all over town head for this large mall, which features a medical center, eight movie theaters, and a bowling alley as well as shops.

Rio Off Price Shopping (⊠ Rua General Severiano 97, Botafogo, ☎ 021/542–5693), just down the street from the Rio Sul shopping center (☞ *below*), is a mall whose prices are 20% lower than normal. The complex has snack bars and two movie theaters.

Rio Sul (⊠ Av. Lauro Müller 116, Botafogo, ☎ 021/295–1332) is one of the city's most popular retail complexes, with more than 400 shops. The shopping is sophisticated, and the food court is endless.

São Conrado Fashion Mall (⊠ Estrada da Gávea 899, São Conrado, ☎ 021/322–0300) sells a wide array of international and domestic fashions, and is Rio's most appealing mall as it's the least crowded and has an abundance of natural light.

Shopping Center Cassino Atlântico (⊠ Av. Nossa Senhora de Copacabana, Copacabana, ☎ 021/247–8709), adjoining the Rio Palace hotel, is dominated by antiques shops, jewelry stores, art galleries, and souvenir outlets.

Shopping Center da Gávea (⊠ Rua Marquês de São Vicente 52, Gávea, ☎ 021/274–9896) has a small but select mix of fashionable clothing and leather goods stores. It also has several top art galleries, of which the best are Ana Maria Niemeyer, Beco da Arte, Borghese, Bronze, Paulo Klabin, Saramenha, and Toulouse.

Via Parque (⊠ Av. Ayrton Senna 3000, Barra da Tijuca, ☎ 021/385–0100) is a 230-store complex popular for its outlets and ample parking (nearly 2,000 spaces). In addition to movie theaters and fast-food restaurants, the mall is home to the Metropolitan Theater.

Markets

The **Feira Hippie** is a colorful handicraft street fair held every Sunday 9–6 in Ipanema's Praça General Osório. Offerings run the gamut from jewelry and hand-painted dresses and T-shirts to paintings and wood carvings, leather bags and sandals, rag dolls, knickknacks, and even furniture. A handful of booths sell samba percussion instruments.

In the evenings and on weekends along the median of **Avenida Atlântica,** artisans spread out their wares. Here you will find paintings, carvings, handicrafts, sequined dresses, and hammocks from the northeast. Saturday (during daylight hours) in Centro sees two **antiques fairs:** an open-air fair near the Praça 15 de Novembro and the Rio Antique Fair on Rua do Lavradio. At both, you can buy china and silver sets, watches, Asian rugs, chandeliers, rare books, records, and all types of objets d'art. The antiques vendors move to the Casa Shopping Center in Barra da Tijuca on Sunday.

The crowded, lively **Feira Nordestino** (Northeastern Fair), held every Sunday 6–1 at the Campo de São Cristóvão, is a social event for northeasterners living in Rio. They gather to hear their own distinctive music, eat regional foods, and buy tools and cheap clothing.

Specialty Shops

Art

Cohn Edelstein (⊠ Rua Jangadeira 14B, Ipanema, ☎ 021/523–0549; Rua Barão da Torre 185A, Ipanema, ☎ 021/287–9933) is an internationally respected contemporary art gallery showing Brazilian works.

Bonino (⊠ Rua Barata Ribeiro 578, Copacabana, ☎ 021/294–7810) is the most traditional, best known, and most visited of Rio's art galleries. It has been around for some 30 years.

Contorno (⊠ Shopping Center da Gávea, Rua Marquês de São Vicente 52, Gávea, ☎ 021/274–3832) is a more eclectic gallery, but the art it displays is certainly Brazilian.

Rio Design Center (⊠ Av. Ataulfo de Paiva 270, Leblon, ☎ 021/274–7893) contains several galleries, including Borghese, Beco da Arte, Montesanti, Museum, and Way.

Beachwear

Blueman (⊠ Rio Sul, Av. Lauro Müller 116, Botafogo, ☎ 021/220–4898), a bikini shop with many mall locations in addition to the Rio Sul branch, carries the bikinis that virtually define Brazil in much of North America's imagination. Tangas are said to have been invented in Ipanema—and they don't take up much room in your luggage.

Bum Bum (⊠ Rua Vinícius de Morais 130, Ipanema, ☎ 021/521–1229) is the market leader in beachwear with locations in Rio Sul and Barra Shopping in addition to its Ipanema branch.

Salinas (⊠ Forum de Ipanema, Visconde de Pirajá 351, Ipanema) is another très chic bikini designer and the label de rigueur with the fashionable in Búzios and other resort areas.

CDs

Toca do Vinícius (⊠ Rua Vinícius de Morais 129, Ipanema, ☎ 021/247–5227) bills itself as a "cultural space and bossa nova salon." The shop, though tiny, does indeed seem like a gathering place for bossa-nova afficionados from around the world. (If you're one of them, there's a good chance you'll leave the shop with an E-mail address for at least one new pal.) Amid the atmosphere of bonhomie, you'll find books (few in English), sheet music, and T-shirts as well as CDs.

Clothing

Alice Tapalos (⊠ Forum de Ipanema, Visconde de Pirajá 351, Ipanema, ☎ 021/247–2594) carries DKNY and other well-known sportswear in its Ipanema, São Conrado Fashion Mall, and Barra Shopping locations.

Ar Livre (⊠ Av. Nossa Senhora de Copacabana 900, Copacabana, ☎ 021/549–8994) has an exceptional selection of good quality T-shirts and beachwear at appealing prices.

Krishna (⊠ Rio Sul, Av. Lauro Müller 116, Botafogo, ☎ 021/542–2443; ⊠ São Conrado Fashion Mall, Estrada da Gávea 899, São Conrado, ☎ 021/322–0437) specializes in classic, feminine dresses and separates—many in fine linens, cottons, and silks.

Mesbla (⊠ Rua do Passeio 42/56, Centro, ☎ 021/534–7720), Rio's largest chain department store, focuses on mostly casual fashions for men, women, and children. But it also has a wide selection of toys, records, cosmetics, musical instruments, and sporting goods.

Handicrafts

Casa do Pequeno Empresario (⊠ Rua Real Grandeza 293, Botafogo, ☎ 021/286–9464) is an exposition center for hand-crafted items made of everything from porcelain to wood and papier-mâché to clay.

Folclore (⊠ Rua Visconde de Pirajá 490, Ipanema, ☎ 021/259–7442). At H. Stern world headquarters (☞ *below*), this handicraft shop bursts with naive paintings, costume jewelry, leather and ceramic crafts, and birds and flowers carved from stone. Quality is high but take note: some items have been imported from other South American nations.

Jewelry

Amsterdam-Sauer (⊠ Rua Visconde de Pirajá 484, Ipanema, ☎ 021/512–9878) is one of Rio's top names (with top prices) in jewelry. Jules

Roger Sauer, the founder of these stores (with branches in Brazil, the United States, and the Caribbean), is particularly known for his fascination with emeralds. The on-site gemstone museum (☎ 021/239–8045) is open Monday–Friday 10–5 and Saturday 9:30–1 (tour reservations are a good idea).

Antonio Bernardo (✉ Gávea, Forum Ipanema, and Fashion Mall shopping malls) has been making gorgeous jewelry with contemporary designs for nearly 30 years.

H. Stern (✉ Rua Visconde de Pirajá 490, Ipanema, ☎ 021/259–7442). Hans Stern started his empire in 1945 with an initial investment of about $200. Today his interests include mining and production operations as well as 170 stores in Europe, the Americas, and the Middle East. His award-winning designers create truly unique and contemporary pieces (the inventory runs to about 300,000 items). At H. Stern world headquarters you can see exhibits of rare stones, and watch craftspeople transform rough stones into sparkling jewels. There's also a museum you can tour (by appointment only). If you feel the prices are too high in the upstairs salons, there are shops downstairs that sell more affordable pieces as well as folkloric items.

Leather Goods

Bottega Veneta (✉ Shopping Center da Gávea, Rua Marquês de São Vicente 52, Gávea, ☎ 021/274–8248) has fine women's shoes and bags.

Formosinho (✉ Av. Nossa Senhora de Copacabana 582, Copacabana, ☎ 021/287–8998) sells men's and women's shoes at low, wholesale prices. In addition to its Copacabana location, it has three other stores along Ipanema's Rua Visconde de Pirajá.

Frankie Amaury (✉ Shopping Center da Gávea, Rua Marquês de São Vicente 52, Gávea, ☎ 021/294–8895) is *the* name in leather clothing.

Mariazinha (✉ Forum de Ipanema, Praça Nossa Senhora da Paztel, Ipanema, ☎ 021/541–6695) carries fashionable footwear.

Nazaré (✉ Shopping Center da Gávea, Rua Marquês de São Vicente 52, Gávea, ☎ 021/294–9849) has bags and fine women's shoes.

Victor Hugo (✉ Rio Sul, Av. Lauro Müller 116, Botafogo, ☎ 021/275–3388) carries women's handbags.

RIO DE JANEIRO A TO Z

Arriving and Departing

By Airplane

All international flights and most domestic flights arrive and depart from the **Aeroporto Internacional Galeão** (☎ 021/398–6060). The airport is about 45 minutes northwest of the beach area and most of Rio's hotels. **Aeroporto Santos Dumont** (☎ 021/524–7070), 20 minutes from the beaches and within walking distance of Centro, serves the Rio–São Paulo air shuttle and a few air-taxi firms.

Nearly three dozen airlines regularly serve Galeão. Several of the international carriers also offer Rio–São Paulo flights. International carriers include: **Aerolineas Argentinas** (☎ 021/398–3520 or 021/224–4931), **American Airlines** (☎ 021/398–4053 or 021/210–3126), **British Airways** (☎ 021/398–3888 or 021/221–0922), **Canadian Airlines** (☎ 021/398–3604 or 021/220–5343), **Delta** (☎ 021/398–3492 or 021/507–7262), and **United** (☎ 021/398–4050 or 021/532–1212).

Several domestic carriers serve international and Brazilian destinations: **Transbrasil** (☎ 021/398–5485 or 021/297–4477), **Varig** (☎ 021/534–0333 or 021/217–4591), and **VASP** (☎ 021/292–2112 or 021/

462–3363). **Nordeste/RioSul** (☎ 021/507–4488 or 021/524–9387) covers domestic routes.

Special airport taxis have booths in the arrival areas of both airports. Fares to all parts of Rio are posted at the booths, and you pay in advance (about $35–$50). Also trustworthy are the white radio taxis parked in the same areas; these charge an average of 20% less. Three reliable special taxi firms are **Transcoopass** (☎ 021/560–4888), **Cootramo** (☎ 021/560–5442), and **Coopertramo** (☎ 021/560–2022).

Air-conditioned *frescão* buses run by **Empresa Real** (☎ 021/290–5665 or 021/270–7041) park curbside outside customs at Galeão and outside the main door at Santos Dumont; for less than $3 they make the hour-long trip into the city, following the beachfront drives and stopping at all hotels along the way. If your hotel is inland, the driver will let you off at the nearest corner. Buses leave from the airport every half-hour from 5:20 AM to 11 PM.

By Bus

Regular service is available to and from Rio. Long-distance buses leave from the **Rodoviária Novo Rio station** (✉ Av. Francisco Bicalho 1, São Cristóvão, ☎ 021/291–5151), near the port. Any local bus marked RODOVIÁRIA will take you to the station. You can buy tickets at the depot or, for some destinations, from travel agents. Buses also leave from the more conveniently located **Menezes Cortes terminal** (✉ Rua São José 35, Centro, ☎ 021/533–7577), near Praça 15 de Novembro.

By Car

Driving in from São Paulo (429 km/266 mi on BR 116) and Brasília (1,150 km/714 mi on BR 040), you enter Rio via Avenida Brasil, which runs into Centro's beachside drive, the Avenida Infante Dom Henrique. This runs along Rio's Baía de Guanabara and passes through the Copacabana Tunnel to Copacabana Beach. Here the beachside Avenida Atlântica continues into Ipanema and Leblon along Avenidas Antônio Carlos Jobim (Ipanema) and Delfim Moreira (Leblon). From Galeão, take the Airport Expressway (known as the Linha Vermelha, or Red Line) to the beach area. This expressway takes you through two tunnels and into Lagoa. Exit on Avenida Epitácio Pessoa, the winding street encircling the lagoon. To reach Copacabana, exit at Avenida Henrique Dodsworth (known as the Corte do Cantagalo). For Ipanema and Leblon, there are several exits beginning with Rua Maria Quitéria.

By Train

Intercity trains leave from *the* central station that starred in the Oscar-nominated movie by the same name, **Estação Dom Pedro II Central do Brasil** (✉ Praça Cristiano Otoni on Avenida President Vargas, Centro, ☎ 021/233–8818). Trains, including a daily overnight train to São Paulo, also leave from the **Estação Leopoldina Barao de Maria** (✉ Av. Francisco Bicalho, São Cristóvão, ☎ 021/273–1122, 575-3399), near Praça 15 de Novembro.

Getting Around

By Bus

Local buses are inexpensive and can take you anywhere you want to go. (Route maps aren't available, but the tourist office has lists of routes to the most popular sights.) Much has been made of the threat of being robbed on Rio's buses. Crime has dropped significantly in the last few years; if you're discreet, you shouldn't have any problems. Just don't wear expensive watches or jewelry, carry a camera or a map in hand, or talk boisterously in English. It's also wise to avoid buses during rush hour. You enter buses at the rear, where you pay an attendant, and pass through a turnstile, then exit at the front. Have your fare in hand when you board to avoid flashing bills or wallets. Be aware that bus drivers speak no English, and they drive like maniacs.

The more upscale, air-conditioned frescão buses run between the beaches, downtown, and Rio's two airports. These vehicles, which look like highway buses, stop at regular bus stops but also may be flagged down wherever you see them. Also recommended are the *jardineira* buses, open-sided vehicles (they look like old-fashioned streetcars) that follow the beach drive from Copacabana to São Conrado as well as beyond to Barra da Tijuca. White posts along the street mark jardineira stops. They offer excellent views of the scenery and drive slowly along the beach avenue, a welcome relief to anyone who has ridden the regular city buses. Green minivans also run back and forth along beachfront avenues, stopping to pick up and drop off people wherever they're flagged. (Fares start at about $2.)

By Car

Driving in Rio isn't for the faint of heart. The carioca style of driving is passionate to the point of abandon, traffic jams are common, the streets aren't well marked, and red lights are often more decorative than functional. Further, despite the fact that the city has opened new parking areas along the beachfront boulevards, finding a spot can still be a problem. If you do choose to drive, exercise extreme caution, wear seat belts at all times, and keep the doors locked. When frustrations get the best of you, the book *How to Be a Carioca* offers some advice: even when you are angry, smile.

Car rentals can be arranged through hotels or agencies and cost about $80–$100 a day for standard models. Agencies include **Hertz** (⊠ Av. Princesa Isabel 334, Copacabana, ☎ 021/275–7440) and **Unidas** (⊠ Av. Princesa Isabel 350, Copacabana, ☎ 021/275–8299). Both also have desks at the international and domestic airports.

Turismo Clássico Travel (☞ Tour Operators and Travel Agents *below*), one of the country's most reliable travel and transport agencies, can arrange for a driver, with or without an English-speaking guide. Classico's owners, Liliana and Vera, speak English and each has 20 years of experience in organizing transportation.

By Metrô

Rio's subway system, the **metrô** (☎ 021/292–6116 or 021/255–5552) is clean, safe, and efficient—a delight to use—but it's not comprehensive. Reaching sights distant from metrô stations can be a challenge, especially in summer when the infamous carioca traffic fans what is already 90° exasperation. Plan your tours accordingly; tourism offices and some metrô stations have maps.

Trains run daily from 6 AM to 11 PM along two lines: Linha 1 runs north from the Cardeal Arcoverde stop in Copacabana, parallel to the coast and into downtown, then west to its terminus at Saens Pena station; Linha 2 starts four stops before Saens Pena at Estacio and heads northwest to Rio's edge at the Pavuna station. A single metrô ticket costs R$1, a 10-pack is R$10 (but there are discounts for riding the subway during the non-rush hours between noon and 4 PM). Combination metrô-bus tickets allow you to take special buses to and from the Botafogo station: The M-21 runs to Leblon via Jardim Botânico and Jóque; the M-22 goes to Leblon by way of Túnel Velho, Copacabana, and Ipanema.

By Taxi
Yellow taxis are just like those in New York, except that even fewer of the drivers speak English. They have meters that start at a set price and have two rates: "1" for before and "2" for after 8 PM. The "2" rate also applies to Sundays and holidays, the month of December, the neighborhoods of São Conrado and Barra da Tijuca, and when climbing steep hills. Drivers are required to post a chart noting the current fares on the inside of the left rear window. Carioca cabbies are, by and large, wonderful people, but there are exceptions. Remain alert and trust your instincts; a few drivers have taken non-natives for a ride.

Radio taxis and several companies that routinely serve hotels (and whose drivers often speak English) are also options. Radio cabs charge 30% more than other taxis but are reliable and, usually, air-conditioned. Other cabs working with the hotels will also charge more, normally a fixed fee that you should agree upon before you leave. Reliable radio cab companies include **Centro de Taxis** (☎ 021/593–2598), **Coopacarioca** (☎ 021/253–3847), and **Coopatur** (☎ 021/290–1009).

Contacts and Resources

Banks and Currency Exchange
The Banco do Brasil branch at Galeão offers good exchange rates, but it won't provide credit-card advances. *Casas do cambio* (exchange houses) are found all over the city, especially along the beaches. Many change money without charging a service fee. Automatic-teller machines (ATMs) throughout town dispense reaís.

Consulates
Australia (⊠ Av. Nilo Pecanha 50, Centro, ☎ 021/240–2294), **Canada** (⊠ Rua Lauro Müller 116, Room 1104, Botafogo, ☎ 021/542–7593), **United Kingdom** (⊠ Praia do Flamengo 284, 2nd Floor, Flamengo, ☎ 021/553–6850), **United States** (⊠ Av. Presidente Wilson 147, Centro, ☎ 021/292–7117).

Emergencies
Ambulance and fire: ☎ 193. **Clinics: Cardio Plus**(⊠ Rua Visconde de Pirajá 330, Ipanema, ☎ 021/521–4899), **Galdino Campos Cardio Copa Medical Clinic**(⊠ Av. Nossa Senhora de Copacabana 492, Copacabana, ☎ 021/548–9966), and **Medtur** (⊠ Av. Nossa Senhora de Copacabana 647, Copacabana, ☎ 021/235–3339). **Dentist: Policlinica Barata Ribeiro**(⊠ Rua Barata Ribeiro 51, Copacabana, ☎ 021/275–4697). **Pharmacies:** Round the clock pharmacies include **Drogario Pacheco** (⊠ Av. Nossa Senhora de Copacabana 534, Copacabana, ☎ 021/548–1525) and **Farmacia do Leme** (⊠ Av. Prado Junior 237, Leme, ☎ 021/275–3847). **Police:** ☎ 190. **Tourism Police** (⊠ Av. Afranio de Melo Franco, Leblon, ☎ 021/511–5112).

English-Language Bookstores
Bookstores that carry some English-language publications include **Livraria Argumento** (⊠ Rua Dias Ferreria 417, Leblon, ☎ 021/239–5294), **Livraria Kosmos** (⊠ Rua do Rosario 155, Centro, ☎ 021/224–8616), and **Sodiler** (⊠ Aeroporto Internacional Galeão, ☎ 021/393–9511; ⊠ Aeroporto Santos Dumont, ☎ 021/393–4377).

Gay & Lesbian Information
Style Travel (Rua Visconde de Piraja 433, 6th floor, Ipanema, ☎ 021/522–0709, FAX 021/522–0617), an offshoot of the established Brasil Plus travel agency, is a great source of information on gay and lesbian lodging, tour, and nightlife options in the area. They can also supply knowledgeable, English-speaking gay and lesbian guides and arrange trips

to outlying areas. Style Travel is a member of the International Gay and Lesbian Travel Association (IGLTA).

Claudio Nascimento runs the **Arco-Iris Association** (☎ FAX 021/293–5322), which educates the public about AIDS and AIDS prevention and gay and lesbian rights (they recently conducted a course for police officers). The group also lobbies for legal reform, and provides general assistance and information to Rio's gay and lesbian community.

Sui Generes is Rio's gay and lesbian glossy magazine. It's available at most newsstands and lists local arts, music, and style events. *Entre Nós* and *O Grito* are Rio's gay newspapers. All of these publications are in Portuguese.

Visit Rio's on-line "Gay Guide" at www.ipanema.com/rio/gay. The site is a wealth of information—from the practical to the downright sexy—on Rio and its lesbian and gay scene. Rio's gay beach scene is at Bolsa on Copacabana Beach in front of the Copacabana Palace and at Ipanema by posts 8 and 9, east of Rua Farme de Amoeda, a.k.a. Farme Gay. Locals on these sandy stretches are usually open to questions about what's happening in the gay and lesbian community.

Health and Safety

You should avoid tap water (note that ice in restaurants and bars is safe as it's usually made from bottled water), and take care not to soak up too much sun. Despite its reputation, crime in Rio is no more dangerous these days than any large city. Most crimes involving visitors occur in crowded public areas: beaches, busy sidewalks, intersections, and city buses. Pickpockets, usually children, work in groups. One will distract you while another grabs a wallet, bag, or camera. Be particularly wary of children who thrust themselves in front of you and ask for money or offer to shine your shoes. Another member of the gang may strike from behind, grabbing your valuables and disappearing into the crowd. Another tactic is for people to approach your car at intersections. Always keep doors locked and windows partially closed. Leave valuables in your hotel safe, don't wear expensive jewelry or watches, and keep cameras out of sight. Walking alone at night on the beach isn't a good idea; neither is getting involved with drugs. Penalties for possession are severe, and dealers are the worst of the worst.

Telephones, the Internet, and Mail

Rio's area code is 021. There are public phones on corners throughout the city. They work with cards that you can buy in a variety of denominations at newsstands, banks, and some shops. (Some phones also work with credit cards.) For long-distance calls, there are phone offices at the main bus terminal, Galeão, downtown at Praça Tiradentes 41, and in Copacabana at Avenida Nossa Senhora de Copacabana 540. To make international calls through the operator, dial 000111. For operator-assisted long-distance within Brazil, dial 101; information is 102.

Brazilians are increasingly joining the Internet community, and the staff at many hotels can arrange Internet access for guests. In addition, you can head to the cybercafé, **El Turf Cyber Bar** (☞ Nightlife and the Arts, *above*) or **CompRio** (✉ Rua da Assembléia 10, basement level, ☎ 021/533–4372), a computer store in the same Centro building as Turisrio. Here you'll find a few computers (note that they're on the slow side) that are available for about $6 an hour weekdays 9–6.

The **main post office** (✉ Av. Presidente Vargas 3077, ☎ 021/503–8222) is in Centro but there are branches all over the city, including one at Galeão and several on Avenida Nossa Senhora de Copacabana in Copacabana and Rua Viscondes de Pirajá in Ipanema. Most branches are open weekdays 8–5 and Saturday 8–noon.

Tour Operators and Travel Agents

You can ride around the Floresta da Tijuca and Corcovado, Angra dos Reis, or Teresópolis in renovated World War II Jeeps (1942 Dodge Commanders, Willys F-75's, and others) with the well-organized **Atlantic Forest Jeep Tours** (☎ FAX 021/495–9827 or ☎ 021/494–4761). Guides speak English, French, German, and Spanish. The company also offers a range of ecological tours, including some on horseback. The superb guides at **Gray Line** (☎ 021/512–9919) speak your language. In addition to a variety of city tours the company also offers trips outside town, whether you'd like to go white-water rafting on the Rio Paraíbuna, tour a coffee plantation, or spend time in Petrópolis. Tours by helicopter are also an option.

Ecology and Culture Tours (☎ 021/522–1620) offers hiking and Jeep tours of Tijuca, Sugar Loaf, Santa Teresa, and various beaches. Guides speak English, and morning and afternoon excursions are available. **Favela Tour** (☎ 021/322–2727) offers a fascinating half-day tour of two favelas. For anyone with an interest in Brazil beyond the beaches, such tours are highly recommended. The company's English-speaking guides can also be contracted for other outings.

Qualitours (☎ 021/232–9710) will take you and yours in a Jeep around old Rio, the favelas, Corcovado, Floresta da Tijuca, and Prainha and Grumari. They can explain everything in English, Hungarian, French, or German. Tandem hang- or paraglide over Pedra da Gávea and Pedra Bonita under the supervision of **São Conrado Eco-Aventura** (☎ 021/522–5586). Folks here will help you, in English, with the finer points of sightseeing by air.

Turismo Clássico Travel (✉ Av. Nossa Senhora de Copacabana 1059, Suite 805, Copacabana, ☎ 021/287–3390) arranges guided tours for English-speaking tourists as well as professionals, and often works with film crews. They also plan more extensive tours around Brazil.

Visitor Information

The Rio de Janeiro city tourism department, **Riotur** (✉ Rua da Assembléia 10, near Praça 15 de Novembro, Centro, ☎ 021/217–7575) has an **information booth** (☎ 021/541–7522) at Avenida Princesa Isabel 183 in Copacabana; it's open 8–5 daily. There are also city tourism desks at the airports and the Novo Rio bus terminal. The Rio de Janeiro state tourism board, **Turisrio** (✉ Rua da Assembléia 10, 7th and 8th floors, Centro, ☎ 021/531–1922), is open weekdays 9–6. You can also try contacting Brazil's national tourism board, **Embratur** (✉ Rua Uruguaiana 174, Centro, ☎ 021/509–6017).

SIDE TRIPS FROM RIO

Rio the state has just as much allure as Rio the city. A scenic northeast road into the mountains leads to Petrópolis, a city that bears testimony to the country's royal legacy. Beyond here, tucked into a lush valley, is charming Nova Friburgo with its Swiss ambience. Due east of the city, dangling off the yacht-frequented coast, are the sophisticated resort towns of Cabo Frio and Búzios, where Rio's chic escape for weekends. And to the southwest along the Costa Verde sit the stunning Angra dos Reis—facing the offshore island of Ilha Grande—and the colonial city of Parati with its 18th century Portuguese architecture and plethora of offshore islets.

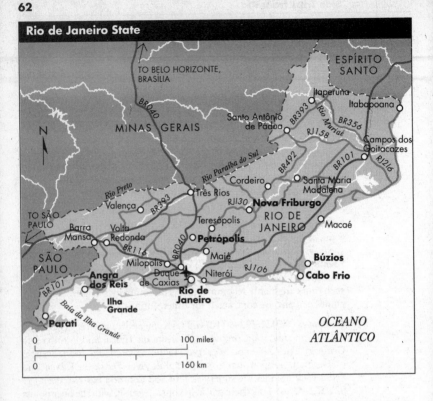

Rio de Janeiro State

Petrópolis

65 km (42 mi) northeast of Rio.

The hilly highway northeast of the city rumbles past forests and waterfalls en route to a mountain town so refreshing and picturesque that Dom Pedro II, Brazil's second emperor, spent his summers in it. (From 1889 to 1899, it was also the country's year-round seat of government.) Horse-drawn carriages shuttle between the sights, passing flowering gardens, shady parks, and imposing pink mansions.

The biggest attraction is the **Museu Imperial,** a museum housed in the magnificent 44-room palace that was Dom Pedro's summer home. The colossal structure is filled with polished wood floors, 19th-century artwork, and grand chandeliers. You can also see the diamond-encrusted gold crown and scepter of Brazil's last emperor, as well as other royal jewels. ⊠ *Rua da Imperatriz 220,* ☎ *0242/427–1023.* ☐ *Admission.* ☉ *Tues.–Sun. noon–5:30.*

From the Imperial Museum, you can walk three long blocks or take a horse-drawn carriage to **São Pedro de Alcantara,** the Gothic cathedral containing the tombs of Dom Pedro II; his wife, Dona Teresa Cristina; and their daughter, Princesa Isabel. ⊠ *Av. Tiradentes,* ☎ *no phone.* ☐ *Free.* ☉ *Weekdays 8–noon, Sun. 8–6.*

The **Palacio de Cristal** (Crystal Palace), a stained-glass and iron structure made in France and assembled in Brazil, was a wedding present to Princesa Isabel. During the imperial years, it was used as a ballroom: it was here the princess held a celebration dance after she abolished slavery in Brazil in 1888. ⊠ *Praça da Confluencia, Rua Alfredo Pacha,* ☎ *no phone.* ☐ *Free.* ☉ *Tues.–Sun. 9–5.*

Dining and Lodging

$$ ✕ **Bauernstube.** German food is the backbone of this log-cabin-style eatery. The bratwurst and sauerkraut are properly seasoned, and the strudel is an excellent choice for polishing off a meal. ⊠ *Dr. Nelson de Sá Earp 297,* ☎ *0242/42–1097. AE, DC, MC, V. Closed Mon.*

$$$$ ✕🖽 **Pousada de Alcobaca.** Just north of Petrópolis, this is considered by many to be the loveliest inn in the area. It sits on the grounds of a large estate and has beautiful gardens and a swimming pool. The kitchen turns out exceptional breakfasts, lunches, and high teas with an emphasis on fresh ingredients. Meals, which include savory pastas, are served in the garden. ⊠ *Agostinho Goulao 298, Correa,* ☎ *0242/ 21–1240,* 🖷 *0242/22–3390. 10 rooms. Restaurant, pool, sauna, tennis court. AE, DC, MC, V.*

$$ ✕🖽 **Pousada Monte Imperial.** A few minutes from downtown, this Euro-style inn has 14 double rooms with private baths, a pool, a lobby with a fireplace, and a restaurant-bar. Drinks and meals can also be taken in the lovely garden. ⊠ *Rua Joséde Alencar 27,* ☎ *0242/37–1664. 14 rooms. Restaurant, bar, pool. AE, DC, MC, V.*

$$$ 🖽 **Hotel Margaridas.** Three chalets and 12 apartments make up this comfortable complex just five minutes from the heart of downtown. You'll find well-tended gardens and a swimming pool. ⊠ *Rua Bispo Pereira Alves 235,* ☎ *0242/42–4686. 12 apartments, 3 chalets. Pool. AE, DC, MC, V.*

En Route If you continue northeast from Petrópolis, you will pass through the town of Teresópolis (named for the empress) as well as the beautiful Serra dos Orgãos National Park on the way to the mountain resort of Nova Friburgo.

Nova Friburgo

131 km (79 mi) northeast of Petrópolis.

This summer resort town was settled by Swiss immigrants in the early 1800s, when Brazil was actively encouraging European immigration and when the economic situation in Switzerland was bad. Woods, rivers, and waterfalls dot the terrain encircling the city. Homemade liquors, jams, and cheeses pack the shelves of the town's small markets. Cariocas come here to unwind in the cool mountain climate.

A cable car rises more than 2,000-ft to **Morra da Cruz,** which offers a spectacular view of the mountainscape. ⊠ *Praça Teleférica,* ☎ *no phone.* 🎫 *Admission.* ☉ *Weekends 9–6.*

Lodging

$$$ 🖽 **Fazenda São João.** Trout fishing and horseback riding are among the draws at this country-house inn, which is surrounded by flowers (including orchids) and fruit trees just a few miles outside town. The owners provide shuttle service to and from Nova Friburgo. ⊠ *Rua Hans Garlipp 28600,* ☎ *0242/42–1304. 21 rooms. Pool, sauna, horseback riding, fishing. AE, DC, MC, V.*

Cabo Frio

168 km (101 mi) east of Rio.

Set up as a defensive port from which to ship wood to Portugal nearly four centuries ago, Cabo Frio has evolved into a resort town renowned for its fresh seafood. It's also a prime jumping off point for the endless number of white sand beaches that crisscross the area around town and the offshore islands. A favorite sailing destination, its turquoise waters are crowded with sailboats and yachts on holidays and weekends. The town itself has attractive baroque architecture.

Praia do Forte is popular thanks to its calm, clear waters and long stretch of sand. On weekends it's jammed with colorful beach umbrellas, swimmers, and sun lovers. Some distance away, **Praia Brava** and **Praia do Foguete** lure surfers to their crashing waves.

Búzios

★   *25 km (15 mi) northeast of Cabo Frio.*

Búzios, a little more than two hours from Rio, is a string of gorgeous beaches that draws resort fans year-round from Europe and South America. This is the perfect place to do absolutely nothing. It was little more than a fishing village until the 1960s, when Brigitte Bardot was photographed here in a bikini. Since then, Búzios's rustic charm has given way to *pousadas,* or inns (some of them luxurious, few inexpensive); restaurants; and bars that are run by people who came on vacation and never left. The balance between the cosmopolitan and the primitive here is seductive.

March through June is low season, when temperatures range from about 27°C (80°F) to 32°C (90°F), and prices often drop 30%–40%. The water is still warm, yet the crowds aren't as great and the area seems much more intimate than in the summer months of October through December. Though not a great deal of English is spoken here, a little Spanish or French will get you a long way.

Each of the beaches offers something different: the lovely, intimate **Azeda** and **Azedinha** are local favorites (and the spots where you may find topless bathing); **Ferradura** is known for the gastronomic excellence of its kiosks and its jet-skiing; **Lagoinha** is referred to by all as a magic beach and has a natural amphitheater where world-class musicians hold concerts; **Brava** is the surfer's beach; **Manguinhos** is popular with windsurfers.

Dining and Lodging

$$$ ✕ **Satyricon.** The Italian fish restaurant famous in Rio has opened up
★   shop here as well. The menu's highlight is the expensive but great seafood, including the restaurant's famous rock-salt-baked whole fish. ⊠ *Rua José Bento Ribeiro Dantas 500,* ☎ *0246/23–1595. AE, DC, MC, V.*

$ ✕ **Chez Michou.** This *crêperie* on the main drag in the center of town is the best place to eat if you want something quick, light, and inexpensive. You can choose from about 500 different crepe fillings and then eat your meal inside or outdoors. At night locals and visitors alike congregate here to drink and people-watch. ⊠ *Rua José Bento Ribeiro Dantas 90,* ☎ *0246/23–6137. No credit cards.*

$ ✕ **Coco Beach.** These kiosks at the far end of Ferradura Beach serve delectable food and drink. Order a *kiwiroska* (a vodka and fresh kiwi drink) and boneless grilled fish. Eat slowly, and you can enjoy a sunset unlike any other. ⊠ *Eastern end of Ferradura Beach. No credit cards.*

$$$ ▨ **Barracuda.** This hotel is included in Brazil's esteemed Roteiros de
★   Charme club, a highly exclusive association of the nation's best places to stay. The view of the sea from the deck is breathtaking. ⊠ *Ponta da Sapata,* ☎ *021/287–3122 ext. 601 for reservations from Rio,* ☎ FAX *0246/23–1314. 23 rooms. Restaurant, pool, sauna, 2 tennis courts. AE, DC, MC, V.*

Angra dos Reis

151 km (91 mi) west of Rio.

Angra dos Reis, the Bay of Kings, anchors the rugged Costa Verde in an area of beautiful beaches, colonial architecture, and clear emerald waters. Schooners, yachts, sailboats, and fishing skiffs thread among the 365 offshore islands, one for every day of the year. Indeed, Angra dos Reis's popularity lies in its strategic location—ideal for exploring those islands, many of which are deserted patches of sand and green that offer wonderful swimming and snorkeling opportunities. Organized boat tours from shore can take you to favored island haunts.

One of the most popular islands is the lush, mountainous **Ilha Grande.** Just 2 km (1 mi) and a 90-minute ferry ride off the shore from Angra dos Reis, it has more than 100 idyllic beaches—sandy ribbons that stretch on and on with a backdrop of tropical foliage. You can roam paths that lead from one slip of sand to the next and negotiate with local boatmen for jaunts to more remote islets.

Dining and Lodging

$$$ ✕🏨 **Hotel Porto Aquarius.** Guest-room balconies overlook the sea and private beach at this modern resort hotel, which has its own marina. Two swimming pools (plus a small pool for children) join the other amenities. The hotel can also arrange boat excursions. Seafood is, by no surprise, the restaurant's specialty, and the menu has a good mix of international and Brazilian dishes. ✉ *Saco Itapirapuan Sapata,* ☎ *0243/65–1642,* 🖷 *0243/65–1766. 138 rooms. Restaurant, bar, 3 pools, sauna, dock. AE, DC, MC, V.*

Parati

100 km (60 mi) southwest of Angra dos Reis.

This stunning colonial city is one of South America's gems. Giant iron chains hang from posts at the beginning of the mazelike grid of cobblestone streets, closing them to all but pedestrians, horses, and bicycles. Until the 18th century, this was an important transit point for gold plucked from the Minas Gerais; a safe harbor protected from pirates by a fort. (The cobblestones are the rock ballast brought from Lisbon, then unloaded to make room in the ships for their golden cargos.) In 1720, however, the colonial powers cut a new trail from the gold mines straight to Rio de Janeiro, bypassing the town and leaving it isolated. It remained that way until contemporary times when artists, writers, and others "discovered" the community and UNESCO placed it on its World Heritage Site list. Brazilian actress Sonia Braga comes here to relax, and Rolling Stone Mick Jagger used it as the backdrop for a music video.

Parati wasn't a city peppered with lavish mansions and opulent palaces; rather it has a simple beauty. By the time the sun breaks over the bay each morning—illuminating the white-washed, colorfully trimmed buildings—the fishermen will have begun spreading out their catch at the outdoor market. The best way to explore is simply to begin walking winding streets banked with centuries-old buildings that hide quaint inns, tony restaurants, shops, and art galleries. Once you've finished your in-town exploration, you can begin investigating what makes this a weekend escape for cariocas: the lush, tropical, offshore islands and not-so-distant strands of coastal beach.

Parati is jammed with churches, but the most intriguing are the trio whose congregations were segregated by race during the colonial era. **Igreja de Nossa Senhora do Rosario** (✉ Rua do Comércio) was built by the town's slaves so they could have their own place of worship. Simple and clean-lined **Igreja de Santa Rita** (✉ Rua Santa Rita), meanwhile, was built in 1722 and earmarked for free mulattos; today it houses a small religious art museum. On the far extreme of the social spectrum, **Igreja de Nossa Senhora das Dores** (✉ Rua Dr. Pereira) was the church of the community's small, but elite, white population. The fortress **Forte Defensor Perpetuo** (✉ Morro da Vila Velha), built in the early 1700s (and rebuilt in 1822) as a defense against pirates and now home to a folk-arts center, sits north of town.

Dining and Lodging

$$ ✕ **Restaurante do Hiltinho.** Seafood reigns at this cozy, quiet spot. It's one of the best eateries in town—both because of the kitchen and because of its prices. ✉ *Rua Marechal Deodoro 233,* ☎ *0243/71–1432. No credit cards.*

$$$$ ▥ **Pousada do Ouro.** Posh and elegant, this is the inn most likely to host celebrities who come to the area for sun and atmosphere. ✉ *Rua da Praia 145,* ☎ *0243/71–1378,* ℻ *0243/71–1311. 18 rooms, 8 suites Restaurant, bar, pool. AE, DC, MC, V.*

$$ ▥ **Porto Pousada Parati.** Rooms in this historic structure in the old-
★   est part of town are wrapped around a series of courtyards and a swimming pool. Rates include breakfast. ✉ *Rua do Comércio,* ☎ *0243/71–1205,* ℻ *0243/71–2111. 51 rooms. Restaurant, bar, pool, sauna. AE, DC, MC, V.*

$$ ▥ **Pousada do Principe.** A prince (the great grandson of Emperor
★   Pedro II) owns this aptly named inn at the edge of the colonial city. The hotel is painted in the yellow and green of the imperial flag, and its quiet, colorful public areas are graced by photos of the royal family. Rooms are small but comfortable (and air-conditioned). The swimming pool in the plant-filled patio beckons. The kitchen here is impressive, too; its chef turns out an exceptional feijoada. ✉ *Av. Roberto Silveira 289,* ☎ *0243/71–2266,* ℻ *0243/71–2120. 34 rooms. Restaurant, pool, sauna, 2 tennis courts. AE, DC, MC, V.*

Side Trips from Rio A to Z

Arriving and Departing

Large, air-conditioned buses leave Rio's Rodoviária Novo Rio bus terminal hourly each day for Petrópolis. (A regional bus service connects Petrópolis with Nova Friburgo.) Each day there are also hourly buses from Rio to Angra dos Reis (3 hrs) and 12 buses to Parati (4 hrs). Nearly hourly buses travel between Parati and Angra dos Reis. Municipal buses connect Cabo Frio and Búzios.

Buses, a shuttle service, and airplanes regularly travel to and from popular Búzios. The best option is the shuttle service, which will pick you up in Rio in the morning and drop you at your pousada before noon. Contact **Turismo Clássico Travel** (☞ Travel Agents and Tour Operators *in* Rio de Janeiro A to Z, *above*) in Rio for reservations.

BR 101 connects the city to the Costa Verde and Parati. You'll need to head north and along BR 040 to reach the mountain towns of Petrópolis and Novo Friburgo. Cabo Frio and other coastal communities east of Rio are along or off RJ 106.

Getting Around

You can rent cars, dune buggies, motorcycles, and bicycles at most of these destinations—or you can simply take taxis around each area. Ask the staff at your hotel or at the tourist offices for recommendations.

Contacts and Resources

BANKS AND CURRENCY EXCHANGE

There are banks and ATMs in each community, but it's best to get reais before leaving Rio. Check in advance with your hotel to make sure credit cards are accepted.

VISITOR INFORMATION

Tourist offices are generally open weekdays from 8 or 8:30 to 6 and Saturday from 8 or 9 till 4; some have limited Sunday hours, too. **Angra dos Reis Tourism Office** (⊠ Across from bus station on Rua Largo da Lapa, ☎ 0243/365–1175, ext. 2186); **Búzios Tourism Office** (⊠ Praça Santos Dumont 111, ☎ 0247/623–2099); **Cabo Frio Tourism Office** (⊠ Av. de Controno, Praia do Forte, ☎ 0246/647–1689); **Nova Friburgo Tourism Office** (⊠ Praça Dr. Demervel B. Moreira, ☎ 0245/523–8000); **Parati Tourism Office** (⊠ Av. Roberto Silveiro, ☎ 0243/371–1266, ext. 217); **Petrópolis Tourism Office** (⊠ Praça da Confluencia 3, ☎ 0242/243–3561).

3　SÃO PAULO

Recognized as the economic capital of Latin America, São Paulo is a place of fancy restaurants and hotels, grand avenues, skyscrapers, and busy folk. It's also a cultural crossroads that has attracted people from all over Brazil as well as from abroad. Elegant cuisine, lively nightlife, abundant arts attractions, and opportunities for a better life are among its magnets. When the hustle-bustle becomes too much, savvy city dwellers escape to the mountains and beaches in surrounding São Paulo State.

CROWDED BUSES GRIND THROUGH streets spouting black smoke, endless stands of skyscrapers block the horizon, and the din of traffic deafens the ear. But

Updated and expanded by Carlos Henrique Severo and Karla Brunet

native *paulistanos* (inhabitants of São Paulo city; inhabitants of São Paulo State are called *paulistas*) love this megalopolis of 17 million. São Paulo now sprawls across 7,951 square km (3,070 square mi), 1,502 square km (580 square mi) of which make up the city proper. The largest city in South America makes New York City look small.

In 1554 Jesuit priests, including José de Anchieta and Manoel da Nóbrega, founded the village of São Paulo de Piratininga and began converting Indians to Catholicism. Wisely set on a plateau, the mission town was protected from attack and was served by many rivers. It remained unimportant to the Portuguese Crown until it became the departure point for the *bandeira* (literally "flag") expeditions, whose members set out to look for gemstones and gold, to enslave Indians, and, later, to capture escaped African slaves (☞ box "Os Bandeirantes," *below*). In the process, these adventurers established inroads to vast portions of previously unexplored territory. São Paulo also saw Emperor Dom Pedro I declare independence from Portugal by the Rio Ipiranga (Ipiranga River), near the city.

In the late 19th century, São Paulo became a major coffee producer, attracting both workers and investors from many countries. Italians, Portuguese, Spanish, Germans, and Japanese put their talents and energies to work here. By 1895, 70,000 of the 130,000 residents were immigrants. Their efforts transformed São Paulo from a sleepy mission post into a dynamic financial and cultural hub. Avenida Paulista was once the site of many a coffee baron's mansion. Money flowed from these private domains into civic and cultural institutions. The arts began to flourish, and by the 1920s, São Paulo was attracting such great artists as Mário and Oswald de Andrade, who introduced modern elements into Brazilian art.

In the 1950s, the auto industry began to develop and contributed greatly to São Paulo's contemporary cityscape. In the last 30 years, people from throughout Brazil have come here seeking jobs, many in the Cubatão Industrial Park—the largest in the developing world—just outside the city limits. Today, like many major European or American hubs, São Paulo struggles to meet its citizens' transportation and housing needs, and goods and services are expensive. Yet, even as the smog reddens your eyes, you'll see that there's much to explore here. As a city committed to making dreams come true, São Paulo offers top-rate nightlife and dining and thriving cultural and arts scenes.

The city faces the Atlantic shore in the southeast region of the state that shares its name. From town it's easy to travel by car or bus to the state's many small, beautiful beaches and beyond to the states of Paraná, Rio de Janeiro, and Minas Gerais. Although most sandy stretches are a couple hours from the city, good side trips can be as close as the 30-minute drive to Embu.

Pleasures and Pastimes

Dining

With more than 12,000 restaurants and a melting-pot of cultures, São Paulo offers a cuisine for every craving. Japanese and Italian restaurants abound. Indeed, paulistanos are very proud of their pizza, especially pies topped with mozzarella, arugula, and sun-dried tomatoes. Establishments that serve Portuguese, German, French, and Spanish dishes are also popular. Be sure to try the *beirute*, a popular Lebanese contribution that's like a Middle Eastern submarine sandwich, served hot in toasted Syrian bread and sprinkled with oregano.

Of course many restaurants offer traditional Brazilian specialities such as *feijoada* (the national dish of black beans and a variety of meats), *churrasco* (barbecued meats), and *moqueca* (fish stew made with coconut milk and *dendê*, or palm oil). Some places specialize in regional food from Bahia (whose spicy dishes are often toned down here), Minas Gerais, and elsewhere. The *virado à paulista* (beans, eggs, and collard greens) is a typical São Paulo dish. Nothing goes better with Brazilian food than a *caipirinha* (a drink with the rum-like *cachaça*, lemon, and sugar). For details on price categories, *see* Dining *in* Smart Travel Tips A to Z.

Lodging

You'll find many world-class hotels in São Paulo. Most of them are in big buildings on or around Avenida Paulista. Regardless of the price category, most hotels have good restaurants and buffet breakfasts. For details on price categories, *see* Lodging *in* Smart Travel Tips A to Z.

Nightlife

True to its eclectic heritage, São Paulo offers a variety of night-time activities: from romantic garden terraces where you can grab a quiet drink to clubs where you can dance to throbbing techno music till dawn. The chic and wealthy head for establishments, many of which serve food, in the Vila Olímpia and Itaim neighborhoods. The Pinheiros neighborhood, near Vila Madalena, has a large concentration of Brazilian clubs and alternative bars. The neighborhood of Jardins has some of the city's best dance clubs as well as a selection of gay and lesbian bars.

São Paulo's music clubs often feature jazz and blues artists. On weekends you'll find samba and *pagode* (musicians sitting around a table playing for a small crowd) in clubs throughout the city. At *forró* (a rhythm from the northeast) clubs, instructors teach you to move like a native.

Parks and Gardens

In Latin America's biggest urban park, Parque Ibirapuera, you can ramble for an entire day without seeing all the grounds and cultural attractions. On Sunday, you may well be accompanied by thousands of paulistanos seeking refuge from all the surrounding concrete. The Fundação Oscar e Maria Luisa Americano has a small forest and a museum. The Parque do Estado (also called the Parque do Ipiranga) surrounds the Museu do Ipiranga and has a beautiful garden.

Side Trips

São Paulo State is full of beaches and towns with artistic and historical treasures. Embu is famous for its furniture stores, and artisans from throughout Brazil sell their wares at its enormous weekend street fair. The historical town of Itu was the stage for many acts in the Brazilian republican movement. In Campos do Jordão you can imagine yourself at a European mountain retreat. On the island called Ilhabela, you can bask on a beautiful beach; swim, snorkel, or dive; or trek to a stunning waterfall.

EXPLORING SÃO PAULO

Each neighborhood seems a testament to a different period of the city's history. The largely pedestrian-only hilltop and valley areas, particularly Vale do Anhangabaú, are where São Paulo's first inhabitants—Jesuit missionaries and treasure-hunting pioneers—lived. Later these areas became Centro (downtown district), a financial and cultural center that's still home to the stock exchange and many banks. It's now the focus of revitalization efforts.

The Bela Vista and Bixiga (really, a subdivision of Bela Vista) neighborhoods, near Centro, are home to many theaters and bars. In the 19th century, many families who made fortunes from coffee built whimsical mansions on the ridge-top Avenida Paulista. Beginning in the post–World War II industrial boom, these homes gave way to skyscrapers. Many of the city's best hotels are also on or near this avenue.

In the growth of the 1970s many businesses moved west and literally downhill to a former swamp. Here you'll find the tall buildings of Avenida Brigadeiro Faria Lima, the stylish homes of the Jardins neighborhood, and the Shopping Center Iguatemi (Brazil's first mall), just off the banks of the Rio Pinheiros. Large-scale construction of corporate headquarters continues just south of here, between the Marginal Pinheiros Beltway and the Avenida Engenheiro Luís Carlos Berrini, not far from the luxurious Shopping Center Morumbi.

Great Itineraries

IF YOU HAVE 3 DAYS

On the first day, plan a walk along Avenida Paulista with its many cultural attractions. Head to Centro on the second day to see such landmarks as the Edifício Itália and Teatro Municipal. Don't miss the Latin arts and crafts exhibits at the Memorial da América Latina. On the third day, head for the Parque do Ibirapuera to visit one of its museums or just relax under the trees.

IF YOU HAVE 5 DAYS

In addition to the attractions outlined in the three-day itinerary, you can take a day to visit the snake museum at Instituto Butantã and/or the Fundação Maria Luisa e Oscar Americano. On your last day tour the Museu do Ipiranga and its environs, where the independence of Brazil was declared.

IF YOU HAVE 7–10 DAYS

With so many days, you can explore the city as detailed above and take a side trip. If shopping is your passion, work in a weekend junket to Embu to hunt for Brazilian crafts in its street fair. If the outdoors beckon, head to Ilhabela, with its beaches, trails, and waterfalls.

When to Tour

Most of the cultural events—film and music festivals and art exhibits—happen between July and December. During the South American summer (January through March) the weather is very rainy, and floods can disrupt traffic. In summer, make reservations for beach resorts as far in advance as possible, particularly for weekend stays. In winter (May through July), follow the same rule for visits to Campos do Jordão.

Centro

Even though São Paulo's downtown district is considered dangerous, it's one of the few places with a historical flavor. Here you can explore the areas where the city began and see examples of architecture, some of it beautifully restored, from the 19th century.

Numbers in the text correspond to numbers in the margin and on the São Paulo Centro map.

A Good Tour

The **Edifício Copan** ①, designed by the great Oscar Niemeyer, seems an appropriate place to begin a tour. Farther up Avenida Ipiranga is the city's tallest building, the **Edifício Itália** ② (you might want to return here at the end of the day for a terrific view of the city). Continue north along the avenue to the **Praça da República** ③. From here, cross Ipiranga and walk down the pedestrian-only Rua Barão de Itapetininga, with its many shops and street vendors. Follow it to the neo-baroque **Teatro Municipal** ④ in the Praça Ramos de Azevedo facing the Mappin department store. Head east across the square to the Viaduto do Chá, a monumental overpass above the Valé do Anhangabaú—the heart of São Paulo. At the end of this viaduct, turn right onto Rua Líbero Badaró and follow it to the baroque **Igreja de São Francisco de Assis** ⑤. A short walk from here along Rua Benjamin Constant will bring you to the **Praça da Sé** ⑥, the city's most central spot and the site of the Catedral Metropolitana da Sé.

From the metro station at the cathedral, you can take the *metrô* (subway) west to the Barra Funda station and the **Memorial da América Latina,** or you can head north out of Praça da Sé and follow Rua Roberto Simonsen to the **Solar da Marquesa de Santos** ⑦, the city's only surviving late-19th-century residence. Nearby is the **Pátio do Colégio** ⑧. From here, walk north along Rua Boa Vista; turn left onto Rua Anchieta and then left onto Rua 15 de Novembro. Number 275, on the left, houses **BOVESPA** ⑨, the São Paulo Stock Exchange. Near the end of Rua 15 de Novembro, at Rua João Brícola 24, stands the 36-floor **Edifício BANESPA** ⑩. To the northwest of here is the **Edifício Martinelli** ⑪. Walk two blocks up on Rua São Bento to the **Basílica de São Bento** ⑫, a church constructed in the beginning of the 20th century. Near it is Café Girondino, a good spot for a break. From the basilica, you can take a train north from the São Bento station to the Luz stop and the **Pinacoteca do Estado** ⑬, the state gallery. On Avenida Tiradentes walk north to the **Museu de Arte Sacra** ⑭ and its religious art.

TIMING AND PRECAUTIONS

This route requires at least five hours on foot and use of the metrô, which is safe and clean. An early start will allow you to be more leisurely should one sight pique your interest more than another. If you're planning to take taxis or hire a driver, bear in mind that traffic jams are common.

Being a tourist in Centro is a bit hazardous. If you keep a low profile and speak at least some Spanish (if not Portuguese) you'll most likely avoid problems. Otherwise you might feel more comfortable touring with a guide (☞ Travel Agents and Tour Operators *in* São Paulo A to Z, *below*). Whatever you do, leave your Rolex back at the hotel.

Sights to See

⑫ **Basílica de São Bento.** This church, constructed between 1910 and 1922, was designed by German architect Richard Berndl. Its enormous organ has some 600 pipes. ⊠ *Largo de São Bento,* ☎ *011/228–3633.* ☞ *Free.* ☉ *Mon., Wed., and Fri. 5–1 and 2–7:45; Thurs. 2–7:45; Sat. 6–1 and 3–7:30; Sun. 5–1 and 3–6. Metrô: São Bento.*

⑨ **BOVESPA.** The busy São Paulo Stock Exchange is a hub for the foreign investment Brazil has attracted in its efforts to privatize state-owned companies. If you leave an ID with the guard at the front desk, you can go up to the mezzanine and watch the hurly-burly; computer terminals in the observation gallery carry the latest stock quotes as well as general information in various languages. BOVESPA offers tours in English, but only to representatives of foreign investment institutions. (If you fit this description, you can make arrangements in advance by faxing the Superintendência Executiva de Desenvolvimento at FAX 011/

São Paulo Centro

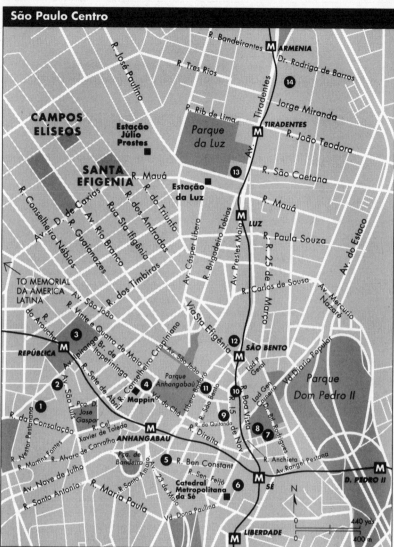

Basílica de São
Bento, **12**
BOVESPA, **9**
Edifício
BANESPA, **10**
Edifício Copan, **1**
Edifício Itália, **2**
Edifício
Martinelli, **11**
Igreja de São
Francisco de Assis, **5**
Museu de Arte
Sacra, **14**

Pátio do Colégio, **8**
Pinacoteca do
Estado, **13**
Praça da
República, **3**
Praça da Sé, **6**
Solar da Marquesa de
Santos, **7**
Teatro Municipal, **4**

239–4981.) ✉ *Rua 15 de Novembro 275,* ☎ *011/233–2000 ext. 516.* 🎫 *Free.* ☉ *Weekdays 9–noon and 2–6. Metrô: São Bento.*

NEED A
BREAK?

Café Girondino is frequented by BOVESPA traders from happy hour until midnight. The bar serves good draft beer and sandwiches. Pictures on the wall depict Centro in its early days. ✉ *Rua Boa Vista 365,* ☎ *011/ 229–4574. Metrô: São Bento.*

⑩ **Edifício BANESPA.** The 36-floor BANESPA Building was constructed in 1947 and modeled after New York's Empire State Building. If you can't fit tea or drinks at the top of the Edifício Itália (☞ *below*) into your Centro tour, this structure offers a no-frills chance for a panoramic look at the city. A radio traffic reporter squints through the smog every morning from here. ✉ *Praça Antônio Prado,* ☎ *no phone.* 🎫 *Free.* ☉ *Weekdays 9–6. Metrô: São Bento.*

❶ **Edifício Copan.** The serpentine Copan Building, an apartment and office block, was designed by renowned Brazilian architect Oscar Niemeyer, who went on to design much of Brasília, the nation's capital. It has the clean, white, undulating curves characteristic of his work. Although many Brazilians prefer colonial architecture, all take pride in Niemeyer's international reputation. The Copan was constructed in 1950, and its 1,850 apartments house about 4,500 people. If you want to shop in the first-floor stores, be sure to do so before dark when the area is overrun by prostitutes and transvestites. ✉ *Av. Ipiranga at Av. Consolação,* ☎ *no phone. Metrô: Anhangabaú.*

★ ❷ **Edifício Itália.** The view of South America's largest city from the top of the Itália Building is astounding. To get to it, you'll have to patronize the bar or dining room of the Terraço Itália restaurant on the 41st floor. As the restaurant is expensive (and isn't one of the city's best), afternoon tea or a drink is the quickest, least expensive option. Tea is served 3–5:30, and the bar opens at 6. ✉ *Av. Ipiranga 336,* ☎ *011/ 257–6566 (restaurant). Metrô: Anhangabaú.*

⑪ **Edifício Martinelli.** Note the whimsical penthouse atop the Martinelli Building, the city's first skyscraper, which was built in 1929 by Italian immigrant-turned-count Giuseppe Martinelli. The rooftop is open weekdays 10:30–4. You need to get permission from the building manager on the ground floor and leave a photo ID at the front desk to take the elevator to the 34th floor and walk up two more flights. ✉ *Avenida São João 35,* ☎ *no phone.* 🎫 *Free. Metrô: São Bento.*

❺ **Igreja de São Francisco de Assis.** The baroque St. Francis of Assisi Church is actually two churches by the same name, one run by Catholic clergy, and the other by lay brothers. One of the city's best-preserved Portuguese colonial buildings, it was built from 1647 to 1790. ✉ *Largo São Francisco 133,* ☎ *011/606–0081.* 🎫 *Free.* ☉ *Daily 7 AM–8 PM; lay brothers' church weekdays 7–11:30 and 1–8, weekends 7 AM–10 AM. Metrô: Sé or Anhangabaú.*

OFF THE
BEATEN PATH

MEMORIAL DA AMÉRICA LATINA – The Latin American Memorial consists of a group of buildings designed by Oscar Niemeyer. The Pavilhão da Criatividade Popular (Popular Creativity Pavilion) has a permanent exhibition of Latin American handicrafts and a model showing all the countries in Latin America. The Salão de Atos building shows the panel *Tiradentes,* about an independence hero from Minas Gerais, painted by Cândido Portinari in 1949 and installed here in 1989. ✉ *Av. Auro Soares de Moura Andrade 664,* ☎ *011/3823–9611.* 🎫 *Free.* ☉ *Tues.–Sun. 9–6. Metrô: Barra Funda.*

⑭ **Museu de Arte Sacra.** The Museum of Sacred Art is a must-see if you can't get to Bahia during your stay in Brazil. It houses an extremely interesting collection of wooden and terra-cotta masks, jewelry, and liturgical objects that date from the 17th century through today. Don't miss the on-site convent, founded in 1774. ✉ *Av. Tiradentes 676,* ☎ *011/227–7694.* 🎫 *Admission.* ⊙ *Tues.–Sun. 9–6. Metrô: Luz.*

❽ **Pátio do Colégio.** The College Courtyard is where, in 1554, São Paulo was founded by the Jesuits José de Anchieta and Manoel da Nóbrega. The church here was constructed in 1896 in the same style as the chapel built by the Jesuits. ✉ *Pátio do Colégio 84,* ☎ *011/3105–6899.* ⊙ *Church: Mon.–Sat. 8:15 AM–midnight, Sun. mass 10 AM. Metrô: Sé.*

⑬ **Pinacoteca do Estado.** The building that houses the State Art Gallery was constructed in 1905 and renovated in 1998. In the permanent collection you can see the work of famous Brazilian artists such as Tarsila do Amaral (whose work consists of colorful somewhat abstract portraits), Anita Malfatti (a painter influenced by fauvism and German expressionism), Cândido Portinari (whose oil paintings have social and historical themes), Emiliano Di Cavalcanti (a multimedia artist whose illustrations, oil paintings, and engravings are influenced by cubism and contain Afro-Brazilian and urban themes), and Lasar Segall (an expressionist painter). ✉ *Praça da Luz 2,* ☎ *011/227–6329.* 🎫 *Admission.* ⊙ *Tues.–Sun. 10–6. Metrô: Luz.*

❸ **Praça da República.** The large, central Republic Square is the site of a huge street fair—with arts and crafts, semiprecious stones, food, and often live music—on Sunday. Some artisans display their work here all week long, so it's worth a peek anytime. *Metrô: República.*

❻ **Praça da Sé.** The large, busy Cathedral Square, under which the city's two major metrô lines cross, is where migrants from Brazil's poor northeast often come to enjoy their music and to sell and buy such regional items as medicinal herbs. It's also the central hangout for São Paulo's street children and the focus of periodic (and controversial) police sweeps to get them off the street. The square and most of the historic area and financial district to its north have been set aside for pedestrians, official vehicles, and public transportation only.

❼ **Solar da Marquesa de Santos.** This 18th-century manor house was bought by Marquesa dos Santos in 1843. It now contains a museum that hosts temporary exhibitions. ✉ *Rua Roberto Simonsen 136,* ☎ *011/3106–2218.* 🎫 *Free.* ⊙ *Tues.–Sun. 9–5. Metrô: Sé.*

❹ **Teatro Municipal.** Inspired by the Paris Opéra, the Municipal Theater was built between 1903 and 1911 with art nouveau elements. *Hamlet* was the first play presented here, and it went on to host such luminaries as Isadora Duncan in 1916 and Anna Pavlova in 1919. Unfortunately, the fully restored auditorium, resplendent with gold leaf, moss-green velvet, marble, and mirrors, is only open to those attending cultural events (☞ Nightlife and the Arts, *below*), but sometimes you can walk in for a quick look at the vestibule. ✉ *Praça Ramos de Azevedo,* ☎ *011/223–3022. Metrô: Anhangabaú.*

Liberdade

At the beginning of the 20th century, a group of Japanese arrived to work as contract farm laborers in São Paulo State. During the next five decades, roughly a quarter of a million of their countrymen followed, forming what is now the largest Japanese colony outside Japan. Distinguished today by a large number of college graduates and successful businesspeople, professionals, and politicians, the colony has made important contributions to Brazilian agriculture and the seafood industry. The Liberdade neighborhood, which is south of Praça da Sé behind the cathedral and whose entrance is marked by a series of red porticoes, is home to many first-, second-, and third-generation Nippo-Brazilians. Here, clustered around Avenida Liberdade, you'll find shops with everything from imported bubble gum to miniature robots to Kabuki face paint. The Sunday street fair here holds many surprises.

Numbers in the text correspond to numbers in the margin and on the São Paulo City map.

A Good Tour

From the **Praça Liberdade** ⑮, by the Liberdade metrô station, walk south along Rua Galvão Bueno. About six blocks from the square is the intriguing **Museu da Imigração Japonesa** ⑯.

TIMING AND PRECAUTIONS

The best time to visit Liberdade is on Sunday during the street fair, when you'll find tents that sell Asian food, crafts, and souvenirs. This tour takes about two hours—a little longer if you linger in the museum. Don't take this tour at night.

Sights to See

⑯ **Museu da Imigração Japonesa.** The Museum of Japanese Immigration has two floors of exhibits about Nippo-Brazilian culture and farm life and Japanese contributions to Brazilian horticulture. (They're credited with introducing the persimmon, the azalea, the tangerine, and the kiwi, among other things, to Brazil.) Call ahead to arrange for an English-language tour. ✉ *Rua São Joaquim 381,* ☎ *011/279–5465.* ✉ *Admission.* ☉ *Tues.–Sun. 1:30–5:30. Metrô: São Joaquim.*

⑮ **Praça Liberdade.** On Sunday morning Liberdade hosts a sprawling Asian food and crafts fair, where the free and easy Brazilian ethnic mix is in plain view; you'll see, for example, Afro-Brazilians dressed in colorful kimonos hawking grilled shrimp on a stick. Liberdade also hosts several ethnic celebrations, such as April's Hanamatsuri, commemorating Buddha's birth. *Metrô: Liberdade.*

Avenida Paulista and Bixiga

Money once poured into and out of the coffee barons' mansions that lined Avenida Paulista, making it, in a sense, São Paulo's financial hub. So it is today, though instead of mansions you'll find many major banks. Like the barons before them, many of these financial institutions greatly support the arts. Numerous places have changing exhibitions—often free—in the Paulista neighborhood. Nearby Bixiga, São Paulo's Little Italy, is full of restaurants.

A Good Tour

Begin the tour at the **Museu de Arte de São Paulo (MASP)** ⑰, which has Brazil's best collection of fine art. Across the street is **Parque Trianon** ⑱, where many businesspeople eat lunch. Leaving the park, veer right onto Avenida Paulista and head for the **Centro Cultural FIESP** ⑲, which frequently has art and theatrical presentations. Farther down Paulista is the **Espaço Cultural Citibank** ⑳, a gallery with temporary exhibitions. Continue a few more blocks along Paulista to the **Instituto Cultural Itaú** ㉑, a great place to see contemporary Brazilian art. In the next block is the **Casa das Rosas** ㉒ with yet another noteworthy gallery. From here you can hop a bus or a taxi to the **Museu Memória do Bixiga** ㉓ with its displays on Italian immigration.

BRAZIL'S MELTING POT

SÃO PAULO IS A MICROCOSM of Brazil's melting pot. The flames of the nation's multiculturalism were ignited the moment that Portuguese discoverer Pedro Álvares Cabral and his sailors saw naked Indians on a beach. To be Brazilian means to share a heritage that's Portuguese, Indian, and African. For some, the mix is seasoned still further by ancestors from other parts of Europe or from Asia or the Middle East.

Most of the Indians encountered by the first Portuguese were members of the Tupi-Guarani language group (2 of an estimated 180 languages spoken by roughly 200 tribes) and were nomadic hunter-gatherers who lived along the coast. Many Brazilian words and place names, such as Copacabana, are Indian. Indeed, the country's name comes from *pau-brasil,* the Indian term for the brazilwood tree (it was used to make a coveted red dye and was the nation's first major export).

The Africans brought to Brazil as slaves were primarily Yoruban (from what are today Liberia, Nigeria, Benin, and parts of Sudan) and Bantu (from Angola, Mozambique, and Zaire). These groups blended their spiritualistic and animist beliefs with the Roman Catholic traditions of their Portuguese masters. Cults arose that likened African gods and goddesses to Catholic saints, creating a completely new pantheon of *orixás* (deities); some groups adopted Indian beliefs as well. Although 70% of Brazilians are Roman Catholic, many are also members of such thriving cults as Candomblé (from Salvador), Macumba (from Rio de Janeiro),

and Xangô (from Recife), to name a few. Those who aren't members are at least respectful of the cults and their traditions (politicians have even been known to court cult leaders). The nation's food and music were also strongly influenced by the Afro-Brazilians. And "samba" is an African word as well as an African rhythm.

When Napoléon invaded Portugal, King João VI and the royal family fled to Brazil. The marriage of his son, Dom Pedro, to the Austrian Archduchess Leopoldina, saw the advent of immigration by German-speaking colonists. Many put down roots in the south, where the climate was similar to that of their homelands. Today, there are southern communities filled with Bavarian-style architecture. After the American Civil War, some U.S. Southerners moved to Brazil; like the Germans, many settled in Brazil's south, though others chose the Amazon.

When Brazil abolished slavery in 1888, the nation actively recruited European agricultural laborers—Germans, Italians, Spanish, Portuguese came to work the fields. They were followed by groups from eastern Europe, Russia, and the Middle East. In 1908, 640 Japanese immigrants arrived in Brazil; by 1969, more than 200,000 of their countrymen and women had followed. Most settled in São Paulo and its environs, and most worked in agriculture. Today, the city has the largest Japanese community outside of Japan. It also has many more varieties of fruits and vegetables than it would have had if the Japanese had not been so successful here.

São Paulo City

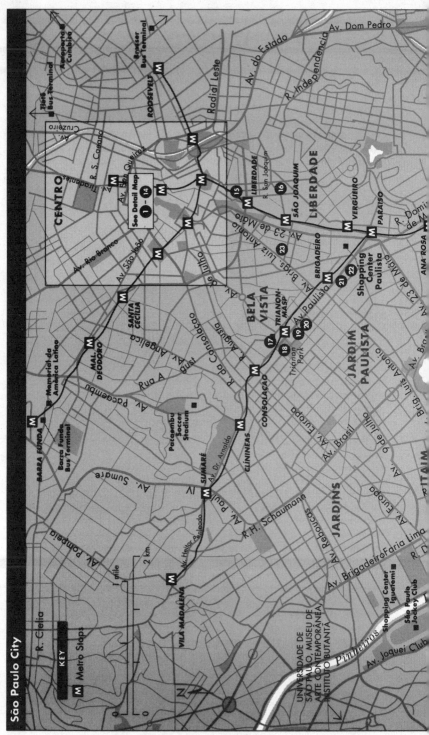

KEY

■ Metro Stops

Ⓜ Metro Stops

— 0 2 km

— 0 1 mile

N

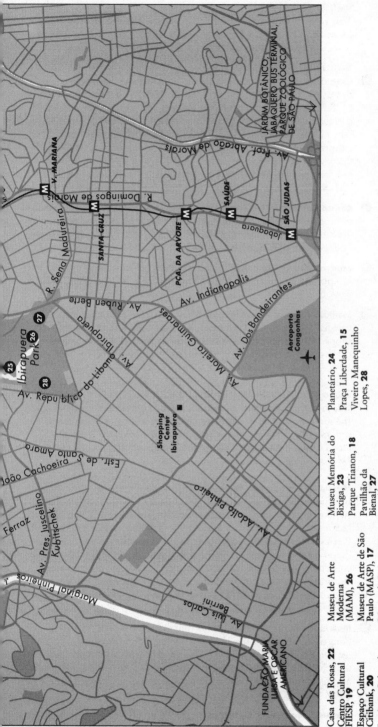

Casa das Rosas, **22**
Centro Cultural
FIESP, **19**
Espaço Cultural
Citibank, **20**
Instituto Cultural
Itaú, **21**

Museu de Arte
Moderna
(MAM), **26**
Museu de Arte de São
Paulo (MASP), **17**
Museu da Imigração
Japonesa, **16**

Museu Memória do
Bixiga, **23**
Parque Trianon, **18**
Pavilhão da
Bienal, **27**
Pavilhão Japonês, **25**

Planetário, **24**
Praça Liberdade, **15**
Viveiro Manequinho
Lopes, **28**

TIMING AND PRECAUTIONS
This tour takes about five hours, including a visit to MASP and the Museu do Bixiga. Busy, well-lit Avenida Paulista may well be the safest place in city. Even so, stay alert, particularly in Parque Trianon.

Sights to See

㉒ Casa das Rosas. The House of the Roses, a French-style mansion, seems out of place next to the skyscrapers of Paulista. It was built in 1935 by famous paulistano architect Ramos de Azevedo for one of his daughters. The building was home to the same family until 1986, when it was made an official municipal landmark. It was opened as a cultural center—with changing fine-arts exhibitions and multimedia displays by up-and-coming artists—in 1991, and it's one of the avenue's few remaining early 20th-century buildings. ⊠ *Av. Paulista 37,* ☎ *011/ 251–5271.* ⊡ *Admission.* ☉ *Tues.–Sun. 2–8. Metrô: Brigadeiro.*

⑲ Centro Cultural FIESP. The cultural center of São Paulo State's Federation of Industry has a theater, a library of art books, and temporary art exhibits. ⊠ *Av. Paulista 1313,* ☎ *011/253–5877.* ⊡ *Free.* ☉ *Tues.– Sun. 9–7. Metrô: Trianon.*

⑳ Espaço Cultural Citibank. Citibank's cultural space hosts temporary exhibitions of Brazilian art. ⊠ *Av. Paulista 1111,* ☎ *011/576–2744.* ⊡ *Free.* ☉ *weekdays 9–7, weekends 10–5. Metrô: Trianon.*

㉑ Instituto Cultural Itaú. Maintained by Itaú, one of Brazil's largest private banks, this cultural institute has art shows as well as lectures, workshops, and films. Its library specializes in works on Brazilian art and culture. ⊠ *Av. Paulista 149,* ☎ *011/238–1700.* ⊡ *Free.* ☉ *Tues.–Sun. 10–7. Metrô: Brigadeiro.*

NEED A
BREAK?

Before heading to the Museu Memória do Bixiga, try a *baurú* at **Ponto Chic** (a block east of Instituto Cultural Itaú and across Avenida Paulista). The restaurant claims to have invented this sandwich, which is made with roast beef, tomato, cucumber, and steam-heated mozzarella. ⊠ *Praça Osvaldo Cruz 26,* ☎ *011/289–1480. AE, DC, MC, V.* ☉ *10 AM–4 AM. Metrô: Paraíso.*

★ ⑰ Museu de Arte de São Paulo (MASP). A striking low-rise elevated on two massive concrete pillars 256 feet apart, the São Paulo Museum of Art contains the city's premier collection of fine arts. The highlights include dazzling works by Hieronymous Bosch, Vincent Van Gogh, Pierre-Auguste Renoir, Edgar Degas, and others. Lasar Segall and Cândido Portinari are two of the many Brazilian artists represented in the collection. The huge open area beneath the museum is often used for cultural events and is the site of a Sunday antiques fair (☞ Shopping, *below*). ⊠ *Av. Paulista 1578,* ☎ *011/251–5644.* ⊡ *Admission.* ☉ *Tues.– Sun. 11–6. Metrô: Trianon.*

㉓ Museu Memória do Bixiga. This museum, established in 1980, contains objects that belonged to Italian immigrants who lived in the Bixiga neighborhood. On Saturday and Sunday, you can extend your tour to include the **Feira do Bixiga**, at Praça Dom Orione, where handicrafts, antiques, and furniture are sold. ⊠ *Rua dos Ingleses 118,* ☎ *011/285– 5009.* ⊡ *Free.* ☉ *Wed.–Sun. 2–5.*

⑱ Parque Trianon. The park was originally created in 1892 as a showcase for local vegetation. In 1968, Roberto Burle-Marx (the Brazilian landscaper famed for Rio's mosaic-tile beachfront sidewalks) renovated it and incorporated new trees. You can escape the noise of the street and admire the flora while seated on one of the benches that are sculpted to look like chairs. ⊠ *Rua Peixoto Gomide 949,* ☎ *011/289–2160.* 🖾 *Free.* ⊙ *Daily 6–6. Metrô: Trianon.*

Parque Ibirapuera

Only 15 minutes by taxi from downtown, Ibirapuera is São Paulo's answer to New York's Central Park, although it's slightly less than half the size and gets infinitely more crowded on sunny weekends. In the 1950s the land, which originally contained the municipal nurseries, was chosen as the site of a public park to honor the city's 400th anniversary. Oscar Niemeyer was called in to head the architects assigned to the project. The park was inaugurated in 1954, and some of the pavilions used for the opening festivities still sit amid its 395 acres. You'll also find jogging and biking paths, a lake, and rolling lawns.

A Good Walk

Enter at Gate 9 and walk around the lake to the starry sights at the **Planetário** ㉔. As you exit the planetarium, veer left for a walk to the **Pavilhão Japonês** ㉕. From here, turn left and follow the path to the Marquise do Ibirapuera, a structure that connects several buildings, including the **Museu de Arte Moderna (MAM)** ㉖ and the **Pavilhão da Bienal** ㉗, which houses the park branch of the Museu de Arte Contemporânea. When you exit the compound, walk toward Gate 7 and the **Viveiro Manequinho Lopes** ㉘, with its many species of Brazilian trees.

TIMING AND PRECAUTIONS
The park deserves a whole day though you can probably do this tour in one afternoon. Avoid the park on Sunday, when it gets really crowded, and after sundown.

Sights to See

㉖ **Museu de Arte Moderna (MAM).** The permanent collection of the Museum of Modern Art includes 2,600 paintings, sculptures (some in a sculpture garden out front), and drawings from the Brazilian modernist movement, which began in the 1920s, when artists were developing a new form of expression influenced by the city's rapid industrial growth. The museum also hosts temporary exhibits that feature the works of new local artists and has a library with more than 20,000 books, photographs, videotapes, and CD-ROMs. In a 1982 renovation, Brazilian architect Lina Bo Bardi gave the building a wall of glass, creating a giant window that beckons you to peek at what's inside. ⊠ *Gate 10,* ☎ *011/573–9932.* 🖾 *Admission (free on Tues.).* ⊙ *Tues.–Wed. noon–6, Thurs. noon–10, Fri.–Sat. 10–8, Sun. and holidays 10–6.*

NEED A BREAK?

The **Bar do MAM,** inside the Museu de Arte Moderna, has sandwiches, pies, soda, coffee, and tea. The comfortable chairs here enable you to thoroughly rest after your walk in the park and your tour of the museum.

㉗ **Pavilhão da Bienal.** From October through November in every even-numbered year, this pavilion hosts the Bienal (Biennial) art exhibition, which draws more than 250 artists from more than 60 countries. The first such event was held in 1951 in Parque Trianon (☞ *above*) and drew artists from 21 countries. It was moved to this Oscar Niemeyer-designed building—with its large open spaces and floors connected by circular slopes—after Ibirapuera Park's 1954 inauguration. The pavilion also houses a branch of the **Museu de Arte Contemporânea** (MAC; Museum of Contemporary Art) whose main branch is at the Universidade de São Paulo (☞ *below*). Exhibits are created from the museum's total collection of 5,400 works by such European artists as Pablo Picasso, Amedeo Modigliani, Wassily Kandinsky, Joan Miró, and Henri

Matisse. Look also for the works of Brazilian artists such as Anita Malfatti, Tarsila do Amaral, Cândido Portinari, and Emiliano Di Cavalcanti. ⊠ *Gate 10,* ☎ *011/573–5255.* ▣ *Museum: Admission (free on Tues.).* ⊘ *Museum: Tues.–Wed. noon–6, Thurs. noon–10, Fri.–Sat. 10–8, Sun. and holidays 10–6.*

㉕ Pavilhão Japonês. An exact replica of the Katsura Imperial Palace in Kyoto, Japan, the Japanese Pavilion is also one of the structures built for the park's inauguration. It was designed by University of Tokyo professor Sutemi Horiguti and built in Japan. It took four months to reassemble here, beside the man-made lake and amid the Japanese-style garden. In the main building you'll find displays of samurai clothes, 11th-century sculptures, and pottery and sculpture from several dynasties. Rooms used for traditional tea ceremonies are upstairs. ⊠ *Gate 10,* ☎ *011/573–6453.* ▣ *Admission.* ⊘ *Weekends and holidays 10–5.*

㉔ Planetário. Paulistanos love the planetarium and frequently fill the 350 seats under its 48-ft-high dome. Here you can see a projection of the 8,900 stars and 5 planets (Mercury, Venus, Mars, Jupiter, and Saturn) that are clearly visible in the Southern Hemisphere. Shows last 50 minutes and always depict the night sky just as it is on the evening of your visit. Be sure to buy tickets at least 15 minutes before the session. ⊠ *Gate 10, Av. Pedro Álvares Cabral,* ☎ *011/575–5206.* ▣ *Admission.* ⊘ *Weekends and holidays, projections at 3:30 and 5:30.*

㉘ Viveiro Manequinho Lopes. The Manequinho Lopes Nursery is where most of the plants and trees used by the city around São Paulo are nurtured. The original was built in the '20s; the current version was designed by Roberto Burle Marx. Here you'll find specimens of such Brazilian trees as *ipê, pau-jacaré,* and *pau-brasil,* the tree after which the country was named (the red dye it produced was greatly valued by the Europeans). The **Bosque da Leitura** (Reading Forest) has a stand that provides books and magazines (all in Portuguese, though) as well as chairs so people can read among the trees. ⊠ *Enter park from Av. República do Líbano,* ☎ *no phone.* ⊘ *Daily 5–5.*

Elsewhere in São Paulo

Several far-flung sights are worth a taxi ride to see. West of Centro is the **Universidade de São Paulo (USP),** which has two very interesting on-site museums: a branch of the Museu de Arte Contemporânea and the Instituto Butantã, with its collection of creatures that slither and crawl. Head southwest of Centro to the **Fundação Maria Luisa e Oscar Americano,** a museum with a forest and garden in the residential neighborhood of Morumbi. In the Parque do Estado, southeast of Centro, are the **Jardim Botânico** and the **Parque Zoológico de São Paulo.**

Sights to See

Fundação Maria Luisa e Oscar Americano. A private, wooded estate is the setting for the Maria Luisa and Oscar Americano Foundation. Exhibits here feature items from the Portuguese colonial and imperial periods as well as modern pieces. You'll find paintings, furniture, sacred art, silver, porcelain, engravings, personal objects of the Brazilian royal family, tapestries, and sculpture. ⊠ *Av. Morumbi 3700,* ☎ *011/842–0077.* ▣ *Admission.* ⊘ *Tues.–Fri. 11–5, weekends 10–5.*

Jardim Botânico. The Botanical Gardens contain about 3,000 plants belonging to more than 340 native species. You'll also find a greenhouse with Atlantic rain forest species, an orchid house, and a collection of aquatic plants. ⊠ *Av. Miguel Stéfano 3031,* ☎ *011/5584–6300.* ▣ *Admission.* ⊘ *Wed.–Sun. 9–5.*

★ ⚉ **Parque Zoológico de São Paulo.** The 200-acre São Paulo Zoo has more than 3,000 animals, and many of its 410 species—such as the *mico-leão-dourado* (golden lion tamarin monkey)—are endangered. Its attractions include a lake with small islands where monkeys live in houses on stilts and the Casa do Sangue Frio (House of Cold Blood) with reptilian and amphibious creatures. ⊠ *Av. Miguel Stéfano 4241,* ☎ *011/276–0811.* ⌨ *Admission.* ⊙ *Tues.–Sun. 9–5.*

Universidade de São Paulo. Consider taking a stroll around the grounds of the country's largest university (founded in 1934), just to soak in the atmosphere of a Brazilian campus. Art lovers can also visit the university branch of the **Museu de Arte Contemporânea,** which consists of a main building and an annex, to see works by world-renowned contemporary European and Brazilian artists (☞ *also* Parque Ibirapuera, *above*). ⊠ *Main building: Rua da Reitoria 109,* ☎ *011/818–3538.* ⌨ *Free.* ⊙ *Weekdays 10–6.* ⊠ *Annex: Rua da Reitoria 160,* ☎ *011/573–9925.* ⌨ *Free.* ⊙ *Tues.–Sun. noon–6.*

In 1888, a Brazilian scientist, with the aid of the São Paulo State government, turned a farmhouse into a center for the production of snake serum. Today, the **Instituto Butantã** has more than 70,000 snakes, spiders, scorpions, and lizards. It still extracts venom and processes it into serum that's made available to victims of poisonous bites throughout Latin America. Unfortunately, the institute has suffered from underfunding; it's somewhat run-down, and its exhibits aren't as accessible to children as they could be. ⊠ *Av. Vital Brasil 1500,* ☎ *011/813–7222.* ⌨ *Admission.* ⊙ *Tues.–Sun. 9–4:30.*

Beaches

São Paulo rests on a plateau 72 km (46 mi) inland. If you can avoid traffic, getaways are fairly quick on the parallel Imigrantes (BR 160) or Anchieta (BR 150) highways, each of which becomes one way on weekends and holidays. Although the port of Santos (near the Cubatão Industrial Park) has *praias* (beaches) in and around it, the cleanest and best beaches are along what is known as the North Shore. Here, mountains and bits of Atlantic rain forest hug numerous small, sandy coves. On weekdays when school is in session, the beaches here are gloriously deserted. Buses run along the coast from São Paulo's Jabaquara terminal near the Congonhas Airport, and there are once-daily trains from the Estação da Luz to Santos and the sands along the North Shore. Beaches often don't have bathrooms or phones right on the sands, nor do they have beach umbrellas or chairs for rent. They do, however, generally have restaurants nearby or at least vendors selling sandwiches, soft drinks, and beer.

Barra do Sahy. Families with young children favor this small, quiet beach 165 km (102 mi) north of the city on the Rio–Santos Highway. Its narrow strip of sand (with a bay and a river on one side and rocks on the other) is steep but smooth, and the water is clean and very calm. Kayakers paddle about and divers are drawn to the nearby Ilha das Couves. Area restaurants serve only basic fish dishes with rice and salad. If you want a special meal head for Camburi (☞ *below*). Note that Barra do Sahy's entrance is atop a slope and appears suddenly—be on the lookout.

Camburi. The young and the restless flock here to sunbathe, surf, and party. At the center of the beach is a cluster of cafés, ice cream shops, bars, and the Tiê restaurant. The service may be slow, but Tiê's menu is extensive and the open-air setup is divine. Another good bet is Bom Dia Vietnã, with its delicious pizzas, sandwiches, sushi, salads, and banana pie. Camburi is just north of Barra do Sahy (☞ *above*). If you're coming from the south, use the second entrance; although it's unpaved, it's in better shape than the first entrance.

Maresias. Some of the North Shore's most beautiful houses line either side of the Rio–Santos road (SP 055) on the approach to Maresias. The beach itself is also nice with its 4-km (2-mi) stretch of white sand and its clean, green waters that are good swimming and surfing. Like Camburi (☞ *above*), just 12 km (7 mi) south, Maresias is popular with a young crowd.

Ubatuba. Many of the more than 30 beaches around Ubatuba are truly beautiful enough to merit the 229-km (148-mi) drive north along the Carvalho Pinto and Oswaldo Cruz highways. For isolation and peace, try Prumirim Beach, which can only be reached by boat; for a little more action try the centrally located Praia Grande, with its many kiosks. Ubatuba itself has a very active nightlife; in nearby Itaguá you'll find several gift shops, a branch of the Projeto Tartarugas Marinhas (Marine Turtles Project), and a large aquarium.

DINING

São Paulo's social life centers on dining out, and there are a great many establishments from which to choose (new ones seem to open as often as the sun rises), particularly in the Jardins district. You'll find German, Japanese, Spanish, Italian, and Portuguese restaurants as well as top-quality French and Indian spots. There are innumerable *churrascarias* (places that serve a seemingly endless stream of barbecued meats), which are beloved by paulistanos. As in other Brazilian cities, many restaurants serve feijoada on Wednesday and Saturday; top restaurants do it up in fancy buffets.

São Paulo restaurants frequently change their credit card policies, sometimes adding a surcharge for their use or not accepting them at all. Though most places don't generally require jacket and tie, people tend to dress up; establishments in the $$ to $$$$ categories expect you to look tidy and elegant (no shorts or muddy or torn jeans).

Brazilian

$$$ ✕ **Baby Beef Rubaiyat.** Galician Belarmino Iglesias was once an employee at this restaurant; today he owns it, and he and his son run it. The meat they serve is from their ranch in Mato Grosso do Sul State. The buffet features charcoal-grilled items—from baby boar (upon request at least two hours in advance) and steak to chicken and salmon—and a salad bar with all sorts of options. Wednesday and Saturday see a feijoada; on Friday the emphasis is on seafood. ⊠ *Alameda Santos 86, Paraíso,* ☎ *011/289–6366. V. No dinner Sun. Metrô: Paraíso.*

$$$ ✕ **Bargaço.** This place has long been considered the best Bahian restaurant in Salvador. If you can't make it to the northeast, be sure to have a meal in the São Paulo branch. Seafood is the calling card. ⊠ *Rua Oscar Freire 1189, Cerqueira César,* ☎ *011/853–5058. AE, DC, MC, V. Metrô: Consolação.*

$$$ ✕ **Dona Lucinha.** Mineiro dishes—from the Minas Gerais State—are the specialties at this modest eatery with plain wooden tables. The classic cuisine is served buffet style, with more than 50 stone pots holding such dishes as *feijão tropeiro* (beans with manioc flour). Save room for a dessert of ambrosia. ⊠ *Av. Chibaras 399, Moema,* ☎ *011/549–2050. AE, DC, MC, V.* ⊠ *Rua Bela Cintra 2325, Jardins,* ☎ *011/282–3797. AE, DC, MC, V.*

$$$ ✕ **Esplanada Grill.** The beautiful people hang out in the bar of this highly
★   regarded churrascaria. The thinly sliced *picanha* steak (similar to rump steak) is excellent; it goes well with a house salad (hearts of palm and

shredded, fried potatoes), onion rings, and creamed spinach. The restaurant's rendition of the traditional *pão de queijo* (cheese bread) is just right. ⊠ *Rua Haddock Lobo 1682, Jardins,* ☎ *011/881–3199. V.*

$$ ✕ **Consulado Mineiro.** During and after the Saturday crafts and antiques fair in Praça Benedito Calixto, it may take an hour to get a table at this homey restaurant set in a house. Among the traditional mineiro dishes are the *mandioca com carne de sol* (cassava with salted meat) appetizer and the *tutu* (pork loin with beans, pasta, cabbage, and rice) entrée. ⊠ *Rua Praça Benedito Calixto 74, Pinheiros,* ☎ *011/3064–3882. AE, DC, MC, V. Closed Mon.*

$ ✕ **Frevo.** Paulistanos of all ilks and ages flock to this Jardins luncheonette for its beirute sandwiches, draft beer, and fruit juices in flavors such as *acerola* (Antilles cherry), passion fruit, and papaya. ⊠ *Rua Oscar Freire 603, Jardins,* ☎ *011/282–3434. No credit cards.*

$ ✕ **Sujinho–Bisteca d'Ouro.** The modest Sujinho serves churrasco without any frills. It's the perfect place for those who simply want to eat an honest, gorgeous piece of meat. ⊠ *Rua da Consolação 2078, Cerqueira César,* ☎ *011/231–5207. No credit cards. Metrô: Consolação.*

Continental

$$$$ ✕ **Cantaloup.** The fact that paulistanos take food seriously has not been lost on the folks at Cantaloup. The two dining areas are in a converted warehouse. Oversize photos decorate the walls of the slightly formal room, and a water fountain and plants make the second area feel more casual. Try the filet mignon with risotto or the St. Peter's fillet with almonds and spinach. Save room for the papaya ice cream with mango soup or the mango ice cream with papaya soup. ⊠ *Rua Manoel Guedes 474, Itaim Bibi,* ☎ *011/866–6445. AE, DC, MC, V.*

$$$ ✕ **Paddock.** Both locations are considered traditional spots for relaxed business lunches. Here, men and women of affairs eat and chat in comfortable armchairs. The Continental cuisine is prepared with finesse; try the lamb with mint sauce or the poached haddock. ⊠ *Av. São Luís 258, Centro,* ☎ *011/257–4768. AE, DC, MC, V. Closed Sun. Metrô: Anhangabaú or República.* ⊠ *Av. Brigadeiro Faria Lima 1541, Loja 109, Itaim Bibi,* ☎ *011/814–3582. AE, DC, MC, V. Closed Sun.*

Eclectic

$$$$ ✕ **La Tambouille.** This Italo-French restaurant with a partially enclosed garden isn't just a place to be seen; many believe it also has the best food in town. Among chef André Fernandes's recommended dishes are the linguini with fresh mussels and prawn sauce and the filet mignon *rosini* (served with foie gras and risotto with saffron). ⊠ *Av. Nove de Julho 5925, Jardim Europa,* ☎ *011/883–6276. AE, V.*

$$ ✕ **Bar des Arts.** A great place for lunch or drinks (it's a favorite with businesspeople), the Bar des Arts is set in a charming arcade near a flower shop, a wine shop, and a water fountain. You'll find both a buffet and à la carte options at lunch. ⊠ *Rua Pedro Humberto 9, at Rua Horacio Lafer, Itaim Bibi,* ☎ *011/829–7828. AE. Closed Mon.*

$$ ✕ **Mestiço.** If you like to eat a late dinner, come here. Tribal masks peer
★ down at you from the walls of the large, modern dining room. Consider the Thai *huan-hin* (chicken with shiitake in ginger sauce and rice) followed by a dessert of lemon ice cream with *baba de moça* (a syrup made with egg whites and sugar). ⊠ *Rua Fernando de Albuquerque 277, Consolação,* ☎ *011/256–3165. AE, V. Metrô: Consolação.*

$$ ✕ **Spot.** The closest thing to a chic diner as you'll find in São Paulo is just one door up from MASP (☞ *Exploring, above*). The salads and the pasta dishes are good bets; come early, though, as it gets crowded

after 10 PM. ⊠ *Alameda Rocha Azevedo 72, Cerqueira César,* ☎ *011/ 283–0946. AE, V. Metrô: Consolação.*

$ ✕ **Milk & Mellow.** Before or after a night of clubbing, stop here for the great sandwiches, hamburgers, and milkshakes in a relaxed atmosphere. It's open weekdays until 4 AM and weekends until 6 AM. ⊠ *Av. Cidade Jardim 1085, Itaim Bibi,* ☎ *011/829–8916. No credit cards.*

French

$$$$ ✕ **Le Coq Hardy.** This award-winning restaurant has two chefs: one is a veteran of the top French kitchens in Brazil and the other spent many years cooking in France. The grilled foie gras and mango, the escargots with mushrooms in an anise and wine sauce, and the roast duck are all highly recommended. ⊠ *Rua Jerônimo da Veiga 461, Itaim Bibi,* ☎ *011/852–3344. AE, DC, MC, V.*

$$$$ ✕ **Freddy.** You'll leave behind the grunge and noise of the streets when you walk through the doors of this long-lived eatery with the feel of an upscale Parisian bistro. Try the duck with Madeira sauce and apple purée, the pheasant with herb sauce, or the hearty cassoulet (white beans, lamb, duck, and garlic sausage). ⊠ *Praça Dom Gastão Liberal Pinto 111, Itaim Bibi,* ☎ *011/829–0977. AE, DC, MC, V.*

$$$$ ✕ **Laurent.** Chef Laurent Suadeau is famous for his use of Brazilian ingredients to create French nouvelle cuisine. Businesspeople from Avenida Paulista appreciate the fine decor and inexpensive (compared with dinner), but still superb, lunch menu. Specialties include the broccoli crepes with a cashew curry and the *bacalhau* (codfish) rolled in spinach leaves. ⊠ *Alameda Jaú 1606, Jardins,* ☎ *011/853–5573. AE, MC, V. No lunch Sat. Closed Sun.*

$$$ ✕ **La Casserole.** Facing a little Centro flower market, this charming bistro has been around for generations. Surrounded by cozy wood-paneled walls decorated with eclectic posters, you can dine on such delights as *gigot d'agneau aux soissons* (roast leg of lamb in its own juices, served with white beans) and cherry strudel. ⊠ *Largo do Arouche 346, Centro,* ☎ *011/220–6283. AE, DC, MC, V. Closed Mon. No lunch Sat.*

$$ ✕ **La Tartine.** This small restaurant has movie posters on its walls and
★ simple but comfortable furniture. The menu changes daily. On Saturday night you'll find the classic coq au vin; on Friday the option is a Moroccan couscous. ⊠ *Rua Fernando de Albuquerque 267, Consolação,* ☎ *011/259–2090. V. Closed Sun.–Mon. Metrô: Consolação.*

Indian

$$$$ ✕ **Ganesh.** Many consider this the best Indian eatery in town. The traditional menu includes curries and tandoori dishes. The decor is all Indian artwork and tapestries. ⊠ *Morumbi Shopping Center, Av. Roque Petroni Jr. 1089, Morumbi,* ☎ *011/240–6768. AE, DC, MC, V.*

Italian

$$$$ ✕ **Ca' D'Oro.** This is a longtime northern Italian favorite among Brazilian bigwigs, many of whom have their own tables in the Old World–style dining room. Quail, osso buco, and veal and raisin ravioli are winners, but the specialty is the Piedmontese *gran bollito misto,* steamed meats and vegetables accompanied by three sauces and served from a cart. ⊠ *Grande Hotel Ca' D'Oro, Rua Augusta 129, Bela Vista,* ☎ *011/236–4300. AE, DC, MC, V. Metrô: Anhangabaú.*

$$$$ ✕ **Fasano.** A family-owned, northern Italian classic, this restaurant is as famous for its superior cuisine as for its exorbitant prices. Ever pay $29 for cream of asparagus soup? How about $49 for a green salad appetizer with foie gras? Here's your chance. Although the decor—marble, mahogany, and mirrors—has seen better days, if you're intent on experiencing the best of the best, this place is a must. The merely upper-middle class can try the gorgeous **Gero** (☎ 011/3064–0005) restaurant, which is just across the street (there's also a branch in the Shopping Center Iguatemi). It's run by the same family, but it's less expensive and attracts a younger, more fun-loving crowd. The mushroom risotto is transcendental. ⊠ *Rua Haddock Lobo 1644, Jardins,* ☎ *011/852–4000. AE, DC, MC, V. No lunch Sat., no dinner Sun.*

$$$$ ✕ **Massimo.** Just off Avenida Paulista, this is the city's prime spot for lunchtime deal-making over such refined Italian pleasures as leg of lamb with leeks or gnocchi with shrimp, tomato, and pesto sauce. Owner Massimo Ferrari, a hefty man in shirtsleeves and suspenders, keeps the best tables on standby for VIPs. ⊠ *Alameda Santos 1826, Jardins,* ☎ *011/284–0311. No credit cards. Metrô: Trianon.*

$$$$ ✕ **La Vecchia Cucina.** Chef Sergio Arno changed the face of the city's Italian restaurants with his *nuova cucina,* exemplified by such dishes as frog risotto and duck ravioli with watercress sauce. Well-to-do patrons feast either in the ocher-color dining room decorated with Italian engravings and fresh flowers or in the glassed-in garden gazebo. ⊠ *Rua Pedroso Alvarenga 1088, Itaim Bibi,* ☎ *011/3060–9822. AE, DC, MC, V. No lunch Sat., no dinner Sun.*

$$$ ✕ **Famiglia Mancini.** A huge provolone cheese is the first thing you see
★ at this warm, cheerful restaurant. An incredible buffet with cheeses, olives, sausages, and much more is the perfect place to find a tasty appetizer. The menu has many terrific pasta options, such as the cannelloni with palm hearts and a four-cheese sauce. ⊠ *Rua Avanhandava 81, Centro,* ☎ *011/256–4320. AE, DC, MC, V. Metrô: Anhangabaú.*

$$$ ✕ **Lellis Trattoria.** Photos of famous patrons (mostly Brazilian actors) hang on the walls, and the doors and bar are made of metal, giving the typical Italian cantina a sophisticated twist. Salmon fillet *marinatta* (in white sauce with potatoes, raisins, and rice) is the best choice on the menu at this spin-off of Gigetto (☞ *below*). ⊠ *Rua Bela Cintra 1849, Jardim Paulista,* ☎ *011/3064–2727. AE, DC, MC, V.*

$$$ ✕ **Santo Colomba.** This Italian restaurant near the Paulista hotels isn't inexpensive, but some say that for the money, you won't find better in the city. It was originally built in Rio de Janeiro's Jóque Clube (Jockey Club) before being brought lock, stock, and barrel (or rather wooden walls, French tiles, and carved wooden bar) to its current São Paulo location. You can feast on pasta with shrimp, squid, tomato, and garlic while listening to live piano music. ⊠ *Alameda Lorena 1165, Jardins,* ☎ *011/3061–3588. AE, DC, MC, V.*

$$ ✕ **Gigetto.** The walls here are adorned with theater posters, a tribute to the actors who dine here after performing at the theater. The modest decor, however, is offset by the elaborate menu's more than 200 delicious options. Try the cappelletti *à romanesca* (with chopped ham, peas, mushrooms, and white cream sauce). ⊠ *Rua Avanhandava 63, Centro,* ☎ *011/256–9804. AE, DC, MC, V. Metrô: Anhangabaú.*

$$ ✕ **Jardim di Napoli.** Appropriately enough, just about everywhere you look in this restaurant you'll see the white, green, and red of the Italian flag. People come for the unmatchable *polpettone alla parmigiana,* a huge meatball with mozzarella and tomato sauce. There are also many other meat dishes as well as pasta selections and pizza. ⊠ *Rua Doutor Martinico Prado 463, Higienópolis,* ☎ *011/3666–3022. No credit cards.*

$$ ✕ **Mamma Mia.** The waiters can't seem to bring you enough food at this eatery, which is known for its grilled chicken. You can also have a salad and pasta dishes. ⊠ *Av. Moema 41, Moema,* ☎ *011/572–5100. AE, DC, MC, V.*

Dining

Almanara, **50**
Amadeus, **29**
Arábia, **27**
Baby Beef Rubaiyat, **54**
Bar des Arts, **48**
Bargaço, **31**
Ca' D'Oro, **4**
Cantaloup, **39**
La Casserole, **1**
Consulado Mineiro, **18**
Le Coq Hardy, **40**
Danang, **46**
Dona Lucinha, **34, 61**
Esplanada Grill, **35**
Famiglia Mancini, **6**
Fasano, **37**
Freddy, **49**
Frevo, **51**
Galpão, **20**
Ganesh, **65**
Gigetto, **5**
Jardim di Napoli, **9**
Komazushi, **58**
Laurent, **22**
Lellis Trattoria, **17**
Mamma Mia, **62**
Massimo, **21**
Mestiço, **11**
Milk & Mellow, **45**
Nagayama, **30, 41**
Oficina
de Pizzas, **19, 32**
Oriental, **23**
Paddock, **3, 38**
Piola, **52**
Pizzaria Camelo, **53**
Ritz, **26**
Roperto, **14**
Roppongi, **47**
Santo Colomba, **25**
Speranza, **55**
Spot, **15**
Sujinho—Bisteca
d'Ouro, **10**
La Tambouille, **42**
La Tartine, **12**
Truta Rosa, **63**
La Vecchia Cucina, **43**
I Vitelloni, **33**

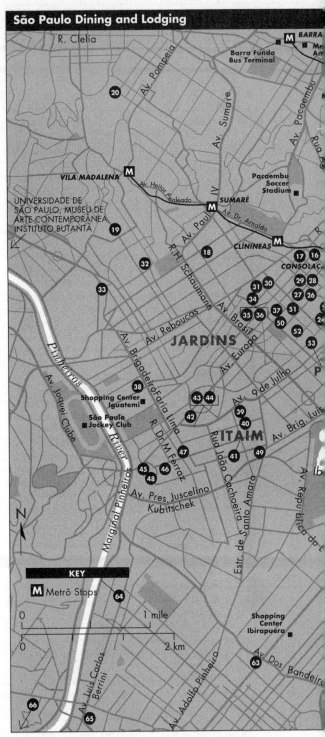

São Paulo Dining and Lodging

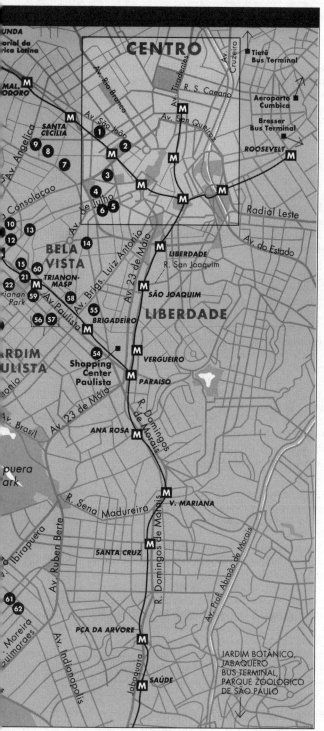

$$ ✗ **Ritz.** Here an animated crowd chatters as contemporary pop music plays in the background. Although each day sees a different special, one of the most popular dishes is the *bife à milanesa* (a breaded beef) with creamed spinach and french fries. ⊠ *Alameda Franca 1088, Cerqueira César,* ☎ *011/280–6808. AE, V. Metrô: Consolação.*

$$ ✗ **Roperto.** Plastic flowers adorn the walls at this typical Bixiga cantina. You won't be alone if you order the traditional and ever-popular fusilli *ao sugo* (with tomato sauce). ⊠ *Rua 13 de Maio 634, Bela Vista,* ☎ *011/288–2573. V.*

Japanese

$$$ ✗ **Komazushi.** Real sushi connoisseurs will appreciate Komazushi. Although master chef Takatomo Hachinohe died in 1998, Jun Sakamoto, the new sushiman in charge, is maintaining the high standards set by his predecessor. The seats at the bar are reserved for customers known to order expensive options. ⊠ *Rua São Carlos do Pinhal 241, Bela Vista,* ☎ *011/287–1820. No credit cards. Closed Mon. Metrô: Trianon.*

$$$ ✗ **Nagayama.** Low key, trustworthy, and well loved, both Nagayama locations consistently serve excellent sushi and sashimi. The chefs like to experiment with unusual recipes (and unusual names), such as the California *uramaki* Philadelphia (rice, cream cheese, grilled salmon, roe, cucumber, and spring onions). ⊠ *Rua Bandeira Paulista 369, Itaim Bibi,* ☎ *011/3064–8937. AE, DC, MC.* ⊠ *Rua da Consolação 3397, Cerqueira César,* ☎ *011/3064–0110. AE, DC, MC.*

$$$ ✗ **Roppongi.** This sushi bar is more about fun than about sushi itself, and fun it does quite well. The nightly clientele includes artists, models, and politicians. There's a private dining area and exit for the fatally chic and amenities for patrons with mobility problems. California rolls are your favorite? Roppongi makes them with mango instead of avocado. For those not fond of raw fish, steaks, pastas, and other international dishes are available. Whatever you order, be sure to refresh yourself with at least one frozen sake before you leave. ⊠ *Rua Jorge Coelho 128, Itaim Bibi,* ☎ *011/883–6991. V.*

Lebanese

$$$ ✗ **Arábia.** For more than 10 years Arábia has been serving traditional Lebanese cuisine in a beautiful, high-ceilinged location. Simple dishes such as hummus and stuffed grape leaves are executed with aplomb. The lamb melts in your mouth with astonishing speed. The "executive" lunch includes one cold dish, one meat dish, a drink, and dessert—all at a (relatively) reasonable price. Don't miss the rose syrup for dessert; it comes over a pistachio delight that may leave you in tears. ⊠ *Rua Haddock Lobo 1397, Jardins,* ☎ *011/3061–2203. AE, D.*

$ ✗ **Almanara.** Part of a chain of Lebanese semi-fast-food outlets, Al-
★ manara is perfect for a quick lunch of hummus, tabbouleh, grilled chicken, and rice. There's also a full-blown restaurant on the premises that serves Lebanese specialties *rodízio*-style (you get a taste of everything until you can ingest no more). ⊠ *Rua Oscar Freire 523, Jardins,* ☎ *011/853–6916. AE, DC, MC, V.*

Pan-Asian

$$$ ✗ **Danang.** This stunningly beautiful restaurant—a huge map of Thailand covers one wall, and a coconut tree grows in the middle of the room—serves a chic, creative mix of Asian cuisines, including Vietnamese, Thai, and Japanese. A recommended dish is *kaeng kung* (prawns with broccoli and other vegetables in a curry-and-coconut-milk sauce). ⊠

Rua Salvador Cardoso 20, Itaim Bibi, ☎ 011/829–4758. DC, MC, V,
No lunch Mon.–Sat. No dinner Sun.

$$$ ✕ **Oriental.** Here, high ceilings and tile floors convey a sense of space
while candles flickering on tables keep things intimate. With such so-
phisticated dishes as shark fin soup, this newcomer is already consid-
ered the best restaurant of its kind. You'll also find less exotic dishes
such as marinated chicken thighs. ⊠ Rua José Maria Lisboa 1000, Jardim
Paulista, ☎ 011/3060–9495. No credit cards. Closed Sun.

Pizza

$$ ✕ **Galpão.** Owned by an architect, this pizzeria has such interesting
★   decor details as lights that shine from behind bottle bottoms embed-
ded in exposed brick walls. Fast service is also a hallmark. The best
menu choice is the arugula, sun-dried tomatoes and mozzarella pizza.
⊠ Rua Doutor Augusto de Miranda 1156, Pompéia, ☎ 011/262–4767.
DC, MC, V. Closed Mon.

$$ ✕ **Oficina de Pizzas.** Both branches of this restaurant look like some-
thing designed by the Spanish artist Gaudí, but the pizzas couldn't be
more Italian and straightforward. Try a pie with mozzarella and toasted
garlic. ⊠ Rua Purpurina 517, Vila Madalena, ☎ 011/816–3749. DC,
MC, V. ⊠ Rua Inácio Pereira da Rocha 15, Vila Madalena, ☎ 011/
813–8399. DC, MC, V.

$$ ✕ **Piola.** Part of a chain started in Italy, this restaurant serves good pasta
dishes as well as pizza. It's frequented by young people who seem to
match the trendy decoration perfectly. ⊠ Rua Oscar Freire 512, Jardins,
☎ 011/3064–6570. AE, DC, MC, V.

$$ ✕ **Pizzaria Camelo.** Though it's neither fancy nor beautiful, the wide-
variety of thin-crust pies served here has kept paulistanos enthralled
for ages. The chopp (draft beer) is great, too. Avoid Sunday nights un-
less you want to wait an hour for a table. ⊠ Rua Pamplona 1873,
Cerqueira César, ☎ 011/887–8764. No credit cards.

$$ ✕ **Speranza.** One of the most traditional pizzerias in São Paulo is famous for its margherita pie. The crunchy pão de linguiça (sausage bread)
appetizers have a fine reputation as well. ⊠ Rua 13 de Maio 1004,
Bela Vista, ☎ 011/573–1229. DC, MC, V.

$$ ✕ **I Vitelloni.** The pizza with arugula, mozzarella, sun-dried tomatoes,
and roasted garlic was invented here and copied by pizzerias all over
town. The place is small, but the service is great. ⊠ Rua Conde Sílvio
Álvares Penteado 31, Pinheiros, ☎ 011/813–1588. No credit cards.

Seafood

$$$$ ✕ **Amadeus.** The quality and preparation of the fish here are consis-
tently superior. Appetizers such as fresh oysters and salmon and en-
dive with mustard, and entrées like shrimp in a cognac sauce, make it
a challenge to find better fruits of the sea elsewhere in town. ⊠ Rua
Haddock Lobo 807, Jardins, ☎ 011/3061–2859. AE, DC. No dinner
weekends. Metrô: Consolação.

$$$ ✕ **Truta Rosa.** Fresh trout, prepared in endless ways, makes this small
restaurant with a huge fish-shape window a hit. You'll cross a metal
bridge over a small lagoon to reach the dining room, where sashimi
and quenelles reel in the customers. ⊠ Av. Vereador José Diniz 318,
Santo Amaro, ☎ 011/247–8629. AE, DC, MC, V. Closed Mon. No
dinner Sun.

LODGING

São Paulo's hotels are almost exclusively geared to business travelers,
both homegrown and foreign. For this reason, most hotels are in the

Avenida Paulista area, with a few in the Marginal Pinheiros and charming Jardins neighborhoods. Many hotels offer discounts of 20%–40% for cash payment or weekend stays. Few include breakfast in the room rate. São Paulo hosts many international conventions, so it's wise to make reservations well ahead of your arrival.

Brazilian "flat" or apartment hotels can accommodate from one to several people and usually have a kitchen and living room, a ground-floor restaurant that serves breakfast, a pool, daily housekeeping, and meeting rooms (rates are in the $$$–$$$$ category). Try **George V** (⊠ Rua José Maria Lisboa 1000, Jardins, ☎ 011/280–9822, ℻ 011/282–7431), **The Landmark** (⊠ Alameda Jaú 1607, Jardins, ☎ 011/282–8677, ℻ 011/282–0167), and **La Résidence** (⊠ Rua Campos Bicudo 153, Itaim Bibi, ☎ 011/3061–5133, ℻ 011/883–6416). For information about youth hostels, contact the **Associação Paulista de Albergues da Juventude** (⊠ Rua 7 de Abril 386, 01320-040, ☎ 011/258–0388). The association sells a book ($2.50) that lists hostels throughout Brazil.

$$$$ ▥ **Gran Meliá São Paulo.** The Meliá is in the same building as São Paulo's
★   world trade center and the D&D Decoração & Design Center (☞ Shopping, *below*). Off the large marble lobby is a bar whose comfortable leather chairs are perfect for unwinding after a day of meetings or shopping. Guest rooms have king-size beds, two phone lines, living rooms with sofas, and small tables that are the perfect places to set up your laptop. The apartment floors have such special amenities as pass-key access and bathroom faucets that can be programmed to record whatever water-temperature you prefer. ⊠ *Av. das Nações Unidas 12559, Brooklin 04578-905, ☎ 011/3043–8000 or 0800/15–5555, ℻ 011/3043–8001. 300 suites. Restaurant, bar, in-room modem lines, in-room safes, room service, indoor pool, beauty salon, massage, sauna, tennis court, exercise room, paddle tennis, business services, meeting rooms. AE, DC, MC, V.*

$$$$ ▥ **L'Hotel.** Close to the major business hubs, this "European-style" hotel has rooms and suites decorated in somewhat sterile floral patterns. The place was modeled after the famous L'Hotel in Paris, and the small number of rooms allows it to focus on providing superior service. Though at its inception L'Hotel wanted to retain an air of exclusivity, reports have been mixed as to its success. ⊠ *Alameda Campinas 266, Jardins 01404-000, ☎ ℻ 011/283–0500. 82 rooms, 5 suites. 2 restaurants, pub, room service, pool, sauna, health club, business services, meeting rooms. AE, DC, MC, V. Metrô: Trianon.*

$$$$ ▥ **Inter-Continental São Paulo.** This exquisite hotel is by far the most
★   attractive of the city's top-tier establishments. Service is attentive, and both the private and public areas are well appointed. Creams and pastels, marble, and unique design elements come together with seamless sophistication and elegance. ⊠ *Av. Santos 1123, Jardins 01419-001, ☎ 011/3179–2600, ℻ 011/3179–2666. 160 rooms, 33 suites. Restaurant, bar, room service, pool, massage, sauna, health club, business services, helipad. AE, DC, MC, V. Metrô: Trianon.*

$$$$ ▥ **Maksoud Plaza.** Ronald Reagan *almost* stayed here on a 1982 presidential visit, but the Secret Service thought the soaring atrium lobby—with its panoramic elevators, fountains, greenery, and shops—posed a security risk. The staff provides professional service, the hotel's restaurants aren't bad, and the in-house theater and the Maksoud 150 nightclub offer entertainment. ⊠ *Alameda Campinas 1250, Jardins 01404-900, ☎ 011/251–2233, ℻ 011/253–4544. 416 rooms, 99 suites. 6 restaurants, 3 bars, room service, indoor pool, health club, nightclub, theater, business services. AE, DC, MC, V. Metrô: Trianon.*

$$$$ ⚄ **Renaissance São Paulo.** A stay at this Jardins hotel, a block from Avenida Paulista, puts you close to both shops and businesses. From the street, it has the appeal of a roll of tinfoil, but its interior is graceful and elegant. There are six Renaissance Club floors of 57 suites that include a buffet breakfast, evening hors d'oeuvres, butler service, express check-in and check-out, and fax machines. If you want to arrive in style, the hotel's helipad is key. ✉ *Alameda Santos 2247, Jardins 01419-002,* ☎ *011/3069–2233 or 800/468–3571 in the U.S.,* Ⓕ *011/ 3064–3344. 452 rooms, 100 suites. 3 restaurants, 3 bars, room service, pool, massage, health club, squash, shops, business services, travel services, helipad, parking (fee). AE, DC, MC, V. Metrô: Consolação.*

$$$$ ⚄ **Sheraton Mofarrej Hotel & Towers.** Just behind Avenida Paulista and
★ next to Parque Trianon, the Mofarrej is part of Sheraton's A-class Luxury Collection hotels. Rooms are done in elegant light hues, and the four floors that have butler service offer other amenities that will make you feel all the more at home. Rooms on the west side overlook the park. ✉ *Alameda Santos 1437, Jardins 01419–905,* ☎ *011/253–5544 or 0800/11–6000,* Ⓕ *011/289–8670. 2 restaurants, 2 bars, room service, indoor pool, outdoor pool, massage, sauna, exercise room, business services, convention center. AE, DC, MC, V. Metrô: Trianon.*

$$$$ ⚄ **Transamérica.** Directly across the Rio Pinheiros from the Centro Empresarial office complex, where many U.S. companies are housed, this hotel is a comfortable and convenient choice for those working outside Centro. The skylit lobby has granite, marble, Persian carpets, palm trees, leather sofas, and oversize modern paintings; the spacious rooms have no special charm, but their pastel colors, wood furnishings, and beige carpeting create a relaxing atmosphere. ✉ *Av. das Nações Unidas 18591, Santo Amaro 04795-901,* ☎ *011/5693–4511 or 0800/12–6060,* Ⓕ *011/5693–4990. 396 rooms, 66 suites. Restaurant, bar, room service, pool, sauna, 9-hole golf course, 2 tennis courts, exercise room, jogging, business services. AE, DC, MC, V.*

$$$ ⚄ **Carillon Plaza.** Walk out of the heated hustle and bustle of the Jardins neighborhood and into this hotel's cool lobby full of mirrors and marble. You can retreat still farther by heading to the roof-top pool for an afternoon of sunbathing or by sinking into a leather chair for a meal in the restaurant. The multilingual staff is very helpful. ✉ *Rua Bela Cintra 652, Jardins 01415-000,* ☎ *011/257–9233,* Ⓕ *011/255– 3346. 39 rooms, 10 suites. Restaurant, bar, in-room safes, room service, pool. AE, DC, MC, V. Metrô: Consolação.*

$$$ ⚄ **Eldorado Higienópolis.** Set in one of the city's oldest and most at-
★ tractive residential neighborhoods, only a five-minute taxi ride from Centro, this hotel has a large pool and a lobby dressed in travertine marble with a pink granite floor. The on-site café is lovely, and the rooms are all pleasant; the noise level is lowest in those at the front above the fifth floor or those in back. ✉ *Rua Marquês de Itu 836, Higienópolis 01223-000,* ☎ *011/224–0666,* Ⓕ *011/222–7194. 152 rooms. Restaurant, bar, room service, pool. AE, DC, MC, V.*

$$$ ⚄ **Grande Hotel Ca' D'Oro.** Owned and run by a northern Italian family for more than 40 years, this Old World–style hotel near Centro has bar-side fireplaces, lots of wood and Persian carpeting, a great variety of room decor (all along classic European lines), ultrapersonalized service, and the beloved Ca' D'Oro restaurant (☞ *Dining, above*). All these amenities attract many repeat customers, including quite a few Brazilian bigwigs. ✉ *Rua Augusta 129, Cerqueira César 01303-001,* ☎ *011/236–4300,* Ⓕ *011/236–4311. 240 rooms, 50 suites. Restaurants, 2 bars, room service, indoor pool, outdoor pool, sauna, exercise room. AE, DC, MC, V. Metrô: Consolação.*

$$ 🏨 Bourbon. Both guests and furnishings are well cared for in this small hotel near the Largo do Arouche, a charming downtown district. A brass-accented basement bar features live piano music. The lobby has upholstered print sofas, an abstract handcrafted black and white wall hanging, and granite flooring. Rooms are done in beige and blue and have marvelously large, sunlit bathrooms. ⊠ *Av. Vieira de Carvalho 99, Centro 01210-010,* ☎ *011/250–0244,* FAX *011/221–4076. 123 rooms. Restaurant, bar, sauna. AE, DC, MC, V. Metrô: República.*

$$ 🏨 La Guardia. If you don't need to be surrounded by luxury, consider this simple, affordable (compared to many São Paulo establishments) hotel. Rooms are small but comfortable and have thick carpets and marble-top tables. The environment is friendly, and the service is good. ⊠ *Rua Peixoto Gomide 154, Cerqueira César 01409-000,* ☎ *011/255–0600,* FAX *011/258–7398. 28 rooms, 14 suites. Restaurant, free parking. AE, DC, MC, V. Metrô: Consolação.*

$$ 🏨 Ville Hotel. Located in the lively Higienópolis neighborhood of apartment buildings, bars, and bookstores abutting Mackenzie University, this hotel costs about $70 a night. The small lobby features a black and pink granite floor, recessed lighting, and leather sofas; rooms are done in pastels with brown carpeting. ⊠ *Rua Dona Veridiana 643, Higienópolis 01238-010,* ☎ *011/257–5288,* ☎ FAX *011/239–1871. 54 rooms. Restaurant, meeting room. AE, DC, MC, V.*

NIGHTLIFE AND THE ARTS

Nightlife

São Paulo is a city beset by trends, so clubs and bars come and go at a dizzying pace. Though these were all thriving spots at press time, it's best to check with hotel concierges and paulistanos you meet to confirm that a place is still open before heading out on the town.

Bars

From the sophisticated to casual, São Paulo has a bar for every taste. The most expensive places are in the Itaim neighborhood. Vila Madalena is full of trendier, alternative places.

Balcão. The word for "balcony" in Portuguese is *balcão,* and true to its name, this place has a sprawling one. If you'd like a little food to accompany your drinks and conversation, try the delicious sandwich with sun-dried tomatoes and mozzarella. ⊠ *Rua Doutor Melo Alves 150, Jardim Paulista,* ☎ *011/280–4630. Metrô: Consolação.*

Barnaldo Lucrécia. Live *música popular brasileira* (MPB; popular Brazilian music) is often a draw here. The crowd is intense, though jovial. ⊠ *Rua Abílio Soares 207, Paraíso,* ☎ *011/885–3425. Metrô: Paraíso.*

Elias. This place is a hangout for fans of the Palmeiras soccer team, whose stadium is just a few blocks away. If you want something to eat, the carpaccio is undoubtedly the best choice on the menu. ⊠ *Rua Cayowaá 70, Perdizes,* ☎ *011/864–4722.*

Empanadas. Most patrons stop here for a beer en route to another Vila Madalena bar. It's a good place to "warm up" for an evening out with a quick drink and a bite to eat. The empanadas are particularly appealing. ⊠ *Rua Wisard 489, Vila Madalena,* ☎ *011/210–2116.*

Frangó. Because it's set in the Freguesia do Ó neighborhood, a stop here makes you feel as if you've been transported to a small town. In addition to a pleasant location, Frangó also offers 90 varieties of beer, including the Brazilian export beer, Xingu. Its rich molasses-like flavor nicely complements the bar's unforgettable *bolinhos de frango com queijo* (chicken balls with cheese). ⊠ *Largo da Matriz de Nossa Senhora do Ó 168, Freguesia do Ó,* ☎ *011/875–7818 or 011/875–9281.*

In case you want to see the world.

At American Express, we're here to make your journey a smooth one. So we have over 1,700 travel service locations in over 130 countries ready to help. What else would you expect from the world's largest travel agency?

do more **AMERICAN EXPRESS**

Travel

Call 1 800 AXP-3429 or visit
www.americanexpress.com/travel

In case you want to be welcomed there.

We're here to see that you're always welcomed at establishments everywhere. That's why millions of people carry the American Express® Card – for peace of mind, confidence, and security, around the world or just around the corner.

do more

Cards

To apply, call 1 800 THE-CARD
or visit www.americanexpress.com

In case you're running low.

We're here to help with more than 190,000 Express Cash
locations around the world. In order to enroll, just call
American Express at 1 800 CASH-NOW before you start
your vacation.

do more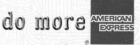

**Express
Cash**

And in case you'd rather be safe than sorry.

We're here with American Express® Travelers Cheques. They're the safe way to carry money on your vacation, because if they're ever lost or stolen you can get a refund, practically anywhere or anytime. To find the nearest place to buy Travelers Cheques, call 1 800 495-1153. Another way we help you do more.

do more **AMERICAN EXPRESS**

Travelers Cheques

Original. This place was a pioneer in the trend of creating bars inspired by Rio de Janeiro's establishments from the '40s. It has good draft beer and snacks. ⊠ *Rua Graúna 137, Moema,* ☎ *011/530–9486.*

Pirajá. The pictures of Rio de Janeiro on the walls here will make you think fondly of Ipanema. The action starts at happy hour after 6 PM. ⊠ *Av. Brigadeiro Faria Lima 64, Pinheiros,* ☎ *011/815–6881.*

Brazilian Clubs

MPB clubs book quiet, largely acoustic instrumental and vocal music in the style of Milton Nascimento, Chico Buarque, and Gilberto Gil. The emphasis tends to be on samba and bossa nova.

Café Soçaite. This is one of the most popular spots for MPB, especially with singles. ⊠ *Rua 13 de Maio 48, Bixiga,* ☎ *011/259–6562.*

Sem Eira Nem Beira. The decor here is inspired by Brazilian bars circa 1940. Previously called Vou Vivendo, the club is famous for its live MPB performances on Friday and Saturday. ⊠ *Rua Elvira Ferraz 966, Itaim Bibi,* ☎ *011/820–6963.*

Cybercafés

Banca Henrique Schaumann. At this newsstand-bar you'll find eight computers connected Monday–Wednesday 7 AM–1 AM and 24 hours Thursday and through Sunday. Access costs about $4 an hour. ⊠ *Av. Henrique Schaumann 159, Pinheiros,* ☎ *011/3063–3292.*

Clube B.A.S.E. The true cyber decor here really puts you in the mood for a little cyber exploration. For $6 per half-hour, you can log onto one of eight computers Tuesday–Friday after 10 PM and Saturday after 11 PM (☞ *also Dance Clubs, below*). ⊠ *Av. Brigadeiro Luiz Antônio 1137, Bela Vista,* ☎ *011/3606–3244.*

Coffee & Book at Saraiva Megastore. This store sells CDs and books and has a café as well as five computers. You can log on Monday–Saturday 10–10 and Sunday 2–8; the cost is $5 for the first half-hour and $4 for each additional 30 minutes. ⊠ *Shopping Eldorado, Av. Rebouças 3970, Pinheiros,* ☎ *011/870–5999.*

Dance Clubs

People tend to go dancing very late in São Paulo. Still, you should arrive early to avoid the lines. Don't worry if the dance floor appears empty at 11 PM; things will start to sizzle an hour or so later.

Avenida Club. Some nights are dedicated to Caribbean rhythms, others to MPB. Regardless, the large, wooden dance floor—one of the finest in town—attracts a crowd of thirtysomethings. ⊠ *Pedroso de Morais 1036, Pinheiros,* ☎ *011/814–7383.*

Blen Blen Brasil. Here you can dance to live music—from reggae to salsa to Brazilian rock. ⊠ *Rua Inácio Pereira da Rocha 520, Pinheiros,* ☎ *011/212–9333.*

Brancaleone. Even if you've always been told that you move to the beat of a different drum, you'll find a suitable rhythm here. Each night brings a new beat, including disco, rock, funk, soul, Brazilian pop, and forró. You can take a break on the patio; refreshments include food as well as drink. ⊠ *Rua Luis Murat 298, Jardim América,* ☎ *011/870–8873.*

Carioca Club. *Carioca* is the word for a person or thing from Rio de Janeiro, and this place has the decor of old-style Rio clubs. Its large dance floor attracts an eclectic mix of college students, couples, and professional dancers who move to samba, *axé* (a type of music from Bahia), and pagode. ⊠ *Rua Cardeal Arcoverde 2899, Pinheiros,* ☎ *011/212–3782.*

Clube B.A.S.E. In the '60s this was a bathhouse, but now it hosts hot dance parties from 9 until the wee hours. Three bars and an enormous dance floor reverberate to a mix of everything from Jimi Hendrix to cutting-edge dance hits. ☒ *Av. Brigadeiro Luís Antônio 1137, Bela Vista,* ☎ *011/605–3162.*

Dado Bier. With a dance floor, a microbrewery, a restaurant, a sushi bar, and a gift shop, this place has something for everyone. No wonder you often have to wait in line to get in. ☒ *Av. Juscelino Kubitschek 1203, Itaim Bibi,* ☎ *011/866–2310.*

Dolores Dolores. DJs spin funk, soul, and hip hop tunes for a crowd in its twenties and thirties. Wednesday and Friday nights are the most popular, and people really do fill up the floor only after the witching hour. ☒ *Rua Fidalga 254, Vila Madalena,* ☎ *011/212–6519.*

Kashmir. If you feel it has been too long since your last magic carpet ride, head for the exclusive Kashmir, one of the longest-lived clubs in town. The decor features pillows to sit on, walls draped in exotic textiles, and indoor and outdoor spaces. There's a belly-dancing show after 10 PM Tuesday through Saturday. ☒ *Rua Fiandeiras 696, Vila Olímpia,* ☎ *011/820–0113.*

KVA. Live or recorded forró is played here every night. There are three stages, two dance floors, and one coffee shop. ☒ *Rua Cardeal Arcoverde 2958, Pinheiros,* ☎ *011/870–2153.*

Lov.e Club & Lounge. The interior design makes you feel like you're in a set from an *Austin Powers* movie. Before 2 AM the music isn't too loud, and you can sit and talk on the '50s-style sofas. Then techno effects keep people on the small dance floor until sunrise. ☒ *Rua Pequetita 189, Vila Olímpia,* ☎ *011/3044–1613.*

Moinho Santo Antonio. With a capacity of about 5,000, this has to be one of the planet's largest nightclubs. In a converted mill far from the center of town, the Moinho (as it's called) has a sushi bar, an Italian restaurant, a juice bar, outdoor and indoor dancing, bungee jumping (from a crane), and a magnificent lighting system. ☒ *Rua Borges de Figueiredo 510, Moóca,* ☎ *011/291–3522.*

Nias. This is one of the few places left in São Paulo where you can still dance to true rock and roll. DJs play tunes from the '60s and '70s and also current international pop-rock tunes. ☒ *Rua dos Pinheiros 688, Pinheiros,* ☎ *011/852–3877.*

The Pool. Ever wish you could fully cool off during a hot night of dancing? Well, this place has a 26-ft-long pool where you can do just that. The club will provide you with a swimsuit, but you can't wear it back on the dance floor. DJs play house music. ☒ *Rua Teodoro Sampaio 1109, Pinheiros,* ☎ *011/881–6604.*

Gay and Lesbian Clubs

Disco Fever. This place is frequented mostly by men between the ages of 18 and 35, and there's room for 1,200 of them. Bodybuilders in swim trunks dance on stages while DJ Mauro Borges and others play '70s and house music until the last patron leaves. ☒ *Av. Ibirapuera 1911, Moema,* ☎ *011/539–5910.*

A Lôca. Here you'll find a large dance floor, a video room, and two bars. A mixed gay and lesbian crowd often dances till dawn and then has breakfast in the club. ☒ *Rua Frei Caneca 916, Cerqueira César,* ☎ *011/3120–2055. Metrô: Consolação.*

Massivo. This fabulous underground disco and club welcomes gay, lesbian, and straight patrons. ☒ *Rua Alameda Itu 1548, Jardins,* ☎ *011/ 883–7505. Metrô: Consolação.*

Nostro 2000. One of São Paulo's oldest gay discos has transvestite and strip shows and an "anything goes" atmosphere. ☒ *Rua da Consolação 2554,* ☎ *011/259–2945. Metrô: Consolação.*

Jazz Clubs

All of Jazz. People come to this small place to actually *listen* to very good jazz and bossa nova. Local musicians jam here weekly. Call ahead to book a table on weekends. ⊠ *Rua João Cachoeira 1366, Vila Olímpia,* ☎ *011/829–1345.*

Blue Night. At this traditional jazz, blues, and soul venue, the audience drinks beer and whiskey and eats french fries with Parmesan cheese. ⊠ *Av. São Gabriel 558,* ☎ *011/884–9356.*

Bourbon Street. With a name right out of New Orleans, one of the world's coolest jazz towns, it's no wonder this is where the best jazz and blues bands play. ⊠ *Rua Dos Chanés 127, Moema,* ☎ *011/5561–1643.*

Café Piu Piu. Although this establishment is best known for jazz, it also hosts groups that play rock, bossa nova, and even tango. ⊠ *Rua 13 de Maio 134, Bixiga,* ☎ *011/258–8066.*

Piratininga. The tiny, round tables at this small bar-restaurant are perfect for a quiet rendezvous. The live jazz and MPB music add to the romance. ⊠ *Rua Wizard 149, Vila Madalena,* ☎ *011/210–9775.*

Sanja Jazz Bar. A few tables (arrive early to get a seat) in an old town house are the setting for live jazz, rock, and blues performances. ⊠ *Rua Frei Caneca 304, Consolação,* ☎ *011/255–2942.*

The Arts

The world's top orchestras, opera and dance companies, and other troupes always include São Paulo in their South American tours. Listings of events appear in the "Veja São Paulo" insert of the newsweekly *Veja*. The arts sections of the dailies *Folha de São Paulo* and *O Estado de São Paulo* also have listings and reviews. In addition, *Folha* publishes a weekly guide on Fridays called "Guia da Folha."

In addition to theater box offices, tickets for many events are available at booths throughout the city, including **Show Ticket at Shopping Center Morumbi** (⊠ Av. Brigadeiro Faria Lima 1191, 3rd floor, ☎ 011/212–7623), open Monday–Saturday 10–10 and Sunday 2–8. Some theaters deliver tickets for a surcharge, as will **Fun by Phone** (☎ 011/867–8687) and **Lucas Shows** (☎ 011/858–5783).

Classical Music, Dance, and Theater

The city is home to both a state and a municipal orchestra, though both suffer from a chronic lack of funds. São Paulo's theater district, in the bohemian Bela Vista neighborhood, has dozens of theaters dedicated mostly to plays in Portuguese. São Paulo has a world-class contemporary dance company, the **Ballet Stagium** (☎ 011/852–3451), and a contemporary music ensemble, **Grupo Novo Horizonte** (☎ 011/256–9766), neither of which have permanent homes.

PERFORMANCE VENUES

Sala São Luiz. This new venue hosts chamber music performances. ⊠ *Av. Juscelino Kubitschek 1830, Itaim Bibi,* ☎ *011/827–4111.*

Teatro da Cultura Artística. Its fine acoustics make this theater perfect for classical music performances. It also hosts dance recitals and plays. ⊠ *Rua Nestor Pestana 196, Cerqueira César,* ☎ *011/258–3616.*

Teatro Faculdade Armando Álvares Penteado (FAAP). The FAAP Theater is the site of concerts and Brazilian plays. ⊠ *Rua Alagoas 903, Pacaembú,* ☎ *011/3662–1992.*

Teatro João Caetano. This theater hosts state-sponsored festivals as well as Brazilian plays. ⊠ *Rua Borges Lagoa 650, Vila Mariana,* ☎ *011/573–3774.* Metrô: Santa Cruz.

Teatro Municipal. Most of São Paulo's serious music, ballet, and opera is performed in the intimate gilt and moss-green-velvet surroundings of this classic theater. There are lyrical performances on Monday at

8:30 and concerts on Wednesday at 12:30. A local cultural organization, the Mozarteum Brasileira Associação Cultural, holds classical music concerts here, which include performances by visiting artists, April–October. ⊠ *Praça Ramos de Azevedo, Centro,* ☎ *011/222–8698. Metrô: Anhangabaú.*

TUCA. The Catholic University theater puts on countercultural concerts as well as plays. ⊠ *Rua Monte Alegre 1024, Sumaré,* ☎ *011/873–3422.*

Via Funchal. With a capacity of more than 3,000 people, this is the site of many large international shows. ⊠ *Rua Funchal 65, Vila Olímpia,* ☎ *011/866–2300 or 011/822–6855.*

Escolas de Samba
From December to February, many *escolas de samba* (samba "schools"; groups that perform during Carnaval) open their rehearsals to the public. The drummers get in sync with the singers, and everyone learns the lyrics to each year's songs. One of the most popular such rehearsals is that of **Rosas de Ouro** (⊠ Av. Cel. Euclides Machado 1066, Freguesia do Ó, ☎ 011/266–0608 or 011/857–4555).

Film
Only foreign children's movies are dubbed; the rest have subtitles with the original dialogue intact. Arrive at blockbuster releases at least 40 minutes early, particularly on Sunday nights. The region near Avenida Paulista, Avenida Consolação, and Rua Augusta has more than 10 movie theaters as well as many cafés and bars where you can hang out before or after the show. Movie theaters in shopping centers are also good options (☞ Shopping, *below*). Call ahead for confirmation because theaters often change their programming without notice.

The **Belas Artes** complex (⊠ Rua da Consolação 2423, ☎ 011/258–4092 or 011/259–6341) offers Hollywood films. **Centro Cultural São Paulo** (⊠ Rua Vergueiro 1000, Paraíso, ☎ 011/277–3611, ext. 279) usually features a series of theme films for free or for very cheap. It also presents plays, concerts, and art exhibits. **Cinearte** (⊠ Av. Paulista 2073, ☎ 011/285–3696) hosts most of the premieres in town. Brazilian, European, and other non-American films are shown at the **Espaço Unibanco** (⊠ Rua Augusta 1470/1475, ☎ 011/288–6780).

Free Shows
Most free concerts—with performances by either Brazilian or international artists—are presented on Sunday in Parque Ibirapuera. City-sponsored events are held in Centro's Vale do Anhangabaú area. State-sponsored concerts take place at the Memorial da América Latina, northwest of Centro. **Serviço Social do Comércio** (SESC, Commerce Social Service; ☎ 011/3179–3400) is very active in cultural programming, and many of its events are free. The organization has units in several neighborhoods. **SESC Anchieta** (⊠ Rua Dr. Vila Nova 245, ☎ 011/256–2322), for example, presents dance and classical theater performances with a contemporary twist.

OUTDOOR ACTIVITIES AND SPORTS

Participant Sports

Bicycling
Parque Ibirapuera has places that rent bicycles for about $8 an hour and a special bike path. There are also bike lanes on Avenida Sumaré and Avenida Pedroso de Morais. **Night Biker's Club** (⊠ Rua Pacheco de Miranda 141, Jardim Paulista, ☎ 011/887–4773) has bike tours in the city at night. **Sampa Bikers** (⊠ Alameda dos Anapurus 1580,

Moema, ☎ 011/9990–0083 or 011/5183–9477) offers tours inside the city and biking side trips outside town; costs start at about $90.

Climbing

Inspired, perhaps, by the skyscrapers on Avenida Paulista, climbers have recently crowded the gyms and rock-climbing schools that have sprung up around town. Most places offer training and rent equipment. Classes start as low as $6 for two hours. Try **Casa de Pedra** (✉ Rua da Paz 1823, Chácara Santo Antônio, ☎ 011/5181–7873), **Guias de Alta Montanha** (✉ Rua Ministro Ferreira Alves 314, Pompéia, ☎ 011/3862–1194), **Jump** (✉ Av. Pompéia 568, Pompéia, ☎ 011/3675–2300), and **90 Graus** (✉ Rua João Pedro Cardoso 107, Aeroporto, ☎ 011/240–8775).

Golf

The greens fee at the 18-hole **Clube de Campo** (✉ Praça Rockford 28, Vila Represa, ☎ 011/5929–3111) is $50. It's open Monday–Tuesday and Thursday–Friday 7–7. The **Golf School** (✉ Av. Guido Caloi 2160, Santo Amaro, ☎ 011/5515–3372) is a driving range that offers 30-minute classes for $20; $10 gets you 100 balls.

Scuba Diving

Most dive schools take people to Ilhabela and other places outside town on weekends and offer NAUI and PADI certification courses. The best-known operations are **Claumar** (✉ Av. Brigadeiro Faria Lima 4440, Itaim Bibi, ☎ 011/866–3032), **Diving College** (✉ Rua Doutor Mello Alves 700, Cerqueira César, ☎ 011/3061–1453), and **Scuba Point** (✉ Rua Pio XII 641, Alto da Lapa, ☎ 011/261–2611).

Tennis

Tênis Coach (✉ Rua Dr. Francisco Tomás de Carvalho, 940, Morumbi) rents courts and gives classes to people of all ages. Court fees at **Play Tênis** (✉ Leopoldo Couto de Magalhães Jr. 1097, Itaim Bibi, ☎ 011/820–7446) are $35 an hour, but they don't rent rackets.

Spectator Sports

Auto Racing

São Paulo hosts a Formula I race every March, bringing this city of 4.5 million cars to heights of spontaneous combustion, especially when a Brazilian driver wins. The race is held at **Autódromo de Interlagos** (✉ Av. Senador Teotônio Vilela 315, Interlagos, ☎ 011/521–9911), which also hosts other kinds of races on weekends. For ticket information on the Formula I race contact the **Confederação Brasileira de Automobilismo** (✉ Rua da Glória 290, 8th Floor, Rio de Janeiro, RJ 20241-180, ☎ 021/221–4895).

Futebol

Futebol (soccer) has always been a Brazilian passion. The nation's love affair with the sport became even stronger after Brazil won the 1994 World Cup and reached the finals during the 1998 World Cup. São Paulo has several well-funded teams with some of the country's best players. The five main teams—São Paulo, Palmeiras, Portuguesa, Corinthians, and Juventus—even attract fans from other states. The two biggest stadiums are **Morumbi** (✉ Praça Roberto Gomes Pedrosa, ☎ 011/842–3377) and the municipally run **Pacaembu** (✉ Praça Charles Miller, ☎ 011/256–9111). Note that covered seats offer the best protection not only from the elements but also from rowdy spectators.

Horse Racing

Thoroughbreds race at the **São Paulo Jockey Club** (✉ Rua Lineu de Paula Machado 1263, Cidade Jardim, ☎ 011/816–4011), which is open

Monday and Wednesday–Thursday 7:30 PM–11:30 PM and weekends 2–9. Card-carrying jockey club members get the best seats and have access to the elegant restaurant.

SHOPPING

People come from all over South America to shop in São Paulo, and shopping is considered an attraction in its own right by many paulistanos. In the Jardins neighborhood, stores that carry well-known brands from around the world coexist with the best Brazilian shops. Prices are high for most items, especially in Jardins and the major shopping centers.

Stores are open weekdays 9–6:30 and Saturday 9–1. A few are open on Sunday (for a list of these shops and their Sunday hours, call ☎ 011/210–4000 or 011/813–3311). Mall hours are generally weekdays 10–10 and Saturday 9 AM–10 PM; during gift-giving holiday seasons malls open on Sunday.

Areas

In **Centro,** Rua do Arouche is noted for leather goods. In **Itaim,** the area around Rua João Cachoeira has evolved from a neighborhood of small clothing factories into a wholesale- and retail-clothing sales district. Several shops on Rua Tabapuã sell small antiques. Also, Rua Dr. Mário Ferraz is stuffed with elegant clothing, gift, and home-decoration stores. **Jardins,** centering on Rua Augusta (which crosses Avenida Paulista) and Rua Oscar Freire, is the most chic area. Double-parked Mercedes-Benzes and BMWs point the way to the city's fanciest stores, which sell leather items, jewelry, gifts, antiques, and art. You'll also find many restaurants and beauty salons. Shops that specialize in high-price European antiques are on or around Rua da Consolação. A slew of lower-price antiques stores line Rua Cardeal Arcoverde in **Pinheiros.**

Department Store

Mappin, one of Brazil's biggest department stores, is especially crowded on Saturday. Lots of *camelôs* (street vendors) offer cassette tapes, T-shirts, and drawings in front of the building. ⊠ *Praça Ramos de Azevedo 131, Centro,* ☎ *011/214–4411. Metrô: Anhangabaú.*

Centers and Malls

D&D Decoração & Design Center. This complex shares a building with the world trade center and the Gran Meliá hotel. It's loaded with fancy decoration stores, full-scale restaurants, and fast-food spots. ⊠ *Av. das Nações Unidas 12555, Brooklin Novo,* ☎ *011/3043–9000.*
Shopping Center Iguatemi. The city's oldest and most sophisticated mall offers the latest in fashion and fast food. Four movie theaters often show American films in English with Portuguese subtitles. The Gero Café, built in the middle of the main hall, has a fine menu. ⊠ *Av. Brigadeiro Faria Lima 2232, Jardim Paulista,* ☎ *011/816–6116.*
Shopping Center Morumbi. Set in the city's fastest-growing area, Morumbi is giving Iguatemi a run for its money. That said, it houses about the same boutiques, record stores, bookstores, and restaurants as Iguatemi, though it has more movie theaters (a total of six). ⊠ *Av. Roque Petroni Jr. 1089, Morumbi,* ☎ *011/553–2444.*
Shopping Paulista. This mall has more than 200 stores and 4 movie theaters and is close to Avenida Paulista. You'll also find a currency exchange office and a tourist information center here. ⊠ *Rua 13 de Maio 1947, Paraíso,* ☎ *011/3178–7300. Metrô: Paraíso.*

Markets

Almost every neighborhood has a weekly outdoor food market (days are listed in local newspapers), complete with loud-mouthed hawkers, exotic scents, and piles of colorful produce.

On Sunday, there are **antiques fairs** near the Museu de Arte de São Paulo and (in the afternoon) at the Shopping Center Iguatemi's (☞ Centers and Malls, *above*) parking lot. Many stall owners have shops and hand out business cards so you can browse throughout the week at your leisure. An **arts and crafts fair**—selling jewelry, embroidery, leather goods, toys, clothing, paintings, and musical instruments—takes place Sunday morning in Centro's Praça da República. Many booths move over to the nearby Praça da Liberdade in the afternoon, joining vendors there selling Japanese-style ceramics, wooden sandals, cooking utensils, food, and bonsai trees. **Flea markets**—with second-hand furniture, clothes, and CDs—take place on Saturday at Praça Benedito Calixto in Pinheiros and on Sunday at the Praça Dom Orione in Bela Vista.

Specialty Shops

Antiques

Arte e Companhia. This collective of three dealers sells Latin American and European antiques. ⊠ *Rua Oscar Freire 146, Jardins,* ☎ *011/3064-1574.*

Patrimônio. Come here for Brazilian antiques at reasonable prices. It also sells some Indian artifacts as well as modern furnishings crafted from iron. ⊠ *Alameda Ministro Rocha Azevedo 1068, Jardins,* ☎ *011/3064-1750.*

Paulo Vasconcelos. Folk art and 18th- and 19th-century Brazilian furniture are among the finds here. ⊠ *Alameda Gabriel Monteiro da Silva 1881, Jardins,* ☎ *011/852-2444.*

Renato Magalhães Gouvêa Escritório de Arte. This shop offers a potpourri of European and Brazilian antiques, modern furnishings, and art. ⊠ *Av. Europa 68, Jardins,* ☎ *011/853-2569.*

Art

Arte Aplicada. For Brazilian paintings, sculptures, and prints, this is the place. ⊠ *Rua Haddock Lobo 1406, Jardins,* ☎ *011/852-5128.*

Camargo Vilaça. The staff here has an eye for the works of up-and-coming Brazilian artists. ⊠ *Rua Fradique Coutinho 1500, Vila Madalena,* ☎ *011/210-7390.*

Espaço Cultural Ena Beçak. Here you can shop for Brazilian prints, sculptures, and paintings and then stop in the café. ⊠ *Rua Oscar Freire 440, Jardins,* ☎ *011/280-7322.*

Galeria Jacques Ardies. If art naïf is your thing, then this place is a must. ⊠ *Rua do Livramento 221, Vila Mariana,* ☎ *011/884-2916. Metrô: Paraíso.*

Galeria Renot. Here you'll find oil paintings by such Brazilian artists as Vicente Rego Monteiro, Di Cavalcanti, Cícero Dias, and Anita Malfatti. ⊠ *Alameda Ministro Rocha Azevedo 1327, Jardins,* ☎ *011/883-5933.*

Galeria São Paulo. This gallery is a leader in contemporary, mainstream art. ⊠ *Rua Estados Unidos 1456, Jardins,* ☎ *011/852-8855.*

Mônica Filgueiras de Almeida. Many a trend has been set at this gallery. ⊠ *Alameda Ministro Rocha Azevedo 927, Jardins,* ☎ *011/282-5292.*

Clothing

Alexandre Herchovitch. Senhor Herchovitch is a famous Brazilian designer. His store has prête-à-porter and tailor-made clothes. ⊠ *Alameda Franca 631, Jardins,* ☎ *011/288-8005.*

Anacapri. This shop sells women's underwear, swimsuits, and clothes in large sizes. ☒ *Rua Juquis 276, Moema,* ☎ *011/532–1154.*

Cori. Everyday outfits with classic lines are the specialty here. ☒ *Rua Haddock Lobo 1584, Jardins,* ☎ *011/881–5223.*

Daslu. Here you can mingle with elite ladies who enjoy personalized attention. It's a "closed" (no storefront) designer-label boutique. ☒ *Rua Domingos Leme 284, Vila Nova Conceição,* ☎ *011/822–3785.*

Elite. Owned by the modeling agency of the same name, this store is a favorite among girls from 13 years old and up for dresses and sportswear. ☒ *Rua Oscar Freire 735, Jardins,* ☎ *011/282–9449.*

Ellus. This is a good place to buy men's and women's jeans, sportswear, and street wear. ☒ *Shopping Eldorado, 3rd Floor, Cerqueira César,* ☎ *011/815–4554.*

Fórum. Although it has a lot of evening attire for young men and women, this shop also sells sportswear and shoes. ☒ *Rua Oscar Freire 916, Jardins,* ☎ *011/853–6269.*

Le Lis Blanc. This shop is Brazil's exclusive purveyor of the French brand, Vertigo. Look for party dresses in velvet and sheer fabrics. ☒ *Rua Oscar Freire 809, Jardins,* ☎ *011/883–2549.*

Maria Bonita/Maria Bonita Extra. If you have a little money in your pocket, shop at Maria Bonita, which has elegant women's clothes with terrific lines. At Maria Bonita Extra, the prices are a little lower. ☒ *Rua Oscar Freire 702, Jardins,* ☎ *011/852–6433.*

Petistil. The younger family members aren't forgotten at this store, which sells clothes for infants and children up to 11 years old. ☒ *Rua Teodoro Sampaio 2271, Pinheiros,* ☎ *011/816–2865.*

Reinaldo Lourenço. The women's clothes here are sophisticated and of a high quality. ☒ *Rua Bela Cintra 2167, Jardins,* ☎ *011/853–8150.*

Richard's. This store carries one of Brazil's best lines of sportswear. Its collection includes outfits suitable for the beach or the mountains. ☒ *Alameda Franca 1185, Jardins,* ☎ *011/282–5399. Metrô: Consolação.*

Uma. Young women are intrigued by the unique designs of the swimsuits, dresses, shorts, shirts, and pants sold here. ☒ *Rua Girassol 273, Vila Madalena,* ☎ *011/813–5559.*

Vila Romana Factory Store. You can't beat the prices for suits, jackets, jeans, and some women's wear (silk blouses, for example) at this store, a 40-minute drive from Centro. The in-town branch is more convenient, but its prices are higher. ☒ *Via Anhanguera, Km 17.5,* ☎ *011/ 7201–2211.* ☒ *Rua Oscar Freire 697, Jardins,* ☎ *011/881–2919.*

Viva Vida. Long evening dresses—many done in shiny, sexy, exotic fabrics—steal the show here. ☒ *Rua Oscar Freire 969, Jardins,* ☎ *011/ 280–0421.*

Zoomp. This shop is famous for its jeans and high-quality street wear. Customers from 13 to 35 mix and match the clothes here, creating some unusual combinations. ☒ *Rua Oscar Freire 995, Jardins,* ☎ *011/ 3064–1556.*

Handicrafts

Alfândega. The owners travel the world collecting things to sell in their shop. Just about every continent is represented here, with such items as Indonesian dolls, painted Spanish bottles, and Brazilian pottery and candles. ☒ *Rua Ceará 124, Higienópolis,* ☎ *011/3662–4651.*

Art Índia. This government-run shop sells Indian arts and crafts made by tribes throughout Brazil. ☒ *Rua Augusta 1371, Loja 119, Cerqueira César,* ☎ *011/283–2102. Metrô: Consolação.*

Casa do Amazonas. As its name suggests, you'll find a wide selection of products from the Amazon in this store. ☒ *Galeria Metropôle, Av. São Luís 187, Loja 14, Centro,* ☎ *011/258–9727. Metrô: São Luís.*

Galeria de Arte Brasileira. This shop specializes in Brazilian handicrafts. Look for objects made of pau-brasil, hammocks, jewelry, T-shirts, *marajoara* pottery (from the Amazon), and lace. ⊠ *Alameda Lorena 2163, Jardins,* ☎ *011/852–9452.*

Jewelry

Antônio Bernardo. This store is owned by one of Brazil's top designers. His work includes both modern and classical pieces that use only precious stones. ⊠ *Rua Bela Cintra 2063, Jardins,* ☎ *011/883–5034.*
Atelier Cecília Rodrigues. This designer crafts unique pieces of gold and precious stones. ⊠ *Rua Horácio Lafer 767, Itaim Bibi,* ☎ *011/829–9394.*
Castro Bernardes. In addition to selling jewelry and precious stones, this store restores old pieces. ⊠ *Rua Jerônimo da Veiga 164, 19th floor, Itaim Bibi,* ☎ *011/280–6812.*

SÃO PAULO A TO Z

Arriving and Departing

By Airplane

São Paulo's international airport, **Cumbica** (☎ 011/6445–2945), is in the suburb of Guarulhos, 30 km (19 mi) and a 45-minute drive (longer during rush hour or on rainy days) northeast of Centro. **Aeroporto Congonhas** (☎ 011/536–3555, ext. 195), 14 km (9 mi) south of Centro (a 15- to 30-minute drive, depending on traffic), serves regional airlines, including the Rio–São Paulo shuttle. From June to September, both airports are sometimes fogged in during the early morning, and flights are rerouted to the **Aeroporto Viracopos** (☎ 0192/247–0909) in Campinas; passengers are transported by bus (an hour's ride) to São Paulo.

Aerolíneas Argentinas (011/214–4233) has daily flights from Buenos Aires and Madrid and twice-a-week service from Auckland, New Zealand, and Sydney, Australia. **Air France** (011/289–2133 or 011/945–2211) has a daily flight from Paris. **American Airlines** (011/214–4000 or 011/258–1244) offers three flights a day from Miami and one a day from both New York and Dallas. **British Airways** (011/259–6144) flies from London every day but Tuesday and Wednesday. **Canadian Airlines** (011/259–9066) flies from Toronto every day but Monday. **Continental Airlines** (0800/55–4777) flies from New York daily; **Delta Airlines** (0800/22–1121) has a daily flight from Atlanta. **United Airlines** (011/253–2323) flies daily from Miami, New York, and Chicago.

Rio Sul (011/231–9164) connects São Paulo with most major Brazilian cities daily. **TAM** (0800/12–3100) flies daily to most Brazilian capitals and major cities in São Paulo State. **Transbrasil** (011/231–1988) has daily flights to major U.S. cities, London, and the main Brazilian cities. **Varig** (011/5561–1161) has daily service to many U.S. and Brazilian cities; it also offers regular service to Toronto, London, Sydney, and Auckland. **VASP** (0800/99–8277) serves New York and many Brazilian cities daily, Miami six times a week, Toronto four times a week, and Los Angeles and Sydney three times a week.

FROM THE AIRPORTS INTO TOWN

EMTU *executivo* **buses** (☎ 011/945–2505)—fancy, green-stripe, "executive" vehicles—shuttle between Cumbica and Congonhas (6 AM–10 PM, every 30 min) as well as between Cumbica and the Tietê bus terminal (5:40 AM–10 PM, every 45 min); the downtown Praça da República (5:30 AM–11 PM, every 30 min); and the Hotel Maksoud Plaza (6:45 AM–11 PM every 35 min), stopping at most major hotels on

Avenida Paulista. The cost is $7. **Municipal buses,** with CMTC painted on the side, stop at the airport and go downtown by various routes, such as via Avenida Paulista, to the Praça da Sé and Tietê bus station.

The sleek, blue-and-white, air-conditioned **Guarucoop radio taxis** (☎ 011/208–1881) will take you from Cumbica to downtown for around $40; the fare to town from Congonhas is about $16. **Comum** (regular) taxis also charge $40 from Cumbica and around $12 from Congonhas. **Fleet Car Shuttle** (counter at Cumbica Airport's arrivals Terminal 1, ☎ 011/945–3030), open daily 6 AM–midnight, serves groups of up to 10 people in a van, stopping at one destination of choice. The fee (for the van load) is about $70.

By Bus

Combined, São Paulo's four **bus stations** (☎ 011/235–0322 for information on all stations) serve 1,105 destinations. The main station—serving all major Brazilian cities (with trips to Rio every half-hour on the half-hour) as well as Paraguay, Argentina, Uruguay, and Chile—is the **Terminal Tietê** (✉ Av. Cruzeiro do Sul) in the north, on the Marginal Tietê Beltway. **Terminal Bresser** (✉ Rua do Hipódromo), in the eastern district of Brás, serves southern Minas Gerais State and Belo Horizonte. **Terminal Jabaquara** (✉ Rua Jequitibas), near Congonhas airport, serves coastal towns. **Terminal Barra Funda** (✉ Rua Mário de Andrade 664) in the west, near the Memorial da América Latina, has buses to and from western Brazil. All stations have or are close to metrô stops. You can buy tickets at the stations; although those for Rio de Janeiro can be bought a few minutes before departure, it's best to buy tickets in advance for other destinations and during holiday seasons.

By Car

The main São Paulo–Rio de Janeiro highway is the Via Dutra (BR 116 North), which has recently been repaved and enlarged in places. The speed limit is 120 kph (74 mph) along most of it, and although it has many tolls, you'll find many call boxes that you can use if your car breaks down. The modern Rodoviária dos Trabalhdores (SP 70) charges reasonable tolls, runs parallel to the Dutra for about a quarter of the way, and is an excellent alternative route. The 429-km (279-mi) trip takes five hours. If you have time, consider the longer, spectacular, coastal Rio–Santos Highway (SP 55 and BR 101). It's an easy two-day drive, and you can stop midway at the colonial city of Parati in Rio de Janeiro State.

Other main highways are the Castelo Branco (SP 280), which links the southwestern part of the state to the city; the Via Anhanguera (SP 330), which originates in the state's rich northern agricultural region, passing through the university town of Campinas; SP 310, which also runs from the farming heartland; BR 116 South, which comes up from Curitiba (a 408 km/265 mi trip); plus the Via Anchieta (SP 150) and the Rodovia Imigrantes (SP 160), parallel roads that run to the coast, each operating one way on weekends and holidays.

By Train

Most travel to the interior of the state is done by bus or automobile. Still, a few places are served by trains. Trains from **Estação da Luz** (✉ Praça da Luz 1, ☎ 011/991–3062), near 25 de Março, run to some metropolitan suburbs and small interior towns. Trains from **Estação Barra Funda** (✉ Rua Mário de Andrade 664, ☎ 011/7082–1100) serve towns in the west of the state. **Estação Júlio Prestes** (✉ Praça Júlio Prestes 148, ☎ 011/223–7211), in Campos Eliseos, has trains to the southeast and some suburbs. **Estação Roosevelt** (✉ Praça Agente Cícero, ☎ 011/292–5417) serves the suburbs only.

Getting Around

By Bus

There's ample **municipal bus service** (0800/12–3133 transit information), but regular buses (white with a red horizontal stripe) are overcrowded at rush hour and when it rains. Stops are clearly marked, but
routes are spelled out only on the buses themselves. The fare is about
60¢. You enter at the front, pay the *cobrador* (fare collector) in the
middle, and exit the back. Often the cobrador has no change, and gives
out *vale transporte* slips, or fare vouchers (with no expiration time).

The green-and-gray **SPTrans executivo** buses (☎ 158), whose numer-
ical designations all end with the letter *E,* are more spacious and cost
around $2 (you pay the driver upon entry). Many *clandestino* (unli-
censed, privately run buses) traverse the city. Although not very pleas-
ing to the eye—most are battered, white vehicles that have no signs—it's
perfectly fine to take them; they charge the same as SPTrans buses.

For bus numbers and names, routes, and schedules for SPTrans buses,
purchase the *Guia São Paulo Ruas,* published by *Quatro Rodas* magazine and sold at newsstands and bookstores for about $10.

By Car

Driving isn't recommended in São Paulo because of the heavy traffic
(nothing moves at rush hour, especially when it rains), dare-devil drivers, and inadequate parking. If, however, you do opt to drive, there
are a few things to keep in mind. Most of São Paulo is between the
Rio Tietê and the Rio Pinheiros, which converge in the western part
of town. The high-speed routes along these rivers are Marginal Tietê
and Marginal Pinheiros. There are also *marginais* (beltways) around
the city. Avenida 23 de Maio runs south from Centro and beneath the
Parque do Ibirapuera via the Ayrton Senna Tunnel. You can take
Avenida Paulista, Avenida Brasil, and Avenida Faria Lima southwest
to the Morumbi, Brooklin, Itaim, and Santo Amaro neighborhoods.
The Elevado Costa e Silva, also called Minhocão, is an elevated road
that connects Centro with Avenida Francisco Matarazzo in the west.

In most commercial neighborhoods you must buy hourly tickets (called
Cartão Zona Azul) to park on the street during business hours. Only
buy them at newsstands, not from people on the street. Booklets of 20
tickets cost $10. Fill out each ticket—you'll need one for every hour
you plan to park—with the car's license plate and the time you initially parked. Leave all tickets in the car's window so that they're visible to the officials from outside. After business hours or at any time
near major sights, people may offer to watch your car. Although paying these "caretakers" about $1 is enough to keep your car's paint job
intact, to truly ensure its safety opt for a parking lot. Rates are $5–$7
for the first hour and $1–$2 each hour thereafter.

Car rental rates range from $50 to $100 a day. Major rental companies include: **Avis** (⊠ Rua da Consolação 335, Centro, ☎ 011/258–
8833), **Hertz** (⊠ Rua da Consolação 439, Centro, ☎ 011/256–9722),
or **Localiza** (⊠ Rua da Consolação 419, Centro, ☎ 011/231–3055).

By Metrô

The **metrô** (☎ 011/284–8877 for general information) is safe, quick,
comfortable, and clean, but unfortunately it doesn't serve many of the
city's southern districts. The blue line runs north–south, the orange line
runs east–west, and the green line runs under Avenida Paulista from
Vila Mariana to the new stations at Sumaré and Vila Madalena, near
Avenida Pompéia. The metrô operates daily 5 AM–midnight. Tickets
are sold in stations and cost 80¢ one way. (You can get discounts on

round-trip fares and when you buy 10 tickets at once; note that ticket sellers aren't required to change large bills.) You insert the ticket into the turnstile at the platform entrance, and it's returned to you only if there's unused fare on it. Transfers within the metrô system are free, and for bus–metrô trips (one bus only), you can buy a *bilhete integração* on buses or at metrô stations for $1.50. Maps of the metrô system are available from the **Departamento de Marketing Institucional** (⊠ Av. Paulista 1842, 19th Floor, ☎ 011/283–4933), or you can pick up the *Guia São Paulo* at newsstands and bookstores.

By Taxi
Most taxis in São Paulo are white. Owner-driven taxis are generally well maintained and reliable as are radio taxis. Fares start at $1.75 and 50¢ for each kilometer (½ mi) or 25¢ for every minute sitting in traffic. After 8 PM fares rise by 20%. You'll also pay a tax if the taxi leaves the city as is the case with trips to Cumbica Airport. Good radio-taxi companies include **Chame Taxi** (☎ 011/865–3033), **Ligue-Taxi** (☎ 011/262–2633), and **Paulista** (☎ 011/846–6555).

Contacts and Resources

Banks and Currency Exchange
Avenida Paulista is the home of many banks (generally open 10–4), including **Citibank** (⊠ Av. Paulista 1111, Jardins, ☎ 011/576–1190). For currency exchange services without any extra fees try **Action** (⊠ Guarulhos Airport, TPS2 arrival floor, ☎ 011/6445–4458; ⊠ Rua Melo Alves 357, Jardins, ☎ 011/3064–2910; and ⊠ Shopping Paulista, Rua 13 de Maio 1947, Paraíso, ☎ 011/288–4222). In Centro, you can exchange money at **Banco do Brasil** (⊠ Av. São João 32, ☎ 011/234–1646) and **Banespa** (⊠ Rua Duque de Caxias 200, ☎ 011/222–7722). Several banks have automatic teller machines (ATMs) that accept international bank cards and dispense reais.

Business Services
At press time, the **U.S. Commercial Center** (☎ 011/853–2811 for Miguel Pardoezela, Senior Commercial Officer), an arm of the U.S. Department of Commerce, was slated to open a state-of-the-art facility for American businesspeople. It will have fully equipped offices with secretarial support, a library, trade events organizers, meeting rooms, and computer and teleconferencing facilities.

Consulates
Australia (⊠ Av. Tenente Negrão 140/121, 12th Floor, Itaim Bibi, ☎ 011/829–6281). **Canada** (⊠ Av. Paulista 1106, 1st floor, Cerqueira César, ☎ 011/285–5099). **New Zealand** (⊠ Rua Pais de Araújo 29, 12th floor, Jardim Europa, ☎ 011/820–5532). **United Kingdom** (⊠ Av. Paulista 1938, 17th floor, Cerqueira César, ☎ 011/287–7722). **United States** (⊠ Rua Padre João Manoel 933, Jardins, ☎ 011/881–6511).

Emergencies
Ambulance: ☎ 192. **Fire:** ☎ 193. **Hospitals: Albert Einstein** (⊠ Av. Albert Einstein 627, Morumbi, ☎ 011/845–1233), **Beneficência Portuguesa** (⊠ Rua Maestro Cardim 769, Paraíso, ☎ 011/253–5022), and **Sírio Libanês** (⊠ Rua. D. Adma Jafet 91, Bela Vista, ☎ 011/234–8877). **Pharmacies:** The three main pharmacies have more than 20 stores, each open 24 hours. Try: **Droga Raia** (⊠ Rua Joaquim Nabuco 84, Brooklin, ☎ 011/240–0584), **Drogaria São Paulo** (⊠ Av. Angélica 1465, Higienópolis, ☎ 011/3667–6291), and **Drogasil** (⊠ Av. Brigadeiro Faria Lima 2726, Cidade Jardim, ☎ 011/212–6276). **Police (Military):** ☎ 190. **Tourist Police:** The **Delegacia de Turismo** (⊠ Av. São Luís 115, Centro, ☎ 011/254–3561 or 011/214–0209) is open weekdays 8–8.

English-Language Bookstores

Most Avenida Paulista newsstands sell major U.S. and European papers as well as magazines and paperbacks in English. **Livraria Cultura** has a large selection of English books of all types in its store at Conjunto Nacional (✉ Av. Paulista 2073/153, Cerqueira César, ☎ 011/285–4033). **Ática Shopping Cultural** (✉ Rua Pedroso de Morais 858, Pinheiros, ☎ 011/867–0022) sells many international books and periodicals. **Laselva** (✉ Shopping West Plaza, Av. Francisco Matarazzo, Água Branca, ☎ 011/864–0037) usually receives magazines from abroad earlier than other bookstores. **Saraiva**'s (✉ Shopping Eldorado, Av. Rebouças 3970, Pinheiros, ☎ 011/870–5999) megastore also has English-language titles.

Health and Safety

Don't drink tap water in São Paulo. Ask for juice and ice made with bottled water in restaurants and bars. Don't eat barbecued meats sold by street vendors; even those made in some bars are suspect. The city's air pollution might irritate your eyes, especially in July and August (dirty air is held in the city by thermal inversions), so pack eye drops. Stay alert and guard your belongings at all times, especially at major sights. Avoid wearing shorts, expensive running shoes, or flashy jewelry—all of which attract attention. Also beware of the local scam in which one person throws a dark liquid on you and another offers to help you clean up while the first *really* cleans up!

Telephones, the Internet, and Mail

Phone booths are bright green and yellow. Most operate using prepaid cards, but some still use tokens. Both cards and tokens are sold at newsstands. Cards with 20 credits are sold for $1.17. Each credit allows you to talk for 3 minutes on local calls and 17 seconds on long-distance calls.

International calls can be made at special phone booths found in Telesp offices around the city. You can choose your own long-distance company. After dialing 0, dial a two-digit company code, followed by the country code and/or area code and number. To call Rio, for example, dial 0, then 21 (for Embratel, a major long-distance provider), then 21 (Rio's area code) and the number. To call the United States, dial 00 (for international calls), 23 (for Bonari, another long-distance company), 1 (country code) and the area code and phone number. For operator assisted (in English) international calls, dial 000111. To make a collect long-distance call (which will cost 40% more than normal calls), dial 9 + the area code and the number. São Paulo's area code is 11; phone numbers in the city and state have six, seven, or eight digits. Most cellular phone numbers have eight digits (a few have seven) and start with the number "9."

Internet access is available at many cybercafés (☞ Nightlife, *above*) around town. There's a branch of the *correio* (post office; ✉ Praça do Correio, ☎ 011/831–5522) in Centro. International couriers include **DHL** (✉ Rua da Consolação 2721, Jardins, ☎ 011/536–2500) and **FedEx** (✉ Av. São Luís 187, Loja 43, Centro, ☎ 011/524–7788).

Tour Operators and Travel Agents

You can hire a bilingual guide through a travel agency or hotel concierge (about $15 an hour with a four-hour minimum), or you can design your own walking tour with the aid of information provided at **Anhembi** (☞ Visitor Information, *below*) booths around the city. Anhembi also offers Sunday tours of museums, parks, and Centro that are less expensive than those offered in hotels. At press time, the **tourist board** (☎ 011/267–2122 ext. 640 or 011/267–0702) was planning to offer three different half-day Sunday bus tours. Officially, none of their guides speaks English, however they may be able to arrange something upon request.

Gol Tour Viagens e Turismo (⊠ Av. São Luís 187, Basement, Loja 12, Centro, ☎ 011/256–2388) and **Opcional Tour and Guide Viagens e Turismo** (⊠ Av. Ipiranga 345, 14th floor, suite 1401, Centro, ☎ 011/259–1007) offer custom tours as well as car tours for small groups. A half-day city tour costs about $40 a person (group rate); a night tour—including a samba show, dinner, and drinks—costs around $100; and day trips to the beach or the colonial city of Embu cost $80–$90. The English-speaking staff at **Savoy** (⊠ Rua James Watt 142, suite 92, Itaim Bibi, ☎ 011/5507–2064 or 011/5507–2065) specializes in personalized tours.

TOURS OUTSIDE SÃO PAULO

Canoar (⊠ Rua Caetés 410, Sumaré, ☎ 011/3871–2282) is one of the best rafting tour operators in São Paulo State. **Trilha Brazil** (⊠ Rua Professor Rubião Meira 86, Jardim América, ☎ 011/282–7089) arranges treks in forests around São Paulo. Reputable operators that offer rainforest, beach, and island excursions include **Biotrip** (⊠ Rua Gama Cerqueira 187, ☎ 011/278–1122), **Pisa Trekking** (⊠ Alameda dos Tupiniquins 202, Moema, ☎ 011/571–2525), and **Venturas e Aventuras** (⊠ Rua Minerva 268, Perdizes, ☎ 011/3872–0362).

Visitor Information

The most helpful contact is the **São Paulo Convention and Visitors Bureau** (⊠ Rua Dom José de Barros 17, Centro, ☎ 011/255–4600). The sharp, business-minded director, Roberto Gheler, speaks English flawlessly and is extremely knowledgeable.

The branches of the city-operated **Anhembi Turismo e Eventos da Cidade de São Paulo** (⊠ Anhembi Convention Center, Av. Olavo Fontoura 1209, ☎ 011/267–0702; ⊠ Praça da República at Rua 7 de Abril, Centro, ☎ 011/231–2922; ⊠ Av. São Luís at Praça Dom José Gaspar, Centro, ☎ 011/257–3422); ⊠ Av. Paulista, across from MASP, Cerqueira César, ☎ 011/231–2922; ⊠ Av. Brigadeiro Faria Limain, in front of Shopping Center Iguatemi, Jardim Paulista, ☎ 011/211–1277) are open daily 9–6.

The bureaucracy-laden **Secretaria de Esportes e Turismo do Estado de São Paulo** (SEST; ⊠ Praça Antônio Prado 9, Centro, ☎ 011/239–5822), open weekdays 9–5:30, has maps and information about the city and state of São Paulo. SEST also has a booth at the arrivals terminal in Cumbica airport; it's open daily 9 AM–10 PM.

SIDE TRIPS FROM SÃO PAULO

Several destinations just outside São Paulo are perfect for short getaways. Itu is a historical city full of museums and churches. Ilhabela is off the coast from São Sebastião on the state's North Shore. The island is part of the Mata Atlântica (Atlantic Rain Forest) and is known for its many waterfalls, trails, and diving spots. Embu's weekend crafts fair and many furniture stores are famous. Although paulistanos often come here for a weekend, you can see all the sights in an afternoon. If you like mountains, try Campos de Jordão; its cafés and clothing stores are often crowded with oh-so chic paulistanos.

Itu

90 km (55 mi) northwest of São Paulo.

This Portuguese colonial town is famous for its 18th-century churches, loads of antiques stores, and a tendency to exaggerate; after a televi-

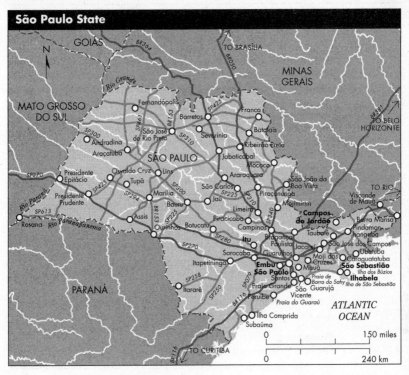

São Paulo State

sion comedian from Itu made his career in the 1960s with a routine about how things in his town were bigger than anywhere else, the local chamber of commerce capitalized on the idea and built an oversize traffic light and pay phone. The gimmick still pays off at local stores, where giant hats, pencils, and other gargantuan items are sold. To make the 50-minute drive to Itu, take the Rodovia Castello Branco to SP 312 west, which runs right through town.

Near the entrance to town is the **Igreja do Bom Jesus** (The Church of the Good Jesus; ⊠ Praça Padre Anchieta, ☎ 011/7822–3871). It's on the site of an earlier chapel that marked the foundation of Itu in 1610. The city grew around this church, and its interior is a gallery of paintings and marble work.

Just two blocks down Rua Paula Souza from Igreja do Bom Jesus is another church, the **Igreja Nossa Senhora de Candelária** (⊠ Praça Padre Miguel, ☎ 011/7823–0638), which was built in 1780. It has paintings by Brazilian artists José Ferraz de Almeida Junior and Padre Jesuíno do Monte Carmelo. The ceiling has 14 paintings by Italian artist Lavínia Cereda.

★ As you leave Praça Padre Miguel you'll come to the **Museu Republicano** (⊠ Rua Barão de Itaim 67, ☎ FAX 011/7823–0240), site of the Itu Convention, the first official republican meeting in Brazi, at which 133 politicians gathered in 1873. The museum keeps furniture from the 19th century and from the office of Prudente de Morais, the first civil Brazilian president. On the first floor, a tiled wall shows some key facts of the country history. The small garden at one side of the building was inspired by those at Versailles.

Just out of the center of town is the ☾ **Parque do Varvito** (☒ Access through Rua Doutor Graciano Geribello), built around a geological site. The park has some small waterfalls, a lake, and an amphitheater.

Dining and Lodging

$$$$ ✕ **Steiner.** This restaurant has been in business since 1902, and today it's managed by the fourth generation of the same family. The *filé à parmegiana* (filet mignon with ham and cheese) attracts people from throughout the area. Lines are frequent on weekends. ☒ *Alameda Jaú 1606,* ☎ *011/853–5573. AE, DC. No lunch Sat. Closed Sun.*

$$$$ ▦ **San Raphael Country.** Large, landscaped lawns surround this Portuguese colonial-style hotel. The reception area has a modern look, with contemporary paintings on the walls; room decor varies, though some rooms have wooden furniture and tapestries. Staff members are very friendly and can speak some English. ☒ *Av. Tiradentes 2223 13300-000,* ☎ *011/7824–2821,* ℻ *011/7824–1915. 87 rooms. Restaurant, bar, indoor-outdoor pool, sauna, tennis court, exercise room, horseback riding, soccer, recreation room. AE, DC, MC, V.*

$$$ ▦ **Maktub.** A Middle Eastern–style decor and a green, beige, and brown color scheme dominate this four-story hotel. It's frequently the site of business meetings. ☒ *Rua Capitão Fleming 135 13309-010,* ☎ *011/7823–2323,* ℻ *011/7823–1013. 36 rooms. Restaurant, bar, air-conditioning, refrigerators, pool, recreation room, convention center. AE, DC, MC, V.*

Shopping

Several shops around Praça da Independência sell the gigantic items that made the town famous: combs, pencils, matches. The antiques and furniture stores are on Rua Paula Souza. **A.R. Antiguidades** (☒ Rua Paula Souza 558, ☎ 011/7823–0347) sells furniture and **Ribeiro Pavani** (☒ Rua Paula Souza 582, ☎ 011/7822–5856) has garden chairs. The staff at these shops can help arrange deliveries abroad.

Ilhabela

São Sebastião is 210 km (130 mi) southeast of São Paulo; Ilhabela is 7 km (5 mi) off the shore (a 15-min boat ride) of São Sebastião.

Ilhabela is favored by those who like the beach and water sports; indeed, many championship competitions are held here. Beaches along the western shore are calm. The hotels are mostly at the north end, though the best sandy stretches are to the south. Scuba divers have six wrecks to explore, and hikers will appreciate the abundance of inland trails that often lead to a waterfall (the island has more than 300 of them). Note that mosquitoes are a problem; bring plenty of insect repellent.

There are two small towns in the island: one is where the locals live, the other is where most visitors stay owing to its hotels, restaurants, and stores. The best way to get around Ilhabela is by car, which you must rent on the mainland. The ferry from São Sebastião transports vehicles as well as passengers to the island.

Praia Grande is 6 km (4 mi) south of the ferry dock and has a long sandy strip with food kiosks, a soccer field, and a small church. At night, people gather 6 km (4 mi) farther south in **Praia do Curral,** where there are many restaurants and bars—some with live music—as well as places to camp. The ship *Aymoré* is sunk off the coast of this beach, near the Ponta do Ribeirão.

A small church and many fishing boats add to the charm of **Praia da Armação,** 14 km (9 mi) north of the ferry dock. The beach was once the hub for processing whales that were caught in the waters around the island. Today, windsurfers stick to capturing the wind and the waves.

To reach **Baía dos Castelhanos,** 22 km (14 mi) east of the ferry dock, you need a four-wheel-drive vehicle; if it rains, even this won't be enough. Consider arriving here by sailboat, a 1½- to 3-hour trip that can be arranged through local tour operators. With such an isolated location, you can see why slave ships once used the bay to unload their illicit cargo after slavery was banned in Brazil. If you're lucky, you might spot a dolphin here.

Dining and Lodging

$$ ★ ✕ **Viana.** This restaurant serves *camarão* (shrimp) prepared in several ways as well as grilled fish. They have few tables, so reservations are recommended. ✉ *Av. Leonardo Reale 1560,* ☎ *012/472–1089. V. Closed Mon.–Thurs. Apr.–June and Aug.–Oct.*

$$$ ★ ▦ **Maison Joly.** Upon arrival here, you're given a "beach kit" complete with mosquito repellent and a hat. Each room is equipped with something that gives it a theme such as a piano, a billiards table, or a telescope. ✉ *Rua Antônio Lisboa Alves 278, Morro do Cantagalo,* ☎ *012/ 472–1201,* ℻ *012/472–2364. 10 rooms. Restaurant, bar, air-conditioning, in-room safes, pool. AE.*

$$ ★ ▦ **Pousada dos Hibiscos.** Set north of the ferry dock, this red house offers mid-size, air-conditioned rooms. The friendly staff serves up a good breakfast and provides pool-side bar service as well. ✉ *Av. Pedro de Paula Morais714,* ☎ ℻ *012/472–1375. 13 rooms. Restaurant, bar, air-conditioning, refrigerators, pool, sauna. DC, MC.*

Outdoor Activities and Sports

BOATING AND SAILING
Because of its excellent winds and currents, Ilhabela is a sailor's mecca. You can arrange boating and sailing trips through **Pesca, Merculho, Náutica & Cia.** (✉ Av. Princesa Isabel 1338, Ilhabela, ☎ 012/974–4704) and **Dick Sail** (✉ Rua Antonio de Macedo Soares 1942, São Paulo, ☎ 011/543–1345).

Ilhabela hosts several annual boating competitions, including a large Sailing Week. For more information on this and other events, contact the **late Club de Ilhabela** (✉ Av. Força Expedicionária Brasileira 299, ☎ 012/472–2300). If you'd like to learn to sail, **Ilha Sailing Ocean School** (✉ Av. Pedro Paula de Moraes 578, Hotel da Praia, ☎ 012/472–1992) has 12-hour courses that cost roughly $120.

HIKING
The **Trilha da Água Branca** (✉ Park administration: Rua do Morro da Cruz 608, Itaguaçú Beach, ☎ ℻ 012/472–2660) is an accessible, well-marked trail. Three of its paths go to waterfalls that have natural pools and picnic areas. You can arrange a guided hike through the park administration. Another option is the **Cachoeira dos Três Tombos** trail. It starts at Feiticeira Beach and leads to three waterfalls.

SCUBA DIVING
Ilhabela has several good dive sites off its shores. In 1894, the British ship *Dart* sank near Itaboca, about 17 km (11 mi) south of the ferry dock; it still contains bottles of wine and porcelain dishes. Recommended for beginners is the sanctuary (which has a statue of Neptune at a depth of 22 ft) off the shore of **Ilha das Cabras,** a nearby islet. The **Ilha de Búzios** is a good place to see a variety of marine life. You can rent equipment and arrange for a dive boat trip through **Discover Dive** (✉ Av. Força Expedicionária Brasileira 147, ☎ 012/472–1999).

SURFING

The best places to surf are Baía de Castelhanos (22 km/14 mi east of the ferry dock) and Pacuíba (20 km/12 mi north of the ferry dock). The **Associação de Surf de Ilhabela** (⊠ Rua Espírito Santo 170, Barra Velha, ☎ 011/534–0737 pager number; the code is 406–8315 and you can leave a message for Daniel or Nino) promotes surfing events on the island.

WINDSURFING

Savvy windsurfers head to Ponta das Canas, at the island's northern tip. Praia do Pinto and Armação (about 12 km/7 mi north of the ferry dock) are also good places. You can take lessons at **BL3** (⊠ Engenho D'Água Beach, ☎ 012/472–1034; ⊠ Armação Beach, ☎ 012/472–1271).

Campos do Jordão

184 km (114 mi) northeast of São Paulo.

Set in the Serra da Mantiqueira at an altitude of 5,576 ft, Campos do Jordão and its fresh mountain air have attracted visitors for years. In July the temperatures drop as low as 32°F (0°C), though it never snows; in warmer months, temperatures linger in the 13°C–16°C (55°F–60°F) range. Some people come here for their health (the town was once a tuberculosis treatment area), others for inspiration, including such Brazilian artists as the writer Monteiro Lobato, the dramatist Nelson Rodrigues, and the painter Lasar Segall. The arts continue to thrive here, especially during July's Festival de Inverno (Winter Festival), which draws classical musicians from around the world.

Boulevard Genéve, in the busy Vila Capivari district, is lined with cafés, bars, and restaurants, making it a nightlife hub. You'll also find many candy shops (particularly those that sell chocolate) and clothing stores.

The **Palácio Boa Vista** (⊠ Rua Dr. Adhemar de Barros 300, ☎ 012/262–1122), the official winter residence of the state's governor, has paintings by such famous Brazilian artists as Di Cavalcanti, Portinari, Volpi Tarsila do Amaral, and Anita Malfatti. The **Capela de São Pedro** (São Pedro Chapel) has sacred art from the 17th and 18th centuries. Admission is free.

The **Horto Florestal** (Forest Park; ⊠ Av. Pedro Paulo, ☎ 012/263–1414) has a trout-filled river, waterfalls, and trails all set among trees from around the world. It's a natural playground for *macacos-prego* (nail monkeys), squirrels, and parrots as well as people.

A chair-lift ride to the top of the **Morro do Elefante** (Elephant Mountain), north of town, is a good way to enjoy the outdoors. You can climb the 370-step iron staircase to the **Pedra do Baú** (Trunk Stone), also north of town. An easy trail starts in São Bento de Sapucaí.

Dining and Lodging

$$$ ✕ **Baden-Baden.** One of the specialties at this charming German restaurant in the heart of town is fondue *misto* (with a variety of meats). ⊠ *Rua Djalma Forjaz 93, Vila Capivari,* ☎ *012/263–3610. AE, MC, V.*

$$ ✕ **Itália Cantina e Ristorante.** As its name suggests, this place specializes in Italian food. The pasta and the meat dishes are delicious. ⊠ *Av. Macedo Soares 306, Capivari,* ☎ *012/263–1140. AE, DC, MC, V.*

$$ ✕ **Linz's Café.** The Austrian fare and the wine list draw an elegant crowd here. Rahm schnitzel (filet mignon in a paprika sauce with champignons and potatoes) is highly recommended. ⊠ *Rua Djalma Forjaz 140, Capivari,* ☎ *012/983–8568. No credit cards.*

OS BANDEIRANTES

I N THE 16TH AND 17TH centuries, groups called *bandeiras* (literally "flags"; it's an archaic term for an assault force) set out on expeditions from São Paulo. Although the *bandeirantes* (bandeira members) are remembered as heroes, their objectives were far from noble. Their initial goal was to enslave Indians. Later, they were hired to capture escaped African slaves and destroy *quilombos*, communities these slaves created deep in the interior. Still, by heading inland at a time when most colonies were close to the shore, the bandeirantes did Brazil a great service.

A fierce breed, they often adopted Indian customs and voyaged for years at a time. Some went as far as the Amazon River; others only to what is today Minas Gerais, where gold was discovered; still others found deposits of precious gems. In their travels, they ignored the 1494 Treaty of Tordesillas, which established a boundary between Spanish and Portuguese lands. (The boundary was a vague north–south line roughly 1,600 km/1,000 mi west of the Cape Verde islands; the Portuguese were to control all lands—discovered and yet to be discovered—east of this line and the Spanish all lands to the west of it.) Other Brazilians followed the bandeirantes, and towns were founded, often in what was technically Spanish territory. These colonists eventually claimed full possession of the lands they settled, and thus, Brazil's borders were greatly expanded.

$$$ 🏨 **Lausanne Hotel.** Set on an enormous green 7 km (4 mi) outside town, this hotel offers plenty of solitude and the chance to commune with nature. ⊠ *Rodovia SP 50, Km 176, Vila Santa Cruz 12460-000,* ☎ *012/262–2900,* FAX *011/883–1016 in São Paulo. 26 rooms. Restaurant, bar, air-conditioning, pool, tennis court, game room. V.*

$$$ 🏨 **Pousada Vila Capivary.** A stay at this cozy guest house puts you in the gastronomic and commercial center of Campos. The friendly staff is helpful and efficient. ⊠ *Av. Victor Godinho 131, Vila Capivari 12460-000,* ☎ *012/263–1746,* FAX *012/263–1736. 10 rooms, 5 suites. Hot tub. AE, DC, MC, V.*

Shopping
Casa de Chocolates Montanhês (⊠ Av. Macedo Soares 123, Loja 08, Capivari, ☎ 012/263–3205) is a well-known chocolate shop. **Geléia dos Monges** (⊠ Rua TadeuRangel Pestana 506, ☎ no phone) sells delicious jellies. You'll find clothing at **Geneve Factory** (⊠ Rod. Floriano R. Pinheiro 1801, Vila Cristina, ☎ 012/262–3466) and the **Geneve Store** (⊠ Rua Djalma Forjaz 100, Lojas 01 and 03, Capivari, ☎ 012/263–2520). For knit items, try **Paloma Malhas** (⊠ Rua Djalma Forjaz 78, Loja 11, Capivari, ☎ 012/263–1218).

Embu

27 km (17 mi) west of São Paulo.

Embu is a Portuguese colonial town of whitewashed houses, old churches, wood-carvers' studios, and antiques shops. A huge downtown handicrafts fair is held here every Saturday and Sunday (on Sunday the streets are so crowded you can barely walk). Embu also has many stores that sell handicrafts and wooden furniture; most of these are close to where the street fair takes place.

🐦 In the Mata Atlântica you can visit the **Cidade das Abelhas** (City of the Bees), a bee farm with a small museum. You can buy honey while your kids climb the gigantic model of a bee. The farm is about 10 minutes from downtown; just follow the signs. ⊠ *Estrada da Ressaca 9,* ☎ *011/493–6460.* 🎟 *Admission.* ⊙ *Tues.–Sun. 8–6.*

The baroque **Igreja Nossa Senhora do Rosário** was built in the 18th century. The church contains many images of saints as well as a museum of sacred art. ⊠ *Largo dos Jesuítas 67,* ☎ *011/494–5333.* 🎟 *Free.* ⊙ *Tues.–Sun.*

Dining

$$ ✕ **Celas.** Pull up one of the wooden chairs here and prepare to feast on the food of either Minas Gerais or Bahia. ⊠ *Largo 21 de Abril 75,* ☎ *011/494–5791. No credit cards.*

$$ ✕ **Churrascaria Gaúcha.** This roadside barbecue place is inspired by the *churrascarias* of Brazil's south. If meat isn't your thing, check out the large, all-you-can-eat salad bar. ⊠ *Via Régis Bittencourt, Km 280,* ☎ *011/494–2961. AE, DC, MC, V.*

Shopping

For art, stop by **Atelier Kavalete** (⊠ Rua Nossa Senhora do Rosário 95, ☎ no phone), which has pieces from throughout Brazil, or **Cantão Galeria** (⊠ Largo dos Jesuítas 169, ☎ no phone), which specializes in works by local artists. For handicrafts and/or furniture, try **Artes e Agrados** (⊠ Largo dos Jesuítas 137, ☎ no phone), **Cabana do Cigano**(⊠ Av. Elias Yazbek 1266, ☎ no phone), **Cantão Móveis e Galeria** (⊠ Largo dos Jesuítas 169, ☎ no phone), **Decorações Mercante** (⊠ Rua Nossa Senhora do Rosário 75, ☎ no phone), and **Guarany Artesanato** (⊠ Largo dos Jesuítas 153, ☎ no phone).

Side Trips from São Paulo A to Z

Arriving and Departing

BY BOAT

The **ferry** (☎ 0800/55–5510) from São Sebastião to Ilhabela accepts reservations. It's worth making them, particularly from December to February. They run every 20 minutes from 5:30 AM to 1 AM weekdays; weekends see 24-hour service. The fare is $5 with a car.

BY BUS

Viação Vale do Tietê (☎ 011/3824–9082) buses run to Itu every hour from São Paulo's Barra Funda station. **Viação Litorânea** (☎ 011/6972–0244) buses leave Tietê station five times for the trip to Ilhabela. **Viação Mantiqueira** (☎ 011/6972–0244) buses travel to Campos do Jordão every two hours from Tietê. Every half-hour **Soamin** (☎ 011/7947–1423) buses depart for Embu from one of several São Paulo locations.

BY CAR

Roads in São Paulo State are in good condition and are well marked; some of them are toll roads. Itu is 1½ hours from town on SP 280 and SP 300. The drive from São Paulo to São Sebastião is about 2½ hours; take the Rodovia Ayrton Senna, followed by the Rodovia Tamoios to Caraguatatuba, and then follow the signs. To reach Campos do Jordão from the city (a 2½-hour drive), take the Rodovia Carvalho Pinto and SP 123. To make the 30-minute drive from São Paulo to Embu, take Avenida Professor Francisco Morato to the Rodovia Régis Bittencourt and then follow the signs.

Getting Around

In Itu, everything is close so the best way to get around is on foot. Although the best way to get around Ilhabela is by car, public buses cross the island from north to south daily.

It's very difficult to get around Campos do Jordão without a car. The attractions are far flung, except for those at Vila de Capivari. Trains depart from the **Estação Ferroviária Emílio Ribas** (☎ 012/263–1531) on tours of the city and its environs (including the 47 km/29 mi trip to Reino das Águas Claras, where there's a park with waterfalls).

On weekends, it's difficult to find a place to park in Embu, and parking lots can be expensive. Although you can easily walk to the town's main sights, the *bondinho* (a "train" whose cars are pulled by a truck) crosses Embu and stops at every main square.

Contacts and Resources

BANKS AND CURRENCY EXCHANGE

In Itu try the **24 Horas** (Rua Floriano Peixoto 761) ATM or the bank, **Bradesco** (Rua Floriano Peixoto 1030). Ilhabela banks include **Banespa** (Rua Dr. Carvalho 98) and **Bradesco** (Praça Cel. Julião M. Negrão 29). In Campos do Jordão, there's a **24 Horas** (Av. Pelinca 166) ATM at the Parque Centro Shop. Banks include **Bradesco** (Rua Boulevard Francisco P. Carneiro 28) and **Itaú** (Av. Pelinca 193). Embu has a branch of **Bradesco** (Rua Maranhão 44).

EMERGENCIES

Hospitals: Pronto Socorro Municipal (⊠ Av. Elias Yazbek 1415, Embu, ☎ 011/7822–5744), **Santa Casa** (⊠ Rua Joaquim Borges 372, Itu, ☎ 011/7822–2000; ⊠ Rua Pe. Bronislau Chereck 15, Ilhabela, ☎ 012/472–1222), **São Paulo** (⊠ Rua Agripino Lopes de Morais 1100, Campos do Jordão, ☎ 012/262–1722). **Police:** ☎ 190.

ENGLISH-LANGUAGE BOOKSTORES

Ponto das Letras (⊠ Rua Dr. Carvalho 146, ☎ 012/472–2104), in Ilhabela, has a small café-bookstore with international magazines.

TOUR OPERATORS AND TRAVEL AGENTS

As its name suggests, **Ilha Tour** (Av. Pedro Paulo de Morais 149, ☎ 012/472–1083) specializes in tours (by boat, bike, horse, or Jeep) of Ilhabela. Another Ilhabela operator is **Mare Mare** (Av. Princesa Isabel 90, ☎ 012/472–1418), which offers scuba-diving, Jeep, horseback-riding and hiking tours. **HS Turismo** (Rua Carlina Antonia Sirin 65, ☎ 012/262–2759) offers five tours in or around Campos do Jordão.

VISITOR INFORMATION

Itu Secretaria de Cultura (⊠ Rua Paula Souza 664, ☎ 011/299–8974), **Ilhabela Secretaria do Turismo** (⊠ Rua Bartolomeu de Gusmão 140, ☎ 012/472–1091), **Campos do Jordão Tourist Office** (⊠ At the entrance to town, ☎ 012/262–2755 ext. 306 or 216), **Embu Secretaria do Turismo** (⊠ Largo 21 de Abril 139, ☎ 011/494–5333).

4   THE SOUTH

Brazil's south is a mosaic of cultures and landscapes. *Gaúcho* (cowboy) traditions flourish in immense fields and rangelands near the border of Uruguay and Argentina. The *colono* (German and Italian colonist) heritage is evident in the cool mountain climes. Spectacular beaches and lush rain forest line the Atlantic coast, vast canyons and eerie sandstone formations dot the interior, and the mighty Foz do Iguaçu beckon with their watery chorus.

THE STATES OF PARANÁ, SANTA CATARINA, and Rio Grande do Sul contain the unexpected. The climate is remarkably cooler (the highest elevations even get a couple of inches of snow every year) and the topography more varied than in the rest of Brazil. Further, you're as likely to find people of German and Italian descent here as you are those with Portuguese ancestry. And, as Brazil's breadbasket, the Região Sul (Southern Region) has a standard of living comparable to many developed nations.

Updated and expanded by Carlos G. Tornquist

The southern section of the Serra do Mar, a mountain range along the coast, stretches well into Rio Grande do Sul. It looks like one green wall—broken only by the occasional canyon or waterfall—separating the interior from the shore. Most of the mountainsides are still covered with the luxuriant Mata Atlântica (Atlantic Rain Forest), which is as diverse and impressive as the forest of the Amazon. The Serra do Mar gives way to hills that roll gently westward to the valleys of the *rios* (rivers) Paraná and Uruguay. Most of these lands were originally covered with forests interspersed with natural rangelands such as the Campos Gerais in the north and the Brazilian pampas in the south.

Although Portugal controlled the continent's Atlantic coast from the Amazon to the Rio de la Plata delta for more than a century after discovering Brazil, the Spanish influence was greatly felt throughout the interior. In the late 1500s, Jesuit missionaries ventured into the valleys of the rios Paraná, Paraguay, and Uruguay, converting (and dominating) the region's native Guarani peoples. The Jesuits and their converts lived in self-sustaining *missões* (mission communities) built around magnificent churches. In the late 1600s, these settlements were increasingly attacked by the *bandeirantes* (slave hunters and adventurers), who sought labor for the gold mines of Minas Gerais. By the time that the Treaty of Madrid—which recognized Portuguese rule of what is roughly today's Brazil—was signed in 1750, the Jesuits were gone, the native peoples were either enslaved or dispersed in the wilderness, and most of the missões were in ruins. As border issues were more or less resolved, Portuguese settlement was stimulated. In these early days, cattle raising was the activity of choice in Paraná and Rio Grande do Sul.

Perhaps the greatest transformation in the region followed the arrival of German and Italian colonos. These immigrants brought along centuries of Old World farming traditions (☞ "Southern Brazil's German Settlers" and "Brazilian Wine" boxes, *below*). Many also contributed greatly to urbanization and industrialization that in turn brought about socioeconomic improvements still evident here today.

Pleasures and Pastimes

Dining

Compared with the dishes of northern Brazil, southern cuisine seems bland. It is, however, eclectic. Rice and beans, Brazilian staples, sit on southern tables beside Italian or German dishes. In the state capitals and larger cities, you can find a variety of international cuisines, though not as readily as you can in São Paulo or Rio. Seafood is very popular along the coast, but don't expect elaborate recipes or seasonings.

The *churrasco* (barbecue), by far the most renowned southern dish and now popular throughout the country, originated in Rio Grande do Sul. A gaúcho's daily rations consisted of beef or mutton—charbroiled on skewers over pit fires—and *mate* (or *chimarrão* as it's called in Rio Grande do Sul), a tea made from the leaves of the *Ilex paraguayensis* tree. (Mate is actually more popular than coffee in the south.) This tradition is carried on in *churrascarias* (steak houses), where waiters bring skewers full of different meats to your table until you can eat no more—a system known as *espeto-corrido* (also known as *rodízio* in the north-central states). The *barreado* is a lesser-known dish from coastal Paraná. The original recipe called for stewing beef, bacon, potatoes, and spices for several hours in a clay pot made air tight with moistened manioc flour.

Café colonial is the elaborate 5 PM tea that's very popular among the Germans and is a dieter's nightmare. Coffee and tea are served—for a set price—with a variety of breads, pies, German kuchen, honey, butter, and several kinds of jelly. For dessert there's ice cream. For price categories, *see* Dining *in* Smart Travel Tips A to Z.

Lodging

The south has a great variety of hotels and inns, though upscale facilities are limited. Except for in the smallest towns and most remote areas, however, you shouldn't have a problem finding comfortable accommodations. *Pousadas,* simple inns usually in vintage houses, are common, particularly in beach towns. A recent trend associated with ecotourism is the *hotel-fazenda,* a farm with guest facilities that often includes meals, horseback riding, and visits to local attractions in its rates.

Southern beaches attract many Argentine tourists, so seaside cities might become crowded from December through March, depending on the exchange rate between the currencies. There's usually enough lodging for this influx of visitors (though you'd be wise to reserve in advance), but traffic on highways and crowding on beaches can be nightmares. For price categories, *see* Lodging *in* Smart Travel Tips A to Z.

Natural Wonders

You can see the power of nature at work at one of Brazil's best known wonders: the Foz do Iguaçu (Iguaçu Falls) at the southwestern tip of Paraná. Vila Velha, a series of strange sandstone formations in the center of Paraná might remind you of the eerily moving landscapes of the western United States. The Serra do Mar and Superagüí regions have Mata Atlântica and almost pristine marine ecosystems. In the Aparados da Serra region of Rio Grande do Sul, gargantuan canyons are the result of millions of years of erosion.

The coastline from Paraná to the city of Tôrres in Rio Grande do Sul has spectacular scenery dotted with great beaches. The landscape is dominated by bays, coves, and hills that end abruptly in the sea. There are a few offshore islands, of which the largest and most visited is Ilha de Santa Catarina. South of Tôrres the terrain changes dramatically: The coastline is basically a 644-km-long (400-mi-long) sandy stretch interrupted only by a few rivers and lagoons.

Wine

The slopes of the Serra Gaúcha (a mountain district in Rio Grande do Sul) were settled by Italians whose winemaking traditions flourished in the region's fertile soil. Recent agricultural and industrial developments have dramatically improved the quality of the wines from Rio Grande do Sul. The best varieties come from Caixas do Sul and Bento Gonçalves and can rightfully compete with their more-renowned Chilean and Argentine counterparts.

Exploring the South

Touring this region, which is roughly the size of France, in a short time is a challenge even though the transportation network is relatively efficient. The major hubs include Curitiba, capital of the region's north-ernmost state of Paraná, and the Foz do Iguaçu, way to the west; Flo-rianópolis, the capital of the central Santa Catarina State; and Porto Alegre, capital of the southernmost state of Rio Grande do Sul.

It's best to divide the region into two large but more or less homoge-neous areas—the coast and the interior—and hit the one that holds the most interest for you. The coast offers great beaches, forested slopes, canyons, the peaks and valleys of the Serra do Mar, and Santa Cata-rina's German colonies. Trips to the interior can include the Iguaçu, the city of Porto Alegre, and the mountains of Rio Grande do Sul.

Great Itineraries

IF YOU HAVE 5 DAYS

Spend two days in Florianópolis for a taste of life on the southern beaches. Then head to the remarkable Foz do Iguaçu—an hour's flight away—for another two days. Return to Florianópolis for the flight home.

IF YOU HAVE 7 DAYS

Spend a day touring the city of Curitiba and take a one-day side trip by car to Vila Velha or by train to Paranaguá. Then head out for a two-day visit to Foz do Iguaçu. From here travel to Florianópolis for a day or two on the beach or visiting the inland German communities be-fore returning to Curitiba for the flight home.

IF YOU HAVE 10 DAYS

Add a day in the city of Porto Alegre and a two-day visit to the Serra Gaúcha to the seven-day itinerary detailed above. If you're truly in-terested in the great outdoors, don't miss the fantastic canyons at Aparados da Serra.

When to Tour

December through March is invariably hot and humid. Rainfall is high and evenly distributed throughout the year. January and Febru-ary are top summer vacation months, so expect crowded beaches, busy highways, and higher prices. Winter (April–November) brings much cooler temperatures, sometimes as low as the upper 20s in the higher elevations at night. Cold fronts blowing in from Patagonia can bring gray, blustery days.

PARANÁ

The state of Paraná is best known for the Foz do Iguaçu, a natural won-der, and the Itaipú Dam, an engineering marvel. At one time, the rolling hills of the state's plateau were covered with forests dominated by the highly prized *Paraná pine,* an umbrella-shape conifer. Most of these pine forests were logged by the immigrants half a century ago, and the cleared land of the immense interior is now where soybeans, wheat, and coffee are grown. (Still, be on the lookout for the occasional Paraná pine.) The state has a very short coastline, but the beaches and the Serra do Mar are spectacular. Curitiba, the upbeat capital, ranks as a top Brazilian city in terms of efficiency, innovative urban plan-ning, and quality of life.

Curitiba

408 km (254 mi) south of São Paulo, 710 km (441 mi) north of Porto Alegre.

Curitiba, with 1.5 million inhabitants, is by far the nation's most pleasant state capital. The 300-year-old city is on the Paraná plateau, at an elevation of 2,800 ft. It owes its name to the Paraná pine cones,

The Southern States

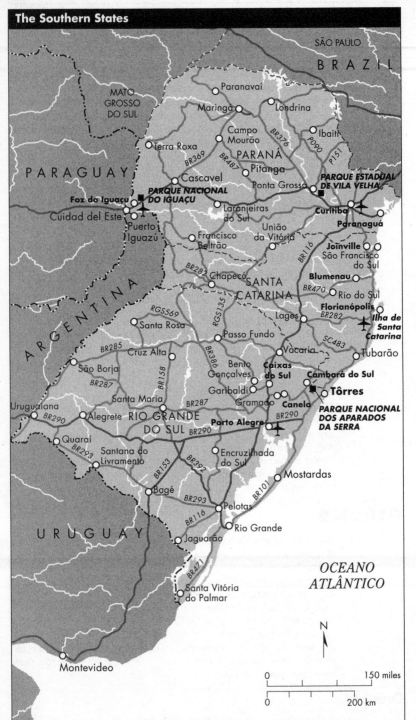

SÃO PAULO

B R A Z I L

MATO
GROSSO
DO SUL

Paranavaí

Maringá
Londrina

Campo
Mourão
Ibaiti

Terra Roxa
BR376
P090
P151

PARANÁ

Pitanga

Cascavel
Ponta Grossa
PARQUE ESTADUAL
DE VILA VELHA

BR369

BR487

PARAGUAY

Foz do Iguaçu
PARQUE NACIONAL
DO IGUAÇU
Larânjeiras
do Sul
Curitiba

Cuidad del Este
Paranaguá

Puerto
Iguazú
Francisco
Beltrão
União
da Vitória
BR116
Joinville

São Francisco
do Sul

BR282
Chapecó
SANTA
CATARINA
Blumenau

BR470
Rio do Sul

RG5569
Florianópolis
BR282

A R G E N T I N A
Santa Rosa
RG5135
Lages
Ilha de
Santa
Catarina

Passo Fundo
SC483
Tubarão

BR285
Cruz Alta
Vacaria

São Borja
BR386
Bento
Gonçalves
Caxias
do Sul
Cambará do Sul

BR287
BR158
Garibaldi
Tôrres

Uruguaiana
Santa Maria
BR287
Gramado
Canela

Alegrete
RIO GRANDE
DO SUL
BR290
Porto Alegre
PARQUE NACIONAL
DOS APARADOS
DA SERRA

BR290
BR290

Quaraí
BR293

Santana do
Livramento
Encruzilhada
do Sul
Mostardas

BR153
BR392

Bagé
BR101

U R U G U A Y
BR293
Pelotas

BR116
Rio Grande

Jaguarão

BR471

Santa Vitória
do Palmar

OCEANO
ATLÂNTICO

N

Montevideo

0   150 miles

0   200 km

which were called *kur-ity-ba* by the native Guaranis. A large number of inhabitants with European ancestry and a temperate climate (with a mean temperature of 16°C/61°F) make the city unique within a region that already differs considerably from the rest of the country.

Curitiba has been given the title of Environmental Capital, and not only because of its geographical features. Since the 1980s, progressive city governments have been innovative in their urban planning, a process that is linked to the former mayor (currently governor of Paraná) and architect, Jayme Lerner. The emphasis on protecting the environment in this town has produced an efficient public transportation system, a comprehensive recycling program, and an array of parks.

Numbers in the text correspond to numbers in the margin and on the Curitiba Setor Histórico map.

Setor Histórico

A GOOD TOUR

Start your tour in the downtown Setor Histórico (Historic District) at the **Museu Paranaense** ①. Then circle the block and take Rua Monsenhor Celso North to the Praça Tiradentes. The **Catedral Metropolitana** ② will be on the opposite side of the square. Continue a couple of blocks north on Rua do Rosário to the Largo da Ordem, site of the **Igreja de São Francisco** ③ and its Museu de Arte Sacra. A block uphill, you'll find **Società Giuseppe Garibaldi** ④ on the northern side of Praça Garibaldi. Right behind the society building are the ruins of São Francisco de Paula Church. Proceed from here on Rua Kellers to the **Museu de Arte do Paraná** ⑤. From here you have several options. You can retrace your steps to the Igreja São Francisco and walk three blocks east on Rua São Francisco and then north on Rua Presidente Faria to the **Passeio Público** ⑥. Alternatively, you can leave the Setor Histórico and explore the **Santa Felicidade** neighborhood—with its many restaurants and shops—or have a bite to eat on the **Rua 24 Horas.**

TIMING

You can follow the Setor Histórico tour in two hours, but allow half a day to fully see the sights. Shopping or people-watching in a park (☞ Parks, Gardens, and Forests, *below*) can fill up the rest of the day.

SIGHTS TO SEE

❷ **Catedral Metropolitana.** The Metropolitan Cathedral is on the site where the city was founded in 1693. The present neo-Gothic structure was finished in 1893 and was built according to the plan of a cathedral in Barcelona, Spain. ⊠ *Rua Barão do Serro Azul 31,* ☎ *041/222–1131.* ☜ *Free.* ☺ *Daily 7 AM–9 PM.*

❸ **Igreja de São Francisco.** St. Francis, Curitiba's oldest church, was built in 1737 and was fully restored in 1981. Check out its gold-plated altar before ducking into the attached **Museu de Arte Sacra** (Sacred Art Museum), with its baroque religious items made of wood and terra-cotta. ⊠ *Largo da Ordem s/n,* ☎ *041/223–7545 for church or 041/322–1525 for museum.* ☜ *Free.* ☺ *Tues.–Fri. 9–6, weekends 9–2.*

❺ **Museu de Arte do Paraná.** Set in what was once a residence, the Art Museum of Paraná displays works by prominent artists from throughout the state. ⊠ *Praça João Cândido 40,* ☎ *041/234–3172.* ☜ *Free.* ☺ *Weekdays 9–6.*

❶ **Museu Paranaense.** The State Museum of Paraná was founded in 1876, but its collections were moved several times before being transferred to this imposing art-noveau building, which served as city hall from 1916 to 1969. The permanent displays contain official documents,

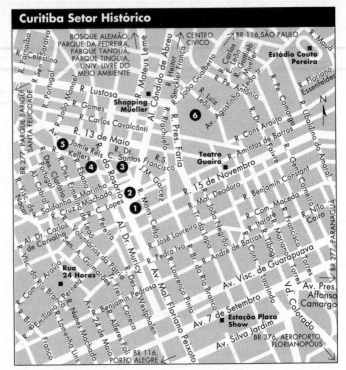

ethnographic materials, coins and photographs, and archaeological pieces related to the state's history. ⊠ *Praça Generoso Marques s/n, Centro,* ☏ *041/323–1411.* 🎟 *Free.* ☉ *Mon.–Fri. 9–5, Sat. 9–10.*

❻ Passeio Público. Opened in 1886, the Public Thoroughfare was designed as a botanical and zoological garden. It soon became a favorite place for the affluent to spend their weekend afternoons. The main gate is a replica of that at the Cimetière des Chiens in Paris. Although it's not the official city zoo anymore, you can observe several Brazilian primates and birds still kept in the park, as well as majestic sycamores, oaks, and the famed Brazilian *ipê amarelo.* ⊠ *Rua Luiz Leão s/n,* ☏ *041/222–2742.* 🎟 *Free.* ☉ *Mon. noon–6, Tues.–Sun. 8–6.*

OFF THE BEATEN PATH

RUA 24 HORAS – To satisfy your hunger or satiate your thirst, head for Rua 24 Horas, a short downtown alley that's sheltered by a glass roof (with interior lighting) supported by a steel structure. The entrance is marked by stylish clocks that hint at the appealing ambience inside. Here you'll find shops and newsstands as well as coffee houses, bars, and restaurants whose tables spill out onto the walkway. All are open 24 hours a day, 7 days a week. ⊠ *Rua Coronel Mena Barreto, between Rua Visconde de Rio Branco and Rua Visconde de Nacar,* ☏ *041/225–1732.*

SANTA FELICIDADE – What was once an Italian settlement (it dates from 1878), is now one of the city's most popular neighborhoods. It has been officially designated as Curitiba's "Gastronomic District" and, indeed, you'll find some fantastic restaurants—as well as some wine and handicrafts shops—along Via Veneto and Avenida Manuel Elias. The area also has several colonial buildings, such as the Igreja Matriz de São José (Saint Joseph Church).

❹ Società Giuseppe Garibaldi. The stately neoclassical mansion housing the Garibaldi Society—a philanthropic organization that once helped a great many Italian immigrants—was built with the help of donations from the Italian government and finished in 1890. Today the society sponsors a folkloric dance group and a choir. ⊠ *Praça Garibaldi s/n,* ☎ *041/222–8843.*

Parks, Gardens, and Forests

It would be a shame to visit Brazil's Environmental Capital without seeing one of its many parks. In addition to the Passeio Público (☞ *above*), you can visit the **Bosque Alemão, Parque Barigüí, Parque da Pedreira, Parque Tangüá, Parque Tingüí,** and **Universidade Livre do Meio Ambiente** (they're clustered northwest of Centro and the Setor Histórico) on your own or as part of the 2½-hour Linha Turismo bus tour (☞ Getting Around, *below*).

PARKS TO SEE

☝ **Bosque Alemão.** The 8-acre German Woods—which, as its name suggests, is a park honoring German colonos—is on a hill in the Jardim Schaffer neighborhood. On its upper side the Bach Oratorium, a small concert hall that looks like a chapel, is the site of classical music performances. The park also has a viewpoint with a balcony overlooking downtown Curitiba, a library with children's books, and a downhill path through the woods called Hanzel and Gretel Trail, named after the Grimm Brothers' tale. The trail ends at the Mural de Fausto (Faust Wall), where there's a stage for music shows. ⊠ *Rua Nicolo Paganini s/n,* ☎ *041/338–6835.* ☞ *Free.* ☉ *Daily sunrise–sunset.*

Parque Barigüí. Curitiba's largest park fills 310 acres. It contains soccer fields, volleyball courts, and jogging and bicycle paths. ⊠ *Av. Candido Hartmann s/n,* ☎ *041/335–2112.* ☞ *Free.* ☉ *Daily sunrise–sunset.*

★ **Parque da Pedreira (Pedreira Paulo Leminski).** The Paulo Leminsky Quarry Park is really a cultural complex that was opened in 1992 in the abandoned João Gava quarry and adjacent wooded lot. The quarry itself was converted to an amphitheater that can accommodate 60,000 people. The 2,400-seat **Opera de Arame** (Wire Opera House), also on the grounds here, is built of tubular steel and wire mesh and is surrounded by a moat. National and international musical events have given this facility world renown. ⊠ *Rua João Gava s/n,* ☎ *041/354–2662.* ☞ *Admission.* ☉ *Tues.–Sun. 8 AM–10 PM.*

Parque Tangüá. Tangüá Park may be the latest addition to Curitiba's recreational scene, but it has become the most visited. Its interesting landscaping includes a pond in an abandoned quarry that creates the backdrop for a tunnel—dug in the rock wall—an artificial waterfall, and a walkway over the water. ⊠ *Rua Dr. Bembem s/n, Pilarzinho,* ☎ *no phone.* ☞ *Free.* ☉ *Daily sunrise–sunset.*

Parque Tingüí. One of the city's most pleasant parks was designed to protect the upper basin of the Rio Barigüí from urban encroachment. It's best known as the site of the Ukrainian Memorial; finished in 1995, this memorial is a reproduction of a Christian-Orthodox church built by Ukrainian immigrants. ⊠ *Rua Fredolin Wolf s/n,* ☎ *041/335–2112.* ☞ *Free.* ☉ *Daily sunrise–sunset.*

Universidade Livre do Meio Ambiente. The Free University of the Environment, set in the Bosque Zaninelli (Zaninelli Woods), opened in 1992, the same year that the UN Conference on the Environment and Development was held in Rio. Its main objective is to promote environmental principles through courses, conferences, and seminars. The impressive main structure is built of eucalyptus wood and has a scenic overlook on its top level. Several paths through the woods make this a popular place to wander. ⊠ *Rua Victor Benato 219,* ☎ *041/254–5548 or 041/254–3734.* ⌷ *Free.* ⊙ *Daily 6 AM–7 PM.*

Dining

$$$ ✕ **Boulevard.** The pleasant atmosphere and excellent wine selection
★ of this highly regarded French restaurant won't fail to impress. The seafood cassoulet is an outstanding appetizer, and the *coté de veau* (veal steak) with lemon sauce and spinach is a fine entrée. ⊠ *Rua Voluntários da Pátria 539, Centro,* ☎ *041/224–8244. AE, DC, MC, V. No lunch Sat. Closed Sun.*

$$$ ✕ **Devon's Baby Beef.** The service is excellent at this rodízio-style churrascaria. It's very popular with businesspeople and those visiting the Centro Cívico area, where most of the public administration buildings are. ⊠ *Rua Lysimaco Ferreira da Costa 436, Centro,* ☎ *048/254–7073. DC, MC, V. No dinner Sun.*

$$$ ✕ **Estrela da Terra.** Set in an old colonial house on the Praça Garibaldi, this is *the* place to try the local barreado dish. The menu also contains choices from other regions. ⊠ *Rua Kellers 95, Setor Histórico,* ☎ *041/335–3492. AE, DC, MC, V.*

$$$ ✕ **Marinheiro.** The setting is simple and old-fashioned, but the seafood is by far the best in Curitiba. The shrimp dishes or the garoupa flambée—served with a spicy cream sauce—deserve your attention. ⊠ *Av. Bispo D. José 2315, Batel,* ☎ *041/243–3828. AE, V. No dinner Sun. Closed Mon.*

$$ ✕ **Madalosso.** The best-known restaurant in Santa Felicidade is in an enormous hangarlike building (the largest structure of its kind in the country). The prix-fixe Italian menu includes an enormous selection of pasta dishes and sauces, meat dishes, and salads. ⊠ *Rua Manoel Ribas 5875, Santa Felicidade,* ☎ *041/372–2121. AE, DC, MC, V. No dinner Sun.*

$$ ✕ **Schwarzwald.** Recognized as one of the city's best German restaurants, Schwarzwald has also carved a name for itself with its great draft beer. Try the house versions of *Eisbein* (pig's leg served with mashed potatoes) and *Kassler* (beef fillet with a cream sauce). ⊠ *Largo da Ordem 63, Setor Histórico,* ☎ *041/223–2585. AE, DC, MC, V.*

$ ✕ **Baviera.** This restaurant is a great choice if you're on a tight budget. It has an interesting location in an imposing house on a hill, and you enter through the cellar. Its menu includes Brazilian-style steak, grilled chicken, and hamburgers. ⊠ *Rua Augusto Stellfeld 18, Setor Histórico,* ☎ *041/232–1955. AE, DC, MC, V.*

Lodging

$$$$ ▥ **Grand Hotel Rayon.** A spacious lobby welcomes you to Curitiba's
★ most sophisticated hotel. Rooms are superbly furnished, the service is impeccable, and the location—in the heart of the financial district and right next to Rua 24 Horas—is convenient. ⊠ *Rua Visconde de Nacar 1424, Centro 80411–201,* ☎ *041/322–6006,* ℻ *041/322–4004. 136 rooms, 11 suites. 2 restaurants, bar, coffee shop, room service, outdoor pool, sauna, exercise room, business services, meeting rooms. AE, DC, MC, V.*

$$$ ▥ **Duomo Park Hotel.** At the small Duomo Park, everything is shiny and new. A stay here puts you close to, but not in the thick of, the action. Rua 24 Horas is nearby. ⊠ *Rua Visconde de Rio Branco 1710, Centro, 80420–200,* ☎ *041/322–6655,* ℻ *041/224–2816. 48 rooms. Restaurant, bar, business services, meeting rooms. AE, DC, MC, V.*

$$ ▥ **Hotel Eduardo VII.** One of Curitiba's traditional downtown hotels is also quite affordable. Its restaurant offers international fare and live Brazilian music. ⊠ *Rua Cândido Leão 15, Centro 80020-050,* ☎

041/322–6767, FAX *041/232–0394. 200 rooms. Restaurant, bar, coffee shop. AE, DC, MC, V.*

$$ ⊡ **Hotel Tivoli.** This downtown hotel—strategically located between Praça Tiradentes and Praça Osório—offers modern, compact, but still comfortable rooms. The tasteful decor transmits a warmth that's complemented by the helpful staff members. ⊠ *Rua Ébano Pereira 139, Centro 80010–050,* ☎ *041/224–0111,* FAX *041/224–0111. 81 rooms. Bar, coffee shop, business services. AE, DC, MC, V.*

$$ ⊡ **Slaviero Braz Hotel.** This hotel is more than 50 years old, but a recent renovation has brought everything up to date. Rooms are large and carefully decorated with colorful spreads and cushions that invite you to relax. Note that rooms in the east wing are smaller and have an odd shape, and elevators are cramped because of the original building plan. The second-floor Getúlio bar-café has a balcony overlooking the walkway of Rua das Flores and is a popular gathering spot for businesspeople. ⊠ *Av. Luiz Xavier 67, Centro, 80020–020,* ☎ *041/ 322–2829,* FAX *041/322–2398. 89 rooms, 2 suites. Restaurant, bar, meeting rooms. AE, DC, MC, V.*

$ ⊡ **Condor Hotel.** The main draw of this basic, low-budget option is its location a block from the bus and rail terminal. Rooms are showing their age but are comfortable enough to be recommended for those en route to other southern destinations. ⊠ *Av. 7 de Setembro 1866, Centro 80060–070,* ☎ *041/262–0322,* FAX *041/262–0322. 95 rooms. AE, DC, MC, V.*

Nightlife and the Arts

Curitiba has a bustling cultural scene, a reflection of the European background of many of its citizens. Complete listings of events are published in the *Gazeta do Povo,* the major daily newspaper.

The **Teatro Guaíra** (⊠ Rua 15 de Novembro s/n, Centro, ☎ 041/322–2628), formerly the Teatro São Teodoro (circa 1884), was totally rebuilt in its present location and reopened in 1974. It has a 2,000-seat auditorium, considered one of the most modern and well-equipped in South America, as well as two smaller rooms. Shows here include plays, popular music concerts, and full-fledged operas.

The **Estação Plaza Show** has something for everyone—night and day. What was once a railway terminal is now a 700,000-square-ft covered area with a colorful and noisy collection of bars and restaurants, amusement parks, and more than 100 shops. A train museum, a cineplex, and daily live musical shows add to the center's charm. ⊠ *Av. 7 de Setembro 2775, Centro,* ☎ *041/322–5356.* ▧ *Admission.* ☉ *Daily 10 AM–2 AM.*

Outdoor Activities and Sports

Curitiba has three professional soccer clubs: Coritiba, Atlético Paranaense, and Paraná. They play either in the old **Estádio Couto Pereira** (⊠ Rua Ubaldino do Amaral 37, Alto da Glória, ☎ 041/362–3234) or the new **Arena da Baixada** (⊠ Rua Engenheiros Rebouças 3113, Água Verde, ☎ 041/333–4747). Check local newspaper listings for upcoming game times and locations.

Parque Barigüi, Parque Tingüi, Parque Tanguá (☞ Exploring, *above*) are good places to go biking and running.

Shopping

Curitiba has several world-class malls, including **Shopping Center Müeller** (Rua Candido de Abreu 127, São Francisco, ☎ 041/224–0510) and **Curitiba Outlet Center** (Rua Brigadeiro Franco 1916, Batel, ☎ 041/224–1900).

Look for traditional crafts of wicker, clay, and leather at **Casa do Artesanato** (⊠ Rua Mateus Leme 22, Centro, ☏ 041/342–4021). You can interact directly with the artisans at the **Feira de Artesanato,** which is held in the Praça Garibaldi every Sunday from 9 to 3.

Paranaguá

90 km (56 mi) southeast of Curitiba.

Most of Brazil's coffee and soybeans are shipped out of Paranaguá, the nation's second-largest port (only Santos is larger), and it also serves as chief port for landlocked Paraguay. The city, which was founded in 1565 by Portuguese explorers, is 30 km (18 mi) from the Atlantic on the Baía de Paranaguá. The northern side of this bay has a great swatch of Mata Atlântica; several islands in the bay also have forest as well as great beaches. You'll find other attractive sandy stretches farther south, toward the Santa Catarina border.

Although you can reach Paranaguá on BR 277, consider taking the more scenic Estrada da Graciosa (Graciosa Road), which follows the route taken by 17th-century traders up the Serra do Mar. This narrow, winding route is some 30 km (18 mi) longer than BR 277, but the breathtaking peaks and slopes covered with rain forest make the extra travel time worthwhile.

Paranaguá's downtown has many examples of colonial architecture and has been designated an official historical area. **Igreja Nossa Senhora do Rosário,** the city's first church, was destroyed, sacked, and rebuilt several times, but its facade (circa 1578) is original. ⊠ *Largo Monsenhor Celso s/n,* ☏ *no phone.* ☞ *Free.* ☉ *Daily 7 AM–9 PM.*

The **Museu de Arqueologia e Etnologia** (Archaeology and Ethnology Museum) occupies a building that was part of a Jesuit school founded in 1752 but closed in 1759 when the Jesuits were expelled from Brazil. (Portuguese authorities of the day feared that the Jesuits would try to take over territory for the Spanish Crown, among other things.) The collection includes pieces found in diggings in the area, most belonging to the Sambaqui peoples. ⊠ *Rua General Carneiro 66,* ☏ *041/422–8844.* ☞ *Admission.* ☉ *Tues.–Sun. noon–5.*

★ The 10-km-long (6-mi-long) **Ilha do Mel** (Honey Island), a state park in the Baía de Paranaguá, is the most popular destination on Paraná's coast. It's crisscrossed by hiking trails—cars aren't allowed and the number of visitors is limited to 5,000 at any one time—and has two villages, Encantadas and Nova Brasília, and several pristine beaches. Local lore has it that the east shore's Gruta das Encantadas (Enchanted Grotto) is frequented by mermaids. On the south shore, check out the great views from Farol das Conchas (Lighthouse of the Shells) and the Forte de Nossa Senhora dos Prazeres (Ft. of Our Lady of Pleasures) built in 1767. Ferries regularly leave from Paranaguá's harbor for the two- to three-hour ride to the island; the cost is about $3.50. Alternatively, you can hop a ferry in Pontal do Paraná, a village 49 km (30 mi) east of Paranaguá; the trip takes 30 minutes and costs $2. To ensure admission in the high season, it's best to book a tour to the island in Curitiba (☞ Travel Agencies and Tour Operators *in* The South A to Z, *below*). ⊠ *Ferry dock: Rua General Carneiro, in front of information kiosk, Paranaguá,* ☏ *041/422–6882.* ⊠ *Ferry dock: Pontal do Sul, Pontal do Paraná,* ☏ *041/455–1316.*

The northern shore of Baía de Paranaguá is also home to the 53,000-acre **Parque Nacional de Superagüi** (Superagüi National Park) and its complex system of coves, saltwater marshes, and forested islands—including Ilha Superagüí and Ilha das Peças. These pristine settings contain animal and bird species unique to the Mata Atlântica. You can visit the continental part of the park from the fishing village of Guaraqueçaba (on the bay's far northern side), a three-hour **ferry ride** (☎ 041/422–6882) from Paranaguá's harbor. It's best to explore the islands on an organized boat tour (☞ Travel Agencies and Tour Operators *in* The South A to Z, *below*).

Beaches

Matinhos, 45 km (28 mi) south of Paranaguá, is a good hub from which to explore a string of pleasant beaches that run south to the border with Santa Catarina. The city has a small permanent population that swells to more than 400,000 people in peak season. The next beach town is **Caiobá,** on the northern side of the delta of the Rio Cubatão; it's well known for its convention center. **Guaratuba** is linked to Caiobá by ferry across the delta.

Dining and Lodging

$$ ✕ **Casa do Barreado.** As its name suggests, this small, homey, family-run restaurant specializes in the traditional barreado. You'll also find *galinha na púcura,* an unusual chicken barreado. Although the restaurant is officially open only on weekends, you can call ahead to arrange a dinner during the week. ⊠ *Rua Antônio Cruz 9, Paranaguá,* ☎ *041/ 423–1830. Reservations essential. No credit cards. Closed weekdays.*

$$$ ✕▦ **Camboa Hotel.** Although it's in the historic district, the Camboa is modern and sophisticated and has a dedicated staff. Rooms on the north side have good bay views. The restaurant is highly recommended for its international dishes with an emphasis on French cuisine. ⊠ *Rua João Estevão s/n, Paranaguá 83203–020,* ☎ *041/423–2121,* ℻ *041/ 423–2121. 114 rooms, 6 suites. Restaurant, 2 bars, coffee shop, 2 pools, sauna, 2 tennis courts, exercise room, shops, recreation room, business services, meeting rooms. AE, DC, MC, V.*

$$ ✕▦ **Hotel Dantas Palace.** This small hotel has comfortable rooms and a convenient location. The on-site restaurant, Le Bistrô, serves excellent international cuisine. ⊠ *Rua Visconde de Nacar 740, Paranaguá 83203–430,* ☎ *041/423–1555,* ℻ *041/422–7075. 45 rooms. Restaurant, bar. AE, DC, MC, V.*

Parque Estadual de Vila Velha

97 km (60 mi) northwest of Curitiba.

The 22 towering rock formations of the 7,670-acre Vila Velha State Park stand in sharp contrast to the green rolling hills of the Campos Gerais, Paraná's central plains. Three-hundred-million years of rain and wind have carved these sandstone formations whose names—"The Lion," "The Cup," "The Mushroom"—reflect their shapes. You can visit these natural monuments on foot or in a tractor-pulled wagon along a well-marked, 2½-km (1½-mi) trail that starts a mile from the visitors center. Traversing the path and viewing the formations on foot takes about two hours. ⊠ *Km 511 on BR 376, 20 km (12 mi) before Ponta Grossa,* ☎ *042/229–2332.* 🎟 *Admission.* ☉ *Daily 8–6.*

Dining and Lodging

$$ ✕ **Pampeana.** This busy, rodízio-style churrascaria is the perfect place to satisfy a hearty appetite acquired after a day of touring Parque Estadual de Vila Velha. It has a great salad bar for those not too crazy about the meat excesses of churrasco. ⊠ *Km 518 on BR 376,* ☎ *042/ 229–2881. DC, MC, V. No dinner Sun.*

$$$ ✕🏨 **Vila Velha Palace.** Considering that this hotel is *the* luxury option in the city, the amenities are limited, but service is friendly and efficient. The basic restaurant serves Brazilian fare. ⊠ *Rua Balduino Taques 123, 84040–000,* ☎ *042/225–2200,* ☎ *042/225–2200. 92 rooms, 2 suites. Restaurant, bar, sauna, meeting rooms. AE, DC, MC, V.*

$$ 🏨 **Hotel Fazenda Capão Grande.** The 150-year-old Fazenda Capão Grande is a fully functional ranch that welcomes guests. Here you can fully experience cowboy traditions—a great way to round out your visit to Vila Velha. Southern-style meals are included in the rates. ⊠ *19 km (12 mi) along an unpaved road off BR 276 (entrance near Km 500 marker),* ☎ *042/229–2216 or 041/244–5957 (reservations),* ☎ *042/ 225–4348. 4 rooms. Horseback riding. No credit cards.*

$$ 🏨 **Planalto Palace.** Although you'll find few facilities here, it's a clean, reliable choice. ⊠ *Rua 7 de Setembro 652, 84010–350,* ☎ *042/225– 3155,* ☎ *042/224–1580. 75 rooms. Bar. AE, DC, MC, V.*

Foz do Iguaçu

637 km (396 mi) west of Curitiba.

The Foz do Iguaçu cascade in a deafening roar at a bend in the Rio Iguaçu, where southwestern Paraná State meets the borders of both Argentina and Paraguay. This avalanche of water actually consists of some 275 separate falls (in the rainy season, they can number as many as 350) that plunge 250 ft onto the rocks below. The backdrop is one of dense, lush jungle; rainbows and butterflies are set off against vast walls of vegetation and ubiquitous red earth. The falls and the lands around them are protected by two nations in Brazil's Parque Nacional Foz do Iguaçu and Argentina's Parque Nacional Iguazú (where the falls are referred to by their Spanish name, the Cataratas de Iguazú).

Allow at least one full day to enjoy the sights within Parque Nacional do Iguaçu, and be sure to set aside time to check out the Argentine side as well. The Brazilians are blessed with the best panoramic view; the Argentine side, where most of the falls are actually situated, offers better up-close experiences. Local travel agencies and tour operators offer trips that will take you to both sides, as well as other notable area sights (☞ Travel Agencies and Tour Operators *in* The South A to Z, *below*). If you want to set your own pace, you can tour the Brazilian side and then take a taxi or one of the regularly scheduled buses across the International Bridge, officially called the Ponte Presidente Tancredo Neves, to Argentina (Canadian, U.K., and U.S. citizens don't need a visa to enter). The main hubs are the Brazilian town of Foz do Iguaçu and the Argentine town of Puerto Iguazú; the Paraguayan town of Ciudad del Este is also nearby. (Note that if you're a Canadian, U.K., or U.S. citizen crossing into Brazil from Argentina or Paraguay, you don't need a visa for a short visit to the falls. You must, however, pay an entry fee and have your passport stamped. Always keep your passport handy as immigration authorities keep the region under close watch.)

The summer months (November–March) are hot and humid, so if you're bothered by the heat plan to visit between April and October. Be aware, however, high waters due to heavy rainfall on the upper Iguaçu River basin might restrict access to some catwalks. Whatever time of year you visit, bring rain gear: some of the catwalks take you right to the falling water, where the spray can leave you drenched.

★ The **Parque Nacional do Iguaçu** is 25 km (16 mi) along a paved highway southwest of downtown Foz do Iguaçu. The **Park Entrance** (⊠ Km 17, Rodovia das Cataratas, ☎ 045/523–8383) is the best place to get information; it's open daily 7 AM–6 PM, and admission is roughly

$3. There's a small museum 1 km (½ mi) beyond the entrance, but most visitors go directly to the falls. Much of the park's 457,000 acres is protected rain forest—off limits to visitors and home to the last viable populations of panthers as well as rare bromeliads and orchids.

The falls are 11 km (7 mi) from the park entrance. The luxurious, historic Hotel das Cataratas (☞ Dining and Lodging, *below*) is near the trailhead. Public parking is allowed on the highway shoulder and in a small lot near the hotel. The path to the falls is 2 km (1 mi) long, and its walkways, bridges, and stone staircases lead through the rain forest to concrete and wooden catwalks.

Salto Macuco (Macuco Falls) is an optional first stop within the park. The crystal clear waters of the Rio Macuco, a tributary of the Iguaçu, fall 60 ft into a natural pool within the forest. The only way to visit this little gem is on a tour (☞ Tour Operators and Travel Agents *in* The South A to Z, *below*) that takes about 2 hours and costs roughly $30 per person. The trip requires a 7 km (5 mi) ride in a four-wheel-drive vehicle, followed by a short hike through the forest; it includes a boat ride to the main falls.

Highlights of the Brazilian side of the falls include first the **Salto Santa Maria,** from which catwalks branch off to the **Salto Deodoro** and **Salto Floriano,** where you'll be doused by the spray. The end of the catwalk puts you right in the heart of the spectacle at **Garganta do Diabo** (Devil's Throat). The tallest and most popular falls extend for 3 km (1½ mi) in a 270-degree arch, and the water thunders down 180 ft. Back on the last section of the main trail, there's a building with facilities, including a panoramic elevator; it's open daily 8:30–6, and there's a very small fee. A balcony brings you close to the far left of **Salto Deodoro.** The trail ends at the road some 35 ft above.

★ In Argentina's **Parque Nacional Iguazú,** there are a couple major *circuitos* (routes). The **Circuito Inferior** (Lower Circuit) is a loop trail that leads to the brink of several falls. It starts off the main path leading from the **Visitors Center** (☎ 0757/20180), which is open daily from 7 AM to 8 PM. Protected promontories, rimmed with wood or metal fences, offer close-ups of the falls. Wear your bathing suit on this route so you can take a dip in the calm pools at the trail's edge. The **Circuito Superior** (Upper Circuit) is a 3,000-ft-long path that borders the ridge on the river's south side, along the top of the falls.

On the Argentine side you'll see the impressive **Salto Lanusse** and **Salto Alvar Nuñez;** up from them is a branch of the river known as the **Braço San Martin.** The large protruding rock surrounded by falls is **Ilha San Martin** (San Martin Island). Farther upstream are **Salto Dois Mosqueteiros** and **Salto Três Mosqueteiros.** The lower part of the river—which is a geological fault—narrows to less than 240 ft. There are several smaller falls along the basalt wall on the opposite side that you may or may not be able to see (it depends on the waterflow at the time of your visit).

The Argentina side also offers the chance to see **Devil's Throat** from a different perspective. From the ½-km-long (¼-mi-long) catwalk over the falls, the mighty waters of the Iguaçu seem to disappear right in front of you. The path starts in **Puerto Canoas,** a settlement 4 km (2½ mi) upriver from the Visitors Center.

There are other notable sights near the Foz do Iguaçu, including the privately funded **Parque das Aves** (Bird Park). Here, on 36 acres of mostly untouched tropical forest right outside the national park, you'll find large aviaries with 160 different species of bird. There are also a butterfly collection, a gift shop, and a restaurant. ⊠ *Km 10.5, Rodovia das Cataratas,* ☎ *045/523–1007.* 🎫 *Admission.* ⊙ *Daily 9–6.*

About 21 km (13 mi) up the Rio Paraná (which flows into the Rio Iguaçu just below the falls) is a great achievement of Brazilian civil engineer-
★ ing: the mighty **Hidrelétrica de Itaipú.** The main structure of the world's largest hydroelectric power plant is 8 km (5 mi) long; its powerhouse (which provides electricity for much of the country) alone is 2 km (1 mi) long. An hour-long guided bus tour of the complex leaves from the visitors center, where you can also watch a 30-minute video about the dam's construction. ⊠ *Km 11, Av. Tancredo Neves,* ☎ *045/520–5252.* 🎫 *Free.* ⊙ *Daily 8–6.*

Not far from the dam is the **Ecomuseu de Itaipú** (Itaipú Ecomuseum), with its six biological refuges. Here you can learn about attempts to preserve local flora and fauna. ⊠ *Km 10, Av. Tancredo Neves,* ☎ *045/520–5817.* 🎫 *Free.* ⊙ *Daily 8–6.*

Dining and Lodging

Owing to its location near the borders of two other countries, the town of Foz do Iguaçu has a cosmopolitan atmosphere that's reflected in its cuisine. For a city of its size, the options are really great. There's also one noteworthy hotel on the Argentina side—the Internacional Cataratas de Iguazú. For convenience, most visitors stay in the establishments that line BR 469 (Rodovia das Cataratas), the highway that runs from the city of Foz do Iguaçu to the national park and the falls.

$$$ ✕ **Zaragoza.** In a quiet neighborhood on a tree-lined street, the cozy
★ restaurant is owned by Paquito, a Spanish immigrant. The fare includes a great paella, the house specialty, as well as several delicious fish op-tions. The *surubi,* a regional fish, definitely merits a try. ⊠ *Rua Quintino Bocaiúva 882,* ☎ *045/574–3084. AE, V.*

$$ ✕ **Cantina 4 Sorelle.** The atmosphere at this Italian restaurant is warm. The staff serves the pasta dishes and the pizzas efficiently. ⊠ *Rua Alm Barroso 1336,* ☎ *045/523–1707. AE, DC, MC, V.*

$$$$ ✕🏨 **Hotel das Cataratas.** Not only is this stately hotel *in* the national
★ park (with wonderful views of the falls), but it also provides the more traditional comforts—large rooms, terraces, hammocks—of a colonial-style establishment. This pink building is surrounded by galleries and gardens; its main section has been declared a Brazilian national her-itage sight. The restaurant serves a traditional Brazilian dinner, featuring *feijoada* (the national dish of black beans and pork), with a variety of side dishes. Anything featuring fish from the Paraná basin is also rec-ommended. ⊠ *Km 25 Rodovia das Cataratas 85850–970,* ☎ *045/523–2266 or 0800/45–2266,* 𝖥𝖠𝖷 *045/574–1688. 200 rooms. 2 restaurants, bar, coffee shop, pool, 2 tennis courts, shops. AE, DC, MC, V.*

$$$ ✕🏨 **Bourbon.** This hotel is a preferred location for conventions. Most of its spacious rooms and its guest facilities are in the main building; suites occupy the top floors of a tower and have superb views of the national park's green expanse. The house restaurant, Tarobá, serves international fare. ⊠ *Km 2½, Rodovia das Cataratas 85863–000,* ☎ *045/523–1313 or 0800/11–8181,* 𝖥𝖠𝖷 *045/574–1110. 300 rooms, 11 suites. 3 restaurants, 2 bars, coffee shop, pool, 2 tennis courts, sauna, health club, shops. AE, DC, MC, V.*

$$$ ✕🏨 **Internacional Cataratas de Iguazú.** Half the rooms in this top-notch
★ Argentina-side hotel have direct views of the falls, so be sure to ask for a view when you make a reservation. Floor-to-ceiling windows let the inspiring scene into the lobby, restaurants, and bars; even the pool has a vista. The handsomely decorated main restaurant serves a mem-orable trout maître d'hôtel wrapped in pastry. ⊠ *Parque Nacional Iguazú, Puerto Iguazú, Argentina,* ☎ *0757/20295 or 0757/20311,* 𝖥𝖠𝖷

0757/21600. 180 rooms, 4 suites. 2 restaurants, 2 bars, pool, 3 tennis courts, meeting rooms. AE, DC, MC, V.

$$$$ ⊞ **Iguaçu Golf Club and Resort.** Even the most demanding visitors will
★ find a stay at the Iguaçu Golf Club unforgettable. The resort has an
18-hole, par-72 course, a driving range, and a practice green. Accommodations are spacious and plush; if you're traveling with family or
a group of friends, ask for one of the separate guest houses. ⊠ *Km 7
Rodovia das Cataratas 6845, 85863–000,* ☎ *045/523–4749,* ℻ *045/
523–5737. 70 rooms, 5 guest houses. Restaurant, 2 bars, pool, golf
course, health club, shops. AE, DC, MC, V.*

$$ ⊞ **Foz Plaza.** This downtown hotel is a reliable budget choice. Although
the rooms are basic—and the decor isn't really tasteful—they're clean.
⊠ *Rua Mal. Deodoro 1819, 85851–030,* ☎ *045/523–1448 or 0800/
11–6768,* ℻ *045/523–1448. 64 rooms. Restaurant, bar, pool. AE, DC,
MC, V.*

SANTA CATARINA

The state of Santa Catarina has almost 485 km (300 mi) of coastline
(with many gorgeous beaches) and a small interior countryside. Its capital, Florianópolis, is on Ilha de Santa Catarina, an island with 42 beaches
and many world-class hotels and resorts. Santa Catarina is also home
to the German settlements of Blumenau and Joinville in the valley of
the Rio Itajaí. This highly industrialized district still retains some of
its German flavor, including a popular Oktoberfest.

Florianópolis and Ilha de Santa Catarina

*300 km (187 mi) southeast of Curitiba, 476 km (296 mi) northeast of
Porto Alegre.*

It's no wonder that every summer around 300,000 Argentines travel
more than 960 km (600 mi) to enjoy the breathtaking beaches and warm
waters off the shore of the Ilha de Santa Catarina. They add to a constant influx of Brazilians, making this one of the country's top tourist
destinations. Called Magic Island by locals and enthusiastic visitors,
Ilha de Santa Catarina is joined to the mainland by two bridges and
has more than 42 charming, easy-to-reach beaches. Lovers of the outdoors will find not only plenty of opportunities for scuba diving, surfing, sailing, and jet-skiing but also plenty of chances to view nature
along trails through tropical forests, from beaches (the whale-watching here is good), or even from the sky strapped into a hang-glider.

But the island isn't only a place of natural wonders. The city of Florianópolis played an important part in history. It was the southernmost
post of Portuguese rule for some time, and it was the site of several
skirmishes with the Spanish before the border disputes were settled.

Although you might be lured by the beaches, downtown Florianópolis offers worthwhile attractions. The **Alfândega** (Old Customs House),
which dates from 1876, is the city's best example of neoclassical architecture. It now houses an artist's association and a handicrafts
shop. ⊠ *Rua Cons. Mafra 141, Centro,* ☎ *048/224–6082.* ☑ *Free.*
⊙ *Weekdays 9–7, Sat. 9–noon.*

Beyond the Alfândega is the picturesque, 100-year old **Mercado Público**
(Public Market), a Portuguese colonial structure with a large central
patio. A recent renovation managed to restore the market—which is
filled with stalls selling fish, fruit, and vegetables—while preserving its
Arabian-bazaar atmosphere. ⊠ *Rua Cons. Mafra 255, Centro,* ☎
048/225–3200. ⊙ *Mon.–Sat. 7 AM–9 PM.*

Box 32 is small and cramped, but it's *the* meeting place for everyone
from businesspeople to students. Here you'll find more than 100 different kinds of liquor including the Brazilian mainstay, *cachaça* (a sugar-
cane-based alcohol). Be sure to try the house specialty, *bolinho de
bacalhau* (a cod appetizer). ⊠ *Rua Cons. Mafra 255, Mercado
Público, Centro,* ☎ *048/224–5588.* ⊙ *Weekdays 10–9, Sat. 10–3.*

The **Museu Histórico** (Historical Museum) is housed in the 18th-cen-
tury Palácio Cruz e Souza (once the governor's home and office), a boxy,
rose-color structure whose stairways are lined with Carrara marble.
The sidewalks around the building are still paved with the original stones
brought from Portugal. The museum's collection includes documents,
personal items, and artwork that belonged to former governors. ⊠ *Praça
15 de Novembro 227, Centro,* ☎ *048/221–3504.* ⊠ *Free.* ⊙ *Tues.–
Fri. 10–7, Sat. 1–7, Sun. 4–7.*

Forts were built to protect the bay and its harbor, which was strategic
to the Portuguese in the early days of the colony. The best way to see
them is on a sailboat tour (☞ Tour Operators and Travel Agents *in*
The South A to Z, *below*) of the bay that separates the continent from
Ilha de Santa Catarina. The best preserved are **Fortaleza de São José**
and the **Forte de Anhatomirim,** which were built in 1744 opposite each
other at the entrance to the Baía Norte (North Bay); the **Fortaleza de
Santo Antônio,** on an islet in the bay; and the **Forte de Santana,** near
the Ponte Hercílio Luz (the first of two bridges built to link the island
to the mainland and now condemned).

Another great sight to visit by sailboat is the **Baía dos Golfinhos** (Dolphin Bay). A few nautical miles up the coast from the island, this bay
is home to hundreds of *botos-cinza* (gray dolphins). They tolerate sailboats moving in very close to them.

Ilha da Santa Catarina has some inland treasures, too. The SC 404 highway travels through its eastern hills to the **Lagoa da Conceição** (Conception Lagoon), 12 km (8 mi) east of downtown Florianópolis. The
region provides a combination of fresh- and saltwater environments
where there are plenty of opportunities for water sports. The village
has a busy nightlife and dining district, and most of its streets are packed
with people on weekend evenings.

Beaches

The island's **northern beaches** are considered the best (and are, hence,
the busiest) owing to their warm waters. You're strongly advised to
explore the sophisticated **Canasvieiras, Jurerê, Ingleses,** and **Santinho**
before choosing a place to drop your beach towel and absorb the sun.

The **Atlantic beaches** have the most impressive seascapes. Surfers have
staked claims to **Joaquina** (where an annual international surfing competition takes place), **Mole,** and **Matadeiro.**

The **southern beaches** have fewer sun worshipers and a much more
laid-back atmosphere. If peace is what you're looking for, make your
first stop **Pântano do Sul.** Secluded **Lagoinha** is a breathtaking beach
that you can only reach by boat or by way of a steep, 3-mi path that
starts at Pântano do Sul.

Dining

$$$ ✕ **Cantábria.** The Spanish fare here is epitomized by an exceptional
paella. The restaurant adds to its already considerable ambience with
live music Thursday through Saturday evenings. ⊠ *Rua Frei Caneca
at Rua Allan Kardec, Centro, Florianópolis,* ☎ *048/228–1202. AE,
DC, MC, V. Closed Mon.*

Ilha de Santa Catarina

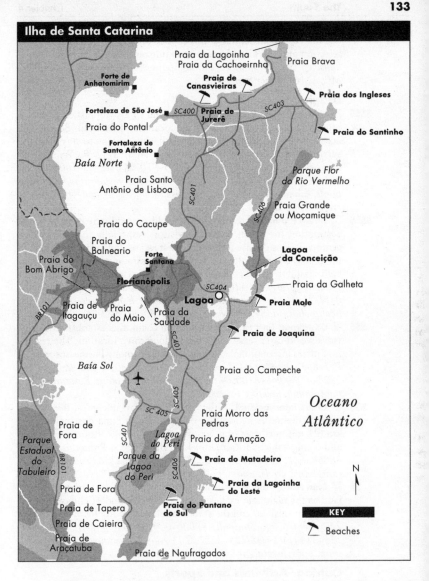

Praia da Lagoinha
Praia da Cachoeirnha
Praia Brava

Forte de Anhatomirim

Praia de Canasvieiras

Praia dos Ingleses

Fortaleza de São José SC400 **Praia de Jurerê** SC403

Praia do Pontal

Praia do Santinho

Fortaleza de Santo Antônio

Baía Norte

Praia Santo Antônio de Lisboa

Parque Flor do Rio Vermelho

SC401

Praia do Cacupe

Praia Grande ou Moçamique

SC406

Praia do Balneario

Forte Santana

Lagoa da Conceição

Praia do Bom Abrigo

Florianópolis

SC404

Lagoa O

Praia da Galheta

Praia de Itagauçu

Praia do Maio

Praia da Saudade

Praia Mole

SC401

Praia de Joaquina

Baía Sol

Praia do Campeche

SC405

Oceano Atlântico

SC405

Praia de Fora

Praia Morro das Pedras

SC401

Parque da Lagoa do Peri

Praia da Armação

Parque Estadual do Tabuleiro

BR101

Lagoa do Peri

SC406

Praia do Matadeiro

N

Praia de Fora

Praia da Lagoinha do Leste

Praia de Tapera

Praia de Caieira

Praia do Pantano do Sul

KEY

Praia de Araçatuba

Praia de Naufragados

Beaches

$$$ ✕ ★ **Marina Ponta da Areia.** A recent addition to the island's roster of fine restaurants, Ponta da Areia offers a grand view of the Lagoa da Conceição. The fare includes a wide variety of seafood, including the island's own *camarão ao bafo,* fresh shrimp steamed with just a little seasoning. ⊠ *Rua Sen. Ivo D'Aquino Neto 133, Lagoa da Conceição,* ☎ *048/232-0759. MC, V. Closed Mon.*

$$$ ✕ **La Pergoletta.** A variety of fresh pasta dishes (try the one with shrimp and white-wine sauce) are the highlights of this highly praised establishment. ⊠ *Trv. Careirão 62, Centro, Florianópolis,* ☎ *048/ 224-6353. Reservations essential. AE.*

$$ ✕ **Arante.** This rustic, beachfront restaurant has a 40-year track record. The menu is flawless; don't pass up the *pirão de caldo de peixe* (black beans cooked with a fish sauce) or the shrimp prepared according to a house recipe. Weekend reservations are advised. ⊠ *Rua Abelardo Gomes 254, Pântano do Sul,* ☎ *048/237-7022. No credit cards.*

$$ ✕ **Ataliba.** With 20-odd years in the business, you can expect nothing less than excellent service at this rodízio-style churrascaria. The meat selection and the salad bar are both outstanding. ⊠ *R. Irineu Born-hausen 5050, Agronomica, Florianópolis,* ☎ *048/333–0990. AE, DC, MC, V. No dinner Sun.*

Lodging

$$$$ 🏨 **Costão do Santinho Resort.** The island's most sophisticated resort
★ offers many facilities and a terrific location on Santinho Beach. The ocean view from rooms that face north is one reason to stay here; the surrounding 100-acre Atlantic forest is another. ⊠ *R. Ver. Onildo Lemos 2505, Praia do Santinho, 88001–970,* ☎ *0800/48–1000 or 048/ 261–1000,* ℻ *048/261–1236. 180 rooms. 3 restaurants, 2 bars, 6 pools, sauna, 4 tennis courts, exercise room, soccer, volleyball, beach, recreation room. AE, DC, MC, V.*

$$$$ 🏨 **Jurerê Praia.** This resort is on the sophisticated Jurerê Beach, a prime destination for South American visitors, especially those from Argentina. It doesn't have traditional guest rooms, but rather guest houses for two to eight people, and requires a minimum stay of one week in high season (December–March). ⊠ *Alameda Carlos Nascimento 200, Praia de Jurerê, 88053–000,* ☎ *048/282–1108 or 0800/48–1530,* ℻ *048/282–1644. 58 guest houses. Restaurant, bar, 2 pools, tennis court, health club, soccer, volleyball, beach. AE, DC, MC, V.*

$$$ 🏨 **Castelmar.** Part of the Best Western chain, this establishment provides world-class service in a prime downtown location. The restaurant offers international fare and is popular among businesspeople. ⊠ *R. Felipe Schmidt 1260, Centro, Florianópolis 88010–002,* ☎ *048/225– 3228 or 0800/48–8100,* ℻ *048/225–0360. 192 rooms. Restaurant, bar, pool, sauna, meeting rooms. AE, DC, MC, V.*

$$$ 🏨 **Lexus Internacional.** Although it has many amenities, this hotel's main attraction is its location on the popular Praia dos Ingleses, 34 km (21 mi) northeast of downtown Florianópolis. Rooms are ample and comfortable. ⊠ *Rua Dom João Becker 859, Praia dos Ingleses, 88058–601,* ☎ *048/269–2622,* ℻ *048/269–2622. 63 rooms. Restaurant, bar, 2 pools, sauna, volleyball, beach. AE, DC, MC, V.*

$$ 🏨 **Baía Norte Palace.** Its location near the bridge that connects the island to the mainland makes this a convenient budget choice. Rooms are well furnished, and the staff is attentive. ⊠ *Av. Beira-Mar Norte 220, Centro, Florianópolis 88000–000,* ☎ *0800/48–0202 or 048/ 225–3144,* ℻ *048/225–3227. 103 rooms. Restaurant, bar, coffee shop, pool, meeting rooms. AE, DC, MC, V.*

Outdoor Activities and Sports

Snorkeling and scuba diving are very popular on the northern beaches. For diving lessons and equipment rentals, check with **Sea Divers** (⊠ Av. Luiz B. Piazza 6562, Ponta das Canas, ☎ 048/284–1535).The cost to rent basic diving gear is about $70 a day.

Hang-gliding and para-sailing are also popular on the island. For equipment and classes try the **Associação de Vôo Ingleses/Santinho** (AVIS; ⊠ Rua João Jose Luz 240, Santinho, ☎ 048/983–6770). A lesson including a tandem flight with an instructor costs about $40.

The warm waters around the island attract whales from Patagonia from July through October. **Projeto Baleia Franca** (☎ 048/973–0977) is a private research organization that offers boat trips to view the cetaceans.

SHOPPING

The local handicrafts *rendas de bilro* (handwoven tapestries) can be found at the **Alfândega** (☞ Exploring *above*). For modern shops in a world-class mall try **Beira-Mar Shopping** (✉ Rua Bocaiúva 2468, Centro, ☎ 048/224–1563).

Blumenau

250 km (156 mi) northwest of Florianópolis.

Blumenau—the cradle of the prosperous Vale do Itajaí region—is a pleasant place, with clean streets and friendly people who take great pride in their community. The name of this city of more than 200,000 inhabitants is indicative of its German origins. Those who settled here brought along their farming culture and transformed the landscape. Some of these colonos started small factories that have grown into today's large textile and electric industries. The city's downtown has been restored to preserve its early German architecture, and the annual Oktoberfest attracts crowds from all over the south. Events spill from the festival site into downtown around Rua 15 de Novembro.

For insight into the history of German immigration, check out the **Museu da Família Colonial** (Colonial Family Museum). The house, which was built in 1864 for the Gaertner family, houses a collection of everyday objects; its garden has many examples of regional flora. ✉ *Av. Duque de Caxias 78,* ☎ *047/326–6990.* 🎫 *Admission.* ☉ *Tues.–Fri. 8–5, Sat. 9–4, Sun. 9–noon.*

Dining and Lodging

$$ ✕ **Frohsinn.** This restaurant is a great choice for German cuisine with a Brazilian flair. The *marreco recheado* (stuffed duck) is the house specialty. ✉ *Rua Gertrud Sierich s/n, Morro do Aipim,* ☎ *047/322–2137. AE, DC, MC, V. No dinner Sun.*

$$$ ✕🏨 **Plaza Blumenau.** Check in here if you're looking for upscale accommodations, spacious rooms, and great facilities. The Terrace restaurant serves international cuisine with an emphasis on things German. ✉ *Rua 7 de Setembro 818, Centro 89010–200,* ☎ *047/326–1277 or 0800/47–1213,* 🖷 *047/322–9409. 123 rooms, 8 suites. Restaurant, bar, pool, exercise room, business services, meeting rooms. AE, DC, MC, V.*

$ ✕🏨 **Hotel Glória.** Rooms here are basic but comfortable, and the staff is attentive. What really makes it popular is the on-site KaffeHaus Glória, a coffee shop that serves the traditional, lavish café colonial. ✉ *Rua 7 de Setembro 954, Centro 89010–280,* ☎ *047/326–1988,* 🖷 *047/326–5370. 97 rooms. Bar, coffee shop. AE, DC, MC, V.*

Shopping

A great variety of clothing, bedding, and bathroom articles can be found here at bargain prices; for the best selection in the downtown district try **Lojas Hering** (✉ Rua 15 de Novembro 759, Centro, ☎ 047/326–2166), or **Flamingo** (✉ Rua 15 de Novembro 367, Centro, ☎ 047/326–0277). The area is home to a growing glassware industry, with high-quality products. Check out **Glaspark** (✉ Rua Rudolf Roedel 147, Salto Weisbach, ☎ 047/327–1261).

Joinville

105 km (65 mi) northeast of Blumenau.

Joinville was founded by German immigrants 150 years ago, and today it's Santa Catarina's largest city. It's a bustling convention, industrial, and international trade center that relies on the nearby seaport of São Francisco do Sul. Although Joinville itself isn't particularly attractive, its surrounding rain-forested hills provide opportunities for some interesting excursions. The **Museu Nacional da Colonização e Imi-**

graçāo (Colonization and Immigration Museum) has a fine collection of objects and crafts from the first immigrants. ⌧ *Rua Rio Branco 229, Centro,* ☎ *047/433–3736.* 🎫 *Free.* ☉ *Tues.–Sun. 9–5.*

Dining and Lodging

$$$ ×🏨 **Tannenhof.** This hotel reigns absolute as the region's best and largest.
★   The architecture imitates the traditional, German, *enxaimel* style (half-timber types of structures). You can dine on international fare in the 11th-floor restaurant, which also serves up a panoramic view of the city and the nearby hills. ⌧ *Rua Visconde de Taunay 340, Centro, 89201–420,* ☎ *047/433–8011 or 0800/99–8011,* 🗛 *047/433–8011. 100 rooms, 3 suites. Restaurant, bar, pool, exercise room, meeting rooms. AE, DC, MC, V.*

$$ 🏨 **Anthurium Park Hotel.** Rooms in this former bishop's residence are small. But the comfort of the hotel and the charm of the setting, which includes a nearby cathedral and a park, won't disappoint. ⌧ *Rua São José 336, Centro, 89200–970,* ☎ *047/433–6229,* 🗛 *047/433–6229. 45 rooms, 4 suites. Restaurant, bar, pool, sauna. AE, DC, MC, V.*

RIO GRANDE DO SUL

The state of Rio Grande do Sul is almost synonymous with the gaúcho, the South American cowboy who is glamorized as much as his North American counterpart. There's more to this state, however, than the idyllic cattle-country lifestyle of early days. As one of Brazil's leading industrial areas, its infrastructure rivals that of any country in the Northern Hemisphere. Its ethnic mix of Portuguese, German, and Italian cultures is evident not only in the food and architecture, but also in the determination of its inhabitants. Indeed, to be gaúcho (which is a term for all people and things from this state) may mean to be a vintner with Italian heritage from Caixas do Sul or an entrepreneur of German descent from Gramado as much as a cattle rancher with Portuguese lineage out on the plains.

The slopes of the Serra Gaúcha were settled by Italian immigrants, who found the region's fertile soil and cold winters appropriate for growing grapes. Thanks to their winemaking skills, the state now produces a couple of nice varieties, particularly in the Caixas do Sul and Bento Gonçalves areas. Along the coast, basaltic cliffs drop into a raging Atlantic and provide an impressive backdrop for the sophisticated seaside resort of Tôrres. Farther inland the Aparados da Serra National Park straddles the state's highest elevations and contains several canyons with breathtaking views.

The state capital, Porto Alegre, is a sophisticated metropolis of 1,300,000 inhabitants that rivals Curitiba in terms of quality of life. This important industrial and business center has universities, museums, and convention centers. It also has plenty of lovely green parks, and many of its streets are lined with *jacarandá* trees that create violet tunnels when they're in full spring bloom.

Porto Alegre

476 km (296 mi) southwest of Florianópolis, 760 km (472 mi) southwest of Curitiba, 1,109 km (690 mi) southwest of São Paulo.

Porto Alegre's hallmark is the hospitality of its people, a trait that has been acknowledged over and over by visitors, earning it the nickname Smile City. The capital of one of Brazil's wealthiest states, Porto Alegre is also an important business center. (Because of its location halfway

SOUTHERN BRAZIL'S GERMAN SETTLERS

IN THE EARLY 1820S, Austrian-born Empress Dona Leopoldina, wife of Dom Pedro I (Brazil's first emperor), envisioned the vast, sparsely populated Brazilian countryside settled with the kind of farmers she knew from Europe. Although European farmers had a poor track record in the tropics, it was felt that southern Brazil's cooler, subtropical climate wouldn't be so inhospitable. Agents hired by the Brazilian crown were dispatched to central Europe, where they touted the wonders of Brazil and the abundance of its "farm land" (actually covered by dense forest and home to native peoples—such as the Guarani and Caigang—and wild animals like the South American puma). Beginning in 1824, and continuing for more than 50 years, thousands of Europeans—many of them German—were lured to central and eastern Rio Grande do Sul and eastern Santa Catarina.

High-end estimates place the number of German *colonos* (colonists) in the 200,000 to 300,000 range (exact figures are hard to come by owing to poor record keeping on the part of Brazilian authorities and the tendency for colonists to indicate the region—Hunsrück, Pommern, Pfalz—from which they came rather than simply "Germany," which only became unified in 1871). Most of those who came were poor or landless farmers who faced famine in their homelands. Some were craftsmen who provided the goods and services needed to truly create settlements. The first New World community was established in São Leopoldo (named after Dona Leopoldina), 31 km (19 mi) north of Porto Alegre on the Rio dos Sinos (Bells River). This and the valley of

the Rio Itajái in Santa Catarina became cradles of Brazil's German immigrants.

The Germans brought their unswerving work ethic, their knowledge of agriculture, and their rich culture—much of which still thrives. Recent studies indicate that at least 500,000 Brazilians speak some German (though it may well be a dialect that speakers of the standard language would find hard to understand). Further, the Lutheran religion is still practiced by many people with German ancestry. Researchers of Rio Grande do Sul's rich folklore are keen to acknowledge that the rhythms of some regional music can be traced back to German polkas. German cuisine is so much a part of the region that hardly anyone here can conceive of a *churrasco* (barbecue) without pork sausages and *Kartofelln Salat* (potato salad). And pastries are an essential part of the German-bred *café colonial* (late-afternoon coffee/tea). Although most small, local breweries have been incorporated into large national companies, prior to the 1970s, the southern states had a long list of them. In addition, German immigrants and their descendants were behind such internationally renowned Brazilian companies as Varig Airlines and Gerdau steel industries.

If you visit such communities as Blumenau, Joinville, São Leopoldo, Novo Hamburgo, Gramado, Lageado, and Santa Cruz do Sul you'll certainly experience a bit of Europe in Brazil. Indeed, Blumenau and Santa Cruz host large Oktoberfests. Crowds of Brazilian-Germans flock to these fests to dance to their traditional rhythms (polkas and waltzes) and indulge in sausages, sauerkraut, and beer.

between Buenos Aires and São Paulo, it has applied to be the seat of the MERCOSUR, the South American Common Market.)

The city was founded on the banks of the Rio Guaíba by immigrants from the Azores in 1772. The Guaíba is actually a 50-km-long (31-mi-long) lagoon formed by four rivers that merge a few miles upstream from the city. The city's port, connected to the Atlantic by the Lagoa dos Patos, has become increasingly active in recent years.

Exploring

From Morro de Santa Teresa (Santa Teresa Hill), you get a grand view of the skyline as it confronts the expanse of the Rio Guaíba. From this spot and the numerous riverfront parks, the great spectacle of Porto Alegre's sunset is inspirational. As local poet Mário Quintana puts it: "Skies of Porto Alegre, how could I ever take you to heaven?" For another great perspective of Centro, consider taking a riverboat tour (☞ Tour Operators and Travel Agents *in* the South A to Z, *below*) of the Rio Guaíba and its islands, which are part of a state park.

The heart of Porto Alegre lies within a triangle formed by Praça da Alfândega, the Mercado Público, and the Praça da Matriz. Not only is this the main business district, but it's also the site of many cultural and historical attractions. Outside this area, Casa de Cultura Mário Quintana and Usina do Gasômetro are very active cultural centers with movies, live performances, art exhibits, and cafés.

Numbers in the text correspond to numbers in the margin and on the Porto Alegre Centro map.

A GOOD WALK

Begin at Praça da Alfândega, the focal point of the Centro area. On the side facing the river are two neoclassical structures: the **Museu de Arte do Rio Grande do Sul** ① and the **Memorial do Rio Grande do Sul** ②. From the square, head north on Avenida 7 de Setembro to the open space in front of the Prefeitura (the Fonte Talavera de la Reina here was donated by the Spanish community of Rio Grande do Sul in 1935). On the opposing side of Avenida Borges de Medeiros is the **Mercado Público** ③. Follow Avenida Borges de Medeiros south to the Viaduto Otávio Rocha, the city's first overpass, and climb the stairway to Avenida Duque de Caixas. One block to your right is the **Museu Júlio de Castilhos** ④ where you can catch a glimpse of gaúcho culture. A couple blocks west are the **Catedral Metropolitana Nossa Senhora Madre de Deus** ⑤ and the adjacent **Palácio Piratini** ⑥.

TIMING

You can follow this tour—and visit the museums–in about four hours.

SIGHTS TO SEE

❺ **Catedral Metropolitana Nossa Senhora Madre de Deus.** Although construction began in 1921, this cathedral wasn't completed until 1986. Its predominant style is Italian Renaissance, but note the twin bell towers, which were inspired by 17th-century Jesuit missions. The facade's mosaic panels were made in the Vatican ateliers. ⊠ *Praça Marechal Deodoro s/n,* ☎ *051/228–6001.* ☜ *Free.* ☉ *Daily 7–noon and 2–7.*

❷ **Memorial do Rio Grande do Sul.** Built at the turn of the century and declared a national architectural landmark in 1981, this structure housed the main post office until recently, when it was set aside to become a state museum. Although the building has an overall neoclassical style, the German-baroque influences are strong; the asymmetrical corner towers, with their bronze rotundas, are said to resemble Prussian army helmets. The lobby and adjoining rooms are currently used

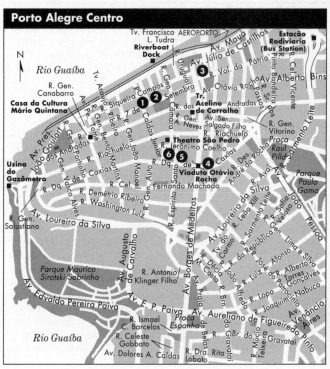

for art and technology exhibits. ✉ *Praça da Alfândega s/n,* ☎ *051/ 221–5214.* 🎟 *Free.* 🕙 *Daily 9–5.*

③ Mercado Público. The Public Market was built in 1869 in the neoclassical style. It has undergone repeated renovations, the last of which (in 1996) added the glass roof that now covers the central inner plaza. With these changes, produce stalls have been replaced by cafés and restaurants making it seem more a modern mall and less a boisterous bazaar. ✉ *Largo Glenio Peres s/n.* 🕙 *Mon.–Sat. 7 AM–11 PM.*

① Museu de Arte do Rio Grande do Sul. In 1997, the old, neoclassical customs building was restored and now houses the Art Museum of Rio Grande do Sul. Here you can see paintings and drawings (in a variety of styles and from several periods) by gaúcho artists. This and several other of the city's neoclassical buildings were designed by renowned German architect Theo Wiederspahn. A collection of his sketches and blueprints is also on display. ✉ *Praça da Alfândega s/n,* ☎ *051/227– 2311.* 🎟 *Free.* 🕙 *Tues.–Sun. 10–5.*

④ Museu Júlio de Castilhos. The small Júlio de Castilhos Museum displays an impressive collection of gaúcho documents, firearms, clothing, and household utensils. The house belonged to Governor Julio de Castilhos, who lived here at the last turn of the century, before the Palácio Piratini (☞ *below*) was built. ✉ *Rua Duque de Caxias 1231,* ☎ *051/221–3959.* 🎟 *Free.* 🕙 *Tues.–Fri. 10–5, weekends 1–5.*

⑥ Palácio Piratini. The Piratini Palace is the stately governor's home and houses some executive offices. The structure's Roman columns convey a solidity and permanence uncommon in official Brazilian buildings. Duck into the main room to see the wall paintings (they depict gaúcho folk tales) by Italian artist Aldo Locatelli. ✉ *Praça da Matriz s/n,* ☎ *051/210–4100.* 🎟 *Free.* 🕙 *Daily 9–5.*

Dining

$$$ ✕ **Al Dente.** This restaurant features northern Italian cuisine. Try the *garganelli* (a Neapolitan variety of pasta) with salmon and wine sauce or the fettucine *negro* (black) with caviar sauce. ⊠ *Rua Mata Bacelar 210, Auxiliadora,* ☎ *051/343–1841. AE, V. Closed Sun.*

$$$ ✕ **Le Bon Gourmet.** The Plaza San Rafael hotel's (☞ *also* Lodging, *below*)
★   restaurant has the best French cuisine in town and is very popular with international visitors. The house highlight is the juicy fillet Camembert with a mushroom sauce. ⊠ *Rua Alberto Bins 514, Centro,* ☎ *051/ 211–5767. AE, DC, MC, V. No lunch Sat. Closed Sun.*

$$$ ✕ **Il Gattopardo Ristorante.** This trendy lunch and dinner spot caters
★   to an upscale crowd. The fare is Italian, so obviously pasta dishes reign supreme. ⊠ *Rua 24 de Outubro 1583, Auxiliadora,* ☎ *051/330– 1972. Reservations essential. AE, DC, MC, V. No lunch Sat. Closed Sun.*

$$ ✕ **Barranco.** One of Porto Alegre's oldest Brazilian restaurants has several dining rooms, but most people head for one of the tables in the open, tree-shaded area. The Argentine beef (it's more tender than local beef) dishes are popular as are the pork ribs au gratin. ⊠ *Rua Protásio Alves 1578, Petrópolis,* ☎ *051/331–6172. AE, DC, MC, V.*

$$ ✕ **Gambrinus.** Generations of politicians, artists, and journalists have flocked to this old-fashioned Mercado Público establishment to debate the city's past and present. The fare is mostly regional; try the stuffed *tainha*, a tasty southern Atlantic fish, or the terrific *mocotó* (cow's knee stewed with vegetables). ⊠ *Rua Borges de Medeiros s/n, Mercado Público, Centro,* ☎ *051/226–6914. Weekday reservations essential. No credit cards. Closed Sun.*

$ **Café do Porto.** This new addition to the city's long list of cafés has a colorful postmodern ambience and a helpful, lively staff. They not only serve 20 different types of coffee, but also drinks, sandwiches, and pastries. ⊠ *Rua Padre Chagas 293, Moinhos de Vento,* ☎ *051/346– 2349. No credit cards.*

Lodging

$$$ 🏨 **Caesar Towers.** Porto Alegre's newest and finest hotel has set high
★   standards to lure well-traveled guests. Rooms are spacious—those at the back have superb views of downtown and the Guaíba—and you can have a basic office set up in them. The on-site Joomon restaurant serves international fare with Japanese accents. ⊠ *Rua Lucas de Oliveira 991, Bela Vista 90940–011,* ☎ *051/333–0333,* 🖷 *051/330– 5233. 131 rooms, 2 suites. Restaurant, bar, pool, sauna, health club, business services. AE, DC, MC, V.*

$$$ 🏨 **Plaza San Rafael.** Conveniently located in the downtown district, the Plaza has long been one of the city's most sophisticated hotels, and recent renovations have brought even more improvements. The restaurant, Le Bon Gourmet (☞ *also* Dining, *above*) has the best French cuisine in town. ⊠ *Rua Alberto Bins 514, Centro 90030–040,* ☎ *051/ 211–5767,* 🖷 *051/221–6883. 262 rooms, 22 suites. Restaurant, bar, pool, sauna, health club, business services. AE, DC, MC, V.*

$$ 🏨 **Umbú.** Although it retains some of its original splendor, location is this traditional hotel's primary draw. It's close to the bus terminal, and access to the airport from here is quick and easy. ⊠ *Av. Farrapos 292, Centro 90035–050,* ☎ *051/228–4355,* 🖷 *051/228–4355. 70 rooms. Restaurant, bar. AE, DC, MC, V.*

Nightlife and the Arts

Porto Alegre has a very active cultural life. Complete listings of entertainment and cultural events are published in the daily papers *Zero Hora* and *Correio do Povo.*

The **Casa de Cultura Mário Quintana** (Mario Quintana Cultural Center) occupies what was Porto Alegre's finest hotel at the turn of the century, the Majestic. The building has two art-film cinemas, one theater, and several exhibit rooms. The popular Café Concerto Majestic, on the seventh floor, has regular music performances. ⊠ *Rua dos Andradas 736,* ☎ *051/221–7147.* ▣ *Admission.* ⊙ *Daily 10 AM–9 PM.*

Dado Bier started off as the city's first microbrewery. Its success among the fashionable led to expansions that have transformed it into an entertainment center. It now includes two restaurants (one serving Japanese cuisine, the other international fare) and a live-music venue, Dado Bier Tambor. ⊠ *Av. Nilo Peçanha 3228,* ☎ *051/334–9111.* ▣ *Admission.* ⊙ *Daily 10 AM–2 AM.*

The **Theatro São Pedro**—a 130-year-old, art nouveau–style theater—is run by a private foundation and hosts musical and stage performances. The popular Café Orquestra das Panelas is in a balcony above the lobby. ⊠ *Praça da Matriz s/n,* ☎ *051/227–5100.* ▣ *Admission.*

Porto Alegre, in an attempt to copy Curitiba's Rua 24 Horas, has revamped a downtown alley called **Travessa Acelino de Carvalho.** Although it's shorter and nowhere near as glitzy as its counterpart in Curitiba, all of its bars, restaurants, and newsstands are open 24 hours a day, 7 days a week.

The **Usina do Gasômetro** (Gas and Power House), with its conspicuous brick smokestack, was the city's first coal-fired power house and was built in the early '20s when the city experienced great growth. Today it's a cultural center housing theaters, meeting rooms, and exhibit spaces right on the banks of the Rio Guaíba. A terrace café overlooking the river—the perfect place to take in a sunset—is the center's newest addition. ⊠ *Av. João Goulart 551,* ☎ *051/227–1738.* ▣ *Admission.* ⊙ *Daily 8 AM–midnight.*

Outdoor Activities and Sports

Internacional, one of the city's major *futebol* (soccer) teams, plays in the **Estádio Beir-Rio** (⊠ Av. Padre Cacique 891, Praia de Belas, ☎ 051/231–4411). Grêmio, the city's other major team, plays in the **Estádio Olímpico** (⊠ Largo dos Campeões s/n, Azenha, ☎ 051/217–4466). The parks **Marinha do Brasil** and **Moinhos de Vento** have great jogging paths that are very busy on weekends.

Shopping

Porto Alegre has several world-class malls, including the popular **Shopping Center Iguatemi** (⊠ Rua João Wallig 1831, Três Figueiras, ☎ 051/223–6455), and the **Praia de Belas Shopping Center** (⊠ Av. Praia de Belas 1181, Praia de Belas, ☎ 051/231–4499).

Look for traditional leather crafts, gaúcho apparel, and souvenirs at **Rincão Gaúcho** (⊠ Rua dos Andradas 1159, Centro, ☎ 051/224–1004). You can also shop for crafts at the **Brique da Redenção** on Rua José Bonifácio in the Bom Fim neighborhood. The entire street is closed to vehicles and taken over by artisans every Sunday from 8 to 3.

Tôrres

205 km (128 mi) northeast of Porto Alegre.

The beaches around the city of Tôrres are among Rio Grande do Sul's most exciting. The sophistication of the seaside areas here attracts international travelers, particularly those from Argentina and Uruguay. The best beaches include Praia da Cal, Praia da Guarita, and Praia Grande. They're separated by outcroppings from which locals like to fish. The Parque da Guarita (Watchtower Park), 3 km (2 mi) south of downtown, was set aside to protect the area's unique vegetation as well as the basaltic hills that end abruptly in the Atlantic.

Dining and Lodging

$$ × **Restaurante Parque da Guarita.** The thatched roof and tropical garden of this restaurant blend in perfectly with its beach setting. Seafood is the specialty here, and you can partake of your meal while enjoying the magnificent view of the park with the surf as a backdrop. ✉ *Estrada do Parque da Guarita,* ☎ *051/664–1056. DC, MC, V. No dinner Mar.–Nov.*

$$ 🏨 **Farol Hotel.** One of the oldest and most traditional hotels on the coast still retains the charm of the days when Tôrres was a small beach town. Guest rooms are simple and comfortable, with up-to-date facilities. ✉ *Rua José Picoral 240, 95560–000,* ☎ *051/664–1240,* FAX *051/664–2670. 90 rooms. Restaurant, bar, pool, nightclub, meeting rooms. AE, DC, MC, V.*

Gramado

133 km (83 mi) northwest of Porto Alegre.

It was no doubt Gramado's mild mountain climate that attracted German settlers to the area in the late 1800s. They left a legacy of German-style architecture and traditions that attract today's travelers. Ample lodging options and a seemingly endless choice of restaurants and café coloniais have given this city a reputation with convention-eers and honeymooners. Every August the city hosts the Festival de Cinema da Gramado, one of Latin America's most prestigious film festivals. At this time it can be difficult to find lodging if you haven't made arrangements in advance.

Twenty kilometers (13 miles) away, on RS 020, is Gramado's smaller, twin city of Canela. Nearby is the **Parque Estadual do Caracol** (Caracol State Park; ✉ Rua Godofredo Raymundo 1747, Estrada Parque do Caracol, ☎ 054/282–2548), with an impressive 400-ft waterfall that flows straight down into a horseshoe-shape valley carved out of the basaltic plateau. The park also includes 50 acres of native forests dominated by the famous Paraná pine.

Dining and Lodging

$$$ × **Gasthof Edelweiss.** Here you'll find German cuisine at its best in a rustic atmosphere. Kassler with orange sauce and duck *à la viennese* (with an orange-flavored cream sauce) are among the specialities. ✉ *Rua da Carriere 1119, Gramado,* ☎ *051/286–1861. AE, DC, MC, V.*

$$ ×🏨 **Bavária.** If you're looking for a peaceful, natural setting this is a good choice—the hotel is within a private park just off some busy areas. The small in-house restaurant of the same name serves German fare and is highly recommended. ✉ *Rua da Bavária 543, Gramado 95670–000,* ☎ *051/286–1362,* FAX *051/286–1362. 56 rooms. Restaurant, bar, pool, sauna. AE, DC, MC, V.*

$$$ 🏨 **Laje de Pedra.** World-class facilities and a unique location are
★   among the draws of this new, luxury hotel. It's built near a cliff, and from its east wing there are impressive views of the Vale do Quilombo (Quilombo Valley). On weekends, the hotel regularly hosts a variety of musical performances. ✉ *Av Pres. Kennedy s/n, Canela 95680-000,* ☎ *054/282–4300,* FAX *054/282–4400. 250 rooms, 8 suites. Restaurant, bar, pool, sauna. AE, DC, MC, V.*

$$$ 🏨 **Serra Azul.** This prestigious, downtown hotel is the preferred choice
★   of Brazilian TV and movie stars during the film festival. Recently, the owners bought a ranch outside the city where you can experience the

gaúcho lifestyle. ⊠ *Rua Garibaldi 152, Gramado 95670-000,* ☎ *054/ 286–1082,* ⅏ *054/286–3374. 151 rooms, 18 suites. Restaurant, bar, indoor pool, sauna. AE, DC, MC, V.*

$ 🏨 **Pousada Zermatt.** For those who are tired of budget hotels that lack charm, this old hotel offers a cozy atmosphere and reasonable rates. ⊠ *Rua da Fé 187, Gramado 95670-000,* ☎ *051/286–2426,* ⅏ *051/ 286–2426. 9 rooms. Bar. AE, DC, MC, V.*

Parque Nacional dos Aparados da Serra

★ *64 km (40 mi) northeast of Gramado.*

This national park was created to protect the great canyons—of which Itaimbezinho is the most famous—that dissect the plateau in the north of Rio Grande do Sul State. Winter (June to August) is the best time to take in the spectacular canyon views as there's less chance of fog. You can hire guides (it's impossible to navigate the trails without them) at the park's main entrance, the Portaria Gralha Azul, which is 20 km (13 mi) southeast of Cambará do Sul, the small town that serves as the park's hub. A new visitors center provides information on regional flora and fauna, as well as the park's history. Beyond the entrance you'll come to grassy meadows that belie the rockiness ahead. The awesome Itaimbezinho canyon, for instance, is cut deep in the basalt bedrock, and, on average, the valley is 3,000 ft below. The longest path takes you into the canyon's interior. The park allows only 1,500 visitors each day, so it's best to arrive early. ⊠ *20 km (12 mi) southeast of Cambará do Sul on unpaved road,* ☎ *051/251–1262.* ⊡ *Admission.* ⊙ *Wed.–Sun. 9–5.*

Dining and Lodging

$ ✗ **Churrascaria Pampa.** It seems fitting that one of Cambará do Sul's few dining options is a churrascaria. ⊠ *Rua J. F. Ritter 584, Cambará do Sul,* ☎ *051/251–1279. No credit cards.*

$$ 🏨 **Pousada das Corucacas.** This pousada is in the main building of an old ranch and is a good place to sample the world of the gaúcho. Guest rooms are small and facilities are basic (though breakfast and dinner are included in the rates), but all this seems in tune with the region's rugged spirit. There are waterfalls and woods in the area; consider exploring them on horseback. ⊠ *Km 3, Estrada Ouro Verde 95481–970,* ☎ *054/251–1128. 7 rooms. Dining room, horseback riding. No credit cards.*

Caixas do Sul

150 km (93 mi) north of Porto Alegre.

Caixas do Sul is the heart of the state's Italian region, where the first immigrants set foot in 1875. The mild climate and fertile soil helped spur development through agriculture; industry followed later. The city and such neighboring communities as Bento Gonçalves and Garibaldi, produce 90% of Brazil's wine, which has acquired some international recognition in recent years (☞ "Brazilian Wine" box, *below*).

The **Museu da Casa de Pedra** (Stone House Museum) is in the house (circa 1878) of the Lucchesi family, one of the first Italian families to arrive in the region. The basalt walls and hewn-wood window frames and doors are testaments to the harshness of the early days. (⊠ *Rua Ludovico Cavinatto s/n.* ⊡ *Free.* ⊙ *Tues.–Sun. 9–5.*)

Dining and Lodging

$$ ✗ **La Vindima.** In business since 1962, this restaurant is nationally recognized for the *galeto al primo canto* (Italian fried chicken). If you're

BRAZILIAN WINE

ALTHOUGH THE FIRST GRAPEVINES were brought to Brazil in 1532 by early Portuguese colonists, the Jesuits who settled in the south decades later were the first to establish true vineyards and wineries (to produce the wine needed for the Catholic mass). It wasn't until much later, however, that Brazil's viticulture gained any importance. In the 1800s a certain Thomas Master introduced American grapes, which did much better in the southern soil and climate than European varieties. At about this time, Italian immigrants—many well-versed in winemaking—began arriving in Brazil. At least 150,000 came to the south, forced from their homelands by overpopulation, war, and famine. These newcomers were the first to produce significant quantities of wine—and to give it its characteristic foxy taste—thereby establishing the Brazilian wine industry. Descendants of these Italian immigrants still produce wines of this kind for themselves and local markets.

Although the Serra Gaúcha is suitable for growing grapes, the rainfall is often excessive in January or March when the grapes reach maturity. This has traditionally made local winegrowers true heroes for being able to produce good wines in spite of difficult conditions.

In recent years, such international industry heavyweights as Moët et Chandon, Almadén, and Heublein have brought modern viticulture to the region. New agricultural techniques and hybridization have enabled European grapes to thrive and wine quality has improved dramatically. (Wines from Rio Grande do Sul have even received prizes in international contests.) In the 1980s, Almadén established new vineyards in the hills near the city of Santana do Livramento (about 480km/300 mi southwest of Porto Alegre on the Uruguay border), where climate and soils are more apt to produce high-quality grapes. Additionally Brazil's wine producers association (UVIBRA) is working on a system similar to that used in European countries for controlled-origin wines.

Today there are more than 100 *cantinas* (winemakers), primarily around the cities of Caixas do Sul and Bento Gonçalves in Rio Grande do Sul. Only a few of these produce wines of superior quality. Vineyards such as Casa Valduga (☎ 054/4338) and Vinícola Miolo (☞ Osteria Mamma Miolo *under* Dining and Lodging *in* Caixas do Sul, *above*) near Bento Gonçalves and Moët et Chandon in Garibaldi offer guided tours and wine-tasting sessions.

The following wines have received mentions in recent contests supervised by the Office International de la Vigne e du Vin (International Bureau of Wine): Chardonnay Brut and Gewürtztraminer (from Casa Valduga); Miolo Reserva Cabernet and Miolo Seleção (from Vinícola Miolo); Grand Philippe Cabernet and Grand Philippe Merlot (from Moët et Chandon).

not driving, try the house wine; if you are driving, the house grape juice is also good. ✉ *Rua Borges de Medeiros 446, Caixas do Sul,* ☎ *051/ 221–1696. No credit cards. Closed Sun.*

$$ ✕ **Osteria Mamma Miolo.** This restaurant is in Bento Gonçalves, adjacent to the Miolo winery. In addition to local versions of Italian fare, you'll also find such game as wild boar on the menu. ✉ *Km 68.5, RS 470, Vale dos Vinhedos, Bento Gonçalves,* ☎ *054/453–2695. MC, V.*

$$$ 🏨 **Reynolds International.** Impeccable service has become a hallmark at this small establishment. Because of this, it has increasingly attracted international businesspeople. ✉ *Rua Dr. Montaury 1441, Caixas do Sul 95100–970,* ☎ *054/223–5844,* 𝖥𝖠𝖷 *054/223–5843. 47 rooms. Bar, health club, business services. AE, DC, MC, V.*

THE SOUTH A TO Z

Arriving and Departing

By Airplane

PARANÁ

Curitiba's **Aeroporto Internacional Afonso Pena** (✉ Av. Rocha Pombo, São José dos Pinhais, ☎ 041/381–1515) is 21 km (13 mi) east of the city. A cab ride to downtown should cost no more than $20.

No international airlines serve Curitiba directly from Canada, the United Kingdom, or the United States. Domestic airlines that fly here include **TAM** (☎ 041/381–1620 or 041/323–5201), **Transbrasil** (☎ 041/381–1579 or 041/322–5655), **Varig** (☎ 041/381–1600 or 322–1343), and **VASP** (☎ 041/382–0345 or 041/221–7422).

The **Aeroporto Internacional Foz do Iguaçu** (✉ Km 13, Rodovia das Cataratas, ☎ 045/523–4244) is 13 km (8 mi) southeast of downtown. The 20-minute taxi ride should cost $12; the 45-minute regular bus ride, about 40¢. Note that several major hotels are on the highway to downtown, so a cab ride from the airport may be less than $12.

Iguaçu is served by **Transbrasil** (☎ 045/523–5205 or 045/523–3836), **Varig**(☎ 045/523–2155 or 523–2111), and **VASP** (☎ 045/523–8678 or 045/523–2212). **TAM** (☎ 0800/12–3100) now serves several destinations in Paraguay, including Ciudad del Este. (The airline offers free transportation to Foz do Iguaçu from Ciudad del Este's airport and back.)

SANTA CATARINA

The **Aeroporto Internacional Hercílio Luz** (✉ Km 12, Av. Deomício Freitas, ☎ 048/236–0879) is 12 km (8 mi) south of downtown Florianópolis. A cab into town will run about $15. Additionally, there's *amarelinho* (minibus) service for $2.

Domestic air carriers that serve the region include **TAM** (☎ 048/236–1812 or 041/323–5201), **Transbrasil** (☎ 048/236–1242 or 048/223–7777), **Varig** (☎ 0800/99–7000), and **VASP** (☎ 048/224–7824 or 0800/99–8277).

RIO GRANDE DO SUL

Porto Alegre's **Aeroporto Internacional Salgado Filho** (✉ Av. dos Estados s/n, ☎ 051/342–5638) is only 8 km (5 mi) northeast of downtown. (The cramped, underequipped, 50-year-old terminal will soon be replaced by a new and much larger facility, whose opening was imminent at press time.) You can prepay ($10) for a ride to town in special airport cars—full-size sedans painted white with a blue stripe—at a booth near the arrivals gate. Regular city cabs (painted a red-orange color) have meters; a ride to downtown should cost around $6. There's also a minibus shuttle into town for 70¢.

Airlines that serve the city include **Aerolíneas Argentinas** (☎ 051/342–4156 or 051/221–3300), **TAM** (☎ 051/358–3000), **Transbrasil** (☎ 051/337–2511 or 051/211–2800), **Varig** (☎ 051/358–7999 or 051/210–3939), and **VASP** (☎ 051/337–3204 or 051/225–6150).

By Bus
For the most part, each city is served by a different company. For long-distance trips, it's best to opt for *executivo* buses, which have air-conditioning, reclining seats, and rest rooms. Regular buses are 20% to 30% less, but aren't nearly as comfortable.

PARANÁ
Curitiba's main bus station is the **Estação Rodoferroviária** (✉ Av. Afonso Camargo s/n, ☎ 041/322–4344). **Catarinense** (☎ 041/222–1298) buses travel to Blumenau (4 hrs) and Joinville (1½ hrs). **Itapemirim** (☎ 041/356–2338) buses run to and from São Paulo (5 hrs). For trips to Porto Alegre (12 hrs), try **Pluma** (☎ 041/223–3641). **Sulamericana** (☎ 041/223–6387) buses make the 10-hour trip to Foz do Iguaçu.

Foz do Iguaçu's **Terminal Rodoviário** (✉ Av. Costa e Silva s/n, ☎ 045/522–3633) is 4 km (2½ mi) northeast of downtown. For trips to Florianópolis (14 hrs), contact **Catarinense** (☎ 045/223–2996). **Pluma** (☎ 045/522–2515) buses make the 16-hour journey to São Paulo. For trips to Curitiba (10 hrs), try **Sulamericana** (☎ 045/522–2050).

SANTA CATARINA
Several bus companies have regular service to and from Florianópolis's **Terminal Rodoviário Rita Maria** (✉ Av. Paulo Fontes 1101, ☎ 048/224–2777). For the 12-hour journey to São Paulo, the 3½-hour trip to Joinville, or the 2-hour trip to Blumenau try **Catarinense** (☎ 048/222–2260). **Pluma** (☎ 048/223–1709) buses travel to Curitiba (5 hrs). For trips to Porto Alegre (6 hrs) try **União Cascavel** (☎ 048/224–2080).

RIO GRANDE DO SUL
For now, all bus lines to the interior and to other states and countries use the ugly, overcrowded **Estação Rodoviária** (✉ Largo Vespasiano Veppo s/n, ☎ 051/145). Some international and interstate routes are slated to use the Aeroporto Salgado Filho building as soon as the new air terminal opens (☞ By Airplane, *above*). **Itapemirim/Penha** (☎ 051/225–0933) has service to São Paulo (19 hrs). **Pluma** (☎ 051/221–5025) buses travel to Curitiba (12 hrs). Florianópolis (6 hrs) is served by **Santo Anjo/Eucatur** (☎ 051/228–8900). To reach Foz do Iguaçu (14 hrs) try **Unesul** (☎ 051/228–0029).

By Car
The southern states have extensive highway systems. Although Rio Grande do Sul has some of the country's best (and safest) roads, those elsewhere aren't always in top condition; several stretches are being renovated, so be prepared for delays. When planning a road trip, ask the nearest Polícia Rodoviária (Highway Patrol) for guidance. Privatized roads (roads that are maintained by private investors rather than the government) are generally in better shape, but you'll have to pay tolls that range from $2–$5.

You can drive from Curitiba to Foz do Iguaçu on BR 277, which traverses Paraná State. It's a long drive (637 km/396 mi), but the highway is in good shape. To visit Vila Velha State Park, a 100 km (62 mi) detour must be made on the BR 376 toward Ponta Grossa. The BR 101 is the most direct route from Curitiba to other southern communities, but it's one of the country's busiest roads (there's lots of truck traffic night and day); it's also undergoing renovation. From Curitiba to Joinville it's 130 km (81 mi), to Blumenau 251 km (156 mi), to Florianópolis 300 km (186 mi), and to Porto Alegre 760 km (470 mi).

BR 116, the so-called Mountain Route, runs from Curitiba to Porto Alegre. Built 40 years ago, it was the first highway connecting the region with the rest of the country. Although it's scenic for much of the way and a little shorter than other routes, it's also narrow, badly kept, and busy.

By Train

One of Brazil's few passenger rail lines runs from Curitiba to Paranaguá—a fabulous trip. Trains pass through the Serra do Mar—where there are great views of the peaks and Atlantic rain forest—and stop in historical towns along the way. There are two kinds of train: the faster *litorina* makes the trip in 3½ hours, departs from Curitiba at 8:30 AM, returns from Paranaguá at 4 PM, and costs $20; the trip by regular train takes 4 hours; it departs at 9 AM, returns at 4:30 PM, and costs $15. To make arrangements contact **Serra Verde Express** (⊠ Estação Rodoferroviária, Gate 8, Curitiba, ☎ 041/323–4007).

Getting Around

By Bus

Within the region's cities, the bus is the preferred form of public transportation. You can reach virtually any neighborhood, and the fares are modest. Still, you must use caution as crime can be a problem on little-traveled routes or during off-peak hours.

PARANÁ

In Curitiba the **Linha Turismo** is a special bus line maintained by the city that follows a 2½-hour circular route. Buses depart every hour from the Praça Tiradentes, and they stop at many attractions. There are taped descriptions of the sights (available in three languages, including English), and the fare is about $3. Timetables are posted at Praça Tiradentes, or you can contact the **Prefeitura-Turismo** (☎ 156 or 041/ 352–4021, ext. 9863) for more information.

In Foz do Iguaçu, Linha Cataratas buses depart hourly from the **Terminal Urbano** (⊠ Av. Juscelino Kubitschek s/n, across from the army barracks, ☎ no phone) for the Hotel das Cataratas, right near the falls. The fare is 30¢. Buses for Puerto Iguazú, Argentina, and Ciudad del Este, Paraguay, depart from the same terminal.

SANTA CATARINA

In Florianópolis, a quick, convenient way to visit the beaches is by amarelinho, or express minibus. They leave regularly from the **Terminal Urbano** (⊠ Praça 15 de Novembro s/n, Centro, ☎ 048/1517).

RIO GRANDE DO SUL

Porto Alegre has an extensive bus system (although there's not one central station) as well as *lotação* (express minibus) service. The lotações leave from several spots in Centro. For more information, call **Informações Municipais** (☎ 051/156).

By Car

Traffic in Curitiba, Florianópolis, and Porto Alegre isn't as hectic as in São Paulo or Rio, so driving won't be overly daunting. Finding a place to park is relatively easy except, of course, in the downtown districts during business hours. Lots are abundant in the cities, and one-hour tickets cost about $1.

Area rental car companies include: **Avis** (✉ Aeroporto Internacional Afonso Pena, Av. Rocha Pombo, São José dos Pinhais, ☎ 041/381–1383; ✉ Av. Salgado Filho 1491, ☎ 041/278–8808) or **Hertz** (✉ Aeroporto Internacional Afonso Pena, Av. Rocha Pombo, São José dos Pinhais, ☎ 041/381–1382; ✉ Av. Nossa Senhora Aparecida 3731, ☎ 041/342–4222).

In Foz do Iguaçu, you can try **Avis** (✉ Km 10, Rodovia das Cataratas, ☎ 045/523–1510) or **Localiza** (✉ Km 10, Rodovia das Cataratas, ☎ 045/523–4800; ✉ Av. Juscelino Kubitschek 2878, ☎ 045/522–1608).

Florianópolis car rental agencies include **Avis** (✉ Aeroporto Internacional Hercílio Luz, Km 12, Av. Deomício Freitas, ☎ 048/236–1426; ✉ Av. Silva Jardim 495, ☎ 048/225–7777), **Hertz** (✉ Aeroporto Internacional Hercílio Luz, Km 12, Av. Deomício Freitas, ☎ 048/236–9955), and **Localiza** (✉ Aeroporto Internacional Hercílio Luz, Km 12, Av. Deomício Freitas, ☎ 048/236–1244; ✉ Av. Paulo Fonte 730, ☎ 048/225–5558).

Car rental agencies in Porto Alegre include **Avis** (✉ Aeroporto Internacional Salgado Filho, Av. dos Estados s/n, ☎ 051/371–4344; ✉ Av. Ceará 341, ☎ 051/342–0400), **Hertz** (✉ Av. dos Estados 75, Loja 3, ☎ 051/337–7755), or **Localiza** (✉ Aeroporto Internacional Salgado Filho, Av. dos Estados s/n, ☎ 051/371–4345; ✉ Av. Carlos Gomes 230, ☎ 051/328–6000).

By Taxi

Taxis in Brazil are normally independently owned, and most are locally organized into cooperatives that maintain phone numbers and dispatchers (hence, the moniker "radio taxis"). These outfits have booths in all airports with posted rates (regulated by city authorities) for specific destinations, and you pay up front for the ride to town. Although it's best to call for a cab in town to avoid delays, you can hail passing taxis. Cabs have meters, but ask for an estimate of the fare to your destination before departing to avoid surprises.

The following are reliable cab companies: **Curitiba radio-taxi service** (☎ 041/262–6262 or 041/276–7676), **Foz do Iguaçu radio-taxi service** (☎ 045/523–4800), **Florianópolis radio-taxi service** (☎ 048/197), **Porto Alegre radio-taxi service** (☎ 051/228–5777).

Contacts and Resources

Banks and Currency Exchange

In general, banks are open weekdays 10–4, though airport branches have extended hours (daily 8 AM–9 PM) just for currency exchange. Exchange houses are usually open weekdays 8–5; some also have Saturday morning hours. ATMs that dispense cash (reais) and work with international bank or credit cards are readily available. Banco 24 Horas ATMs are linked with Cirrus; Banco do Brasil ATMs are affiliated with Plus.

In Curitiba, try **Banco ABN-AMRO** (Av. Candido de Abreu 304, Centro Cívico, ☎ 041/252–2233) or **Banco do Brasil** (✉ Aeroporto Internacional Afonso Pena, Av. Rocha Pombo, São José dos Pinhais, ☎ 041/223–1350).

In Foz do Iguaçu, try **Banco do Brasil** (Av. Brasil 1377, ☎ 045/523–2288) or **Omegatur Turismo e Câmbio** (Av. Juscelino Kubitschek 245, ☎ 045/572–2837).

SANTA CATARINA

In Florianópolis your choices include **Banco do Brasil** (✉ Praça 15 de Novembro 20, ☎ 048/222–7000) and **Ilhatur** (✉ Rua Jeronimo Coelho 185, ☎ 041/224–6333).

RIO GRANDE DO SUL

In Porto Alegre, try **Banco do Brasil** (✉ Rua Uruguai 185, Centro, ☎ 051/228–7877; ✉ Aeroporto Internacional Salgado Filho, Av. dos Estados s/n, ☎ 051/371–4154), **Citibank** (✉ Praça Maurício Cardoso 176, ☎ 051/222–4488), or **Turispres** (✉ Rua dos Andradas 1091, suite 104, ☎ 051/225–3054; ✉ Estação Rodoviária, Largo Vespasiano Veppo s/n, ☎ 051/225–3565).

Consulate

United Kingdom (✉ Rua Itapeva 110, Suite 505, Porto Alegre, ☎ 051/341–0720).

Emergencies

PARANÁ

Ambulance: ☎ 192. **General emergencies:** ☎ 100. **Hospital: Hospital Cajuru** (✉ Av. São José 300, Curitiba, ☎ 041/362–1100). **Police:** ☎ 190.

Hospital: Hospital Internacional (✉ Av. Brasil 1637, Foz do Iguaçu, ☎ 045/523–1404). **Pharmacy: FarmaRede** (✉ Av. Brasil 46, Foz do Iguaçu, ☎ 045/523–1929). **Police:** ☎ 190.

SANTA CATARINA

Hospital: Hospital Universitário (✉ Av. Beira-Mar Norte, Trindade, Florianópolis, ☎ 048/231–9100). **Pharmacy:** the **Farmácia Rita Maria** (✉ Av. Paulo Fontes 1101, Terminal Rita Maria, Florianópolis, ☎ 048/224–3249 is open 24-hours a day. **Police:** ☎ 190.

RIO GRANDE DO SUL

Ambulance: ☎ 192. **Fire:** ☎ 193. **Hospital: Hospital Pronto Socorro** (✉ Av. Osvaldo Aranha s/n, Porto Alegre, ☎ 051/330–9888). **Pharmacy:** the **Farmácia PanVel** (✉ Av. 24 de Outubro 722, Moinhos de Vento, Porto Alegre, ☎ 051/222–0188) is open 24-hours a day. **Police:** ☎ 190.

English-Language Bookstores

Few bookstores stock English-language books. When they're available, expect only a limited selection of paperbacks. Foreign newspapers are rarely available; you might have more success with popular international magazines.

In Curitiba try **Livraria O Livro Técnico** (✉ Shopping Center Itália, Rua João Negrão 129, ☎ 041/232–6621). Florianópolis has the **Livraria Alemã** (✉ Rua Felipe Schmidt 14, ☎ 041/224–0178).

In Porto Alegre good bets are **Prosa i Verso** (✉ Quinta Avenida Shopping Center, Av. Mostardeiro 120, ☎ 051/222–1155), which has a limited selection of classics and run-of-the-mill paperbacks, and **Siciliano** (✉ Iguatemi Shopping Center, Rua João Wallig 1800, ☎ 051/338–1833), which carries paperbacks, travel guides, and some popular magazines.

Health and Safety

Here, in Brazil's most developed region, tap water is safe to drink in most areas; it's usually highly chlorinated, however, so you may prefer the taste of bottled water. As in the rest of Brazil, avoid eating unpeeled fruit. Crime is low compared with the northern parts of the country. However, you should guard your belongings on city buses and in crowded public spaces—especially bus terminals, which are havens for pickpockets.

Telephones, the Internet, and Mail

Area codes in the region include 041 for Curitiba, 045 for Foz do Iguaçu, 048 for Florianópolis, and 051 for Porto Alegre. Outside hotels, you can make long-distance calls from *posto telefônicos* (central phone offices), kept by phone companies in all cities. Fax services, and more recently Internet services, are also provided at most of these offices.

PARANÁ

Curitiba: Teleposto TELEPAR (⊠ Av. Pres. Afonso Camargo 330, Centro, ☎ 041/322–9848). **Correios** (Post Office; ⊠ Av. Marechal Deodoro 298, ☎ 041/310–2100). **FedEx** (⊠ Rua Nossa Senhora da Penha 435, ☎ 041/362–5155). **Foz do Iguaçu: Posto Telefônico TELEPAR** (Rua E. Barros s/n, Centro, ☎ 045/523–2449). **Correios** (Praça Getúlio Vargas 72, ☎ 045/574–2381).

SANTA CATARINA

Florianópolis: Posto Telefônico TELESC (⊠ Praça Pereira Oliveira 20, ☎ 048/106). **Correios** (⊠ Praça 15 de Novembro 242, ☎ 048/159). **FedEx** (⊠ Rua Coronel Américo 912, ☎ 048/240–6232).

RIO GRANDE DO SUL

In Porto Alegre, you can make long-distance calls from some phone booths or try the **CRT Phone Center** (⊠ Av. Sen. Salgado Filho 27, ☎ 051/228–0505), which has fax and Internet services, too.

Correios (⊠ Rua Siqueira Campos 1100, Porto Alegre, ☎ 051/228–9102 or 051/159 for toll-free information on other city branches). **FedEx** (⊠ Av. Ceará 255, Porto Alegre, ☎ 051/343–5424). **UPS** (⊠ Rua Visc. Rio Branco 279, Porto Alegre, ☎ 051/346–6655).

Tour Operators and Travel Agents

PARANÁ

In Curitiba try **Best Ways** (⊠ Estação Rodoferroviária, Gate 8, ☎ 041/323–4007).

Reliable companies in Foz do Iguaçu include **Golden Foz Turismo** (⊠ Rua Tarobá 557, Centro, ☎ 045/523–2121); **Macuco Boat Safari** (⊠ Km 21, Rodovia das Cataratas, ☎ 045/574–4244), which arranges trips to Salto Macuco and onto the main falls; and **Helisul Táxi Aéreo** (⊠ Km 16.5, Rodovia das Cataratas, ☎ 045/523–1190), which arranges helicopter tours of the falls and, if you like, of Itaipú dam. The shortest flight (10 min) costs $50 per person.

SANTA CATARINA

In Florianópolis try **Ilhatur** (Rua Jeronimo Coelho 185, ☎ 041/224–6333). **ScunaSul** (⊠ Pier under Ponte Hercílio Luz, ☎ 048/225–1806) is a reliable boat-tour operator, with well-kept sailboats and an informed staff.

RIO GRANDE DO SUL

In Porto Alegre, **Cisne Branco** (⊠ Port of Porto Alegre, Main Gate, Av. Mauá 1050, ☎ 051/224–5222) runs day and night boat trips on the Guaíba.

Tours to the Serra Gaúcha and the coast can be arranged by several Porto Alegre operators including **Socaltur** (⊠ Rua Senhor dos Passos 235, ☎ 051/228–3955) and **Unesul** (⊠ Rua Vigário José Inácio 621, ☎ 051/228–8111).

Caá-Etê Expeditions (⊠ Av. Protásio Alves 2715, suite 905, Porto Alegre, ☎ 051/338–3323) is a good choice for adventure trips such as rafting or hiking excursions to the state parks.

Visitor Information

PARANÁ

Paraná Turismo (State Tourism Board; ⊠ Rua Dep. Mário de Barros, 290, Curitiba, ☎ 041/224–7273 or 041/1516 [24-hr hotline]). **FozTur** (⊠ Rua Alm. Barroso 1300, Foz do Iguaçu, ☎ 045/574–2196 or 041/1516 [24-hr hotline]).

SANTA CATARINA

SanTur (⊠ Rua Felipe Schmidt 249, 9th floor, Florianópolis, ☎ 048/224–6300).

RIO GRANDE DO SUL

Secretaria de Turismo (State Tourism Authority; ⊠ Av. Borges de Medeiros 1501, 10th floor, Porto Alegre, ☎ 051/228–7377 or 051/228–7749; ⊠ Aeroporto Internacional Salgado Filho, Av. dos Estados s/n, ☎ 051/228–7377 ext. 248; ⊠ Estação Rodoviária, Largo Vespasiano Veppo s/n, ☎ 051/228–7377 ext. 247).

5 MINAS GERAIS

In the early 18th century gold was discovered in the rich, red earth of Minas Gerais. The legacies of this discovery are historic cities with narrow, cobblestone streets that wind past baroque churches; mineral spa towns made mystical with therapeutic waters and mountainous surroundings; and a type of Brazilian like no other. The traditional, proud *mineiros* have sent forth some of the nation's most famous artists and politicians.

Updated and
expanded by
Shane
Christensen

BRAZIL'S CENTRAL MOUNTAINOUS REGION is dominated by the state of Minas Gerais, a name (meaning "general mines") inspired by the area's great mineral wealth. In the 18th century, its vast precious-metal reserves made the state, and particularly the city of Ouro Prêto, the de facto capital of the Portuguese colony. That period of gold, diamond, and semiprecious stone trading is memorialized in the historic towns scattered across the mountains and remains a tremendous source of pride for the *mineiros* (inhabitants of the state). Minas Gerais is a calmer, more conservative, more thoughtful Brazil. Yet it has also been a hotbed for movements that have triggered political, economic, and cultural development.

Exploration of Minas Gerais began in the 17th century, when *bandeirantes* (bands of adventurers) from the coastal areas came in search of slaves and gold. Near the town of Vila Rica, they found a black stone that was later verified to be gold (the coloring came from the iron oxide in the soil). Vila Rica thus came to be called Ouro Prêto (Black Gold), and at the beginning of the 18th century, Brazil's first gold rush began. Along with the fortune seekers came Jesuit priests, who were later exiled by the Portuguese (for fear that they would try to manipulate the mineral trade) and replaced by *ordens terceiros* ("third" or lay orders). By the middle of the century, the Gold Towns of Minas were gleaming with new churches built first in the baroque-rococo style of Europe and, later, in a baroque style unique to the region.

Minas was also blessed with a local artistic genius. The son of a Portuguese architect and a former slave, Antônio Francisco Lisboa was born in 1738 in what is today Ouro Prêto. Nicknamed Aleijadinho, "the little cripple," he was left deformed as an adult by an illness. Working in cedarwood and soapstone, Aleijadinho carved the passion of his beliefs in sculptures that grace churches throughout the state (☞ "The Passion of Aleijadinho" box, *below*).

By the end of the 18th century, the gold began to run out, and Ouro Prêto's population and importance decreased. The baroque period ended at the start of the 19th century, when the Portuguese royal family, in flight from the conquering army of Napoléon Bonaparte, arrived in Brazil, bringing with them architects and sculptors with different ideas and artistic styles. Twisted, ornate columns and walls adorned with lavish carvings gave way to straight, simple columns and walls painted with murals or simply washed in white.

Though you'll always be awed by the Gold Towns, Minas Gerais has other attractions. Roughly six hours south of Belo Horizonte, the state capital, several mineral spa towns form the Circuito das Aguas (Water Circuit). Thought to have healing powers, the natural springs of places like São Lourenço and Caxambu have drawn the Brazilian elite for more than a century. Close by is the unusual town of São Tomé das Letras—a place where UFOs are said to visit, and where mystics and bohemians wait for the dawn of a new world.

While justifiably proud of their state's artistic accomplishments, mineiros are also passionate about their politics. Minas Gerais has produced many of Brazil's most famous leaders, including Tiradentes, who led Brazil's first attempt at independence; Juscelino Kubitschek, the president who made Brasília happen; and Tancredo Neves, who helped restore Brazilian democracy in the mid 1980s.

Today, Minas is Brazil's second most industrialized state, after São Paulo. The iron that darkened the gold of Ouro Prêto remains an important source of state income, along with steel, coffee, and auto manufacturing. Although some of its once heavily wooded areas have been stripped bare—the heavy price of development—Minas still has diverse and amazingly pristine ecosystems, including Atlantic forests, rain forests, wetlands, and grasslands. The traffic that the mines brought here in the 17th century thrust Brazil into civilization, and now, well into the wake of the gold rush, a steady sense of progress and a compassion for the land remains.

Pleasures and Pastimes

Architecture

Minas Gerais has Brazil's finest examples of baroque architecture. The elaborate, oft-gilded carvings in Ouro Prêto's churches are largely attributed to the legendary Aleijadinho. All told, more than 3,000 of its buildings—which have not only baroque and rococo but also neoclassical and eclectic characteristics—are under preservation orders.

Dining

Comida mineira (Minas cuisine) offers distinctive flavors and specialties. Pork, particularly *lombo* (pork tenderloin), is used in many dishes and is often served with white rice and/or corn porridge. Typical specialties include *tutu a mineira* (mashed beans with roast pork loin, pork sausage, chopped collard greens, and boiled egg), *feijão tropeiro* (beans mixed with manioc flour, roast pork loin, fried egg, chopped collard greens, and thick pork sausage), *frango com quiabo* (chicken cooked in broth with chopped okra), and *frango ao molho pardo* (chicken cooked in a black sauce—the chicken's blood). Of course *caipirinhas* (drinks of crushed ice; crushed lime; sugar; and *cachaça,* a sugarcanebased liquor) go well with all the regional dishes. Mineiros tend to eat dinner after 8 (often closer to 10). Restaurants are busiest on weekends and may require reservations; many close on Monday. For price categories, *see* Dining *in* Smart Travel Tips A to Z.

Gemstones

Minas Gerais produces most of the world's colored gemstones, including imperial topaz (found nowhere else and available in pink and tangerine hues, with the best stones being as clear as possible), the grande dame of them all. The state's mines also produce amethysts, aquamarines, tourmalines, and emeralds. The stones are cut, polished, and incorporated into jewelry in cities like Ouro Prêto and Belo Horizonte, where you can buy authenticated pieces—often at heavily discounted prices—from top jewelers. Note that gems vary widely in quality and value; don't buy them on the streets, and be wary about buying them from smaller shops (get recommendations first).

Shopping

Hand-carved wood and soapstone figures and objects are sold by street vendors in all the historic cities. Other typical handicrafts include pottery and tapestries, in particular the hand-woven *arraiola* tapestries for which the area around Diamantina is famous. Of course you should always be on the lookout for interesting jewelry (☞ Gemstones, *above*).

Lodging

Mineiro hotel, *pousada* (inn), and *fazenda* (farm) owners are paying more and more attention to the quality of their rooms and service. That said, most hotels remain small, lack English-speaking staffs, and have few of the amenities common in American and European chains. When you book, you'll likely be given a choice between a standard and luxury room; the *apartamento de luxo* (luxury room) may be slightly larger, offer air-conditioning, and have a better-equipped bathroom. In most cases, breakfast is included in the rate. Significant weekend discounts are common in Belo Horizonte. For price categories, *see* Lodging *in* Smart Travel Tips A to Z.

Exploring Minas Gerais

The peaks of the Serra do Mantiqueira separate Minas from Rio de Janeiro and give way to the Paraiba Valley. Although Minas is large, its major attractions, including Belo Horizonte, Ouro Prêto, and the mineral spa towns, are in the state's southeast, within driving distance of one another. The key historic cities—called the Gold Towns—are in the Serra do Espinhaço range, with Ouro Prêto at 4,000 ft above sea level.

Great Itineraries

IF YOU HAVE 5 DAYS

Rest from your journey by staying overnight in Belo Horizonte, the gateway city and hub for trips to the Gold Towns. On the second day, head to Sabará, a short local bus ride away. On the third day, travel to Ouro Prêto, a two-hour drive or bus ride from the capital, for two days of exploring its rich architecture, shopping for its unique handicrafts, and absorbing its folklore.

IF YOU HAVE 7 DAYS

Spend a day in Belo Horizonte. On the second day, rent a car and head to Ouro Prêto for two days of sightseeing. On the fourth day, visit neighboring Mariana, the state's oldest city. For your remaining days you can either head north to Diamantina or south through Congonhas and on to the charming town of Tiradentes.

IF YOU HAVE 10 DAYS

Follow the seven-day itinerary. On the eighth day head to the spa towns south of Belo Horizonte for the remainder of your trip. Be aware that innkeepers in places like São Lourenço and Caxambu will do their best to convince you that a few days in their towns aren't nearly enough—the waters' curative properties are said to only take effect after 20 or so days.

When to Tour

The busiest and often most exciting times to travel are during the Christmas, Easter, and Carnaval (Carnival) periods—although Carnaval is much more subdued here than in Bahia or Rio. July, when the weather is cool and dry, is winter break month and another peak season. To avoid crowds, travel from April to June or August to December. Discounts may be available during these months, although fewer services will be offered.

BELO HORIZONTE AND THE HISTORIC CITIES

Brazil's first planned state capital, Belo Horizonte (often called the Garden City or just simply "Belo") has tree-lined streets and an intimate small-town atmosphere that belies its size. Although it has few tourist attractions, it's the gateway to the region's historic cities, and its citizens are warm, gracious, and helpful.

Two hours southeast of Belo is Ouro Prêto, a UNESCO World Heritage Site. The country's de facto capital during the gold-boom years, it was also the birthplace of Brazil's first independence movement: the Inconfidência Mineira. Today, a vibrant student population ensures plenty

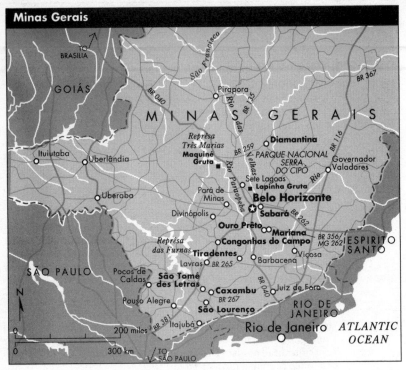

Minas Gerais

of year-round activity, and there are many lodging, dining, and shopping options.

All the Gold Towns are characterized by winding cobblestone streets, brilliant baroque churches, impressive mansions and museums, and colorful markets. Smaller but no less charming than Ouro Prêto is Tiradentes, which truly seems to have stopped in time about midway through the 18th century. Between Ouro Prêto and Tiradentes lies Congonhas, whose basilica is guarded by Aleijadinho's extraordinary sculptures of the 12 Old Testament prophets. In each of the towns you visit, from Sabará to Mariana to Diamantina, you'll discover a rich cultural history that sheds considerable light on colonial Brazil.

Belo Horizonte

444 km (276 mi) northwest of Rio, 741 km (460 mi) southeast of Brasília.

With a population of almost 2.4 million, Belo Horizonte is Brazil's third-largest city and the capital of Minas Gerais, a state renowned as much for its love of tradition as for its mineral wealth. For visitors, Belo Horizonte is primarily a jumping-off point for trips to the surrounding region, as the city itself offers little of historic value. (It is, in fact, relatively young, having been founded in 1897.)

The well-maintained **Parque Municipal** is in the heart of the business district and close to several hotels. Its tree-lined walks, small lakes, and rustic bridges make it an example of the passion for orderliness that's characteristically mineiro. This same trait has helped make Belo Horizonte one of the cleanest and safest of Brazil's leading cities. Within the park is the **Palácio das Artes** (Palace of the Arts; ⊠ Av. Afonso Pena 1537, ☎ 031/237–7286), a cultural center with a theater; a library;

art galleries; exhibition halls; and the Centro de Artesenato Mineiro, with such contemporary Minas handicrafts as carvings of wood and soapstone, pottery, and tapestries—all for sale. Admission is free.

Ironically, though most people come to Belo for the nearby historic region, one of the city's principal attractions is the Pampulha neighborhood, famed for its examples of modern Brazilian architecture. Foremost among these is the **Capela de São Francisco** (Chapel of Saint Francis), completed in 1943 and considered one of the most important works of Brazil's famed architect Oscar Niemeyer. Inside the small but distinctive chapel, with its undulating roof, are frescoes—of St. Francis and of the Stations of the Cross—by Cândido Portinari, a famous Brazilian modernist. To reach the chapel, take a taxi or Bus 2004 (it goes north on Avenida Presidente Antônio Carlos). The chapel is on the edge of an artificial lake a half-hour from downtown; the drive to it is lovely. ⊠ *Av. Otacílio Negrão de Lima, Km 12, Pampulha,* ☎ *031/ 491–2319.* 🎟 *Admission.* ⊘ *Weekdays 8:30–noon and 1:30–6, weekends 9–6.*

Dining

$$$$ ✕ **Restaurante Verandão.** On the 25th floor of the Othon Palace hotel (☞ Lodging, *below*), this romantic restaurant offers spectacular urban vistas. Start off with a cocktail at one of the outdoor candlelit tables before coming inside for dinner, where a generous buffet acts as the dining room's centerpiece. The weekend sees the chef's innovative "soapstone barbecue," where you choose thinly sliced meats to grill on a hot soapstone; your meal also comes with potatoes, sauces, and toast. Live Brazilian music accompanies dinner nightly. ⊠ *Av. Afonso Pena 1050, Centro,* ☎ *031/273–3844. AE, DC, MC, V.*

$$$$ ✕ **Splêndido Ristorante.** The food and the service at this cosmopolitan restaurant are exceptional; the prices are also on the "splendid" side. The kitchen blends northern Italian and French cuisines, and it's assured that anyone who's anyone will show up here at some point during a visit to Belo Horizonte. ⊠ *Rua Levindo Lopes 251, Savassi,* ☎ *031/227–6446. AE, DC, MC, V.*

$$$$ ✕ **Vecchio Sogno.** What is widely considered Belo Horizonte's best Italian restaurant attracts a well-heeled clientele. Tuxedo-clad waiters serve selections from the extensive wine list as well as steak, seafood, and pasta dishes. Consider the grilled fillet of lamb with saffron risotto in a mushroom and garlic sauce; the gnocchi *di mare,* made with spinach and potatoes and served with a white-clam and scallop sauce; or the *badejo,* a local white fish baked and dressed in a seafood sauce. Reservations are highly recommended. ⊠ *Rua Martim de Carvalho 75, Santo Agostinho,* ☎ *031/292–5251 or 031/290–7585. AE, DC, MC, V. No lunch Sat. No dinner Sun.*

$$$ ✕ **Amici Miei.** This casual Italian eatery is popular with Brazilians celebrating the end of the workday. The restaurant is often packed both inside and on the large outdoor patio; you may need to wait a minute for the staff to find you a table. Start with the *champignon Recheado* (a large mushroom stuffed with shrimp and prosciutto), followed by *tournedo Amici Miei* (filet mignon wrapped in bacon and marinated in garlic and olive oil). ⊠ *Rua Tome de Souza 1331, Centro,* ☎ *031/ 282–4992. DC, MC, V.*

$$$ ✕ **Chalezinho.** There's only one reason to come here: romance. The dimly lit chalet, with its elegant piano music (accompanied by the occasional saxophone), is a magical retreat in the hills above town. The specialty is fondue; the filet mignon cooked in a bowl of sizzling oil and paired with any one of eight delicious sauces is a treat. Afterward, order a chocolate fondue, which comes with a mouth-watering selection of fruits waiting to be dipped. When you finish, step outside to

the Praça dos Amores (Lovers' Plaza) for a kiss under the moonlit sky. ⊠ *Alameda da Serra 18, Vale do Soreno–Nova Lima,* ☎ *031/286–3155. AE, DC, MC, V. No lunch.*

$$ ✕ **Casa dos Contos.** The menu at this gathering place for local journalists, artists, and intellectuals is unpretentious and varied, ranging from fish and pasta to comida mineira. In keeping with its bohemian clientele, Casa dos Contos serves well past midnight. ⊠ *Rua Rio Grande do Norte 1065, Funcionários,* ☎ *031/222–1070. AE, DC, MC, V.*

$$ ✕ **Restaurante Top Beer.** This trendy restaurant-bar makes an ideal launching pad for your evening. The large outdoor patio offers great people-watching, as students and executives alike plan their night out while sipping caipirinhas. The inside dining room is an inviting tropical enclave, with fountains and trees surrounding the tables. The pasta dishes and grilled steaks are commendable. ⊠ *Rua Tomé de Souza 1121, Savassi,* ☎ *031/221–1116. AE, DC, MC, V.*

$ ✕ **Chico Mineiro.** Dining Minas Gerais–style means ample portions of
★ such hearty dishes as tutu a mineira, the local equivalent of meat and potatoes. Nowhere is it better prepared than at this traditional restaurant in the Savassi neighborhood, home to Belo's liveliest night spots. ⊠ *Rua Alagoas 626, Savassi,* ☎ *031/261–3237. AE, DC, MC, V.*

$ ✕ **Dona Lucinha II.** Traditional Minas dishes are offered in this cafeteria-style eatery. Though there's not much charm, the "self-service" concept helps to keep the prices down. ⊠ *Rua Sergipe 811, Savassi,* ☎ *031/261–5930. AE, DC, MC, V.*

Lodging

$$$$ 🏨 **Ouro Minas Palace Hotel.** Though not centrally located, this hotel
★ truly deserves a star. Rooms are comfortably decorated and appealing, with large beds and well-appointed bathrooms; minibars and modem hook-ups are standard. The hotel offers numerous amenities uncommon in Belo Horizonte: a pool with waterfalls, a fitness center, tennis courts, and a multilingual staff. ⊠ *Av. Christiano Machado 4001, Ipiranga, 31910-810,* ☎ *031/429–4001,* FAX *031/429–4002. 343 rooms, 44 suites. Restaurant, bar, café, in-room modem lines, minibars, pool, massage, Turkish bath, 2 tennis courts, health club, business services, car rental. AE, DC, MC, V.*

$$$ 🏨 **Brasilton Contagem.** This modern member of the Hilton chain is popular with business travelers because of its proximity to the Contagem industrial district (it is, however, quite far from the center of town). Guest rooms face a central courtyard with a pool and tropical gardens, creating an atmosphere of total relaxation. ⊠ *BR 381, Km 3.65, Contagem 32241-410,* ☎ *031/396–1100,* FAX *031/396–1144. 144 rooms. Restaurant, bar, pool. AE, DC, MC, V.*

$$$ 🏨 **Hotel Wimbledon.** An elegant yet warm atmosphere and a central
★ location are two of this hotel's draws. Guest rooms are well decorated, with polished hardwood floors, local artwork, and modern bathrooms; luxury rooms have Jacuzzis. Attentive service makes this hotel feel more like a bed-and-breakfast. There's a rooftop pool and bar—the perfect spot for an afternoon drink. ⊠ *Av. Afonso Pena 772, Centro 30130-002,* ☎ *031/222–6160,* FAX *031/222–6510. 69 rooms, 1 suite. Restaurant, bar, pool, sauna. AE, DC, MC, V.*

$$$ 🏨 **Merit Plaza.** Located downtown, this hotel offers excellent value,
★ particularly for business travelers in need of modern amenities and a convenient location. Granite covers the contemporary atrium lobby, and guest rooms have sound-proof walls, large beds, well-appointed bathrooms, and phones equipped for computer and fax use. ⊠ *Rua dos Tamoios 341, Centro 30130-002,* ☎ *031/201–9000,* FAX *031/271–*

Finally, a travel companion that doesn't snore on the plane or eat all your peanuts.

MCI WORLDCOM   *WorldPhone®*

123 456 7891 2345
J.D. SMITH

When traveling, your MCI WorldCom Card is the best way to keep in touch. Our operators speak your language, so they'll be able to connect you back home—no matter where your travels take you. Plus, your MCI WorldCom Card is easy to use, and even earns you frequent flyer miles every time you use it. When you add in our great rates, you get something even more valuable: peace-of-mind. So go ahead. Travel the world. MCI WorldCom just brought it a whole lot closer.

You can even sign up today at www.mci.com/worldphone or ask your operator to make a collect call to 1-410-314-2938.

EASY TO CALL WORLDWIDE

1 Just dial the WorldPhone access number of the country you're calling from.
2 Dial or give the operator your MCI WorldCom Card number.
3 Dial or give the number you're calling.

Argentina	
To call using Telefonica	**0-800-222-6249**
To call using Telecom	**0-800-555-1002**
Brazil	**000-8012**
Mexico	
Avantel	**01-800-021-8000**
Telmex ▲	**001-800-674-7000**
Collect access in Spanish	**980-9-16-1000**
Morocco	**00-211-0012**

For your complete WorldPhone calling guide, dial the WorldPhone access number for the country you're in and ask the operator for Customer Service. In the U.S. call 1-800-431-5402.

▲ When calling from public phones, use phones marked LADATEL.

EARN FREQUENT FLYER MILES

American Airlines®
AAdvantage®

Continental Airlines
OnePass

▲ Delta Air Lines
SkyMiles®

MILEAGE PLUS®
United Airlines

U·S AIRWAYS
DIVIDEND MILES

MCI WorldCom, its logo and the names of the products referred to herein are proprietary marks of MCI WorldCom, Inc. All airline names and logos are proprietary marks of the respective airlines. All airline program rules and conditions apply.

MCI WORLDCOM

The first thing you need overseas is the one thing you forget to pack.

FOREIGN CURRENCY DELIVERED OVERNIGHT

Chase Currency To Go® delivers foreign currency to your home by the next business day*

It's easy–before you travel, call 1-888-CHASE84 for delivery of any of 75 currencies

Delivery is free with orders of $500 or more

Competitive rates– without exchange fees

You don't have to be a Chase customer–you can pay by Visa® or MasterCard®

CHASE

THE RIGHT RELATIONSHIP IS EVERYTHING.®

1•888•CHASE84
www.chase.com

5700. 115 rooms, 2 suites. Restaurant, bar, café, in-room modem lines, business services. AE, DC, MC, V.

$$$ ☐ **Othon Palace.** The Othon has the best location of any hotel in Belo Horizonte. Although aging (it opened in 1978), renovations are on-going, and the level of service remains high. Rooms provide little special character, but are comfortable and enjoy spectacular city views, including the tree-lined Parque Municipal. The rooftop pool and bar is the best in town, and the on-site Restaurante Verandão (☞ *Dining, above*) is excellent. ✉ *Av. Afonso Pena 1050, Centro 30130-002,* ☎ *031/273–3844,* FAX *031/212–2318. 266 rooms, 19 suites. Restaurant, bar, pool, massage, sauna, tennis court, exercise room, concierge floor, business services, meeting rooms. AE, DC, MC, V.*

$$ ☐ **Grandville Hotel.** The lobby of this centrally located hotel, one of the city's older establishments, is often crowded with conventioneers. Rooms are comfortable, if a bit dark; many, however, have the same view of the city and surrounding mountains that you'll find from the small rooftop pool and bar. ✉ *Rua Espírito Santo 901, Centro 30160-031,* ☎ *0800/31–1188,* FAX *031/248–1100. 247 rooms, 8 suites. Restaurant, bar, pool, sauna, exercise room, business services, meeting rooms. AE, DC, MC, V.*

$$ ☐ **Wembley Palace.** This aging high-rise offers clean (albeit small) rooms, reliable service, and a central location. ✉ *Rua Espírito Santo 201, Centro 30160-031,* ☎ *031/273–6866,* FAX *031/224–9946. 105 rooms, 2 suites. Restaurant, bar, minibars. AE, DC, MC, V.*

$ ☐ **Amazônas.** You'll find clean, simply furnished, reasonably priced rooms at this downtown hotel. There's a good restaurant on the 11th floor. ✉ *Av. Amazônas 120, Centro 30160-031,* ☎ *031/201–4644,* FAX *031/202–4236. 76 rooms. Restaurant, bar. AE, DC, MC, V.*

$ ☐ **Palmeiras da Liberdade.** Although it's in the chic Savassi neighborhood, this comfortable hotel is very affordable. Rooms count cable TV and direct-dial phones among their many amenities, all of which make this place a good bet if you lack deep pockets. ✉ *Rua Sergipe 893, Savassi 30130–171,* ☎ FAX *031/261–7422. 62 rooms. Restaurant, bar, air-conditioning, minibars, refrigerators. AE, DC, MC, V.*

Nightlife and the Arts

The center of cultural life in Belo Horizonte is the downtown **Palácio das Artes** (✉ Rua Afonso Pena 1537, Parque Municipal, ☎ 031/237–7286), where ballet companies and symphony orchestras sporadically perform. The box office is only open when performances are coming up.

Much of Belo's nightlife is in the Savassi neighborhood, with its inviting cafés and bars as well as a handful of clubs with live Brazilian music. For some of Brazil's best cachaças and one of the city's best views, try **Alambique** (✉ Av. Raja Gabaglia 3200, Chalé 1D, São Bento, ☎ 031/296–7188). The oh-so-chic **Café** (✉ Rua Cláudio Manoel 583, Funcionários, ☎ 031/261–6019) is open late every night but Monday (when it's closed completely). A traditional bar with live popular Brazilian music is the **Cervejaria Brasil** (✉ Rua Aimorés 78, Savassi, ☎ 031/225–1099). A popular bar for "GLS" (gays, lesbians, and sympathizers) is **Excess** (✉ Rua Antonio de Albuquerque 729, Savassi, ☎ 031/227–5133). **Restaurante Top Beer** (☞ *Dining, above*) is an ideal spot to begin your evening.

Outdoor Activities and Sports

FUTEBOL

The **Estádio Mineirão** (✉ Av. Antônio Abrão Carão 1001, Pampulha, ☎ 031/441–6133) is Brazil's third-largest stadium and the home field for Belo's two professional *futebol* (soccer) teams: Atletico Mineiro and Cruzeiro.

Nossa Tropa (☎ 031/9972–8505, 031/9952–7152, or 031/583–0005) arranges day treks on horseback into the mountains surrounding Belo.

Most of the city's parks offer good, if small, jogging paths, and running is common during the day. The best place to jog is probably the Parque Municipal, with its shaded lawns and sparkling lake.

For amateur spelunkers, the mountains of Minas are replete with caves to be explored, though they must be seen with a guided tour (☞ Tour Operators and Travel Agents in Minas Gerais A to Z, *below*). The largest and most popular cavern is the **Maquiné Gruta** (☎ 031/771–7877), 113 km (70 mi) northwest of Belo Horizonte near the town of Cordisburgo, with six large chambers. The **Lapinha Gruta** (☎ 031/681–1958) is only 36 km (22 mi) north of Belo, near the city of Lagoa Santa, on the road leading from Confins airport.

Shopping

In the fashionable Savassi and Lourdes neighborhoods you'll find the city's best antiques, handicrafts, and jewelry stores. For clothing, head to one of the major shopping centers. On Saturday morning, Avenida Bernardo Monteiro (between Rua Brasil and Rua Otoni) is the site of an **antiques fair and food market**, offering a taste of mineiro cuisine. On Sunday morning, head for the large (nearly 3,000 vendors) **arts-and-crafts fair** in front of the Othon Palace hotel on Avenida Afonso Pena.

Arte Sacra Antiguidades (✉ Rua Alagoas 785, Savassi, ☎ 031/261–7256) offers a fine selection of Minas antiques.

The centrally located **Bahia Shopping** (✉ Rua de Bahia 1022, Centro, ☎ 031/201–7966) is a good place to shop for clothing. Many shops sell designer togs for men and women in Belo Horizonte's most exclusive mall, **BH Shopping** (✉ BR 040, Belvedere, ☎ 0800/31–9001).

Brasarts (✉ Rua Curitiba 2325, Lourdes, ☎ 031/291–5220) has a good selection of handicrafts. The **Centro de Artesanato Mineiro** (✉ Av. Afonso Pena 1537, Parque Municipal, ☎ 031/222–2400), in the Palácio das Artes, offers a wide range of regional crafts.

Gems are the obvious focus in an area famous for its mines; just be sure to buy only from reputable dealers. (If you're going to Ouro Prêto, wait to buy until you get there.) **Amsterdam Sauer** (✉ Av. Afonso Pena 1050, Centro, ☎ 031/273–3844) is a good place to begin your search. The **Gem Center** (✉ Av. Afonso Pena 1901, 5th Floor, Centro, ☎ 031/222–8189) is another good bet. **H. Stern** (✉ BH Shopping Center, Loja 105–106, BR 040, Belvedere, ☎ 031/286–1568) is one of Brazil's leading names for gems. **Raymundo Vianna** (✉ BH Shopping Center, BR 040, Belvedere, ☎ 031/286–6635; ✉ Rua Bernardo Guimarães 2412, ☎ 031/292–2655) has a fine reputation.

Parque Nacional Serra do Cipó

96 km (60 mi) northeast of Belo Horizonte.

Highlights of the Serra do Cipó National Park include the roaring Cachoeira da Farofa, a waterfall, and the sprawling Canyon das Bandeirantes. Numerous bird species as well as wolves, jaguars, anteaters, monkeys, and the poisonous *sapo de pijama* (colored pajama frog) make up the area's wildlife. Although difficult to reach and lacking in infrastructure, the park's beautiful landscape and ecological wealth make it worth the trip along MG 010 north from Belo toward Lagoa Santa.

Facilities are poor, so consider visiting the area as part of an organized tour. If you're an intrepid traveler you can rent a car, call the park's **visitors center** (☎ 031/651–1000) for some information, and head out on your own. The area's best hotel is **Cipó Veraneio** (✉ MG 010, Km 95, Jaboticatubas, ☎ 031/651–1000). The **Fazenda Monjolas Pousada** (✉ MG 010, Km 100, Santana do Riacho, ☎ 031/984–9848) offers simple, affordable accommodations. Camping facilities are available at **Véu da Noiva** (✉ MG 010, Km 101, Santana do Riacho, ☎ 031/201–1166).

Diamantina

290 km (180 mi) northeast of Belo Horizonte.

Diamantina took its name from the diamonds that were extracted in great quantities here in the 18th century. Perhaps because of its remote setting in the barren mountains close to the *sertão* (remote, arid region), Diamantina is extremely well preserved, although its churches lack the grandeur of those in other historic towns. Its white-walled structures stand in pristine contrast to the iron red of the surrounding mountains. The principal attraction in Diamantina is the simple pleasure of walking along the clean-swept cobblestone streets surrounded by colonial houses—note the covered overhanging roofs with their elaborate brackets.

The city was the home of two legendary figures of the colonial period: diamond merchant João Fernandes and his slave mistress Xica da Silva, today a popular figure in Brazilian folklore. According to legend, Xica had never seen the ocean, so her lover built her an artificial lake and then added a boat. Two area attractions are linked with her; to see them you should contact the Casa da Cultura (☞ Visitor Information *in* Minas Gerais A to Z, *below*) to arrange a guided tour. The **Casa de Xica da Silva** (✉ Praça Lobo Mesquita 266, ☎ no phone) contains colonial furniture and Xica's private chapel. The **Igreja Nossa Senhora do Carmo** (✉ Rua do Carmo, ☎ no phone) is a church built in 1751 as a gift from Fernandes to his mistress. Supposedly Xica ordered that the bell tower be built onto the back of the building so that the ringing wouldn't disturb her.

The **Museu do Diamante,** the city's diamond museum, is in a building that dates from 1789 and displays equipment used in colonial-period mines. ✉ *Rua Direta 14,* ☎ *038/531–1382.* ☐ *Free.* ☉ *Tues.—Sat. 10–noon, Sun. noon–4.*

The **Casa de Juscelino Kubitschek** was the first home of one of Brazil's most important 20th-century presidents and the man who built Brasília. ✉ *Rua São Francisco 241,* ☎ *no phone.* ☐ *Free.* ☉ *Tues.–Fri. 10–noon; weekends noon–4.*

On Rua da Glória, notice the covered wooden **footbridge** connecting the second stories of two buildings that once served as the headquarters of the colonial governors.

Dining and Lodging

$–$$ ✕ **Cantina do Marinho.** This well-respected restaurant specializes in comida mineira. Favorites are pork steak with tutu and pork tenderloin with feijão tropeiro. ✉ *Rua Direta 113,* ☎ *038/531–1686. No credit cards.*

$–$$ 🏨 **Tijuco.** Surprisingly, this historic-district inn is housed in an Oscar Niemeyer–designed structure. It's considered the best hotel in town; the views from it are certainly outstanding. ⊠ *Rua Macau do Meio 211, 39100,* ☎ *038/531–1022. 26 rooms. Restaurant, bar. AE, DC, MC, V.*

Nightlife

Diamantina enjoys a special distinction as Brazil's center of serenading. At night, particularly on the weekends, the city's romantics gather in a downtown alley known as Beco da Mota, the former red-light district and now home to several popular bars frequented by students and young professionals. Strolling guitar players also gather on Rua Direita and Rua Quitanda.

Sabará

19 km (12 mi) east of Belo Horizonte.

Sabará's churches drive home the enormous wealth of Minas Gerais during the gold rush days. In this former colonial town, today a sprawling suburb of 90,000, historic buildings are scattered about, requiring you either to join a tour or drive. The interiors of the baroque churches are rich in gold-leaf paneling.

In the main square sits the unfinished **Igreja de Senhora do Rosário dos Pretos** (Our Lady of the Rosary of the Blacks Church; circa 1767), which was built, like its counterpart in Ouro Prêto, by slaves. Here, however, they ran out of gold before the project could be completed. When slavery was abolished in 1888, the church was left as a memorial. ⊠ *Praça Melo Viana s/n,* ☎ *no phone.* 🎟 *Admission.* ☉ *Daily 8–noon and 2–6.*

The ornate **Igreja de Nossa Senhora da Conceição** (Our Lady of the Immaculate Conception), though small, is Sabará's main church and an outstanding example of Portuguese baroque architecture combined with elements of Asian art. Its simple exterior gives no indication as to the wealth inside, typified by its luxurious gold altar and lavishly decorated ceiling. ⊠ *Praça Getúlio Vargas s/n,* ☎ *031/671–1724.* 🎟 *Admission.* ☉ *Wed.–Fri. 10–noon and Sun. mass.*

Igreja de Nossa Senhora de Ó (Our Lady of Ó), one of Brazil's oldest and smallest churches, contains paintings said to have been completed by 23 Chinese artists brought from the former Portuguese colony of Macau. Other signs of Asian influence include the Chinese tower and the gilded arches. ⊠ *Largo do Ó s/n,* ☎ *031/671–1724.* 🎟 *Admission.* ☉ *Wed.–Sat. 9–noon and 2–5, Sun. 9–1 and 3–5.*

In the **Igreja de Nossa Senhora do Carmo** (Our Lady of Carmel Church), Brazil's famed artist, Aleijadinho, designed the pulpits, choir loft, and doorway. This is one of several Minas churches on which Aleijadinho and the painter Manuel da Costa Ataíde, a brilliant artist in his own right, collaborated. ⊠ *Rua do Carmo s/n,* ☎ *031/671–1523.* 🎟 *Admission.* ☉ *Wed.–Sun. 9–noon and 1–5.*

Ouro Prêto

97 km (60 mi) southeast of Belo Horizonte.

The former gold-rush capital is the best place to see the legendary Aleijadinho's artistry. Now a lively university town, it has been preserved as a national monument and a World Heritage Site. The surrounding mountains, the geometric rows of whitewashed buildings, the cobblestone streets and red-tile roofs that climb the hillsides, and the morn-

THE PASSION OF ALEIJADINHO

IT'S A TESTAMENT TO the creative spirit that Brazil's most famous artist couldn't use his hands or feet. Born in 1738 in Vila Rica (today's Ouro Prêto) to a Portuguese architect and a black slave, Antônio Francisco Lisboa developed a passion for art through exposure to his father's projects. In his mid-thirties, he developed an illness (some say leprosy, others syphilis; most assume it was arthritis) that led to a life of torment. Nicknamed Aleijadinho (Little Cripple), he shunned human contact, going out only at night or before dawn. With the help of some assistants, he traveled between towns, sculpting and overseeing church construction. He died on November 18, 1814, and was buried in the church he attended as a child.

There's no hint of Aleijadinho's pain in the delicate, expressive features of his soapstone and cedarwood figures. Indeed, his art is distinguished by a striking liveliness and deep religious faith. His most cherished works, such as the larger-than-life Old Testament Prophets at the church in Congonhas, were created with a hammer and chisel strapped to his wrists, a feat often compared to the suffering of Christ. After those in Congonhas his best works are in Ouro Prêto, where he designed the brilliant Igreja São Francisco de Assis, among other things.

ing mist and evening fog—all give Ouro Prêto an evocative air, as if at any moment it could be transported back three centuries.

In its heyday, Ouro Prêto was one of Brazil's most progressive cities and the birthplace of the colony's first stirrings of independence. A movement called the Inconfidência Mineira was organized to overthrow the Portuguese rulers and establish an independent Brazilian republic. It was to have been led by a resident of Ouro Prêto, Joaquim José da Silva Xavier, a dentist known as Tiradentes (Tooth Puller). But the Minas rebellion never got off the ground. In 1789, word of Tiradentes's intentions reached the capital of Rio de Janeiro; he was hanged, drawn, and quartered, and his followers were either imprisoned or exiled.

Exploring Ouro Prêto

Ouro Prêto has several museums as well as 13 colonial *igrejas* (churches), which are highly representative of mineiro baroque architecture. The Minas style is marked by elaborately carved doorways and curving lines. Most distinctive, though, are the interiors, richly painted and decorated lavishly with cedarwood and soapstone sculptures. Many interiors are unabashedly rococo, with an ostentatious use of gold leaf, a by-product of the region's mineral wealth.

All the town's sights are within easy walking distance of the central square, Praça Tiradentes, which teems with gossiping students, eager merchants, and curious visitors. From here, the longest walk you'll make takes about 15 minutes. Note that many museums and churches are closed on Monday.

Numbers in the text correspond to numbers in the margin and on the Ouro Prêto map.

Begin at Praça Tiradentes. Two blocks east stands the distinctive twin-tower **Igreja de São Francisco de Assis** ①. Two blocks farther east is the **Igreja de Nossa Senhora da Conceição** ② and its small Aleijadinho museum. From here, head east on Rua da Conceição, which becomes Rua Santa Efigênia to the **Igreja de Santa Efigênia** ③. Retrace your steps to Praça Tiradentes, and visit the **Museu do Oratório** ④ and its neighboring **Museu da Inconfidência** ⑤. Walk north across the plaza to **Museu da Mineralogia e das Pedras** ⑥, inside the Escola de Minas.

West of Praça Tiradentes and off Rua Brigadeiro Musqueira is the **Teatro Municipal** ⑦. Next door is the **Igreja de Nossa Senhora do Carmo** ⑧, with major works by Aleijadinho and Ataíde. Ouro Prêto's original mint, the **Casa dos Contos** ⑨, is a short distance northwest on Rua São José. Continuing south on the same street, which becomes Rua Rondolfo Bretas, you'll come to the **Igreja de Nossa Senhora do Pilar** ⑩ with its baroque interior. Head northwest on Rua Rondolfo Bretas followed by Rua Dr. Getúlio Vargas to the less-ornate but equally intriguing **Igreja de Nossa Senhora do Rosário dos Pretos** ⑪.

This is an all-day tour. Start out early as some churches are only open in the morning. Unless you're an ecclesiastic, plan to spend about 20 minutes in each church and 30–45 minutes in each museum.

⑨ **Casa dos Contos.** The colonial coinage house contains the foundry used to mint the coins of the gold-rush period as well as examples of coins and period furniture. The museum building is considered among the best examples of Brazilian colonial architecture. ⊠ *Rua São José 12,* ☎ *031/551–1444.* ☜ *Admission.* ☉ *Tues.–Sat. 12:30–5:30, Sun. 8:30–1:30.*

⑧ **Igreja de Nossa Senhora do Carmo.** Completed in 1772, the impressive Our Lady of Carmel Church contains major works by Aleijadinho and Ataíde. It was originally designed by Aleijadinho's father, himself an architect, but was later modified by the son, who added more baroque elements, including the characteristic soapstone sculptures of angels above the entrance. ⊠ *Praça Tiradentes s/n,* ☎ *031/551–1209.* ☜ *Admission.* ☉ *Tues. and Thurs.–Sun. 1:30–5.*

② **Igreja de Nossa Senhora da Conceição.** The lavishly gilded Our Lady of the Conception Church, completed in 1760, contains the tomb of Aleijadinho as well as a small museum dedicated to the artist. ⊠ *Praça Antônio Dias s/n,* ☎ *031/551–3282.* ☜ *Admission.* ☉ *Tues.–Sun. 8–11:30 and 1–5.*

⑩ **Igreja de Nossa Senhora do Pilar.** Built around 1711 on the site of an earlier chapel, this is the most richly decorated of Ouro Prêto's churches and one of Brazil's best examples of baroque religious architecture. It's said that 400 pounds of gold leaf were used to cover the interior. ⊠ *Rua Brigador Mosqueira Castilho Barbosa s/n,* ☎ *031/551–4735.* ☜ *Admission.* ☉ *Tues.–Sun. noon–4:30.*

⑪ **Igreja de Nossa Senhora do Rosário dos Pretos.** The small, intriguing Our Lady of the Rosary of the Blacks was built by slaves, some of whom bought freedom with the gold they found in Ouro Prêto. According to legend, the church's interior is bare because the slaves ran out of gold after erecting the baroque building. ⊠ *Largo do Rosário s/n,* ☎ *031/551–1209.* ☜ *Admission.* ☉ *Tues.–Sun. noon–4:30.*

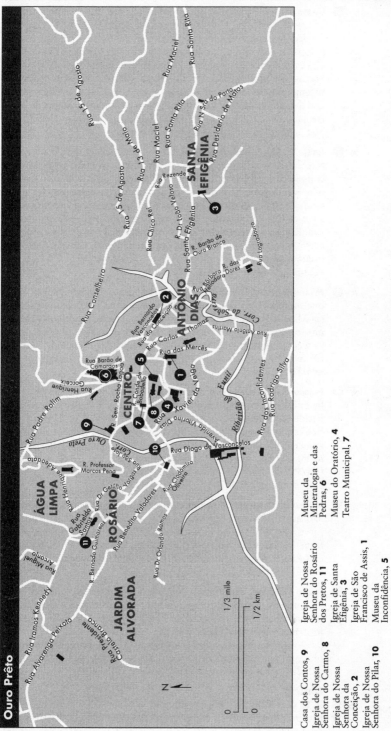

❸ Igreja de Santa Efigênia. This interesting slave church is on a hill east of Praça Tiradentes. Construction lasted 60 years (1730–90) and was funded by Chico-Rei. (This African ruler was captured during Brazil's gold rush and sold to a mine owner in Minas Gerais. Chico eventually earned enough money to buy his freedom—in the days before the Portuguese prohibited such acts—and became a hero among slaves throughout the land.) The clocks on the facade are the city's oldest, and the interior contains cedar sculptures by Francisco Xavier de Brito, Aleijadinho's teacher. ⊠ *Just off Rua de Santa Efigênia,* ☎ *031/551–5047.* 🎫 *Admission.* ⊙ *Tues.–Sun. 8–noon.*

★ **❶ Igreja de São Francisco de Assis.** Considered Aleijadinho's masterpiece, this church was begun in 1766 by the Franciscan Third Order and not completed until 1810. In addition to designing the structure, Aleijadinho was responsible for the wood and soapstone sculptures on the portal, high altar, side altars, pulpits, and crossing arch. The panel on the nave ceiling representing the Virgin's glorification was painted by Ataíde. Cherubic faces, garlands of tropical fruits, and allegorical characters are carved into the main altar, and are still covered with their original paint. ⊠ *Largo de Coimbra s/n,* ☎ *031/551–3282.* 🎫 *Admission.* ⊙ *Tues.–Sun. 8–11:30, 1:30–4:45.*

★ **❺ Museu da Inconfidência.** A former 18th-century prison as well as the one-time city hall, this museum commemorates the failed Inconfidência Mineira rebellion with many artifacts. Among the displays are furniture, clothing, slaves' manacles, firearms, books, and gravestones, as well as works by Aleijadinho and Ataíde. The museum also holds the remains of the unlucky revolutionaries. ⊠ *Praça Tiradentes 139,* ☎ *031/551–1121.* 🎫 *Admission.* ⊙ *Tues.–Sun. noon–5.*

★ **❻ Museu da Mineralogia e das Pedras.** Housed opposite the Museu da Inconfidência in the former governor's palace and inside the current Escola de Minas (School of Mines), the Museum of Minerals and Rocks contains an excellent collection of precious gems (including diamonds), gold, and crystals. The minerals have been organized according to their rarity, color, and crystallization. ⊠ *Praça Tiradentes 20,* ☎ *031/559–1530 or 031/559–1531.* 🎫 *Admission.* ⊙ *Weekdays noon–4:45, weekends 9–1.*

❹ Museu do Oratório. This museum established in the old house of the St. Carmel Novitiate celebrates sacred art from the 18th and 19th centuries. Some of the oratories, which reflect ideas of religious beauty from the period, have been displayed at the Louvre. ⊠ *Rua Costa Senna and Rua Antônio Pereira,* ☎ *031/551–5369.* 🎫 *Admission.* ⊙ *Daily 9:30–11:50, 1:30–5:30.*

❼ Teatro Municipal. The former opera house, built between 1746 and 1769, still presents shows and plays, making it Latin America's oldest municipal theater still in operation. There's no regular schedule for performances, however; check with the Associação de Guias de Turismo (☞ Visitor Information *in* Minas Gerais A to Z, *below*) for information on events. ⊠ *Rua Brigadeiro Mosqueira s/n,* ☎ *031/551–1544, ext. 224.* 🎫 *Admission.* ⊙ *Daily 1–6.*

Dining

$$$$ ✕ **Le Coq d'Or.** The finest restaurant in Minas Gerais and one of the
★ best in Brazil is in Ouro Prêto's Solar Nossa Senhora do Rosário hotel (☞ Lodging, *below*). An elegant atmosphere with formal place settings, attentive service, and soft Brazilian music make it ideal for a quiet, romantic dinner. The executive chef trained in Paris at the renowned Cordon Bleu culinary institute before introducing creative, French-inspired cuisine to Brazilian gourmands. The ever-changing menu always in-

cludes an innovative selection of meat and fish dishes, and the wine list is excellent. ⊠ *Rua Dr. Getúlio Vargas 270,* ☎ *031/551–5200. AE, DC, MC, V.*

$$$ ✕ **Casa do Ouvidor.** Atop a jewelry store in the heart of the historic
★ district, this popular restaurant has garnered several awards for such regional dishes as tutu a mineira, feijão tropeiro, and frango com quiabo. Portions are huge, so come with an empty stomach, and be prepared for a noisy, ever-crowded dining room. ⊠ *Rua Conde de Bobadela 42,* ☎ *031/551–2141. AE, DC, MC, V.*

$$ ✕ **Casa Grande.** Here you can dine with a view of the 18th-century buildings that line Praça Tiradentes. Among the regional dishes are tutu a mineira, frango ao molho pardo, and, for dessert, *dôce de leite com queijo* (fresh white cheese with caramelized milk). ⊠ *Praça Tiradentes 84,* ☎ *031/551–2976. No credit cards.*

$ ✕ **Café Geraes.** This cozy, bi-level café is at the center of Ouro Prêto's
★ artistic and intellectual life. Students sip wine and feast on delicious sandwiches, soups, and other snacks. The pastries and the coffees are equally appealing. ⊠ *Rua Direita 122,* ☎ *031/551–0128 or 031/551–1405. DC, MC.*

$ ✕ **Chafariz.** Regional cuisine is served buffet-style in this informal
★ eatery near the Casa dos Contos. The small, colorful dining room has hard-wood floors, wood-beam ceilings, and wood tables draped with blue, green, or white tablecloths. ⊠ *Rua São José 167,* ☎ *031/551–0128. AE, DC, MC.*

Lodging

Some families in Ouro Prêto rent rooms in their homes, although usually only during Carnaval and Easter, when the city's hotels fill up. For a list of rooms to rent, contact the **Associação de Guias de Turismo** (☞ Visitor Information *in* Minas Gerais A to Z, *below*). The association also provides information on places to camp.

$$$$ ⬚ **Pousada do Mondego.** This small, intimate inn is next to the Igreja
★ de São Francisco de Assis in a house that dates from 1747. You'll find period furnishings, a colonial ambience, and highly personalized service. The hotel also offers two-hour city tours in a minibus from the 1930s, and it has its own antiques store and art gallery. ⊠ *Largo de Coimbra 38, 35400,* ☎ *031/551–2040 or 021/287–3122 ext. 601 (reservations in Rio),* 𝔽𝔸𝕏 *031/551–3094. 23 rooms. Restaurant, bar, travel services. AE, DC, MC, V.*

$$$$ ⬚ **Solar Nossa Senhora do Rosário.** Superior service and the world-
★ class Le Coq d'Or restaurant (☞ Dining, *above*) are among this hotel's draws. The beautiful 19th-century building feels like a bed-and-breakfast, with elegant yet comfortable decor, quiet floors, and charming guest rooms. When you're not exploring the town, have a swim in the luxurious hilltop pool or stop by the atrium for afternoon tea. The hotel even has its own section of an original mine, discovered during renovations. ⊠ *Rua Dr. Getúlio Vargas 270, 35400,* ☎ *031/551–5200,* 𝔽𝔸𝕏 *031/551–4288. 28 rooms, 9 suites. Restaurant, bar, pool, sauna, business services, convention center. AE, DC, MC, V.*

$$$ ⬚ **Grande Hotel.** As its name suggests, the Grande is Ouro Prêto's largest hotel (with 35 rooms, it's immense by local standards). It's also the town's premier modernist structure—a curving two-story building on concrete pillars designed by world-acclaimed architect Oscar Niemeyer. Cultural purists and aesthetes, however, consider it an eyesore. ⊠ *Rua Senador Rocha Lagoa 164, 35400,* ☎ 𝔽𝔸𝕏 *031/551–1488. 35 rooms. Restaurant, bar. AE, DC, MC, V.*

$$$ ⬚ **Luxor Ouro Prêto.** With stone walls that date back 200 years, beautiful wood floors, and gracious antique furnishings, this hotel has the feeling of a 19th-century lodge. The lobby leads to a small, romantic restaurant: typical "mineira" cooking is served to the lucky few tables. Guest rooms enjoy views of the city, and some have original paintings by famous Minas artist Chanina. ✉ *Rua Dr. Alfredo Baeta 16, 35400,* ☎ FAX *031/551–2244. 16 rooms. Restaurant, bar. AE, DC, MC, V.*

$–$$ 🏨 **Pousada Ouro Prêto.** Popular with backpackers, this pousada has
★ small rooms that are individually decorated with local art. Its openair halls have flowers and paintings of Ouro Prêto; the terrace in front of the lobby offers a peaceful view of the city center. The English-speaking staff will do laundry for free. ✉ *Largo Musicista José dos Anjos Costa 72, 35400,* ☎ FAX *031/551–3081. No credit cards.*

$ 🏨 **Colonial.** Close to the main square, this is a good example of the small, no-frills inns found in most of the historic cities. What you'll get is a very basic, clean room for a low price. Room 1 has a loft and can sleep up to five people. ✉ *Rua Camilo Veloso 26, 35400,* ☎ *031/ 551–3133,* FAX *031/551–3361. 18 rooms. AE, DC, MC, V.*

Nightlife and the Arts

Even if the food and the barman at **Acoso 85** (✉ Largo do Rosário, ☎ 031/551–2397) don't impress you, the incredibly high ceilings, stone walls, and medieval ambience will. It's popular with the late-night crowd. **Bardobeco** (✉ Trv. do Arieira 15, ☎ no phone) is the city's best *cachaçaria,* with more than 40 brands of cachaça, including the owner's own Milagre de Minas.

The best place for information about theater, arts, and musical performances is at the **Associação de Guias de Turismo** (☞ Visitor Information *in* Minas Gerais A to Z, *below*). **Fundação das Artes de Ouro Prêto** (FAOP; ✉ Rua Dr. Getúlio Vargas 185, ☎ 031/551–2014), the local arts foundation, hosts various art and photographic exhibitions throughout the year.

Outdoor Activities and Sports

HIKING

The best source of information about hiking and hiking tours in the region is the **Associação de Guias de Turismo** (☞ Visitor Information *in* Minas Gerais A to Z, *below*). The association also rents sports equipment.

Shopping

HANDICRAFTS

There are numerous handicrafts stores on Praça Tiradentes and its surrounding streets. At the daily **handicrafts fair,** in front of the Igreja de São Francisco de Assis, vendors sell soapstone and wood carvings, paintings, and other items. For authentic Minas antiques as well as handicrafts, visit **Bureau d'Art** (✉ Largo do Rosário 41). **Seleiro** (✉ Rua Direita 191, ☎ 031/551–1774) has a good selection of traditional crafts.

JEWELRY AND GEMSTONES

Amsterdam Sauer (☎ 031/551–3383) has a branch in Praça Tiradentes. One of the best places in Brazil to purchase gems, especially the rare and beautiful imperial topaz, is **Ita Gemas** (✉ Rua Conde de Bobadela 139, ☎ 031/551–4895). Another excellent store for authenticated gems—including imperial topaz, emeralds, and tourmalines—is **Raymundo Vianna** (✉ Rua Conde de Bobadela 48, ☎ 031/551–2487).

En Route Between Ouro Prêto and Mariana lies **Mina de Ouro de Passagem,** Brazil's oldest gold mine. During the rush, thousands of slaves perished here owing to its dangerous, back-breaking conditions. Although the mine is no longer in operation, you can ride an old mining car through 11 km (7 mi) of tunnels and see exposed quartz, graphite, and black tourmaline. Buses travel here from Ouro Prêto (catch them beside the Escola de Minas) and cost about $1; taxis are less than $10. ✉ *4 km*

(3 mi) from Ouro Prêto on road to Mariana, ☎ 031/557–1255 or 031/ 557–5000. 🎫 Admission. ⏱ Daily 9–6.

Mariana

11 km (7 mi) east of Ouro Prêto.

The oldest city in Minas Gerais (founded in 1696) is also the birth-place of Aleijadinho's favorite painter, Manuel da Costa Ataíde. Mariana, like Ouro Prêto, has preserved much of the appearance of an 18th-century gold-mining town. Its three principal churches all show-case examples of the art of Ataíde, who intertwined sensual romanticism with religious themes. The faces of his saints and other figures often have mulatto features, reflecting the composition of the area's population at the time. Today, Mariana is most visited for the weekly organ concerts at its cathedral.

The **Catedral Basílica da Sé,** completed in 1760, contains paintings by Ataíde, although it's best known for its 1701 German organ, transported by mule from Rio de Janeiro in 1720. This unique instrument— there are only two of its kind in the world—was a gift from Dom João V. Concerts take place Friday at 11 AM and Sunday at 12:15 PM. ⊠ *Praça Cláudio Manoel s/n, ☎ 031/557–1237. 🎫 Admission. ⏱ Tues.– Sun. 8–noon and 2–6:30.*

Behind the cathedral is the **Museu Arquidiocesano,** which claims to have the largest collection of baroque painting and sculpture in the state, including the wood and soapstone works by Aleijadinho and paintings by Ataíde. ⊠ *Rua Frei Durão 49, ☎ 031/557–1237. 🎫 Admission. ⏱ Tues.–Sun. noon–1.*

Although the 1793 **Igreja de São Francisco de Assis** (Church of St. Francis) features soapstone pulpits and altars by Aleijadinho, its most impressive works are the sacristy's ceiling panels, which were painted by Ataíde. They depict, in somber tones, the life and death of St. Francis and are considered by many to be the artist's masterpiece. Sadly, however, they've been damaged by termites and water. ⊠ *Praça João Pinheiro, ☎ no phone. 🎫 Admission. ⏱ Daily 8–noon and 1–5.*

The **Igreja da Nossa Senhora do Carmo** (Our Lady of Carmel Church), with works by Ataíde and Aleijadinho, is noteworthy for its impressive facade and sculpted soapstone designs. Ataíde is buried at the rear of the church. ⊠ *Praça João Pinheiro, ☎ 031/557–1635. 🎫 Admission. ⏱ Daily 8–5.*

Congonhas do Campo

50 km (31 mi) west of Mariana; 94 km (58 mi) south of Belo Horizonte.

To see Aleijadinho's crowning effort, head to the small Gold Town of Congonhas do Campo. Dominating Congonhas is the hilltop pilgrimage church, **Igreja Bom Jesus do Matosinho,** built in 1757 and the focus of great processions during Holy Week. At the churchyard entrance, you'll see Aleijadinho's 12 life-size Old Testament prophets carved in soapstone, a towering achievement and one of the greatest works of art anywhere from the baroque period. The prophets appear caught in movement, and every facial expression seems marked with the sculptor's own pain during his final years. Leading up to the church on the sloping hillside are 6 chapels, each containing a scene from the Stations of the Cross. The 66 figures in this remarkable procession were carved in cedar by Aleijadinho and painted by Ataíde. ⊠ *Praça da Basílica s/n, ☎ 031/731–1590. 🎫 Admission. ⏱ Tues.–Sun. 10–5.*

Tiradentes

129 km (80 mi) south of Congonhas do Campo.

Probably the best historic city to visit after Ouro Prêto, Tiradentes was the birthplace of a martyr who gave it its name (it was formerly called São José del Rei) and retains much of its 18th century charm. Life in this tiny village—nine streets with eight churches set against the backdrop of the Serra de São José—moves slowly. This quality attracts wealthy residents of Belo Horizonte, Rio, and São Paulo, who have sparked a local real estate boom by buying up 18th-century properties as weekend getaways.

Besides the excellent selection of handicrafts—some 20 shops line Rua Direita in the town center—the principal attraction is the **Igreja de Santo Antônio.** Built in 1710, it contains extremely well-preserved, gilded carvings of saints, cherubs, and biblical scenes. The church's soapstone frontispiece—a celebration of baroque architecture—was sculpted by Aleijadinho. ⊠ *Rua Padre Toledo,* ☎ *no phone.* 🎟 *Admission.* ☉ *Daily 9–noon and 2–5.*

Dining and Lodging

$$ ✕ **Estalagem.** The Estalagem draws rave reviews for its feijão tropeiro
★   and frango ao molho pardo. Although it's small and cozy, its atmosphere is elegant; light music and quiet, attentive service make for a relaxing meal. ⊠ *Rua Gabriel Passos 280,* ☎ *032/355–1144. No credit cards. Closed Mon.*

$$ ✕ **Teatro da Villa.** On the site of an old Greek-style amphitheater, this restaurant offers dinner theater, Tiradentes' style. The menu features international fare, including meat and fish dishes. Most of the performances involve local folk music and dance. ⊠ *Rua do Sol 157,* ☎ *no phone. No credit cards. Closed weekdays.*

$–$$ ✕ **Canto do Chafariz.** This center of regional cuisine is rated tops for its tutu. ⊠ *Largo do Chafariz 37,* ☎ *032/355–1377. Reservations not accepted. No credit cards. Closed Mon.*

$$$$ 🏨 **Solar da Ponte.** In every respect—from the stunning antiques to the
★   comfortable beds to the elegant place settings—this inn is a faithful example of regional style. Breakfast and afternoon tea (included in the rate) are served in the dining room, overlooking well-tended gardens. With advance notice, the English owner and his Brazilian wife can arrange historical, botanical, and ecological tours on foot or horseback. ⊠ *Praça das Mercês s/n 36325,* ☎ *032/355–1255 or 021/287–1592 (reservations in Rio),* 🖷 *032/355–1201. 12 rooms. Bar, dining room, pool, sauna. MC, V.*

$$$ 🏨 **Pousada Alforria.** Alforria enjoys a quiet, peaceful location with a
★   fabulous view of the São José mountains. The light-filled lobby—with its stone floors, high ceilings, and beautiful Brazilian artwork (some of it from Bahia)—leads to a charming breakfast space and courtyard. Rooms have considerable natural light and are individually decorated; mattresses are firm, and bathrooms modern. ⊠ *Rua Custódio Gomes 286, 36325,* ☎ 🖷 *032/355–1536. 9 rooms. Pool. No credit cards.*

$$ 🏨 **Pousada Três Portas.** This pousada is in an adapted colonial house—with hardwood floors and locally made furniture and artwork—in the historic center of Tiradentes. The owner runs a small puppet theater adjacent to the breakfast room. Rooms are clean and modern. ⊠ *Rua Direita 280A, 36325,* ☎ *032/355–1444,* 🖷 *032/355–1184. 8 rooms, 1 suite. Pool, steam room. No credit cards.*

The Arts

Cultural life in Tiradentes revolves around the **Centro Cultural Yves Alves** (⊠ Rua Direita 168, ☎ 032/355–1503), which has theatrical performances, films, concerts, and art exhibitions. On weekends, the **Teatro da Villa** (☞ Dining and Lodging, *above*) has musical shows that accompany dinner.

Shopping

Local artwork is the biggest draw here, with painters and sculptors famous throughout Brazil working in their gallery-like studios. The main street for galleries and antiques shops is Rua Direita.

ART

Atelier Fernando Pitta (✉ Beco da Chácara s/n, ☎ 032/355–1475) is set up like Michelangelo's studio, with wild, abstract variations on religious themes. **Atelier José Damas** (✉ Rua do Chafariz 130, ☎ 032/9961–0735) belongs to Tiradentes's most famous artist. He paints local scenes—such as a train through the mountains or a dusty afternoon street—on canvas and on stones.

JEWELRY AND GEMSTONES

Although not as upscale as the stores in Ouro Prêto, **Artstones** (✉ Rua Ministro Gabriel Passos 22, ☎ 032/464–4595) carries imperial topaz, emeralds, quartz, and tourmaline, and has some finished jewelry.

THE MINERAL SPA TOWNS

Known for the curative properties of their natural springs, a collection of mineral spa towns in southern Minas Gerais form the Circuito das Aguas (Water Circuit). For more than a century, people in need of physical, mental, and spiritual rejuvenation have flocked to these mystical towns, bathing in the pristine water parks and drinking from the bubbling fountains. Today, they're especially popular among older, wealthier Brazilians, who come to experience the fresh air and beautiful landscapes, and to relieve their hypertension, arthritis, allergies, diabetes, and various stomach problems.

You'll be told that a minimum of three weeks drinking the waters is required for their healing powers to take hold (don't try drinking three weeks' worth of water in a day, unless you want to leave with more ailments than when you arrived). Usually, a one- or two-day visit is enough to experience a helpful placebo effect.

São Lourenço

387 km (240 mi) south of Belo Horizonte.

The most modern of the mineral spa towns is a good base from which to visit the other Circuito das Aguas communities. From here, taxis and tour operators will happily negotiate a day rate for the circuit, usually around $50.

São Lourenço's **Parque das Aguas** (Water Park) includes a picturesque lake with art deco pavilions, fountains, and gorgeous landscaping. The center activity is its *balneário,* a hydrotherapy spa where people from around the world immerse themselves in bubbling mineral baths and marble surroundings. There are separate bath and sauna facilities for men and women, and you can also get a massage. ✉ *Praça Brasil s/n,* ☎ *035/332–3066.* 💷 *Admission.* ☉ *Park: daily 8–6. Balneário: daily 8:30–11:30 and 2–5.*

If your experience at the park fails to rid you of all physical and mental illness, head to the **Templo da Euboise,** the temple of a spiritual organization dedicated to wisdom and perfection through yoga. The temple is open to the public only on weekend afternoons. In any case, get yourself here before the end of the world—the Euboise believe this will be the only place to survive. ⊠ *Praça da Vitória s/n,* ☎ *035/331–1333.* 🎫 *Donation suggested.* ⊙ *Weekends 2–4.*

Dining and Lodging

$$ ✕ **Le Sapê.** This restaurant is quite popular in a city where most visitors prefer to eat in their hotels. The eclectic menu includes typical mineira food, as well as pizza, pasta, and fondue. ⊠ *Av. Comendador Costa 589,* ☎ *035/331–1142. No credit cards.*

$$$ ✕🏨 **Fazenda Emboaba.** About a half-hour's walk from the Parque das
★   Aguas, this gracious fazenda is more like a private estate than a rural farm. Its carefully decorated rooms have gorgeous bucolic views; at night, the only sounds you'll hear are of various animals roaming through the countryside. Occasional performances are offered in the fazenda's theater, and there are numerous other activities, such as horseback riding, to keep you amused. ⊠ *Rua Jorge Amado 350, Solar dos Lagos, 37440,* ☎ *035/332–4600,* 🅵🅰🆇 *035/332–4392. 20 rooms. Restaurant, massage, sauna, tennis court, horseback riding, soccer, theater. AE, DC, MC, V.*

$$$ ✕🏨 **Hotel Brasil.** This luxury hotel is just across from the Parque das Aguas at the Praça Duque de Caixas. It has its own pools, fountains, and mineral waters, and the rate includes full-board. Ask for a room with a park view. ⊠ *Alameda João Lage 87, 37440,* ☎ *033/332–1313,* 🅵🅰🆇 *033/331–1536. 145 rooms. Restaurant, bar, pools. AE, DC, MC, V.*

Caxambu

30 km (19 mi) northeast of São Lourenço.

A 19th-century town once frequented by Brazilian royalty, Caxambu remains a favorite getaway for wealthy and retired *cariocas* (residents of Rio). Although most people spend their time here relaxing in bath houses and drinking curative waters, you can also browse in the markets where local sweets are sold or take a horse-and-buggy ride to a fazenda.

In Caxambu's **Parque das Aguas,** you'll find towering trees, shimmering lakes, and fountains containing various minerals—each believed to cure a different ailment. Lavish pavilions protect the springs, and the balneário—a beautiful Turkish-style bath house—offers saunas and massages. In addition, hundreds of thousands of liters of mineral water are bottled here daily and distributed throughout Brazil. ⊠ *Town center,* ☎ *035/341–1298.* 🎫 *Admission.* ⊙ *Park: daily 7–6. Balneário: Wed.–Sat. 8:30–noon and 3–5.*

Overlooking the springs is the **Igreja Isabel da Hungria.** The small Gothic church was built by Princess Isabel, daughter of Dom Pedro II, after the springs were believed to restore her fertility. ⊠ *Rua Princesa Isabel s/n,* ☎ *no phone.* 🎫 *Donation suggested.* ⊙ *Daily 9–4.*

Horse-and-buggy rides start at the park's entrance and explore the streets of Caxambu as well as old farms in the surrounding area. The best of these fazendas is Chácara Rosalan, with its beautiful flower and fruit orchards. Rides cost about $20. Alternatively, you could take a **chair lift** (it operates daily 7–6) from near the bus station to the peak of Cristo Redentor, where there's a small restaurant and an impressive city view.

Dining and Lodging

$$$–$$$$ ✕ **La Forelle.** The best restaurant in town is Danish, not Brazilian. The
★   filet mignon, the salmon, and the trout are among the extensive menu's stellar entrées. You'll also find delicious fondues and freshly made breads. ⊠ *BR 354, 3 km (2 mi) south of Caxambu,* ☎ *035/341–1961. AE, DC, MC, V. No lunch.*

$$–$$$ ⊞ **Hotel Glória.** Although it's just across from Caxambu's Parque das Aguas, this luxury resort has its own rehabilitation pool and sauna as well as a variety of sports amenities. Rooms are well equipped and have marble baths; the rate includes full-board, and meals are served in an antiques-filled dining room. ⊠ *Av. Camilio Soares 590, 37440,* ☎ FAX *035/341–3000. 120 rooms. Bar, dining room, minibars, pool, sauna, tennis court, basketball, exercise room. AE, DC, MC, V.*

São Tomé das Letras

54 km (33 mi) northwest of Caxambu.

With its tales of flying saucers, its eery stone houses that resemble architecture from outer space, and its 7,500 inhabitants who swear by years of friendship with extraterrestrials, São Tomé das Letras may be one of the oddest towns on earth. Set in a stunning mountain region, it attracts mystics, psychics, and flower children who believe they've been spiritually drawn here to await the founding of a new world. Most visitors make São Tomé a day trip from Caxambu, smartly escaping nightfall's oncoming UFOs.

A center of religious activity and one of the few non-stone buildings in São Tomé, **Igreja Matriz** is in the main square and contains frescoes by Brazilian artist Joaquim José de Natividade. Next to the Igreja Matriz is the **Gruta de São Tomé,** a small cave which, in addition to its small shrine to São Tomé, features some of the mysterious inscriptions for which the town is famous. Just 3 km (2 mi) from São Tomé, two caverns, **Carimbado** and **Chico Taquara,** both display more indecipherable hieroglyphics. A short walk from the caves will put you in view of **Veu da Noiva** and **Veu da Euboise,** two powerful waterfalls.

MINAS GERAIS A TO Z

Arriving and Departing

By Airplane

Belo Horizonte is the gateway to Minas Gerais. **Aeroporto Internacional Tancredo Neves** (☎ 031/689–2700)—also known as Aeroporto Confins—is 39 km (24 mi) north of Belo Horizonte and serves domestic and international flights. Taxis from Confins to downtown cost about $40 and take roughly a half hour. There are also *executivo* (air-conditioned) buses that leave every 45 minutes and cost $11. **Aeroporto Pampulha** (☎ 031/490–2001) is 9 km (5 mi) northwest of downtown and serves domestic flights. Taxis from here to downtown cost about $10.

American Airlines (☎ 0800/12–4001) flies from Miami to Rio and on to Confins. **TAM** (☎ 031/490–5500) has domestic flights to and from Pampulha. **Transbrasil** (☎ 031/273–6722, 031/689–2480, or 0800/15–1151) has domestic service to both airports. In addition to connecting Belo Horizonte with other Brazilian cities, **Varig** (☎ 031/339–6000) has service to Confins from New York. **VASP** (☎ 0800/99–8277 or 031/689–5360) also offers domestic flights into both airports.

By Bus

Frequent buses (either air-conditioned executivos or warmer, less comfortable, yet cheaper, coaches) connect Belo Horizonte with Rio ($25–$40; 7 hrs), São Paulo ($25–$50; 9 hrs), and Brasília ($25–$40; 12 hrs). Advance tickets are recommended at holiday times. All buses arrive at and depart from (punctually) the **Rodoviário** (⊠ Av. Afonso Pena at Av. do Contorno, Belo Horizonte, ☎ 031/201–8111 or 031/271–3000).

Bus companies include **Cometa** (☎ 031/201–5611) for Rio and São Paulo, **Gontijo** (☎ 031/201–6130) for São Paulo, **Itapemirim** (☎ 031/271–1027) for Brasília, **Penha** (☎ 031/271–5621) for Brasília, and **Útil** (☎ 031/201–7744) for Rio and São Paulo.

By Car
BR 040 connects Belo Horizonte with Rio (444 km/276 mi) to the southeast and Brasília (741 km/460 mi) to the northwest; BR 381 links the city with São Paulo (586 km/364 mi). The roads are in good condition, although exits aren't always clearly marked.

Getting Around

By Bus
Belo Horizonte's municipal bus system is safe and runs efficiently, although buses are crowded during rush hour (7–9 and 5–7). Buses are clearly numbered, and you can get route information in the *Guia do Ônibus,* a guide that's available in bookstores. All city buses have a chord to pull or a button to press to request a stop. Fares depend on the distance traveled, but are always less than $1.

Buses are a fabulous way to travel throughout the region. Coaches connect Belo Horizonte with Ouro Prêto ($7; 2–3 hrs), Diamantina ($18; 6 hrs), and São João del Rei ($11; 4 hrs). Mariana can be reached from Ouro Prêto ($1; 30 min), Tiradentes from São João del Rei ($2; 30 min). From Belo Horizonte, a bus to São Lourenço or Caxambu takes roughly 6½ hours and costs about $10. To reach São Tomé das Letras, you must change buses in Três Coracões; the entire journey takes 5½ hours.

Bus companies with regular service from Belo Horizonte include **Cisne** (☎ 031/201–8660) for Sabará; **Gardenia** (☎ 031/271–2111) for São Lourenço; **Pássaro Verde** (☎ 031/272–1811) for Ouro Prêto, Diamantina, and Mariana; and **Sandra** (☎ 031/201–2927) for Congonhas.

By Car
Belo Horizonte's rush-hour traffic can be heavy, and parking can be difficult (for on-street parking you need to buy a sticker at a newsstand or bookshop). Narrow cobblestone streets inside the historic cities, however, weren't designed for cars, and some alleys can make for a tight squeeze. Parking isn't a problem in the smaller communities, except during holidays.

The historical cities and spa towns are, for the most part, connected by fairly decent minor routes to one of the region's main highways. There's no ideal direct route from Belo Horizonte to Diamantina; your best bet is north on BR 040 and then east on BR 259. Sabará is slightly east of Belo, just off BR 262. From Belo you can take BR 040 south and BR 356 (it becomes MG 262) east to Ouro Prêto and beyond to Mariana. To reach Tiradentes from Belo, take BR 040 south (Congonhas do Campo is on this route) and then BR 265 west. São Lourenço, Caxambu, and São Tomé das Letras are south of Belo off BR 381, parts of which are under construction. As an alternative, you can take BR 040 south to BR 267 west.

Rental cars cost between $20 and $50 per day, depending on whether or not mileage is included. Agencies include **Localiza** (✉ Aeroporto Confins, Belo Horizonte, ☎ 031/689–2070; ✉ Rua Bernardo Monteiro 1567, Belo Horizonte, ☎ 0800/99–2000 or 031/247–7957) and **Lokamig** (✉ Aeroporto Confins, Belo Horizonte, ☎ 031/689–2020; ✉ Av. Contorno 8639, Belo Horizonte, ☎ 031/335–8977).

By Taxi

Taxis in Belo Horizonte are white and can be hailed or called. The meter starts at about $1 and costs about 50 cents for every kilometer traveled (slightly higher at night and on weekends). Two reputable companies are **BH Taxi** (☎ 031/215–8081) and **Rádio Taxi** (☎ 0800/31–2288 or 031/421–505).

In the historic towns, it's hard to drive along narrow, cobblestone streets, so taxis aren't abundant. Besides, these towns are small enough to explore on foot. You'll find plenty of eager taxis in both Caxambu and São Lourenço waiting to take you around the Circuito das Aguas. A taxi between São Lourenço and Caxambu runs about $25; $50 to São Tomé das Letras.

Contacts and Resources

Banks and Currency Exchange

Outside Belo Horizonte, currency exchange can be challenging and/or expensive, so change money before you arrive or plan to do it at your hotel. You can change money at Confins airport weekdays 10–6, and Saturday 10–4 (you're out of luck if you arrive Sunday). **Banco Sudameris** (✉ Av. João Pinheiro 214, Centro, Belo Horizonte, ☎ 031/277–3134) has good exchange rates. **Banco do Brazil** (✉ Rua Rio de Janeiro 750, Centro, Belo Horizonte) also offers exchange services, though the rates aren't the best.

Consulates

The U.S. has no consulate in Belo Horizonte, but it does have the **U.S. Commercial Service** (✉ Rua Timbiras, 7th floor, ☎ 031/213–1571), which assists companies that are doing business in Minas Gerais. **British Consulate** (✉ Rua Inconfidentes 1075, Belo Horizonte, ☎ 031/261–2072).

Emergencies

Ambulance and Police: ☎ 190. **Fire:** ☎ 193. **Hospital: Hospital João XXIII** (✉ Av. Alfredo Balena 400, Sta. Efigênia, Belo Horizonte, ☎ 031/239–9200). **Pharmacy: Drogaria Araujo** (☎ 031/270–5000) is a 24-hour Belo Horizonte pharmacy that makes deliveries.

Health and Safety

There are no major health concerns in Minas Gerais, although you should drink bottled rather than tap water. (Despite the curative properties of the mineral waters in the spa towns, don't drink too much when you first arrive unless you want to cleanse your system thoroughly.) Petty crime is an issue in Belo Horizonte, though not as much as it is in Rio or São Paulo. Use common sense: avoid waving your money around or wearing expensive jewelry. The historic cities and mineral spa towns are among Brazil's safest places.

Telephones, the Internet, and Mail

The area code for the region is 031. If you don't want to place long-distance calls from your hotel, you can make them from the *posto telefônicos* (phone offices) found in airports and bus stations throughout Minas. Office hours are generally 7 AM–10 PM. In Belo Horizonte, the main **TELEMIG** (✉ Av. Afonso Pena 744, Centro) office is open 24 hours. The **main post office** (✉ Av. Afonso Pena 1270, Centro, Belo Horizonte, ☎ 031/201–9833) is open weekdays 9–7, weekends 9–1. Internet service is slowly making its way to the region and may be available at your hotel's business center. In Belo Horizonte, the **Cybernet Café** (✉ Av. Cristóvão Columbo 596, ☎ 031/261–5166) lets you hook up for about $10 an hour.

Tour Operators and Travel Agents

AMETUR (✉ Rua Alvarenga Peixoto 295/102, Lourdes, Belo Horizonte, ☎ FAX 031/275–2139), the Association of Rural Tourism, is a group of respected, trustworthy ranch owners who have converted their fazendas into accommodations with luxurious, yet down-home, surroundings. You can visit one or more of these ranches, where relaxation, swimming, horseback riding, walks in the woods, and home-cooked meals are the orders of the day. Suzana Sousa Lima runs AMETUR as well as her own fazenda, Boa Esperança, which has been rated among the top accommodations in the country.

AMO-TE (✉ Rua Professor Morais 624, Apartamento 302, Centro, Belo Horizonte, ☎ 031/344–8986), Minas's Association of Ecological Tourism, offers many fascinating tours. A great way to get acquainted with the history and topography of Minas is on a one- to five-day horseback trip with AMO-TE's Tulio. His English is perfect, his knowledge impressive, and his horses—native Mineiros themselves—have a unique step (not unlike a lambada) that makes extensive trips more comfortable than you might imagine.

CLN Tourism and Transportation Services (✉ Rua Dr. Antônio Ibrahim 103A, Belo Horizonte, ☎ FAX 031/551–6311 or 031/9961–1220) offers exceptional tours of Ouro Prêto and the historic cities. CLN's Cláudio Neves speaks fluent English, knows a great deal about the region's history, and can arrange airport pickup and other transportation. **Companhia Trekking** (✉ Rua Pernambuco 1389, Belo Horizonte, ☎ 031/281–6618) organizes spelunking, hiking, rafting, and mountain-biking trips throughout Minas.

Sangetur (✉ Rua Inconfidentes 732, Belo Horizonte, ☎ 031/261–1055) is an all-purpose agency that can help you rent a car, make travel arrangements or hotel reservations, and book city tours. **YTUR Turismo** (✉ Av. do Contorno 8000, Belo Horizonte, ☎ 031/275–3233) can arrange hotel bookings, transportation plans, and tours of Belo Horizonte and beyond.

Visitor Information

In Belo Horizonte **Belotur** (✉ Rua Pernambuco 284, ☎ 031/277–9797; ✉ Mercado das Flores at Av. Afonso Pena at Rua da Bahia, Centro, ☎ 031/277–7666; ✉ Rodoviária, Av. Afonso Pena at Av. do Contorno, Centro, ☎ 031/277–6907; ✉ Confins airport, ☎ 031/689–2557), the municipal tourist board, is open daily 8 AM–10 PM at the airports and weekdays 8–7 elsewhere. **Turminas** (✉ Praça Rio Branco 56, Lourdes, Belo Horizonte, ☎ 031/212–2134), the state tourism authority, has been undergoing administrative changes, and its future is uncertain. At press time, however, it was still supplying information on the historic cities and other attractions weekdays 12:30–6:30.

Diamantina's **Casa da Cultura** (✉ Praça Antônio Eulálio 53, ☎ 038/531–1636) has information on the town, including all cultural events. It's open weekdays 8–6, Saturday 9–5, and Sunday 9–noon.

In Mariana, contact the **Associação de Guias** (✉ Praça Tancredo Neves s/n, ☎ 031/557–9000) for general information on the city. Its hours are Tuesday–Saturday noon–5:30.

The **Associação de Guias** (✉ Praça Tiradentes 41, ☎ 031/551–2655), formed by Ouro Prêto's professional tour guides, can provide general information on the city weekdays 8–6. Its well-informed, courteous guides also conduct 6- to 7-hour walking tours (in English) of the historic area. Be prepared for some stiff hiking up and down numerous hills.

In Tiradentes the **Secretária de Turismo** (✉ Rua Resende Costa 71, ☎ 032/335–1212) is the best place to go for information weekdays 8–6.

São Lourenço has a small **tourist kiosk** (✉ Praça João Lage s/n, ☎ 033/332–4455) in front of the water park. It's open weekdays 8–11 and 1–6. In Caxambu, there's an equally small **tourist desk** (✉ Praça Cônego José de Castilho Moreira s/n, ☎ 035/341–3977) that's open weekdays 8–6.

6 BRASÍLIA AND THE WEST

In 1960, when Brasília replaced Rio de Janeiro as the capital, Brazil finally turned from its coastline to face its interior. The temperate climate and the government jobs have attracted many people to this futuristic city. West of it are the sparsely populated states of Goiás, Mato Grosso, and Mato Grosso do Sul, which are best known for their frontier feel and for the Pantanal— South America's largest swamp.

VISITING BRASÍLIA IS LIKE LEAPING HEADLONG into the middle of the 21st century. Rising from the red earth of the 914-m (3,000-ft) Planalto Central (Central Plateau) and surrounded by the *cerrado* (Brazilian savanna) is one of the world's most singular cities. Its structures crawl and coil along the flat landscape and then shoot up in shafts of concrete and glass that capture the sun's rays.

Updated and expanded by Carlos G. Tornquist and Charles Runnette

The idea of moving the capital to the interior dates back to the early days of Brazil's independence, but it wasn't until 1955 that the scheme became more than just a possibility. Many said Brasília couldn't be built; others simply went ahead and did it. The resolute Juscelino Kubitschek made it part of his presidential campaign platform. Upon taking office, he organized an international contest for the city's master plan. A design submitted by urban planner Costa was selected, and he and his contemporaries—including architect Oscar Niemeyer and landscape artist Roberto Burle Marx—went to work. With a thrust of energy, the new capital was built less than five years later quite literally in the middle of nowhere.

Costa once mused, "The sky is the sea of Brasília." He made sure that the city had an unhindered view of the horizon, with buildings whose heights are restricted, wide streets and avenues, and immense green spaces. The sky here is an incredible blue that's cut only by occasional clusters of fleecy clouds. The earth is such an amazing shade of red that it seems to have been put here just for contrast. At night, it's hard to tell where the city lights end and the stars begin.

All around this wonderland of modernity nestles the old Brazil—the land of soybean plantations, beef cattle, and sluggish rivers. Nevertheless, those who flock to the rugged yet beautiful west have their eyes on the future. The surreal collection of migrants includes opportunists with get-rich-quick schemes; frontier folk with hopes of a solid, stable tomorrow; mystics and prophets, who swear by the region's spiritual energy; and dreamers who are convinced that extraterrestrials visit here regularly. For most earthly visitors, however, the high point of the west is the Pantanal, a flood plain the size of Great Britain that's home to an amazing array of wildlife and the ever-present possibilities for adventure.

Pleasures and Pastimes

Design

Urban planning, engineering, architecture, and landscape design were applied so harmoniously in Brasília that the city seems like one gigantic sculpture. Costa had a simple, original concept: "Brasília was conceived by the gesture of those who mark a place on a map: two axis intersecting at a right angle, that is, the sign of a cross mark." From above, his original Plano Piloto (Pilot or Master Plan) portion of the city looks like an airplane (it has also been described as a bow and arrow). It's built around the straight Eixo Monumental (Monumental Axis), which runs northwest–southeast and forms the "fuselage." This is crossed by the Eixo Rodoviário (Highway Axis), which curves roughly north–south and forms the *asas* ("wings").

Costa had several objectives, among them: do away with centralization (i.e., a central "downtown" with all the commercial and government facilities separate from residential areas); design highways that were as accident-free as possible; and ensure that the vast horizon would always be visible. The latter goal complemented Oscar Niemeyer's idea of architecture as "a manifestation of the spirit, imagination, and poetry." Though Niemeyer's buildings are often massive, they're generally low, linear, and set in grand spaces—conveying a sense of both light and lightness. To complete the package, the Plano Piloto's most important gardens (some are more like "waterscapes") were planned by renowned landscape designer Roberto Burle Marx, who emphasized the use of Brazilian vegetation in natural arrangements.

Dining

As the capital, Brasília attracts citizens from throughout the country as well as dignitaries from around the world. Hence, you'll find restaurants offering a variety of regional cuisines—particularly that of the northeast—as well as international fare. In the west, the cuisine isn't as interesting or as flavorful as that found elsewhere in the country. That said, however, the food is hearty, and the meals are large; affordable, all-you-can-eat buffets are ubiquitous. For price categories, see Dining in Smart Travel Tips A to Z.

Lodging

Brasília's master plan called for its hotels to be built amid banking and commercial sections and close to government offices. As they cater primarily to businesspeople and government officials, few hotels fall into budget categories. A recent ordinance has allowed new development along the shores of Lago Paranoá; at press time, several more upscale hotels were in the works here. Such budget options as *pousadas* (inns) are far from these hubs; many are in neighboring *cidades-satélite* (satellite cities), the communities where many city workers reside.

The frontier towns west of Brasília have few deluxe accommodations. Inside the Pantanal, the *fazendas* (farms) where most people stay are quite spartan; pack a pillow and bug spray (not all fazendas have netting for their beds). For price categories, see Lodging in Smart Travel Tips A to Z.

Natural Wonders

Brazil's vast cerrado has small trees, shrubs, and grasses that are amazingly well adapted to the harshness of the dry season, when temperatures in some parts rise well above 38°C (100°F) and humidity drops to a desert low of 15%. Several palm species grow around natural springs and watering holes. Cacti and bromeliads are also abundant. Look also for the *pequi,* a shrub that produces berries used in local cuisine. Since development, it has become harder to spot such indigenous cerrado wildlife as deer, emus, and jaguars. In the lush Pantanal wetlands, on the other hand, it's easy to spot birds (more than 600 species flock here), monkeys, *jacarés* (caiman alligators), and fish—including the famous piranha. You may also catch a glimpse of *capivaras* (capybaras; the world's largest, and reportedly sweetest, rodents), wild boar, giant anteaters, and many types of snakes (including the *sucuri,* or anaconda). Of the elusive panthers, jaguars, and pumas, however, the most you'll probably see are some tracks.

Exploring Brasília and the West

Brasília is 1,600 km (1,000 mi) from the Atlantic, on the flat plateau known as the Planalto Central. This is the domain of the vast cerrado, whose climate and vegetation are akin to those of the African savanna. The capital is actually in the Distrito Federal (Federal District), a 55,000 sq km (21,000 sq mi) administrative region carved out of Goiás State. Also in this district are the cidades-satélite, which were originally intended merely as residential areas for Brasília workers, but which now qualify as cities in their own right.

The Distrito Federal is flanked by Goiás State, part of the country's agricultural heart and the starting point for two massive Amazon tributaries, the rios Araguaia and Tocantins. Here, civilization consists of small towns. Although a few date from colonial times, many have sprung up in recent years as farmers from Brazil's south have settled in the region. Still farther west, the states of Mato Grosso and Mato Grosso do Sul have their share of Brazil's agribusiness. They also contain the Pantanal, an area whose watery terrain and rich, unique wildlife have escaped being paved over by the modern world—for now.

Great Itineraries

IF YOU HAVE 5 DAYS

Spend two days exploring Brasília's Plano Piloto, including the Eixo Monumental, the Praça dos Três Poderes, the shores of the Lago Paranoá, and the Parque da Cidade. On the third morning fly to Cuiabá and sign up for an overnight trip into the Pantanal to spot wildlife and maybe to fish for piranha.

IF YOU HAVE 7 DAYS

For Brasília, set aside two days to explore the Plano Piloto and to tour the Parque Nacional da Brasília, the Jardim Botânico, and the Catetinho. On the third day take an overnight trip to Pirenópolis, a well-preserved colonial town just outside the capital. On the following day, return to Brasília for a flight to Cuiabá and yet another overnight trip, this one into the Pantanal.

IF YOU HAVE 10 DAYS

Spend four leisurely days in Brasília exploring the Plano Piloto and visiting the Parque Nacional, the cult communities, and the nearby town of Pirenópolis. On the fifth day fly to either Cuiabá or Campo Grande and schedule a four-day (three-night) trip into the Pantanal with a small tour group. Such treks include riverboat rides, horseback rides, fishing, bird-watching (during the day and, sometimes, at night), and cooking your very own piranha stew.

When to Tour

In Brasília and much of the west, you can count on clear days and comfortable temperatures from March to July (the mean temperature is 22°C/75°F). The rainy season runs from December to February; in August and September, the mercury often rises to 38°C (100°F). When congress is in session, Brasília is quite busy during the week. When congress adjourns (July and January–February), the city's pulse slows noticeably.

In the Pantanal, peak season is synonymous with the dry season (July–October; it's also called "winter," though temperatures rarely drop below 27°C/80°F). At this time, the rivers have receded, the roads (what few there are) are passable, the mosquito population has dwindled, and the birds are nesting. You won't see as much wildlife during the wet season, but you will experience the swamp in all its impenetrable glory.

BRASÍLIA

By Carlos G. Tornquist

Brazil's capital was moved from Salvador to Rio in 1763 so that the Portuguese court could be near the center of all the mining and exporting activity. In 1960, it was moved from coastal Rio to Brasília in an attempt to awaken the center of this sleeping giant.

As far back as 1808, Brazilian newspapers ran articles discussing Rio's inadequacies and proposing a new interior capital: "Our present capital is in a corner of Brazil and contact between it and Pará or other far removed states is extremely difficult. Besides, Rio subjects the government to enemy invasion by any maritime power." In 1892 congress authorized the overland Cruls Expedition to find a central locale where "a city could be constructed next to the headwaters of big rivers" and where "roads could be opened to all seaports." Within three months the expedition leaders had chosen the plateau region of Goiás. However, despite this and several other attempts to establish a location and to move the capital, nothing was done for more than 60 years.

In the mid-1950s a sharp politician named Juscelino Kubitschek made the new capital part of his presidential campaign agenda. When he was elected president in 1956, he set the wheels in motion. After a site was selected (in Goiás, as proposed by the 1892 expedition) and Lúcio Costa's master plan was chosen, President Kubitschek flew to the Planalto Central—where there was nothing but the inhospitable cerrado—had mass said on the building site, stayed the night, and set up work committees. Loans and grants came in from all over the world.

To build a new seat of power for Latin America's largest nation—complete with a modern infrastructure as well as ministries and offices, banks, shops, houses, schools, hospitals, churches, and theaters—was a monumental undertaking. In the first days of the construction, few of the necessary materials could be obtained on the Planalto Central. An airfield was constructed and planes loaded with supplies flew in continuously from Rio and São Paulo. Thousands of workers came to the region from the northeast. Most were unskilled; all were willing to face any hardship for a paycheck. They learned fast and worked hard, often up to 15 hours a day. A collection of wooden shacks sprang up and became a city of 100,000 laborers known as Freetown. It was a rough place where anything went as long as there was money to pay for it.

Back in Rio, opposition to the new capital was loud and heated. Debates in the senate turned into fist fights, and committees were continuously conducting investigations into all the spending. Government employees were unhappy about the impending move. Some feared that Rio's business would drastically decline and its real estate values would dramatically drop once the city ceased to be the capital. Others simply didn't want to leave the glorious beaches and the many and familiar services. Kubitschek's government countered all this with inducements: 100% salary increases, tax breaks, earlier-than-usual retirement ages, free transportation and moves to the capital, ridiculously low rents on Brasília's new apartments and houses, and even discounts on new home furnishings.

Kubitschek had set a date for the city's inauguration: April 21, 1960. Despite all the odds, it was ready. The day began with mass in the uncompleted cathedral and ended with a fireworks display, during which the president's name burned in 5-m-high (15-ft-high) letters. In spite of its high cost and the criticism it received in its early days, Brasília has become a comfortable, functional capital. Highways run directly from it to several regions, including the farther flung states that once were so isolated from the capital. It has also forced the nation to look westward from the coast, launching a new era of pioneering and colonization.

Exploring Brasília

Addresses in the airplane-shape Plano Piloto might make even surveyors scratch their heads. There are the usual streets, avenues, and plazas with numbers or letters. There are sometimes compass points: *norte* (north), sul (south), este (east), oeste (west). And there are also such things as *setors* (S.; sectors), *quadras* (Q.; squares), *blocos* (Bl.; blocks, but really more akin to buildings), *lotes* (Lt.; lots), lojas (Lj.; literally, "shops" or "stores," but here a type of subdivision within a larger building), and *conjuntos* (Cj.; yet another type of building subdivision). Although the original layout is very logical, it can be hard to get chapter-and-verse addresses, making them seem illogical.

The Eixo (pronounced *ay*-shoo) Monumental, the city's "fuselage," is lined with government buildings, museums, and monuments as well as banks, hotels, and shops. It runs roughly from the Praça do Cruzeiro to the Esplanada dos Ministérios, at the tip of which is the Praça dos Três Poderes. Intersecting the Eixo Monumental, near the Esplanada dos Ministérios, is the Eixo Rodoviário. It and the areas just off it form the city's "wings." The Asa Sul, or South Wing, is almost totally built up; the Asa Norte, or North Wing, still has spaces for development.

The Eixo Rodoviário has a double line of *superquadras* (supersquares) made up of two (usually) quadras numbered from 100 to 399 and consisting of eight six-story blocos. Four superquadras make up one self-sufficient Unidade de Vizinhança (Neighborhood Unit), with shops, schools, police stations, and post offices. New quadras numbered 400 and above have been added outside the initial plan. In and around the two main axes are streets and avenues that connect still more residential–commercial areas, parks and gardens, and the Lago Paranoá (formed by a dam built about 16 km/10 mi southeast of the Plano Piloto and divided into Lago Sul and Lago Norte shores/districts). Along the outer shores of this lake are several residential areas. These include the Setores de Habitações Individuais (Individual Habitation Sectors) and the Setores de Mansões (Mansion Sectors).

It's best to tackle the Eixo Monumental and the Esplanada dos Ministérios first, and then visit the Praça dos Três Poderes. The sights in these areas are easy to reach by bus, cab, or organized tour. Staying at a hotel in the nearby Setor Hotel Norte or Setor Hotel Sul (SHN or SHS; Hotel Sector North or South) will keep traveling time to a minimum. If you have time get a taxi to the cidades-satélite. Before heading out, get as detailed an address as possible, check that your cabbie knows where to go, and agree on a fare up front.

Eixo Monumental

Most of the Plano Piloto's major sights are along or just off the grand, 8-km-long (5-mi-long) Eixo Monumental and its multilane boulevards. The distances are too far to see everything on foot, so if you want to explore on your own rather than as part of a tour, you'll have to combine walking with bus and/or cab rides.

Numbers in the text correspond to numbers in the margin and on the Brasília map.

A GOOD TOUR
Start at the **Praça do Cruzeiro** ① at the Eixo Monumental's northwestern end. It's an easy 180-m (200-yd) walk to Niemeyer's **Memorial JK** ②, where you can learn about the man who made Brasília happen. From here it's another short walk to the **Memorial dos Povos Indígenas** ③, a round structure containing indigenous artifacts. If you're interested in history and geography, hop a cab for the **Instituto Histórico e Geográfico** and then take a break in the nearby **Parque da Cidade.** Alternatively, you can continue (by taxi or bus) to the other Eixo Monumental sights, starting with the **Torre de TV** ④.

Head southeast and cross the Eixo Rodoviário to the pyramid that houses the **Teatro Nacional Cláudio Santoro** ⑤. At the other side of the Eixo

Brasília

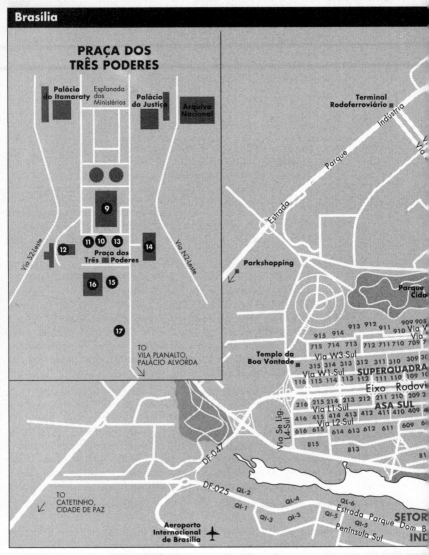

PRAÇA DOS TRÊS PODERES

Palácio do Itamaraty
Esplanada dos Ministérios
Palácio da Justiça
Arquivo Nacional

Via S2-Leste
Via N2-Leste

Praça dos Três Poderes

TO VILA PLANALTO, PALÁCIO ALVORDA

Terminal Rodoferroviário

Indústria

Parque

Estrada

Parkshopping

Parque Cida

Templo da Boa Vontade

Via W3-Sul
Via W1-Sul

SUPERQUADRA

Eixo Rodovi

ASA SUL

Via Se Lig.
Via L1-Sul
Via L2-Sul
L4-Sul

TO CATETINHO, CIDADE DE PAZ

DF-047

DF-025

QL-2
QL-1
QL-3
QL-4
QL-5
QL-6
QL-5

Estrada Parque Dom B
Península Sul

SETOR
IND

Aeroporto Internacional de Brasília

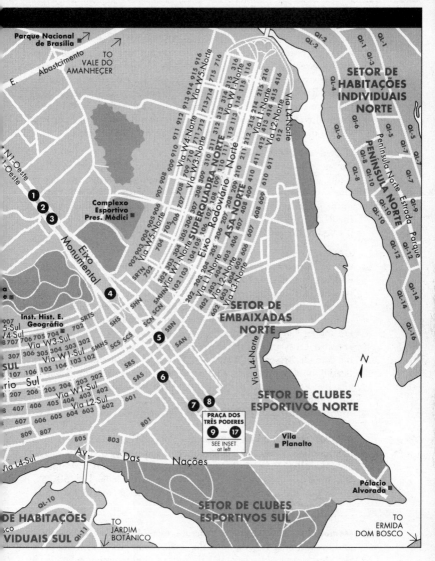

Parque Nacional de Brasília →

TO
VALE DO
AMANHEÇER

E. Abastcimento

QI-2
QI-2
QI-1 QI-3
QI-1

SETOR DE
HABITAÇÕES
INDIVIDUAIS
NORTE

Complexo
Esportivo
Pres. Médici ■

Eixo
Monumental

916
913 914 915 916
Via W5-Norte
715 716
316
315 316
Via W1-Norte
215 216
415 416

911 912
910 911 912
Via W4-Norte
711 712
713 714
313 314
Via W2-Norte
112 113
114 115 116
213 214
413 414 415 416
Via L2-Norte

907 908
909 910
Via W3-Norte
710 711
210 211 212
111
110 111
211 212
410 411 412
611 612
Via L1-Norte

905 906
903 904 905 906
Via W5-Norte
707 708
706 707 708
SUPERQUADRA NORTE
306 307
304 305 306 307
Eixo Rodoviário Norte
ASA NORTE
108 109
107 108 109
208 209 210
207 208
405 406 407 408
609 610
607 608
Via L3-Norte

SRTN
702
302 303 304
102 103 104 105
SMHN
Via W1-Norte
403 404 405
602 603 604
402
202 203 204 205
Via L1-Norte
Via L2-Norte

Inst. Hist. E.
Geográfio
907
5-Sul
74-Sul

SRTS
SHN
SHS
SCN
SHM
SCS
SBN
SAN
SAIN

SETOR DE
EMBAIXADAS
NORTE

8 707 706 705 704 ■
Via W3-Sul
307 306 305 304 303 302
Via W1-Sul
SMHS
SCS
SBS
SAS
Via L4-Norte

107 106
105 104 103 102
SUL

rio Sul

207 206 205 204 203 202
Via W1-Sul
8 407 406 405 404 403 402
Via L2-Sul
607 606 605 604 603 602
601
809 807
805 803 801

SETOR DE CLUBES
ESPORTIVOS NORTE

Via L4-Sul
Av. Das Nações

PRAÇA DOS
TRÊS PODERES
⑨ — ⑰
SEE INSET
at left

Vila
■ Planalto

Pálacio
Alvorada ■

QL-10

DE HABITAÇÕES
sco
VIDUAIS SUL
QL-11

TO
JARDIM
BOTÂNICO

SETOR DE CLUBES
ESPORTIVOS SUL

TO
ERMIDA
DOM BOSCO

① ② ③ ④ ⑤ ⑥ ⑦ ⑧

Monumental and a little farther southeast is the unique **Catedral Metropolitana de Nossa Senhora da Aparecida** ⑥, a Niemeyer masterpiece. You're just a few steps from the Esplanada dos Ministérios, a gigantic corridor formed by 17 identical buildings lined up along either side of the Eixo Monumental. (They house several government ministries, and most have annex buildings of equal or larger size behind and connected to them by glassed-in passageways.) The buildings that face each other at the far end of the Esplanada (just before the Praça dos Três Poderes) are two more world-renowned Niemeyer works: the **Palácio do Itamaraty** ⑦ and **Palácio da Justiça** ⑧.

TIMING AND PRECAUTIONS

You need at least a day (6–8 hours) to visit and fully appreciate all the sights. Although you'll probably ride as well as walk, wear comfortable shoes and drink plenty of water, particularly if you're exploring in the hotter months. Note that some government buildings, such as the Palácio do Itamaraty, frown on shorts, tank tops, and the like, so it's best to dress conservatively.

SIGHTS TO SEE

★ ⑥ **Catedral Metropolitana de Nossa Senhora da Aparecida.** The city's cathedral is a Niemeyer masterpiece that was finished in 1967. The circular structure consists of 16 reinforced concrete "fingers" that arch skyward. They support huge panes of glass that shelter a subterranean church. Inside, *Os Anjos* (*The Angels*)—an aluminum sculpture by Brazilian modern artist Alfredo Ceschiatti—hovers above the altar. The *cruzeiro* (cross) used at the city's first mass is also here. Above ground, the cathedral resembles a crown of thorns and is surrounded by a reflecting pool. Its entrance is guarded by four majestic bronze statues, also by Ceschiatti, of *Os Evangelistas* (*The Evangelists*). The outdoor carillon is a gift of the Spanish government. ✉ *Esplanada dos Ministérios,* ☎ *061/224–4073.* 🎫 *Free.* ⊙ *Daily 8–5.*

OFF THE BEATEN PATH   **INSTITUTO HISTÓRICO E GEOGRÁFICO** – The small collection of photographs and memorabilia in the saucer-shape History and Geography Institute document the city's history. The exhibition includes a vintage Jeep used by Kubitschek to visit the construction site in the late '50s. ✉ SEPS 703/903, Lt. C/D/E, ☎ 061/226–7753. 🎫 Free. ⊙ Tues.–Sun. 8–noon and 2–6.

★ ② **Memorial JK.** This Niemeyer structure resembles an Egyptian pyramid and has a similar function: It's the final resting place of former president Juscelino Kubitschek (JK), the city's founding father, who died in 1981. The mortuary chamber has a lovely stained-glass roof by local artist Marianne Peretti. The bronze statue of JK—his hand raised as if in blessing—looks down upon the Eixo Monumental and makes this one of Brasília's most moving monuments. Permanent and changing exhibits here document the story behind the city's construction. ✉ *Eixo Monumental Oeste,* ☎ *061/225–9451.* 🎫 *Admission.* ⊙ *Tues.–Sun. 9–6.*

③ **Memorial dos Povos Indígenas.** Initially slated to contain an art museum, this building was abandoned for several years until it was literally taken over by indigenous peoples' organizations. It now houses a small museum with crafts by such peoples as the Kayapó and the Xavante, which once lived on the cerrado and now dwell in the Xingu area of the Amazon. Traditional dance performances and ritual celebrations are sometimes held in the memorial's central arena. ✉ *Eixo Monumental Oeste,* ☎ *061/223–3760.* 🎫 *Free.* ⊙ *Tues.–Sun. 9–5.*

Palácio do Itamaraty. For the home of the Foreign Ministry, Niemeyer surrounded a glass rectangular structure with a detached stone shelter whose facade is a series of elegant, elongated arches. The whole complex is, in turn, surrounded by a Burle Marx–designed reflecting pool (more like a lake) that augments the sense of spaciousness. The building and the water create a perfect backdrop for the *Meteoro* (*Meteor*), a round, abstract, Carrara-marble sculpture by Brazilian-Italian artist Bruno Giorgi. On the guided tour of the interior, you'll see an astounding collection of modern art—including paintings by such Brazilian artists as Candido Portinari—and a tropical garden, also the work of Burle Marx. ⊠ *Esplanada dos Ministérios,* ☎ *061/211–6640.* ☜ *Free.* ☉ *Tours weekdays at 4* PM.

❽ **Palácio da Justiça.** The exterior of Niemeyer's Justice Ministry has waterfalls that cascade between its frontal columns. Inside there's an important library (not open to the public) that contains one of the few complete, original sets of Shakespeare's works—a gift from Queen Elizabeth to Kubitschek. ⊠ *Esplanada dos Ministérios,* ☎ *061/218–3223 or 061/218–3224.* ☉ *Weekdays 8–noon and 2–7.*

OFF THE BEATEN PATH **PARQUE DA CIDADE** – A few blocks from the Instituto Histórico and Geográfico, you can relax in the shade of City Park, a collaborative effort by Costa, Niemeyer, and Burle Marx. Recent improvements include a state-of-the-art lighting system and more security guards, making an evening walk, run, or bike ride along a path more agreeable than ever. ⊠ *Entrances at Q. 901 S and Q. 912 S,* ☎ *061/225–2451 or 061/ 223–0702 (park administration office).* ☉ *Dawn–dusk.*

❶ **Praça do Cruzeiro.** Set at a commanding height above the Eixo Monumental, this small, solemn plaza is where the city's first mass was held on May 3, 1957. The site's original cross is now at the Cathedral Metropolitana (☞ *above*).

❺ **Teatro Nacional Cláudio Santoro.** Another of Niemeyer's "pyramid projects," the sides of this theater have an array of concrete cubes and rectangles designed by Brazilian architect Athos Bulcão. Its three stages host a variety of performances, and its several small art galleries offer changing exhibits. ⊠ *SBN, Via N2,* ☎ *061/325–6105 or 061/321–3738 ext. 160.* ☜ *Free.* ☉ *Tues.–Sun. 2–6.*

❹ **Torre de TV.** The *salão panorâmico* (observation room) of this 204-m (670-ft) TV tower offers spectacular views, particularly at night. On a lower level, the small **Museu Nacional das Gemas** has an impressive collection of Brazilian gems as well as a shop that sells stones and crafts and a café. ⊠ *Eixo Monumental,* ☎ *061/322–3227 (museum).* ☜ *Deck: free. Museum: admission.* ☉ *Deck: Mon. 2–9 and Tues.–Sun. 9–9. Museum: daily 9–7.*

NEED A BREAK? From the Torre de TV, it's only a couple of blocks to the Patio Brazil shopping mall, with its **Expresso Pão de Queijo** (⊠ Pátio Brazil Shopping, 4th floor, ☎ 061/314–7400). This is a great place to sample a delicacy from the state of Minas Gerais—the *pão de queijo* (cheese bread)—as well as other pastries, coffee, and freshly squeezed juices.

Praça dos Três Poderes

Buildings housing the government's three branches symbolically face each other in the Plaza of the Three Powers, the heart of the Brazilian republic. Here both power and architecture have been given balance as well as a view of Brasília and beyond. Indeed, the cityscape combined with the planalto's endless sky have made the plaza so unusual that Russian cosmonaut Yuri Gagarin once remarked, "I have the impression of landing on a different planet, not on Earth!"

A GOOD TOUR

Start at the plaza's western end, where twin high-rises and two bowl-shape structures make up the **Congresso Nacional** ⑨. Directly in front of it is the **Museu Histórico de Brasília** ⑩, whose facade is adorned with a sculpture of Kubitschek. To one side of the museum and beneath the plaza is the **Espaço Lúcio Costa** ⑪, with exhibits depicting the planner's ideas for the city, beyond which you'll find the **Supremo Tribunal Federal** ⑫. To the other side of the museum is Giorgi's famous sculpture, **Os Candangos** ⑬, which sits in front of the **Palácio do Planalto** ⑭, the executive office. Heading eastward across the plaza you'll come to the **Mastro da Bandeira** ⑮ and the **Panteão da Pátria** ⑯. Head eastward along the path in the lawn to the **Espaço Cultural Oscar Niemeyer** ⑰, where several of the renowned architect's projects are displayed and explained. From here you can head beyond the plaza by cab to the **Vila Planalto** neighborhood and on to the **Palácio da Alvorada.**

TIMING

All the sights in the plaza are close to one another, so you can easily complete this tour on foot in about four hours. Trips by taxi or bus to the Vila Planalto and the Palácio da Alvorada will make this a full-day tour.

SIGHTS TO SEE

⑬ **Os Candangos.** This 8-m-tall (25-ft-tall) bronze sculpture by Giorgi has become the symbol of Brasília. The laborers, many from the northeast, who built the city from scratch were called *candangos*; today the moniker applies to anyone who settles here. The recently restored statue, which consists of graceful, elongated figures holding poles, is right across from Palácio do Planalto (☞ *below*).

⑨ **Congresso Nacional.** One of Niemeyer's most audacious projects consists of two 28-story office towers for the 500 representatives of the Câmara dos Deputados (House of Representatives) and the 80 members of the Senado (Senate); a convex structure, where the câmara meets; and a concave structure, where the senado convenes. The complex is connected by tunnels to several *anexos* (office annexes) and contains a collection of works by such Brazilian artists as Di Cavalcanti, Bulcão, and Ceschiatti as well as French designer Le Corbusier. The indoor gardens were done by Burle Marx. ⊠ *Praça dos Três Poderes,* ☎ *061/318–5107 or 061/311–3344.* 🎟 *Free.* ☉ *Weekdays 9–noon and 2–5, weekends 10–2.*

⑰ **Espaço Cultural Oscar Niemeyer.** This branch of the Oscar Niemeyer Foundation—which is based in Rio and was created to preserve and present the architect's work—opened in 1988 and houses a library and database with text and images from Niemeyer's archives. The small auditorium hosts a variety of presentations, which have included talks by the architect himself—after all, this is also the site of his Brasília office (at press time he was 92 and still active). ⊠ *Praça dos Três Poderes, Lt. J.,* ☎ *061/224–3255 or 061/224–3556.* 🎟 *Free.* ☉ *Weekdays 9–6.*

⑪ **Espaço Lúcio Costa.** As a tribute to the urban planner who masterminded Brasília, this underground complex was added to the plaza in the late '80s. It has a 139-sq-m (1,500-sq-ft) display of the city's blueprint, and you can read Costa's original ideas for the project (the text is in Portuguese and English). ⊠ *Praça dos Três Poderes,* ☎ *061/321–9843.* 🎟 *Free.* ☉ *Daily 9–6.*

⑮ Mastro da Bandeira. At what is also known as the Pavilhãao Nacional (National Pavilion), you'll find a 242-sq-m (2,600-sq-ft) Brazilian flag on a 92-m (300-ft) steel flagpole. At noon on the first Sunday of the month, members of the armed forces take part in a Troca da Bandeira (Flag Change) ceremony. This is a good spot to contemplate the Brazilian flag's elements. The green background symbolizes the forests that spanned most of the country in the early days. The yellow diamond represents the gold-mining period that so influenced the country's history. The blue circle in the center is a homage to the grĕat blue skies that dominate the territory; inside it are 26 stars—one for each state—from the southern skies and a white band with the national motto *"Ordem e Progresso"* ("Order and Progress").

⑩ Museu Histórico de Brasília. The city's first museum has a small collection of pictures of the city and writings about it by such luminaries as Pope Pius XII, Kubitschek, and Niemeyer. The building is a reinforced concrete and marble structure with a statue of Kubitschek on its facade, a 1960 work of Brazilian sculptor José Pedrosa. ⊠ *Praça dos Três Poderes,* ☎ *061/325–6244.* ☐ *Free.* ☉ *Daily 9–6.*

OFF THE BEATEN PATH

PALÁCIO DA ALVORADA – At the tip of a peninsula formed by Lago Paranoá, the president's official residence—with its trademark slanting supporting columns—was Niemeyer's first project and was finished in June of 1958. Although you can't go inside, you can explore the grounds, whose gardens incorporate the cerrado's flora as well as some of its fauna (be on the lookout for emus and armadillos). ⊠ *SHTN, Via Presidencial s/n,* ☎ *061/411–4000.* ☉ *Dawn–dusk.*

⑭ Palácio do Planalto. Although you can't enter the executive office building you should pause to study its facade. Niemeyer gave the highly acclaimed structure an unusual combination of straight and slanting lines. ⊠ *Praça dos Três Poderes,* ☎ *061/411–1221 or 061/411–1355.*

★ **⑯ Panteão da Pátria.** Designed by Niemeyer in 1985, this building honors the nation's heroes, including the beloved Tancredo Neves (it's also known as the Panteão Tancredo Neves), whose untimely death prevented him from being sworn in as Brazil's first democratically elected president after the military dictatorship ended. Inside the curved structure, which resembles a dove, you'll find works by Athos Bulcão and João Camara. One set of panels, the *Inconfidentes,* depicts the martyrs of the 18th-century Inconfidência Mineira movement, which was organized in Minas Gerais State to overthrow the Portuguese and establish an independent Brazilian republic. ⊠ *Praça dos Três Poderes,* ☎ *061/224–3255 or 061/224–3556.* ☐ *Free.* ☉ *Daily 8–5.*

⑫ Supremo Tribunal Federal. The Brazilian Supreme Court has the structural lightness that is the backbone of Niemeyer's work. The Tribunal Pleno, the highest court in Brazil, convenes on the ground floor. The top floor houses an 80,000-volume library. The 3-m (10-ft) granite statue set amid the reflecting pool is *The Justice* by Ceschiatti. (Note that shorts and tank tops aren't appropriate attire here.) ⊠ *Praça dos Três Poderes,* ☎ *061/319–6561 or 061/319–8000.* ☐ *Free.* ☉ *Weekdays 9–6.*

OFF THE BEATEN PATH

VILA PLANALTO – Set between the Praça dos Três Poderes and the Palácio da Alvorada, this neighborhood was where the architects, engineers, topographers, accountants, and other professionals lived (in prefabricated wooden houses) while Brasília was under construction. Today it's a down-to-earth, middle- to low-income residential area that maintains the boomtown spirit of the early days. It's the perfect place to find a *buteco* (bar) for an evening *seresta* (impromptu musical soirée), a national pastime.

Beyond the Plano Piloto

If you have the time, step outside the Plano Piloto and explore the outer perimeter of Lago Paranoá, where you'll find parks, gardens, and several interesting neighborhoods. You'll also encounter the cult communities that reflect Brasília's mystical side. In 1883 an Italian priest named Dom Bosco (St. John Bosco) had a vision of a new civilization rising around a lake between the 15th and 20th parallels. "This will be the promised land," he proclaimed. The futuristic architecture; the location between the 15th and 16th parallels in the vast, eerie cerrado; and the formation of the Lago Paranoá have led many to believe that Brasília is the realization of Bosco's vision. (Bosco never actually set foot in Brazil, making his vision seem even more mysterious.) Since its inception, the city has attracted a variety of religious groups.

★ **Catetinho.** When Rio was the capital, the president resided in the Palácio Catete. While the new capital was being built, Kubitschek's temporary lodging was called the Catetinho (Little Catete). Niemeyer built the barracks-like wooden edifice in 10 days in the summer of 1956. A nearby landing strip allowed the president to fly in directly from Rio. The building, which is 16 km (10 mi) southeast of the bus terminal in the Plano Piloto, was abandoned for several years. A recent renovation, however, has restored and transformed it into a must-see museum for those interested in the city's history. It's surrounded by woods in which there's a small springwater pool where the president and his entourage once bathed. ⊠ *Km 0, BR 040,* ☎ *061/380–1921.* 🎟 *Free.* ☉ *Tues.–Sun. 9–5.*

Cidade da Paz. Partly subsidized by the Federal District government, the City of Peace is home to a branch of the Universidade Holística Internacional (International Holistic University), whose goal is to "contribute to the awakening of a new conscience and a new world view." The community occupies the 500-acre Granja do Ipé, 26 km (16 mi) southeast of the Plano Piloto and once the country manor of General Golbery do Couto e Silva, who many consider the éminence grise behind the military regime (1964–85). The buildings on the grounds now accommodate university offices, meditation rooms, art galleries, and artisans shops. There are also three thermal pools and waterfalls. ⊠ *Km 30, BR 040,* ☎ *061/380–1202.* 🎟 *Free.* ☉ *Weekdays 9–noon and 3–6.*

Ermida Dom Bosco. This lakefront sanctuary 24 km (15 mi) east of the Plano Piloto is dedicated to the saint who inspired so many of those who settled in the new capital. A scenic overlook with an outstanding view of the Plano Piloto and a tranquil Burle Marx–designed garden make it an ideal place to watch the sun set. ⊠ *Lago Sul, Setor de Mansões Dom Bosco, Cj. 12,* ☎ *061/366–2141.* 🎟 *Free.* ☉ *Tues.–Sun. 9–5.*

Jardim Botânico. The Botanical Gardens are in a 9,000-acre ecological reserve 27 km (17 mi) south of the Plano Piloto that is only partially open to the public. Three marked trails educate you about different types of Brazilian vegetation, and there's an herb garden with almost 100 different types of native medicinal species. ⊠ *Lago Sul, Setor de Mansões Dom Bosco, Cj. 12,* ☎ *061/366–2141.* 🎟 *Free.* ☉ *Tues.–Sun. 9–5.*

Parque Nacional de Brasília. The 60,000-acre Brasília National Park is in the northeastern area of the Federal District. The typical cerrado

WITHOUT KODAK MAX
photos taken on 100 speed film

Ever see someone

waiting for the sun to come out

while trying to photograph

a charging rhino?

New!
Kodak Max film:

Now with better color,
Kodak's maximum
versatility film gives
you great pictures in
sunlight, low light,
action or still.

WITH KODAK MAX
photos taken on Kodak Max 400 film

**It's all you need
to know about film.**

www.kodak.com

vegetation includes grasslands, woodland savannas, and taller gallery woods on the bottomlands. A 5-km (3-mi) trail through mostly flat cerrado terrain starts at the visitor center, where you can pick up maps and brochures. The park also has two pools (fed by natural springs), dressing rooms, and picnic and barbecue areas. ⊠ *EPIA, 9 km (6 mi) from bus terminal,* ☎ *061/233–4055 or 061/234–9057.* ☒ *Admission.* ⊙ *Tues.–Sun. 8–4.*

Templo da Boa Vontade. This temple 8 km (5 mi) south of the Eixo Monumental is adjacent to the national headquarters of the Legião da Boa Vontade (Goodwill Legion), a philanthropic organization. The pyramid-shape building is open to all denominations for worship or meditation. At the top of it sits a 21 kg (46 lb) quartz crystal, the largest ever found in Brazil. ⊠ *SGAS 915, Lt. 75/6,* ☎ *061/245–1070 or 061/245–1389.* ☒ *Free.* ⊙ *Daily 24 hours.*

Vale do Amanhecer. The most famous of the cult communities, the Valley of the Dawn is near Planaltina, a cidade-satélite 40 km (25 mi) north of the Plano Piloto. The community was established in 1969 by Neiva Zelay, known as Tia Neiva, a one-time truck driver who died in 1985 and who reportedly had extrasensory powers. Each day, the community's grounds are the site of many rituals conducted by followers of a variety of faiths and philosophies. About 1,000 people live in the community. ⊠ *Km 10, DF 15,* ☎ *061/389–1258.* ☒ *Donation suggested.* ⊙ *Grounds: daily 10 to midnight. Services: daily 12:30–2:30.*

Dining

Brazilian

$$$ ✕ **Antigamente Lago Sul.** The location—in a neocolonial house on the
★ shore of the Lago Sul—is superb, and the *comida mineira* (food typical of Minas Gerais) dishes have won many awards—both factors make reservations a good idea. Try the *galinha á D. Carlota Joaquina* (chicken with red sauce) or the *ouro velho de Goiás* (butter-fried chicken nuggets). Brazilian music performances accompany your meal. ⊠ *Lago Sul, SHIS, Q. 06, Cj. 11, Casa 19,* ☎ *061/248–2233. DC, MC, V. No dinner Sun. Closed Mon.*

$$ ✕ **Cabana da Árvore.** The chef at this simple, unique restaurant—in a log house built around a 12-m (40-ft) ficus tree—uses a traditional clay oven to prepare dishes from the states of Minas Gerais and Goiás. Any one of the regional *cachaças* (a liquor made from sugarcane) goes well with the rice with pequi berries. ⊠ *Rua 1, Lt. 2, Vila Planalto,* ☎ *061/224–7765. DC, MC, V. No dinner Sun.*

$$ ✕ **Churrascaria do Lago.** At this *churrascaria* (barbecue restaurant), waiters bring meats to your table until you tell them to stop. It has been here, in this superb lakefront location near the Palácio da Alvorada, since the city's early days. Reservations are advised. ⊠ *Lago Norte, SHTN, Cj. 1-A,* ☎ *61/223–9365. AE, DC, MC, V.*

$$ ✕ **Cumê na Roça.** This restaurant on a small farm outside the Plano Piloto, 16 km (10 mi) north of the bus terminal, specializes in lunches (dinner is served only on Friday) of comida mineira. Try the *leitão pururuca* (roasted piglet with regional seasonings) while you take in the view of the Lago Norte. ⊠ *Fazenda Brejo, Chácara 8T, Ólhos d'Água,* ☎ *061/500–1600. Reservations essential. No credit cards.*

Eclectic

$$$ ✕ **The Falls.** As its name suggests, this restaurant in the basement of the Naoum Plaza Hotel (☞ Lodging, *below*) has a decor that includes artificial waterfalls that cascade amid tropical vegetation. The ambience is as much of a draw as the food, which includes such exquisite dishes as the *sinfonia de peixes,* the "fish symphony" of Brazilian

seafood, rice, and *pirão* (beans and cassava flour). ⊠ *Setor Histórico, Rua Kellers 95*, ☎ *061/322–4545 or 0800/61–4844. AE, DC, MC, V.*

$$$ ✕ **La Via Vechia.** The restaurant in the Bonaparte Hotel (☞ Lodging,
★ *below*) is favored by the powers-that-be for its quiet atmosphere and superb decor. Chefs Dudu and Eduardo will do all they can to please even the most demanding customer. Specialties include the *cordeiro á la Via Vechia* (mutton with a cream sauce made with cassis and Port) and the award-winning grilled seafood combination served with a fruit risotto. It's best to make reservations for dinner. ⊠ *SHS Q. 02, Bl. I,* ☎ *061/322–2288. AE, DC, MC, V.*

$$ ✕ **Papaguth.** Its location in the Academia de Tênis resort (☞ Lodging, *below*) gives this restaurant the relaxed, casual atmosphere that makes it so popular with busy executives, particularly at lunch time (reservations are advised). The fare includes everything from Brazilian-style steak to grilled chicken to hamburgers. ⊠ *SCES, T. 4, Lt. 1–B,* ☎ *061/316–6254. AE, DC, MC.*

French

$$$ ✕ **La Chaumière.** The pleasant atmosphere of this highly regarded 30-
★ year-old restaurant won't fail to impress. The fare is classical French, the fillet with green pepper sauce a mainstay entrée. ⊠ *SCLS, Q. 408, Bl. A, Lt. 13,* ☎ *61/242–7599. AE. No dinner Sun. Closed Mon.*

German

$$ ✕ **Fritz.** In Brasília, this is *the* place for German cuisine. The *Eisbein* (pig's leg with mashed potatoes) and *Kassler* (fillet with cheese) are standouts on the varied menu. ⊠ *SCLS, Q. 404, Bl. D, Lj. 35,* ☎ *061/223–4622. AE, DC, MC, V. No dinner Sun. Closed Mon.*

Italian

$$$ ✕ **Vila Borghese.** The cantina ambience and fantastic cuisine (including many freshly made pastas) make you feel as if you're in Italy. The *tagliatelli negro* (tagliatelli pasta made with squid ink) served with a garlic, herb, and shrimp sauce is divine. ⊠ *SCLS, Q. 201, Bl. A, Lj. 33,* ☎ *061/226–5650. AE, DC, MC, V. No dinner Sun. Closed Mon.*

Spanish

$$ ✕ **Salamanca.** Don't let looks fool you at this restaurant. The decor may not be very sophisticated, but the paella certainly is. ⊠ *SCLS 112, Bl. B, Lj. 33,* ☎ *061/346–8212. AE, MC, V. Closed Sun.*

Lodging

$$$$ 🏨 **Bonaparte Hotel Residence.** Stylish decor (with plush carpeting,
★ wood paneling, and accent lighting in the lobby), spacious rooms (all could be considered suites), and outstanding business services have made the Bonaparte the preferred choice for many. The on-site restaurant, La Via Vechia (☞ Dining, *above*), is one of the best in town. ⊠ *SHS, Q. 02 Bl. J 70322–900,* ☎ *061/322–2288 or 0800/61–9991,* 𝙵𝙰𝚇 *061/ 322–9092. 128 rooms. 2 restaurants, bar, coffee shop, room service, pool, sauna, exercise room, business services, meeting rooms. AE, DC, MC, V.*

$$$$ 🏨 **Hotel Nacional.** The upscale Nacional—one of the city's first hotels—has accommodated such important guests as Queen Elizabeth, who stayed here in the '60s. Even after almost 40 years, it's still one of the city's finest lodging options. Echoing Brasília's modern architecture, lightness of form and functionality dominate the decor here. The Taboo Grill is a great place for grilled meat or seafood. ⊠ *SHS, Q. 01, Bl. A 70322–900,* ☎ *061/321–7575,* 𝙵𝙰𝚇 *061/ 223–9213. 346 rooms. Restaurant, bar, coffee shop, room service, indoor pool, sauna,*

exercise room, business services, meeting rooms, travel services. AE, DC, MC, V.

$$$$ 🏨 **Kubitschek Plaza.** High-caliber service and upscale amenities are the
★ hallmarks here. The lobby is decorated with antiques, Persian rugs, and original paintings by renowned Nippo-Brazilian artist Tomie Otake. Rooms are comfortable and have a sedate, modern decor. After a hard day conducting affairs of state and/or business, many people head for the on-site Plaza Club, a restaurant–bar with a dance floor. ✉ *SHN, Q. 02, Bl. E 70710–908,* ☎ *061/329–3333,* 𝔽𝔸𝕏 *061/328–9366. 265 rooms. 2 restaurants, bar, coffee shop, room service, indoor pool, sauna, exercise room, business services, meeting rooms, travel services. AE, DC, MC, V.*

$$$$ 🏨 **Naoum Plaza Hotel.** Brasília's most sophisticated hotel attracts
★ heads of state (during their official visit in 1990, Prince Charles and Princess Diana stayed in the Royal Suite) and their diplomats. Rooms are luxuriously appointed, with tropical-wood furniture and beige color schemes. The service is impeccable. Two upscale restaurants, The Falls (☞ Dining, *above*) and Mitsubá (with Japanese fare), add to the hotel's appeal. ✉ *SHS, Q. 05, Bl. H/I 70322–914,* ☎ *061/322–4545 or 0800/61–4844,* 𝔽𝔸𝕏 *061/322–4949. 171 rooms, 16 suites. 2 restaurants, bar, coffee shop, room service, pool, sauna, exercise room, business services, meeting rooms, travel services. AE, DC, MC, V.*

$$$ 🏨 **Academia de Tênis Resort.** What was once merely a tennis club on the shores of Lago Paranoá has, over the course of 30 years, become a resort with all the usual amenities. Rooms are in chalets that dot the gardens and woods of the grounds, which also contain several restaurants and bars. ✉ *SCES, T. 4, Lt. 1-B, 70200–000,* ☎ *061/316–6252,* 𝔽𝔸𝕏 *061/316–6268. 228 rooms. 6 restaurants, 3 bars, coffee shop, room service, 5 outdoor pools, 3 indoor pools, sauna, 22 tennis courts, exercise room, business services, meeting rooms. AE, DC, MC, V.*

$$$ 🏨 **Aracoara Hotel.** One of Brasília's oldest and most traditional hotels played a role in the country's history: João Figueiredo made this the *de facto* presidential residence for a while in the late '70s. Although it's starting to show its age, it is still a worthy choice. The on-site restaurant offers international fare and live Brazilian music. ✉ *SHN, Q. 05, Bl. C, 70710–300,* ☎ *061/328–9222 or 0800/61–4881,* 𝔽𝔸𝕏 *061/328–9067. 114 rooms, 16 suites. Restaurant, bar, coffee shop, sauna. AE, DC, MC, V.*

$$$ 🏨 **Eron Brasília Hotel.** This hotel offers such high-tech in-room amenities as Internet connections and complete stereo systems; you can even have a desktop computer installed. Rooms are carefully decorated in pastel color schemes. The Restaurante Panorâmico and its piano bar afford a grand view of the Eixo Monumental, making it a popular gathering spot for politicians. ✉ *SHN, Q. 05, Bl. A, 70710–300,* ☎ *061/329–4100,* 𝔽𝔸𝕏 *061/326–2698. 170 rooms, 10 suites. Restaurant, bar, in-room modem lines, nightclub, meeting rooms, travel services. AE, DC, MC, V.*

$$$ 🏨 **Metropolitan Hotel Residence.** This low-key hotel has a lower price tag than its sister property, the Bonaparte (☞ *above*). It's also conveniently close to the Brasília Shopping Mall, and offers special rates for extended stays. ✉ *SHN Q. 02, Bl. J, 80020–020,* ☎ *061/327–3939 or 0800/61–3939,* 𝔽𝔸𝕏 *061/327–3738. 115 rooms. Restaurant, bar, pool, sauna, exercise room, meeting rooms. AE, DC, MC, V.*

$$ 🏨 **Península Hotel.** Although it has few frills, this new hotel is a good budget choice. Rooms have a tasteful decor that makes them feel cozy; bathrooms are large; and the staff is dedicated. *SHN, Q. 03, Bl. B, 71710–911,* ☎ *061/328–4144,* 𝔽𝔸𝕏 *061/328–4144. 191 rooms, 4 suites. Restaurant, bar, pool, sauna, exercise room, meeting rooms. AE, DC, MC, V.*

$$ 🏨 **San Marco.** If you're looking for functionality and reliability, stay at the San Marco. You can bask in the central Brazilian sun, taking in the Eixo Monumental, beside its rooftop pool. The adjacent restaurant, La Gondola, serves delicious international fare. ⊠ *SHS, Q. 05, Bl. C, 70710–300,* ☎ *061/321–8484,* 🆇 *061/223–6552. 191 rooms, 4 suites. Restaurant, bar, pool, sauna, exercise room, meeting rooms, travel services. AE, DC, MC, V.*

$ 🏨 **Hotel das Nações.** You can spend some of the money you save by staying at this budget hotel, which has been around since the city's early days, at the nearby Patio Brasil mall. (Who needs abundant facilities and imaginative decor when you can go shopping?) ⊠ *SHS, Q. 04, Bl. I, 70300–300,* ☎ *061/322–8050,* 🆇 *061/225–7722. 120 rooms. Bar. AE, DC, MC, V.*

Nightlife and the Arts

Nightlife

BARS

Beirute (⊠ SCLS 109, Bl. A, Lj. 02/04, ☎ 061/244–1717), an eclectic bar-restaurant with an Arabian flair, has been in business since 1966. During its first decade, it drew politicians for post-session discussions; today it attracts intellectuals and the alternative-minded. Embassy personnel gather at the stylish **Café Cassis** (⊠ SCLS 214, Bl. B, Lj. 22., ☎ 061/346–7103). For a classical ambience, try **Café Colonial à Capitú,** (⊠ SCLS 403, Bl. D, Lj. 20., ☎ 061/225–9791), which has performances of baroque music. **Gates Pub** (⊠ SCLS 403 Bl. B, lj. 34, ☎ 061/322–9301) is popular with those who appreciate jazz and blues.

DANCE CLUBS

In Brasília's clubs, some nights are devoted to such northeastern Brazilian rhythms as *forró*—the result of the large percentage of northeasterners who settled here. A mixed clientele gathers at the **Café Cancun** (⊠ Liberty Mall, SCN, Q. 2, Bl. D, ☎ 061/328–8915). The **Universal Diner** (⊠ SCLS 210, Bl. B, Lj. 30, ☎ 061/443–2089) caters to a young, trendy crowd.

The Arts

THEATER

The **Teatro Nacional Cláudio Santoro** (⊠ SBN, Via N2, ☎ 061/321–3738 ext. 160 or 061/226–0766 for symphony ticket information) has three stages and several practice rooms used by the National Symphony Orchestra, which performs here from March through November. **Concha Acústica** (⊠ SHTN, ☎ 61/321–3738), an amphitheater on Lago Paranoá, was thoroughly renovated in time for Y2K celebrations. The main building of the **Fundação Brasileira de Teatro** (Brazilian Theatrical Foundation; ⊠ SDS, Bl. C., Lj. 30, ☎ 061/226–0182) has two theaters: the Teatro Dulcina de Moraes and the Teatro Conchita de Moraes.

Outdoor Activities and Sports

Participant Sports

GOLF

At the tip of Eixo Monumental, not far from the Palácio da Alvorada, you can golf on the 18-hole course at the **Clube de Golfe de Brasília** (⊠ SCES, Trecho 2, Cj. 2, ☎ 061/223–7194 or 061/224–2718). Guests at some hotels have free access to the course; all others pay.

HIKING

If you just want to wander along a trail, head to the **Parque Nacional de Brasília** (⊠ EPIA, 9 km/6 mi from bus terminal, ☎ 061/233–4055 or 061/234–9057). If you're interested in learning about local vegetation while you walk, try one of the three trails at the **Jardim Botânico** (✉ Lago Sul, Setor de Mansões Dom Bosco, Cj. 12, ☎ 061/366–2141). You can also arrange longer treks into the cerrado (☞ Tour Operators and Travel Agents *in* Brasília and the West A to Z, *below*).

SWIMMING

The **Parque Nacional de Brasília** (✉ EPIA, 9 km/6 mi from bus terminal, ☎ 061/233–4055 or 061/234–9057) has pools filled with mineral water. It is best to take your dip in the morning to beat the crowds. Some 35 km (22 mi) south of the Eixo Monumental is the **Cachoeira da Saia Velha** (✉ BR 040, Saida Sul, ☎ 061/223–5838), a natural preserve with cerrado vegetation and several waterfalls that cascade into pools. Admission is free.

TENNIS

You can get in a match or take classes at the **Academia de Tênis Resort** (✉ SCES, T. 4, Lt. 1-B, ☎ 061/233–4055) daily from 8 to 4. Court fees are about $15 an hour (equipment included); lessons cost $17 an hour.

Spectator Sports

Most sporting events are held in the Centro Desportivo Presidente Medici, a complex on the north side of the Eixo Monumental. The **Estádio Mané Garrincha** (☎ 061/224–9860) is where Gama FC, a B-league *futebol* (soccer) team, plays. **Ginásio Cláudio Coutinho** (☎ 061/225–5977) and the larger, 17,000-seat **Ginásio Nilson Nelson** (☎ 061/224–4775) are the arenas used for volleyball and basketball games as well as for musical events. The **Autódromo Internacional Nelson Piquet** (☎ 061/273–6586), named after a Formula I champion and a native of Brasília), has a 5-km (3-mi) racetrack that hosts several Brazilian motor sports events.

Shopping

There are two major shopping districts along the Eixo Monumental: the Setor Commercial Norte (SCN; Northern Commercial Sector) and the Setor Commercial Sul (SCS; Southern Commercial Sector). In addition, almost every superquadra has its own central commercial district.

Centers and Malls

Brasília Shopping. Housed in an odd, arch-shape building, Brasília's newest mall has several international chain stores, as well as movie theaters, restaurants, and snack bars. ✉ SCN, Q. 05, ☎ 061/328–2122. ☯ *Mon.–Sat. 10–10, Sun. 2–10.*

Conjunto Nacional Brasília. The Conjunto is one of the nation's first malls. Its central location (across from the Teatro Nacional) and glitzy neon facade make it one of the most visited. ✉ SDN, Cj. A, ☎ 061/316–9700. ☯ *Mon.–Sat. 10–10.*

Parkshopping. Brasília's largest and most sophisticated shopping center has 183 shops as well as gardens by landscape designer Burle Marx. It also hosts many cultural events in its central plaza; the annual Verão Cultural (Cultural Summer) program, for example, attracts major Brazilian musical talents. ✉ SAIS, Q. A-1, Lt. 6580, ☎ 061/233–1412. ☯ *Mon.–Sat. 10–10.*

Crafts

The last weekend of each month sees the **Feira de Antiguidades** (Antiques Fair; ✉ Pedestrian mall of Brasília Design Center, STRVS). At the **Feira de Artesanato** (Artisans Fair) you'll find semiprecious-stone ornaments and jewelry, bronze items, and wood carvings. It's held at

the foot of the Torre de TV on the Eixo Monumental Saturday and
Sunday from 9 to 6.

Gemstones
For quality stones head to the shop next to the Museu Nacional das
Gemas at the **Torre de TV** (⊠ Eixo Monumental, ☎ 061/322–3227,
ext. 201). It is open Tuesday–Friday 2–8, weekends 10–6.

THE WEST

Updated and
expanded by
Charles
Runnette

The vast, virtually untamed west consists of the frontier states of
Goiás, Mato Grosso, and Mato Grosso do Sul. Agriculture and ranching are the mainstays here, and the landscape is dotted only by a handful (though growing number) of small towns and even fewer cities. The
main hubs—such as Goiânia, Cuiabá, and Campo Grande—are, for
the most part, sophisticated trading outposts, where farmers and ranch-
ers bring their goods to market. Tourism has only begun to flourish
here as more and more people discover the charms of such places as
the colonial town of Pirenópolis; the quasimystical mesa of Chapada
dos Guimarães; and, of course, the mysterious Pantanal.

Goiânia

209 km (130 mi) southwest of Brasília.

Built in the 1930s as the capital of Goiás, an important agriculture and
farming state, today Goiânia is one of Brazil's 10 largest cities. Although
it's a 20th-century planned metropolis of more than 1 million people,
unlike its more famous neighbor, Goiânia will never make it to UN-
ESCO's short list of World Heritage Sites. Its primary importance to
visitors is as a gateway to the west.

If you find yourself with some time to kill en route to elsewhere, consider visiting Goiânia's **Museu Antropológico da UFG** (University Anthropology Museum), which has a large collection of Indian artifacts.
*Praça Universitário 1166, Sector Universitário, ☎ 062/261–6898. ⊠
Admission. ☉ Tues.–Fri. 9–5.*

Near the middle of town is the **Bosque dos Burtis,** a large, wooded park.
You can leisurely stroll beside its man-made lakes, sit by its fountains
(wear bug spray; the mosquitoes can be fierce), or visit the small
Museu de Arte (Art Museum) in its northwestern corner. ⊠ *Setor
Oeste, ☎ 062/824–1190 to museum. ⊠ Free. ☉ Park: daily 9–6. Mu-
seum: Tues.–Sun. 9–6.*

OFF THE
BEATEN PATH

POUSADA DO RIO QUENTE/HOTEL TOURISMO – This resort complex 175
km (109 mi) south of Goiânia consists of two hotels and a very popular,
beautifully landscaped water park with 10 naturally heated pools and
water rides galore. The park itself makes a nice day trip from Goiânia
(admission is charged). On a longer stay, you can take advantage of
the hotels' ($$–$$$) many activities such as tennis, horseback riding,
and fishing; there are also on-site restaurants and bars. Consult the well-
informed staff about transportation options to the complex. ⊠ *Off GO
507, ☎ 062/452–8000, ℻ 062/452–8575. AE, DC, MC, V.*

Dining and Lodging
$$ ✕ **Piquiras.** This popular, upscale seafood place—known for its *peixe
na telha* (fish with pine nuts)—has two locations. The original is in the
quiet Piquiras neighborhood down the street from the Castro's Park
hotel (☞ *below*); the new branch is in the chic Marista section of town.
Be prepared for the automatic spritzer designed to help keep you cool

during the day with periodic mists of water. At night, your biggest concern will be making reservations. ⊠ *Av. República do Líbano 1758, Setor Oeste,* ☎ *062/251–8168. AE, DC, MC, V.* ⊠ *Rua 146, 464R 139, Setor Marista,* ☎ *062/281–4344. AE, DC, MC, V.*

$ ✕ **Tacho de Cobre.** Although it's a ways from the middle of town, the excellent Goiás cuisine makes it worth the hike. Try the roasted ham with *farofa* (cassava-meal browned in butter), raisins, and olives. ⊠ *Rua 72, 550, Setor JD (near Estádio Serra Dourada),* ☎ *062/242–1241. AE, DC, MC, V. No dinner Sun.*

$$–$$$ ✕🖃 **Castro's Park.** Goiânia's top-of-the-line hotel caters to wealthy busi-
★ nesspeople during the week. On the weekends the clientele and the mood change—things are a little less harried, and there are more families by the pool. Rooms are very modern with all the amenities you'd expect at a luxury establishment, and the staff is helpful and friendly. One of the on-site restaurants serves a noteworthy *feijoada* (traditional Brazilian dish of pork, black beans, and rice). ⊠ *Av. República do Líbano 1520, Setor Oeste 74115-30,* ☎ *062/223–7766,* ℻ *062/225–7070. 161 rooms, 16 suites. 2 restaurants, bar, air-conditioning, minibars, pool, sauna, business services, convention center, travel agency. AE, DC, MC, V.*

$ 🖃 **Bandeirantes.** Rooms in this hotel—which is cheaper than it ought to be because it doesn't have a pool—are pleasant enough and have TVs and decent bathrooms. Its location is both a draw and a disadvantage: it's conveniently near the center of town, but it is in a neighborhood that can be noisy and unsafe at night. ⊠ *Av. Anhangüera 5106, Setor Central,* ☎ ℻ *062/212–0066. 70 rooms, 3 suites. Restaurant, bar, meeting rooms. AE, DC, MC, V.*

Shopping

Across from the Estação Rodoviária (Bus Station) you'll find the massive **Centro de Tradições e Artesanato** (⊠ Av. Goiás at Praçado Trabalhador, Setor Norte Ferroviário, ☎ 062/229–3676), which has a wide selection of locally made ceramics, baskets, and wood carvings as well as stalls upon stalls of rocks. It's open daily 8–8. On Saturday a crafts market, the **Feria da Lua,** is held in the Praça Tamanadré. On Sunday, you can shop for a variety of goods at the **market** in the Praça Cívica.

Pirenópolis

131 km (81 mi) north of Goiânia, 159 km (99 mi) west of Brasília.

Settled in the 18th century, at the height of the Goiás gold rush, this town was abandoned soon after it was built because area mines turned out to have very little gold. Some locals say that the years of isolation were a blessing as they've helped to preserve the town's character. In 1989, the federal government gave what was once virtually a ghost town National Monument status. On weekends people now flee from the modern concrete and glass of nearby Goiânia and Brasília to immerse themselves in Pirenópolis's colonial flavor. You'll find historic churches; charming restaurants; quaint resorts; and several well-respected jewelers, whose stunning pieces are often made of silver and semiprecious stones.

Slightly above town is the **Praça da Matriz** with several historical structures. The handsome, colonial **Igreja Nossa Senhora do Rosário–Matriz** (c. 1728–32) is the oldest church in Goiás. Across the plaza is the recently restored theater with the odd spelling, the **Teatro de Pyrenópolis** (c. 1899).

Just down the street from the Praça da Matriz is the **Museu das Cavalhades,** with displays of the outlandish medieval costumes worn by participants in the Festo do Divino Espírito Santo. First celebrated in 1891, this three-day event has the atmosphere of a Renaissance fair

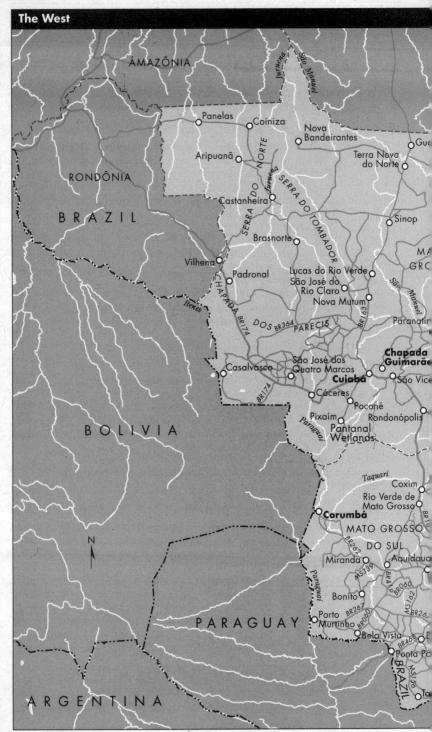

ÁMAZÔNIA

RONDÔNIA

B R A Z I L

Panelas

Coiniza

Nova
Bandeirantes

Aripuanã

Terra Nova
do Norte

Gu

Castanheira

SERRA DO NORTE

SERRA DO TOMBADOR

Sinop

Brasnorte

MA
GRO

Vilhena

Padronal

Lucas do Rio Verde

São José do
Rio Claro

Nova Mutum

Paranatin

CHAPADA BR174

Tenes

DOS   BR364

PARECIS

Chapada
Guimarãe

Casalvasco

São José dos
Quatro Marcos

Cuiabá

São Vic

BR174

Cáceres

Pixaím

Poconé

Rondonópolis

B O L I V I A

Paraguai

Pantanal
Wetlands

Taquari

Coxim

Rio Verde de
Mato Grosso

N

Corumbá

MATO GROSSO

DO SUL

BR262

Miranda

Aquidaua

MS339

BR1

Bonito

Porto
Murtinho

Paraguai

BR267

BR060

Bela Vista

BR060

P A R A G U A Y

Ponta Pc

BRAZIL

MS 13

A R G E N T I N A

MARANHÃO

PARÁ

PIAUÍ

Xingu

arantã do Norte

Vila Rica
Projeto Santa Cruz
Bonsucesso
Santa Terezinha
BR060
Porto Alegre
do Norte
Parque
Indígena
do Xingu

TOCANTINS

B R A Z I L

Tocantins

Xingu

TO
SSO

BR060

SERRA DO RONCADOR

Rio das Mortes

Araguaia

BAHIA

Dona Rosa
Canarana
Matinha
Água Boa

BR158

São Miguel do Araguaia
Porangatu

Bandeirantes

Posse
Alto Paraíso
de Goiás

Cocalinho
Uruaçu
ga
Campinápolis

GO164

Maranhão

BR153

BR414

BR010

São Francisco

BR020

dos
s
Rio das Mortes
BR070

Araguaia

Aruanã

GOIÁS

Rialma

Formosa

GO18

ante
Barra do Garças

BR070
Goiás
Pirenópolis
DISTRITO
★ Brasília
FEDERAL

BR364

São Luís de
Montes Belos
GO326
BR153
BR060

Alto
Araguaia

SERRA DO CAIAPÓ

GO174

Paraúna
Anápolis
Goiânia
Cristalina

Mineiros
Rio Verde
BR060

Rio Quente
Caldas Novas
BR153

Taquari

Itumbiara
Catalão

MINAS GERAIS

São Simão

BR060
Cassilândia
MS324
Paranaíba

Paranaíba

Grande

Bandeirantes
a

Campo
Grande
Três Lagoas
BR262

SÃO PAULO

BR267
Bataguassu
urados

Paraná

Paranapanema

RIO
DE
JANEIRO

PARANÁ

B R A Z I L

0   200 miles

0   300 km

and virtually takes over the town six weeks after Easter Sunday. Among the roster of activities is a staged battle between Moors and Christians (the Christians win every year). ⊠ *Rua Direita 39,* ☎ *062/331–1166.* ⊡ *Admission.* ⊙ *Fri.–Sun. 9–5.*

The most striking of all the town's churches is the **Igreja Nosso Senhor do Bonfim** (c. 1750–54). Outside it's a fine example of the area's colonial architecture. Most of its stunning interior (the altars are particularly beautiful), however, was brought over from Portugal in the 18th century. ⊠ *Rua do Bonfim near intersection of Rua Aurora,* ☎ *no phone.* ⊡ *Free.*

Dining and Lodging

$ ✕ **Arravinda.** The first eatery on the main strip of restaurants and bars is also a "spiritual" center whose raspy-voiced, aging-hippie owner is the town's mother figure. The food is good, though not daring (pizza, sandwiches, and big bottles of beer); try one of the delicious fish dishes, particularly the peixe na telha. (A few words of warning: if you feed the cats, they won't leave you alone.) There's live music—anything from blues to salsa—here on weekends. ⊠ *Rua do Rosário 25,* ☎ *no phone. No credit cards. Closed Mon.–Tues.*

$ ✕ **As Flor.** This eatery is popular with locals, though both the lunch and the dinner menu consist mostly of cured meats and beans. Still, everything here is cooked in view and is very tasty, and lunch has an incredible price tag: $3 buys as much food as you can eat, though drinks are extra. ⊠ *Sizenando Jaime 16,* ☎ *no phone. No credit cards. Closed weekends.*

$ ✕ **Tabla.** A cute young couple (Gabriel and Mariana) are the proprietors of this small, brightly decorated restaurant. Although seafood is a specialty, the menu offers delicious pizzas and a chicken pot pie (of sorts). The seasoned cod sticks—fried and served with a spicy, homemade salsa—are delicious. On summer weekends, bands play Brazilian tunes here. ⊠ *Rue do Rosário 31,* ☎ *062/969–3039. MC, V. Closed Mon.–Tues.*

$ ✕⊡ **Hotel Quinta de Santa Bárbara.** Across from the Igreja Nosso Senhor do Bonfim sits this rustic, family-oriented resort with colonial-style bungalows. Each has two rooms with TVs, comfortable beds, and fantastic flagstaff floors; out front a veranda offers views of the town that are particularly beautiful at sunset. The open-air, all-you-can-eat restaurant serves excellent Goiás specialties cooked in a massive kiln-like stove. ⊠ *Rua do Bonfim 1,* ☎ ℻ *062/331–1304. 20 rooms. Restaurant, bar, minibars, 2 pools, sauna, fishing. V.*

$$$ ⊡ **Pousada dos Pireneus.** Some people come here on weeklong quests
★   to lose weight; others bring their families for weekend retreats. The main lodge—which is reminiscent of an adobe structure from the southwestern United States—contains the restaurant and bar, which looks out at the pools, tennis courts, and beyond the beautifully landscaped grounds to town. Rooms are in what can only be described as a 17th-century condo complex; ground-floor quarters have decks and hammocks. ⊠ *Chácara Mata do Sobrato,* ☎ *062/331–1345,* ℻ *062/ 331–1462. 103 rooms. Restaurant, bar, 2 pools, massage, sauna, spa, tennis court, aerobics, horseback riding, bicycles, shops, recreation room, convention center. AE, DC, MC, V.*

Nightlife

Most of the nightlife is along or just off the **Rua do Rosário,** which is closed to vehicular traffic on weekends. The liveliest bars are Âlveria, Varanda, and Bar Central. Of these, Bar Central is the cheapest with beers for less than $1. For a late-night snack head to **Pizza Trotramundos**

(✉ Rua do Rosário 32, ☎ no phone) where the best pie has olives, mushrooms, and ham.

Outdoor Activities and Sports

Around Pirenópolis are several parks, some with wonderful waterfalls, swimming holes, and trails. The **Santuário de Vida Silvestre–Fazenda Vagafogo** (✉ Rua do Carmo, 6 km/4 mi north of town center, ☎ no phone) is a large ecological preserve with 57 acres of untouched cerrado flora and fauna, a medium-size waterfall that crashes into a natural pool, a small forest, hiking trails, and a little café near the visitors center at the entrance. The preserve is open Tuesday–Sunday 8–5; there's an admission fee.

For a small fee, you can refresh yourself in the spray of waterfalls or in swimming holes daily 8:30–5 at the **Reserva Ecológica Vargem Grande** (✉ 13 km/8 mi along road to Parque Estadual da Serra dos Pireneus, ☎ 062/331–1171). The historic (c. 1800) sugar mill and grounds of **Fazenda Babilônia** (✉ GO 431, 24 km/15 mi west of town, ☎ no phone) are open Wednesday–Sunday 8–5; admission is charged. There's also a small café for a snack or a coffee. If you're a fan of waterfalls, the **Cachoeiras Bonsucesso** (✉ Rua do Carmo, 7 km/4 mi north of town, ☎ no phone) are must-sees. You can stop by daily 7–5. There's a small admission fee.

Shopping

All the best shops are easy to find in the center of this small town. **Alexandre Sidou** (✉ Rua dos Pireneus 43, ☎ 062/331–1519) sells interesting gold and silver jewelry. **Pica Pedra** (✉ Beira Rio at Rua do Rosário, ☎ no phone) specializes in stones and rocks. At **Shanti** (✉ Rua do Bonfim 20, ☎ no phone) you can shop for local handicrafts and indulge in an ice cream or an espresso.

Cuiabá

934 km (580 mi) west of Goiânia.

The capital of Mato Grosso State isn't exactly in the middle of nowhere, but you can certainly see the middle of nowhere from here. Just to give you an idea of how far it is from here to just about anywhere: São Paulo is 1,615 km (1,000 mi) to the southwest; Brasília, 1,130 km (700 mi) to the west; Porto Velho, 1,456 km (900 mi) to the northeast. Originally settled in the 18th century when gold was found nearby, Cuiabá is now mostly known as the southernmost gateway to the Amazon and, more importantly, as the northern gateway to the Pantanal. You can visit one of several museums while you're waiting for a tour into these wetlands (arrangements take only about a day; ☞ Tour Operators and Travel Agents *in* Brasília and the West A to Z, *below*).

The **Museu História Natural e Antropologia e Museu Histórico,** close to the center of town, is really a complex of museums with displays of everything from ancient Indian artifacts to contemporary art. ✉ *Palácio da Instrução, Praça da República,* ☎ *065/321–3391.* 🎟 *Admission.* ☾ *Weekdays 12:30–5:30.*

Northeast of the town's main square is the **Museu de Pedras Ramis Bucair,** with a stunning collection of area fossils and stones (including what's purportedly a meteorite). ✉ *Rua Galdino Pimentel 195.* 🎟 *Admission.* ☾ *Weekdays 7–11 and 1–4.*

Slightly out of town is the **Museu do Indio/Museu Rondon.** Its displays include photos of and objects from area indigenous groups, including the Bororo, Pareci, Xavante, and Txukarramae. The museum is at a university, whose grounds also contain a zoo populated by Pantanal

THE PANTANAL

I T'S WIDELY HELD THAT THE Pantanal is the best place to view wildlife in all of South America. A flood plain of the Rio Paraguay and its tributaries, it covers about 225,000 square km (140,000 square mi), two-thirds of which is in Brazil and is owned by ranching families who have been here for generations. The Portuguese began colonizing the area about 200 years ago; today it's home to more than 21 million head of cattle and some 4 million people. Yet there's still abundant wildlife in this mosaic of swamp, forest, and savanna. From your hub of an area *fazenda* (ranch) or lodge—where air-conditioning, swimming pools, and well-cooked meals are possibilities—you can experience local flavor as well as area flora and fauna.

More than 600 species of birds live in the Pantanal during different migratory seasons, including *araras* (hyacinth macaws), fabulous blue and yellow birds that can be as long as 1 m (3 ft) from head to tail; larger-than-life rheas, which look and walk like aging modern ballerinas; fantastically colored vultures (and you thought they were all black); as well as cormorants, ibises, herons, kingfishers, hawks, egrets, to name a few. You're also sure to spot *capivaras* (capybaras; large South American rodents), tapirs, giant anteaters, marsh deer, maned wolves, otters, and one of the area's six species of monkey.

The countless *jacarés* (caiman alligators) would never dream of attacking, unless provoked. Blind, deaf, and lacking a sense of smell, caimans catch the fish they eat by following vibrations in the water. Poaching put these creatures on the verge of extinction—it takes four animals to make one pair of shoes—but this is no longer a problem as farmers have begun raising them. Although it's hard to spot jaguars and pumas, finding their tracks isn't uncommon. One native guide reported having spotted no more than six big felines in his life. Though all trade in wild species has been illegal since 1967, poachers still prize these cats for their skins. Don't let the *sucuri* (anaconda) snakes, which can grow up to 9 m (30 ft) in length, worry you. They've only eaten a couple humans since people started keeping track.

October is the beginning of the Pantanal's rainy season, which peaks in February but lasts through March. The land is much greener and more ravishing than at other times of the year, but the wildlife is harder to spot. In the dry season (July–October), when leaves fall and grasses die, land animal sightings are more frequent. As the waters continue to dry, fish get caught in the remaining pools and attract a great variety of birds. The best fishing season is May through October, and considering the more than 230 varieties of fish in the area, anglers won't be disappointed.

wildlife. ⊠ *Av. Fernando Correiada Costa, 4 km/2 mi east of town,* ☎ *065/315–5511.* ☜ *Admission.* ⊘ *Weekdays 8–5.*

Dining

$$ ✕ **Morro de St. Antonio.** This surf-and-turf place has a Polynesian vibe and caters to a yuppie crowd. Many of the entrées are enough for two people. Dinner is served nightly until 1 AM; on weekends this is a good place to drink and be merry into the wee hours. ⊠ *Av. Isaac Póvoas 1167, Centro, Cuiabá,* ☎ *065/622–0502. AE, DC, MC, V.*

$$ ✕ **Papagaio Grill.** The menu here has some decent regional fare of simple meat and fish dishes, but the pasta is the big draw. The drinks are good, too—particularly the *caipirinhas* (cachaça, crushed lime, crushed ice, and sugar)—which may be why this place hops until almost dawn on weekends. (Dinner is served nightly until 2 AM.) The huge TV screen that looms over the tables, however, makes decent conversation hard. ⊠ *Av. Mato Grosso 764, Centro, Cuiabá,* ☎ *065/621–1020. AE, DC, MC, V.*

$ ✕ **Choppão.** Although it's a little out of the way, locals regularly fill this open-air restaurant to feast on tasty meat dishes that are large enough to share. The beef fillet with mushrooms is particularly juicy and delicious. ⊠ *Av. Getúlio Vargas at Praça 8 de Abril, Centro, Cuiabá,* ☎ *065/322–9101. DC, MC, V.*

$ ✕ **Panela de Barro.** This little *comida-por-kilo* (food-by-the-kilo) joint is good for a filling, affordable lunch or dinner. Its buffet has one regional specialty after another, and you pay (by weight) only for what you eat. Don't be shy about asking a staffer to explain the dishes to you. ⊠ *Rua Cândido Mariano at Comandante Costa, Centro, Cuiabá,* ☎ *065/321–5443. MC, V.*

$ ✕ **Regionalíssimo.** Set in the same building as the Casa do Atesão (☞ Shopping, *below*), this self-service eatery offers regional cuisine. After a hearty meal, you can browse through the shop filled with ceramics, baskets, and wood handicrafts. ⊠ *13 de Junho 314, Porto, Cuiabá,* ☎ *065/322–4523. AE, DC, MC. No dinner.*

Lodging

CUIABÁ

$$ 🏨 **Eldorado.** A vision of glass and brass (no gold, as the name would suggest), this hotel has some of the best rooms in the center of town. You'll appreciate the pleasant decor, air-conditioning, and cable TV—particularly after staying at a sparse Pantanal fazenda. Don't miss the giant bird cage beside the pool; it's an easy way to see toucans and macaws up close. ⊠ *Av. Isaac Póvoas 1000, Centro 78045–640,* ☎ *065/624–4000,* 🖷 *065/624–1480. 141 rooms, 6 suites. Restaurant, bar, air-conditioning, pool, shops, convention center. AE, DC, MC, V.*

$$ 🏨 **Mato Grosso Palace.** This Best Western hotel is also the crown jewel of the local "Mato Grosso" mini-chain. Rooms, although lacking in charm, have modern baths, cable TV, and layouts that can accommodate families—all of which make them a good deal for the price. Staff members, however, aren't as friendly as they could be. ⊠ *Rua Joaquim Murtinho 170, Centro,* ☎ *065/624–7747,* 🖷 *065/321–2386. 118 rooms, 12 suites. Restaurant, bar, air-conditioning, in-room safes, minibars, business services. AE, DC, MC, V.*

$ 🏨 **Jaguar Palace.** Location is key at this high-rise: it's close enough to everything, but far enough removed to offer a peaceful night's sleep. Rooms are small but clean; all have air-conditioning and TV (no cable). Ask for one on a higher floor so you can take in a view of Cuiabá and beyond. ⊠ *Av. Getúlio Vargas 600, Centro,* ☎ *065/624–4404,* 🖷 *065/ 623–7798. 90 rooms, 9 suites. Restaurant, bar, air-conditioning, minibars, pool, meeting room, travel agency. DC, MC, V.*

$ ⊞ **Mato Grosso.** If you're looking for a cheap, clean, in-town hotel, this member of the local "Mato Grosso" chain is the place. It's housed in what was once a prison, so you must decide whether to take one of the more expensive, yet cell-like, lower-floor rooms (they have little light but are air-conditioned) or one of the more affordable, higher-level rooms (they're bright but are cooled only by fans). One very good institution here is the simple but delicious breakfast that's included in the rate. ⊠ *Rua Comandante Costa 2522, Centro,* ☎ *065/321–9121,* FAX *065/614–7053. 67 rooms. Restaurant, bar. DC, MC, V.*

THE PANTANAL

$$ ⊞ **Cabanas do Pantanal.** This Pantanal resort offers two- to three-night packages that include transportation to and from Cuiabá, all meals, and guided hikes and fishing trips. (If you're traveling in the off-season try to negotiate on the price.) Though not very charming, the cabins are fairly modern and have private baths. The resort's location on a major river makes it an excellent base for exploring the wetlands and for spotting wildlife. ⊠ *42 km (26 mi) south of Poconé (144 km/90 mi south of Cuiabá) on Rio Piraim,* ☎ *065/623–4141 in Cuiabá,* FAX *065/623–8880. 18 cabins. Restaurant, minibars, pool, hiking, boating, fishing. AE, DC, MC, V.*

$$ ⊞ **Pantanal Mato Grosso.** Set on the Transpantaneira Highway, this member of the local "Mato Grosso" chain is one of the northern Pantanal's more upscale choices. Its rooms may be sparsely decorated, but they're all air-conditioned, and its staff can arrange fishing expeditions (for piranha if you like), guided treks on horseback or on foot, and trips by small airplane for a bird's-eye view of the wetlands. Two- to four-night packages are available; just be sure to book ahead, particularly in high season, and have the hotel arrange transportation to and from Cuiabá. ⊠ *Km 65, Rodovia Transpantaneira, Poconé,* ☎ FAX *065/968–6205. 33 rooms. Restaurant, air-conditioning, pool, hiking, horseback riding, boating, fishing. AE, DC, MC, V.*

$ ⊞ **Pousada Pixaim.** This small, relatively low-key pousada isn't always accessible by road, making small planes your only transport option. The wooden cabins, which are on stilts, sleep three people and are far from deluxe (though they do have private baths). Still, this is a good hub for exploring the swamp by boat or on foot. ⊠ *Km 61, Rodovia Transpantaneira, Pixaim,* ☎ *065/721–2091 or 065/721–1172 reservations in Cuiabá,* FAX *065/721–2091. 10 cabins. Restaurant, hiking, boating. No credit cards.*

Nightlife

On weekends two restaurants, Morro de St. Antonio and Papagaio (☞ Dining, *above*), stay open late just to serve drinks and encourage revelry. Toward the newer part of the city, along Avenida C.P.A., you'll find many happening sports bars and nightclubs. If you're looking for a more wholesome evening try one of the many ice cream parlors, such as **Alaska** (⊠ Rua Pedro Celestino 215).

Shopping

For Indian handicrafts try the **Casa do Artesão** (⊠ 13 de Junho at Rua Senador Metello, ☎ 065/321–0603). For rocks and fossils visit the shop inside the **Museu de Pedras Ramis Bucair** (⊠ Rua Galdino Pimentel 195). If you're beginning to feel the power of South America's geodesic center radiating from the Chapada dos Guimarães (☞ *below*), head for **Flora Guarani** (⊠ Av. Duarte 689-B, ☎ 067/983–7109). The proprietor, Everaldo, sells candles, herbal remedies, and stuff that seems an awful lot like magic potions.

Chapada dos Guimarães

64 km (40 mi) north of Cuiabá.

This quasimystical mesa is the area's most popular attraction after the Pantanal. Along the road to the town from Cuiabá, you'll pass the **Portão do Inferno** (Gates of Hell), a scenic viewpoint over the chasm that was created when the mesa was formed. Beyond the Portão do Inferno, you'll come to the **Parque Nacional Véu de Noiva.** Of its five waterfalls, the eponymous Cachoeira Véu da Noiva (Bridal Veil Falls) is the most impressive. There's a small entrance fee to the park, which is open daily 8–6, and you can enjoy lunch at the open-air restaurant near the falls.

In town, the **Igreja de Nossa Senhora de Santana** (✉ Praça Central) is a handsome colonial church (c. 1799) with some exceptional interior flourishes. Just 8 km (5 mi) beyond the center of town, you'll come to a site that has made this chapada a spiritual mecca for the New Age set, the **Mirante do Ponto Geodésico.** In 1972, a satellite photograph proved that the continent's true center was not in Cuiabá, where a monument had been built, but right here on the edge of the mesa. If the geodesic center doesn't hold spiritual meaning for you, come for the fantastic vista; on a clear day, you can see as far as the Pantanal. If you have time, arrange a guided visit to the **Caverna do Francês,** an enormous sandstone cave (one of the largest in Brazil) that's 45 km (30 mi) to the east.

Dining and Lodging

$ ✕ **Nivo's Tour Restaurant.** The restaurant is true to its motto *"Qualidad: Ingrediente Fundamental de Boa Cozinha"* ("Quality: the Basic Ingredient of Good Cooking"). The *pratos típicos* (typical dishes) here are as delicious—particularly the fish entrées—as they are reasonably priced. About $4 buys an all-you-can-eat lunch (drinks are extra); the central location is another draw. ✉ *Praça Bispo dom Wunibaldo,* ☎ *065/791–1284. V. No dinner. Closed Mon.*

$ ✕ **O Mestrinho.** Both day-trippers and locals pack this self-service, all-you-can-eat restaurant, making it the liveliest place in town. Everyone in the split-level dining room seems to get up at once whenever something new is brought from the kitchen (try to avoid a table near the buffet). The feijoada here is especially tasty. ✉ *Rua Quinco Caldes 119,* ☎ *065/791–1181. V. No dinner Sun.–Tues.*

$$ ▥ **Pousada Penhasco.** Clinging to the edge of the mesa, this small resort may be far from the Chapada dos Guimarães's town center but it has tremendous views of the cerrado. The sunny rooms are in cabins scattered about the property. All rooms have access to verandas with great vistas. As this place caters to families and tour groups, the staff frequently arranges soccer matches on the on-site field and en masse outings to area sights. If you want to explore on your own, you can borrow a bike. ✉ *Av. Perimetreal,* ☎ *065/624–1000 in Cuiabá,* ☎ FAX *065/791–1555. 20 rooms. Restaurant, bar, minibars, pool, sauna, hiking, soccer, bicycles. AE, DC, MC, V.*

Campo Grande

694 km (430 mi) south of Cuiabá.

Nicknamed the Cidade Morena (Brunette City) because of the reddish-brown earth on which it sits, this relatively young (founded in 1899) city was made the capital of Mato Grosso do Sul in the 1970s when the huge state of Mato Grosso was divided into Mato Grosso and Mato Grosso do Sul. Campo Grande's economy has traditionally relied on farming, but now ecotourism is booming in this southern gateway to the Pantanal. The wetlands have become a trendy spot not only for foreign visitors, but also for the wealthy of São Paulo and Rio. At press time, the currency devaluation made it wise for Brazilians to seek vacation destinations within their country. Further, some of the nation's beloved evening *telenovelas* (soap operas), featured characters who disappeared into the vast, mysterious swamp—adding to its appeal.

If you have time on your hands before heading into the Pantanal, visit the **Museo Dom Bosco,** whose taxidermy exhibits and displays of Indian artifacts will educate you on Pantanal animals and the region's social history. Don't miss the bug room, whose walls are covered—from floor to ceiling—with insects of every type. If you find these critters more horrifying than fascinating, retreat to the room full of only butterflies. ⊠ *Rua Barão do Rio Branco 1843, facing Praça do República,* ☎ *067/721–1090.* 🎫 *Admission.* ☉ *Weekdays 8–6, Sat. 8–5, Sun. 8–11:30 and 1:30–5.*

OFF THE
BEATEN PATH
CORUMBÁ – Eight hours by bus from Campo Grande and just 30 minutes from Bolivia is the colonial-style port city of Corumbá. Unlike the other gateway cities, it's actually inside the Pantanal, overlooking the Rio Paraguay. You can arrange river trips or wetland treks upon arrival, but choose your tour operator carefully (☞ Tour Operators and Travel Agents in Brasília and the West A to Z, *below*). Consider staying at the reasonably priced **Nacional Palace** (⊠ Ria América 936, ☎ 067/231–6868, FAX 067/231–6202, AE, DC, MC, V), which has all the amenities you could want (including air-conditioning) in a steamy swamp town. The **Santa Mônica Palace** (⊠ Rua Antônio Maria Coelho 345, ☎ 067/231–3001, FAX 067/231–7880, AE, DC, MC, V) is another good hotel with all the necessary comforts.

Dining

$$ ✕ **Madellena.** Campo Grande's best restaurant fills up quickly on the
★ weekends, so make a reservation or plan to arrive early. All the entrées are flavorful, but the *peixe com bananas* (fish served with bananas and hearts of palm) is a standout. ⊠ *Rua Pedro Celestino 1641,* ☎ *067/ 725–8339. AE, DC, MC, V.*

$$ ✕ **Radio Clube.** One of the fancier places in town, this restaurant-nightclub adds some energy to the somewhat lifeless Praça da República. You can stop by for a drink or a meal of Continental fare. ⊠ *Rua Pedro João Cripa 1280,* ☎ *067/721–0131. AE, DC, MC, V. Closed Sun.– Mon.*

$ ✕ **Restaurant da Gaúcha.** Across from the Hotel Internacional (☞ Lodging, *below*) and right near the bus depot, this small, self-serve restaurant offers an array of meat, fish, and vegetable platters for lunch (note that the meat dishes are generally tastier than those with vegetables). Seating is at picnic-style tables with attractive red-gingham tablecloths. ⊠ *Rua Allan Kardec 238,* ☎ *067/724–8851. No credit cards.*

$ ✕ **Sabor En Quilo.** Air-conditioned dining rooms are what set this chain of pay-by-the-kilo lunch spots apart from all the others. The bright lighting and the family-run feel add some cheer as well. Be sure to try the oh-so cheesy lasagna. ⊠ *Rua Dom Aquino 1786,* ☎ *067/721–4726. AE, DC, MC, V. No dinner.* ⊠ *Av. Afonso Pena 2223,* ☎ *067/721– 4726. AE, DC, MC, V. No dinner.* ⊠ *Rua Barão do Rio Branco 1118,* ☎ *067/383–3911. AE, DC, MC, V. No dinner.*

$ ✕ **Vitório's.** This cavernous, churrascaria fills up quickly at mealtimes. The rowdy regulars sing right along with the Brazilian and Paraguayan bands that play here almost nightly. ⊠ *Av. Afonso Pena 1907,* ☎ *067/ 724–5001. DC, MC, V.*

Close-Up

OTHERWORLDLY VISITORS

MANY BELIEVE THAT THE PANTANAL is the landing spot of choice for visitors from outer space. In 1996, officials in Barra do Garcas, 480 km (300 mi) west of Cuiabá in Mato Grosso State, even designated 12 acres of the town's property for the world's first UFO "airport"—the Interspace Aerodrome. During his nationwide tour, the official who initiated the project, Valdon Vargão, said, "They can call me mad. But I'm doing humanity a service . . . My main concern is to maintain a cordial and official relationship with the extraterrestrials." Though the aerodrome was never built, the publicity it received fueled the notion that the Pantanal is a hotbed of UFO activity.

In mid-1997, members of a small farming community 258 km (160 mi) northeast of Cuiabá were convinced that a local farmer and his son were hiding aliens after a fiery ball was seen to crash on their property. The next year people all over the west, from Campo Grande to Cuiabá, reported seeing a large, shiny cylinder pass overhead; it made no noise and, thankfully, harmed no one. Other mass and individual sightings have been reported, as have alien abductions. Many Pantanal area locals will warn you to be wary of nighttime attacks . . . not by jaguars, but by aliens.

Lodging
CAMPO GRANDE

$$$ 🏨 **Jandaia.** The Jandaia is so thoroughly modern that it almost seems out of place in this wild-west town. Though it has little character, it does have all the facilities and amenities you'd expect of a deluxe hotel as well as a convenient central location. Note that the staff, like the decor, lacks charm. ⊠ *Rua Barão do Rio Branco 1271, 79002–174,* ☎ *067/721–7000,* 🖷 *067/721–1401. 130 rooms, 10 suites. 2 restaurants, bar, air-conditioning, minibars, pool, exercise room, meeting rooms. AE, DC, MC, V.*

$$ 🏨 **Campo Grande Hotel.** This futuristic, concrete, Brasília-like structure has the friendliest staffers in town (they *love* to practice their English). Rooms are as comfortable and appealing as any in the more expensive hotels, and they have air-conditioning and cable TV. ⊠ *Rua 13 de Maio 2825, 79002–351,* ☎ *067/384–6061 or 067/384–6961,* 🖷 *067/724–8349. 84 rooms, 4 suites. Restaurant, bar, air-conditioning, minibars, business services, meeting rooms. AE, DC, MC, V.*

$ 🏨 **Hotel Internacional.** Though modest, this budget option is clean and well-maintained; what's more, management doesn't feel compelled to jack up the rates just because there's a pool. The dormitory-like rooms have firm single beds, TVs, and en-suite bathrooms. It's worth spending an extra $5 a night for air-conditioning. The only problem here is the location near the bus station—a part of town that can be scary at night. ⊠ *Rua Alan Kardac 223, 79008–330,* ☎ *067/784–4677,* 🖷 *067/ 721–2729. 100 rooms. Restaurant, bar, pool. AE, DC, MC, V.*

THE PANTANAL

$$$$ ✕🔲 **Caiman Ecological Refuge.** This ranch pioneered the idea of sus-
★   tainable land use and ecological awareness in the early 1980s, and it
remains one of the Pantanal's top lodges. The service is excellent—from
the professional manner of the kitchen and bar staffs to the knowledgeable guides, all of whom hold a degree in biology or a related science and most of whom speak excellent English. (They clearly love what
they do and are sincerely interested in your well being.) Rooms, which
have such amenities as private baths and air-conditioning, are in one
of four lodges. Opt for a room in the main lodge, which has the nicest
common areas and the best location (the lodge surrounded almost entirely by water has its charms, too, though). Activities include horseback rides through the wetlands, boat trips to islands on the refuge's
vast holdings, night rides in open vehicles to see nocturnal animals, and
video and slide shows. Excursions are accompanied by at least one multilingual staffer who can answer most questions about flora and fauna,
and a local guide who knows the terrain. The schedule of activities also
allows ample time for relaxation and dips in the pool. Though steep,
the price includes meals and bus transfers in and out of Campo Grande's
airport. ✉ *North of Miranda, 235 km (146 mi) west of Campo Grande,*
☎ *067/687–2102 or 011/883–6622 reservations in São Paulo,* FAX
011/883–6037 in São Paulo. 30 rooms. Restaurant, bar, air-conditioning,
pool, hiking, horseback riding, boating. AE, DC, MC, V.

$$$$ **Fazenda Rio Negro.** You can stay in the rustic but charming century-
old farm house here, where the food is good (meals are included in the
rates) and all rooms have baths. Although other amenities may not quite
be up to North American standards, at press time the ranch had just
been bought by the Washington D.C.–based Conservation International,
and plans for improvements were on the table. Further, the wildlife is
abundant, the guides are knowledgable, and a stay here gives you a
feel for life on a Pantanal ranch at the Rio Negro. The only way to
reach this 25,000-acre property is by plane (a roughly $650 flight) from
either Campo Grande or Corumbá. ✉ *About 200 km (125 mi) north-*
west of Campo Grande, ☎ FAX *067/751–5191 or 067/751–5248 reser-*
vations in Campo Grande. 10 rooms. Restaurant, hiking, horseback
riding, boating. No credit cards.

Nightlife

Campo Grande is wilder than Cuiabá; parts of town (particularly the
area near the bus station) are downright dangerous and best avoided
at night. On the better side of the tracks is **4 Mil** (✉ Av. Afonso Pena
4000, ☎ no phone), a bar frequented by the town's young hipsters.
Another hotspot in the safe part of town is the nightclub, **Nix** (✉ Av.
Afonso Pena near corner of 25 de Dezembro, ☎ no phone).

Chip's (✉ Av. Afonso Pena 1977, near corner of Rua 14 de Julho, ☎
no phone), a 24-hour snack shop on the main drag, serves terrific hamburgers. Indulge in a few of them (they're very thin) while taking in
the scene from the stainless-steel counter or a table out front. Next door
is what may be Mato Grosso do Sul's only cybercafé, **Iris** (✉ Av.
Afonso Pena 1975, ☎ 067/784–6002). You can surf the Web (for
about $10 per hour) every night till 10 or leaf through one of the week-
old English-language magazines.

Shopping

For baskets of all shapes, beautiful wood handicrafts, and interesting
ceramics made by Pantanal Indians, head to **Casa de Artesão** (✉ Rua
Calógeras 2050 at Av. Afonso Pena, ☎ 067/383–2633). It's open
weekdays 8–6 and Saturday 8–noon. The **Feria Indígena,** adjacent to
the Mercado Central and just across Avendia Afonso Pena from the

Casa de Artesão, is also a good place to shop for locally made crafts. It operates Tuesday–Sunday 8–5. The massive **Shopping Campo Grande** (⊠ Av. Afonso Pena 4909) has everything you'd expect in an American- or European-style mall—from a Carrefour department store to a food court with McDonald's. The many boutiques are what make this place shine, though.

BRASÍLIA AND THE WEST A TO Z

Arriving and Departing

By Airplane

BRASÍLIA

The **Aeroporto Internacional de Brasília** (⊠ EPAR-Lago Sul, ☏ 061/365–1941), 10 km (6 mi) west of the Eixo Monumental, is considered South America's first "intelligent" airport, with computer-controlled communications and baggage-handling operations.

Airlines that serve the city include **American Airlines** (☏ 061/321–3322), **Nordeste** (☏ 061/365–1022), **Rio-Sul** (☏ 061/242–4099), **TAM** (☏ 061/365–2529), **Transbrasil** (☏ 061/365–1296 or 061/243–6133), **Varig** (☏ 061/365–1550 or 061/327–3455), and **VASP** (☏ 061/365–1552 or 061/321–3636).

From the Airport into Town. Taxis are your only real options (city buses, which cost about 60¢, don't have room for your luggage). Trips to the hotel sectors along the Eixo Monumental take roughly 15 minutes and cost about $10. Double-check costs at the dispatcher booth near the arrival gate, and reconfirm the fare with your driver.

THE WEST

Major western airports include **Aeroporto Santa Genoveva** (⊠ Praça Cap. Frazão, ☏ 062/207–1288), 6 km (4 mi) northeast of Goiâna; **Aeroporto Marechal Rondon** (☏ 065/682–2213), 7 km (4 mi) south of Cuiabá; **Aeroporto International de Campo Grande** (⊠ Av. Duque de Caxias, ☏ 067/763–2444), 7 km (4 mi) west of Campo Grande.

Three of the regional carriers serve all three hubs: **TAM** (☏ 062/207–4539 in Goiânia, 065/682–3650 in Cuiabá, or 067/763–0000 in Campo Grande), **Varig** (☏ 062/207–1743 in Goiânia, 065/682–1140 in Cuiabá, 067/763-0000 in Campo Grande, or 0800/99–7000 nationwide), and **VASP** (☏ 062/207–1350 in Goiânia, 065/682–3737 in Cuiabá, 067/763–2389 in Campo Grande, or 0800/99–8277 nationwide).

From the Airports into Town. None of the airports is very far from any of these cities, so cabs are your best bets. The fare into Goiânia and Campo Grande is about $7; into Cuiabá it's more like $9. Though buses (about 75¢) serve the airports, they often pull up well away from the terminals, and to use them you need to understand each city's layout fairly well.

By Bus

BRASÍLIA

Brasília's interstate bus station, the **Estação Rodoferroviária** (☏ 061/233–7200), is at the westernmost tip of the Eixo Monumental. For trips to Goiânia (3 hrs), try **Araguaina** (☏ 061/233–7566 or 0800/62–1011). **Expresso São Luiz** (☏ 061/233–7961) buses make the 12-hour journey to Cuiabá. To make the 14-hour trip to São Paulo, try **Real** (☏ 061/361–4555). **Itapemirim** (☏ 061/361–4505 or 0800/99–2627) buses run to and from Rio de Janeiro (17 hrs) and Belo Horizonte (11 hrs).

THE WEST

Although the distances in the west are great, buses remain the primary mode of transportation owing to high airfares and limited air service. **Goiânia's Rodoviária** (Bus depot; ✉ Av. Goiás, ☎ 062/224–8466) is in the Norte Ferroviário sector. **Cuiabá's Rodoviária** (✉ Av. Mal. Deodoro, ☎ 065/621–2429) is in the Alvorada neighborhood north of the city center. **Campo Grande's Rodoviária** (☎ 067/383–1678) is at the corner of Dom Aquino and Joaquim Nabuco.

A dazzling array of companies offers regular bus service connecting Brasília and Goiânia (3 hrs/$12), Goiânia and Cuiabá (13 hrs/$40), Goiânia and Goís Velho (2½ hrs/$11), Cuiabá and Campo Grande (10 hrs/$30), Cuiabá and Chapada dos Guimarães (2 hrs/$5), and Campo Grande and Corumbá (7 hrs/$25). There's less frequent service between Brasília and Pirenópolis (2½ hrs/$4) and Pirenópolis and Goiânia (2 hrs/$10).

Andorinha (✉ Corner of Dom Aquino and Joaquim Nabuco, upstairs inside Rodoviária, Campo Grande, ☎ 067/383–5314) has frequent service between Campo Grande and Corumbá. **Auto Viação Goinésia** (✉ Terminal Rodoviário "L" Norte, Brasília, ☎ 061/562–0720), which operates most of the buses between Pirenópolis and both Brasília and Goiânia.

BY CAR

Brasília is connected with the rest of the country by several major highways. BR 050 is the shortest way south to São Paulo (1,015 km/632 mi). From the city of Cristalina (113 km/70 mi south of Brasília), it is another 612 km (380 mi) to Belo Horizonte on BR 040. The westbound route, BR 060, runs to Goiânia and the Pantanal and intersects with BR 153, the north–south Transbrasiliana Highway, which stretches another 1,930 km (1,200) mi north to Belém. BR 020 runs northeast from Brasília to Salvador (1,450 km/900 mi).

Most routes within the west aren't paved, and Brazilian drivers— known for their wild abandon—usually pack onto those that are. Further, getting around on your own by car is difficult without a very good working knowledge of Portuguese. Outside the cities, few people speak English, making it hard to get directions if you get lost. In short, it's best to avoid traveling to and within the west by car. With the exception of the paved BR 163, which skirts the Pantanal's eastern edge from Cuiabá to Campo Grande and is in fairly good condition, the roads near the Pantanal aren't in great shape. The Transpantaneira Highway traverses the Pantanal from Campo Grande in the south to Porto Jofre, a dead-end smack in the middle of the wetlands. Saying that this is a dirt road doesn't convey how rough and time-consuming a journey on it is. In summer, it's completely closed owing to the flooding.

Getting Around

By Subway

At press time, Brasília's short, new *metrô* (subway) was open only at rush hour for test runs. When it's fully operational, it will be a great way to travel beneath the southern portion of the Eixo Rodoviário and above ground to some of the cidades-satélite.

By Bus

BRASÍLIA

Virtually all city buses depart from Estação Rodoviária at the Eixo Monumental. Route names (usually coinciding with the final destination) and departing times appear on digital displays. Rides within the Plano Piloto cost about 60¢. There are also a few air-conditioned express buses, which make fewer stops and cost about $1. Of these, the Terminal Rodoferroviário and Palácio da Alvorada buses are good for sightseeing along the Eixo Monumental.

The major western cities are fairly compact, so you won't need to worry about taking a bus except perhaps to the airport or the interstate bus depot. The one exception is Campo Grande, where the shopping area is quite a distance east along Afonso Pena. Bus fares in all the western cities are about 75 ¢. Try to have small change available when you board because the space between the door and the area where the conductor takes your money gets crowded and claustrophobic quickly.

By Car
BRASÍLIA
The capital was originally designed for cars. Until recently, wide north–south and east–west multilane highways—with their nifty cloverleafs, overpasses, and exits—allowed quick access to all major points. Nowadays, you can expect traffic jams at rush hour. Parking is easy in the residential areas but can be tricky in the commercial sectors.

A compact car with air-conditioning will cost about $70 a day. Area rental agencies include **Avis** (⊠ Aeroporto Internacional,, ☎ 061/365–2344), **Hertz** (⊠ Aeroporto Internacional, ☎ 061/362–2818), **Localiza** (⊠ Aeroporto Internacional, ☎ 061/365–3260), and **Unidas** (⊠ SIA Trecho 08 lt 1280, ☎ 061/234–3266; ⊠ Aeroporto Internacional, ☎ 061/365–1418).

THE WEST
Driving isn't recommended in most western cities as Brazilian drivers are frightening in their disregard for signs, stop lights, and basic rules of the road. If you do rent a car, expect to pay about $60–$70 per day for a VW Gol (very popular in this part of Brazil) with unlimited mileage. Insurance is necessary (opt for the most comprehensive coverage possible), so be sure to ask about it when getting a quote. Note that many of the larger urban hotels have free parking.

Rental companies with offices in the region include **Avis** (☎ 0800/55–8066), **Hertz** (☎ 0800/14–7300), **Localiza** (☎ 0800/99–2000), and **Unidas** (☎ 0800/12–1211).

By Taxi
BRASÍLIA
Fares in Brasília are lower than in the rest of the country, and most cabs are organized into cooperatives with dispatchers. It's best to call for one of these "radio taxis," particularly in the evening; unlike those in other Brazilian cities, some offer discounted rates for cabs ordered by phone. **Rádio Taxi Cidade** (☎ 061/321–8181 or 061/321–3030) offers 30% off the meter fare. **Rádio Taxi Alvorada** (☎ 061/321–3030) charges 50% of the regular fare.

THE WEST
As most of the tourist areas in western cities are compact, you'll rarely need a cab except for trips to the airport, the bus depot, or to and from your hotel at night. Cabs in the region are somewhat expensive, but they're all metered, so you shouldn't have to haggle. They're safe and comfortable, and you can generally hail them on the street. Tips aren't expected though a small gratuity (less than 10%) is greatly appreciated.

Contacts and Resources

Banks and Currency Exchange
You'll find major banks equipped with ATMs (dispensing reais) in the capital and most parts of the west (Pirenópolis and the Chapada dos

Guimarães are notable exceptions). Note, however, that they run primarily on the Plus network; if your card is only affiliated with Cirrus, plan accordingly. Banco do Brasil is the best for travelers checks, with relatively low fees and decent exchange rates. Throughout the region, the better hotels will either exchange money for you (though rates aren't always great) or tip you off to the area's best *casas de câmbio* (exchange houses).

BRASÍLIA

Try **American Express** (⊠ Buriti Travel, CLS 402, Bl. A, Lj. 27/33, ☎ 061/225–2686), **Banco do Brasil** (⊠ SBN Q. 01, Bl. A, ☎ 061/224–4353; ⊠ Aeroporto Internacional, ☎ 061/365–1183), **Citibank** (⊠ SCS Q. 06, Bl. A, Lj. 186, ☎ 061/225–9250), or **BankBoston** (⊠ SCS Q. 06, Bl. A, Lj. 200, ☎ 061/321–7714).

THE WEST

In Goiânia, the **BankBoston** across from the Castro's Park Hotel has an ATM. Goiânia's main **Banco do Brasil** (⊠ Av. Goiás 980, Centro) is open weekdays 10–6; there's also one at the airport.

Cuiabá has a large **Banco do Brasil** (⊠ Av. Getúlio Vargas and Rua Barão de Melgaço) in the middle of town that's open weekdays 10–4 and has quite a few 24 hour ATMs. Several little câmbios line Rua Cândido Mariano, including **Guimel He Tour** (⊠ Rua Cândido Mariano 402), which is open weekdays 8:30–6 and offers good rates on cash exchanges.

All the major banks have offices in the center of Campo Grande, along Avenida Afonso Pena. Try **Banco do Brasil** (⊠ Av. Afonso Pena at Rua 13 de Maio), which is open weekdays 10–5; there's also a branch at the airport.

Embassies

In Brasília, embassies have their own sectors (Setors das Embaixadas), and most of them are south of the Eixo Monumental, hence the abbreviation "SES" in their addresses. **Australia** (⊠ SHIS, Q 9, Cj. 01, Casa 1, ☎ 061/248–5523 or 061/248–5569), **Canada** (⊠ SES, Av. da Nações, Lt. 16, ☎ 061/321–2171), **United Kingdom** (⊠ SES, Av. da Nações, Q. 801, Cj. K, Lt. 8, ☎ 061/225–2710 or ☎ 061/225–2625), **United States** (⊠ SES, Av. da Nações, Q. 801, Lt. 3, ☎ 061/321–7272).

Emergencies

Ambulance: ☎ 192. **Fire:** ☎ 193. **Police:** ☎ 190. **Hospitals: Hospital de Base do Distrito Federal** (⊠ Setor Hospitalar Sul, Brasília, ☎ 061/225–0070), **Hospital Ernestina Lopes Jayme** (⊠ Rua dos Pirineus, Pirenópolis, ☎ 062/331–1530), **Hospital Santo Antônio** (⊠ Rua Quinco Caldas, Chapada dos Guimarães, ☎ 065/791–1116), **Hospital Santa Casa** (⊠ Rua Eduardo Santos Pereira 88, Campo Grande, ☎ 067/721–5151) **Hospital Santa Casa** (⊠ Praça Seminário 141, Cuiabá, ☎ 065/624–4222), and **Hospital Santa Helena** (⊠ Rua 95, 99, Sector Sul, Goiânia, ☎ 062/219–9000).

Pharmacies: In Brasília, **Drogaria Rosário** (⊠ SHCS 102, Bl. C, Lj. 05, ☎ 061/323–5901 or 061/323–1818 for deliveries) is open 24 hours a day and has delivery service. There's a **late-night pharmacy** in Cuiabá near the corner of Avenida Getúlio Vargas and Rua Joaquim Murtinho. In Campo Grande try the **late-night pharmacy** at the corner of Avenida Afonso Pena and Rua 14 de Julho. Elsewhere in the region, use the **24-Hour Pharmacy Hotline:** ☎ 132. **Tropical Disease Control Hotline:** ☎ 061/225–8906.

English-Language Bookstores

In Brasília, **Livraria Sodiler** (✉ SCN, Conjunto Nacional, ☎ 061/225–3940; ✉ Aeroporto Internacional, Upper Concourse, EC 14, ☎ 061/365–1967) has the best selection of English-language books, magazines, and newspapers. Elsewhere in the west, English-language reading material is hard to come by.

Health and Safety

Although Brasília doesn't have as much crime as Rio and São Paulo, be cautious at night and at any time on buses or in bus terminals. For the most part, the western cities are safe, but—as in Brasília—you should always be cautious when going out at night, particularly near bus terminals. The southern and western parts of Goiânia are safest. In Cuiabá, steer clear of the embankment at night.

In Brasília and throughout the west, stick to bottled water (and check that restaurants use it to make juice and ice). You should have a long chat with your doctor before heading to the west. Malaria is a concern; yellow fever even more so. It's best to get a yellow-fever shot before arriving, but if you decide to travel at the last minute, there's a clinic in Cuiabá's airport that offers free vaccinations. (It's on the second floor, right near the stairwell, and is open 8:45–5). Dengue fever—for which there is no vaccination or preventative medication—is also a concern in the cities around the Pantanal. Taking Vitamin B supplements a few days before and during your stay will help to fend off mosquitoes. Also, be sure to use insect repellant with DEET, preferably from home (word is that area mosquitoes aren't fended off by local sprays).

Telephones, the Internet, and Mail

Area codes in the region are as follows: Brasília, 061; Goiânia and Pirenópolis, 062; Cuiabá, 065; and Campo Grande, 067.

BRASÍLIA

You can make long-distance calls from TeleBrasília's *postos telefônicos* (phone centers) on the lower concourse at the airport (open 24 hours) and at the Terminal Rodoferroviário. For long-distance calls you can choose from two companies: Embratel (access code 021) and Telebrasília (access code 014). Fax services are available at major *correio* (post office) branches. Unlike other large Brazilian cities, Internet services are nonexistent outside hotels. **Correio** (✉ SBN, Q. 1, Bl. A, ☎ 061/317–1900). **DHL** (✉ SCS, Q. 06, Bl. A, Suite 1A, ☎ 061/225–9263).

THE WEST

Brazil recently deregulated its phone system, resulting in marginally lower rates for domestic calls and an increase in confusion for visitors: Before making a long-distance call from a pay phone in the west you must dial 014 or 021 to connect to a carrier. Goiânia's phone office is at the corner of Rua 3 and Rua 7. In Cuiabá, you'll find such an office on Rua Barão de Melgaço, near the Praça Jaudy. Campo Grande's phone office is at the corner of Rua Rui Barbosa and Rua Dom Aquino.

Although there are more Brazilians on the Internet than any other single country in South America, most of them don't live in the west. The few hotels with business centers have only the slowest Internet dial-up connections; cybercafés are virtually nonexistent (there is one in Campo Grande). Each of the region's major cities has a post office. **Goiânia's post office** (✉ Praça Civica 11) is northeast of the civic center, just off Avenida Tocantins. The **Cuiabá post office** (✉ Praça da República) is in the middle of town, just south of the tourist office; there's also a small branch on the second floor of the airport. There are two centrally located branches of the **Campo Grande post office**

(✉ Av. Calógeras 2309, at corner of Rua Dom Aquino; ✉ Rua Barão do Rio Branco, across from bus depot).

Tour Operators and Travel Agents

BRASÍLIA

Most hotels have an associated travel agency that will arrange tours. Popular excursions include a basic day trip along the Eixo Monumental, a shorter night version with stops at clubs, and an uncanny "mystical tour" to the cult communities around town. **ESAT Aero Táxi** (✉ Monumental Axis at TV Tower, ☎ 61/323–8777) can arrange helicopter tours of the Plano Piloto and other Distrito Federal sights. The shortest flight (10 min) costs $40 per person (minimum of four people per flight). **MS Turismo** (✉ SHCS/EQS 102/103, Bl. A, Lj. 04/22, ☎ 061/224–7818) offers city tours as well as trips into the Cerrado. **VoeTur** (✉ Brasília Shopping, SCN Q. 5, Bl. A, Lj. 235-A, ☎ 061/328–4400) offers a variety of tours.

THE WEST

In Pirenópolis, **Agência Tilapatur** (✉ Rua da Prata 17, ☎ 062/331–1551) has bus, bike, or horseback tours of the ecological spots surrounding the town. Diniz of **Ecotur** (✉ Rua Emílio, ☎ 062/331–1392) is another good Pirenópolis guide who offers similar "ecological" trips.

Arriving in one of the Pantanal's gateway cities without having a tour already booked isn't a problem. Just be careful when choosing a guide upon arrival—some budget travelers have had bad experiences. To avoid being overcharged compare prices. Also be sure your guide has adequate equipment, sufficient knowledge about area wildlife, and good English-language skills. **Anaconda** (✉ Rua Commandante Costa 649, Cuiabá, ☎ 065/624–4142 or 065/624–5128) runs large tours into the Pantanal and around Cuiabá. In Cuiabá many guides will vie for your attention but none will be as persistent or as personable as Joel Souza of **Joel Safari Tours** (✉ Av. Getúlio Vargas 155-A, Cuiabá, ☎ 065/623–4696). Although he does treks to the Chapada dos Guimarães, he specializes in taking groups of four to six people on three- to four-day Pantanal tours. You'll stay in various fazendas and travel by horseback, car, boat, and on foot—whatever it takes to get the best animal sightings. The cost is about $60 per person per day, everything included.

The owner of **Impacto Turismo** (✉ Rua Padre João Crippa 686, Campo Grande, ☎ FAX 067/725–1333), Adnésio Junior (call him Junior), speaks serviceable English and will send you on one of four trips that he sells to everyone who comes through. In the Campo Grande area, Geni Barbier of **Panbratour,** (✉ Rua Estevão Alves Corrêa 586, Aquidauana, ☎ FAX 067/241–3494) really does take your budget and interests into account when planning a tour. In Corumbá, **Corumbátur** (✉ Rua Antônio Maria Coelho 852, ☎ 067/231–1532 or 067/231–1260) is a reliable operator that can arrange boat trips on the Rio Paraguay or van trips into the wetlands.

Visitor Information

BRASÍLIA

The **Brasília Convention and Visitors Bureau** (✉ SRTVN, Centro Empresarial Norte, Q. 701, Cj. C, Bl. A, suite 616–618, ☎ 061/329–5616) has tourist information. The main office of the Federal District Tourism Authority, **SETUR** (✉ SDC, Centro de Convenções Ulisses Guimarães, 1st floor, ☎ 061/325–5716 or 061/225–5717) is another good place for information. At press time, its branches at the airport and Praça dos Três Poderes (across from the Panteão da Pátria) were being renovated, and rumor had it that they may be handed over to the convention and visitors bureau.

Goiânia's **DIRTUR** (✉ Rua 30 at Rua 4, Centro de Convenções, ☎ 062/217–1121) has a lot of information, but it's far from comprehensive. The staff members in Campo Grande's **Centro de Informação Turística e Cultura** (✉ Av. Noroeste at Afonso Pena, ☎ 067/724–5830) can give you information about everything under the sun in Campo Grande and environs, but don't look for any smiles. In Cuiabá, the staffers at **SEDTUR** (✉ Praça da República 131, ☎ 065/624–9060) are personable and helpful, but they don't have much information.

7 SALVADOR, RECIFE, AND FORTALEZA

These colonial cities are the triple crown of Brazil's northeast. Salvador at once startles you with its African rhythms and soothes you with its salty breezes. Recife, cut by rivers and edged by an ocean laden with reefs, is called the "Venice of Brazil." Fortaleza is set on a coast blessed with constant cooling breezes and amazingly warm waters.

THE NORTHEASTERN CITIES of Salvador, Recife, and Fortaleza are imbued with the very essence of Brazil. Their churches, villas, and fortresses tell the tale of Portuguese settlers who fought Dutch invaders and amassed fortunes from sugar. The beaches in and around these cities evoke Brazil's playful side and its love affair with sun, sand, and sea. West of the cities, the rugged, often drought-stricken *sertão* (bush) seems a metaphor for Brazil's darker side—one where many people struggle for survival. This warp and weave of history and topography is laced with threads of culture: Indian, European, African, and the unique blend of all three that is essentially Brazilian.

Updated and expanded by Karen Bressler, Marilene Felinto B. de Lima, and Wilma Felinto B. de Lima

The area known as the northeast begins in the state of Bahia and extends to the edge of the Amazon. In addition to Bahia, the region is composed of the states of Sergipe, Alagoas, Pernambuco, Paraiba, Rio Grande do Norte, Ceará, Piauí, and Maranhão. In Bahia, the historical and cultural influence is predominately African; northward, it's more European. Throughout the region, the Indian influence is a mere shadow of long ago days when they first worked with the Portuguese to harvest *pau-brasil* (brazilwood) trees. Later they either fled inland to escape slavery or were integrated into the European and African cultures.

Although the Spanish and Portuguese had established rough territorial boundaries in the New World with the 1494 Treaty of Tordesillas, the French, English, and Dutch weren't inclined to respect the treaty, which was made by Papal decree. In the 16th century, the Portuguese Crown established 15 "captaincies" (the forerunners of today's states), as a way to protect Brazil from invaders. Each captaincy was assigned a "captain," who governed the territory and collected taxes while also defending it and ensuring its colonization. During this period, many northeasterners made huge profits either from sugar grown on plantations they had established or in the trade of African slaves, who were forced to work the cane fields and *engenhos* (mills).

Under the leadership of Duarte Coelho, the northeastern captaincy of Pernambuco thrived. Coelho adeptly established good relations with area Indians and was among the first to employ African labor. At one point, Pernambuco had more sugar engenhos than any other captaincy. Olinda, its capital, was filled with the elegance and luxury that only true sugar-barons could finance. Recife, the capital of what is now Pernambuco state, also began to evolve as a major port.

By 1549 it became clear to Portugal's monarch, Dom João III, that his New World captaincies were, for the most part, failing. He appointed Tomé de Sousa as Brazil's first governor general and ordered him to establish a colonial capital in the central captaincy of Bahia. Hence, the city of Salvador was established on a bluff overlooking the vast Bahia de Todos os Santos (All Saints' Bay).

In 1611, Martim Soares Moreno was dispatched from Portugal to a captaincy farther in the northeast with orders to fend off the French who were threatening the area. Captain Moreno fell in love with the place—parts of which became the state of Ceará and its capital, Fortaleza—as well as its people. He was especially taken with an Indian woman, whom he married. (The love affair was immortalized in the 19th-century classic Brazilian novel *Iracema,* named for the Indian woman, by José de Alencar. Contemporary Fortaleza's Mucuripe Bay has a famous statue of Iracema by Corbiano Lins, a sculptor from Pernambuco.)

Although the French had posed an early threat to Brazil, it was the Dutch who truly tested its mettle. In 1602, they set up the powerful Dutch East India Company, which demolished Portugal's Asian spice-trade monopoly. Soon the Dutch began to look toward Brazil and its profitable sugar enterprises (they even sent botanists to catalog the nation's flora). In 1621, after the Dutch West Indian Company was established, Dutch attacks in northeastern Brazil began. They invaded and took over several captaincies, but the Portuguese drove them from one after another, finally ousting them entirely in 1654.

The coveted northeast still has much to offer. In today's Salvador, the music, art, dance, religions, and cuisine of the millions of Africans who were forced to settle in the region are well preserved. Farther north, Recife is a city of water and bridges, and nearby Olinda is still a beautiful enclave of colonial architecture, though bohemians have replaced sugar barons. Fortaleza sits along Ceará state's 570-km-long (354-mi-long) coast, which provides a backdrop of fantastic beaches full of white dunes.

Pleasures and Pastimes

Beaches
Urban sands are often lined by wide walkways and filled with beach-goers and food and beverage vendors that lend both atmosphere and attitude. The farther from the cities you go, the more pristine the beaches. On many stretches, fishermen still head out for the high seas in *jangadas* (hand-crafted log rafts with beautiful sails), clusters of palm trees provide natural shade, and the dunes are so high you can ski down them. What's more, the Atlantic waters are warm here year-round.

Dining
African culture was the catalyst for much of the region's cuisine, particularly that of Bahia. When the slaves arrived, they brought their own knowledge of how to cook using tropical ingredients. Coconut milk, *dendê* (palm) oil, and hot spices were insinuated into Portuguese and Indian dishes, transforming them into something quite new. Regional dishes often feature seafood; most are well-seasoned if not fiery hot. *Moqueca* is a regional seafood "stew" made with fish and/or shellfish, dendê oil, coconut milk, onions, and tomatoes. Other classics include *vatapá* (a thick, purée-like stew made with fish, shrimp, cashews, peanuts, and a variety of seasonings) and *ximxim de galinha* (chicken marinated in lemon or lime juice, garlic, and salt and pepper, and then cooked with dendê and peanut oil, coconut milk, tomatoes, and seasonings). For details on price categories, *see* the chart *in* How to Use this Book, at the front of the guide.

Lodging
Lodging options range from swank, modern high-rises with an international clientele and world-class service to cozy, family run *pousadas* (inns) on remote beaches or in small fishing villages. "Flat" or apartment hotels—where guest quarters have kitchens and living rooms as well as bedrooms—are also options. In peak season, especially during Carnaval (Carnival), rates are higher and reservations are a must. For details on price categories, *see* the chart *in* How to Use this Book at the front of the guide.

Exploring Bahia, Fortaleza, and Recife

Several good main and secondary roads, some of them right along the coast, run north–south through the region. Still, considering the distances you must travel, it's best to fly between the cities. From each,

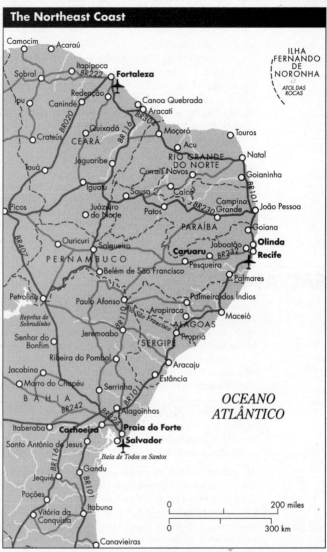

The Northeast Coast

you can rent a car and explore other parts of the coast or make your way inland and slightly off the beaten path.

Great Itineraries

IF YOU HAVE 5 DAYS

For such a short stay, you'll have to pick one of the cities and explore it and its environs thoroughly. To really get the feel of the region, your best bet is Salvador. Spend two days seeing the historic in-town sights and visiting the Ilha de Itaparica or the Península Itapagipe. On the third day drive to Praia do Forte for a day on the beach and a night in a resort, or head west to Cachoeira for a day of spiritual exploration and a night in a pousada.

IF YOU HAVE 7 DAYS

Fly into Salvador, and spend two days exploring the city. On the third day, fly to Recife. Spend a day in Recife Velha and another on the beach. On the sixth day, visit Olinda—staying late enough to catch the sunset from the Alto da Sé—before flying back to Salvador for the return flight home.

You can see all three cities, though your schedule will be very full. Fly into Salvador, and spend two days there. On the third day, take a side trip to one of the beaches outside town. Fly to Recife on the fourth day, and spend the next two days exploring the in-town sights and Olinda. On the seventh day, fly to Fortaleza; spend a day in town and another shopping for lace in nearby Aquiraz or sunbathing on the beach at Canoa Quebrada. On the 10th day, fly back to Salvador for the journey home.

When to Go

Peak season is December–March (the South American summer) and the month of July when schools have breaks. Make reservations far in advance for stays during these months, especially if you plan to visit during Carnaval (February or March). As the weather is sunny and warm year-round, consider a trip in the off-season, when prices are lower and the beaches less crowded.

SALVADOR

Bahia's state capital is a city of 2 million people, at least 80% of whom are Afro-Brazilian. It captivates visitors with African rhythms that roll forth everywhere—from buses and construction sites to the rehearsals of the Ilê Aiyê percussion group. The scents of coriander, coconut, and palm oil waft around corners that also host white-turbaned women who cook and sell deep-fried spicy shrimp and bean cakes. Baroque church interiors covered with gold leaf hark back to the riches of the Portuguese colonial era, when slaves masked their religious beliefs under a thin Catholic veneer. And partly thanks to modern-day acceptance of those beliefs, Salvador has become the fount of Candomblé, a religion based on personal dialogue with the *orixás*, a family of African deities closely linked to both nature and the Catholic saints.

The influence of Salvador's African heritage on Brazilian music has turned this city into one of the most stirring places to spend Carnaval, the bacchanalian fling that precedes Lent (and only one of more than 20 festivals punctuating the local calendar). As Bahia's distinctive *axé* music has gained popularity around the country, the city has begun to compete with Rio de Janeiro's more traditional celebration. Salvador's Carnaval means dancing night after night in the street to the ear-splitting, bone-rattling music of *trios elétricos* (bands on special sound trucks), and watching the parades of outlandish Carnaval associations. This movable feast formally lasts a week in February or March but begins in spirit at New Year's and continues even into Lent in small towns outside Salvador, with street festivals called *micaretas*.

Exploring Salvador

Salvador was founded on a cliff overlooking Bahia de Todos os Santos, and occupies a triangle that's sided by the bay and the ocean and which comes to a point at the Farol da Barra (Barra Lighthouse). The original city, called the Cidade Histórica (Historical City), is divided into *alta* (upper) and *baixa* (lower) districts and has buildings that date as far back as the 16th century. The Cidade Baixa occupies a space between the cliff's drop-off and the bay; it's a commercial district where you'll find the fully enclosed handicrafts market, the Mercado Modelo, and the port. Sleepy Ilha Itaparica is the largest of the harbor's 38 islands. Northwest around the bay lies the Península Itapagipe, site of the Nossa Senhora do Bomfin church and the Mont Serrat Fort.

Tree-lined Avenida 7 de Setembro runs south through the Vitória neighborhood and past the Iate Club to the Barra neighborhood, a mix of beach, good cheap restaurants, low-life cafés, and moderately priced hotels. At the Farol da Barra the city runs east and north again on the oceanside leg of the triangle. The next beaches, Ondina and Rio Vermelho, are home to Salvador's most expensive resorts; the latter is quite bohemian. Going north along the so-called Orla Marítima (connecting avenues along the coast), there are many restaurants, the cleanest beaches, and, at the city's northernmost point, the Lagoa de Abaeté—a deep, black, freshwater lagoon.

The baroque churches, museums, colonial houses, and narrow, cobbled streets of the Cidade Histórica are best seen on foot. To travel between the Cidade Alta and the Cidade Baixa you can take the room-size Lacerda Elevator or the more utilitarian funicular railway. Inexpensive *comum* (common) taxis are a good way to get around the rest of the city.

Numbers in the text correspond to numbers in the margin and on the Salvador Cidade Histórico map.

Cidade Alta

A GOOD WALK

Begin your walk at the most famous of the city's 176 churches, the 18th-century baroque **Igreja de São Francisco** ① and its neighboring **Igreja da Ordem Terceira de São Francisco** ②. From here, cross Rua Inácio Accioli (which becomes Rua São Francisco) and head through the Praça Anchieta to Rua da Oração João de Deus and the **Igreja São Domingos de Gusmão da Ordem Terceira** ③. Just beyond this church is the large square called **Terreiro de Jesus** ④. At the Terreiro's northwest end is the 17th-century **Catedral Basílica** ⑤. From the cathedral head up to Rua Francisco Muniz Barreto and take a left onto Rua Alfredo de Brito. Two blocks up this street on your right is the **Fundação Casa de Jorge Amado/Museu da Cidade** ⑥, where you can see memorabilia of the author of such famous titles as *Dona Flor e Seus dos Maridos* (*Dona Flor and Her Two Husbands*), as well as exhibits on Candomblé.

Rua Alfredo de Brito leads into the famed **Largo do Pelourinho** ⑦. To the north stands the baroque **Igreja de Nossa Senhora do Rosário dos Pretos** ⑧. Walk up the hill past ancient pastel-color houses and African handicrafts shops and art galleries to the **Igreja e Museu do Convento do Carmo** ⑨.

TIMING

Simply walking this route will take about three hours. Pelourinho, with its music, cafés, restaurants, and shops, is a place that can be explored several times over a period of days and yet always seems new.

SIGHTS TO SEE

⑤ Catedral Basílica. Hints of Asia permeate this 17th-century masterpiece: Note the intricate ivory and tortoiseshell inlay from Goa on the Japiassu family altar, third on the right as you enter; the Asian facial features and clothing of the figures in the transept altars; and the 16th-century tiles from Macao in the sacristy. A Jesuit who lived in China painted the ceiling over the cathedral entrance. ⊠ *Terreiro de Jesus,* ☎ *no phone.* ⊡ *Free.* ⊙ *Tues.–Sat. 8–11 and 3–6; Sun. 5–6:30.*

⑥ Fundação Casa de Jorge Amado/Museu da Cidade. The Jorge Amado House contains the writer's photos, book covers, and a lecture room.

Salvador Cidade Histórico

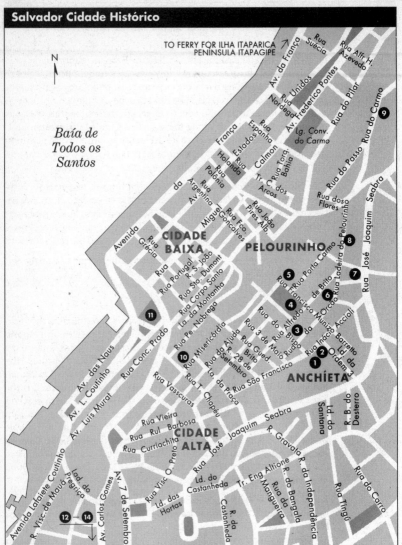

N

TO FERRY FOR ILHA ITAPARICA
PENÍNSULA ITAPAGIPE

Baía de
Todos os
Santos

CIDADE
BAIXA

PELOURINHO

ANCHÍETA

CIDADE
ALTA

Catedral Basílica, **5**
Elevador Lacerda, **10**
Fundação Casa de
Jorge Amado/Museu
da Cidade, **6**
Igreja e Museu do
Convento do
Carmo, **9**
Igreja de Nossa
Senhora do Rosário
dos Pretos, **8**
Igreja da Ordem
Terceira de
São Francisco, **2**
Igreja São Domingos
de Gusmão da Ordem
Terceira, **3**

Igreja de São
Francisco, **1**
Largo do
Pelourinho, **7**
Mercado Modelo, **11**
Museu de Arte
Moderna da
Bahia, **13**
Museu de
Arte Sacre, **12**
Museu Carlos Costa
Pinto, **14**
Terreiro de Jesus, **4**

Amado lived in the Hotel Pelourinho when it was a student house, and he set many of his books in this part of the city. Next door is the **Museu da Cidade,** with exhibitions of the costumes of the orixas of Candomblé. ⊠ *Corner of Rua Alfredo Brito and Largo do Pelourinho,* ☎ *071/321– 0122.* 🎟 *Free.* ☉ *Fundação: weekdays 9:30 AM–10 PM. Museum: Tues.–Fri. 10–5, weekends 1–5.*

❾ Igreja e Museu do Convento do Carmo. The 17th-century Carmelite Monastery Church and Museum is famous for its restored French organ and carved cedar figure of Christ, the latter kept in the sacristy. Studded with tiny Indian rubies to represent blood, the figure was once carried through the streets in a silver-handled litter during Holy Week, but is now too fragile to be moved. The monastery, which was occupied by the Dutch when they invaded in 1624, features a small church built in 1580 and a chapel with Portuguese *azulejos* (tiles) that recount the story of the Jesuit order. ⊠ *Largo do Carmo s/n,* ☎ *071/242–0182.* 🎟 *Free.* ☉ *Church: Daily for mass only, 7 AM, but accessible from museum. Museum: Mon.–Sat. 8–noon, 2–6; Sun. 8–noon.*

❽ Igreja de Nossa Senhora do Rosário dos Pretos. Guides tend to skip over the Church of Our Lady of the Rosary of the Blacks, which was built in a baroque style by and for slaves between 1704 and 1796. It's worth a look at the side altars, to see statues of the Catholic church's few black saints. Each has a fascinating story. ⊠ *Ladeira do Pelourinho s/n,* ☎ *no phone.* 🎟 *Free.* ☉ *Weekdays 8–5, weekends 8–2.*

❷ Igreja da Ordem Terceira de São Francisco. The Church of the Third Order of St. Francis has an 18th-century Spanish plateresque sandstone facade—carved to resemble Spanish silver altars made by beating the metal into wooden molds—that's unique in all Brazil. The facade was hidden for decades under a thick coat of plaster, until, the story goes, a drunk electrician went wild with a hammer in the 1930s. ⊠ *Praça Padre Anchieta s/n,* ☎ *071/242–7046.* 🎟 *Free.* ☉ *Mon.–Sat. 8–noon and 2–5; Sun. 8–noon.*

❸ Igreja São Domingos de Gusmão da Ordem Terceira. The baroque Church of the Third Order of St. Dominic (1723) houses a fascinating collection of carved processional saints and other sacred objects. Such sculptures often had hollow interiors used to smuggle gold into Portugal to avoid government taxes. You'll see Asian features and details in the church decoration, evidence of long-ago connections with Portugal's Asian colonies of Goa and Macao. Upstairs are two impressive rooms with carved wooden furniture used for lay brothers' meetings and receptions. ⊠ *Terreiro de Jesus,* ☎ *071/242–4185.* 🎟 *Free.* ☉ *Mon.– Sat. 8–noon and 2–5.*

★ ❶ Igreja de São Francisco. The most famous of the city's churches, the 18th-century baroque Church of St. Francis has an active monastery. Listen for the sound of African drums in the square outside as you appreciate the ceiling painted in 1774 by José Joaquim da Rocha, a mulatto who founded Brazil's first art school. The ornately carved cedar and rosewood interior virtually writhes with images of mermaids, acanthus leaves, and caryatids—all bathed in shimmering gold leaf. Guides will tell you that there's as much as a ton of gold here, but restoration experts say there's actually much less, as the leaf used is just a step up from a powder. A super Sunday morning alternative to crowded beaches is Mass here (9–11, 11–11:45); stay until the end, when the electric lights go off, to catch the wondrous subtlety of gold leaf under natural light. ⊠ *Praça Padre Anchieta,* ☎ *no phone.* 🎟 *Free.* ☉ *Mon.– Sat. 8–noon and 2–5; Sun. 8–noon.*

★ ❼ **Largo do Pelourinho.** Named for the pillory where slaves were punished, this plaza is now the setting for one of the largest and most charming groupings of Brazilian colonial architecture and a thriving cultural renaissance. There are four public stages in Pelourinho, at least two of which have music nightly, all named after characters in Jorge Amado novels. **Dia & Noite** (☎ 071/322–2525) is the association that organizes the music; they publish a monthly schedule widely available in the area, at most tourist offices, and in hotels.

❹ **Terreiro de Jesus.** A large square with three churches and a small handicrafts fair, Terreiro de Jesus opens the way to exotic, historic Salvador. Where nobles once strolled under imperial palm trees, protected by their slaves, you'll now see men practicing *capoeira*, a stylized, dancelike foot-fight with African origins, to the thwang of the *berimbau*, a rudimentary but mesmerizing bow-shape musical instrument.

Cidade Baixa and Beyond

You can travel between the Cidade Alta and the Cidade Baixa aboard the popular **Elevador Lacerda** ⑩. Exiting the elevator at the Cidade Baixa, cross the Praça Visconde de Cairú to the **Mercado Modelo** ⑪ for some shopping and some people-watching. From here you have several options. Heading north, away from the ocean and along the bay, you pass the port and the terminal where you can catch a ferry for **Ilha de Itaparica.** Or you can head south by cab to one of several museums: the **Museu de Arte Sacra** ⑫; the **Museu de Arte Moderna da Bahia** ⑬; or the **Museu Carlos Costa Pinto** ⑭, which is in the Vitória neighborhood.

TIMING

You could start late in the morning and make a relaxed day of this tour. Navigating the elevator and the market takes a little more than an hour, though you'll probably want to spend more time browsing. The trip to either Ilha de Itaparica or to one or more of the museums will fill up a leisurely afternoon.

SIGHTS TO SEE

⑩ **Elevador Lacerda.** Costing about 2¢ and covering 236 ft in a minute, the elevator runs between the Praça Municipal in the Cidade Alta and Praça Visconde de Cairú and the Mercado Modelo. Built in 1872, the elevator ran on steam until its 1930 restoration. Bahians joke that the elevator is the only way to "go up" in life.

OFF THE BEATEN PATH   **ILHA DE ITAPARICA** – Originally settled because of its ample supply of fresh water, Brazil's largest maritime island doesn't have notable beaches, but there are some quiet shady cobbled streets lined with pastel-color colonial homes sure to charm you. As the complete schooner tour can be tiresome, one option is to take it one way, get off at Itaparica, skip the cattle-call lunch, take a taxi to a good restaurant, enjoy a postprandial afternoon stroll, and ride the ferry back to Salvador.

⑪ **Mercado Modelo.** This enclosed market (closed Sun. afternoon) may not be the cheapest place to buy handicrafts—and you do have to bargain—but it must be experienced. It assaults the senses, with its *cachaça* (a strong Brazilian liquor made from sugarcane), cashew nuts, pepper sauces, cigars, the dried shrimp that are an integral part of Bahian cooking, manioc flour, leather goods, hammocks, lace, musical instruments, African sculptures, and gems. Outside, you'll hear the nasal-voiced *repentistas*, regional folk singers who make up songs on the spot. Notice the blue azulejos on the building with Gothic-style windows, once a sort of chamber of commerce, now a supermarket. Be prepared for extraordinarily persistent salespeople in and around the building. At the rear of the market, boys practice *capoeira* (a sport that's half fighting, half dancing) and sell monkeys; the harbor excursion boats are moored across the way.

13 **Museu de Arte Moderna da Bahia.** A mid-16th-century waterfront mill set between the Cidade Alta and Cidade Baixa houses the Bahian Museum of Modern Art's permanent collection of work by some of Brazil's top modern painters, including Cândido Portinari, Alfredo Volpi, Siron Franco, and Hector Carybé. The museum building is part of a complex that includes the **Solar do Unhão,** a former sugar mill/residential complex that dates from the 18th century. ✉ *Av. Contorno s/n,* ☎ *071/ 329–0660.* 🎫 *Free.* 🕐 *Tues.–Fri. 1–9, Sat. 11–9, Sun. 2–7.*

12 **Museu de Arte Sacra.** Housed in a former Carmelite monastery near the Cidade Alta, the Sacred Art Museum and its adjoining **Igreja de Santa Teresa** (Church of St. Teresa) are two of the city's best-cared-for repositories of religious objects. An in-house restoration team has worked miracles that bring alive Bahia's 1549–1763 golden age as Brazil's capital and main colonial port. See the silver altar in the church, moved here from the demolished Sé church, and the blue-and-yellow-tiled sacristy replete with a bay view. ✉ *Rua do Sodré 276,* ☎ *071/243–6310.* 🎫 *Admission.* 🕐 *Weekdays 11:30–5:30.*

14 **Museu Carlos Costa Pinto.** The collection is the fruit of one wealthy couple's fascination with art and antiques and a rare example of private support for the arts in Brazil. Among the museum's 3,000 objects fashioned around the world over the last three centuries is Costa Pinto's collection of oversize gold and silver jewelry worn by favored slave women. Here are some prime examples of the *balangandã* (also called the *penca*), a chain of large charms—in the shape of tropical fruits, fish, perhaps a berimbau—worn by slave women around the waist. Prized slaves were initially given the chain and the clasp by their masters, who, over time, continued to reward loyalty and service with gifts of the charms (many jewelry and crafts stores sell replicas of these pieces). The balangandã usually includes a *figa,* a closed fist with a thumb sticking out of the top. According to African legend, the figa can increase warriors' fertility. In Brazil, however, it's considered simply a good-luck charm (in order for it to work, though, it must always be a gift). It's also used as a good-luck gesture, sort of like crossing your fingers. ✉ *Av. 7 de Setembro 2490,* ☎ *071/336–6081.* 🎫 *Admission.* 🕐 *Mon. and Wed.– Fri. 2:30–7, weekends 3–6.*

Península Itapagipe

A GOOD DRIVE

A 20-minute taxi ride from the Mercado Modelo, around the bay to the northwest, brings you to the Itapagipe Peninsula and the **Igreja de Nosso Senhor do Bonfim.** Here or in the square facing the church you'll be accosted by someone selling a printed ribbon, willing to tie it around your wrist with three knots (and sell 20 more to take home to friends), each good for one wish if you wear the ribbon until it falls off and throw it into the ocean. Each color stands for a paired Catholic saint and Candomblé deity. A five-minute drive from the church is the dazzling white **Mont Serrat Fort.**

TIMING

One and a half hours ought to suffice for travel to and from Itapagipe, a tour of the church, and a visit to the fort. The morning mass on the first Friday of the month draws a huge congregation, most wearing white, Candomblé on one side and Catholic on the other.

SIGHTS TO SEE

Igreja de Nosso Senhor do Bonfim. A procession of women dressed in petticoat-puffed Empire-waist white dresses, turbans, and ritual neck-

SPIRITUAL SALVADOR

EVIDENCE THAT BRAZIL is officially a Roman Catholic country can be found everywhere. There are beautiful churches and cathedrals—from the colonial to the baroque to the modern—across the nation. Most Brazilians wear a religious medal or two, bus and taxi drivers place pictures of St. Christopher prominently in their vehicles, and two big winter celebrations (in June) honor St. John and St. Peter. For many Brazilians, however, the real church is that of the spirits.

When the Africans were forced aboard slave ships, they may have left their families and possessions behind, but they brought along an impressive array of gods. Foremost among them were Olorum, the creator; Iemanjá, the goddess of the rivers and water; Oxalá, the god of procreation and the harvest; and Exú, a trickster spirit who could cause mischief or bring about death. Of lesser rank but still very powerful were Ogun, Obaluayê, Oxôssi, and Yansan to name a few.

The Catholic Church, whose spiritual seeds were planted alongside the rows of sugarcane and cotton, was naturally against such religious beliefs. As a compromise, the Africans took on the rituals of Rome and kept their old gods. Thus, new religions—Candomblé in Bahia, Macumba in Rio, Xangó in Pernambuco, Umbanda in São Paulo—were born. Iemenjá had her equivalent in the Virgin Mary and was queen of the heavens as well as queen of the seas; the powerful

Oxalá became associated with Jesus Christ; and Exú, full of deception to begin with, became Satan. Other gods were likened to saints: Ogun to St. Anthony, Obaluayê to St. Francis, Oxôssi to St. George, Yansan to St. Barbara. On their altars crosses and statues of the Virgin, Christ, and saints sat beside offerings of sacred white feathers, magical beads, and bowls of cooked rice and cornmeal.

Salvadorans are eager to share their rituals with visitors, though often for a fee (you can make arrangements through hotels or tour agencies). The Candomblé temple ceremony, in which believers sacrifice animals and become possessed by gods, is performed nightly except during Lent. Temples, usually in poor neighborhoods at the city's edge, don't allow photographs or video or sound recordings. You shouldn't wear black (white is preferable) or revealing clothing. The ceremony is long and repetitive, there's no air-conditioning, and often no chairs; men and women are separated.

A *pãe de santo* or *mãe de santo* (Candomblé priest or priestess) can perform a reading of the *búzios* for you; the small brown shells are thrown like jacks into a circle of beads—the pattern they form tells about your life. Don't select your mãe or pãe de santo through an ad or sign, as many shell-readers who advertise are best not at fortune-telling but at saying "One hundred dollars, please" in every language.

laces comes here the Thursday before the third Sunday in January to wash the steps with holy flower water. Built in the 1750s, the simple church is filled with ex-votos—wax, wooden, and plaster replicas of body parts—objects of devoted prayer and believed to be capable of miraculous cures. Many figures in Catholicism have a counterpart deity in Candomblé; Nosso Senhor do Bonfim's is Oxalá, the father of all the gods and goddesses. Thus the seemingly bizarre mixture of figurines found in the shops opposite the church: St. George and the Dragon, devils, Indians, monks, sailors, and warriors, plus ex-votos that include house keys and Volkswagens for the devotees of consumerism. ⊠ *Praça do Senhor do Bonfim, Alto do Bonfim, Itapagipe,* ☎ *no phone.* 🎫 *Free. Closed Tues.–Sun. noon–2:30 and Mon.*

Mont Serrat Fort. Built in 1500 and named for the shrine of the Black Virgin at Montserrat, near Barcelona, the white fort is still used by the Brazilian military. It's not open to the public. There's a church by the same name nearby, rarely open, with a renowned carving of St. Peter.

Beaches

Beaches are wall-to-wall people on the weekends, but if you don't mind a crowd it's fun to soak up both sun and beach culture, which includes sand sports, firewater drinks, spicy seafood snacks (don't miss the *acarajé*, a deep-fried bean cake with dried shrimp and sauce) at beachside kiosks, live music, and the briefest of swimwear.

At most local beaches the food and drink kiosks provide chairs and umbrellas free of charge; you pay only for what you consume. Some also offer rudimentary bathroom, changing, and shower facilities free of charge for patrons. Aside from these, there are no functioning bathrooms on the beaches, but some have public showers that run on one-minute tokens costing less than 25¢. Don't leave belongings unattended.

The *jardineira* bus stops at all the beaches along the coast, from downtown north as far as the Stella Maris beach. A more comfortable *ônibus executivo* (executive bus; marked ROTEIRO DAS PRAIAS) runs from Praça da Sé to Flamengo beach, stopping at all the same stops. As a rule, the farther away from the port, the better the beach.

Barra do Jacuípe. A river runs down to the ocean at this long, wide, pristine beach lined with coconut palms, about 40 km (25 mi) north of Salvador. There are beachfront snack bars. The **Santa Maria/Catuense bus company** (☎ 071/359–3474) operates six buses (marked PRAIA DO FORTE) daily that stop at this beach.

Guarajuba. With palm trees and calm waters banked by a reef, this is the nicest beach of them all, though it's 60 km (38 mi) north of Salvador. The bus to Barra do Jacuípe (☞ *above*) continues on to Guarajuba. There are snack kiosks, fishing boats, surfing, dune buggies, and a playground.

Itapuã. Frequented by artist types who live nearby, Itapuã is at the end of the string of beaches that stretch north from Salvador, about a half-hour drive from downtown. Although it's polluted in some places, this beach has a terrific atmosphere. Around K and J streets there are food kiosks, music bars, and amusement park rides, too. A mystical freshwater lagoon, the **Lagoa de Abaeté** lies inland from Itapuã. Set in lush greenery, its black depths provide a startling contrast with the fine white sand of its shores. No one knows the source of these waters, where Bahian women often wash clothes in the morning. City buses going to the lagoon leave from Campo Grande or Estação da Lapa and cost less than 50¢. If you're driving, take the Orla Marítima north out of the city until Itapuã. At the Largo da Sereia (a square with a mermaid statue), follow signs for the lagoon. Tour operators include the lagoon on their beach tours, which cost about $25.

Jaguaribe. This is the "in crowd" hangout, frequented by singles on Saturday and good for surfing, windsurfing, and sailing. There are plenty of snack bars. This beach is just before Piatã (☞ *below*), 16 km (10 mi) north of downtown.

Piatã. Heading north and leaving the more built-up areas of the city behind, the first truly clean beach you'll come to is the wide oceanside Piatã (20 km/13 mi from downtown). Its calm waters and golden sand attract families.

Porto da Barra and Farol da Barra. Some Salvadorans, especially singles, swear by the urban beaches Porto da Barra and Farol da Barra, which are frequented by a colorful mix of people who live nearby and tourists staying at neighboring hotels. Petty thievery is a problem here. There are no bathrooms or kiosks, but you can rent a beach chair for about $1. The corner of Porto da Barra closest to the Grande Hotel da Barra is a gay hangout. Toward the other end, around the corner from the lighthouse, lie the hotel districts of **Ondina** and **Rio Vermelho**, where the beaches intermittently suffer pollution problems.

Stella Maris. The Stella Maris beach (18 km/11 mi north of downtown), *the* beach in Salvador, is popular with surfers and beautiful girls, but it's most famous for its kiosks.

Dining

You can easily find restaurants serving Bahian specialties in Barra, a neighborhood full of bars and sidewalk cafés. There are also many good spots in bohemian Rio Vermelho and a slew of places along the beachfront drive beginning around Jardim de Alah. It's wise to order meat only in *churrascarias* (barbecued-meat restaurants), avoiding it in seafood places.

Brazilian

$$$ ✕ **Casa da Gamboa.** A longtime favorite of Bahian writer Jorge
★ Amado, this is an institution of Bahian cooking. *Casquinha de siri* (breaded crab in the shell) comes as a complimentary starter; then try the *peixe com risoto de ostras* (grilled fish with oyster risotto), followed by the very good traditional desserts. ⊠ *Rua João de Deus 32, Pelourinho,* ☎ *071/321–3393. AE, MC, V. No lunch.*

$$$ ✕ **Maria Mata Mouro.** At this intimate restaurant, you almost feel as if you're at a friend's house for dinner. The Bahian food is served with an extra creative twist, and you're assured of a good meal. The *badejo* (grouper) in ginger is delicious. ⊠ *Rua Inácio Acciole 8, Pelourinho,* ☎ *071/321–3929. AE, V. Closed Sun.*

$$$ ✕ **Tempero da Dadá.** This is one of the best-loved restaurants in town.
★ The original location, in Federação, where the famous Dadá herself usually cooks, is better-liked, but the newer branch in Pelourinho is just as good. Dadá has been cooking since she was eight, when she stood on stools to get to the stove. Though the house specialty is *bobó de camarão* (shrimp), the grilled fish, the vatapá, and the moquecas are every bit as good. Dadá first started attracting artists and musicians who had heard about her fabulous cooking years ago and just stopped by her home for a meal. On occasion you'll still find local luminaries—like musician Carlinhos Brown—at tables on the veranda. ⊠ *R. Teixeira Mendes 55, Federação,* ☎ *071/331–4382. AE, MC, V. Closed Mon.* ⊠ *R. Frei Vicente 5, Pelourinho,* ☎ *071/321–5883. AE, MC, V. Closed Mon.*

$$ ✕ **Dona Celina.** This Bahian restaurant in Pelorinho offers alfresco as well as indoor dining, and a good selection of vegetarian dishes. The

ambience will charm you. ✉ *Rua Francisco Muniz Barreto 15,* ☎ *071/ 321–1721. No credit cards.*

$$ ✕ **Uauá.** You'll find cuisine representative of many Brazilian regions here. The clientele, which includes most of the city, are die-hard fans. There are two locations, one in Pelourinho and one at Itapuã Beach. ✉ *R. Gregório de Matos 36, Pelourinho,* ☎ *071/321–3089. AE, DC, MC, V. Closed Mon.* ✉ *Av. Dorival Caymi 46, Itapuã,* ☎ *071/249– 9579. AE, DC, MC, V. Closed Mon.*

$ ✕ **Arroz de Hauçá.** Two unemployed brothers convinced their family's 70-year-old cook to go public, and turned their plant-filled house into a restaurant. The restaurant, in turn, put the home-cooked dish it's named for on the map of Bahian cuisine. This hefty plate of rice, in coconut milk and covered with a sauce of shrimp paste and onions, has a circle of fried jerked beef and onions in the middle. And while the *arroz de hauçá* is the star here, you can also find the usual Bahian specialties on the menu. The management doesn't frown on sharing dishes. ✉ *Rua Sabino Silva 598, Jardim Apipema,* ☎ ⅢⅩ *071/247–3508. AE, DC, MC, V.*

Eclectic

$$ ✕ **Extudo.** Young professionals and singles jam-pack this bar and restaurant just about every night. Bahian and international dishes include camarão *comodoro,* shrimp and prunes gratinéed in a creamy tomato sauce; Finnegan's steak with black pepper sauce; and *frango flambado,* flambéed chicken. ✉ *Rua Lídio Mesquita 4, Rio Vermelho,* ☎ *071/334–4669. No credit cards. Closed Mon.*

French

$$$$ ✕ **Chez Bernard.** Discerning *soteropolitanos* (the pompous but nonetheless correct term for natives of the city) say this is undoubtedly the best, as well as one of the oldest, French restaurants in town. There are no particular specialties: everything is worth trying. ✉ *Gamboa de Cima 11, Aflitos,* ☎ *071/329–5403. AE, V. Closed Sun.*

Seafood

$$$ ✕ **Bargaço.** Typical Bahian food is served in this oversize, brightly lit shed, a 20-minute drive along the beach from downtown, once a must in Salvador that now caters mostly to tour groups. Starters such as *pata de caranguejo* (vinegared crab claw) are hearty and plentiful, but they may do more than take the edge off your appetite for the requisite moqueca de *camarão* (shrimp) or moqueca *de siri mole* (soft-shell crab); try the *cocada baiana* (sugar-caked coconut) for dessert, if you have room. ✉ *Rua P, Lote 1819, Quadra 43, Jardim Armação, Boca do Rio,* ☎ *071/231–5141 or 071/231–3900. AE, DC, MC.*

$$ ✕ **Frutos do Mar.** This plain, traditional seafood spot in the hopping Barra neighborhood is a favorite among cash-conscious locals for its shrimp moquecas and *ensopados* (catch-of-the-day stews resembling bouillabaisse), which come with a typical, sweet-flavored bean called *feijão de leite.* ✉ *Rua Marquês de Leão 415, Barra,* ☎ *071/245–6479 or 071/254–6322. AE, DC, MC, V.*

$$ ✕ **Iate Clube da Bahia.** From your captain's chair in this informal air-conditioned yacht club restaurant, set on the cliff between Barra and the Vitória neighborhood, you get a spectacular view of boats bobbing in the bay. You also get honest Continental and Bahian cooking, such as double gratinéed fish and moquecas. ✉ *Av. 7 de Setembro 3252, Barra,* ☎ *071/336–9011. AE, DC, MC, V. Closed Mon.*

$$ ✕ **Iemanjá.** Probably the best value for regional cooking, Iemanjá is also a place with a bubbly, underwater atmosphere, replete with aquamarine sea-goddess murals and aquariums. The service is somewhat slow and there's no air-conditioning, but most patrons don't seem to mind, concentrating instead on plowing through mountainous portions

of moqueca or ensopado. ⊠ *Av. Otávio Mangabeira 929, Jardin Armação,* ☎ *071/231–5770. No credit cards.*

Lodging

There are only a few hotels in the historic Cidade Alta, overlooking the bay. Going south into the Vitória neighborhood along Avenida 7 de Setembro, there are many inexpensive hotels, convenient both to the Barra area beaches and to historic sights. In the yuppie Barra neighborhood, many hotels are within walking distance of cafés, bars, restaurants, and clubs. The resort-hotel district lies farther north, a 20-minute taxi ride from downtown and historic areas, on and around the Ondina and Rio Vermelho beaches.

$$$$ 🏨 **Enseada das Lajes.** Perched on a cliff overlooking the ocean, this
★ hotel is the most exclusive in town, though guests have reported that the standards don't merit the exorbitant rate. Both private and public areas are decorated in antiques, and the hotel is surrounded by gardens that descend to the sea. The owners have a second property by the same name on Ilha de Itaparica. ⊠ *Av. Oceânica 511, Morro da Paciência, Rio Vermelho,* ☎ *071/336–1027,* FAX *071/336–0654. 9 rooms. Restaurant, bar, pool. AE, DC, MC.*

$$$$ 🏨 **Transamérica Salvador.** As far as big hotels go, the Transamérica is doubtless among the best. The standard rooms are small but they have terrific views east toward the bay. Although it's in Rio Vermelho, the hotel retains an isolated feel, because it's atop a mountain. Nearby, however, you'll find great restaurants that are open 24 hours. ⊠ *Rua Monte do Conselho 505, Rio Vermelho,* ☎ *071/330–2233,* FAX *071/ 330–2200. 202 rooms. Restaurant, bar, pool, tennis court, health club, shops, business services, meeting rooms. AE, DC, MC, V.*

$$$$ 🏨 **Tropical Hotel da Bahia.** Owned by Varig Airlines and often included in package deals, this centrally located hotel is a bit tattered, but practical for those whose priority is Salvador's history and culture, not beach-combing (although there's a free beach shuttle). Some rooms overlook the square where Carnaval begins; the Concha Acústica do Teatro Castro Alves, site of many big musical shows, is within walking distance, and performers there often stay here. ⊠ *Praça Dois de Julho 2, Campo Grande,* ☎ *071/336–0102,* FAX *071/336–9725. 282 rooms, 10 suites. Restaurant, bar, coffee shop, 2 pools, massage, sauna, dance club. AE, DC, MC, V.*

$$$ 🏨 **Bahia Othon.** A short drive from most historic sights, nightlife, restaurants, and in-town beaches, this busy modern business and tourist hotel offers an ocean view from all rooms, whose ceramic-tile floors and wood furniture are a bit worn. Top local entertainers often perform at the hotel's outdoor park, and in high season, the staff organizes poolside activities as well as trips to better beaches. ⊠ *Av. Presidente Vargas 2456, Ondina,* ☎ *071/247–1044,* FAX *071/245–4877. 300 rooms, 25 suites. Restaurant, bar, coffee shop, pool, sauna, health club, dance club, concierge floor. AE, DC, MC, V.*

$$$ 🏨 **Caesar Towers.** This Caesar has comfortable apartments only 8 km (5 mi) from Centro and 15 km (10 mi) from the best beaches. It's close to Barra district restaurants and bars. ⊠ *Av. Oceânica 1545, Ondina,* ☎ *071/331–8200,* FAX *071/237–4668. 120 rooms. Restaurant, coffee shop, pool, sauna, health club, meeting rooms. AE, DC, MC, V.*

$$$ 🏨 **Catussaba Hotel.** Close to the airport and 40 km (25 mi) from the
★ city, this hotel opens directly onto a good swimming beach. All the comfortable, simple rooms have an ocean view, and there's a large, attractive pool area. ⊠ *Alameda Praia de Guarita 101, Alamedas da Praia, Itapuã,* ☎ *071/374–0555,* FAX *071/374–4749. 133 rooms. Restaurant, bar, pool, sauna, tennis court, health club, meeting room. AE, MC, V.*

$$$ ⊞ **Fiesta Bahia Hotel.** Though neither on the beach nor close to the historical center, this hotel is a great choice for business travelers. Located in the city's financial district and close to the convention center, the Fiesta offers rooms with direct phone lines, fax and PC terminals, and queen-size beds—amenities that distinguish it from its competitors. ⊠ *Av. Antônio Carlos Magalhães 711, Itaigara,* ☎ *071/352–0000,* FAX *071/352–0050. 239 rooms. Restaurant, bar, coffee shop, room service, 2 pools, health club, shops, nightclub, business services. AE, DC, MC, V.*

$$$ ⊞ **Hotel Sofitel Salvador.** Just beyond the city's northern perimeter, this resort and convention hotel near good beaches is a world unto itself, decorated with local art and oversize, old-fashioned farm implements. The green-and-blue-accented rooms all have a view of the spacious grounds and the ocean beyond. Amenities include a gallery, on-site boutiques, crafts demonstrations, and free minibus service to downtown. ⊠ *Rua da Pasárgada s/n, Farol de Itapuän,* ☎ *071/374–9611, 800/ 763–4835 in U.S.,* FAX *071/374–6946. 197 rooms, 9 suites. 2 restaurants, 3 bars, room service, 2 pools, beauty salon, massage, 9-hole golf course, 3 tennis courts, health club, boating, shops. AE, DC, MC, V.*

$$$ ⊞ **Ondina Apart-Hotel Residência.** In the resort hotel district, a short drive from the sights, nightlife, and restaurants, this apartment-hotel complex on the beach has simple, modern furniture and kitchenettes. Many businesspeople and families opt for this hotel when they're staying in Salvador for extended periods. ⊠ *Av. Presidente Vargas 2400, Ondina,* ☎ *071/203–8000,* FAX *071/203–8112. 100 apartments. Restaurant, bar, coffee shop, beauty salon, 2 tennis courts, health club, dance club. AE, DC, MC, V.*

$$ ⊞ **Grande Hotel da Barra.** Near the downtown beaches and convenient to the historic center, the Grande has comfortable, well-maintained rooms with such decorative touches as pink-and-green floral bedspreads, latticework screens, and lots of wood carvings. The front rooms have verandas. Though not all rooms have an ocean view, they do all have VCRs. ⊠ *Av. 7 de Setembro 3564, Porto da Barra,* ☎ *071/ 247–6506,* FAX *071/264–6011. 112 rooms, 5 suites. Restaurant, bar, pool, beauty salon, sauna. AE, DC, MC, V.*

$$ ⊞ **Hotel Bahia do Sol.** This hotel's low rates and prime location, close to museums and historic sights, may make up for its battered wooden furniture. Front rooms have a partial ocean view, but those in the back are quieter. ⊠ *Av. 7 de Setembro 2009, Vitória,* ☎ *071/336–7211,* FAX *071/336–7776. 86 rooms, 4 suites. Restaurant, bar, meeting rooms, free parking. AE, DC, MC, V.*

$$ ⊞ **Hotel Catharina Paraguaçu.** The sleeping areas at this intimate,
★ charming hotel—set in a 19th-century mansion—are small but comfortable, and include six split-level suites. It's family-run and in a neighborhood of good restaurants and bars. ⊠ *Rua João Gomes 128, Rio Vermelho,* ☎ FAX *071/247–1488. 23 rooms, 6 suites. Minibars. MC, V.*

$ ⊞ **Hotel Vila Romana.** On a quiet street minutes from the beach and not far from many upscale bars and cafés, this Bahian version of a Roman palazzo has seen better days. Still, it's favored by many Italian visitors, who don't seem to mind the rudimentary plumbing. Try for one of the back rooms, which are better ventilated. ⊠ *Rua Prof. Leme de Brito 14, Barra,* ☎ *071/336–6522,* FAX *071/247–6748. 60 rooms, 3 suites. Restaurant, bar, pool. AE, DC, MC, V.*

$ ⊞ **Pousada das Flores.** A great location (within walking distance of
★ Pelourinho), combined with simple elegance conspire to make this one of the city's best budget options. Rooms are large and have high ceilings, a stylish blue and white decor, and hardwood floors. For peace and quiet as well as a view of the ocean, opt for a room on an

upper floor. ⊠ *Rua Direita de Santo Antônio 442, Cidade Histórico,* ☎ FAX *071/243–1836. 6 rooms, 3 suites. AE, DC, MC, V.*

Nightlife and the Arts

Pelourinho has music every night and more bars and clubs than you can count. It's perfectly safe to walk around until late here, as practically every corner has at least one police officer. Activity also centers on the neighborhoods of Barra and Rio Vermelho, and both areas are near many hotels.

Salvador is considered by many artists as a laboratory for the creation of new rhythms and dance steps. As such this city has a lively—almost electric—performing arts scene. See the events calendar published by Bahiatursa or local newspapers for details on live music performances as well as the rehearsal schedules and locations of the *blocos* (Carnaval percussion bands). Gay and lesbian information is available from the **Grupo Gay da Bahia** (⊠ Rua do Sodré 45, ☎ 071/322–2552), which publishes an entertainment guide to Salvador's gay scene, *Guia para Gays,* that costs about $5.

Nightlife

BARS

Good bar bets include **Bambara** (⊠ Av. Otávio Mangabeira, Jardim de Alá, ☎ no phone), which sometimes has live music; **Bananas Beet** (⊠ Rua 3, Jardim Iracema, Patamares, ☎ 071/363–5656); and **Estação do Pelo** (⊠ Rua João de Deus 25, Pelourinho, ☎ no phone), which serves food as well as drink.

DANCE SHOWS

Shows at the **Moenda** (⊠ Jardim Armação, Rua P, Quadra 28, Lote 21, ☎ 071/231–7915 or 071/230–6786) begin daily at 8 PM. There are Afro-Brazilian dinner shows (the shows are much better than the dinners) at the **Solar do Unhão** (⊠ Av. do Contorno s/n, ☎ 071/321–5551), which opens Monday to Saturday at 8 PM. The Afro-Bahian show at the **Teatro Miguel Santana** (⊠ Rua Gregório de Mattos 47, ☎ 071/321–0222) in Pelourinho has the best folkloric dance troupes in town.

NIGHTCLUBS

Many of the best dance clubs are along the beaches of Amaralina and Pituba. Live bands play on stages to dance floors thronging with people all night long. Try **Kalamazoo** (⊠ Av. Otávio Mangabeira s/n, ☎ 071/363–5151), **Queops** (⊠ Hotel Sol Bahia Atlântico, Rua Manoel Antônio Galvão 100, ☎ 071/370–9000), or **Rock in Rio Café** (⊠ Av. Otávio Mangabeira 6000, Boca do Rio, ☎ 071/371–0979).

The Arts

CAPOEIRA REHEARSALS

Capoeira, the hypnotic African sport-cum-dance accompanied by the *berimbau* (a bow-shape musical instrument), can be seen Tuesday, Thursday, and Saturday evenings at 7 at the 17th-century Forte Santo Antônio Além do Carmo, just north of the Museu do Carmo in the Cidade Alta, a 5- to 10-minute taxi ride from downtown. Two schools practice here. The more traditional is the Grupo de Capoeira Angola. Weekday nights are classes; the real show happens on Saturday.

CARNAVAL REHEARSALS

Afro-Brazilian percussion groups begin rehearsals—which are really more like creative jam sessions—for Carnaval around mid-year. **Ilê Aiyê,** which started out as a Carnaval bloco, has turned itself into much more in its 25-year history and now has its own school, promotes the study and practice of African heritage, religion, and history and is involved

---

Close-Up

CAPOEIRA: THE FIGHT DANCE

THE SPORT OF *CAPOEIRA*—dance and martial arts all in one—
is purely Brazilian. The early days of slavery often saw fights
between Africans from rival tribes who were thrust together on
one plantation. When an owner caught slaves fighting, both
sides were punished. To create a smoke screen, the Africans incorporated music and song into the fights. They brought a traditional *berimbau* "string-drum" instrument (a bow-shape piece of wood with a metal
wire running from one end to the other, where there's a hollow gourd
containing seeds) to the battles. Its mesmerizing reverberations were
accompanied by singing and chanting, and when the master appeared,
the fighters punched only the air and kicked so as to miss their op-
ponent.

The fights have been refined into a sport that was once practiced primarily in Bahia and Pernambuco but has now spread throughout Brazil.
Today's practitioners swing and kick—keeping their movements tightly
controlled—to the mood and beat of the berimbau without touching
their opponents. (Tapped with a stick or a coin, the berimbau's taut
wire produces a throbbing, twanging sound, whose rhythm is enhanced
by the rattling seeds.) The back-bending all the way to the floor, the
agile foot movements (to avoid an imaginary knife), and the compelling
music make capoeira a fascinating sport to watch.

---

with many social issues. The work this bloco is undertaking in the name
of Afro-Brazilian pride and prosperity is both vast and inspirational.
Practices are held every Saturday night at Fort St. Antônio and should
not be missed. Olodum, Salvador's most commercial percussion group,
has its own venue, the **Casa do Olodum** (⊠ Rua Gregório de Matos
22, Pelourinho, ☎ 071/321–5010).

MUSIC, THEATER, AND DANCE VENUES
Casa do Comércio (⊠ Av. Tancredo Neves 1109, ☎ 071/371–8700)
hosts music performances and some theatrical productions. All kinds
of musicians play at the **Concha Acústica do Teatro Castro Alves** (⊠
Ladeira da Fonte s/n, ☎ 071/247–6414), a band shell. The **Teatro ACBEU**
(⊠ Av. 7 de Setembro 1883, ☎ 071/247–4395 and 071/336–4411) hosts
contemporary and classic music, dance, and theater performances by
both Brazilian and international talent. **Teatro Castro Alves** (⊠ Ladeira
da Fonte s/n, ☎ 071/247–6414) is a top venue for theater, music, and
dance. Small theater groups perform at the German-Brazilian Cultural
Institute's **Teatro ICBA** (⊠ Av. 7 de Setembro 1809, ☎ 071/237–0120),
which also screens German films. You can see theatrical, ballet, and
musical performances at the **Teatro Iemanjá** (⊠ Jardim Armacão s/n,
Centro de Convenções).

Outdoor Activities and Sports

Participant Sports
BICYCLING AND RUNNING
For bicycling and running, the best places are **Dique do Tororó** (⊠ En-
trances at Av. Presidente Costa e Silva and Av. Vasco da Gama, Tororó),

a park round a lake; **Jardim dos Namorados** (⊠ Av. Otavio Mangabeira, Pituba), a park where you'll find places to rent bikes; there are also volleyball courts and soccer fields; **Parque Metropolitano de Pituaçu** (⊠ Facing Praia do Corsário, Pituaçu); and **Parque Jardim de Alá** (⊠ between Pituba and Boca do Rio, Costa Azul).

GOLF AND TENNIS
Cajazeira Golfe & Country Club (⊠ Av. Genaro Carvalho s/n, Castelo Branco, ☎ 071/246–8007) is an option for golf. **Hotel Sofitel Salvador** (⊠ Rua Passárgada s/n, Farol de Itapoã, ☎ 071/374–9611) offers day passes to its golf course and its tennis courts.

SURFING, WINDSURFING, AND SAILING
For surfing, windsurfing, and sailing, contact **Iate Clube da Bahia** (⊠ Av. 7 de Setembro, Barra, ☎ 071/336–9011 or 071/336–9693).

WATER PARK
Wet'n Wild Bahia (⊠ Av. Luiz Viana s/n, also known as Av. Paralela, ☎ 071/367–7000), 22 km (14 mi) north of Salvador, has a wave pool and water slides and chutes. Admission is roughly $20 for a whole day; it's open daily 10–5 in summer (Mar.–Sept.).

Spectator Sport
FUTEBOL
Bahia and Vitória are the two best local teams, and they play year-round (except at Christmastime) Wednesday night and Sunday at 5 PM at the **Estádio da Fonte Nova** (⊠ Av. Vale do Nazaré, Dique do Tororó, ☎ 071/243–3322, ext. 237). Tickets are sold at the stadium a day in advance. Avoid sitting behind the goals, where the roughhousing is worst. The best seats are in the *arquibancada superior* (high bleachers).

Shopping

Local art and such handicrafts as lace, hammocks, wood carvings, and percussion instruments are good buys in the city.

Areas
The city's most traditional shopping area, for a variety of everyday goods at lower prices than in the malls, is **Avenida 7 de Setembro.** For paintings, especially art naïf, visit the many galleries in the Cidade Alta in and around the **Largo do Pelourinho.** For local handicrafts, the **Mercado Modelo** is your best bet.

Centers and Malls
Two big shopping malls have cinemas; restaurants; boutiques that sell locally manufactured clothing; and franchise outlets or branch stores of Rio, São Paulo, and Minas Gerais retailers. **Shopping Center Iguatemi** (⊠ Av. Antônio Carlos Magalhães 148), the older and more traditional of the two malls, is near the bus station. **Shopping Barra** (⊠ Av. Centenário 2992), in the Barra neighborhood back from the beach, is newer and glitzier. The top hotels provide free transportation to it.

Specialty Stores
ART
Top local artists (many of whom use only first names or nicknames) include Totonho, Calixto, Raimundo Santos, Joailton, Nadinho, Nonato, Maria Adair, Carybé, Mário Cravo, and Jota Cunha. **Atelier Portal da Cor** (⊠ Ladeira do Carmo 31, Pelourinho, ☎ 071/242–9466) is run by a cooperative of local artists.

HANDICRAFTS
The **Casa Santa Barbara** (⊠ Rua Alfredo de Brito, ☎ 071/244–0458) sells Bahian clothing and lacework of top quality, albeit at prices

slightly higher than elsewhere. Note that it's closed Saturday afternoon and Sunday. **Kembo** (✉ Rua João de Deus 21, ☎ 071/322–1379), a shop in Pelourinho, carries handicrafts from many different Brazilian Indian tribes. The owners travel to reservations all over the country and buy from the Pataxós, Kiriri, Tupí, Karajá, Xingú, Waiwai, Tikuna, Caipós, and Yanomami among others.

Salvador has several state-run handicrafts stores, with lower prices and smaller selections. One of the best is the **Instituto Mauá** (✉ Praça Azevedo Fernandes 2, ☎ 071/235–5440). **Artesanato Fieb-Sesi** (✉ Rua Borges dos Reis 9, ☎ 071/245–3543) also carries woven and lace goods, musical instruments, sandals, and pottery.

JEWELRY AND GEMSTONES

Salvador has a branch (actually there are several, most of them in malls and major hotels) of the well-known, reputable **H. Stern** (✉ Largo do Pelourinho, ☎ 071/322–7353) chain. At **Simon** (✉ Rua Ignácio Accioli, ☎ 071/242–5218) the city's most famous jewelers, you can peer through a window into the room where goldsmiths work.

Side Trips from Salvador

Praia do Forte
80 km (50 mi) north of Salvador.

This small fishing village takes its name from the castle built here in 1556 by a Portuguese settler. It's now a tranquil resort where the preservation of flora and fauna takes precedence. Praia de Arembebe, 40 km (25 mi) north of Praia do Forte, is the site of the **Projeto Tamar** (☎ 071/824–1193), an ecological project set up to protect the giant sea turtles that emerge at night from September to March to lay their eggs along Brazil's northeastern coastline. Visitors are welcome.

The 1,500-acre **Reserva Sapiranga,** which preserves a remnant of the forest that once lined most of the Brazilian coast, has a great diversity of flora and fauna (including monkeys that will eat from your hands). Other attractions include the ruins of the Portuguese Garcia D'Avila family's stone castle and chapel, dating from 1600; a fishing village full of great snack bars and restaurants; the Pojuca River falls and rapids; and the Timeantube Lake, with many bird species. The best way to visit the area is on a Jeep tour.

LODGING

$$$$ ⊞ **Praia do Forte Resort Hotel.** This beachfront complex is not only a complete resort but is also right next door to part of the Tamar sea-turtle preservation project. Public areas are decorated in deluxe Robinson Crusoe style using natural materials; rooms are like hideaways with verandas, hammocks, and ceiling fans. Activities include kayaking, sailing, and bird-watching. Room rates include breakfast and dinner. (Note: some travelers have reported that the allure of this resort has diminished.) ✉ *Rua do Farol s/n, Praia do Forte, Mata de São João,* ☎ *071/876–1111,* ᴾᴬˣ *071/876–1112. 210 rooms. 2 restaurants, 3 bars, 4 pools, 2 tennis courts, health club, snorkeling, windsurfing, boating, dance club, children's programs. AE, DC, MC, V.*

Cachoeira
121 km (70 mi) west of Salvador.

This riverside Portuguese colonial town is the site of some of Brazil's most authentic Afro-Brazilian rituals and festivals. Every August 14–16, the **Irmandade da Boa Morte** (Sisterhood of the Good Death, once a slave women's secret society) holds a half-Candomblé, half-Catholic festival honoring the spirits of the dead. It features a solemn procession and a spinning samba street dance.

However, an excursion to Cachoeira is worthwhile any time of the year. You can walk through the colorful country market, see architecture preserved from an age when Cachoeira shipped tons of tobacco and sugar downriver to Salvador, and visit the sisterhood's **small museum** (✉ Largo D'Ajuda s/n, ☎ 075/725–1343) to meet these elderly but energetic women. It's recommended that you make a small donation; hours are weekdays 10–1 and 3–5.

DINING AND LODGING

$–$$ ✕⌷ **Pousada Convento.** You can stay overnight or have lunch at this former Carmelite monastery. It dates from the 17th-century. ✉ *Praça da Aclamação s/n,* ☎ FAX *075/725–1716. 26 rooms. Restaurant, air-conditioning, minibars, pool, playground, meeting rooms, free parking. AE, MC, V.*

RECIFE

The most violent battles between the Dutch and the Portuguese took place in the captaincy of Pernambuco. Under the Portuguese, the capital city had been Olinda; but, beginning in 1637 and through the Dutch turn at the reigns (under the powerful count Maurício de Nassau) both Olinda and Recife were greatly developed. The Dutch had hoped that Brazilian sugar planters wouldn't resist their rule, but many took up arms. In 1654, after a series of battles around Recife, the Dutch finally surrendered. In the 17th century, Pernambuco maintained much of the affluence of the earlier sugar age by also cultivating cotton. With several rivers and offshore reefs, Recife proved to be an excellent port and began to outgrow Olinda.

Today 1.4 million people call Recife, the capital of Pernambuco state, home. It's a vibrant metropolis whose spirit is halfway between the modern cities of the south and the traditional northeastern centers; a combination of old and new makes it an example of the past and a window on the future. Known as the Venice of Brazil because it's built on three rivers and connected by a host of bridges, Recife got its name from the *arrecifes* (reefs) that line the coast. In the mornings, when the tide is in along the city's most popular beach, Boa Viagem, the water comes up almost to the road. As the tide recedes, the rocks of the reefs slowly reappear; pools of water are formed, fish flap around beach-goers, and the rock formations dry into odd colors in the afternoon sun.

Exploring Recife

Recife is large and somewhat hard to negotiate. The Centro (city center)—with its mixture of high-rises, colonial churches, and markets—is always busy during the day. The crowds and the narrow streets, especially in the Santo Antônio district, can make finding your way around even more confusing.

Centro consists of three areas: Recife Velho (Old Recife); Recife proper, with the districts of Santo Antônio and São José; and the districts of Boa Vista and Santo Amaro. The first two areas are on islands formed by the Rivers Capibaribe, Beberibe, and Pina; the third is made into an island by the Canal Tacaruna. All the islands are connected by bridges.

Six kilometers (4 miles) south of Centro is the upscale residential and beach district of Boa Viagem, reached by bridge across the Bacia do Pina. Praia da Boa Viagem (Boa Viagem Beach), the Copacabana of

AFRO-BRAZILIAN HERITAGE

THERE ARE FEW OTHER COUNTRIES with such a symphony of skin tones grouped under one nationality. This rich Brazilian identity began when the first Portuguese sailors were left to manage the new land. From the beginning, Portuguese migration to Brazil was predominantly male, a fact that unfortunately led to unbridled sexual license—ranging from seduction to rape—involving Indian women and, later, African women.

The first Africans arrived in 1532, along with the Portuguese colonizers, who continued to buy slaves from English, Spanish, and Portuguese traders until 1855. All records pertaining to slave trading were destroyed in 1890, making it impossible to know exactly how many people were brought to Brazil. Still it's estimated that 3–4.5 million Africans were captured and transported from the Sudan, Gambia, Guinea, Sierra Leone, Senegal, Liberia, Nigeria, Benin, Angola, and Mozambique. Many were literate Muslims who were better educated than their white overseers and owners.

In Brazil, miscegenation and cohabitation between white men and women of other races was practiced openly. In the great houses of sugar plantations, which relied on slave labor, it was common for the master to have a white wife and slave mistresses. A master might free the mother of his mixed-race offspring and allow a son of color to learn a trade or inherit a share of the plantation. The legendary Xica da Silva—a slave concubine elevated to mistress of the manor by her wealthy master (and then consigned to oblivion and abandonment when he was

ordered back to Portugal)—vividly demonstrates the nexus of Brazilian sexual and racial politics.

When the sugar boom came to an end, it became too expensive for slave owners to support their "free" labor force. Abolition occurred gradually, however. It began around 1871, with the passage of the Law of the Free Womb, which liberated all Brazilians born of slave mothers. In 1885, another law was passed freeing slaves over age 60. Finally, on May 13, 1888, Princess Isabel signed a law freeing all slaves.

Often unskilled, the former slaves became Brazil's unemployed and underprivileged. Although the country has long been praised for its lack of discrimination, this veneer of racial equality is deceptive. Afro-Brazilians still don't receive education on par with that of whites nor are they always paid equally for equal work. There are far fewer black or mulatto professionals, politicians, and ranking military officers than white ones. Although a civil rights movement like that of the United States is unlikely, subtle activism to bring about racial equality and educate all races about the rich African legacy continues. For many people, the most important holiday isn't September 7 (Brazilian Independence Day) but rather November 20 (National Black Consciousness Day). It honors the anniversary of the death of Zumbi, the leader of the famous *quilombo* (community of escaped slaves) of Palmares, which lasted more than 100 years and was destroyed by *bandeirantes* (adventurers who tracked runaway slaves) in one final great battle for freedom.

Recife, is chockablock with trendy nightclubs and restaurants as well as most of the city's moderately priced and expensive hotels.

Numbers in the text correspond to numbers in the margin and on the Recife map.

A Good Tour

Begin at the **Fortaleza do Brum** ①. After viewing the fort, follow Rua do Brum south to Praça Tiradentes where it becomes Rua do Apolo. The streets between Apolo and Rua do Bom Jesus form the heart of **Recife Velho** ②. After wandering through Old Recife, and stopping at a café for a break, hop a cab for the short ride to **Praça da República** ③ in the Santo Antônio district. From the square, you can either take another cab to the **Museu de Arte Moderna Aloísio Magalhães**—across the Rio Capibaribe in the Boa Vista district—or follow Rua do Imperador to the **Igreja da Ordem Terceira de São Francisco** ④.

From the church continue along Rua do Imperador and turn right; walk one block to Rua Duque de Caxias and the **Igreja do Santíssimo Sacramento** ⑤ (also called Igreja de Santo Antônio or Matriz de Santo Antonio) in the Praça da Independência. West of the square, follow Avenida Dantas Barreto south for two blocks; turn left onto Avenida Nossa Senhora do Carmo and follow it to the **Igreja e Convento do Carmo** ⑥. From here, take Rua Direita south to Rua Tobias Barreto and turn right; follow Tobias Barreto (it becomes Travessa do Mecedo) to the Praça Dom Vital and the **Mercado de São José** ⑦. After browsing in the market, return to Travessa do Macedo/Tobias Barreto and follow it back to Avenida Dantas Barreto and the **Catedral de São Pedro dos Clérigos** ⑧. From the cathedral, follow Dantas Barreto south. Turn left onto Rua Passo da Pátria, right onto Rua Vidal de Negreiros, and left onto Rua de São João and the **Forte das Cinco Pontas** ⑨ in the São José district. If you have any energy left after the tour, consider taking a taxi to the **Museu do Homem do Nordeste.**

TIMING AND PRECAUTIONS

The tour takes five to six hours, longer if you linger at a café or a sight or if you head to an out-of-the-way museum. Unfortunately, theft is common in the streets of Recife. Be on guard against pickpockets, keep a tight hold on purses and cameras, and leave jewelry in the hotel safe.

SIGHTS TO SEE

❽ **Catedral de São Pedro dos Clérigos.** The facade of this cathedral, which was built in 1782, has fine wood sculptures; inside is a splendid trompe-l'oeil ceiling. The square surrounding the cathedral is a hangout for artists who often read their poetry or perform folk music. It's lined with many restaurants, shops, and bars; you'll also find a museum containing exhibits on Carnaval and an art gallery. ✉ *Pátio de São Pedro, São José,* ☎ *081/224–2954.* 🎟 *Free.* ☉ *Tues.–Sat. 9–5.*

❶ **Fortaleza do Brum.** To safeguard their control, the Dutch wisely, yet futilely, built more than one fortress. In this one (circa 1629) you'll find reminders of those precarious days in the on-site **Army Museum,** with its collection of old cannons, infantry weapons, and soldiers' utensils; there's even a skeleton of a soldier that dates from 1654. On a lighter note, the fort also contains a restaurant. ✉ *Praça Luso-Brasileiro, Recife Velho,* ☎ *081/224–4620.* 🎟 *Free.* ☉ *Tues.–Fri. 9–4, weekends 2–4.*

❾ **Forte das Cinco Pontas.** The Dutch built this fortress in 1630 (it was then rebuilt in 1677). Inside is the **Museu da Cidade,** where maps and photos illustrate the history of Recife. ✉ *Largo das Cinco Pontas, São José,* ☎ *081/224–8492.* 🎟 *Free.* ☉ *Weekdays 9–6, weekends 1–5.*

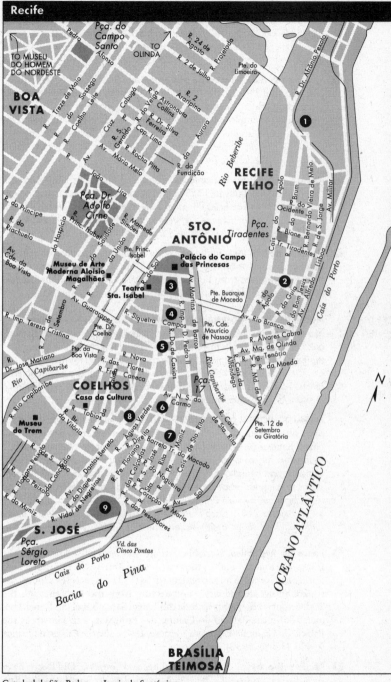

⑥ **Igreja e Convento do Carmo.** This church and convent are constructed of wood and white gold. ⊠ *Praça do Carmo s/n, Santo Antônio,* ☎ *081/224–3341.* 🎟 *Free.* ⊙ *Weekdays 6:30–8 (mass at 6:30 AM, 6 PM, and 7 PM); Sat. 7–8 (mass at 7 AM); Sun. 10–8:30 (mass at 10 AM and 7 PM).*

④ **Igreja da Ordem Terceira de São Francisco.** Built in 1606, this church has beautiful Portuguese tilework. Don't miss the adjoining **Capela Dourada** (Golden Chapel), which was constructed in 1697 and is an outstanding example of Brazilian baroque architecture. The church complex also contains a convent, the **Convento Franciscano de Santo Antônio.** ⊠ *Rua do Imperador 206, Santo Antônio,* ☎ *081/224–0530.* 🎟 *Free.* ⊙ *Weekdays 7–6 (mass at 7).*

⑤ **Igreja do Santíssimo Sacramento.** Also called Matriz de Santo Antônio, this church was built in 1753 in the baroque and neoclassical styles. It was rebuilt in 1864. ⊠ *Praça da Independência s/n, Santo Antônio,* ☎ *081/224–5076.* 🎟 *Free.* ⊙ *Weekdays 7–7 (mass at 7 AM and 6 PM), Sat. 7–7 (mass at 6 PM), Sun. 9–8 (mass at 9 AM and 7 PM).*

⑦ **Mercado de São José.** In the city's most traditional market vendors sell handicrafts and food. It's housed in a beautiful cast-iron structure that was imported from France in the 19th century. ⊠ *Trv. do Macedo s/n, São José.* ⊙ *Mon.–Sat. 6–6, Sun. 6–noon.*

OFF THE
BEATEN PATH

MUSEU DE ARTE MODERNA ALOÍSIO MAGALHÃES – The Aloísio Magalhães Modern Art Museum has a good collection of paintings by Pernambuco artists. Each of its three exhibit halls contains art from a different region or phase; one room, for example, is dedicated to avant-garde art. The museum also hosts changing exhibits of works by international artists. ⊠ *Rua da Aurora 265, Boa Vista,* ☎ *081/423–2761.* 🎟 *Admission.* ⊙ *Tues.–Sun. noon–6.*

MUSEU DO HOMEM DO NORDESTE – With three museums—one with displays about sugar, one with anthropological exhibits, and one with regional handicrafts—under one roof, the Museum of the Northeastern Man offers great insight into Brazil's history. You'll find everything from utensils made by indigenous peoples, European colonizers, and African slaves to religious articles used in Catholic and Candomblé rituals to ceramic figurines by such artists as Mestre Vitalino and Mestre Zé. ⊠ *Av. 17 de Agosto 2187, Casa Forte,* ☎ *081/441–5500.* 🎟 *Free.* ⊙ *Tues. and Fri. 11–6, Thurs. 8–6, weekends 1–6.*

③ **Praça da República.** Republic Square was originally known as the Camp of Honor, a nod to those who were drawn and quartered here during the Republican movement of 1817. The structures around the square showcase the city's architecture from the 19th through the 20th century. Highlights include the **Teatro Santa Isabel** (St. Isabel Theater, 1850); the **Palácio do Campo das Princesas,** also known as the Palácio do Governo (Governor's House, 1841); and the **Palácio da Justiça** (Court House, 1930).

② **Recife Velho.** Many of the old buildings and houses of Old Recife have recently been restored. The area between Rua do Bom Jesus and Rua do Apolo is full of shops, cafés, restaurants, and bars, making it the hub of downtown life both day and night.

Beaches

The 8-km-long (5-mi-long) **Praia da Boa Viagem** is often crowded but is always beautiful. Its warm, calm, aquamarine waters form small pools near reefs. Abundant coconut trees and rows of beached jangadas add still more charm. The main beachfront drag, Avenida Boa Viagem, is lined with elegant apartment buildings, the best hotels, and a wide *calçadão* (sidewalk)—the perfect place to bike, run, or simply promenade. Although Boa Viagem is one long sandy stretch, it has several sections: its northern area is called Pina because of its proximity to the Pina district; its southern areas are called Piedade and Candeias, after two nearby districts that are actually part of the neighboring town of Jaboatão dos Guararapes. Note that the waters around Pina are polluted and aren't good for swimming. Other areas are dangerous because of sharks, which come close to the shore, particularly in January.

About 30 km (19 mi) south of Recife, quiet, beautiful **Gaibu** is surrounded by palm trees. Its blue waters are good for surfing, and it's also the site of volleyball competitions and fishing and sailing events. Just 5 km (3 mi) east of Gaibu is **Cabo de Santo Agostinho,** one of the Pernambuco's finest beaches. It's good for swimming and diving, although surfing has been banned owing to the danger of shark attacks. In the town of Cabo de Santo Agostinho you can walk around the ruins of the Forte Castelo do Mar, which is next to the church.

You'll find cool, clean waves at **Porto de Galinhas,** 70 km (43 mi) south of Recife. The beach, which follows the curve of a pretty bay lined with coconut-palm and cashew trees, gets very crowded on weekends, even in the off season. There are plenty of jangadas for rent; other boats can take you to the island of Santo Aleixo. Three kilometers (two miles) southwest of Porto de Galinhas is the more secluded **Maracaípe,** where surfing championships take place.

Although **Tamandaré,** 110 km (68 mi) south of Recife, is in the middle of an important nature reserve, development plans are in the works. Come quick, before its beaches—such as Praia dos Carneiros and Praia de Guadalupe—become one big resort area.

Ilha de Itamaracá. This island is off the coast of the historic city of Igarassu, 39 km (24 mi) north of Recife. Surrounded by canals, the ocean, and mangrove swamps, it's ideal for boat, catamaran, and canoe rides. The best beach is Forte Orange, next to Coroa do Avião.

Dining

Brazilian

$$ ✕ O Buraco de Otília. One of the city's most traditional restaurants has been in business for 40 years. The menu offers regional fish and meat dishes. ✉ *Rua da Aurora 1231, Santo Amaro,* ☎ *081/231–1528. DC, MC, V.*

$$ ✕ Da Mira. The owner has transformed three rooms of his house into this restaurant. In addition to a pleasant, homey atmosphere, you'll also find delicious regional dishes. ✉ *Av. Dr. Eurico Chaves 916, Casa Amarela,* ☎ *081/268–6241. No credit cards.*

Eclectic

$$ ✕ Leite. Established in 1882, Leite is one of Brazil's oldest restaurants. Some of the tables are filled by the same people each day, and several waiters are following in the footsteps of generations of family members who worked here before them. Recent restorations added the coolness of air-conditioning to the already pleasant ambience. ✉ *Praça Joaquim Nabuco 147, Santo Antônio,* ☎ *081/224–7977. AE, DC, MC, V.*

Italian

$$ ✕ Barbarico Bongiovani. This restaurant offers a sophisticated setting and a high-quality Italian menu. ✉ *Av. Engenheiro Domingos Ferreira 2655, Boa Viagem,* ☎ *081/325–4268. AE, DC, MC, V.*

Seafood

$$$ ✕ **Bargaço.** People come to this pleasant restaurant for the moquecas *pernambucanas* (Pernambuco style). ☒ *Av. Boa Viagem 670, Pina,* ☎ *081/465–1847. AE, DC, MC, V.*

$$ ✕ **Biruta.** The fresh seafood and regional preparations make the dishes here winners. Your choices range from steamed shrimp to paella. Meat and pasta dishes are also options. ☒ *Rua Bem-te-vi 15, Pina,* ☎ *081/ 325–5321. AE, DC, MC, V.*

Lodging

Recife's best hotels are in Boa Viagem, just 15 minutes south of the city center and close to the airport. There are very few good places to stay downtown.

$$$$ ▥ **Sheraton Recife.** At the sophisticated Sheraton, each floor has two rooms that directly face the sea; the rest have a lateral sea view. The two business floors have computers, fax/modem lines, and secretarial assistance. One restaurant serves French food, the other regional cuisine; both are excellent and have panoramic views. ☒ *Av. Bernardo Vieira de Melo 1624, Piedade, Jaboatão dos Guararapes,* ☎ *081/468– 1288,* FAX *081/468–1118. 275 rooms. 2 restaurants, bar, pool, sauna, tennis court, business services, meeting rooms. AE, DC, MC, V.*

$$$ ▥ **Mar Hotel Recife.** Location is one of this hotel's main draws: it's a five-minute drive from the airport, a 15-minute drive from Recife Velho, and is also very close to Praia Boa Viagem. Rooms have desks with swivel chairs, two phone lines, and fax/modem lines. When you're ready to call it a day, you can relax by the pool—with its soothing waterfall—or feast on international, Italian, or Japanese cuisine at one of the three on-site restaurants. Afterward, you can retire to the bar for drinks or maybe a little dancing on the small dance floor. ☒ *Rua Barão de Souza Leão 451, Boa Viagem, Recife, 51030-300,* ☎ *081/ 462–4446,* FAX *081/462–4444. 207 rooms. 3 restaurants, bar, pool, sauna, exercise room, meeting rooms. AE, DC, MC, V.*

$$$ ▥ **Parthenon Golden Beach.** At one of the best flat hotels in town, each unit has one or two bedrooms, a living room, and a fully equipped kitchen. ☒ *Av. Bernardo Vieira de Melo 1204, Piedade, Jaboatão dos Guararapes,* ☎ *081/468–3002,* FAX *081/468–1941. 175 apartments. 2 restaurants, 2 bars, air-conditioning, kitchenettes, pool, sauna, exercise room. AE, DC.*

$$ ▥ **Hotel do Sol.** This hotel faces the beach in Boa Viagem. Each unit has a TV and a phone. ☒ *Av. Boa Viagem 978, Pina, Recife,* ☎ *081/ 465–9898,* FAX *081/465–5278. 69 rooms. Bar, air-conditioning, pool. DC, MC, V.*

$$ ▥ **Navegantes Praia Hotel.** A stay at this small, affordable hotel puts you a block from the beach. Each room has a phone and a TV. ☒ *Rua dos Navegantes 1997, Boa Viagem, Recife 51020-011,* ☎ *081/326– 9609,* FAX *081/325–2689. 25 rooms. Air-conditioning, pool. AE.*

$$ ▥ **Recife Plaza.** Overlooking the Rio Capibaribe, this modern downtown hotel is simple and functional. Rooms have TVs and phones. ☒ *Rua da Aurora 225, Boa Vista, Recife 50060-000,* ☎ FAX *081/231–1200. 68 rooms. Restaurant, air-conditioning, minibars, pool, sauna. AE, DC, MC, V.*

Nightlife and the Arts

Nightlife

Pólo Pina, the calçadão in the Pina district, is a popular night spot near the beach. In the streets off Rua Herculano Bandeira, you'll find close to two dozen bars and restaurants. Between Rua do Apolo and Rua do Bom Jesus (or Rua dos Judeus) in Recife Velho, people gather in a seemingly endless variety of bars, cafés, and nightclubs. On Saturday, the market in Praça de Boa Viagem comes alive with dancers moving to *forró*, the traditional music of Pernambuco.

BARS

At **Arsenal do Chopp** (✉ Praça Arthur Oscar at Rua do Bom Jesus, Recife Velho, ☎ 081/224–6259) you can sit inside or watch the world go by from a comfortable chair at one of the tables along the sidewalk. The trendy **Depois do Escuro** (✉ Av. Rio Branco 66, Recife Velho, ☎ 081/424–7451) is in an old building at the heart of a bohemian neighborhood. A lively crowd frolics to older tunes at the well-decorated **Espaço Antônio Maria** (✉ Rua do Bom Jesus 63, Recife Velho, ☎ 081/224–6132).

CYBERCAFÉS

To enter cyberspace, head for the **Cyber Café do Shopping Guararapes** (✉ Av. Barreto de Menezes 800, Piedade, Jaboatão dos Guararapes, ☎ 081/464–2488), or **Recife Internet Café** (✉ Av. Barreto de Menezes 800, Loja 128, Piedade, ☎ 081/464–2107).

DANCE AND MUSIC CLUBS

The **Calypso Bar** (✉ Rua do Bom Jesus 147, Recife Velho, ☎ 081/224–4855) is *the* place to dance to live music in Recife Velho. You can fortify yourself with appetizers, including seafood, as well as drinks. To dance to forró head for **Catedral da Seresta** (✉ Rua Real da Torre 1435, Bairro Torre, ☎ 081/228–0567). You'll find Latin music and Mexican appetizers at **El Paso** (✉ Rua do Bom Jesus 237, Recife Velho, ☎ 081/224–7804). The **Gafieira Clube das Pás** (✉ Rua Odorico Mendes 263, Campo Grande, ☎ 081/241–0751), founded in 1887, is a good place to dance to *gafieira*, another type of traditional Pernambuco music. **Maria Bonita** (✉ Rua Jack Ayres s/n, Boa Viagem, ☎ 081/325–5402) is a forró hot spot.

GAY AND LESBIAN BARS

Galeria Joana D'Arc (✉ Rua Herculano Bandeira 500, Pina) is a cluster of small bars and snack bars, among them Café Poire, Anjo Solto, Barnabé, and Oriente Médio.

The Arts

GALLERY

The **Oficina Cerâmica Francisco Brennand** (✉ Engenho Santos Cosme e Damião s/n, Várzea, ☎ 081/271–2466) is the workshop and gallery (with exhibits of more than 2,000 pieces) of Francisco Brennand, one of Brazil's most important sculptors. Brennand, who is also known for his painting and pottery, studied in France and was influenced by Pablo Picasso and Joan Miró, among others. The building is set in thickly forested surroundings, a rare landscape for suburban Recife, and the gallery exhibits are open weekdays.

THEATERS

Recife's biggest theater, the **Teatro da Universidade Federal de Pernambuco** (✉ Av. dos Reitores s/n, Cidade Universitária, ☎ 081/222–1200), has almost 2,000 seats and a splendid architectural design. It's known for its performances of contemporary works. The city's more traditional theaters include **Teatro Santa Isabel** (✉ Praça da República s/n, Santo Antônio, ☎ 081/224–1020), which was built in 1850; the **Teatro do Parque** (✉ Rua do Hospício 81, Boa Vista, ☎ 081/423–6044), which has been beautifully restored; and **Teatro Apolo** (✉ Rua do Apolo 121, Recife Velho, ☎ 081/224–1114).

Outdoor Activities and Sports

Participant Sports

SAILING

You can arrange sailing and/or fishing trips on jangadas with fishermen at Boa Viagem. Boating and sailing trips are also available through the **Cabanga Iate Clube** (⊠ Av. Engenheiro José Estelita s/n, Pina, ☎ 081/428–4277) and **Forte Náutica** (⊠ Rua Cais de Santa Rita 645, Santo Antônio, ☎ 081/424–4664 or 081/224–1614).

SCUBA DIVING

There are some 20 wrecks, including those of Portuguese galleons, off Recife's shores, and the waters are rich in marine life. Though diving is practiced year round, visibility is best between October and May when the wind and water are at their calmest. Several reputable dive operators offer instruction and guided dives and rent equipment. Try **Expedição Atlântico** (⊠ Rua Comendador Bento Aguiar 520/101, ☎ 081/227–0458 or 081/424–4664), or **Taverna do Mar** (⊠ Av. Beira Mar 1200, Piedade, Jaboatão dos Guararapes, ☎ 081/341–1097).

Spectator Sport

FUTEBOL

Recife's main *futebol* (soccer) teams are Sport Clube do Recife, Náutico Sport Clube, and the very popular Santa Cruz Sport Clube. Matches take place at one of the city's three stadiums: **Estádio da Ilha do Retiro** (⊠ Praça da Bandeira, Ilha do Retiro, ☎ 081/227–1213), **Estádio dos Aflitos** (⊠ Av. Cons. Rosa e Sliva 1086, Aflitos, ☎ 081/423–8900), and **Estádio do Arruda** (⊠ Av. Beberibe 1285, Arruda, ☎ 081/258–1811).

Shopping

Vendors in the **Mercado de São José** (⊠ Trv. do Macedo, São José) sell clothes and regional handicrafts as well as fish, meat, and other foodstuffs. It's closed Sunday afternoon. The **Feira Hippie** (Hippie Fair) held in the seafront Praça Boa Viagem on Saturday and Sunday afternoons starting at 4, also sells local handicrafts.

The enormous **Shopping Center Recife** (⊠ Rua Padre Carapuceiro 777, Boa Viagem, ☎ 081/464–6000) has a good variety of Brazilian and international shops. **Shopping Center Boa Viagem** (Av. Presidente Dutra 298, Imbiribeira, 081/472–7201) and **Shopping Guararapes** (⊠ Av. Barreto de Menezes 800, Piedade, Jaboatão dos Guararapes, ☎ 081/464–2211) are other options.

The **Casa da Cultura** (⊠ Rua Floriano Peixoto s/n, Santo Antônio, ☎ 081/224–2850) is set in a 19th-century building that was once a prison. The old cells, with their heavy iron doors, have been transformed into shops that, every day but Sunday, sell clay figurines, wood sculptures, carpets, leather goods, and articles made from woven straw. One of the cells has been maintained to give you an idea of how the prisoners lived. There are also areas for exhibitions and shows, such as the Monday, Wednesday, and Friday performances of local dances like the *ciranda*, the forró, and the *bumba-meu-boi*.

Side Trips from Recife

Olinda

7 km (4 mi) north from Recife.

Once the capital of Pernambuco and today a suburb of Recife, Olinda is a stunning slice of the old northeast. The city was founded by the Portuguese in 1535 and was developed further by the Dutch during their brief turn at running Pernambuco in the 1600s. The narrow, winding streets of this UNESCO World Cultural Site snake up and down hills that, at every turn, offer views of the Atlantic and Recife. The scene is just as picturesque up close: Many of the houses have latticed balconies, heavy doors, and pink-stucco walls evocative of the colonial era. The zoning laws are strict, resulting in a beautiful, compact city where the white, pink, and red of the homes and tile roofs stand against the rich green of the hills and the blue of the ocean.

Give yourself plenty of time to explore Olinda on foot. To deter potential thieves, it's best to take a guided tour. Official guides (look for those with ID cards) congregate in the Praça do Carmo. They're former street children, and half the fee (about $20) for a full city tour goes to a home for street children. The highlights include the **Igreja do Carmo** (1653–54) and its neighboring Convento de Santo Antônio do Carmo, the oldest Carmelite building in Brazil; the **Semináio de Olinda,** an old Jesuit seminary; the **Museu de Arte Sacreda,** a museum full of religious relics; and the **Mosteiro de São Bento,** which housed Brazil's first law school. Two other noteworthy churches—the **Igreja da Misericórdia** and the **Igreja da Sé**—are on the Alto da Sé, from which there's a fabulous view of the city. If you can, be here for the sunset; you won't soon forget it.

SHOPPING

In the **Mercado da Ribeira,** the former slave market, you'll find more than a dozen handicraft shops. Regional art is also sold in shops on the **Rua do Amparo,** better known as Rua dos Artistas.

Caruaru
134 km (83 mi) west of Recife.

Busy, modern Caruaru is famous for its many crafts *feiras* (markets). Vendors at the **Feira Livre,** held on Wednesday and Saturday, sell local handicrafts, including pottery and leather and straw items. In a separate area, you'll find the feira *do troca-troca,* where junk and treasures alike are traded. The **Feira da Sulanca,** on Tuesday and Thursday, is a textile and clothing fair. **Feira de Artesanato,** at Parque 18 de Maio, is a great place to find leather goods, ceramics, hammocks, and baskets.

The local specialties are little clay figures originally created by Mestre Vitalino (1901–63). Most of the area's potters live in **Alto do Moura,** 6 km (4 mi) south of Caruaru, where a house once owned by Vitalino is now the Casa Museu Mestre Vitalino, a museum that's open Monday–Saturday 9–noon and 2–5 and Sunday 9–noon.

FORTALEZA

The city of Fortaleza sprung up around the Forte de Schoonemborch, a Dutch fortress built in 1649. After the Portuguese defeated the Dutch, the small settlement was called Fortaleza Nossa Senhora da Assunção (Fortress of Our Lady of the Assumption). The city didn't fully burgeon until 1808, when its ports were opened and the trade of cotton with the United Kingdom commenced.

Today, this community of more than 2 million inhabitants is Brazil's fifth largest city and is the capital of Ceará state. The beaches here are cooled by constant breezes and lapped by waters with an average temperature of 20°C/68°F. The coastline stretches far beyond town; to the east, along the Litoral Leste or the Costa Sol Nascente (Sunrise Coast), you'll find many towns and fishing villages. To the west, along the Litoral Oeste or the Costa Sol Poente (Sunset Coast) there are beautiful pristine stretches.

Exploring Fortaleza

Fortaleza is a flat city whose streets are laid out in a grid. Its business center lies above the Centro Histórico (Historical Center), and includes the city's major market, several shopping streets, and government buildings. East of the center, urban beaches are lined with high-rise hotels and restaurants. Beyond are the port and old lighthouse, from which Praia do Futuro runs 5 km (3 mi) along Avenida Dioginho.

Numbers in the text corresponds to numbers in the margin and on the Fortaleza Centro Histórico map.

A Good Walk (Or Two)

For a tour of the Centro Histórico, start at the **Fortaleza de Nossa Senhora da Assunção** ① at Rua João Moreira. East of the fortress follow Avenida Alberto Nepomuceno (Rua Conde D'Eu) south one block to the **Catedral da Sé** ②. From the church, cross Rua Conde D'Eu to Rua General Bezerril and the **Mercado Central** ③. Just beyond the market is the **Praça dos Leões** ④ with the Igreja Nossa Senhora do Rosário and the Palácio da Luz as well as the Museu do Ceará. From the museum, follow Rua Floriano Peixoto south, passing the Praça do Ferreira on your right, to Rua Liberato Barroso. Follow it until you cross Rua General Sampaio to the **Theatro José de Alencar** ⑤. Return to Rua General Sampaio and follow it to Rua Castro e Silva and the **Centro de Turismo** ⑥; nearby is the **Passeio Público** ⑦.

On another day—or if you have some energy left after your tour of the historical center—consider a stroll along the seaside, palm-lined walkway, east of the Passeio Público. From Praia Formosa you can walk to Praia de Iracema, an older beach area with some late-19th-century houses. Along the way you'll pass the Ponte Metálica (also called the Ponte dos Ingleses), a pier from which you might spot dolphins. Farther east are Praia do Meireles and Praia do Mucuripe with the **Farol do Mucuripe** ⑧ and its Museu de Fortaleza. You can continue all the way to Praia do Futuro for a total seashore walk of 8 km (5 mi).

TIMING AND PRECAUTIONS

The tour of the Centro Histórico will take three hours, much longer if you browse in the Mercado Central or explore the Centro de Turismo. Although a straight walk along the shore moving at a good clip would take roughly three hours, you'll want to move at a more leisurely pace, stopping to enjoy the view and to rest. Be on guard against pickpockets—particularly in the historical district.

SIGHTS TO SEE

❷ **Catedral da Sé.** Inspired by the cathedral in Cologne, Germany, this one was built between 1937 and 1963 and has a dominant Gothic look. Its two spires are 75 meters (250 ft) high, and it can accommodate 5,000 worshippers, who are no doubt inspired by its beautiful stained-glass windows. ✉ *Praça da Sé s/n, Centro,* ☎ *085/231–4196.* 🎫 *Free.*

❻ **Centro de Turismo.** This simple, neoclassical structure (circa 1866) was once a prison. Today it will hold you captive with its **Museu de Arte e Cultura Popular** (Popular Art and Culture Museum), whose displays of local handicrafts and sculptures are quite interesting; its mineralogy museum; and its many shops that sell hand-crafted items. As its name suggests, you'll also find a tourist information office here. ✉ *Rua Senador Pompeu 350, Centro,* ☎ *085/212–3566.* 🎫 *Admission to museum.* 🕐 *Mon.–Sat. 7–6, Sun. 7–noon.*

❽ **Farol do Mucuripe.** Erected by slaves and dedicated to Princess Isabel, this lighthouse was inaugurated in 1846. Surrounded by a system of

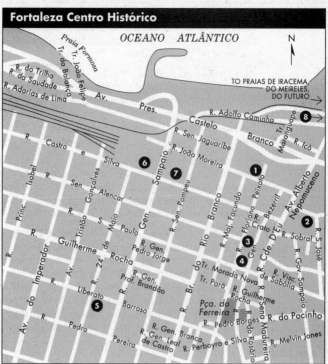

Fortaleza Centro Histórico

battlements, it operated for 111 years and was not deactivated until 1957. In 1982 it underwent restoration and was designated a municipal historic monument. It now houses the **Museu de Fortaleza,** better known as the Museu do Farol, with exhibits on the city's history. ✉ *Av. Vicente de Castro, Mucuripe,* ☎ *085/263–1115.* 🎫 *Free.* ☉ *Weekdays 7–6, weekends 7–noon.*

❶ **Fortaleza de Nossa Senhora da Assunção.** The city originated at the Fortaleza Nossa Senhora da Assunção (1649), which was built on the site of the old Dutch Forte Schoonemborch in 1816. ✉ *Av. Albert Craveiro, Centro,* ☎ *085/231–5155.* 🎫 *Free.* ☉ *Open daily 8–5.*

❸ **Mercado Central.** With four floors and more than 500 stores, this is *the* place to find handicrafts. If you really want to shop, set aside a few hours and wear comfortable shoes. Although most items here are quite affordable, don't let that stop you from comparing prices. ✉ *Av. Alberto Nepomuceno 199, Centro,* ☎ *085/454–8766 or 085/454–8273.* ☉ *Weekdays 7:30–6:30, Sat. 8–4, Sun. 8–noon.*

❼ **Passeio Público.** Also called the Praça dos Mártires, this landmark square dates from the 19th century. It has a central fountain and is full of century-old trees and statues of Greek deities. Look for the ancient baobab tree.

❹ **Praça dos Leões (Praça General Tibúrcio).** Built in 1817, this square is officially named after a Ceará general who fought in Brazil's war against Paraguay. However, it's also commonly referred to as the Praça de Leões owing to its bronze lions, which were brought over from Paris in the early 20th century.

On the square at Rua Rosário, you'll see the **Igreja Nossa Senhora do Rosário** (☎ *085/231–1998*). Built by slaves in the 18th century, it's one of the city's oldest churches and has a typical Brazilian colonial design. As the slaves who built it also worshipped in it, it's an important piece of African heritage in Ceará, a state considered a pioneer in the liberation of slaves. You can duck inside weekdays 7 AM–6:30 PM and Sunday 7:30 AM–10 PM.

Also on Rua do Rosário is the late-18th-century **Palácio da Luz** (☎ 085/231–5600). What was originally the home of the Portuguese Crown's representative, Antônio de Castro Viana, was built by Indian laborers. In 1814, it became property of the imperial government and has since served as the residence of the president of the province and then as the site of the state's cultural council.

The **Museu do Ceará** (✉ Rua São Paulo s/n, ☎ 085/251–1502) is also on the square. Housed in the former Assembléia Provincial (Provincial Assembly Building), its exhibits are devoted to the history and anthropology of Ceará state. It's open Wednesday–Friday 8:30–5:30, Saturday 10–4, and Sunday 2–5; there's a small admission fee.

⑤ **Theatro José de Alencar.** The José de Alencar Theater is a pastel-color mixture of neoclassical lines and art-nouveau detail. It was built in 1910 of steel and iron (many of its cast-iron sections were imported from Scotland) and was restored in 1989. It's still used for a variety of cultural events—including concerts, plays, and dance performances—and houses a library and an art gallery. If you'd like to take a tour, some of the guides speak English; call ahead for reservations. ✉ *Praça do José Alencar, Centro,* ☎ *085/252–2324.* ⬚ *Free.* ☾ *Weekdays 10–noon and 2–5.*

Beaches

Fortaleza's enchanting coast runs 22 km (14 mi) along the Atlantic between the Rio Ceará to the west and the Rio Cocó to the east. The scenery and the feel of this great urban stretch of sand vary as often as its names: Ceará, Pirambu, Formosa, Iracema, Beira-Mar, Meireles, Mucuripe, Mansa, Titanzinho. In the city center and its immediate environs, feel free to soak up the sun and the ambience of the beaches, but stay out of the water; it is, unfortunately, too polluted for swimming. However, you'll find clean waters and amazing sands just a little ways from Centro and beyond into Ceará State. The surfing is fine at several beaches, including those near the towns of Paracuru and Pecém, to the west of Fortaleza, and Porto da Dunas, to the east.

Canoa Quebrada. Hidden behind dunes 164 km (101 mi) east of Fortaleza, the stunning Canoa Quebrada beach was "discovered" a little more than 30 years ago by French doctors working in the area. The spectacular scenery includes not only dunes but also jangadas, red cliffs, and groves of palm trees. Although it was originally settled by Italian hippies, the village itself has moved on with the times slightly and now has good roads and a couple pousadas if you want to stay overnight.

Dois Coqueiros. On weekends, people come to this small beach, 28 km (17 mi) west of Fortaleza, to see and to be seen. The setting is spectacular: white sands, coconut trees, and strong waves.

Futuro. This 8-km (5 mi) stretch is the most beautiful beach on the city's east coast. It starts at Ponta do Mucuripe and goes up to the Rio Cocó.

Icaraí. Set 17 km (11 mi) west of Fortaleza, this white-sand beach includes snack bars and other facilities on its list of attributes.

Iguape. The white sand dunes at this beach, 50 km (31 mi) east of Fortaleza, are so high that people actually ski down them. The water is calm and clean. In the nearby village, you'll find both fishermen and lacemakers (lace is sold at the Centro de Rendeiras). There's also a lookout at Morro do Enxerga Tudo.

Outro. You won't find any natural shade at this 8-km-long (5-mi-long) beach 8 km (5 mi) southeast of Centro, but you will find glorious sand dunes, fresh-water showers, and vendors selling local dishes. On Thursday night the atmosphere is festive with live music and forró dancing. (Avoid the south end of this beach, known as Caça e Pesca; the water is polluted because of the outflow of the Rio Cocó.)

Porto das Dunas. Its water sports options, including surfing, and its sand dunes are enough to draw many people to this beach 29 km (18 mi) southeast of Centro. Its main attraction, however, may well be the Beach Park—South America's largest water park, with pools, water slides, sports fields, and helicopter rides. You can get here on the jardineira bus from Centro or from along Avenida Beira Mar.

Sabiaguaba. The village here, 20 km (12 mi) southeast of Centro, is known for its seafood; the beach for its unusual flat rocks that jut from the sea, its calm waters, its coconut trees, and its white sand dunes. The area also has mangrove swamps.

Tabuba. For tranquility, head to this west coast beach, 35 km (22 mi) from the city. It's a straight sandy stretch, with high dunes, rough waters, and lots of coconut trees.

Dining

You'll find several good seafood restaurants along Praia de Iracema and Praia do Mucuripe. Be sure to try the *lagosta ao natural* (langouste simply cooked in water and salt and served with homemade butter), which is available in most restaurants. Sun-dried meat with *paçoca* (manioc flour seasoned with herbs and red onions) is another popular regional dish.

Brazilian

$$ ✕ **Caçuá.** Regional items decorate this restaurant and create an agreeable setting. The house specialty is sun-dried meat and paçoca, though dishes of chicken and lamb are also recommended. ⊠ *Av. Engenheiro Santana Jr. 970, Papicu,* ☎ *085/234–1915. AE, V.*

$ ✕ **Colher de Pau.** Here the sun-dried meat is served not only with paçoca but also with banana and *baião-de-dois* (rice and beans). The shellfish dishes, many prepared using regional recipes, are also standouts. ⊠ *Rua Frederico Borges 204, Varjota,* ☎ *085/267–3773. AE, DC, MC, V.* ⊠ *Rodovia dos Tabajaras 412, Praia de Iracema,* ☎ *085/219–4097. AE, DC, MC, V.*

Eclectic

$$ ✕ **Le Dinner.** The savvy mix of French and Asian cuisine blend well with this restaurant's sophisticated ambience and personalized service. The menu includes beef, poultry, and seafood selections. Reservations are recommended. ⊠ *Rua Afonso Celso 1020, Aldeota,* ☎ *085/224–2627. AE. Closed Sun. and last two weeks of Feb.*

French

$$$ ✕ **Le Marine.** Candles flicker on each table, and violin and cello music fills the air-conditioned dining room and sitting room. The flambéed dishes are the best: try the King Jorge shrimp or the langouste in champagne. ⊠ *Av. Marechal Castelo Branco 400, Centro,* ☎ *085/252–5253. AE, DC, MC, V.*

Italian

$$ ✕ **Pulcinella.** You can feast on this restaurant's classic Italian fare (sometimes given a regional twist) in either the air-conditioned dining room, which has a smoking section, or in the alfresco seating area. Among the most popular dishes are spaghetti in garlic sauce with shrimp and pimiento and veal in a mushroom-and-herb sauce. ⊠ *Rua Osvaldo Cruz 640, Aldeota,* ☎ *085/261–3411. AE, DC, MC, V.*

Seafood

\$\$\$ ✕ **Al Mare.** Facing as it does out to the sea, it seems appropriate that the building housing this establishment is shaped like a ship. The grilled seafood *al mare*—a medley of fish, langouste, shrimp, octopus, and squid in an herb sauce—is the house specialty. ✉ *Av. Beira-Mar 3821, Mucuripe,* ☎ *085/263–3888. AE, DC, MC, V.*

\$\$ **Cemoara.** A sophisticated decor with clean lines add to the appeal of what is one of Fortaleza's traditional seafood restaurants. Although the *bacalão* (salt cod) selections are fabulous, you won't go wrong with the grilled lobster in a caper sauce or any of the flambéed dishes. Air-conditioning and smoking/no-smoking areas ensure that your meal will be a comfortable one. ✉ *Av. da Abolição 3340-A, Meireles,* ☎ *085/ 263–5001. AE, DC, MC, V.*

Lodging

Most hotels are along Avenida Beira-Mar (also known as Avenida Presidente John Kennedy). Those in the Praia de Iracema are generally less expensive than those along Praia do Mucuripe; Iracema is also a more interesting area to explore.

\$\$\$\$ 🏨 **Caesar Park Hotel Fortaleza.** On Praia do Mucuripe, just a 15-minute drive from either the airport or the city center, this luxury hotel can certainly include "convenient location" in its list of features. Marble and black granite give the building a modern, sleek, look, and all the rooms have terrific sea views. One of the on-site restaurants serves Brazilian fare, another French; the third, Mariko, is noteworthy for Japanese food, particularly its buffets of lobster, shrimp, sushi, sashimi, and oysters. The view from the pool area on the 20th floor is fantastic. (Note that hotel has facilities for travelers with disabilities.) ✉ *Av. Beira-Mar 3980, Mucuripe, 60165-050,* ☎ *085/263–1133 or 085/800–2202,* 🖷 *085/263–1444. 185 rooms, 45 suites. 3 restaurants, 2 bars, air-conditioning, in-room safes, minibars, room service, pool, hot tub, massage, sauna, steam room, health club, business services, convention center, free parking. AE, DC, MC, V.*

\$\$\$ 🏨 **Esplanada Praia.** At this recently renovated, top-end Praia do Meireles hotel, rooms have hammocks on balconies that face the sea. You'll feel inclined to unwind amidst beige-colored linens and basic furnishings that offer all the comforts of home. The multilingual staff is very efficient. ✉ *Av. Beira-Mar 2000, Meireles, 60165-121,* ☎ *085/248– 1000,* 🖷 *085/248–8555. 230 rooms. Restaurant, bar, pool, beauty salon, shops, nightclub. AE, DC, MC, V.*

\$\$\$ 🏨 **Imperial Othon Palace.** The Palace has a lively beachfront location, at the center of Avenida Beira-Mar and right in front of *feirinha de artesanato* (artisans fair; ☞ Shopping, *below*). Standard rooms are large, conservatively decorated, and well-equipped; suites face the sea. If you're here on business, consider a stay on one of the executive floors, which offer such perks as private breakfasts, meeting rooms, and secretarial services. Service throughout the hotel is world class. ✉ *Av. Beira-Mar 2500, Meireles 60165-121,* ☎ *085/242–9177,* 🖷 *085/242–7777. 222 rooms, 14 suites. 2 restaurants, coffee shop, bar, air-conditioning, in-room safes, minibars, room service, pool, beauty salon, massage, sauna, children's programs, business services, meeting room, free parking. AE, DC, MC, V.*

\$\$\$ 🏨 **Marina Park.** This resort complex looks like a huge ship, an appropriate design as it overlooks a calm bay and is connected to a marina. Rooms and suites have cream-color drapes, simple wooden dressers, and exotically patterned comforters. You can always find a place to relax beside the enormous free-form pool. The top-notch staff provides highly professional service. ✉ *Av. Presidente Castelo Branco*

400, Praia de Iracema 60312-060, ☎ 085/252–5253, FAX *085/253–1803. 259 rooms, 13 suites. 6 restaurants, bar, coffee shop, air-conditioning, in-room modem lines, in-room safes, minibars, room service, pool, beauty salon, massage, sauna, 4 tennis courts, volleyball, dock, shops, dance club, children's programs, playground, business services, meeting rooms, helipad, free parking. AE, DC, MC, V.*

$$$ 🏨 **Praia Centro.** Shoppers take note: this pleasant hotel is on a street famous for its clothing, shoe, and jewelry stores. It's also only three blocks from the Praia de Iracema, and close to many good restaurants and bars. Rooms are comfortable, and have such touches as Asian-inspired area carpets and honey-color wooden furniture. ✉ *Av. Monsenhor Tabosa 740, Iracema, 60165-011, ☎ 085/219–1122,* FAX *085/ 219–1122. 190 rooms. Restaurant, bar, air-conditioning, room service, pool. AE, DC, MC, V.*

$$$ 🏨 **Parthenon Golden Flat.** The comfortable apartments here are perfect for families and those in the city on a long stay. Each unit has one or two bedrooms as well as a living room and a fully equipped kitchen. If you get tired of preparing your own meals, you can head for the restaurant or the coffee shop; kids will appreciate the pool and the playground. ✉ *Av. Beira-Mar 4260, Mucuripe, 60165-121, ☎ 085/263–1413,* FAX *085/263–1413. 132 apartments. Restaurant, bar, coffee shop, pool, sauna, playground. AE, DC, MC, V.*

$$$ 🏨 **Seara Praia.** The lobby of the modern Seara Praia is decorated with works by local artists. It's set on Praia do Meirles; for an ocean view, however, be sure to ask for a deluxe room or suite. ✉ *Av. Beira-Mar 308, Meireles, 60165-121, ☎ 085/248–9000,* FAX *085/242–5955. 203 rooms, 14 suites. Restaurant, bar, pool, beauty salon, recreation room. AE, DC, MC, V.*

$$ 🏨 **Praiano Palace.** This hotel is a surprisingly affordable option in the chic Praia do Meirles area. Its rooms are simple but comfortable, and all of them have sea views. ✉ *Av. Beira-Mar 2800, Meirles, 60165-121, ☎ 085/242–9333,* FAX *085/242–3333. 169 rooms. Restaurant, bar, pool. AE, DC, MC, V.*

Nightlife and the Arts

Nightlife

Fortaleza is renowned for its lively nightlife, particularly along Avenida Beira-Mar. The action often includes live forró, the traditional and very popular music and dance of the northeast.

BARS AND CLUBS

At **Alambique Cachaçaria** (✉ Rua dos Potiguares 192, Praia de Iracema, ☎ 085/219–0656) you'll find more than 400 types of cachaça. Line 'em up. For *música popular brasileira,* commonly referred to as MPB (popular Brazilian music), head to **Aldeia In** (✉ Av. Dom Luís 879, Aldeota, ☎ 085/261–3227). **Cais Bar** (✉ Av. Beira-Mar 696, Praia de Iracema, ☎ 085/219–4963) is a known hangout for artists and intellectuals. **Chico do Caranguejo** (✉ Av. Zezé Diogo 4930, Praia do Futuro, ☎ 085/234–6519) is the place to feast on crabs while enjoying live samba and axé music shows. On Monday night—the most popular night for forró—consider checking out the **Pirata Bar** (✉ Rua dos Tabajaras 325, Praia de Iracema, ☎ 085/219–8030), where as many as 2,000 people can move to the forró beat on the dance floor and in other areas inside or out. For exotic drinks try **Siriguela Banana** (✉ Rua dos Tremembés 100, Loja 6, Praia de Iracema, ☎ 085/219–6111).

CYBERCAFÉ

You can plug into the Internet at **Mirante Cyber Bar** (✉ Av. Beira-Mar 4430, Mucuripe, ☎ 085/263–1006).

GAY BAR

Broadway (⊠ Rua Carolina Sucupira 455, Aldeota, ☎ 085/261–2074) is Fortaleza's premier gay nightclub. A dance floor, bars, and open as well as intimate seating areas fill its great space.

DANCE SHOWS AND RODEOS

Just outside Fortaleza, you'll find establishments that blend forró shows with *vaquejada*, a traditional rodeo in which farm hands try to wrangle bulls and wild horses. **Cajueiro Drinks** (⊠ BR 116, Km 20, Eusébio, ☎ 085/275–1482) is a highly recommended spot for rodeo shows.

For a lively mix of vaquejada with samba, reggae, forró, and other types of music, try **Clube do Vaqueiro** (⊠ Quarto Anel Viário de Fortaleza, BR 116, Km 14, Eusébio, ☎ 085/278–2000), or **Parque do Vaqueiro** (⊠ BR 020, Km 10, after the loop in the intersection, Caucaia, ☎ 085/296–1159).

NIGHTCLUBS

A young crowd grooves to MPB and rock-and-roll at **Boite Domínio Público** (⊠ Rua Dragão do Mar 212, Praia de Iracema, ☎ 085/219–3883). A sophisticated, over-25 crowd fills the two dance floors and the bars at **Boite Mustike** (⊠ Mucuripe Club, Av. Beira-Mar 4430, Mucuripe, ☎ 085/263–1006). In Praia do Futuro, Tuesday nights are hottest at **Oásis** (⊠ Av. Santos Dumont 6061, Papicu, ☎ 085/262–2326), a large dance hall with plenty of room for the masses.

The Arts

The **Centro Cultural Banco do Nordeste** (⊠ Rua Floriano Peixoto 941, Centro, ☎ 085/488–4100) often hosts plays, concerts, and art exhibitions. Opened in 1998, the **Centro Dragão do Mar de Arte e Cultura** (⊠ Rua Dragão do Mar 81, Praia de Iracema, ☎ 085/488–8600) is Fortaleza's largest cultural center. This majestic complex has art museums and workshops, cinemas, an amphitheater, and an auditorium. The beautiful, early 19th-century **Theatro José de Alencar** (⊠ Praça José de Alencar, Centro, ☎ 085/252–2324) is still the site of many concerts, plays, and dance performances. Alongside the main theater is a smaller venue (it seats about 120 people) for more intimate events. There's also a small stage in the theater's garden.

Outdoor Activities and Sports

Participant Sports

A good way to get out and about is on a walk, run, or bike ride along the beachfront Avenida Beira-Mar's calçadão. On the sands themselves, you'll find volleyball courts and soccer fields. There are also sport fields in the Parque do Cocó, the city's main park.

HIKING

You can hire guides to take you on a variety of hikes through **Eco Turismo Fundação Maria Nilva Alves** (⊠ Av. Monsenhor Tabosa 314, ☎ 085/254–4011), **Rota do Sol** (⊠ Rua Pedro Coelho 986, Aldeota, ☎ 085/226–1657), and **Trip Trekking** (⊠ Rua Capitão Francisco Pedro 768, Loja 1, Rodolfo Teófilo, ☎ 085/281–2869).

SCUBA DIVING

The coast of Ceará has several good dive sites. To rent equipment and arrange lessons and/or trips contact **Atividades Subaquáticas e Pesquisas Ambientais** (ASPA; ⊠ Rua Eduardo Garcia 23, Loja 13, Aldeota, ☎ 085/268–2966 or 085/231–5378), or **Projeto Netuno** (⊠ Rua do Mirante 165, Mucuripe, ☎ 085/263–3009).

WINDSURFING

Open seas and constant trade winds make Ceará's beaches perfect for windsurfing. You can arrange lessons and rent equipment at **Windcenter/Hi-Winds** (✉ Av. Beira-Mar 3222, Loja 20, ☎ 085/242–2611) and **Windclub** (✉ Av. Beira-Mar 2120, Praia dos Diários, ☎ 085/982–5449).

Spectator Sport

FUTEBOL

Fortaleza's two futebol teams, Ceará and Fortaleza, play in the **Estádio Plácido Castelo** (✉ Av. Alberto Craveiro s/n, ☎ 085/295–2466), also known as Castelão, or **Estádio Presidente Vargas** (✉ Av. Marechal Deodoro s/n, ☎ 085/281–3225).

Shopping

Fortaleza is one of the most important centers for crafts—especially bobbin lace—in the northeast. You'll find shops that sell a good variety of handicrafts—as well as those offering clothing, shoes, and jewelry—along **Avenida Monsenhor Tabosa** in Praia de Iracema.

Fortaleza's shopping centers, both large and small, house branches of the best Brazilian stores. The biggest and most traditional center is **Shopping Center Iguatemi** (✉ Av. Washington Soares 85, Água Fria, ☎ 085/273–3577). **Avenida Shopping** (✉ Av. Dom Luís 300, Meireles, ☎ 085/264–9444) and **North Shopping** (✉ Av. Bezerra de Menezes 2450, São Geraldo, ☎ 085/287–6000) are other options.

Markets and fairs are the best places to look for lacework, embroidery, leather goods, hammocks, and carvings. The large, warehouse-style **Central de Artesanato do Ceará** (CEART; ✉ Av. Santos Dumont 1589, Aldeota, ☎ 085/268–2970) sells all types of handicrafts, though at higher prices than elsewhere. The handicraft stores at **Centro de Turismo** (✉ Rua Senador Pompeu 350, Centro, ☎ 085/231–3566 or 085/253–1522) are also good options. More than 600 artisans sell their work at the nightly **crafts fair** (✉ Av. Beira-Mar, in front of Imperial Othon Palace) on Praia do Meireles.

For lace aficionados a trip to the town of **Aquiraz,** 30 km (19 mi) east of Fortaleza, is a must. Ceará's first capital (1713–99) is today a hub for artisans who create the famous *bilro* (bobbin) lace. On the beach called Prainha (6 km/4mi east of Aquiraz) is the Centro de Rendeiras Luiza Távora. Here, seated on little stools, dedicated and patient women lacemakers explain how they create such items as bedspreads and tablecloths using the bilro technique.

SALVADOR, RECIFE, AND FORTALEZA A TO Z

Arriving and Departing

By Airplane

SALVADOR

The **Aeroporto Deputado Luís Eduardo Magalhães** (☎ 071/204–1010), 37 km (23 mi) northeast of the city, accommodates international and domestic flights. Airlines that serve the city include **Air France** (071/351–6631), **American Airlines** (071/245–0477), **Lufthansa** (071/341–5100), **Rio-Sul** (071/204–1253), **TAM** (071/204–1367), **Transbrasil** (071/377–2467), **Varig** (071/204–1070), and **VASP** (071/377–2495).

From the Airport into Town. Avoid taking comum taxis from the airport; drivers often jack up the fare by refusing or "forgetting" to turn on the meter. Instead opt for a prepaid *cooperativa* (co-op) taxi (they're white with a broad blue stripe); the cost is $30–$45 for the 20- to 30-minute drive downtown. The *ônibus executivo*, an air-conditioned bus, runs daily from 6 AM to 9 PM at no set intervals; it costs about $1.10 and takes about an hour to reach downtown, stopping at hotels along the way. (Drivers don't speak English, but will stop at a specific hotel if shown a written address). Several companies operate these buses, the largest being **Transportes Ondina** (✉ Av. Vasco da Gama 347, ☎ 071/245–6366). The municipal Circular buses, operated by both Transportes Ondina and **Transportes Rio Vermelho** (✉ Av. Dorival Caymmi 18270, ☎ 071/377–2587), cost about a quarter and run along the beaches to downtown, ending up at São Joaquim, where ferries depart for Ilha de Itaparica.

RECIFE

The **Aeroporto Internacional Guararapes** (✉ Praça Ministro Salgado Filho s/n, Imbiribeira, ☎ 081/464–4188) is 10 km (6 mi) south of Recife, just 5 minutes from Boa Viagem and 15 minutes from the city center. The main airlines operating here are **American Airlines** (☎ 081/465–2156 or 081/465–2876), **Rio Sul Nordeste** (☎ 081/465–6799), **TAM** (☎ 081/465–8800), **Transbrasil** (☎ 081/423–1366 or 081/423–4040), **Varig** (☎ 081/464–4440 or 081/464–4499), and **VASP** (☎ 081/421–3611 or 081/421–1427).

From the Airport into Town. Tourist taxis from the airport cost about $5 to Boa Viagem and $10 to downtown; the trip in a regular taxi will cost a little less. The ride from the airport to Olinda will cost $12–$15. From the airport there are regular buses and microbuses (more expensive). The bus labeled AEROPORTO runs to Avenida Dantas Barreto in the center of the city, stopping in Boa Viagem on the way. To reach Olinda, take the AEROPORTO bus to Avenida Nossa Senhora do Carmo in Recife and pick up the CASA CAIADA bus from there.

FORTALEZA

Opened in 1998, the **Aeroporto Internacional Pinto Martins** (✉ Av. Senador Carlos Jereissati, ☎ 085/477–1200) is 6 km (4 mi) south of downtown. No international carriers serve the airport, but there are regular flights to all major Brazilian cities on the national carriers: **Transbrasil** (☎ 085/477–1800 or 085/477–1818), **TAM** (☎ 085/477–6261 or 085/477–1881), **Varig** (☎ 085/477–1710 or 085/477–1720), and **VASP** (☎ 085/477–5353).

From the Airport into Town. The fixed-price *especial* (special) taxis charge about $7 for trips from the airport to downtown on weekdays, $14 on weekends. Highly recommended is the Guanabara Top-Bus, a *frescão* (air-conditioned bus) that loops from the airport through the center and on to Praia Iracema and Praia Meireles. It leaves the airport every 25 minutes, 7 AM–10 PM daily, and costs about $1. City buses also run from here to the nearby bus station (☞ Getting Around by Bus, *below*) and Praça José de Alencar in Centro.

By Bus

SALVADOR

You can purchase bus tickets (no need to buy in advance except during Carnaval season) at the **Terminal Rodoviário** (✉ Av. Antônio Carlos Magalhães, Iguatemi, ☎ 071/358–6633). The **Itapemirim** (☎ 071/358–0037) company has three buses a day to Recife (13 hrs, $35–$45), Fortaleza (19 hrs, $55), and Rio (28 hrs, $80–$155).

The **Santa Mana Catuense** (☎ 071/359–3474) company has hourly service from the Terminal Rodoviário to Praia do Forte starting at 7:30 AM, with the last bus returning to the city at 5:30 PM; tickets cost about

$3. The **Camurujipe** (☎ no phone) company has hourly service from the Terminal Rodoviário to Cachoeira between 5:30 AM and 7 PM. You can also reach Cachoeira by a combination of boat and bus: Boats depart weekdays at 2:30 PM from the **Terminal Marítimo** (✉ Behind the Mercado Modelo, Av. França s/n, ☎ 071/243–0741) for the three-hour trip to Maragojipe; you then board a bus for the bumpy half-hour ride to Cachoeira.

RECIFE

The **Terminal Integrado de Passageiros** (TIP; ✉ Rodovia BR 232, Km 15, Curado, Jaboatão dos Guararapes, ☎ 081/452–1999), a *metrô* (subway, although here the trains run above ground) terminal and a bus station 14 km (9 mi) from the city center, handles all interstate bus departures and some connections to local destinations. To reach it via metrô, a 30-minute ride, enter the subway through the Museu do Trem, opposite the Casa da Cultura, and take the train marked RODOVIÁRIA. Several buses a day go to Salvador (12–14 hrs, $37) and Fortaleza (12 hrs, $41); there are also daily departures to Rio (40 hrs, $108), and frequent service to Caruaru (2 hrs, $6).

In Boa Viagem, you can take the PIEDADE/RIO DOCE bus to Olinda. Buses to Igarassu and Ilha de Itamaracá leave from the center of Recife, at Avenida Martins de Barros, in front of Grande Hotel.

FORTALEZA

The main bus station, **Terminal Rodoviário João Tomé** (✉ Av. Borges de Melo 1630, Fátima, ☎ 085/256–1566) is 6 km (4 mi) south of Centro. In low season, you can buy tickets at the station right before leaving; it's best to make reservations for weekend travel to major northeastern cities and, in high season, for trips to well-known beach destinations. **São Benedito** (☎ 085/256–1999) runs five buses daily to Beberibe and Morro Branco beach (2½ hrs; $2) and three daily to Aracati and Canoa Quebrada (3½ hrs; $7). **Expresso Guanabara** (☎ 085/227–0214 or 085/227–0215) and **Itapemirim** (☎ 085/272–4511) have five daily buses to Recife (12 hrs; $30–$61) and three daily to Salvador (21 hrs; $55); in addition, Itapemirim has daily buses to Rio de Janeiro. **Penha** (085/272–4511) also runs buses to Rio de Janeiro (48 hrs; $129–$160) and São Paulo (52 hrs; $130–$160).

By Car

SALVADOR

Two highways—BR 101 and BR 116—run between Rio de Janeiro and Salvador. If you take the BR 101, get off at the city of Santo Antônio/Nazaré and follow the signs to Itaparica, 61 km (38 mi) away. At Itaparica, you can either take the 45-minute ferry ride to Salvador or continue on BR 101 to its connection with BR 324. If you opt for the BR 116, exit at the city of Feira de Santana, 107 km (67 mi) from Salvador and take the BR 324, which approaches the city from the north. Follow the signs marked IGUATEMI/CENTRO for downtown and nearby destinations. To reach Praia do Forte by car, take the Estrada do Coco north and follow the signs; there's a short stretch of unpaved road at the end. To reach Cachoeira, take BR 324 north for about 55 km (34 mi), then head west on BR 420 through the town of Santo Amaro. The trip takes 1½ hours.

RECIFE

The main north–south highway is BR 101. To the north, it travels through vast sugar plantations; it's mostly straight, with only slight slopes and downgrades. To travel south, you can also take the scenic coastal road, the PE 060, which passes through Porto de Galinhas Beach. To reach Caruaru take BR 232 west; the trip takes 1½ hours.

FORTALEZA

The main access roads are the BR 304, which runs southeast to Natal and Recife and which is paved and in good condition; the BR 222, which travels west to the state of Piauí and onto Brasília and is paved with a few poor sections; the BR 020 southwest, which goes to Picos in Piauí state and on to Brasília and is fully paved; and the BR 116, which runs south to Salvador and is paved, though it has several stretches in poor condition. The fully paved CE 004, or Litoránea, links the coastal towns to the southeast as far as Aracati. Many of the state's secondary roads are paved, though there are also some dirt roads in fair condition.

Getting Around

By Boat

SALVADOR

Itaparica and the other harbor islands can be reached by taking a ferry or a launch, by hiring a motorized schooner, or by joining a harbor schooner excursion—all departing from the docks behind the Mercado Modelo. Launches cost about $1 and leave every 45 minutes from 7 AM to 6 PM from **Terminal Turístico Marítimo** (⌧ Av. França s/n, ☎ 071/243–0741). The ferry takes passengers and cars and leaves every half hour between 6 AM and 10:30 PM from the **Terminal Ferry-Boat** (⌧ Terminal Marítimo, Av. Oscar Ponte 1051, São Joaquim, ☎ 071/321–7100). The fare is around $1 for passengers, $6–$8 for cars, and takes 45 minutes to cross the bay.

RECIFE

Catamaran rides along the Rio Capibaribe pass Recife's grand houses, historic monuments, old bridges, and mangrove swamps. There are two such excursions: The hour-long afternoon trip goes through the old rotating bridge and passes Recife Velho and São José, the customs quay, the Santa Isabel Bridge, and the Rua da Aurora quays to the area near the Casa da Cultura. The two-hour-long night tour is aboard a slower—though more lively—vessel. The boat has room for 60 people, and the trip is like a party, with live music, drinks, and snacks. It passes the quays of São José Estelita (a set of restored warehouses) and then goes back by the Calanga Iate Clube, passing the ruins of the old Casa de Banhos and running to the Rio Beberibe, from where there's a beautiful view of Olinda. Boats leave from near the Praça do Marco Zero in Recife Velho; for reservations call ☎ 081/436–2220.

By Bus and Metrô

SALVADOR

Buses are crowded, dirty, and dangerous, but they serve most of the city and cost a pittance (50¢). The fancier executivo buses ($1.20) serve tourist areas more completely but have been subject to a spate of robberies. The glass-sided green, yellow, and orange jardineira bus (marked PRAÇA DA SÉ)—which runs from the downtown Praça da Sé to the Stella Maris beach along the beachfront Orla Marítima series of avenues—is fine for getting to the beach.

RECIFE

City buses cost 50¢; they're clearly labeled and run frequently until about 10:30 pm. Many bus stops have signs indicating the routes. Recife also has above-ground metrô trains that leave from its central station and also travel to the main bus station, the TIP (☞ *also* Getting Around by Bus, *above*). To reach Boa Viagem via metrô from the station, get off at the Joana Bezerra stop (a 20-min ride) and take a bus or taxi ($10) from here. Combination bus-metrô tickets cost about $1; routes are explained in a leaflet issued by **CBTU Metrorec** (081/251–5256).

FORTALEZA

The fare on city buses is 65¢. Those marked 13 DE MAIO or AGUANAMBI 1 or 2 run from Avenida General Sampaio and pass the Centro de Turismo; from here (Rua Dr. João Moreira) you can take the bus labeled CIRCULAR to Avenida Beira-Mar and Praia de Iracema and Praia do Meireles. From Avenida Castro e Silva (close to Centro de Turismo), PRAIA DO FUTURO and SERVILUZ buses run to Praia do Futuro. For beaches west of the city, take a CUMBUCO bus from Praça Capistrano Abreu on Avenida Tristão Gonçalves or from along Avenida Beira-Mar. For the eastern beach of Porto das Dunas and the Beach Park, take a BEACH PARK from Praça Tristão Gonçalves or from along Avenida Beira-Mar.

By Car

SALVADOR

The dearth of places to park makes rental cars impractical for sightseeing in the Cidade Alta (although the government plans to build more parking areas). Further, many soteropolitanos are reckless drivers (they often ignore even the most basic traffic rules), making driving a dangerous proposition, especially if you don't know your way around. That said, cars are handy for visits to outlying beaches and far-flung attractions. Rental companies include **Avis** (⊠ Av. 7 de Setembro 1796, ☎ 071/237–0155 or 071/377–2276 at the airport), **Hertz** (071/377–3633 at the airport), or **Localiza** (071/377–2272 at the airport).

RECIFE

Because of horrible rush-hour traffic jams and careless drivers, it's best to rent a car only for side trips out of Recife. The best companies include **Localiza** (⊠ Guararapes Airport, ☎ 081/341–2082 or 081/461–1931), **Interlocadora** (⊠ Av. Fernando Simões Barbosa 644, Boa Viagem, ☎ 081/465–1041), and **Unidas** (⊠ Av. Engenheiro Domingos Ferreira 3641, Boa Viagem, ☎ 081/465–0200).

FORTALEZA

Fortaleza is an easy city in which to drive. Major routes take you easily from one side of town to the other. Although rush hour sees traffic jams, they're nowhere near as bad as in other big cities. To rent a car, contact **Avis** (⊠ Av. Barão de Studart 1425, Aldeota, ☎ 085/261–6785), **Hertz** (⊠ Rua Oswaldo Cruz 175, Meireles, ☎ 085/242–5425), or **Localiza** (⊠ Av. Antônio Justa 2400, Meireles, ☎ 085/242–4255).

By Taxi

SALVADOR

Taxis are metered, but you must convert the unit shown on the meter to Brazilian currency using a chart posted on the window. Tipping isn't expected. You can hail a comum taxi (white with a red and blue stripe) on the street (they often line up in front of major hotels) or summon one by phone. If you bargain, a comum taxi can be hired for the day for as little as $50. Try **Ligue Taxi** (☎ 071/358–0733). The more expensive, though usually air-conditioned, *especial* (special) taxis also congregate outside major hotels, though you must generally call for them. Reliable companies include **Coometas** (☎ 071/244–4500) and **Contas** (☎ 071/245–6311).

RECIFE

Taxis are cheap in Recife (fares double on Sunday), but drivers seldom speak English. You can either hail a cab on the street or call for one. Recommended taxi services are **Coopertáxi** (☎ 081/224–8441), **Radiotáxi Recife** (☎ 081/423–7777), and **Teletáxi** (☎ 081/421–4242).

FORTALEZA

You can either hail a taxi on the street or call for one. Fares are affordable, though you should note that they double on Sunday, and few drivers are English speakers. Reliable taxi services include **Coopertáxi** (☎ 085/227–0480), **Disquetáxi** (☎ 085/287–7222), **Ligue Táxi** (☎ 085/231–7333), and **Rádio Táxi** (☎ 085/287–5554).

Contacts and Resources

Banks and Currency Exchange

SALVADOR

Never change money on the streets, especially in the Cidade Alta. All major banks have exchange facilities, but only in some of their branches. Try **Citibank** (✉ Rua Miguel Calmon 555, Comércio), which has good rates; **Banco Económico** (✉ Rua Miguel Calmon 285); and **Banco do Brasil** (✉ Av. Estados Unidos 561, Comércio), which also offers exchange services at its branches in the Shopping Center Iguatemi and at the airport.

RECIFE

Recommended *casas de câmbio* (exchange houses) in the city center include **Mônaco Câmbio** (✉ Praça Joaquim Nabuco 159) and **Norte Câmbio Turismo** (✉ Rua Mathias de Albuquerque 223, Sala 508). In Boa Viagem try **Norte Câmbio Turismo** (✉ Rua dos Navegantes 691, Loja 10) or **Colmeia Câmbio & Turismo** (✉ Rua dos Navegantes 784, Loja 4).

Banco do Brasil (✉ Av. Dantas Barreto 541, Santo Antônio; ✉ Av. Conselheiro Aguiar 3600, Boa Viagem) offers exchange services in several in-town locations as well as at its airport branch.

FORTALEZA

Banco do Brasil's (✉ Rua Floriano Peixoto) Centro branch is open weekdays 10–3; the Meireles branch on Avenida Abolição has the same hours. There are lots of casas de câmbio in Meireles as well.

Consulates

SALVADOR

United Kingdom (Av. Estados Unidos 15, Comércio, 071/243–9222 or 071/243–7399). **United States** (✉ Rua Pernambuco 568, Pituba, ☎ 071/345–1545).

RECIFE

United Kingdom (✉ Av. Engenheiro Domingos Ferreira 4150, Boa Viagem, ☎ 081/465–0230 or 081/465–0247). **United States** (✉ Rua Gonçalves Maia 163, Boa Vista, ☎ 081/421–2441).

FORTALEZA

United Kingdom (✉ Sede Grupo Edson Queiroz, Praça da Imprensa, ☎ 085/224–8888). **United States** (✉ Instituto Brasil Estados Unidos, Rua Nogueira Acioly 891, ☎ 085/252–1539).

Emergencies

SALVADOR

General emergencies: ☎ 192. **Hospitals: Aliança Hospital** (✉ Av. Juracy Magalhães Jr. 2096, ☎ 071/350–5600), **Hospital Português** (✉ Av. Princesa Isabel 2, Santa Isabel, ☎ 071/203–5555), **Hospital Jorge Valente** (✉ Av. Garibaldi 2135, ☎ 071/203–4333).

Police: The office of the **Delegacia de Proteção do Turista** (☎ 071/320–4103), the tourist police, is down the steps at the back of the Belvedere at the Praça da Sé. This office deals as best it can (on a shoe-string budget) with tourist-related crime after the fact. There are also military police foot patrols; officers, some of whom have rudimentary second-language skills, wear armbands that say POLÍCIA TURÍSTICA.

RECIFE

Ambulance: ☎ 081/465–5566. **Hospitals: Centro Hospitalar Albert Sabin** (⊠ Rua Senador José Henrique 141, Ilha do Leite, ☎ 081/421–5411 or 071/421–6155) and **Real Hospital Português** (⊠ Av. Agamenon Magalhães, Derby, ☎ 081/416–1122 or 081/416–1112). **Pharmacies:** Recommended 24-hour drugstores include **Farmácia dos Pobres** (⊠ Av. Conselheiro Aguiar 3595, Boa Viagem, ☎ 081/325–5998) and **Farmácia Casa Caiada** (⊠ Rua Padre Carapuceiro 777, Boa Viagem, ☎ 081/465–1420).

FORTALEZA

Ambulance: ☎ 085/254–5592, 085/221–2873, or 085/257–3322. **Hospitals: Hospital Antônio Prudente** (⊠ Av. Aguanambi 1827, Fátima, ☎ 085/277–4000), **Hospital Batista** (⊠ Rua Prof. Dias da Rocha 2530, Aldeota, ☎ 085/261–2999), **Hospital Génesis** (⊠ Av. Santos Dumont 1168, Aldeota, ☎ 085/255–8500). **Surfing Emergencies:** ☎ 193.

English-Language Bookstores

SALVADOR

Graúna (⊠ Av. 7 de Setembro 1448; ⊠ Rua Barão de Itapoã, Porto da Barra) has many books in English. **Livraria Brandão** (⊠ Rua Rui Barbosa 15B, Centro, ☎ 071/243–5383) sells second-hand books in foreign languages. **Livraria Planeta** (Aeroporto Deputado Luís Eduardo Magalhães) has English-language books, magazines, and newspapers.

RECIFE

Livraria Brandão (⊠ Rua da Matriz 22) has used English-language books; the shop also sells books from stalls on Rua do Infante Dom Henrique. **Livro 7** (⊠ Rua 7 de Setembro 329a) is a large emporium with a huge stock, including many foreign-language titles. You can find English-language books, magazines, and newspapers at **Sodiler**, which has branches at the Guararapes airport and in the Shopping Center Recife.

FORTALEZA

You'll find English-language publications at **Livros e Letras** (⊠ Avenida Shopping, Av. Dom Luís 300, Loja 232, Meireles, ☎ 085/264–9376) and **Edésio** (⊠ Shopping Iguatemi, Av. Washington Soares 85, Loja 62, Água Fria, ☎ 085/273–1466).

Health and Safety

As in any large city, discretion and a low-key approach will more than likely ensure a hassle-free trip to Salvador, Recife, or Fortaleza. Leave valuables at home, and don't wear expensive watches. Potential thieves are unlikely to know the difference between a real Rolex and a fake one, so it's better not to try to fool anyone. Wear your purse bandolier style (with the strap over one shoulder) and keep your wallet out of easy reach for thieves (a money belt isn't a bad idea). Never leave belongings unattended. Carry only a photocopy of your passport, leaving the original in the hotel safe.

Fortaleza is generally safe. Watch out for pickpockets in the city center and keep an eye on your belongings at the beach. You should also avoid the Serviluz *favela* (slum) between the old lighthouse Mucuripe (Avenida Vicente de Castro) and Praia do Futuro; the favela behind the railway station; the Passeio Público at night; Avenida Abolição at its eastern (Nossa Senhora da Saúde Church) and western ends.

Telephones, Internet, and Mail

SALVADOR

Salvador's area code is 071. The city's main **post office** (☎ 071/243–9383) is in the Praça Inglaterra in the Cidade Baixa. You'll also find branches on the Avenida Princesa Isabel in Barra and the Rua Marques de Caravelas in Ondina, at the Barra and Iguatemi shopping centers, and at the airport. The airport branch is open 24 hours; all others are open weekdays 8–5. All branches offer express-mail service.

RECIFE

Express-mail service is available at all post offices. The main **post office** (⊠ Av. Gurarapes 250) is downtown; its *posta restante* (held mail) counter is in the basement. There are also branches at the airport, the TIP, and in Boa Viagem at Avenida Conselheiro Aguiar and Rua Coronel Sérgio Cardim. The area code for Recife is 081. You can make international calls from booths on the first floor at the airport and from **phone offices** (⊠ Rua do Hospício 148, Centro; ⊠ Rua Diário de Pernambuco 38). For Internet access try one of the city's cybercafés (☞ Nightlife and the Arts, *above*).

FORTALEZA

Fortaleza's area code is 085. Public phones take cards, which are sold in a variety of denominations at many shops. You can make international calls from offices of **Teleceará** (⊠ Rua Floriano Peixoto 99, corner of Rua João Moreira, Centro; ⊠ Rua José Vilar 375, Aldeota; ⊠ Av. Beira-Mar 736, Iracema; ⊠ Av. Beira-Mar 3821, Meireles; ⊠ Av. César Cals 1297, Praia do Futuro). For Internet service try **Company Office Rede de Negócios** (Av. Beira Mar 3980, Mucuripe 085/263–1119), which also has fax and secretarial services, and **Mirante Cyber Bar** (☞ Nightlife, *above*). All branches of the **post office** (⊠ Rua Senador Alencar 38, Centro; ⊠ Monsenhor Tabosa 1109, Iracema) offer express-mail services.

Tour Operators and Travel Agents

SALVADOR

The city's large group tours are fairly cursory, and their guides often speak minimal English; such tours are also targeted by hordes of street vendors at almost every stop. Several travel agencies offer half-day minibus tours with hotel pickup and drop-off for about $20–$25. Agencies also offer daylong harbor tours on motorized schooners ($30–$35) and night tours ($40–$45) that include dinner and an Afro-Brazilian music and dance show. A beach tour that includes the Lagoa de Abaeté can be arranged as well, with a car and guide provided for about $30 a head (minimum 2 people).

Another option is a private tour with a Bahiatursa guide (they carry the proper credentials), hired through your hotel, a travel agency, or at a Bahiatursa kiosk (☞ Visitor Information, *below*). Prices vary depending on the size of the group (it costs about $100 for one person, $80 each for two people, and so on) and include a car, which picks you up and drops you off at your hotel. Beware of guides who approach you at church entrances; they overcharge for telling tall tales.

Though it specializes in African heritage tours of Bahia, **Tatur Tours** (⊠ Ave. Antônio Carlos Magalhães 2573, Edifício Royal Trade, S. 1308, ☎ 071/358–7216) also offers personalized, special-interest city tours. The staff can also arrange top-notch excursions from Salvador.

Other leading agencies include **Globe Turismo** (⊠ Rua Dra. Praguer Fróes 97, ☎ 071/245–9611), **Lilás Viagens e Turismo Ltda.** (⊠ Av. Tancredo Neves 274, Bloco B, Centro Empresarial Iguatemi II, ☎ 071/358–7133), and **L. R. Turismo** (⊠ Av. Otávio Mangabeira 2365, ☎ 071/248–3333).

If you'd like to tour Praia do Forte, **Odara Turismo** (⊠ Praia do Forte Resort Hotel, Av. do Farol s/n, Mata de São João; ⊠ mailing address,

Visconde do Rosário 114, Sobreloja 103, Comércio, Salvador, Bahia, 40015, ☎ 071/876–1080) offers half- and full-day Jeep tours for $110–$150 with hotel pickup in Salvador.

RECIFE

To make tour and travel arrangements, including excursions from Recife, try **Andratur** (⊠ Av. Conselheiro Aguiar 3150, Loja 7, Boa Viagem, ☎ 081/465–8588), **Evatour** (⊠ Av. Conselheiro Aguiar 1360, Loja 14, Boa Viagem, ☎ 081/465–1164 or 081/325–5426), or **Souto Costa Viagens e Turismo Ltda.** (⊠ Rua Félix de Brito Melo 666, ☎ 081/465–5000).

FORTALEZA

For plane tickets, airport transfers, and city and beach tours, try **Alpha Viagens and Turismo** (⊠ Av. Santos Dumont 1687, Loja 9, Aldeota, ☎ 085/261–8633), **Lafuente Turismo** (⊠ Av. Senador Virgílio Távora 496, Meireles, ☎ 085/244–8558 or 085/242–1010), **L' Avilatur Viagens e Turismo** (⊠ Av. Rui Barbosa 1055 A, Aldeota, ☎ 085/261–4777), **Nettour Viagem e Turismo** (⊠ Rua Tenente Benévolo 1355, Praia de Iracema, ☎ 085/268–3099), or **Petrelli Turismo** (⊠ Rua Barbosa de Freitas 1440, Aldeota, ☎ 085/261–1222). For cruises, good operators include **Ernanitur** (Av. Barão de Studart, 1165, suites 101–104, Meireles, 085/244–9363) and **Mundial Tur** (Av. Barão de Studart 277, Meireles, 085/244–9293).

Visitor Information

SALVADOR

The main office of the state tourist board, **Bahiatursa** (⊠ Centro de Convenções, Jardim Armação s/n, 41750–270, ☎ 071/370–8400) is far from tourist attractions. However, there are five other conveniently located branches: the **airport** (⊠ Aeroporto Internacional, 2 de Julho s/n, ☎ 071/204–1244); the **bus station** (⊠ Av. Antônio Carlos Magalhães s/n, Terminal Rodoviário, ☎ 071/358–0871); the **downtown historic center** (⊠ Terreiro de Jesus s/n, ☎ 071/321–0388); the **Mercado Modelo** (⊠ Praça Visconde de Cairú s/n, ☎ 071/241–0240); and in the **Cidade Alta** (⊠ Porto da Barra s/n, ☎ 071/247–3195). All offices are open daily 8–6, except for the main branch, which is open 7–7, and the airport branch, which is open 8:30 AM–10 PM.

Emtursa (⊠ Largo do Pelourinho 12, ☎ 071/243–6555 or 071/243–5738; ⊠ Trv. da Ajuda 2, 2nd floor, ☎ 071/321–4346 or 071/321–9307), the municipal tourist board, is open weekdays 8–6.

RECIFE

The official state tourist board is **Empetur** (⊠ Guararapes Airport, ☎ 081/462–4960; ⊠ Centro de Convenções, Complexo Rodoviário de Salgadinho s/n, ☎ 081/241–3119; ⊠ TIP, Rodovia BR 232, Km 15, Curado, Jaboatão dos Guararapes, ☎ 081/452–1999). In Olinda contact the **Secretaria de Turismo** (⊠ Rua de São Bento 160, ☎ 081/429–1927; ⊠ Rua Bernardo Vieira de Melo, Mercado da Ribeira, Praça do Carmo, ☎ 081/439–1660).

FORTALEZA

A tourist information hotline, **Disque Turismo** (☎ 1516) operates weekdays 8–6; English is spoken. You can also get information through the **Secretaria de Segurança Pública do Estado do Ceará** (⊠ Trv. José Napoleão 82, Meireles, ☎ 085/263–5904).

Branches of Ceará state's tourist board, **Setur** (⊠ Centro Administrativo Virgílio Távora, Cambeba, ☎ 085/218–1177; ⊠ Aeroporto Internacional Pinto Martins, Av. Senador Carlos Jereissati, ☎ 085/477–

1667; ⊠ Centro de Turismo, Rua Senador Pompeu 350, Centro, ☎ 085/212–2493), are open weekdays 8–6, except for the one at the airport, which is open 24 hours a day. The municipal tourist board, **Fortur** (Av. Santos Dumont 5335, Papicu, 085/265–1177; Av. Beira-Mar, in front of Clube Náutico, 085/242–4447) has booths that are open weekdays 8 AM–10 PM and weekends 8–6.

8 THE AMAZON

Adventure awaits you in the Amazon. You can travel by riverboat—perhaps accompanied by pink dolphins—and bask on the soft, white sands of a river beach. You can stay in a jungle lodge—fishing for piranha by day, searching for alligators at night. You can witness the violent meeting of the world's most voluminous river with the Atlantic. And you can dock in cities whose mansions are a testament to wealth and ostentation of the bygone age of rubber.

Updated and
expanded by
Brad Weiss

AFLIGHT OVER THE AMAZON region is unforgettable. The world's largest rain forest seems an endless carpet of green that's sliced only by the curving contours of rivers. Its statistics are as impressive: The region covers more than 10 million square km (4 million square mi) and extends into eight other countries (French Guiana, Suriname, Guyana, Venezuela, Ecuador, Peru, Bolivia, and Colombia). It takes up roughly 40% of Brazil in the states of Acre, Rondônia, Amazonas, Roraima, Pará, Amapá, and Tocantins. The rain forest produces ⅓ of the world's oxygen and is home to ⅕ of its freshwater supply as well as 500,000 catalogued species of plants and animals. Yet it's inhabited by only 16 million people—that's less than the population of metropolitan São Paulo.

Life here centers on the rivers, the largest of which is the Amazon itself. From its source in southern Peru, it runs 6,300 km (3,900 mi) to its Atlantic outflow. It's second in length only to the Nile, and of its hundreds of tributaries, 17 are more than 1,600 km (1,000 mi) long. In places the Amazon is so wide that you can't see the shore, earning it the appellation of Rio Mar (River Sea). Although there has been increasing urbanization, 45% of the Amazon's residents live in rural settlements along the riverbanks, where the trees are full of fruit, the waters teem with fish, and the soil—whose nutrients are leached by heavy rainfall—is suited to the hearty, multipurpose manioc root.

The Spaniard Vincente Pinzon is credited with having been the first to sail the Amazon in 1500. But the most famous voyage was undertaken by Spanish conquistador Francisco de Orellano, who set out from Ecuador on a short mission to search for food in 1541. Orellano was also, no doubt, familiar with the legend that started it all—that of El Dorado (The Golden One), a monarch whose kingdom was so rich in gold he covered his naked body in gold dust each day. Instead of gold or a lost kingdom, however, Orellano ran into natives, heat, and disease. When he emerged from the jungle a year later, his crew told a tale of women warriors they called the Amazons (a nod to classical mythology). This captivating story lent the region its name.

Much later, Portuguese explorer Francisco Raposo claimed to have found the ruins of a lost civilization in the jungle. He wrote: "We entered fearfully through the gateways to find the ruins of a city. . . We came upon a great plaza, a column of black stone and on top of it the figure of a youth was carved over what seemed to be a great doorway." Whatever Raposo saw was never again found. For, unlike the highly organized Indian kingdoms and cities of Mexico and Peru, the Amazon natives were primarily nomadic hunter-gatherers.

Documented accounts indicate that early Portuguese contacts with the Indians were relatively peaceful. But it wasn't long before the peace ended, and the indigenous populations were devastated. Diseases brought by the Europeans and against which the Indians had no resistance took their toll; the Portuguese attempts to enslave them did the rest. When the Portuguese arrived in Brazil, there were roughly 4.5 million Indians, many of them in the Amazon; today there are just over 300,000 in the nation and fewer than 200,000 in the Amazon (☞ box "The Vanishing Indians," *below*). Although the Portuguese conducted expeditions into the Amazon and established forts to protect the territory against other Europeans, they found neither gold nor a viable labor force. Official interest in the region waned until the rubber era of the late 19th century.

Rubber, needed for bicycle and automobile tires, practically trans-formed Belém and Manaus from outposts to cities. Rubber barons con-structed mansions and monuments and brought the most modern trappings of life into the jungle. As money poured in and out of the Amazon, the area attracted a colorful array of explorers, dreamers, and opportunists. On the Rondon-Roosevelt expedition of 1913, Brazil-ian adventurer Cândido Mariana da Silva Rondon (for whom the state of Rondônia is named) and former president Theodore Roosevelt came across a then-unknown river (Rondon named it for Roosevelt). In 1925, British adventurer Colonel Percy Fawcett, who had been seek-ing Raposo's lost city for years, made one more trip into the jungle and then disappeared. In 1928, Henry Ford began to pour millions of dollars into vast rubber plantations. After much struggle and few re-sults, the projects were scrapped 20 years later.

Since the rubber era, huge reserves of gold and iron have been discovered. Land-settlement schemes and development projects, such as hydroelectric plants and major roadworks, have followed. Conservation has not al-ways been a priority. Vast portions of the "world's lung" have been indiscriminately deforested; tribal lands have again been encroached upon; and industrial by-products, such as mercury used in gold min-ing, have poisoned wildlife and people. The 1988 murder (by a wealthy cattle rancher) of Brazilian activist Chico Mendes, who had made a name for himself lobbying for environmental issues abroad, brought still more global attention to the region. Although the Brazilian gov-ernment has established reserves and made other efforts to preserve the territory, conservationists aren't satisfied.

And yet, 500 years after the first Europeans arrived, much of the Ama-zon has not been thoroughly explored by land. It's still a place where simple pleasures are savored and the mystical is celebrated. You can still hear stories of lost cities and of unearthly creatures (☞ box "Tales from the Mist: Amazon Legends," *below*). You can still stand on a river-boat deck and be astounded by the vastness of the mighty Rio Ama-zonas or charmed by wooden huts along a narrow waterway. You can wave at locals fishing from canoes and gawk at trees that tower 150 feet. You can count stars in a clear night sky and spot birds over sun-dappled waters. For more direct contact with the inhabitants (human, animal, and mythical) you can step ashore, beyond the dense vegeta-tion. You, too, can have an unforgettable experience.

Pleasures and Pastimes

Dining

Who needs regular old beef or poultry when you can have water-buf-falo steak or wild Amazon duck? If you have even more intrepid taste buds you can even try armadillo (beware of ordering alligator and tur-tle, which are still found on some menus although it's against the law). In addition to piranha, you'll find river fish with such exotic Indian names as *tucunaré, pirarucu, tambaquí, curimatá, jaraquí,* and *pacú.* The *pimenta-de-cheiro,* a local hot pepper oil, seriously spices things up. Side dishes often include *farofa* (coarsely ground manioc), *farinha* (finely ground manioc), black beans, and rice.

For dessert, try some of the region's famed fruits, such as *cupuaçu* (a yellow, sweet, extremely fragrant fruit the size of a basketball), *guaraná* (a small, red fruit used in the popular Brazilian soft drink of the same name), and *açaí* (another small, red fruit; it's bitter but is commonly found in sweetened, energy-enhancing sorbets that are beloved by ath-letes). The region's most popular beers are Antarctica and Cerpa.

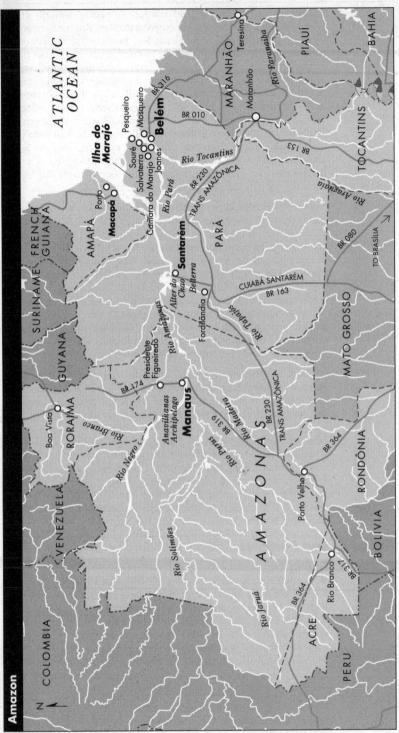

Reservations and dressy attire are rarely needed (indeed, reservations are rarely taken). Tipping isn't customary. For price categories, *see* the chart *under* Dining *in* Smart Travel Tips A to Z at the front of this guide.

Handicrafts

Handicrafts made by indigenous groups include wooden furniture, woven items, bows and arrows, and jewelry and headdresses of seeds and feathers. (Note: U.S. Customs prohibits the import of certain feathers; ask the storekeeper about such items before you buy.) In Belém, you'll find *marajoara* pottery, which has the intricate designs used by the tribe of the same name. Vases and sculptures in Macapá often contain manganese—a black, shiny mineral mined locally.

Lodging

Regardless of whether you stay in a resort, a hotel, a *pousada* (inn), or a jungle lodge, expect prices to be on the high side. Further, service and amenities may not match the price tags, and such extras as laundry service can be outrageously expensive (always ask about costs beforehand). All that said, there are bargains to be found, and most places include breakfast in their rates. Further, many establishments offer discounts of as much as 20%—don't be shy about asking for a reduced rate, especially in low season. Rooms in hotels, particularly in the cities, generally have air-conditioning, phones, and TVs. Unless otherwise noted, all rooms have baths. For price categories, *see* the chart *under* Lodging *in* Smart Travel Tips A to Z at the front of this guide.

Exploring the Amazon

Although there are regular flights throughout the Amazon, many visitors still opt for the area's primary mode of transportation—boat. The region encompasses hundreds of navigable rivers, but vessels tend to follow only a few well-charted waterways, mainly the Amazon, Negro, Solimões, Madeira, Pará, and Tapajós rivers. A trip along the Amazon itself—especially the 1,602 km (993 mi) three- to five-day journey between Belém and Manaus—is a singular experience. Averaging more than 3 km (2 mi) in width, but reaching up to 48 km (30 mi) in the rainy season, there are many spots where it's impossible to see either bank. At night, the moon and stars are the only sources of light, reinforcing the sense of being in true wilderness.

Cruises

Whatever your style of travel, your budget, or the length of your stay, there's a boat plying the river to suit your needs. You can sleep in a hammock on the deck of a thatch-roofed riverboat or in the air-conditioned suite of an upscale tour operator's private ship. (For Brazilian companies that arrange boat transportation, *see* Tour Operators and Travel Agents *in* the Amazon A to Z *below*). Note that, owing to the dense riverbank vegetation, it's not easy to spot wildlife from a boat. Further, some craft travel far from shore, defeating any chance you have of seeing the flora or the fauna. It's best to plan a boat trip that includes a stop or two, so that you can explore the rain forest.

ENASA BOATS

The state-run **Empresa de Navegação da Amazônia S/A (ENASA)** has an enormous, first-rate catamaran that travels between Belém and Manaus once or twice a month. All of its 62 cabins have air-conditioning, music, phones, and baths with hot water. Other shipboard amenities include a pool, a bar, and a restaurant that serves regional food. The four- to five-day trip costs roughly $500. Unfortunately, the schedule isn't regular, and you can't make reservations through travel agencies. ENASA has other ships that travel more frequently, but they don't offer the same standard of luxury.

OCEAN-GOING SHIPS

Some cruise ships call at Manaus as part of itineraries that may include stops in Santarém, Rio de Janeiro, and southern Caribbean islands. Most trips take place during the North American winter; they range in length from 11 to 29 days and costs start at $2,500. The major lines making such journeys are Princess Cruises and Royal Olympic Cruises (☞ Tour Operators *in* Smart Travel Tips at the front of this guide).

SPEEDBOATS

Two high-speed catamarans run between Manaus and Santarém (12 hours, $50) and between Macapá and Belém (7 hours, $40). Traveling at 40–50 knots per hour, they arrive in about a third of the time as other boats, but they travel far from the riverbanks, so you won't see much on the journey. They have cushioned seats and air-conditioning.

STANDARD RIVERBOATS

If you think that comfort should take a back seat to adventure, consider a leisurely trip by standard double- or triple-decker boats, which carry both freight and passengers. Although you may not get a close-up view of the riverbank, you will get the real feel of life along the river. Frequent stops at small towns are opportunities for interesting interactions and observations.

You might be able to get a cabin, but expect it to be claustrophobic. Cabins cost $100 to $200 between Manaus and Belém and about half that to or from Santarém. The real adventure, however, is out on the deck, where most passengers sleep in hammocks ($50–$75 between Manaus and Belém), often with little or no space between them. You must bring your own hammock (they're sold onshore for about $15) as well as a few yards of rope to tie it up.

Clusters of booths sell tickets at the docks. Even if you don't speak Portuguese, you can ascertain the necessary information from the signs alongside the booths. Inspect the vessel you will travel on closely (sanitary conditions vary from boat to boat), and, if you plan to sleep in a hammock, board early to secure a good spot (away from the engine and toilets). Travel as light as possible, and keep your gear secure at all times. Bring plenty of sunscreen and insect repellent. Nights can be surprisingly cool, so pack a light blanket. Food is served, but the quality ranges from okay to deplorable. At best, the diet of meat, rice, and beans can become monotonous. Experienced Brazilian travelers bring their own food, bottled water, small stoves, and pans; you can also buy fresh fruit at stops along the way (just be sure to peel or wash it thoroughly with bottled water before eating it).

TOURIST BOATS

Tourist boats, which are used by tour operators and can be hired for private groups, are more comfortable than standard riverboats. They generally travel close to the riverbank and have open upper decks from which you can observe the river and forest. The better tour operators have a regional expert—usually an ecologist or botanist—on board, who's fluent in English. You can either sleep out on the deck in a hammock or in a cabin, which will usually have air-conditioning or a fan. Meals are generally provided.

Organized Trips

From 3 to 19 days, from hammocks in the open air to luxurious wood-paneled boat cabins and/or jungle lodges, from Belém to Manaus, most tour operators offer a variety of itineraries. Along the route, you may visit indigenous villages, explore tributaries by small craft, and learn about the flora and fauna. (For specific operators, *see* Tour Operators *in* Smart Travel Tips, at the front of this guide.)

CANOEING AND FISHING

Paddling local wooden canoes by day and camping at night, you may explore the rain forest that lines the banks of the Rio Negro (Negro River) and perhaps continue along smaller tributaries. En route, you'll see monkeys, iguanas, river dolphins, and alligators, and you'll visit with local river people. (Trips generally run 7–10 days.) Some 20 species of fish inhabit the Amazon. But it's the legendary peacock bass, described as the "ultimate adversary," that lures most anglers. Mobile safari camps allow you to reach obscure, unpopulated watersheds, or you can opt for an air-conditioned stateroom aboard a boat.

CULTURE

Although Brazil limits visits to Indian reservations to researchers, if you have an interest in indigenous cultures, you can learn about the Yanomami people on 11- or 15-day itineraries. Operators take you in small boats along the Rio Negro to visit small Yanomami communities that aren't part of a reservation, and to spend several days with the people of one village. One operation, Amizade Limited, takes its cultural trips a step farther. You can help the organization's volunteers and Brazilian students construct a self-sustaining silk-screening workshop where Amazonian street children can learn a viable skill.

TREKKING AND CAMPING

Inland jungle adventures last 3–15 days, and most begin with a boat trip up the Rio Negro from Manaus. Some trips are based at Ariaú Jungle Towers where four-story accommodations, linked by catwalks, stand atop stilts. Other programs combine cruises with jungle lodge stays. All include rain forest walks, usually led by a naturalist. If you're more adventurous, consider a trekking and camping trip. By day, you'll spend an average of six hours traveling through thick vegetation. At night, you'll no doubt sleep well—perhaps in a hammock and certainly serenaded by wildlife.

Great Itineraries

Because of the Amazon's immense size and wealth of natural wonders, even 10 days is a short time to explore the region. Still, during a week-long stay, you can see some urban highlights and spend a little time on the river as well. The following independent itineraries start in Belém and end in Manaus, but it's fine to follow them in reverse.

IF YOU HAVE 7 DAYS

Fly into Belém and spend two days exploring the Cidade Velha and the natural reserves in and around the city. Then fly to Manaus for two days—enough time for the short boat ride to the meeting of the waters and to take a city tour that includes the Teatro Amazonas. Then head out for a stay of a day or two at one of the famed jungle lodges.

IF YOU HAVE 10 DAYS

Spend two days in Belém exploring the city and its environs. On your third day, travel by boat to Ilha do Marajó for a two-day *fazenda* (ranch) stay. Return to Belém for a flight to Manaus; two days is enough to see the urban sights and to see the meeting of the waters. Spend your last few days at a jungle lodge outside Manaus.

IF YOU HAVE 15 DAYS

After spending two days exploring Belém and a couple more on a fazenda in Ilha do Marajó, hop either a luxury or standard riverboat for the two-day journey to Santarém. Spend a day strolling the city before heading to Alter do Chão, an hour away. Then fly from Santarém into Manaus, where you should spend a day or two sightseeing before heading to a jungle lodge.

When to Tour

In summer (winter in the Northern Hemisphere) it's often brutally hot. During the winter, it's hot but bearable. The average temperature is 80°F (27°C); nights are always cooler. The rainy season (high water) runs from December to June; the dry season (low water) is from July to November. Although travel during both seasons is good, high water means better access to some areas and better wildlife spotting. On the flip side, it also means that some river beaches will be flooded.

BELÉM

Belém, the capital of Pará State, is a river port of more than 1.5 million people on the southern bank of the Rio Guamá, 120 km (74 mi) from the Atlantic and 2,933 km (1,760 mi) and 3,250 km (1,950 mi) north of Rio de Janeiro and São Paulo, respectively. The Portuguese settled here in 1616, using it as a gateway to the interior and an outpost to protect the area from invasion by sea. Because of its ocean access, Belém became a major trade center. Like the upriver city of Manaus, it rode the ups and downs of the Amazon booms and busts, alternately bursting with energy and money and slumping into relative obscurity. Its first taste of prosperity was during the rubber era in the late 19th and early 20th centuries. Almost overnight it became an opulent, extravagant city. Architects from Europe were brought in to build churches, civic palaces, theaters, and mansions, often using fine, imported materials. Monuments were erected to honor magnates. When Malaysian rubber supplanted that of Brazil in the 1920s, wood, and later, minerals, provided the impetus for growth.

In the past 20 years, Belém has experienced rapid expansion, pushed by major projects in the surrounding area, including the Tucuruvi hydroelectric dam, Brazil's second-largest, and the development of the Carajás iron-ore mining region. Modern high-rises are replacing the colonial structures. Recently, however, local governments have launched massive campaigns to preserve the city's rich heritage.

Exploring Belém

Belém is more than just a jumping-off point for the Amazon. It has several good museums and restaurants and lots of extraordinary architecture. Several distinctive buildings—some with Portuguese *azulejos* (tiles) and ornate iron gates—survive along the downtown streets and around the Praça Frei Caetano Brandão, in the Cidade Velha (Old City). East of here, in the Nazaré neighborhood, colorful colonial structures mingle with new ones housing trendy shops.

Numbers in the text correspond to numbers in the margin and on the Belém map.

Cidade Velha

A GOOD WALK

Begin at the **Igreja Nossa Senhora das Mercês** ①, a large, pink church just northeast of the **Ver-o-Peso** ② market. Walking southwest through the market, you'll pass the small dock where fishermen unload the day's catch. Turn left on Avenida Portugal (past the municipal clock, crafted in the image of Big Ben), which borders Praça Dom Pedro II. Follow it to the large, baby-blue Palácio Antônio Lemos, which houses the **Museu de Arte de Belém (MABE)** ③. Next door is the even larger, white Palá-

cio Lauro Sodré, in which you'll find the **Museu do Estado do Pará** ④.
Just behind this museum, the golden church, **Igreja de São João Batista** ⑤, looms. From here, head back toward Praça Dom Pedro II along
Rua Tomásia Perdigão, and turn left onto Travessa Félix Roque. This
takes you to the rear of the **Catedral da Sé** ⑥ (the entrance faces Praça
Frei Caetano Brandão). To your right as you exit the cathedral is the
Museu de Arte Sacra ⑦, and just beyond is the **Forte do Castelo** ⑧.

TIMING

This tour will take two to three hours—longer if you linger in the museums. It's best to start at 8 AM or 9 AM and finish by lunchtime. Next
to the Forte do Castelo is the Círculo Militar restaurant (☞ Dining,
below), the perfect place to enjoy a meal and the view of Bahía de Guajará (Guajará Bay).

SIGHTS TO SEE

⑥ **Catedral da Sé.** In 1771 Bolognese architect Antônio José Landi, whose
work can be seen throughout the city, completed the cathedral's construction on the foundations of an older church. It has an interesting
mix of baroque, colonial, and neoclassical styles. Its interior is richly
adorned with Carrara marble, and the high altar was a gift from Pope
Pius IX. *Praça Frei Caetano Brandão.* ☒ *Free.* ☉ *Tues.–Fri. 8–noon
and 2–5, Sat. 6 PM–8 PM, Sun. 4 PM–9 PM.*

⑧ **Forte do Castelo.** The birthplace of Belém was originally called Forte
do Presépio (Fort of the Crèche). It was from here that the Portuguese
founders launched their conquests of the Amazon. The fort's role in the
region's defense is evidenced by the English- and Portuguese-made cannons. ☒ *Praça Frei Caetano Brandão.* ☒ *Free.* ☉ *Daily 8 AM–9 PM.*

① **Igreja Nossa Senhora das Mercês.** Our Lady of Mercy Church is another baroque creation attributed to Antônio Landi. Notable for its
pink color and its convex facade, it's part of a complex that includes the
Convento dos Mercedários, which has served as a convent and, less mercifully, as a prison. ☒ *Largo as Mercês.* ☒ *Free.* ☉ *Mon.–Sat. 8–1.*

⑤ **Igreja de São João Batista.** The prodigious architect Antônio Landi
finished the small, octagonal St. John the Baptist Church in 1777. It
was completely restored in 1997 and is considered the city's purest example of baroque architecture. ☒ *Rua Dr. Tomásia Perdigão at Largo
de São João.* ☒ *Free.*

③ **Museu de Arte de Belém (MABE).** When you arrive at the Metropolitan Art Museum, don't be surprised if a security guard hands you large,
brown, furry objects—these are slippers that you must wear over your
shoes to protect the wooden floors. The bottom level has temporary
expositions. Shuffle up to the second level and the permanent collection of furniture and paintings that date from the 18th century through
the rubber boom. The museum is housed in the recently renovated Palácio Antônio Lemos (circa 1883), a municipal palace built in the Imperial Brazilian style with French influences. ☒ *Praça Dom Pedro II,*
☎ *091/241–1398.* ☒ *Free.* ☉ *Tues.–Fri. 10–6, Sat.–Sun. 9–1.*

⑦ **Museu de Arte Sacra.** The first part of a guided Sacred Art Museum
tour (call to reserve an English-speaking docent 48 hours in advance)
takes you through the early 18th-century, Amazon baroque **Igreja de
Santo Alexandre** (St. Alexander Church), which is distinguished by intricate woodwork on its alter and pews. On the second half of the tour,
you'll see the museum's collection of religious sculptures and paintings. The first floor has temporary exhibitions, a gift shop, and a café.
☒ *Praça Frei Caetano Brandão,* ☎ *091/225–1125.* ☒ *Admission; free
on Tues.* ☉ *Tues.–Sun. 10–6.*

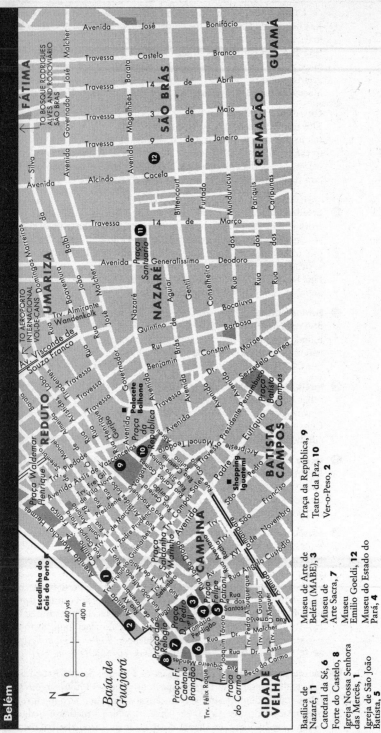

Belém

N

Baía de
Guajará

Escadinha do
Cais do Porto

0   440 yds
0   400 m

FÁTIMA

TO BOSQUE RODRIGUES
ALVES AND RODOVIÁRIO
SÃO BRÁS

GUAMÁ

CREMAÇÃO

SÃO BRÁS

Avenida   José   Bonifácio

Travessa   Castelo   Branco

Travessa   14   de   Abril

Travessa   3   de   Maio

Travessa   9   de   Janeiro

Alcindo   Cacela   ⑫

Travessa   14   de   Março

Avenida   Generalíssimo   Deodoro

Praça ⑪
Santuário

NAZARÉ

UMARIZA

TO AEROPORTO
INTERNACIONAL
VAL-DE-CANS Domingos Marreiros

Av. Visconde de
Souza Franco

REDUTO

Praça Waldemar
Henrique

Palacete
Bolonha ■

Praça
da
República

⑩ ⑨

Praça
Batista
Campos

**BATISTA
CAMPOS**

Shopping
Iguatemi ■

CAMPINA

① ② ③ ④ ⑤ ⑥ ⑦ ⑧

**CIDADE
VELHA**

Praça do
Carmo

Praça Fr.
Caetano
Brandão

Praça
D. Pedro
II

Praça do
Relógio

Basílica de
Nazaré, **11**
Catedral da Sé, **6**
Forte do Castelo, **8**
Igreja Nossa Senhora
das Mercês, **1**
Igreja de São João
Batista, **5**

Museu de Arte de
Belém (MABE), **3**
Museu de
Arte Sacra, **7**
Museu
Emílio Goeldi, **12**
Museu do Estado do
Pará, **4**

Praça da República, **9**
Teatro da Paz, **10**
Ver-o-Peso, **2**

❹ Museu do Estado do Pará. The Pará State Museum is in the sumptuous Palácio Lauro Sodré (circa 1771), an Antônio Landi creation with Venetian and Portuguese elements. The first floor hosts consistently outstanding visiting exhibitions; the second floor contains the permanent collection of furniture and paintings. ✉ *Praça Dom Pedro II,* ☎ *091/ 225–3853.* 🎫 *Free.* ☉ *Permanent collection: Tues.–Fri. 10–5:45. Temporary exhibits: Tues.–Sun. 10–5:45.*

★ **❷ Ver-o-Peso.** Literally meaning "See the Weight" (a colonial-era sales pitch), this market is a hypnotic confusion of colors and voices. Vendors hawk tropical fruits, "miracle" jungle roots, and charms for the body and soul. There are jars filled with animal eyes, tails, and even heads as well as a variety of herbs—each with its own legendary power. A regional oddity are the sex organs of the river dolphin, supposedly unrivaled cures for romantic problems. In the fish market, you'll get an up close look at pirarucu, the Amazon's most colorful species; the *mero,* which can weigh more than 91 kilos (200 pounds); and the silver-scale *piratema.* Across the street from Ver-o-Peso is the small arched entrance to the municipal meat market. Duck in and glance at the pink and green painted ironwork, imported from Britain and done in a French style. Be sure to visit Ver-o-Peso before noon, which is when most vendors leave, and be careful of pickpockets.

Nazaré

Just east of the Cidade Velha, Nazaré's mango tree–lined streets create the sensation of walking through tunnels. Among the historic buildings there's a tremendous variety of pastel colors and European styles. Many of the newer buildings house elegant shops.

A GOOD TOUR

Begin at the south end of the **Praça da República** ⑨. Across Avenida da Paz is the large, pink **Teatro da Paz** ⑩. After leaving the theater, veer left onto Avenida Governador José Malcher; look for the sign for Lá em Casa, one of Belém's best restaurants (☞ Dining, *below*). Just behind it is the elaborate Palacete Bolonha, from which you should continue east along Governador José Malcher (note the burgundy and gold designs painted on the road at several intersections; they're styled after those on marajoara pottery). Turn right onto Travessa Benjamin Constant and right again onto Avenida Nazaré. Just beyond Avenida Generalíssimo Deodoro is the **Basílica de Nazaré** ⑪. Continue east three more blocks to the **Museu Emilio Goeldi** ⑫. After touring the museum, consider taking a short ($5) taxi ride northeast to the **Bosque Rodrigues Alves,** a chunk of jungle right in the middle of town.

TIMING

It should take about 1½ hours to reach the Museu Emilio Goeldi. Plan to spend an hour or two here owing to the quantity (and quality) of the displays. If you need a break, the museum has a restaurant and a snack bar. Count on at least an hour at Bosque Rodrigues Alves.

SIGHTS TO SEE

★ **⑪ Basílica de Nazaré.** It's hard to miss this opulent, Roman-style basilica. Not only does it stand out visually, but in the plaza out front, there's an enormous tree filled with screeching parakeets. It was built in 1908 on the site where a *caboclo* (rural inhabitant) named Placido saw a vision of the Virgin in the early 1700s. The basilica's ornate interior is constructed entirely of European marble and contains elaborate mosaics, detailed stained-glass windows, and intricate bronze doors. In the small, basement-level **Museu do Círio,** displays explain the Círio de Nazaré festival, which is held each October to honor the city's patron saint. ✉ *Praça Justo Chermont s/n,* ☎ *091/224–9614 for museum.*

TALES FROM THE MIST: AMAZON LEGENDS

THE IMMENSE AMAZON region is fertile ground not only for flora and fauna, but also for legends. They're an integral part of local culture and are remarkably consistent throughout the region.

Many are based on strange creatures that inhabit the rivers and jungle. One of the most widespread legends is that of the *cobra grande* (giant snake), which strikes fear into the hearts of many a river dweller. Popularized by the movie, *Anaconda*, which was filmed near Manaus, the story involves *sucuri* (anaconda) snakes of epic proportions that terrorize jungle creatures. They're said to cause shipwrecks and to eat fleeing passengers whole. According to one version, the snakes originated from a human baby whose mother discarded it in the river.

Another extremely popular (and considerably less gruesome) legend is that of the *botos* (dolphins) that take human form. Always dressed immaculately in white, they appear at parties and dance with the youngest, most beautiful girls. They lure the girls outside, where they seduce them and then return to the water just before dawn. You can always tell a boto from its slightly fishy smell and the hole in the top of its head, which is covered by a hat.

Curupira is said to lure people into the jungle, causing them to become irreversibly lost. He appears as a nude and savage indigenous child, about six or seven years old, whose feet are turned backward. As the story goes, white men cut off his feet before killing him. A god sewed Curupira's feet back on backwards and returned him to the forest to exact revenge.

Some people claim that you can solicit Curupira's help for hunting and crop failures. As payment, you must bring him tobacco, matches, and a bottle of liquor, the latter of which he will down in one swig to seal the pact. If you ever tell anyone about the agreement, Curupira will hunt you down and stab you to death with his long, sharp fingernails. As he approaches to do this deed, you'll purportedly develop a sense of remorse.

Several tales explain the origins of important fruits and vegetables. Guaraná, for example, was the name of a young child beloved by all. As the story goes, he was killed by the jealous god, Jurupari, who disguised himself as a snake. Lightning struck as the village gathered around Guaraná's body and wept. At that moment the lightning god, Tupã, ordered the villagers to bury the child's eyes. The *guaraná* fruit (which actually resembles eyes) sprouted from the burial spot.

In the legend of Açaí, the chief of a starving tribe ordered all babies to be sacrificed to end the famine. The chief's daughter, Iaça, had a beautiful baby. Before its sacrifice, she found the child holding a palm tree, and then he suddenly vanished. The tree then became full of *açaí* (Iaça backwards) fruit, from which a wine was made that saved the tribe and ended the sacrifices.

🖾 *Free to both basilica and museum.* ⊘ *Basilica: Mon. 6–11 and 3–5, Tues.–Sat. 6–11 and 3–7, Sun. 3–7. Museum: weekdays 8–6.*

OFF THE
BEATEN PATH
BOSQUE RODRIGUES ALVES – In 1883, this 40-acre plot of rain forest was designated an ecological reserve. Nowadays, you'll find an aquarium and two amusement parks as well as natural caverns, a variety of animals (some in the wild), and mammoth trees. ⊠ *Av. Almirante Barroso,* ☎ *091/226–2308.* 🖾 *Admission.* ⊘ *Tues.–Sun. 8–5.*

★ ⑫ **Museu Emílio Goeldi.** Founded by a naturalist and a group of intellectuals in 1866, this complex contains one of the Amazon's most important research facilities. Its museum has an extensive collection of Indian artifacts, including the distinctive and beautiful pottery of the Marajó Indians, known as marajoara. An adjacent tract of rain forest has reflection pools with giant Victoria Régia water lilies. But the true highlight is the wide collection of Amazon wildlife, including manatees, rare blue alligators, sloths, and various species of monkeys. ⊠ *Av. Magalhães Barata 376,* ☎ *091/249–1233.* 🖾 *Admission.* ⊘ *Weekends and Tues.–Thurs. 9–noon and 2–5; Fri. 9–noon.*

⑨ **Praça da República.** Here you'll find a large statue that commemorates the proclamation of the Republic of Brazil, an amphitheater, and several French-style iron kiosks.

⑩ **Teatro da Paz.** Greek-style pillars line the front and sides of this neoclassical theater, which was completed in 1878 and is the third-oldest in Brazil. Inside, note the imported details such as the Italian marble pillars and the French chandeliers. Opera and classical music performances are still held in the theater, which seats more than 800 people. English-speaking guides are available to give 20-minute tours. ☎ *091/224–7355.* 🖾 *Admission.* ⊘ *Weekdays 9–noon and 2–5.*

Beaches

The closest ocean beach is **Salinas,** a four-hour drive from Belém. The river beaches are much closer. Depending on the season and time of day, they're either expansive stretches or narrow strips of soft, white sand. Currents are rarely strong, and there's usually a large area of shallow water. Although **Outerio** is an easy half-hour bus ride from town, it's not very scenic; it's also generally crowded and a little dirty.

Most people head for one of the 18 beaches on Ilha Mosqueiro, along the Rio Pará. Connected to the mainland by a large bridge, it's just an hour's drive from the city. Although **Farol** is close to Ilha Mosqueiro's hub, Vila, and is often crowded, it's still pretty. Stands sell fresh fish dishes, and at low tide you can walk to tiny, rocky Ilha do Amor (Love Island). In October, the waves are high enough for river-surfing competitions. **Morubira,** also close to Vila, has beautiful colonial houses and many restaurants and bars.

The water is clear and the shore is clean at **Marahú.** Several stands sell food and drink. The bus from Belém doesn't travel here directly; you have to disembark in Vila and hop another bus. You must also catch a second bus in Vila to reach the aptly named **Paraíso.** It's lined with trees and has soft white sands and clear emerald waters. If you can't bear to leave this paradise at day's end, consider a stay at the Hotel Fazenda Paraíso (☞ Lodging, *below*).

Dining

$$–$$$ ✕ **Au Bon Vivant.** With its soft, blue, neon lighting and abstract art, this French establishment is as chic as it gets in the Amazon. The menu offers a refreshing dose of creativity, which is generally lacking in the region's restaurants. There's also an antipasto bar with premium meats, cheeses, and seafood. ⊠ *Trv. Quintino Bacaiúva 2084, Cremação,* ☎ *091/225–001. AE, DC, MC, V. Closed Mon.*

$$ ✕ **Círculo Militar.** The specialty here, one block from Ver-o-Peso market and near the Forte do Castelo, is fresh fish. Try the *filhote ao leite de coco* (river fish sautéed in a coconut milk). Come for lunch so that you can enjoy the river view. ⊠ *Praça Frei Caetano Brandão s/n, Cidade Velha,* ☎ *091/223–4374. AE, DC, MC, V.*

$$ ✕ **Dom Giuseppe.** From gnocchi to ravioli, the flawless preparation of basics distinguishes this Italian eatery from all the others. Everyone in town knows this, too, so reservations are a good idea, particularly on weekends. Don't leave without ordering a scrumptious *dolce Paula* (an ice cream and brownie dessert). ⊠ *Av. Conselheiro Furtado 1420, Batista Campos,* ☎ *091/241–1146. AE, DC, MC, V.*

$$ ✕ **Lá em Casa.** Not only are the Amazon specialties here superb, but
★ the owner, Dona Ana Maria, has a smile for everyone. Consider trying Belém's premier dish, *pato no tucupi,* duck in a yellow herb sauce made from manioc root and served with the mildly intoxicating *jambu* leaf. The *casquinha de caranqueijo* (stuffed crab shells with coconut sauce) is another good choice, as is the açaí sorbet. There are attractive seating areas indoors (with air-conditioning) and outside on a deck. ⊠ *Av. Governador José Malcher 247, Nazaré,* ☎ *091/223–1212. AE, DC, MC, V.*

$$ ✕ **Miako.** Belém has a large Japanese community (second only to that of São Paulo), so there's no lack of Japanese restaurants. This one, however, is a tried-and-true favorite for its excellent service, attractive wooden decor, and consistently good food. The sushi is terrific. ⊠ *Rua 1 de Março 76, Centro,* ☎ *091/242–2355. AE, DC, MC, V.*

$ ✕ **Casa Portuguesa.** Although it's in the heart of the commercial district, this restaurant does its best to replicate the charm of a Portuguese country home. The specialties are dishes with chicken and, of course, cod. ⊠ *Rua Senador Manoel Barata 897, Centro,* ☎ *091/242–4871. AE, DC, MC, V.*

$ ✕ **Rodeio.** Devoted carnivores take note: there's nothing like a meal in a *churrascaria* after a few days on a riverboat with little to eat but fish and rice. The reasonable fixed-price menu here not only includes as many servings of grilled and roasted meats as you can eat, but also salads and dessert. ⊠ *Trv. Padre Eutíqiu 1308, Batista Campos,* ☎ *091/212–2112. AE, DC, MC, V. No dinner Sun. and Mon.*

Lodging

$$$ 🏨 **Hilton International Belém.** The Hilton's reliability and amenities are topped only by its location right on the Praça da República. Although not very distinguished, the rooms are well equipped and comfortable. Executive rooms have the nicest views as well as access to a lounge with a VCR, a meeting area, and complimentary food and drink. ⊠ *Av. Presidente Vargas 882, Centro 66017–000,* ☎ *091/242–6500 or 800/445–8667 in U.S.,* ℻ *091/225–2942. 361 rooms. 2 restaurants, 2 bars, pool, beauty salon, sauna, health club, convention center. AE, DC, MC, V.*

$$–$$$ 🏨 **Equatorial Palace.** Its Nazaré location, within walking distance of the port and the Cidade Velha, is the best thing about this hotel. Although it's something of an institution (often featured in package deals) and has a few remnants of a more luxurious past, its rates are

hardly consistent with the facilities and services offered. ✉ *Av. Braz de Aguiar 612, Nazaré 66035–000,* ☎ *091/241–2000,* 🖷 *091/223–5222. 204 rooms, 7 suites. Restaurant, bar, pool. AE, DC, MC, V.*

$$ 🏨 **Hotel Regente.** This hotel offers excellent service and a prime location for a reasonable price. Stained-glass windows and soft leather couches welcome you in the attractive lobby. Rooms on the 12th floor are nicer and more modern than those on other floors, yet cost the same. ✉ *Av. Governador José Malcher 485, Nazaré 66035–100,* ☎ *091/241–1222,* 🖷 *091/242–0343. 196 rooms, 6 suites. Restaurant, bar, pool. AE, DC, MC, V.*

$$ 🏨 **Itaoca Hotel.** It comes as no surprise that this reasonably priced hotel has the highest occupancy rate in town. Its rooms are extremely comfortable, well equipped, and modern, and most have a fantastic view of the dock area and river. ✉ *Av. Presidente Vargas 132, Centro 66010–902,* ☎ 🖷 *091/241–3434. 36 rooms. Restaurant, in-room safes, meeting room. AE, DC, MC, V.*

$ 🏨 **Hotel Fazenda Paraíso.** Just a few feet from one of the most beautiful beaches on Ilha Mosqueiro, this hotel is the ideal place to spend a day or two just outside the city. Wooden and brick chalets with red-tile roofs accommodate as many as five people. Similarly designed apartments, which house up to three people, are more economical for singles and couples. The pool is configured in the shape of a clover. Be sure to make reservations as the hotel is very popular on weekends. ✉ *Beira-Mar, Praia do Paraíso, Ilha Mosqueiro 66915–000,* ☎ *091/772–2444 or 091/228–3950 in Belém. 12 rooms, 10 chalets. Restaurant, pool, horseback riding, beach, boating. AE, DC, MC, V.*

$ 🏨 **Manacá Hotel.** This small, bright-red hotel with a slanted, brown-
★ tile roof looks like a cross between a Monopoly hotel piece and a pagoda. With cozy, softly lighted common rooms, it offers more charm than larger places at about a quarter of the price. It's a clean, simple alternative if you can live without a pool or a bar. ✉ *Trv. Quintino Bocaiuva 1645, Nazaré 66033–620,* ☎ *091/223–3335. AE, DC, MC, V.*

$ 🏨 **Zoghbi Apart Hotel.** The only apartment hotel in town has suites with fully equipped kitchens that are great for families or for those who plan on being in Belém for a while. The already reasonable rate is reduced nearly 50% for stays that exceed 15 days. ✉ *Rua Ferreira Cantão 100, Centro 66017–110,* ☎ *091/241–1800. 55 apartments. Kitchenettes. V.*

Nightlife and the Arts

Nightlife

The *doca* (dock) area—about eight blocks east of the *escadinha,* the dock used for boat trips—has many bars and dance clubs. The main strip is Avenida Visconde de Souza Franco, but there are several locales a few blocks off it as well.

BARS

The clientele at the open-air **Bar do Parque** (✉ Praça República s/n, ☎ 091/242–8798) consists of a truly interesting cross-section of people, and the view of the Praça da República is beautiful. Popular dock area bars include **Bora Bora** (✉ Rua Bernal do Couto 38, ☎ 091/241–5848); **Colarinho Branco** (✉ Av. Visconde de Souza Franco 80, ☎ 091/242–1007); and **Roxy Bar** (✉ Av. Senador Lemos 231, ☎ 091/224–4514), which tops nearly everyone's list of hip spots.

DANCE AND MUSIC CLUBS

Africa Bar (✉ Praça Kennedy s/n, next to Paratur, ☎ 091/241–1085) consistently attracts some of the biggest names in Brazilian music. The **Zeppelin Club** (✉ Av. Senador Lemos 108, ☎ 091/223–8936) is the undisputed king of *boates* (dance clubs) and has prices to match. The cover charge on Friday and Saturday (the only nights the club is open) is about $15. For jazz, try **Zolt** (⌗ Rua Domingos Morreiros 470, ☎ 091/242–5771).

The Arts

For information about cultural events, contact the state-run **Secretaria de Cultura** (SECULT; ⌗ Av. Governador Magalhães Barata s/n, ☎ 091/249–3001). The **Teatro da Paz** often hosts plays, Philharmonic concerts, and dance recitals. Outstanding theatrical productions (in Portuguese) are held at the **Teatro Experimental Waldemar Henrique** (⌗ Av. Presidente Vargas 645, Praça da República, ☎ 091/222–4762).

Outdoor Activities and Sports

Participant Sports

FISHING

Pará state is renowned for the quality and variety of its fish. For information about fishing trips, contact the **Secretaria de Estado de Ciência, Tecnologia e Meio Ambiente** (SECTAM; ⌗ Trv. Lomas Valentinas 2717, ☎ 091/266–5000).

JUNGLE AND RIVER EXCURSIONS

On one- to several-day trips from Belém, you can explore the Guamá, Acará, and Mojú rivers. You can also catch a boat in the city at 4:30 AM and be at Ilha dos Papagaios (Parrot Island) by sunrise, when thousands of *papagaios* (parrots) leave in an unforgettable flight. Larger tour operators can make all the necessary arrangements (☞ Tour Operators and Travel Agents *in* the Amazon A to Z, *below*).

As you travel by Jeep along rain forest trails to the **Crocodile Safari Zoo** (☎ 091/222–9102), images of *Jurassic Park* may come to mind. Although the focus at this research station, a half-hour northwest of the city, is crocodiles (more than 500 of them are contained here), it also has a museum with prehistoric fossils and a large collection of shells. There's also river access, so you can take short canoe trips. Call ahead to arrange an afternoon visit accompanied by an English-speaking guide. The cost is roughly $20 per person, including transportation.

Spectator Sports

FUTEBOL

Belém's two *futebol* (soccer) teams are Payssandú and Remo—neither of which is currently in the premier league. Still, attending a Brazilian match, regardless of the quality of the team, is a memorable experience. Payssandú plays at **Estádio Leônidas de Castro** (⌗ Av. Almirante Barroso s/n, ☎ 091/241–1726). For Remo games, head to **Estádio Evandro Almeida** (⌗ Av. Almirante Barroso s/n, ☎ 091/223–2847).

HORSE RACING

If you like the horses, try your luck at the **Centro Hípico de Belém** (⌗ Rodovia do Coqueiro 36, ☎ 091/235–1252). It's open daily 7–6.

Shopping

Areas and Malls

Belém's main shopping street is **Avenida Presidente Vargas,** particularly along the Praça da República. There are also many boutiques and specialty shops in **Nazaré.** To shop in air-conditioning, head for the upscale **Shopping Center Iguatemi** (⌗ Trv. Eutíquio 1078), a mall in the truest sense of the word. In **Icoaraci,** a riverside town 18 km (11 mi) northeast of Belém, shops make and sell marajoara pottery.

Specialty Shops

Artesanato Paruara (✉ Rua Sezedelo Correo 15, ☎ 091/248–4555) specializes in oils, stones, and other "mystical" items. At **Artindia** (✉ Av. Presidente Vargas 762, Loja 6, ☎ 091/223–6248) you'll find a good selection of jewelry, painted wooden shields, bows and arrows, and other crafts—all handmade by Indians. (Note: Be careful about items that have feathers; some are prohibited by U.S. Customs.) Several places sell marajoara pottery, painted coconut shells, and straw baskets including **Cacique** (✉ Av. Presidente Vargas 692, ☎ 091/242–1144); the small shop at **Paratur** (✉ Praça Kennedy s/n, ☎ 091/224–9633), the state tourist board; and **Vitoria Régia** (✉ Presidente Vargas 552, ☎ 091/241–1113).

BETWEEN BELÉM AND MANAUS

The smaller communities between the Amazon's two major cities give the best picture of pure Amazonian culture. Life tends to be even more intertwined with the river, and the center of activity is the dock area in village after village. Even a brief stop in one of these towns provides an interesting window into the region's day-to-day life.

Ilha do Marajó

Soure is 82 km (49 mi) northwest of Belém.

With an area of roughly 49,600 square km (18,900 square mi), Ilha do Marajó is reputedly the world's largest river island. Its unspoiled environment and abundant wildlife make it one of the few accessible places in the Amazon that seems truly isolated. The island was once inhabited by the Aruã tribes. It was only after attempts by both the British and the Dutch that the Portuguese, through trickery, finally conquered them.

Ilha do Marajó's western half is dominated by dense rain forest, its eastern half by expansive plains and savannah—ideal spots for raising cattle and the famous water buffalo. According to local lore, the arrival of the buffalo was an accident, the result of the wreck of a ship traveling from India to the Guianas. Today, the island has ½ million of these creatures as well as more than 1 million head of cattle; the human head count is only 250,000. A day trip to a local ranch or a stay at Fazenda Carmo Camará (☞ Dining and Lodging, *below*), the only ranch that currently hosts overnight guests, will give you a close-up look at the unique lifestyle of the island's people as well as the chance to view some of its animals—both domesticated and wild. You may see alligators, monkeys, and the *capybara* (the world's largest and most adorable rodent).

Camará is the island's most important port and is where most boats from Belém dock. With almost 20,000 people, picturesque **Soure,** on the northeast coast, is Ilha do Marajó's largest town. Its many palm and mango trees, its simple but brightly painted houses, and its shore full of fishing boats make it seem more Caribbean than Amazon. **Salvaterra,** a short boat ride south across the narrow Rio Paracauari, is smaller than Soure but equally charming. Near these two towns, you'll find enchanting river beaches—all a short (and cheap) taxi ride away.

Praia do Pesqueiro, 14 km (8 mi) north of Soure, is understandably the island's most popular beach. When you stand on its white-sand expanse, looking out at the seemingly endless watery horizon and feeling the waves lap your feet, it's hard to believe that you're not on the ocean. There are several thatch-roof restaurant-bars, making this an even more ideal place to spend an afternoon. You can travel here from Soure by taxi, moto-taxi, or even bike.

The beach at **Caju Una,** a secluded fishing village, is breathtaking: a long strip of white sand with no vendors and few people. The village and its neighbor, Vila do Céu, are about a 45-minute drive (19 km/11 mi north) from Soure. Buses don't travel here, but for about $15 you can hire a taxi for an afternoon; a moto-taxi (which holds only one passenger) costs about half that. A 20-minute, 4-km (2-mi) taxi ride northeast of Soure is **Praia do Araruna.** Rather than sandy stretches, it has a red-mangrove forest. In this eerie setting of twisted trees jutting from the misty swamp, you almost expect Yoda to appear. More likely, it will be a flock of scarlet ibis. **Joanes,** 23 km (14 mi) southwest of Soure, was the island's first settlement. You can poke around the ruins of its 16th-century Jesuit mission, bask in the sun on its pretty beach, and have a meal in one of its good seafood restaurants. A taxi from Soure will cost about $20.

Dining and Lodging

Local cuisine invariably involves the water buffalo, whether in the form of a succulent steak or in cheeses and desserts made with buffalo milk. There's also an array of fish that are unique to the area. Bring cash (credit cards are rarely accepted) in small bills as breaking large ones can be a challenge. (In a pinch, beer vendors can usually make change.)

$ ✕ **Minha Deusa.** As you sit in your small, private, thatch-roof bunga-
★ low, you're serenaded by a symphony of jungle creatures and enticed by the wondrous smells of the food. The *file á marajoara* is an enormous cut of buffalo so tender and delicious that it could tempt even the most steadfast vegetarian. Fish dishes here are also outstanding; best to avoid the chicken, which doesn't measure up. ⊠ *Trv. 14, No. 1193, Soure,* ☎ *no phone. No credit cards.*

$ ✕ **Pousada Búfalo.** This small restaurant is probably your best dining option in "downtown" Soure. The decor is drab, but the fish dishes are tasty; try the *peixe com molho de camarão* (fish with shrimp sauce). ⊠ *Trv. 17, No. 134, Soure,* ☎ *091/741–1475. No credit cards.*

$$$$ ✕▥ **Fazenda Carmo Camará.** Reading through the guest book, it
★ seems as if a spiritual awakening is the standard result of a stay here. As a guest in the small, antiques-filled farm house, you're privy to simple comforts, wonderful hospitality, outstanding home-style meals prepared with farm-fresh ingredients, and fascinating activities galore. You can take an early morning canoe trip in search of howler monkeys; set off on horseback through wildlife-rich pastures; hop in a Jeep for a muddy ride to the newly discovered archaeological site; or take a dip in the small lake surrounded by hundreds of large, affectionate fish. The fazenda can accommodate 8–10 people, and stays are generally part of a package that includes meals, transportation to and from the fazenda (a half-hour van ride and an hour boat ride from Camará), and accompaniment by an English-speaking guide. A three-day, two-night stay costs roughly $250 per person. ⊠ *Contact Amazon Star Tours: Rua Henrique Gurjão 236, Belém 66053–360,* ☎ *091/212–6244.*

$–$$ ✕▥ **Hotel Ilha do Marajó.** This hotel offers solid creature comforts and excellent facilities, including a lovely pool. Rooms are clean, but during the rainy season, mosquitoes tend to infiltrate them. At the attractive outdoor restaurant you can partake of decent, reasonably priced food and enjoy the river view. Every Saturday evening, the hotel hosts a performance of *carimbo,* local music that combines African and Indian rhythms. Package deals, which you can arrange at any travel agency in Belém (☞ Tour Operators and Travel Agents *in* the Amazon A to Z, *below*), are highly recommended. They include van transport to and from the dock in Camará and day trips to nearby fazendas and beaches. English-speaking guides are available for the excursions. ✉ *Trv. 2, No. 10, Soure 68870–000,* ☏ *091/741–1315. 32 rooms. Restaurant, bar, minibars, pool, tennis court, game room. No credit cards.*

$–$$ ✕🏨 **Pousada dos Guarás.** With private bungalows and its own beach, this Salvaterra pousada has a serene, intimate atmosphere. Because of its isolated location, though, you're limited to meals at the on-site restaurant. Still, the pousada is a good deal, particularly if you opt for the package that includes transportation to and from the docks and trips to Soure shops, local fazendas, and beaches; it's best to make arrangements with a travel agent in Belém (☞ Travel Agents and Tour Operators *in* the Amazon A to Z, *below*). ✉ *Av. Beira-Mar (Praia Grande), Salvaterra 66860–000,* ☏ 𝔽𝔸𝕏 *091/765–1133. 20 rooms. Restaurant, bar, air-conditioning, minibars, pool, horseback riding, beach, game room. AE, DC, MC, V.*

$ ✕🏨 **Pousada Bosque dos Aruãs.** This pousada offers very simple wooden bungalows with river views. The bungalows aren't long on comfort or ambience, but if your budget is tight, this isn't a bad bet. ✉ *Rua 2 at Av. Beira Mar, Salvaterra 68860–000,* ☏ *091/765–1115 or 091/223–0628 in Belém. 10 bungalows. Restaurant, bar, bicycles.*

Nightlife

The carimbo group that performs at the Hotel Ilha do Marajó (☞ *above*) on Saturday sometimes puts on a show in Soure on Wednesday or Friday. Ask a staffer at your hotel or a taxi driver for details. On Friday night, there's usually live music at **Badalué** (✉ Trv. 14, Soure). One of the most popular types of music in the region is *brega*, which means "tacky." The name for this accordion-influenced music is appropriate, but don't be surprised if the music grows on you.

Shopping

There are a few stores that sell sundries along Travessa 17 and Rua 3 in Soure. For marajoara pottery and ceramic figurines, try **Arte Caboclo** (✉ Trv. 5, between Rua 8 and Rua 9, Soure). You can even see how the ceramics are made in the workshop at the back of the store, which is open daily 8–6. For sandals, belts, and other leather goods, head to **Curtume Marajó** (✉ Rua 1, Bairro Novo, ☏ no phone), a five-minute walk from the center of Soure (and next to the slaughterhouse). The workers here will be happy to give you a tour that demonstrates the month-long process of turning cowhide into tanned leather. The shop's hours are 7–11 and 1–5 Monday through Saturday.

At **Núcleo Operário Social Marilda Nunes** (✉ Rua 3 between Trv. 18 and Trv. 19, Soure) you'll find stalls with everything from marajoara pottery and woven items to T-shirts and liquor. In theory, its hours are daily 7–noon and 2:30–6; the reality may be something else entirely.

Macapá

330 km (198 mi) northwest of Belém.

Macapá is on the northern channel of the Amazon Delta, and like Belém, was built by the Portuguese as an outpost from which to explore and protect the region. Today it's the capital of and largest city (150,000 people) in Amapá State. It's also one of only five metropolises in the world that sits on the equator.

Macapá's main lure, however, is as a base for trips to see an extraordinary phenomenon—the *pororoca* (meeting of the waters). Each day from March to May, when the Amazon is in flood stage, the incoming ocean tide crashes against the outflowing waters of the Rio Araguari 200 km (120 mi) north of Macapá. The violent meeting of the waters produces waves as high as 15 ft; in the final stage of this event, you can hear what sounds like thunder. It gradually builds in intensity until the waters sweep into the forest along the riverbanks. The trip to the site of the pororoca takes nearly two days by boat and costs about $200 per person (which gets you a private cabin, meals, and an English-speaking guide). For more information, contact **Amapá Tours** (☞ Tour Operators and Travel Agents *in* the Amazon A to Z, *below*).

Macapá's top man-made attraction is Brazil's largest fort, **Fortaleza de São José de Macapá.** It was completed in 1782, after 18 grueling years, and is constructed of stones brought from Portugal as ship ballast. Its well-preserved buildings house a visitors center, an art gallery, a meeting room, and dance/music recital room. ⊠ *Av. Cândido Mendes s/n,* ☎ *096/212–5118.* ☎ *Free.* ☉ *Daily 4 PM–7 PM.*

The **Marco Zero do Equador** is a modest monument to the equatorial line that passes through town. Although it consists only of a tall, concrete sundial and a stripe of red paint along the equator, there's a distinct thrill to straddling the line or hopping between hemispheres. The soccer stadium across the street uses the equator as its centerline. ⊠ *Av. Equatorial 0288,* ☎ *096/241–1951.* ☎ *Free.* ☉ *Daily 7:30–6.*

Dining and Lodging

$$ ✕ **Martinho's Peixaria.** This riverfront eatery, while far from fancy, offers a nice view and the city's best sampling of river fish. Try the grilled tucunaré, which is large enough for two people. ⊠ *Av. Beira-Rio 810,* ☎ *no phone.* V.

$–$$ ✕ **Cantinho Baiano.** Due to the conservative tastes of the locals, the Salvador-born owner is phasing in the famed specialties from the state of Bahia. These dishes, especially the seafood or shrimp *moquecas* (fish stews) are a highlight. The excellent river view, soft music, and colorfully clad waiters add to the pleasure of the meal. ⊠ *Av. Acelino de Leão 01,* ☎ *096/223–4153. AE, DC, MC, V. No dinner Sun.*

$–$$ ✕ **Soho Restaurante.** Beyond its sliding door is an attractive dining room—replete with authentic Japanese lanterns and wall-hangings—that offers a variety of skillfully prepared Chinese and Japanese dishes. For an inexpensive treat, try the mini-*yakisoba,* Asian noodles served with your choice of meats cooked on a hibachi (don't be deceived by the "mini"; one serving is enough for two people). The large, open-air terrace fills up on Friday and Saturday at around 11 PM, when a local band starts to play. You'll need to take a taxi to reach this restaurant, which is about 15 blocks from the central riverfront area. ⊠ *Av. Pedro Baião 2201, Trem,* ☎ *096/223–8525. V. No dinner Sun.*

$$–$$$ ⊞ **Hotel Atalanta.** Painted a garish pink and supported by towering Roman columns, this hotel seems out of place in its surroundings. Indeed, its inconvenient location 10 blocks from the river in an otherwise nondescript residential neighborhood is its only drawback. Inside, you'll find such charming details as stained-glass windows; small pink columns; and immaculate, comfortable guest rooms. *Av. Coaracy Nunes 1148 68900–010,* ☎ FAX *096/223–1612. 30 rooms, 3 suites. Air-conditioning, minibars, sauna, exercise room. AE, DC, MC, V.*

$$ ⊞ **Hotel Macapá.** Partially obscured by palm trees, this three-story, white, colonial-style hotel—topped by a classic red-tile roof—is set on well-manicured grounds. The interior, however, is slightly worn, and the guest rooms aren't very impressive—despite their modern amenities. Opt for one of the suites, which have balconies with exceptional river views. ⊠ *Av. Engenheiro Azarias Neto 17, 68900–080,* ☎ *096/223–1144,* FAX *096/223–1115. 74 rooms, 2 suites. Restaurant, bar, air-conditioning, in-room safes, minibars, pool, tennis court. AE, DC, MC, V.*

$$ ★ 🖼 **Pousada Ekinox.** Although it has a less than desirable location, this guest house has many charms. Some of its comfortable, attractive rooms have balconies that look out on a flower-lined patio. There's also an extensive library that has some books in English—a rarity in this region—and movies that you can watch in your room. Breakfast is included in the rates; full-board costs $15 more per person. ✉ *Rua Jovino Dinoá 1693, 68906–420,* ☎ *096/222–4378 or 096/224–2440,* FAX *096/223–7554. 14 rooms. Restaurant, bar, library. No credit cards.*

Nightlife and the Arts

NIGHTLIFE

Macapá has a surprisingly active nightlife. If you like to bar hop, head for the riverfront, where about 10 bars—some with music—are busy nearly every night. True night owls will appreciate the **Arena** (✉ Rua Hamilton Silva s/n, ☎ no phone) nightclub, which doesn't open until midnight. To get the most out of the $10 cover charge, come on Saturday, the most popular night. On weekend evenings, the **Soho Restaurante** (☞ Dining and Lodging, *above*) has live music.

THE ARTS

On most weekends, there's a play (in Portuguese), a Philharmonic concert, or dance recital in the **Teatro das Bacabeiras** (✉ Rua Cândido Mendes 368, ☎ 096/212–5121). Other presentations are held in the Fortaleza de São José (☞ *above*).

Shopping

Although Macapá has a free-trade zone, neither the prices nor the selection are anything to write home about. The largest concentration of shops is on Rua Cândido Mendes and Rua São José.

The **Núcleo Artesanal** (✉ Av. Engenheiro Azarias Neto 2201, Trem, ☎ 096/212–8528), an outstanding arts center, has two distinct parts. The **Casa do Artesão** sells works by local craftspeople and artists—everything from tacky souvenirs to exquisite paintings and pottery. It's open 9–9 Monday–Saturday and 8 AM–10 PM Sunday, and Visa is accepted. The **Associação dos Povos Indígenas do Tumucumaque (APITU)** has an excellent selection of textiles, baskets, and other objects made by Indian tribes. Its hours are 8–noon and 2–6 every day but Sunday, when it's open 5–9. In addition, an artisan fair is held outside the center on Sunday from 8 AM to 10 PM.

Santarém

836 km (518 mi) west of Belém, 766 km (475 mi) east of Manaus.

Since its founding in 1661, Santarém has ridden the crest of many an economic wave. First wood, then rubber, and today mineral wealth have been the lures for thousands of would-be magnates hoping to carve their fortunes from the jungle. The most noteworthy of these may well be Henry Ford. Although he never actually came to Brazil, Ford left his mark on it in two rubber plantations southwest of Santarém—Fordlândia and Belterra (☞ "Henry Ford's Impossible Dreams," *below*). Today, Santarém, a laid-back city of 242,000, is a traditional port of call.

The city is situated at the confluence of the aquamarine Rio Tapajós and the muddy brown Amazon. Seeing the meeting of these waters is second only to witnessing the pororoca outside Macapá (☞ *above*). Although you can see the confluence from throughout the city, it's best viewed from the **Praça Mirante do Tapajós,** on the hill in the center of town and just a few blocks from the waterfront.

Close-Up

HENRY FORD'S IMPOSSIBLE DREAM

HENRY FORD SPENT MILLIONS of dollars to create two utopian company towns and plantations to supply his Model-T's with rubber tires. In 1927, he chose an area 15 hours southwest of Santarém. A year later, all that was needed to build a small town and its infrastructure was transported from Michigan to the Amazon by boat. Small, Midwestern-style houses were built in row after row. *Seringueiros* (rubber harvesters) were recruited with promises of good wages, health care, and schools for their children. Fordlândia was born. Despite all the planning, the scheme failed. The region's climate, horticulture, and customs weren't taken into account. Malaria and parasites troubled the workers; erosion and disease plagued the trees.

Convinced that he had learned valuable lessons from his mistakes, Ford refused to give up. In 1934 he established another community in Belterra, just 48 km (30 mi) outside Santarém. Although some rubber was extracted from the plantation, production fell far short of original estimates. World War II caused further disruptions as German boats cruised the Brazilian coast and prevented food and supplies from arriving. Advancements in synthetic rubber struck the final blow. Today, some rusted trucks and electric generators, a few industrial structures, and many empty bungalows are all that remains of Ford's impossible dreams.

To learn more about Santarém's culture and history, head for the **Centro Cultural João Fona** (João Fona Cultural Center). This small museum has a hodgepodge of ancient ceramics, indigenous art, and colonial-period paintings. ✉ *Praça Barão de Santarém,* ☎ *091/522–1383.* 🎫 *Free.* ⊙ *Weekdays 8–5.*

★ You can take several cruises from Santarém on specially outfitted boats. The trip down the Rio Tapajós to the village of **Alter do Chão,** on the Lago Verde (Green Lake), is one of the best. The area has been called "the Caribbean of the Amazon," and when you see its clear green waters and its white-sand beach, it's easy to understand why. Buses also make the hour-long journey from Santarém to Alter do Chão regularly. From the village, it's a short canoe ride across a narrow channel to the beach. (Note that from April to July, when the water is high, the beach disappears.)

While you're in the village, be sure to visit the outstanding **Centro de Preservação da Arte, Cultura, e Ciências Indigena** (Center for the Preservation of Indigenous Arts). An American ex-pat sculptor has assembled a collection of more than 1,600 remarkable pieces from 57 Amazon tribes. Videos and photo displays help to teach you more about the indigenous cultures and their plight, and an on-site cooperative store sells Indian art. ✉ *Rua Dom Macedo Costa,* ☎ *091/527–1110.* 🎫 *Admission.* ⊙ *Daily 10–noon and 2–5.*

Dining and Lodging

$ ✕ **Alter Nativo.** Despite its clever name, this Alter do Chão establishment doesn't offer alternative dishes. Rather it prepares typical fish dishes as well as, if not better, than many of the fish restaurants in town. Try the tucunaré or pirarucú with the *molho de escabeche*, a savory tomato and onion sauce. ⊠ *Praça da Nossa Senhora da Saude s/n, Alter do Chão,* ☎ *091/527–1160.* V. ☉ *No dinner Sun.*

$ ✕ **Lumi.** The cuisine and decor of this open-air restaurant are an interesting mix of Japanese and Pará State. The sushi and sashimi are pricy, but the *pratos econômicos* (economical dishes) are cheap, tasty (and large) portions of fried fish or steak accompanied by rice and vegetables. ⊠ *Av. Cuiabá s/n, Santarém,* ☎ *091/522–2174. No credit cards.*

$ ✕ **Mascote.** The vine-draped entrance, flanked by lamps that glow softly at night, beckons you through to the patio. Here you'll find an enchanting dining area with a great view of both the river and the plaza. The extremely varied menu includes pizza, sandwiches, steaks, and seafood. Generally the food is good, but the service is lackadaisical at times. ⊠ *Praça do Pescador s/n, Santarém,* ☎ *091/523–2844. AE, DC, V.*

$ ✕ **Mutunuy II.** This meat-lover's paradise close to the center of town is a great place for a bargain lunch. Try the *churrasco misto*, a beef-, chicken-, and sausage-filled skewer accompanied by rice, farofa, potato salad, and a garden salad—all for about $4. ⊠ *Trv. Turiano Meira 1680, Santarém,* ☎ *091/522–7909.* V.

$–$$ 🏨 **Amazon Park Hotel.** The only "luxury" hotel in town has a decent location (a short taxi ride from the center of town), a gorgeous pool, and such in-room amenities as TVs and minibars. Still, with little in the way of competition, it doesn't seem to have much incentive to improve itself, as evidenced by the aging facilities and the scantily furnished rooms. ⊠ *Av. Mendonça Furtado 4120, Santarém 68040–050,* ☎ *091/523–2800,* ℻ *091/522–2631. 122 rooms. Restaurant, bar, air-conditioning, minibars, pool. AE, DC, MC, V.*

$ 🏨 **Pousada Tupaiulândia.** If you're planning an overnight visit to Alter do Chão, this pousada three blocks from the beach is one of the best places to stay. Its large rooms are comfortable; those with air-conditioning, as opposed to just fans, cost slightly more. (As this hotel is popular and has few rooms, reserve as far in advance as possible.) ⊠ *Rua Pedro Teixeira s/n, Alter do Chão 68109–000,* ☎ *091/527–1157. 7 rooms. Restaurant, minibars. V.*

$ 🏨 **Rio Dourado.** This new hotel—bathed in peach paint—is a good deal.
★ In addition to reasonable rates, your money gets you simple but attractive accommodations, a convenient location, and friendly service. ⊠ *Rua Floriano Peixoto 799, Santarém 68005–080,* ☎ ℻ *091/522–3764. 33 rooms. Air-conditioning, airport shuttle. No credit cards.*

$ 🏨 **Santarém Palace.** With all-new everything, this centrally located hotel has reasserted itself as one of the finest in town. The rooms are very clean, comfortable, and well equipped; some even have a good view of the river. ⊠ *Av. Rui Barbosa 726, Santarém 68005–080,* ☎ *091/ 523–2820,* ℻ *091/522–1779. 44 rooms. Restaurant, air-conditioning, minibars, meeting room. No credit cards.*

Nightlife

One of the most popular bars, and certainly the one with the nicest view of the meeting of the waters, is **Mascotinho** (⊠ Praça Manuel de Jesus Moraes s/n, ☎ 091/523–2399). Come for the scene and the scenery; eat elsewhere. Santarém's dance clubs play a mix of Brazilian and international music. On Friday, **La Boom** (⊠ Av. Cuiabá 694, Liberdade, ☎ 091/522–3632) is *the* place to be. Curiously, Sunday, not Saturday, is a very big night at some clubs, particularly **Zoom** (⊠ Av. Presidente Vargas 1721, Santa Clara, ☎ 091/522–1787).

Shopping

There are several artisan shops in Santarém, but by far the best place for gifts and souvenirs is the Center for the Preservation of Indigenous

Arts (☞ *above*) in Alter do Chão. The prices are on the high side, but it offers the region's best selection of authentic Indian artwork.

MANAUS

Manaus, the capital of Amazonas state, is a sprawling, hilly city of more than 1 million. It's on the banks of the Rio Negro and surrounded by dense jungle, 766 km (475 mi) southwest of Santarém, 1,602 km (993 mi) southwest of Belém. Taking its name from the Manaó tribe, which means "Mother of the Gods," the city was founded in 1669. It has long flirted with prosperity. Of all the Amazon cities and towns, Manaus is most identified with the rubber boom. In the late 19th and early 20th centuries, the city supplied the world with 90% of its rubber. The immense wealth that resulted was monopolized by a few rubber barons, never numbering more than 100, who lived in the city, spent enormous sums on ostentatious lifestyles (and structures to match), and dominated the region like feudal lords. *Seringueiros* (rubber tappers) were recruited; a few were Indians, but most were transplants from Brazil's crowded and economically depressed northeast. Thousands flocked to the barons' huge plantations, where they lived virtually as slaves. As work progressed, conflicts erupted between barons and Indians over encroachment on tribal lands. Stories of cruelty abound: One baron is said to have killed more than 40,000 Indians during his 20-year "reign." Another boasted of having slaughtered 300 Indians in a day.

The 25-year rubber era was brought to a close thanks to Englishman Henry A. Wickham, who smuggled rubber-tree seeds out of Brazil in 1876. The seeds were planted in Malaysia, where new trees flourished; within 30 years, Asian rubber ended the Brazilian monopoly. Although several schemes were launched to revitalize the Amazon rubber industry and many seringueiros continued to work independently in the jungles, the high times were over. Manaus entered a depression that lasted until 1967, when it was made a free-trade zone. Its economy was revitalized, and its population jumped from 200,000 to 900,000 in less than 20 years. Today, it's the Amazon's most popular destination, due in large part to the many accessible jungle lodges in the surrounding region. Manaus's principal attractions are its lavish, brightly colored houses and civic buildings—vestiges of an opulent time when the wealthy sent their laundry to be done in Europe and sent for Old World artisans and engineers to build their New World monuments.

Exploring Manaus

Manaus is a fairly spread out city with few true high-rises. Although many hotels and sights are in its Centro (City Center) neighborhood, it lacks a truly concentrated downtown like that found in Belém. Centro isn't particularly large and is set on a slight hill above the river. The biggest problem to getting around town is that many streets don't have signs, especially in the free-trade zone.

Numbers in the text correspond to numbers in the margin and on the Manaus Centro map.

Centro
A GOOD WALK

Begin as early in the day as possible at the **Mercado Adolfo Lisboa** ①. Exit at its northeast end and continue along the waterfront. You'll pass fishing and trading boats until you reach the Porto Flutuante, the British-made floating dock where most large ships anchor. To the right of the dock, a path runs to the **Alfândega** ②. Avenida Eduardo Ribeiro continues where the path leaves off; follow it to the municipal clock,

on your left, and the stairs that lead to the **Catedral da Nossa Senhora da Conceição** ③. From here, you can turn right on Avenida 7 de Setembro and visit one of several interesting museums, including the **Palácio Rio Negro** ④ and the **Museu do Índio** ⑤.

Alternatively, you can continue north from the cathedral on Avenida Eduardo Ribeiro to the pink **Teatro Amazonas** ⑥. Turn right, just before the theater, onto Rua José Clemente and follow it to the plaza dominated by the **Igreja São Sebastião** ⑦. From here, head around the other side of the theater, along Rua 10 de Julho, and back onto Avenida Eduardo Riberio to the Praça do Congress. Cross the plaza and Avenida Ramos Ferreira and turn left; follow Ramos Ferreira to the **Praça da Saudade** ⑧—a good place to relax, eat, and people-watch.

TIMING

Plan to spend 3–4 hours following the walk from start to finish. The tour that continues to Avenida 7 de Setembro will probably take 1½ hours; if you opt to veer off from the rest of the walk here, count on spending up to 3 hours reaching and visiting the museums.

SIGHTS TO SEE

② **Alfândega.** The Customs House was built by the British in 1902 with bricks imported as ship ballast. It stands alongside the floating dock that was built at the same time to accommodate the annual 40-ft rise and fall of the river. The Customs House is now home to the regional office of the Brazilian tax department; although it's not officially open to the public, the guards may let you in upon request. ⊠ *Rua Marquês de Santa Cruz s/n,* ☎ *092/234–5481.*

③ **Catedral da Nossa Senhora da Conceição.** Built originally in 1695 by Carmelite missionaries, the Cathedral of Our Lady of the Immaculate Conception (also called Igreja Matriz) burned down in 1850 and was reconstructed in 1878. It's a simple, predominantly neoclassical structure with a bright, colorful interior. ⊠ *Praça da Matriz,* ☎ *no phone.*

❼ Igreja São Sebastião. Neoclassical St. Sebastian's (circa 1888), with its charcoal-gray color and medieval characteristics, seems foreboding. Its interior, however, is luminous and uplifting, with an abundance of white Italian marble, stunning stained-glass windows, and beautiful ceiling paintings. The church has a tower on only one side. Explanations for this asymmetrical configuration include that the second tower wasn't built due to lack of funds; that it was intentionally not added as symbolic gesture toward the poor; or that the ship with the materials for its construction sank. ⊠ *Praça São Sebastião,* ☎ *no phone.*

❶ Mercado Adolfo Lisboa. This market, built in 1882, is a wrought-iron replica of the market (now destroyed) in Les Halles in Paris; the ironwork is said to have been designed by Gustave Eiffel himself. Vendors sell Amazon food products and handicrafts daily from around dawn until noon. ⊠ *Rua do Barés 6,* ☎ *092/234–8441.*

❺ Museu do Índio. The Indian Museum was constructed and is maintained by Salesian sisters, an order of nuns with eight missions in the upper Amazon. It displays handicrafts, weapons, ceramics, ritual masks, and clothing from the region's tribes. ⊠ *Rua Duque de Caxias 356,* ☎ *092/234–1422.* ⊠ *Admission.* ⊙ *Weekdays 8:30–11:30 and 2–4:30, Sat. 8:30–11:30.*

❹ Palácio Rio Negro. The extravagant Rio Negro Palace was built at the end of the 19th century as the home of a German rubber baron. Later, it was used as the governor's official residence. Today, it hosts some of the city's finest art exhibits and houses a cultural center. ⊠ *Av. 7 de Setembro 1546,* ☎ *092/622–2834.* ⊠ *Free.* ⊙ *Tues.–Sun 3–9.*

❽ Praça da Saudade. This bustling, energetic square is a great place to sit back and soak up the local culture. There's a small amusement park, an amphitheater, and several food stalls that serve such dishes as *vatapá* (shrimp in coconut oil) and *tacacá* (shrimp stew).

★ **❻ Teatro Amazonas.** The city's lavish opera house was completed in 1896 after 15 years. The Italian Renaissance–style interior provides a clear idea of the wealth that marked the Amazon rubber boom: marble doorways from Italy, wrought-iron banisters from England, crystal chandeliers from France, and striking panels of French tiles and Italian frescoes depicting Amazon legends. In April 1997, after a 90-year hiatus, the theater reopened with a two-week long international music festival. Recently, a wide variety of entertainers—from José Carreras to the Spice Girls—have performed here. Half-hour tours are conducted daily between 9 and 4. ⊠ *Praça São Sebastião s/n,* ☎ *092/622–2420.* ⊠ *Admission.* ⊙ *Mon.–Sat. 9–4.*

Elsewhere in and Around Manaus

If you have a little energy left after your Centro tour, you can take a cab to one of several far-flung in-town sights. The **INPA–Bosque da Ciência** ⑨ is northeast of the center, and beyond it is the **Museu de Ciências Naturais da Amazônia** ⑩. To the center's northwest is the **Mini-Zoo do CIGS** ⑪. If you have another day or two, consider an excursion to the **Amazon Ecopark** or the town of **Presidente Figuereido,** both outside the city limits.

OFF THE BEATEN PATH

AMAZON ECOPARK – It's a half-hour boat ride from the Tropical Hotel (☞ Dining and Lodging, *below*) along the Tarumã bayou to the Amazon Ecopark, with its monkey jungle, waterfalls, and Amazon birds. The park offers half- and full-day tours ($30 and $60 respectively) with professional guides. ☎ *092/234–0939.*

THE VANISHING INDIANS

IN 1500, WHEN THE PORTUGUESE arrived in Brazil, the Indian population was 4.5 million, and there were an estimated 1,400 tribes. From the beginning, the Portuguese fell into two camps in terms of their attitudes toward the natives: the missionaries, who wanted to "tame" them and convert them to Catholicism, and the colonizers, who wished to first exploit and then enslave them. The missionaries lost, and when it became apparent that the Indians couldn't be enslaved, the infamous *bandeirantes* (members of *bandeiras* or assault forces) relentlessly persecuted the Indians to "liberate" tribal lands. Although many Indians lost their lives defending their way of life, the greatest killers were smallpox and influenza—European diseases against which they had no immunity. A slow but steady integration into Portuguese society also caused the native population to dwindle.

Today, of Brazil's 328,000 remaining Indians, about 197,000 live in the Amazon. There are about 220 societies, each with its own religious beliefs, social customs, and economic activities. The larger groups include the Manaó, Yanomami, Marajó, Juma, Caixana, Korubo, and Miranha. They speak one of 170 distinct languages; Tupi (with seven in-use derivations, including Tupi-Guarani) is the most widely spoken, followed by Macro Jê, Aruák, Karíb, and Arawá.

Throughout Brazil's history, sporadic efforts were made to protect the Indians, but it was only in 1910 that the government established an official advocacy agency. Founded by Cândido Mariana da Silva Rondon, the Service for the Protection of the Indians (SPI), supported Indian autonomy, ensured that their traditional practices were respected, and helped them to ac-

quire Brazilian citizenship. In 1930, however, the SPI was abolished after funds were exhausted and administrative corruption became apparent. It was replaced in 1967 by the current governmental Indian advocacy group, FUNAI (Fundação Nacional do Indio, or the National Indian Foundation). Although it has been highly criticized, FUNAI helped to get the first (and, thus far, only) Indian elected into office: Mario Juruna, a FUNAI member and Indian chief, served as federal deputy from 1983 to 1987. The foundation has also defended the rights of Indians to protect their lands (it allows only legitimate researchers to visit reservations), which are increasingly targeted for logging, rubber extraction, mining, ranching, or the building of industrial pipelines and hydroelectric plants.

The Indians have always respected and understood their environment; hence, it's easy to understand how their plight and that of the rain forest have become linked. On his worldwide 1989 tour with the rock musician Sting, Chief Raoni of the Megkroniti garnered support for Brazil's Indians and raised overall environmental consciousness. At the same time, conservation efforts to preserve the rain forest have called attention to some of FUNAI's issues. For the Brazilian government, however, the issue is complicated: rainforest conservation often takes second place to economic development. Further, the Indians still lack many basic human rights, and violence (such as the 1998 murder of prominent activist Francisco de Assis Araujó) still sporadically occurs as the Indians continue to defend their way of life against outsiders.

—By Melisse Gelula and
Althea Gamble

⑨ INPA–Bosque da Ciência. Used as a research station for the INPA (Instituto Nacional de Pesquisa da Amazônia), this slice of the rain forest is home to a great diversity of flora and fauna. Some highlights include manatee tanks, alligator ponds, a botanical garden, and nature trails. ⊠ *Rua Otávio Cabral s/n, Aleixo,* ☎ *092/643–3293.* 🎫 *Admission.* ⊙ *Tues.–Fri. 9–11 and 2–4, weekends 9–4.*

⑪ Mini-Zoo do CIGS. At this zoo you can see some 300 animals native to the Amazon. The Brazilian army also operates a jungle-survival training school here. Soldiers from around the globe come to participate in the two-year program. At the end of it, men (no women yet) are tested by being air-dropped into the jungle with only a pack of matches, a gun, and five bullets. ⊠ *Estrada do São Jorge 750,* ☎ *092/671–6903.* 🎫 *Admission.* ⊙ *Tues.–Sun. 9–4:30.*

⑩ Museu de Ciências Naturais da Amazônia. The Natural History Museum has displays of insects and butterflies. You can also view Amazon river fish in large tanks. ⊠ *Estrada Belém s/n, Aleixo,* ☎ *092/644–2799.* 🎫 *Free.* ⊙ *Mon.–Sat. 9–5.*

OFF THE BEATEN PATH

PRESIDENTE FIGUEREIDO – One of the Amazon's best-kept secrets is a 2-hour, 107-km (64-mi) drive north of Manaus. This small, 12-year-old town has been the jumping off point for mineral exploration and extraction in recent years. Expeditions for these minerals have led to the discovery of such natural wonders as waterfalls (there are 45 of them in the area, some as high as 140 ft) and caves and caverns, some with prehistoric drawings and pottery fragments. There's also an archaeology museum near town. Call the **Secretaria de Turismo** (☎ 092/324–1158), whose office is next to the bus station, ahead of time to arrange for an English-speaking guide.

Beaches

Known to locals as the Copacabana of the Amazon, **Praia do Ponta Negra** is next to the Hotel Tropical (☞ Lodging, *below*), a 20-minute bus ride from Centro. With numerous restaurants, bars, and sports and nightlife facilities, it's busy day and night.

Crescent-shape **Praia da Lua** is 23 km (14 mi) southwest of Manaus. You can only reach it by boat on the Rio Negro, so it's clean and less crowded than other beaches. **Praia do Tupé,** another Rio Negro beach accessible only by boat, is 34 km (20 mi) northwest of Manaus. It's popular with locals and tends to fill up on Sunday and holidays, when a special ship makes the trip from the city.

Dining

$$–$$$ ✕ **La Barca.** You usually have to wait for a table here, a testament to this fish restaurant's popularity. The menu offers many options, but the specialty is pirarucú. Meals are accompanied by live music. ⊠ *Rua Recife 684, Parque 10,* ☎ *092/236–7090. AE, DC, MC, V.*

$$ ✕ **Canto da Paixada.** Few eateries can claim to be fit for a pope; when
★ Pope John Paul II came to Manaus in 1981, this restaurant was chosen to host him. The dining areas aren't elegant, but the fish dishes are outstanding. One platter feeds two. ⊠ *Rua Emilio Moreira 1677, Praça 14,* ☎ *092/234–3021. V. No dinner Sun.*

$$ 🍴 **Fiorentina.** The green awning and red-and-white check table cloths hint that this restaurant serves authentic Italian. The pasta dishes are delicious, especially the simple lasagna *fiorentina* (with a marinara and ground-beef sauce). Saturday sees a *feijoada* (black beans, rice, meats, and farofa or farinha) that costs about $10. ⊠ *Praça da Polícia 44, Centro,* ☎ *092/232–1295. AE, DC, MC, V.*

$$ ✗ **Suzuran.** For more than 20 years this festive restaurant has served the town's best Japanese food. If you can't decide between raw fish and your fried favorites, don't. The *suzuran teishoku* contains sushi, sashimi, tempura, and fried fish. ⊠ *Boulevard Álvaro Maia 1683, Adrianópolis,* ☎ *092/234–1693. No credit cards. Closed Tues.*

$ ✗ **Churrascaria Búfalo.** Twelve waiters, each offering a different type
★ of meat, scurry around this large, crowded restaurant. As if all of the delectable meats weren't enough, the table is also set with about 10 side dishes, including two types of manioc root, pickled vegetables, and caramelized bananas. ⊠ *Rua Joaquim Nabuco 628–A, Centro,* ☎ *092/ 633–3773. AE, DC, MC, V. No dinner Sun.*

$ ✗ **Coqueiro Verde.** Don't bother asking for a menu—everybody who comes here orders the *carne de sol,* beef cured in the sun for a day or two. This delicious, affordable treat is served with rice, beans, farofa, and salad. All this and you can even pet the restaurant's mascot—a cute, woolly monkey—out in the garden. ⊠ *Rua Ramos Ferreira 1920, Centro,* ☎ *092/232–0002. AE, DC, MC, V. No dinner Sun.*

Lodging

Although there are several decent in-town hotels, the jungle lodges— actually small hotels—outside town are far more exciting. They usually have guides on staff and offer treks, alligator "hunts," canoe trips, and opportunities to fish and swim. Many lodges are near the Rio Negro, where mosquitoes aren't a problem because of the water's acidity level. (Price categories for lodges are based on 2 day/1 night packages, which include meals and transportation to and from the lodge.)

Hotels

$$$$ 🏨 **Tropical.** Nothing in the Amazon can match the majesty of this resort. The sprawling complex is 20 km (12 mi) northwest of downtown and overlooking the Rio Negro, with a short path that leads to the beach. In addition to the on-site zoo, numerous sports facilities, and two gorgeous pools, the Tropical also has its own dock. One drawback here is the staff, whose members aren't always helpful (they can be apathetic). You can book rooms here through Varig Airlines, and if you fly Varig you'll receive a 40% room discount. The on-site Tarumã restaurant is a reliable choice for dinners of regional and international fare. ⊠ *Estrada da Ponta Negra s/n, Ponta Negra 69037–060,* ☎ *092/659– 5000,* 🗏 *092/658–5026. 610 rooms. 2 restaurants, bar, coffee shop, in-room safes, 2 pools, sauna, 4 tennis courts, basketball, exercise room, jogging, beach, dock, boating, shops, dance club, recreation room, travel services, helipad. AE, DC, MC, V.*

$$$ 🏨 **Taj Mahal.** When this hotel recently became a member of the Holiday Inn chain, it was a mixed blessing. Meeting the strict new quality standards transformed it into a more modern, more luxurious hotel than before. But much of the original, charming East Indian artwork— some of which you can still see in the lobby—didn't make the cut. Although the Taj Mahal seems more standardized now, it's still a pleasant option with a rooftop pool, a revolving restaurant, and convenient location. Request a room with a river view. ⊠ *Av. Getúlio Vargas 741, Centro 69020–020,* ☎ 🗏 *092/633–1010. 144 rooms, 26 suites. Restaurant, bar, pool, beauty salon, massage, sauna, meeting rooms. AE, DC, MC, V.*

$$–$$$ 🏨 **Lord Best Western.** Although it's clean and comfortable, this hotel in the heart of the free-trade zone shows signs of wear. Request a room on the recently renovated fourth floor, which has much nicer, more modern furnishings and novel amenities such as electronic DO NOT DISTURB

signs. The staff is helpful and efficient. On Wednesday, the restaurant has live jazz and a feijoada. ⊠ *Rua Marcílio Dias 217, Centro 69005–270,* ☎ *092/622–2844,* ℻ *092/622–2576. 95 rooms, 8 suites. Restaurant, bar. AE, DC, MC, V.*

$$–$$$ 🏨 **St. Paul.** If you are planning an extended stay, this apartment-hotel (or "flat hotel" as they're called in Brazil) in Centro is your best bet. Accommodations are immaculate and have living rooms and fully-equipped, modern kitchens. For stays of more than a week, you can get a discount of as much as 50%. ⊠ *Av. Ramos Ferreira 1115, Centro 69010-120,* ☎ *092/622–2131,* ℻ *092/622–2137. 45 apartments. Pool, sauna, exercise room. AE, DC, MC, V.*

$$ **Ana Cássia.** The rooftop pool and most of the rooms at this 10-story hotel offer the city's best river and market views. Entering the lobby— with red leather couches, highly polished green and white floors, and multiple mirrors—you may feel as if you've stepped into the early '80s. The well-equipped rooms aren't nearly as distinguished. ⊠ *Rua dos Andradas 14, Centro 69005–180,* ☎ *092/622–3637,* ℻ *092/622–4812. 88 rooms, 12 suites. Restaurant, coffee shop, pool, beauty parlor, sauna, meeting room. AE, DC, MC, V.*

$ 🏨 **Central.** Located in the free-trade zone, this hotel is good if you're on a tight budget. Rooms are simple, clean, and have all the standard amenities. ⊠ *Rua Dr. Moreira 20, Centro 69005-250,* ☎ *092/622–2600,* ℻ *092/622–2609. 50 rooms. Minibars. AE, DC, MC, V.*

Jungle Lodges

$$$$ 🏨 **Amazon Lodge.** Three hours by boat from Manaus, this lodge consists of rustic, floating cabins with air-conditioning and baths. Because of its remote location, the chances for wildlife spotting are terrific. The English-speaking guides are knowledgeable and friendly. ⊠ *Contact Nature Safaris: Conjunto Parque Aripuanã, Rua 12, Casa 02, Planalto, Manaus 69040–180,* ☎ *092/656–5464 or 092/656–3357,* ℻ *092/656–6101. 14 rooms. Restaurant, fishing, hiking. No credit cards.*

$$$$
★ 🏨 **Ariaú Jungle Tower.** This lodge's four-story wooden towers are on stilts and are linked by catwalks. The effect is more dramatic in the rainy season when the river covers the ground below. Although the idea is to make you feel integrated with nature, the size of this complex generally prevents such a sentiment—or much contact with wildlife. The exceptions are the adorable, semi-wild monkeys that often visit and inevitably make mischief. Three hours by boat from Manaus on the Rio Ariaú, the lodge offers excellent food and comfortable rooms. Its most popular accommodation—sought by honeymooners and celebrities—is the Tarzan House in the treetops 100 feet up. ⊠ *Mailing address: Rua Silva Ramos 41, Centro, Manaus 69010–180,* ☎ *092/234–7308,* ℻ *092/233–5615. 134 rooms. Restaurant, bar, 2 pools, hiking, dock, fishing, helipad. AE, DC, MC, V.*

$$$$ 🏨 **King's Island.** To reach this ever-so remote lodge you can either spend a week on a boat or 3½ hours on a plane. Your experience here will be very distinct from one at the other lodges, mostly because it's in the São Gabriel da Cachoeira mountains. The area is awash in gorgeous waterfalls and also offers the opportunity to hike in beautiful cloud forests. Exotic-travel enthusiasts will be hard-pressed to find a more fascinating place from which to explore the Amazon. ⊠ *Contact Nature Safaris: Conjunto Parque Aripuanã, Rua 12, Casa 02, Planalto, Manaus 69040–180,* ☎ *092/656–5464 or 092/656–3357,* ℻ *092/656–6101. 14 rooms. Restaurant, hiking, fishing. No credit cards.*

$$$$
★ 🏨 **Lago Salvador.** Although it's only a 45-minute boat ride from Manaus, this lodge still offers a serene, secluded atmosphere. Four cabanas, with three apartments each, are set on the banks of the lake from which the lodge receives its name. The rooms, which have fans and

running water, are simple but comfortable. Each cabana has a radio so that you can contact one of the staff members who are on call 24-hours a day to pick you up in a canoe or bring you food. Ask for Cabana 2, which has the nicest facilities. ✉ *Contact Amazônia Expeditions: Tropical Hotel, Estrada da Ponta Negra, Manaus,* ☎ *092/658–4221,* FAX *092/659–5308. 4 cabanas, each with 3 apartments. Restaurant, room service, hiking, boating. V.*

Nightlife and the Arts

The night-time highlight in Manaus is the Boi-Bumbá. Live, pulsating music is played while men and women in Indian costumes tell stories and perform a fascinating, sensual dance. These performances, and others, are held regularly in the large amphitheater at Ponta Negra Beach. In addition, the Teatro Amazonas still draws some of the biggest names in theater, opera, and classical music.

Many bars and clubs have live music or a DJ. **Coraçao Blue** (✉ Estrada da Ponta Negra 3701 (Km 6), ☎ 092/984–1391) often has rock bands. Two large clubs in Cachoerinha, **Nostalgia Clube** (✉ Av. Ajuricaba 800, ☎ 092/233–9460) and **Mixtura Brasileira** (✉ Av. Ajuricaba, ☎ 092/232–3503) have both live music and a DJ. Another popular, but somewhat more high-brow dance club, is the Tropical Hotel's **Estudio Tropical** (✉ Estrada da Ponta Negra s/n, ☎ 092/658–5000), open only on Friday and Saturday.

Outdoor Activities and Sports

Participant Sports

JET SKIING

How many of your friends can say they've jet skied in the Amazon? **Clube do Jet** (✉ Rua Praiana 13, access through Av. do Turismo, ☎ 092/245–1332) rents equipment for about $40 an hour.

JUNGLE AND RIVER EXCURSIONS

The most common excursion is a half- or full-day tourist-boat trip 15 km (9 mi) east of Manaus, where the jet-black water of the Rio Negro flows beside the yellowish-brown water of the Rio Solimões for 6 km (4 mi) before merging into one as the Rio Amazonas. (It's also common to see pink dolphins in this area.) Many of these meeting-of-the-waters treks include motor boat side trips along narrow streams or through bayous. Some also stop at the Parque Ecológico do January, where you can see Amazon birds and a lake filled with giant Victoria Régia water lilies.

Overnight boat trips into the rain forest follow the Rio Negro, exploring flooded woodlands and narrow waterways, and stop for a hike on a trail. At night, guides take you by canoe on an alligator "hunt." They shine flashlights into the alligators' eyes, momentarily transfixing them, after which they grab the reptiles, hold them for photographs, and then release them. Longer trips to the Negro's upper reaches—where the river is narrower and life along the banks easier to observe—are also options. Such trips usually stop at river settlements where you can visit with local families. They can also include jungle treks; fishing (with equipment supplied by boat operators); and a trip to Anavilhanas, the world's largest freshwater archipelago. It contains some 350 islands with amazing Amazon flora. Because of the dense vegetation, however, you won't see much wildlife other than birds and monkeys. To arrange any of these excursions, contact an area tour operator (☞ Tour Operators and Travel Agents *in* the Amazon A to Z, *below*).

Spectator Sports

Manaus's professional soccer teams, Rio Negro and Nacional, play at **Estádio Vivaldo Lima** (⊠ Av. Constantino Nery, ☎ 092/236–1640). A taxi ride to the stadium and tickets should each cost about $10.

Shopping

Areas and Malls

If you're not from South America, you probably won't find too much of interest in the free-trade zone. Still, you might want to duck into a couple of the endless shops scattered throughout the downtown district—just to have a look. The largest, most upscale mall is **Amazonas Shopping** (⊠ Av. Djarma Batista 482, Chapad, ☎ 092/642–3555).

Specialty Stores

You'll find such regional crafts as straw baskets, hats, and jewelry at the **Museu do Índio** (⊠ Rua Duque de Caxias 356, ☎ 092/234–1422), the **Central de Artesanato Branco e Silva** (⊠ Rua Recife 1999, ☎ 092/236–1241), and **Ecoshop** (⊠ Amazonas Shopping, 2nd floor, ☎ 092/642–2026).

THE AMAZON A TO Z

Arriving and Departing

By Airplane

BELÉM

All flights are served by **Aeroporto Internacional Val-de-Cans** (⊠ Av. Julio Cesár s/n ☎ 091/257–0522), which is 11 km (7 mi) northwest of the city. **Varig** (☎ 091/224–3344) has three flights a week to and from Miami and daily flights to and from Rio, São Paulo, Brasília, and Manaus. Other domestic carriers fly daily to Rio, São Paulo, Brasília, and Manaus including **TAM** (☎ 092/257–1745), **Transbrasil** (☎ 091/224–3677, and **VASP** (☎ 091/224–5588).

From the Airport: The easiest route from the airport is south on Avenida Julio Cesár and then west on Avenida Almirante Barroso. The 20-minute taxi ride costs $15. There are also buses; look for those labeled MAREX/PRES. VARGAS (for the Hilton and other hotels), MAREX/PRAÇA KENNEDY (Paratur and the docks), or MAREX/VER-O-PESO (Cidade Velha).

BETWEEN BELÉM AND MANAUS

Although plans for a new Ilha do Marajó airport—one that can handle planes from large domestic carriers—are in the works, 30-minute flights between Belém and the existing airport are infrequent and expensive. For now, it's best to contact **Amazon Star Tours** (☞ Tour Operators and Travel Agents *below*) to arrange a flight, or plan to take a boat (☞ *below*).

Macapá is a 40-minute flight from Belém, and **VASP** (☎ 096/224–1016) and **Varig** (☎ 096/223–4612) offer regular service. Between Santarém and both Belém and Manaus, **Varig** (☎ 091/523–2488) and **Penta** (☎ 091/522–2220) offer daily hour-long flights. **Tavaj** (☎ 091/522–1418) flies three times a week.

From the Airport: Aeroporto de Macapá (⊠ Rua Hildemar Maia s/n, Santa Rita, ☎ 096/223–2323) is 4 km (2 mi) northwest of town. Although buses make the journey regularly, hopping a taxi for the short, inexpensive ride is your best bet. **Aeroporto Maria José** (⊠ Rodovia Fernando Guilhom, ☎ 091/523–1021) is 14 km (23 mi) west of Santarém. Buses and taxis are plentiful.

MANAUS

The international **Aeroporto Brigadeiro Eduardo Gomes** (☎ 092/621–1210), 17 km (10 mi) south of downtown, no longer has direct flights to or from the United States. Indirect flights may be cheapest on **LAB** (☎ 092/633–4200) via La Paz or **Aeropostale** (☎ 092/233–7685) via Caracas.

TAM (☎ 092/652–1381), **Transbrasil** (☎ 092/622–1705), **Varig** (☎ 092/622–3161), and **VASP** (☎ 092/622–3470) offer daily flights to and from Santarém, Belém, Brasília, Rio, and São Paulo.

From the Airport: The trip to Centro takes about 20 minutes and costs $20–$25 by taxi. A trip on one of the city buses, which depart regularly during the day and early evening, costs less than a dollar.

By Boat

BELÉM

Most ships arrive and depart in the general dock area called the escadinha. **ENASA** (✉ Av. Presidente Vargas 41, ☎ 091/242–3165 or 091/212–2479) ships and standard riverboats head upriver from here to Santarém and Manaus. Many excursions depart from the new tourist-boat terminal 20 minutes south of town on Avenida Alcindo Cacela (Praça Princesa Isabel). If you're bringing a car to Ilha do Marajó, you must take it on one of the **ferries** (☎ 091/296–7472) that depart from Icoaraci, a town 18 km (11 mi) to the northeast.

From the Docks: The docks are quite close to the town center. A taxi ride shouldn't cost more than $5.

BETWEEN BELÉM AND MANAUS

Boats (including ENASA vessels) travel daily between Belém and Camará on Ilha do Marajó. Only ENASA goes to Soure; it makes the four-hour, $4 trip twice a week. **Arapari** (092/212–2492) also operates boats between Belém and Camará daily; although they're slightly more expensive than other lines, they cut the time down to three hours.

Although Macapá is very close to Ilha do Marajó's western side, all boats traveling to Macapá originate in Belém. Standard riverboats regularly make the 24-hour trip. If time is of the essence, high-speed boats cut the journey down to 7 hours and cost only $40. Another option is the "party boat," which makes the run five times a week. Its restaurant, bars, and many decks make the 24-hour trip very enjoyable. You can rent hammock space for $20 (hammocks aren't provided), or reserve a fairly luxurious cabin in advance for $100. Contact **Bom Jesus** (✉ Av. Mendonça Junior 12, Macapá, ☎ 096/223–2342).

Only standard riverboats make the trip from Macapá to Santarém and onward to Manaus (a two-day journey). The journey on a standard riverboat from Belém to Santarém is roughly two days.

From the Docks: On Ilha do Marajó **vans** (☎ 091/741–1441) run from Camará, where many boats dock, to Soure and cost about $4. For Macapá, you dock in the nearby port town of Santana, where taxis await. The fare will range from $5–$15 (it depends on how many other passengers the driver can gather). Buses, which cost $1, run hourly. In Santarém, taxis are always at the docks; the journey to anywhere in town will be less than $5.

MANAUS

In front of the Porto Flutuante there's a group of stands where people sell tickets for everything from high-speed cruisers to standard riverboats. **ENASA** (✉ Rua Marechal Deodoro 61, ☎ 092/633–2307 or 091/633–2563) also has a reservation office in town.

From the Docks: The docks are in Centro, so most hotels are quite close. A taxi, if necessary, shouldn't be very expensive.

By Bus

BELÉM

The bus station, **Rodoviário São Bras** (⊠ Av. Almirante Barroso s/n, Praça Floriano Peixoto), is east of Nazaré. Reservations for buses are rarely needed. **Boa Esperança** (☎ 091/266–0033) makes the 209-km (125-mi) journey to Salinas Beach six times a day. The slow bus (4 hrs) costs $5; the faster bus (3 hrs) costs $7. **Beira-Dão** (☎ 091/226–1162) leaves every half-hour on the 60-km (36-mi), 2-hour, $2 journey to Ilha Mosqueiro. Clearly marked buses to Outeiro Beach and the town of Icoaraci pass the bus station regularly and cost about 50¢.

MANAUS

The bus station, **Terminal Rodoviário Huascar Angelim** (⊠ Rua Recife 2784, Flores, ☎ 092/236–2732) is 7 km (4 mi) north of the center. You'll probably only use it to get to Presidente Figueiredo: take the bus labeled ARUANÃ, which runs regularly and costs $5.

By Car

The BR 316 begins on the outskirts of Belém and runs eastward toward the coast and then south, connecting the city with Brazil's major northeastern hubs. To reach the beaches at Ilha Mosqueiro outside Belém, take BR 316 and then head north on PA 391. To reach Salinas Beach, take BR 316 to PA 324 and head north on PA 124. From Manaus, BR 174 runs north to Boa Vista and BR 319 travels south to Porto Velho. Unfortunately, both routes are in terrible condition and are often closed, especially during the rainy season.

Getting Around

By Bike

On Ilha do Marajó one of the best ways to reach the beaches or to explore Soure is on bike, as the locals do. Rates are less than $1 an hour. Try **Bimba** (⊠ Rua 4, between Trv. 18 and Trv. 19, ☎ no phone).

By Boat

To reach most Manaus area beaches, catch a boat from the Porto Flutuante. The only day with regularly scheduled trips is Sunday, when boats transport great crowds for about $3 per person. To the beaches and other attractions—such as the meeting of the waters—you can hire small craft near the Porto Flutuante or the escadinha area closer to the market. You can also make arrangements through tour operators.

By Bus

BELÉM

The city's bus service is safe, efficient, and comprehensive, but a little confusing—ask a local for guidance. You board buses at the rear, where you pay an attendant the equivalent of 50¢ and pass through a turnstile to take your seat.

BETWEEN BELÉM AND MANAUS

All buses in the region are entered from the rear and cost 50¢–$1. In Soure, buses to Camará pass by the riverside fairly regularly. In Macapá, there's an outdoor terminal on Rua Antônio Coelho de Carvalho, a block from the fort. Here you can catch the bus labeled B. NOVO/UNIVERSIDADE to the Marco Zero, a 20-minute ride. Buses from Santarém to Alter do Chão depart from Praça Tiradentes in the city center or from Avenida Cuiabá (near the Amazon Park Hotel). They make the journey back and forth five or six times a day.

MANAUS

The city bus system is extensive and fairly easy to use. The fare is about 50¢. Most of the useful buses run along Avenida Floriano Peixoto, including Bus 120, which goes to Ponta Negra and stops near the Tropical Hotel. The Fontur bus, which costs about $5, travels between Centro and the Tropical Hotel several times a day.

By Car

BELÉM

Although Belém has the most traffic of any Amazon city and what seems like more than its fair share of one-way streets, in-town driving is relatively easy. Parking is only tricky in a few areas, such as Avenida Presidente Vargas and the escadinha. Rental cars cost between $40 and $70 a day. Several companies have offices at the airport and in town. Try: **Localiza** (⊠ Av. Pedro Álvares Cabral 200, ☎ 091/212–2700) and **Norauto** (⊠ Av. Gentil Bittencourt 2086, ☎ 091/249–4900).

BETWEEN BELÉM AND MANAUS

Traffic and parking problems don't exist in the region. There aren't any car rental companies on Ilha do Marajó, but you can rent a car in Belém and transport it to the island on the ferry that leaves from Icoaraci. In Macapá, you can rent through **Locvel** (⊠ Av. Fab 2093, ☎ 096/223–7999). **Sanvel Locadora** (⊠ Av. Mendonça Furtado 2085, ☎ 091/522–3428) is a reliable agency in Santarém.

MANAUS

There are no major traffic or parking problems in the city, and you can rent a car at the airport through **Unidas Rent a Car** (☎ 092/621–1575).

By Taxi

BELÉM

There are plenty of taxis, and they're easy to flag down on the street (you only need call for them at odd hours). All taxis have meters; tips aren't necessary. Reliable companies include **Coopertaxi** (☎ 091/257–1720) and **Taxi Nazaré** (☎ 091/242–7867).

BETWEEN BELÉM AND MANAUS

Except on Ilha do Marajó, where you have to bargain for a price, taxis have meters. In Soure, call ☎ 091/741–1336 for either a regular cab or a moto-taxi, which only fits one person but is much cheaper. In Macapá and Santarém taxis are plentiful, and you can hail them on the street or call **Rádio Taxi** (☎ 096/223–5656) in Macapá and **Rádio Táxi Piauí** (☎ 091/523–2725) in Santarém.

MANAUS

Taxis, all equipped with meters, are easy to flag down on the streets. At odd hours, you can call **Tucuxi** (☎ 092/622–4040).

Contacts and Resources

Banks and Currency Exchange

BELÉM

The airport branch of the **Banco do Brasil** (☎ 091/257–1983) charges a $20 commission to exchange travelers checks. In town, you'll find the best rates at **Banco Amazônia** (⊠ Av. Presidente Vargas 800, ☎ 091/216–3252), which is open weekdays 10–4. **Casa Francesa Câmbio e Turismo** (⊠ Trv. Padre Prudêncio 40, ☎ 091/241–2716) is one of several exchange houses that offer comparable rates.

BETWEEN BELÉM AND MANAUS

There are no exchange facilities on Ilha do Marajó. In Macapá, you can exchange money at **Banco do Brasil** (⊠ Rua Independência 250,

☎ 096/223–2155), which is open weekdays 11–2:30. You'll probably get a better rate at **Casa Francesa Câmbio e Turismo** (✉ Rua Independência 232, ☎ 096/224–1418). In Santarém, you can exchange money at **Banco do Brasil** (✉ Av. Rui Barbosa 794, ☎ 091/523–2600), which is open weekdays 10–1.

MANAUS

At the airport, you can exchange money at **Banco do Brasil** and **Banco Real.** In town, you'll probably get the best rates at **Cortez Câmbio** (✉ Av. 7 de Setembro 1199, ☎ 092/622–4222).

Consulates

BELÉM

United Kingdom (✉ Av. Governador José Malcher 815, rooms 410–411, ☎ 091/223–0990 or 091/222—0762). **United States** (✉ Rua Oswaldo Cruz 165, ☎ 091/223–0613 or 091/223–0810).

MANAUS

United Kingdom (✉ Rua Poraquê 240, Distrito Industrial, ☎ 092/237–7869 or 092/237–7186). **United States** (✉ Rua Recife 1010, Adrianópolis, ☎ 092/633–4907).

Emergencies

BELÉM

Ambulance: ☎ 192. **Fire:** ☎ 193. **Hospital: Hospital e Maternidade Dom Luiz I** (✉ Av. Generalíssimo Deodoro 868, ☎ 091/241–4144). **Pharmacy: Big Ben** (✉ Av. Gentil Bittencourt 1548, ☎ 091/241–3000) has many branches and offers 24-hour delivery service. **Police:** ☎ 190.

BETWEEN BELÉM AND MANAUS

Ambulance: ☎ 1520 in Macapá. **Fire:** ☎ 193 in Macapá and ☎ 091/522–2530 in Santarém. **Hospitals: Santa Severa** (✉ Rua 8 and Trv. 17, Soure, Ilha do Marajó, ☎ 091/741–1459), **Pronto Socorro** (✉ Rua Milton Silva s/n, Macapá, ☎ 096/421–1499), **Hospital e Maternidade Sagrada Familia** (✉ Av. Presidente Vargas 1606, Santarém, ☎ 091/522–1988).

Pharmacies: Farmácia Teixeira (✉ Rua 2 s/n, Soure, Ilha do Marajó, ☎ 091/741–1487) may be one of the Soure pharmacies that's open 24 hours (they rotate 24-hour duty). In Macapá **Farmácia Globo** (✉ Rua Leopoldo Machado 1902, ☎ 096/223–1378) is open 24 hours a day. There's also a 24-hour rotation among Santarém's pharmacies; try **Droga Farma** (✉ Av. Rui Barbosa 763, ☎ 091/522–7981).

Police: ☎ 147 in Macapá and ☎ 091/523–2633 in Santarém.

MANAUS

Ambulance: ☎ 192. **Fire:** ☎ 092/611–5040. **Hospital: Hospital e Pronto Socorro Municipal 28 de Agosto** (✉ Rua Recife s/n, Adrianópolis, ☎ 092/236–0326). **Pharmacy: Drogaria Angelica** (✉ Av. Djarma Batista 428, ☎ 092/233–6100) offers 24-hour delivery service. **Police:** ☎ 190.

Health and Safety

Dengue and malaria exist in the Amazon, although they aren't common concerns in the cities. Throughout the region, avoid drinking tap water and using ice made from it. In Belém, watch out for pickpockets at Ver-o-Peso market and avoid walking alone at night, particularly in the Cidade Velha. Manaus also has some crime problems; again solitary night-time walks aren't recommended, especially around the port. On the sleepy Ilha do Marajó, the greatest personal safety concern may well be getting hit on the head by a fallen mango.

Telephones, the Internet, and Mail

BELÉM

The area code for Belém is 091. Public phones, operated with cards (sold in newsstands), are found on many corners. You can make long distance calls at **Telepará** (✉ Av. Presidente Vargas 610), which is open daily 7 AM–midnight. **Convert** (✉ Shopping Iguatemi, Trv. Padre Eutíquio 1078, third floor, ☏ 091/250–5566) provides internet service for $2 an hour and is open daily 10–10. The central branch of the **post office** (✉ Av. Presidente Vargas 498, ☏ 091/212–1155) is open weekdays 8–noon and 2–6. You can send faxes from here and, as in all Brazilian post offices, SEDEX international courier service is available.

BETWEEN BELÉM AND MANAUS

Santarém's area code is 091; in Macapá, it's 096. Throughout the region, there are a number of card-operated public phones. In Santarém, you can make long-distance calls at **Telepará** (✉ Av. Rua Siqueira Campos 511, ☏ 091/523–2974), which is open weekdays 7 AM–9:30 PM and Sunday 8 AM–9 PM. The Internet is not yet available in the region.

On Ilha do Marajó, the **Soure post office** (☏ 091/741–1207) is on Rua 2 between the Travessa 13 and Travessa 14. The **Macapá central post office** (✉ Av. Coroliano Jucá 125, ☏ 096/223–0196) is open weekdays 9–noon and 2–5. You can mail a letter at the **Santarém post office** (✉ Praça da Bandeira 81, ☏ 091/523–1186) weekdays 8–4.

MANAUS

In Manaus, the area code is 092. Public phones, which take cards, are plentiful in Centro but aren't easy to find elsewhere in town. For long distance calls, go to **Telamazon** (✉ Av. Getúlio Vargas 950, Centro, ☏ 092/621–6339), which is open on weekdays 7–6:30 and Saturday 8–2. **Argo Internet** (✉ Rua Emílio Moreira 1769, Praça 14, ☏ 092/633–1236) charges $15 per hour to use the internet. The most central **post office** (✉ Rua Marechal Deodoro 117, Centro, ☏ 092/622–2181) is open weekdays from 9 to 5 and on Saturday from 9 to 1.

Tour Operators and Travel Agents

BELÉM

Some of the better operators are **Amazon Star Tours** (✉ Rua Henrique Gurjão 236, ☏ 091/212–6244), **Fontenele** (✉ Av. Assis de Vasconcelos 199, ☏ 091/241–3218), and **Lusotur** (✉ Equatorial Palace hotel, Av. Braz de Aguiar 612, ☏ 091/241–2000). For excursions as well as help with plane and hotel reservations, contact **Angel Turismo** (✉ Hilton International Belém, Av. Presidente Vargas 882, Praça da República, ☏ 091/224–2111).

BETWEEN BELÉM AND MANAUS

Tour operators that arrange trips to Ilha do Marajó are based in Belém. **Amapá Tours** (✉ Hotel Macapá, Av. Azarias Neto 17, Macapá, ☏ 096/223–2553) offers city and river tours and is the only company that arranges trips to see the pororoca. **Santarém Tur** (✉ Amazon Park Hotel, Rua Adriano Pimentel 44, Santarém, ☏ 091/522–4847) can arrange boat trips of varying lengths on the Amazon and Arapiuns rivers, day trips to Alter do Chão, and city tours. **Amazon Tours** (✉ Trv. Turiano Meira 1084, Santarém, ☏ 091/522–1928), run by knowledgeable, friendly American Steven Alexander, offers tailor-made river, city, and Alter do Chão tours; he also conducts half-day trips to a patch of forest he owns a half-hour's drive southeast of Santarém.

MANAUS

Some of the better tour operators include: **Amazônia Expeditions** (✉ Tropical Hotel, Estrada da Ponta Negra s/n, ☏ 092/658–4221), **Ama-**

zon Explorers (⊠ Rua Nhamundá 21, ☎ 092/633–3319), and **Anaconda Tours** (⊠ Rua Dr. Almínio 36, ☎ 092/233–7642). Another operation, **Tarumã** (⊠ Av. Eduardo Ribeiro 620, ☎ 092/633–3363), can also help with hotel and transportation arrangements.

Visitor Information

BELÉM

Belemtur (⊠ Av. Governador José Malcher 592, Nazaré, ☎ 091/242–0900 or 091/242–0033), the city tourist board, is open weekdays 8–noon and 2–6. Pará State's tourist board, **Paratur** (⊠ Praça Kennedy, on the waterfront, ☎ 091/223–7029 or 091/212–0669), is open weekdays 8–6. Both agencies are well organized and extremely helpful.

BETWEEN BELÉM AND MANAUS

On Ilha do Marajó contact the **Secretária Municipal de Turismo** (⊠ Rua 2 between Trv. 14 and Trv. 15, Soure, ☎ 091/741–1326). For information in Macapá, contact the state tourism authority, **DETUR** (⊠ Rua Raimundo Álvares da Costa 18, ☎ 096/223–0627). In Santarém, contact **COMTUR** (⊠ Rua Floriano Peixoto 343, ☎ 𝔽𝔸𝕏 091/523–2434).

MANAUS

Amazonas State's tourism authority, the **Secretaria de Estado da Cultura e Turismo** (⊠ Av. 7 de Setembro 1546, Centro, ☎ 092/234–2252), is open weekdays 8–6. The Manaus tourism authority is **Fundação Municipal de Turismo (FUMTUR)** (⊠ Praça Dom Pedro III, Centro, ☎ 092/622–4986 or 092/622–4886); it's open weekdays 8–5.

PORTUGUESE VOCABULARY

Words and Phrases

	English	Portuguese	Pronunciation
Basics			
	Yes/no	Sim/Não	**see**ing/nown
	Please	Por favor	pohr fah-**vohr**
	May I?	Posso?	**poh**-sso
	Thank you (very much)	(Muito) obrigado	(**moo**yn-too) o-bree **gah**-doh
	You're welcome	De nada	day **nah**-dah
	Excuse me	Com licença	con lee-**ssehn**-ssah
	Pardon me/what did you say?	Desculpe/O que disse?	des-**kool**-peh/o.k. **dih**-say?
	Could you tell me?	Poderia me dizer?	po-day-**ree**-ah mee dee-**zehrr**?
	I'm sorry	Sinto muito	**seen**-too **moo**yn-too
	Good morning!	Bom dia!	bohn **dee**-ah
	Good afternoon!	Boa tarde!	**boh**-ah **tahr**-dee
	Good evening!	Boa noite!	**boh**-ah **noh**ee-tee
	Goodbye!	Adeus!/Até logo!	ah-**deh**oos/ah-**teh loh**-go
	Mr./Mrs.	Senhor/Senhora	sen-**yor**/sen-**yohr**-ah
	Miss	Senhorita	sen-yo-**ri**-tah
	Pleased to meet you	Muito prazer	**moo**yn-too prah-**zehr**
	How are you?	Como vai?	**koh**-mo **vah**-ee
	Very well, thank you	Muito bem, obrigado	**moo**yn-too **beh**-in o-bree-**gah**-doh
	And you?	E o(a) Senhor(a)?	eh oh sen-**yor**(**yohr**-ah)
	Hello (on the telephone)	Alô	ah-**low**

Numbers

	1	um/uma	oom/**oom**-ah
	2	dois	**doh**ees
	3	três	**treh**ys
	4	quatro	**kwa**-troh
	5	cinco	**seen**-koh
	6	seis	**seh**ys
	7	sete	**seh**-tee
	8	oito	**oh**ee-too
	9	nove	**noh**-vee
	10	dez	**deh**-ees
	11	onze	**ohn**-zee
	12	doze	**doh**-zee
	13	treze	**treh**-zee

14	quatorze	kwa-**tohr**-zee
15	quinze	**keen**-zee
16	dezesseis	deh-zeh-**sehys**
17	dezessete	deh-zeh-**seh**-tee
18	dezoito	deh-**zoh**ee-toh
19	dezenove	deh-zeh-**noh**-vee
20	vinte	**veen**-tee
21	vinte e um	**veen**-tee eh **oom**
30	trinta	**treen**-tah
32	trinta e dois	**treen**-ta eh **doh**ees
40	quarenta	kwa-**rehn**-ta
43	quarenta e três	kwa-**rehn**-ta e **treh**ys
50	cinquenta	seen-**kwehn**-tah
54	cinquenta e quatro	seen-**kwehn**-tah e **kwa**-troh
60	sessenta	seh-**sehn**-tah
65	sessenta e cinco	seh-**sehn**-tah e **seen**-ko
70	setenta	seh-**tehn**-tah
76	setenta e seis	seh-**tehn**-ta e **seh**ys
80	oitenta	ohee-**tehn**-ta
87	oitenta e sete	ohee-**tehn**-ta e **seh**-tee
90	noventa	noh-**vehn**-ta
98	noventa e oito	noh-**vehn**-ta e **oh**ee-too
100	cem	**seh**-ing
101	cento e um	**sehn**-too e **oom**
200	duzentos	doo-**zehn**-tohss
500	quinhentos	key-**nyehn**-tohss
700	setecentos	seh-teh-**sehn**-tohss
900	novecentos	noh-veh-**sehn**-tohss
1,000	mil	meel
2,000	dois mil	**doh**ees meel
1,000,000	um milhão	oom mee-lee-**ahon**

Colors

black	preto	**preh**-toh
blue	azul	a-**zool**
brown	marrom	mah-**hohm**
green	verde	**vehr**-deh
pink	rosa	**roh**-zah
purple	roxo	**roh**-choh
orange	laranja	lah-**rahn**-jah
red	vermelho	vehr-**meh**-lyoh
white	branco	**brahn**-coh
yellow	amarelo	ah-mah-**reh**-loh

Days of the Week

Sunday	Domingo	doh-**meehn**-goh
Monday	Segunda-feira	seh-**goon**-dah **fey**-rah
Tuesday	Terça-feira	**tehr**-sah **fey**-rah
Wednesday	Quarta-feira	**kwahr**-tah **fey**-rah

Thursday	Quinta-feira	**keen**-tah **fey**-rah
Friday	Sexta-feira	**sehss**-tah **fey**-rah
Saturday	Sábado	**sah**-bah-doh

Months

January	Janeiro	jah-**ney**-roh
February	Fevereiro	feh-veh-**rey**-roh
March	Março	**mahr**-soh
April	Abril	ah-**bree**l
May	Maio	**my**-oh
June	Junho	gy**oo**-nyoh
July	Julho	gy**oo**-lyoh
August	Agosto	ah-**ghost**-toh
September	Setembro	seh-**tehm**-broh
October	Outubro	owe-**too**-broh
November	Novembro	noh-**vehm**-broh
December	Dezembro	deh-**zehm**-broh

Useful Phrases

Do you speak English?	O Senhor fala inglês?	oh sen-**yor fah**-lah een-**glehs**?
I don't speak Portuguese.	Não falo português.	nown **fah**-loh pohr-too-**ghehs**
I don't understand (you)	Não lhe entendo	nown ly**eh** ehn-**tehn**-doh
I understand	Eu entendo	**eh**-oo ehn-**tehn**-doh
I don't know	Não sei	nown say
I am American/British	Sou americano (americana)/ inglês/inglêsa	sow a-meh-ree-**cah**-noh (a-meh-ree-**cah**-nah/ een-**glah**s (een-**glah**-sa)
What's your name?	Como se chama?	**koh**-moh seh **shah**-mah
My name is . . .	Meu nome é . . .	mehw **noh**-meh eh
What time is it?	Que horas são?	keh **oh**-rahss **sa**-ohn
It is one, two, three . . . o'clock	É uma/São duas, três . . . hora/horas	eh **oom**-ah/**sa**-ohn **oo**mah, **doo**-ahss, **treh**ys **oh**-rah/**oh**-rahs
Yes, please/No, thank you	Sim por favor/ Não obrigado	seing pohr fah-**vohr**/ nown o-bree-**gah**-doh
How?	Como?	**koh**-moh
When?	Quando?	**kwahn**-doh
This/Next week	Esta/Próxima semana	**ehss**-tah/**proh**-see-mah seh-**mah**-nah
This/Next month	Este/Próximo mêz	**ehss**-teh/**proh**-see-moh mehz
This/Next year	Este/Próximo ano	**ehss**-teh/**proh**-see-moh **ah**-noh
Yesterday/today tomorrow	Ontem/hoje amanhã	**ohn**-tehn/**oh**-jeh/ ah-mah-**nyan**
This morning/afternoon	Esta manhã/ tarde	**ehss**-tah mah-**nyan** / **tahr**-deh

Tonight	Hoje a noite	**oh**-jeh ah **noh**ee-tee
What?	O que?	oh **keh**
What is it?	O que é isso?	oh **keh** eh **ee**-soh
Why?	Por quê?	pohr-**keh**
Who?	Quem?	**keh**-in
Where is . . . ?	Onde é . . . ?	**ohn**-deh **eh**
the train station?	a estação de trem?	ah es-tah-**sah**-on deh train
the subway station?	a estação de metrô?	ah es-tah-**sah**-on deh meh-**tro**
the bus stop?	a parada do ônibus?	ah pah-**rah**-dah doh **oh**-nee-boos
the post office?	o correio?	oh coh-**hay**-yoh
the bank?	o banco?	oh **bahn**-koh
the hotel?	o hotel . . . ?	oh oh-**tell**
the cashier?	o caixa?	oh **kahy**-shah
the museum?	o museo . . . ?	oh moo-**zeh**-oh
the hospital?	o hospital?	oh ohss-pee-**tal**
the elevator?	o elevador?	oh eh-leh-vah-**dohr**
the bathroom?	o banheiro?	oh bahn-**yey**-roh
the beach?	a praia de . . . ?	ah **prah**y-yah deh
Here/there	Aqui/ali	ah-**kee**/ah-**lee**
Open/closed	Aberto/fechado	ah-**behr**-toh/feh-**shah**-doh
Left/right	Esquerda/ direita	ehs-**kehr**-dah/ dee-**ray**-tah
Straight ahead	Em frente	ehyn **frehn**-teh
Is it near/far?	É perto/ longe?	eh **pehr**-toh/**lohn**-jeh
I'd like to buy . . .	Gostaria de comprar . . .	gohs-tah-**ree**-ah deh cohm-**prahr** . . .
a bathing suit	um maiô	oom mahy-**owe**
a dictionary	um dicionário	oom dee-seeoh-**nah**-reeoh
a hat	um chapéu	oom shah-**peh**oo
a magazine	uma revista	**oo**mah heh-**vees**-tah
a map	um mapa	oom **mah**-pah
a postcard	cartão postal	kahr-**town** pohs-**tahl**
sunglasses	óculos escuros	**ah**-koo-loss ehs-**koo**-rohs
suntan lotion	um óleo de bronzear	oom **oh**-lyoh deh brohn-zeh-**ahr**
a ticket	um bilhete	oom bee-**lyeh**-teh
cigarettes	cigarros	see-**gah**-hose
envelopes	envelopes	eyn-veh-**loh**-pehs
matches	fósforos	**fohs**-foh-rohss
paper	papel	pah-**pehl**
sandals	sandália	sahn-**dah**-leeah
soap	sabonete	sah-bow-**neh**-teh
How much is it?	Quanto custa?	**kwahn**-too **koos**-tah
It's expensive/ cheap	Está caro/ barato	ehss-**tah kah**-roh / bah-**rah**-toh

A little/a lot	Um pouco/muito	oom **pohw**-koh/ **moo**yn-too
More/less	Mais/menos	**mah**-ees /**meh**-nohss
Enough/too much/too little	Suficiente/ demais/ muito pouco	soo-fee-see-**ehn**-teh/ deh-**mah**-ees/ **moo**yn-toh **pohw**-koh
Telephone	Telefone	teh-leh-**foh**-neh
Telegram	Telegrama	teh-leh-**grah**-mah
I am ill.	Estou doente.	ehss-**tow** doh-**ehn**-teh
Please call a doctor.	Por favor chame um médico.	pohr fah-**vohr shah**-meh oom **meh**-dee-koh
Help!	Socorro!	soh-**koh**-ho
Help me!	Me ajude!	mee ah-**jyew**-deh
Fire!	Incêndio!	een-**sehn**-deeoh
Caution!/Look out!/ Be careful!	Cuidado!	kooy-**dah**-doh

On the Road

Avenue	Avenida	ah-veh-**nee**-dah
Highway	Estrada	ehss-**trah**-dah
Port	Porto	**pohr**-toh
Service station	Posto de gasolina	**pohs**-toh deh gah-zoh-**lee**-nah
Street	Rua	**who**-ah
Toll	Pedagio	peh-**dah**-jyoh
Waterfront promenade	Beiramar/ orla	behy-rah-**mahrr**/ **ohr**-lah
Wharf	Cais	**kah**-ees

In Town

Block	Quarteirão	kwahr-tehy-**rah**-on
Cathedral	Catedral	kah-teh-**drahl**
Church/temple	Igreja	ee-**greh**-jyah
City hall	Prefeitura	preh-fehy-**too**-rah
Door/gate	Porta/portão	**pohr**-tah/porh-**tah**-on
Entrance/exit	Entrada/ saída	ehn-**trah**-dah/ sah-**ee**-dah
Market	Mercado/feira	mehr-**kah**-doh/ **fey**-rah
Neighborhood	Bairro	**buy**-ho
Rustic bar	Lanchonete	lahn-shoh-**neh**-teh
Shop	Loja	**loh**-jyah
Square	Praça	**prah**-ssah

Dining Out

A bottle of . . .	Uma garrafa de . . .	**oo**mah gah-**hah**-fah deh

A cup of . . .	Uma xícara de . . .	**oo**mah **shee**-kah-rah deh
A glass of . . .	Um copo de . . .	oom **koh**-poh deh
Ashtray	Um cinzeiro	oom seen-**zeh**y-roh
Bill/check	A conta	ah **kohn**-tah
Bread	Pão	**pah**-on
Breakfast	Café da manhã	kah-**feh** dah mah-**nyan**
Butter	A manteiga	ah mahn-**teh**y-gah
Cheers!	Saúde!	sah-**oo**-deh
Cocktail	Um aperitivo	oom ah-peh-ree-**tee**-voh
Dinner	O jantar	oh **jyahn**-tahr
Dish	Um prato	oom **prah**-toh
Enjoy!	Bom apetite!	bohm ah-peh-**tee**-teh
Fork	Um garfo	**gahr**-foh
Fruit	Fruta	**froo**-tah
Is the tip included?	A gorjeta esta incluída?	ah gohr-**jyeh**-tah ehss-**tah** een-clue-**ee**-dah
Juice	Um suco	oom **soo**-koh
Knife	Uma faca	**oo**mah **fah**-kah
Lunch	O almoço	oh ahl-**moh**-ssoh
Menu	Menu/ cardápio	me-**noo** / kahr-**dah**-peeoh
Mineral water	Água mineral	**ah**-gooah mee-neh-**rahl**
Napkin	Guardanapo	gooahr-dah-**nah**-poh
No smoking	Não fumante	nown foo-**mahn**-teh
Pepper	Pimenta	pee-**mehn**-tah
Please give me	Por favor me dê	pohr fah-**vohr** mee **deh**
Salt	Sal	sahl
Smoking	Fumante	foo-**mahn**-teh
Spoon	Uma colher	**oo**mah koh-ly**ehr**
Sugar	Açúcar	ah-**soo**-kahr
Waiter!	Garçon!	gahr-**sohn**
Water	Água	**ah**-gooah
Wine	Vinho	**vee**-nyoh305

INDEX

NOTES

NOTES